The Complete FreeBSD®

Important notice

A list of errata and addenda is available for this book on the first CD-ROM in the file /book/errata. The most up-to-date list is on ftp://ftp.lemis.com/pub/cfbsd/errata-2. Please check these lists before reporting problems.

If you find errors in this book, please report them to Greg Lehey <grog@lemis.com> *for inclusion in the errata list.*

The Complete FreeBSD®

Third Edition

Greg Lehey

Walnut Creek CDROM

The Complete FreeBSD®

by Greg Lehey <grog@FreeBSD.ORG>

Published by Walnut Creek CDROM

Suite 260, 1547 Palos Verdes Mall

Walnut Creek CA 94596 USA

- Sales +1-925 674-0783
- Technical support +1-925 603-1234
- Fax +1-925 674-0821
- Email: info@cdrom.com
- Web: http://www.cdrom.com/

See page xxxiii for the list of the RCS IDs which was previously printed on this page.

Printed in Canada
ISBN 1-57176-246-9
UPC 7-47851-15102-3

Printed on acid-free paper.

This book was written in *troff* and formatted on 17 May 1999 with GNU *groff* version 1.11 running under FreeBSD 4.0-CURRENT. It was set in ITC Garamond.

Contents

Chapter 4: Quick Installation 57

Chapter 5: Installing FreeBSD 63

Chapter 6: Shared OS Installation 91

Chapter 7: Installation Problems 99

Chapter 11: Making friends with FreeBSD   157

Chapter 12: Starting and stopping the system 189

Chapter 13: File systems   223

Chapter 14: Disks   243

Chapter 15: Tapes, backups and floppy disks 281

Chapter 16: Printers 293

Chapter 27: The Domain Name Service 477

Chapter 28: Firewalls and IP aliasing 499

Chapter 29: Network debugging 509

Chapter 30: The Network File System 523

Chapter 31: Basic network access 531

Part II: Selected man pages 591

Appendix A: Terminology 717

•

Tables and Figures

Preface

FreeBSD is a high-performance operating system derived from the *Berkeley Software Distribution*, or *BSD*, the version of UNIX developed at the University of California at Berkeley between 1975 and 1993. FreeBSD is not a UNIX clone. Historically and technically, it has greater rights than UNIX System V to be called *UNIX*. Legally, it may not be called UNIX, since UNIX is now a registered trade mark of The Open Group.

This book is intended to help you get FreeBSD up and running on your system and to familiarize you with it. It can't do everything, but plenty of UNIX books and online documentation are available, and a large proportion of them are directly applicable to FreeBSD. In the course of the text, I'll repeatedly point you to other documentation.

I'm not expecting you to be a guru, but I do expect you to understand the basics of using UNIX. If you've come from DOS, however, I'll try to make the transition a little less rocky.

The third edition

Depending on the way you count, this is the third or fourth edition of *The Complete FreeBSD*: the first edition of the book was called *Installing and Running FreeBSD*, and was published in March 1996. Since then, FreeBSD has changed continually, and it's difficult for a book to keep up with the change. This doesn't mean that FreeBSD has changed beyond recognition, but people have done a great job of working away those little rough edges which make the difference between a usable operating system and one which is a pleasure to use. If you come to FreeBSD from System V, you'll certainly notice the difference.

In the second edition, I omitted some text which had become obsolete particularly quickly. For example, in the first edition I went to a lot of trouble to tell people how to install from an ATAPI CD-ROM, since at the time the support was a little wobbly. Almost before the book was released, the FreeBSD team improved the support and rolled it into the base release. The result? Lots of mail messages to the `FreeBSD-questions` mailing list saying, "Where can I get *ATAPI.FLP*?". Even the frequently posted errata list didn't help much.

This kind of occurrence has brought home to me the difference in time scale between software releases and book publication. FreeBSD CD-ROMs are released every three months. A new edition of a book every year is considered very frequent, but it obviously can't hope to keep up with the software release cycle. Still, we're going to try to bring out more frequent editions of the book.

Another thing that we discovered was that the book was too big. The Second Edition contained 1,100 pages of man pages, the FreeBSD manual pages which are also installed online on the system. These printed pages were easier to read, but they had two disadvantages: firstly, they were slightly out of date compared to the online version, and secondly they weighed about 1 kilogram (2.2 lbs). The book was just plain unwieldy, and many people reported that they had physically torn out the pages from the book to make it more manageable.

So this edition has undergone some weight loss. The man pages aren't completely gone, but I have limited them to about the same ones we had in "Installing and Running FreeBSD": I have included the ones you need when you're having trouble installing the operating system or starting the machine. It also tells you (on page 591) how to print out any other man pages you may like to have in printed form.

Conventions used in this book

In this book, I use **bold** for the names of keys on the keyboard. We'll see more about this in the next section.

I use *italic* for the names of UNIX utilities, directories, filenames and *URL*s (*Uniform Resource Locators*, the new file naming technology which you'll know from the World-Wide Web), and to emphasize new terms and concepts when they are first introduced. I also use this font for comments in the examples.

I use `constant Width` in examples to show the contents of files, the output from commands, program variables, actual values of keywords, for mail IDs, for the names of *Internet News* newsgroups, and in the text to represent commands.

I use `constant Italic` in examples to show variables for which context-specific substitutions should be made. For example, the variable `filename` would be replaced by an actual filename.

I use `constant Bold` in examples to show commands or text that would be typed in literally by the user.

In this book, I recommend the use of the Bourne shell or one of its descendents (*sh*, *bash*, *pdksh*, *ksh* or *zsh*). *sh* is in the base system, and the rest are all in the Ports Collection. I personally use the *bash* shell.

This is a personal preference, and a recommendation, but it's not the standard shell. The standard BSD shell is the C shell (*csh*), which has a fuller-featured descendent *tcsh*. In particular, the standard installation sets the *root* user up with a *csh*. See page 179 for details of how to change the shell.

In most examples, I'll show the shell prompt as $, but it doesn't normally matter which shell you use. In some cases, however, it does:

- Sometimes you need to be super-user, which I'll indicate by using the prompt #.

- Sometimes the commands only work with the Bourne Shell and derivatives (*zsh*, *bash*), and they won't work with *csh*, *tcsh*, and friends. In these cases I'll show the *csh* alternative with the standard *csh* prompt %.

In the course of the text I'll occasionally touch on a subject which is not of absolute importance, but which may be of interest. I'll print them in smaller text, like this.

Describing the keyboard

One of the big differences between UNIX and other operating systems concerns the way they treat so-called "carriage control codes."

When UNIX was written, the standard interactive terminal was still the Teletype model KSR 35. This mechanical monstrosity printed at 10 characters per second, and the control characters really did cause physical motion. The two most important characters were *Carriage Return*, which moved the carriage (which carried the print head) to the left margin, and *Line Feed*, which turned the platen to advance the paper by the height of a line. To get to the beginning of a new line, you needed to issue both control characters. We don't have platens or carriages any more, but the characters are still there, and in systems like DOS, a line of text will be terminated by a carriage return character and a line feed character. UNIX only uses a "new line" character, which corresponds to the line feed.

It's surprising how many confusing terms exist to describe individual keys on the keyboard. My favourite is the *any* key ("Press any key to continue"). We won't be using the *any* key in this book, but there are a number of other keys whose names need understanding.

- The *Enter* or *Return* key. I'll call this **ENTER**.

- Control characters (characters produced by holding down the **CTRL** key and pressing a normal keyboard key at the same time). I'll show them as, for example, **CTRL-D** in the text, but these characters are frequently echoed on the screen as a caret (^) followed by the character entered, so in the examples, you may see things like ^D.

- The **ALT** key, which Emacs afficionados call a **META** key, works in the same way as the **CTRL** key, but it generates a different set of characters. These are sometimes abbreviated by prefixing the character with a tilde (~) or the characters **A-**. I personally like this method better, but to avoid confusion I'll represent the character generated by holding down the **ALT** key and pressing D as **ALT-D**.

- **NL** is the *new line* character. In ASCII, it is **CTRL-J**, but UNIX systems generate it when you press the **ENTER** key. UNIX also refers to this character as \n, a usage which comes from the C programming language.

- **CR** is the *carriage return* character, in ASCII **CTRL-M**. Most systems generate it with the **ENTER** key. UNIX also refers to this character as \r—again, this comes from the C programming language.

- **HT** is the ASCII *horizontal tab* character, **CTRL-I**. Most systems generate it when the **TAB** key is pressed. UNIX and C also refer to this character as \t.

Acknowledgements

This book is based on the work of many people, first and foremost the FreeBSD documentation project. Significant parts of the first edition were derived from the FreeBSD handbook, in particular Chapter 11, *Making friends with FreeBSD*. The FreeBSD handbook is supplied as on-line documentation with the FreeBSD release—see page 11 for more information.

Book reviewers

This book wouldn't be the same without the help of a small group of dedicated critics who tried out what I said and pointed out that it didn't work. In particular, I'd like to thank Jack Velte of Walnut Creek CDROM, who had the idea of this book in the first place, Jordan Hubbard and Gary Palmer for tearing the structure and content apart multiple times, and also Bob Bishop, Julian Elischer, Stefan Esser, John Fieber, Glen Foster, Poul-Henning Kamp, Michael Smith, and Nate Williams for valuable contributions ("what, you expect new users to know that you have to shut down the machine before powering it off?"). [See page 220 for details on how to shut down the system]. Finally, special thanks to Josef Möllers, Andreas Ritter, and Jack Velte, who put drafts of this book through its paces and actually installed FreeBSD with their help.

The second edition had much more review than the first. A number of dedicated reviewers held through for several months as I gradually cranked out usable copy. In particular, special thanks to:

Annelise Anderson <andrsn@andrsn.stanford.edu>, Sue Blake <sue@we-learn.com.au>, Jonathan M. Bresler <jmb@FreeBSD.ORG>, William Bulley <web@merit.edu>, Mike Cambria <MCambria@lucent.com>, Brian Clapper <bmc@WillsCreek.COM>, Paul Coyne <pcoyne@br-inc.com>, Lee Crites <leec@adam.adonai.net>, Jerry Dunham <dunham@dunham.org>, Stefan Esser <se@FreeBSD.org>, Patrick Gardella <patrick@cre8tivegroup.com>, Gianmarco Giovannelli <gmarco@scotty.masternet.it>, David Kelly <dkelly@HiWAAY.net>, Andreas Klemm <andreas@klemm.gtn.com>, John Lind <john@starfire.MN.ORG>, Andrew MacIntyre <andymac@bullseye.apana.org.au>, Jonathan Michaels <jlm@caamora.com.au>, Jörg Micheel <joerg@begemot.org>, Marco Molteni <molter@logic.it>, Charles Mott <cmott@snake.srv.net>, Jay D. Nelson <jdn@qiv.com>, Daniel J. O'Connor <doconnor@gsoft.com.au>, Andrew Perry <andrew@python.shoal.net.au>, Kai Peters <kpeters@silk.net>, Wes Peters <softweyr@xmission.com>, Mark Prior <mrp@connect.com.au>, Guido van Rooij <guido@gvr.org>, Stephen J. Roznowski <sjr@home.net>, Andrew Rutherford <AndrewR@iagu.net> Thomas Vickery <tvickery@iol.ie>, Don Wilde <don@PartsNow.com>.

Many of the Second Edition reviewers came back for the Third Edition. In addition, thanks to John Birrell <jb@cimlogic.com.au> for his help with the Alpha architecture, and Michael A. Endsley <al7oj@customcpu.com> for ferreting out bugs, some of which had been present since the days of "Installing and Running FreeBSD".

How this book was written

This book was written and typeset almost entirely with tools supplied as standard with the FreeBSD system. The only exception was the Garamond font, which we can't supply with FreeBSD because it requires a license. **Without this font, the book would look much the same: it would just be in Times Roman, like this sentence here.**

The text of this book was written with the GNU *Emacs* editor, and it was formatted with the GNU *groff* text formatter, version 1.11, and some heavily modified *mm* macros. The man pages were formed with *an* and *doc* macros, slightly modified to produce a table of contents entry, an index entry, and correct page sizing. The process was performed under FreeBSD 4.0-CURRENT.[1] Even the development versions of FreeBSD are stable enough to perform heavy-duty work like professional text formatting.

The source files for this book are kept under *RCS*, the *Revision Control System* (see the man page *rcs(1)*). Here are the RCS Version IDs for the chapters of this particular book. If you have a comment about a particular chapter, it will help if you can tell me the version ID.

```
$Id: title.complete,v 3.3 1999/05/17 03:00:20 grog Exp $
$Id: preface.mm,v 3.4 1999/05/17 03:50:00 grog Exp $
$Id: introduction.mm,v 3.4 1999/05/16 03:18:00 grog Exp $
$Id: concepts.mm,v 3.4 1999/05/17 03:56:30 grog Exp $
$Id: version3.mm,v 3.2 1999/05/15 06:37:46 grog Exp $
$Id: quickinstall.mm,v 3.2 1999/05/15 06:37:56 grog Exp $
$Id: install.mm,v 3.4 1999/05/17 03:13:49 grog Exp $
$Id: shareinstall.mm,v 3.2 1999/05/15 06:38:10 grog Exp $
$Id: problems.mm,v 3.3 1999/05/17 03:02:47 grog Exp $
$Id: ports.mm,v 3.3 1999/05/17 03:26:00 grog Exp $
$Id: xsetup.mm,v 3.3 1999/05/16 01:48:00 grog Exp $
$Id: xtheory.mm,v 3.2 1999/05/15 06:39:02 grog Exp $
$Id: unixref.mm,v 3.5 1999/05/17 03:03:18 grog Exp $
$Id: starting.mm,v 3.4 1999/05/17 03:51:00 grog Exp $
$Id: filesys.mm,v 3.2 1999/05/15 06:47:42 grog Exp $
$Id: disks.mm,v 3.2 1999/05/15 06:47:54 grog Exp $
$Id: tapes.mm,v 3.4 1999/05/17 03:04:18 grog Exp $
$Id: printers.mm,v 3.2 1999/05/15 06:48:09 grog Exp $
$Id: desktop.mm,v 3.3 1999/05/17 03:04:47 grog Exp $
$Id: building.mm,v 3.3 1999/05/17 03:08:42 grog Exp $
$Id: current.mm,v 3.3 1999/05/16 01:25:44 grog Exp $
$Id: emulate.mm,v 3.2 1999/05/15 06:49:07 grog Exp $
$Id: netintro.mm,v 3.2 1999/05/15 06:49:14 grog Exp $
$Id: netsetup.mm,v 3.2 1999/05/15 06:49:21 grog Exp $
$Id: isp.mm,v 3.2 1999/05/15 06:49:42 grog Exp $
$Id: modems.mm,v 3.2 1999/05/15 06:49:54 grog Exp $
$Id: ppp.mm,v 3.5 1999/05/17 03:10:29 grog Exp $
$Id: slip.mm,v 3.2 1999/05/15 06:50:03 grog Exp $
$Id: dns.mm,v 3.2 1999/05/15 06:50:13 grog Exp $
$Id: firewall.mm,v 3.2 1999/05/15 06:50:19 grog Exp $
```

---

1. See Chapter 19, *Keeping up to date with FreeBSD*, for a description of -CURRENT.

```
$Id: netdebug.mm,v 3.3 1999/05/16 01:26:03 grog Exp $
$Id: nfs.mm,v 3.2 1999/05/15 06:50:31 grog Exp $
$Id: netbasics.mm,v 3.2 1999/05/15 06:50:38 grog Exp $
$Id: email.mm,v 3.4 1999/05/17 03:11:07 grog Exp $
$Id: www.mm,v 3.3 1999/05/17 03:36:12 grog Exp $
$Id: fax.mm,v 3.3 1999/05/17 03:12:34 grog Exp $
$Id: micronet.mm,v 3.2 1999/05/15 06:51:03 grog Exp $
$Id: terminology.mm,v 3.2 1999/05/15 06:51:17 grog Exp $
$Id: commands.mm,v 3.3 1999/05/16 01:55:37 grog Exp $
$Id: biblio.mm,v 3.2 1999/05/15 06:51:42 grog Exp $
$Id: licenses.mm,v 3.2 1999/05/15 06:51:47 grog Exp $
$Id: tmac.M,v 1.20 1999/05/14 04:14:31 grog Exp $
```

1

Introduction

FreeBSD is a state of the art operating system derived from AT&T's *UNIX* operating system.[1] It runs on the following platforms:

- Personal computers based on the Intel i386 CPU architecture, including the 386, 486 and Pentium families of processors, and compatible CPUs from AMD and Cyrix.

- The Compaq/Digital Alpha processor.

- In addition, significant development efforts are going towards porting FreeBSD to other hardware, notably the MIPS R4000 series and the Sun Sparc.

This book only describes the released versions of FreeBSD for Intel and Alpha processors.

How to use this book

This book is divided into five parts:

1. The first part, chapters 1 to 8, tells you how to install FreeBSD and what to do if things go wrong.

2. Chapters 9 to 20 introduce you to life with FreeBSD, including setting up optional features, building custom kernels and keeping up to date with FreeBSD.

3. Chapters 21 to 35 introduce you to FreeBSD's rich network support.

4. Starting on page 591 you'll find selected *man pages*, the definitive documentation for most of the system. I have chosen those pages most likely to be needed before the system is installed, or while upgrading. Once the system is running, it's easier to read them on-line.

5. The appendices start on page 717 and include a large amount of reference material.

In more detail, we'll discuss the following subjects:

---

1. FreeBSD no longer contains any AT&T proprietary code, so it may be distributed freely. See page 7 for more details.

- In the rest of this chapter, we'll look at what FreeBSD is, what you need to run it, and what resources are available:

  ☞ On page 4 we'll look at FreeBSD's features.

  ☞ Starting on page 7 we'll look at how FreeBSD came to be.

  ☞ On page 9 we'll compare FreeBSD to other free UNIX-like operating systems.

  ☞ On page 11 we'll look at other sources of information about FreeBSD.

  ☞ On page 14, we'll look at the world-wide FreeBSD community.

  ☞ On page 15 we'll consider what kinds of support are available for FreeBSD.

  ☞ Finally, on page 17 we'll look at the BSD's emblem, the dæmon on the cover of this book.

- Chapter 2, *Before you install*, discusses the installation requirements and theoretical background of installing FreeBSD. You don't *really* need to read this chapter, but it'll make you feel a whole lot more confident if you do.

- Chapter 3, *FreeBSD version 3*, describes the changes that have taken place in FreeBSD since the introduction of version 3.

- Chapter 4, *Quick Installation*, presents a quick installation overview. If you're reasonably experienced, this may be all you need to install FreeBSD. Otherwise, read on...

- In Chapter 5, *Installing FreeBSD*, we'll walk through a typical installation. Read this chapter if you are installing FreeBSD on a disk by itself.

- In Chapter 6, *Shared OS Installation*, we'll look at the differences you will encounter if you install FreeBSD on a system which already contains another operating system.

- Chapter 7, *Installation Problems*, discusses what to do if you run into problems during or after installation.

- Chapter 8, *The Ports Collection*, describes the thousands of free software packages which you can optionally install on a FreeBSD system.

- Chapter 9, *Setting up X11*, tells you how to set up XFree86, the Intel 386 architecture implementation of the industry standard X11 Windowing System.

- In Chapter 10, *XFree86 configuration in depth*, we'll look at the theory behind getting X11 working.

- Chapter 11, *Making friends with FreeBSD*, presents a number of aspects of FreeBSD which are of interest to newcomers (particularly from a Microsoft environment), in particular the concepts of *users* and *processes*. We'll also consider the basics of using the *shell*, as well as the importance of timekeeping.

- Chapter 12, *Starting and stopping the system*, describes how to start and stop a FreeBSD system and all the things you can do to customize it. In particular, we'll look at the more common configuration files and what they should contain.

- Chapter 13, *File systems*, contains information about the FreeBSD directory structure and device names. You'll find the section on device names (starting on page 231) interesting even if you're an experienced UNIX hacker.

- Chapter 14, *Disks*, describes how to format and integrate hard disks, and how to handle disk errors.

- FreeBSD provides professional, reliable data backup services as part of the base system. Don't ever let yourself lose data because of inadequate backup provisions. Read all about it in Chapter 15, *Tapes, backups and floppy disks*.

- Chapter 16, *Printers*, describes the BSD spooling system and how to use it both on local and networked systems.

- Chapter 17, *Setting up your FreeBSD desktop*, describes the user's viewpoint of FreeBSD. UNIX has come a long way in the last few years—make yourself comfortable.

- Chapter 18, *Configuring the kernel*, discusses how to build a customized version of FreeBSD.

- In Chapter 19, *Keeping up to date with FreeBSD*, we'll discuss how to ensure that your system is always running the most appropriate version of FreeBSD.

- FreeBSD can run software written for a number of other operating systems. Read about it in Chapter 20, *Emulating other operating systems*.

- Starting at Chapter 21, *Networks and the Internet*, we'll look at the Internet and the more important services.

- Chapter 22, *Configuring the local network*, describes how to set up local networking.

- Chapter 23, *Connecting to the Internet*, discusses the issues in selecting an Internet Service Provider (ISP) and establishing a presence on the Internet.

- Chapter 24, *Serial communications and modems*, discusses serial hardware and the prerequisites for PPP and SLIP communications.

- In Chapter 25, *Configuring PPP*, we look at FreeBSD's two PPP implementations and what it takes to set them up.

- In Chapter 26, *UUCP and SLIP*, we look at two older serial communication protocols.

- In Chapter 27, *The Domain Name Service*, we'll consider the use of names on the Internet.

- Security is an increasing problem on the Internet. In Chapter 28, *Firewalls and IP aliasing*, we'll look at some things we can do to improve it. We'll also look at *IP aliasing*, since it goes hand-in-hand with firewalls.

- Networks sometimes become *notworks*. In Chapter 29, *Network debugging*, we'll see what we can do to solve network problems.

- Chapter 30, *The Network File System*, describes Sun's classic system for sharing file systems between networked computers.

- We'll look at the basic network access programs in Chapter 31, *Basic network access*.

- Despite the World Wide Web, traditional two-way personal communication is still very popular. We'll look at it in Chapter 32, *Electronic Mail*.

- Most people think the World Wide Web *is* the Internet. We'll look at both client and server access in Chapter 33, *The World-Wide Web*.

- Computers can send faxes a lot more cheaply and flexibly than fax machines. We'll look at how to do that with FreeBSD in Chapter 34, *HylaFAX*.

- Before Microsoft and Novell discovered the Internet, they created a number of less powerful networking systems, some of which are still in use. We'll look at them in Chapter 35, *Connecting to non-IP networks*.

- Appendix A, *Terminology*, explains some of the terms used in this book.

- In Appendix B, *Command equivalents*, we'll look at Microsoft's MS-DOS commands and how to perform similar functions with FreeBSD.

- Appendix C, *Bibliography*, suggests some books for further reading.

- Finally, Appendix D, *License agreements*, contains the licence agreements under which FreeBSD software is distributed.

FreeBSD features

As we have seen, FreeBSD runs on Intel and compatible processors. It is derived from "Berkeley UNIX", the flavour of UNIX developed by the Computer Systems Research Group at the University of California at Berkeley and previously released as the *Berkeley Software Distribution* (BSD) of UNIX.

> For copyright reasons, FreeBSD may not be called UNIX. You be the judge of how much difference this makes.

FreeBSD provides you with many advanced features previously available only on much more expensive computers, including:

- FreeBSD on the Intel platform is a *32-bit operating system*. Unlike some commercial so-called "32 bit operating systems", it contains no 16-bit code whatsoever. The Intel i386 architecture runs significantly faster in 32 bit mode than in 16 bit mode, so this translates to a significantly higher performance.

- On the Alpha platform, FreeBSD is a 64 bit operating system.

- FreeBSD uses *preemptive multitasking* with dynamic priority adjustment to ensure smooth and fair sharing of the computer between applications and users.

- FreeBSD is a *multi-user system*: many people can use a FreeBSD system simultaneously for unrelated purposes. The system shares peripherals such as printers and tape drives properly between all users on the system.

- FreeBSD provides complete *TCP/IP networking* including SLIP, PPP, NFS and NIS support. This means that your FreeBSD machine can interoperate easily with other systems and also act as an enterprise server, providing vital functions such as NFS (remote file access) and e-mail services, or putting your organization on the Internet with WWW, ftp, routing and firewall (security) services. In addition, the Ports Collection includes software for communicating with proprietary protocols—see Chapter 35, *Connecting to non-IP networks* for more details.

- *Memory protection* ensures that neither applications nor users can interfere with each other. If an application crashes, it cannot affect other running applications.

- FreeBSD includes the *XFree86* implementation of the industry standard *X Window System (X11R6) graphical user interface (GUI)*.

- FreeBSD can run most programs built for SCO UNIX and UnixWare, Solaris on the i386 platform, BSD/OS, NetBSD, 386BSD, and Linux.

- The FreeBSD ports and packages collection includes over two thousand ready-to-run applications.

- Thousands of additional and easy-to-port applications are available on the Internet. FreeBSD is source code compatible with most popular commercial UNIX systems and thus most applications require few, if any, changes to compile. Most freely available software was developed on BSD-like systems. As a result, FreeBSD is one of the easiest platforms you can port to.

- Demand paged *virtual memory (VM)* and "merged VM/buffer cache" design efficiently satisfies applications with large appetites for memory while still maintaining interactive response to other users.

- *Shared libraries* (the UNIX equivalent of Microsoft's DLLs) provide for efficient use of disk space and memory.

- The base system contains a full complement of C, C++ and Fortran development tools. Many additional languages for advanced research and development are also available in the ports and packages collection.

- FreeBSD comes with *source code* for the entire system, so you have the greatest degree of control over your environment.

- Extensive *online documentation*, including traditional *man pages* and a hypertext-based *online handbook*.

FreeBSD is based on the 4.4BSD-Lite release from the Computer Systems Research Group (CSRG) at the University of California at Berkeley, and carries on the distinguished tradition of BSD systems development. Building on the excellent base provided by CSRG, the FreeBSD Project has spent many thousands of hours fine tuning the system for maximum performance and reliability in real-life load situations. FreeBSD's features, performance and reliability compare very favourably with those of commercial operating systems.

The applications to which FreeBSD can be put are truly limited only by your own imagination. From software development to factory automation, inventory control to azimuth correction of remote satellite antennae: with FreeBSD, you can do just about anything that you could do with a commercial UNIX product. FreeBSD benefits significantly from thousands of high quality applications developed by research centers and universities around the world, often available at little or no cost. Commercial applications are also available and appearing in greater numbers every day.

Because the source code for FreeBSD itself is generally available, the system can easily be customized for special applications or projects, in ways not generally possible with operating systems from commercial vendors. You can easily start out small with an inexpensive 386 class PC and upgrade as your enterprise grows. Here is just a sampling of some of the applications in which people currently use FreeBSD:

- *Internet Services*: the Internet grew up around Berkeley UNIX. The original TCP/IP implementation, released in 1982, was based on 4.2BSD, and nearly every current TCP/IP implementation has borrowed from it. FreeBSD includes this implementation, the most mature TCP/IP available at any price. This makes it an ideal platform for a variety of Internet services such as FTP servers, World Wide Web servers, Gopher servers, Electronic Mail servers, USENET News servers, and Bulletin Board Systems. Need a new router? A DNS name server? A firewall to keep people out of your internal network? FreeBSD can easily turn that unused 386 or 486 PC sitting in the corner into an advanced router with sophisticated packet filtering capabilities.

- *Education:* Are you a student of computer science or a related engineering field? There is no better way of learning about operating systems, computer architecture and networking than the hands on, under the hood experience that FreeBSD can provide. A number of freely available CAD, mathematical and graphic design packages also make it highly useful to those whose primary interest in a computer is to get *other* work done.

- *Research:* With source code for the entire system available, FreeBSD is an excellent platform for research in operating systems as well as other branches of computer science. FreeBSD's freely available nature also makes it possible for remote groups to collaborate on ideas or shared development without having to worry about special licensing agreements or limitations on what may be discussed in open forums.

- *X Window workstation:* FreeBSD makes an excellent choice for an inexpensive X terminal solution, either using the freely available XFree86 server or one of the excellent commercial servers provided by XI Graphics, Inc.[1] Unlike an X terminal, FreeBSD allows many applications to be run locally, if desired, thus relieving the burden on a central server. FreeBSD can even boot "diskless", making individual workstations even cheaper and easier to administer.

---

1. See *http://www.xig.com* for further information about XI Graphics.

- *Software Development:* The basic FreeBSD system comes with a full complement of development tools included the renowned GNU C/C++ compiler and debugger.

A little history

FreeBSD is a labour of love: big commercial companies produce operating systems and charge lots of money for them. The FreeBSD team produces a professional-quality operating system and gives it away. That's not the only difference.

In 1981, when IBM introduced their Personal Computer, the microprocessor industry was still in its infancy. The PC had a minimum of 16 kB and a maximum of 64 kB on-board memory. UNIX wouldn't run on this hardware, so Microsoft, who at the time marketed their own version of UNIX, went looking for something simpler. The "operating system" they chose was correspondingly primitive: a clone of Digital Resarch's successful CP/M operating system, written by Tim Patterson of Seattle Computer Products and originally called *QDOS* (*Quick and Dirty Operating System*). At the time, it seemed just the thing: it would run just fine without a hard disk (in fact, the original PC didn't *have* a hard disk, not even as an option), and it didn't use up too much memory. The only thing that they really had to do was to change the name. Since the operating system was for IBM, they named it PC-DOS after DOS/360, an operating system of the mid-60s. Microsoft marketed its version under the name MS-DOS.

By this time, a little further down the West Coast of the USA, the Computer Systems Research Group (*CSRG*) of the University of California at Berkeley had just modified AT&T's UNIX operating system to run on the new DEC VAX 11/780 machine, which sported virtual memory, and had turned their attention to implementing some new protocols for the ARPANET: the so-called *Internet Protocols*. The version of UNIX that they had developed was now sufficiently different from AT&T's system that it had been dubbed *Berkeley UNIX*.

As time went on, both MS-DOS and UNIX evolved. Before long MS-DOS was modified to handle hard disks—not well, but it handled them, and for the PC users, it was so much better than what they had before that they ignored the inefficiencies. After all, the PC gave you your own hard disk on your desk, and you didn't have to share it with all the other people in the department. Microsoft even tried to emulate the UNIX directory structure, but only succeeded in implementing the concept of nested directories. At Berkeley, they were developing a higher performance disk subsystem, the *Fast File System*, now known as the *UNIX File System*.

By the late 80s, it was evident that Microsoft no longer intended to substantially enhance MS-DOS. New processors with support for multitasking and virtual memory had replaced the old Intel 8088 processor of the IBM PC, but they still ran MS-DOS by emulating the 8088 processor, which was now completely obsolete. The 640 kB memory limit of the original PC, which once appeared bigger than anybody would ever need, became a serious problem. In addition, people wanted to do more than one thing at a time with their computers.

A solution to both problems was obvious: move to the 32 bit address mode of the new Intel 80386 processor and introduce real multitasking, which operating systems on larger machines had had for decades. Of course, these larger machines were only physically larger. The average PC of 1990 had more memory, more disk and more processing power than just about any of the large computers of the 70s. Nevertheless, Microsoft still hasn't solved these problems for its desktop "operating system", Windows 95.

UNIX, on the other hand, was a relatively mature operating system at the time when the PC was introduced. As a result, Microsoft-based environments have had little influence on the development of UNIX. UNIX development was determined by other factors: changes in legal regulations in the USA between 1977 and 1984 enabled AT&T first to license UNIX to other vendors, noticably Microsoft, who announced XENIX in 1981, and then to market it itself. AT&T developed System III in 1982, and System V in 1983. The differences between XENIX and System V were initially small, but they grew: by the mid-80s, there were four different versions of UNIX: the *Research Version*, used only inside AT&T, the *Berkeley Software Distribution* (BSD) from Berkeley, the commercial *System V* from AT&T, and XENIX, which no longer interested Microsoft, and was marketed by the company which had developed it, the *Santa Cruz Operation*, or *SCO*.

One casualty of UNIX's maturity was the CSRG in Berkeley. UNIX was too mature to be considered an object of research, and the writing was on the wall: the CSRG would close down. Some people decided to port Berkeley UNIX to the PC—after all, SCO had done it years ago. In the Berkeley tradition, however, they wanted to give it away. The industry's reaction was not friendly. In 1992, AT&T's subsidiary *USL* (*UNIX Systems Laboratories*) filed a lawsuit against *Berkeley Software Design Inc.* (*BSDI*), the manufacturer of the BSD/386 and (later) the BSD/OS operating systems, both very similar to FreeBSD, for alleged distribution of AT&T source code in violation of licence agreements. They subsequently extended the case to the University of California at Berkeley. The suit was settled out of court, and the exact conditions were not all disclosed. The only one that became public was that BSDI would migrate their source base to the newer 4.4BSD-Lite sources, a thing that they were preparing to do in any case. Although not involved in the litigation, it was suggested to FreeBSD that they should also move to 4.4BSD-Lite, which was done with the release of FreeBSD version 2.0 in late 1994.

Now, in the late 1990s, FreeBSD is the best-known of the BSD operating systems, one that many consider to follow in the tradition of the CSRG. I can think of no greater honour for the development team. It was developed on a shoestring budget, yet it manages to outperform commercial operating systems by an order of magnitude.

Things have changed elsewhere as well. In 1992, AT&T sold USL to Novell Inc., who had introduced a product based on System V.4 called UnixWare. Although UnixWare has much better specifications than SCO's old System V.3 UNIX, it was never a success, and Novell finally sold their UNIX operation to SCO, who now markets both systems. Most FreeBSD users don't see that either system has any significant advantage over FreeBSD, especially since FreeBSD can run applications designed for either SCO system.

Other free UNIX-like operating systems

FreeBSD isn't the only free UNIX-like operating system available—it's not even the best-known one. The best-known free UNIX-like operating system is undoubtedly Linux, but there are also a number of other BSD-derived operating systems. We'll look at them first:

- *386/BSD* was the original free BSD operating system, introduced by William F. Jolitz in 1992. It never progressed beyond a test stage: instead, two derivative operating systems arose, FreeBSD and NetBSD. As far as anybody can tell, 386/BSD is dead.

- *NetBSD* is an operating system which, to the casual observer, is almost identical to FreeBSD. The main differences are in the fact that NetBSD runs on just about any hardware, whereas FreeBSD concentrates on mainly Intel hardware. FreeBSD tries harder to be easy to understand for a beginner. For a comparison of FreeBSD and NetBSD, somewhat biased towards NetBSD, and now also somewhat dated, see *http://www.cons.org/cracauer/bsd-net-vs-free.html*.

- *OpenBSD* is a spinoff of NetBSD which focuses on security. You can find more information at *http://www.openbsd.org*.

You might get the impression that there are lots of different, incompatible BSD versions. In fact, they're all very similar.

FreeBSD and Linux

Linux is a clone of UNIX written by Linus Torvalds, a student in Helsinki, Finland. At the time, the BSD sources were not freely available, and so Linus wrote his own version of UNIX.

Linux is a superb example of how a few dedicated, clever people can produce an operating system that is better than well-known commercial systems developed by a large number of trained software engineers. It is better even than a number of commercial UNIX systems.

Obviously, I don't think Linux is as good as FreeBSD, or I wouldn't be writing this book, but the differences between FreeBSD and Linux are more a matter of philosophy rather than of concept. Here are a few contrasts:

Table 1-1. Differences between FreeBSD and Linux

FreeBSD is a direct descendent of the original UNIX, though it contains no residual AT&T code.	Linux is a clone and never contained any AT&T code
FreeBSD is a complete operating system, maintained by a central group of software developers. There is only one distribution of FreeBSD.	Linux is a kernel, personally maintained by Linus Torvalds. The non-kernel programs supplied with Linux are part of a *distribution*, of which there are several.

FreeBSD aims to be a stable production environment.

Linux is still a "bleeding edge" development environment, though many distributions aim to make it more suitable for production use.

As a result of the centralized development style, FreeBSD is straightforward and easy to install.

The ease of installation of Linux depends on the "distribution". If you switch from one distribution of Linux to another, you'll have to learn a new set of installation tools.

FreeBSD is still relatively unknown, since its distribution was restricted for a long time due to the AT&T lawsuits.

Linux did not have any lawsuits to contend with, so for a long time it was the only free UNIX-type system available.

As a result of the lack of knowledge of FreeBSD, not much commercial software is available for it.

A growing amount of commercial software is becoming available for Linux.

As a result of the smaller user base, FreeBSD is less likely to have drivers for brand-new boards than Linux.

Just about any new board will soon have a driver for Linux.

Because of the lack of commercial applications and drivers, FreeBSD will run most Linux programs, whether commercial or not. It's also relatively simple to port Linux drivers to FreeBSD.

Linux appears not to need to be able to run FreeBSD programs or drivers.

FreeBSD has a large number of afficionados who are prepared to flame anybody who dares suggest that it's not better than Linux.

Linux has a large number of afficionados who are prepared to flame anybody who dares suggest that it's not better than FreeBSD.

In summary, Linux is also a very good operating system. For many, it's better than FreeBSD. It's a pity that so many people on both sides are prepared to flame[1] each other. There are signs that both sides are learning to appreciate each other, and a number of people are now running both systems.

---

1. To quote Eric Raymond's "The New Hacker's Dictionary":

:flame: 1. /vi./ To post an email message intended to insult and provoke. 2. /vi./ To speak incessantly and/or rabidly on some relatively uninteresting subject or with a patently ridiculous attitude. 3. /vt./ Either of senses 1 or 2, directed with hostility at a particular person or people. 4. /n./ An instance of flaming. When a discussion degenerates into useless controversy, one might tell the participants "Now you're just flaming" or "Stop all that flamage!" to try to get them to cool down (so to speak).

Other documentation on FreeBSD

People occasionally complain that there are so few books on FreeBSD—currently, this is about the only one in the English language, and it can't do everything. That looks like a pretty meagre offering, even if you do like this book.

This impression is incorrect. In fact, FreeBSD users have access to probably more top-quality documentation than just about any other operating system. Remember that word UNIX®. Sure, the lawyers tell us that we can't refer to FreeBSD as UNIX, because UNIX belongs to the Open Group. That doesn't make the slightest difference to the fact that just about any book on UNIX will apply more directly to FreeBSD than any other flavour of UNIX. Why is this?

Commercial UNIX vendors have a problem, and FreeBSD doesn't help them: why should people buy their products when you can get it free from the FreeBSD Project (or, for that matter, from other free UNIX-like operating systems such as NetBSD, OpenBSD and Linux)? One obvious reason would be "value-added features". So they add features or fix weak points in the system, put a copyright on the changes, and help lock their customers in to their particular implementation. As long as the changes are really useful, this is legitimate, but it does make the operating system less compatible with "standard UNIX", and the books about standard UNIX are less applicable.

In addition, many books are written by people with an academic background. In the UNIX world, this means that they are more likely than the average user to have been exposed to BSD. Many general UNIX books handle primarily BSD, possibly with an additional chapter on the commercial System V version.

In Appendix C, *Bibliography*, you'll find a list of books which I find particularly worthwhile. I'd like to single out some which I find particularly good, and which I frequently use myself:

- The FreeBSD *online handbook* contains a lot of information specifically about FreeBSD, including a deeper discussion of many topics in this book. It is available on the World Wide Web at *http://www.FreeBSD.org/handbook.html*, and it is also available on each FreeBSD system in the directory */usr/share/doc/handbook*. Before installation, you can access it from the *Live Filesystem* CD-ROM. We'll look at how to do that in the next section.

- The FreeBSD *FAQ* (*Frequently Asked Questions*) is just what it says it is: a list of questions that people frequently ask about FreeBSD, with answers of course. It is located in the directory */usr/share/doc/FAQ*. If you run MS-DOS, you can view it before installation with the *VIEW* program. Check the CD-ROM booklet for the location, which could change.

- *UNIX Power Tools*, by Jerry Peek, Tim O'Reilly, and Mike Loukides, is a superb collection of interesting information, including a CD-ROM. Recommended for everybody, from beginners to experts.

- *UNIX for the Impatient*, by Paul W. Abrahams and Bruce R. Larson, is more similar to this book, but it includes a lot more material on specific products, such as shells and the *Emacs* editor.

- The *UNIX System Administration Handbook*, by Evi Nemeth, Garth Snyder, Scott Seebass, and Trent R. Hein, is one of the best books on systems administration I have seen. It covers six different UNIX systems, including BSD/OS, which is very close to FreeBSD.

- There are a large number of active Internet groups which deal with FreeBSD. Read about them in the online handbook.

Reading the handbook

If you're running X, you can use a browser like *netscape* to read the handbook. If you don't have X running yet, use *lynx*. Both of these programs are included on the CD-ROM. To install them, enter:

```
# pkg_add /cdrom/packages/All/netscape-communicator-4.5.tgz
or
# pkg_add /cdrom/packages/All/lynx-2.8.1.1.tgz
```

The numbers after the name (4.5 and 2.8.1.1) may change after this book has been printed. Use *ls* to list the names if you can't find these particular versions.

Note that *lynx* is not a complete substitute for *netscape*: since it is text-only, it is not capable of displaying the large majority of web pages correctly. It will suffice for reading most of the handbook, however. See page 112, for more information on *pkg_add*.

In either case, you start the browser with the name of the handbook:

```
$ lynx /usr/share/doc/handbook/handbook.html
$ netscape /usr/share/doc/handbook/handbook.html &
```

You enter the & after the invocation of *netscape* to free up the window in which you invoke it: *netscape* opens its own window.

You can look at the FAQ in the same way—just substitute the name *FAQ/freebsd-faq.html* for *handbook/handbook.html*.

If you haven't installed the handbook, you can still access it from the Live Filesystem CD-ROM. Assuming the CD-ROM is mounted on */cdrom*, choose the directory */cdrom/usr/share/doc/handbook/handbook.html*.

Alternatively, you can print out the handbook. This is a little more difficult, and of course you'll lose the hypertext references, but you may prefer it in this form. To format the handbook for printing, you'll need a PostScript printer or *ghostscript*. See page 300 for more details of how to print PostScript.

You can download handbook from *ftp://ftp.FreeBSD.ORG/pub/FreeBSD/doc/handbook.ps.gz*. Use *ftp* (page 535) to transfer the document.

The online manual

The most comprehensive documentation on FreeBSD is in the form of *man pages*. Nearly every program on the system comes with a short reference manual explaining the basic operation and various arguments.

When online, you view the man pages with the command *man*. For example, to learn more about the command *ls*, type:

```
$ man ls
LS(1)                        FreeBSD Reference Manual                       LS(1)

NAME
     ls - list directory contents

SYNOPSIS
     ls [-ACFLRTacdfiloqrstu1] [ file ... ]

DESCRIPTION
     For each operand that names a file of a type other than directory, ls
     displays its name as well as any requested, associated information.  For
     each operand that names a file of type directory, ls displays the names.
(etc)
```

In this particular example, with the exception of the first line, the text in **constant width bold** is not input, it's the way it appears on the screen.

The online manual is divided up into sections numbered:

1. User commands

2. System calls and error numbers

3. Functions in the C libraries

4. Device drivers

5. File formats

6. Games and other diversions

7. Miscellaneous information

8. System maintenance and operation commands

9. Kernel interface documentation

In some cases, the same topic may appear in more than one section of the on-line manual. For example, there is a user command *chmod* and a system call chmod(). In this case, you can tell the man command which you want by specifying the section number:

```
$ man 1 chmod
```

This will display the manual page for the user command chmod. References to a particular section of the on-line manual are traditionally placed in parentheses in written documentation. For example, *chmod(1)* refers to the user command *chmod*, and *chmod(2)* means the system call.

This is fine if you know the name of the command and forgot how to use it, but what if you can't recall the command name? You can use man to search for keywords in the command descriptions by using the -k option, or by starting the program *apropos*:

```
$ man -k mail
$ apropos mail
```

Both of these commands do the same thing: they show the names of the man pages that have the keyword *mail* in their descriptions.

Alternatively, you may browse through */usr/bin* and see all these file names, but you don't have any idea what they do. To find out, enter one of the lines:

```
$ cd /usr/bin; man -f *
$ cd /usr/bin; whatis *
```

Both of these commands do the same thing: they print out a one-line summary of the purpose of the program:

```
$ cd /usr/bin; man -f *
a2p(1)            - Awk to Perl translator
addftinfo(1)      - add information to troff font files for use with groff
apply(1)          - apply a command to a set of arguments
apropos(1)        - search the whatis database for strings
...etc
```

GNU *info*

The Free Software Foundation has its own on-line hypertext browser called *info*. Many FSF programs come with either no man page at all, or with an excuse for a man page (*gcc*, for example). To read the online documentation, you need to browse the *info* files with the *info* program, or from *Emacs* with the *info* mode. To start *info*, simply type:

```
$ info
```

In *Emacs*, enter **CTRL-h i** or **ALT-X** info. Whichever way you start *info*, you can get brief introduction by typing h, and a quick command reference by typing ?.

The FreeBSD community

FreeBSD was developed by a world-wide group of developers. It could not have happened without the Internet. Most of the key players have never even met each other in person: the main communication is via the Net. If you have any kind of Internet connection, you can participate as well. If you don't have an Internet connection, it's about time you got one. The connection doesn't have to be complete: if you can receive email, you can participate. On the other hand, FreeBSD includes all the software you need for a complete Internet connection, not the very limited subset that most PC-based "Internet" packages offer you.

Support

As it says in the copyright, FreeBSD is supplied as-is, without any support liability. If you're on the Net, you're not alone, however. Liability is one thing, but there are plenty of people prepared to help you, most for free, some for fee. A good place to start is with the mailing lists FreeBSD-newbies@FreeBSD.org and freebsd-questions@FreeBSD.org. In conversation they are typically abbreviated to -newbies and -questions respectively. To sign up, send a mail message to majordomo@FreeBSD.org with the text

```
subscribe FreeBSD-newbies
```
or
```
subscribe FreeBSD-questions
```

You'll get a reply back saying that the request must be authenticated: it'll look something like this:

```
Please be sure to read the charters before subscribing or sending
mail to any FreeBSD mailing list for an explanation of which topics
are relevant for a given list and what types of postings are and
are not allowed.  They may be found at:

        http://www.freebsd.org/handbook/eresources.html#ERESOURCES-MAIL

Someone (possibly you) has requested that your email address be added
to or deleted from the mailing list "freebsd-newbies@FreeBSD.ORG".

If you really want this action to be taken, please send the following
commands (exactly as shown) back to "Majordomo@FreeBSD.ORG":

        auth 7e06ee31 subscribe freebsd-newbies grog@example.org

If you do not want this action to be taken, simply ignore this message
and the request will be disregarded.

If your mailer will not allow you to send the entire command as a single
line, you may split it using backslashes, like so:

        auth 7e06ee31 subscribe freebsd-newbies \
        grog@example.org

If you have any questions about the policy of the list owner, please
contact "freebsd-newbies-approval@FreeBSD.ORG".

Thanks!

Majordomo@FreeBSD.ORG
```

Just reply to that message, removing all the text except the auth line:

```
        auth 7e06ee31 subscribe freebsd-newbies grog@example.org
```

Send this message to `majordomo@FreeBSD.org` (which is what you do if you just reply), not to the list itself. You'll get another reply back:

```
Welcome to the freebsd-newbies mailing list!

Please save this message for future reference.  Thank you.

If you ever want to remove yourself from this mailing list,
you can send mail to <Majordomo@FreeBSD.ORG> with the following
command in the body of your email message:

    unsubscribe freebsd-newbies

or from another account, besides grog@example.org:

    unsubscribe freebsd-newbies grog@example.org

If you ever need to get in contact with the owner of the list,
(if you have trouble unsubscribing, or have questions about the
list itself) send email to <owner-freebsd-newbies@FreeBSD.ORG> .
This is the general rule for most mailing lists when you need
to contact a human.

 Here's the general information for the list you've subscribed to,
 in case you don't already have it:

FREEBSD-NEWBIES

Welcome to FreeBSD!
This list is a gathering place for people new to FreeBSD.
Please feel free to share your experiences with others on this list.

Support questions should be sent to freebsd-questions@freebsd.org
(NOT to the newbies list please)

Full info and FAK   http://www.welearn.com.au/freebsd/newbies/
Resource list       http://www.FreeBSD.org/projects/newbies.html
```

As the welcome message says, `-newbies` is a discussion group for people new to FreeBSD; it's not intended for real technical problems. Use `-questions` for that.

When submitting questions to `-questions`, remember that people are under no obligation to answer your question. Make them want to answer it: submit the question in a clear, understandable manner. For more details, see *http://www.lemis.com/questions.html*. You may also like to check out the FreeBSD World Wide Web (WWW) site at *http://www.FreeBSD.org*, in particular the support page at *http://www.FreeBSD.org/support.html*.

In addition, Walnut Creek CDROM supplies limited basic installation support for purchasers of the Walnut Creek CDROM edition of FreeBSD. Here's how to contact Walnut Creek CDROM:

- By phone. Call +1 925 603 1234[1]

---

1. If you live in North America, you may not recognize the +1. This is the international dialing code for North America; replace the + symbol with your national prefix code for international calls. For example, in most parts of Europe you replace the + with 00; in Australia, you replace it with 0011, so the complete number becomes 0011 1 925 603 1234.

- By fax. Fax to +1 925 674 0821.

- By email. Send email to `support@cdrom.com`.

Remember, too, that if all else fails you can return your CD-ROM to Walnut Creek CDROM for an unconditional refund. If you do have to go to this step, please let us know what went wrong. You'll get your refund either way, but if you have problems with FreeBSD, we want to know why and how we can improve the product.

Reporting bugs

If you find something wrong with FreeBSD, we want to know about it. There are two ways to report a bug:

- Report it via the World Wide Web at *http://www.FreeBSD.org/send-pr.html.*

- Use the *send-pr* program to send it as a mail message.

The Berkeley dæmon

The little dæmon on the cover of this book symbolizes BSD. It is included with kind permission of Marshall Kirk McKusick, one of the leading members of the former Computer Sciences Research Group at the University of California at Berkeley, and owner of the dæmon's copyright.

The dæmon has occasionally given rise to a certain amount of confusion. In fact, it's a joking reference to processes which run in the background—see Chapter 11, *Making friends with FreeBSD*, page 183, for a description. The outside world occasionally sees things differently, as the following story indicates:

Newsgroups: alt.humor.best-of-usenet
Subject: [comp.org.usenix] A Great Daemon Story

From: Rob Kolstad <kolstad@bsdi.com>
Newsgroups: comp.org.usenix
Subject: A Great Daemon Story

Linda Branagan is an expert on dæmons. She has a T-shirt that sports the dæmon in tennis shoes that appears on the cover of the 4.3BSD manuals and *The Design and Implementation of the 4.3BSD UNIX Operating System* by S. Leffler, M. McKusick, M. Karels, J. Quarterman, Addison-Wesley Publishing Company, Reading, MA 1989.

She tells the following story about wearing the 4.3BSD dæmon T-shirt:

Last week I walked into a local "home style cookin' restaurant/watering hole" in Texas to pick up a take-out order. I spoke briefly to the waitress behind the counter, who told me my order would be done in a few minutes.

So, while I was busy gazing at the farm implements hanging on the walls, I was approached by two "natives." These guys might just be the original Texas rednecks.

"Pardon us, ma'am. Mind if we ask you a question?"

Well, people keep telling me that Texans are real friendly, so I nodded.

"Are you a Satanist?"

Well, at least they didn't ask me if I liked to party.

"Uh, no, I can't say that I am."

"Gee, ma'am. Are you sure about that?" they asked.

I put on my biggest, brightest Dallas Cowboys cheerleader smile and said, "No, I'm positive. The closest I've ever come to Satanism is watching Geraldo."

"Hmmm. Interesting. See, we was just wondering why it is you have the lord of darkness on your chest there."

I was this close to slapping one of them and causing a scene—then I stopped and noticed the shirt I happened to be wearing that day. Sure enough, it had a picture of a small, devilish-looking creature that has for some time now been associated with a certain operating system. In this particular representation, the creature was wearing sneakers.

They continued: "See, ma'am, we don't exactly appreciate it when people show off pictures of the devil. Especially when he's lookin' so friendly."

These idiots sounded terrifyingly serious.

Me: "Oh, well, see, this isn't really the devil, it's just, well, it's sort of a mascot."

Native: "And what kind of football team has the devil as a mascot?"

Me: "Oh, it's not a team. It's an operating—uh, a kind of computer."

I figured that an ATM machine was about as much technology as these guys could handle, and I knew that if I so much as uttered the word "UNIX" I would only make things worse.

Native: "Where does this satanical computer come from?"

Me: "California. And there's nothing satanical about it really."

Somewhere along the line here, the waitress noticed my predicament—but these guys probably outweighed her by 600 pounds, so all she did was look at me sympathetically and run off into the kitchen.

Native: "Ma'am, I think you're lying. And we'd appreciate it if you'd leave the premises now."

Fortunately, the waitress returned that very instant with my order, and they agreed that it would be okay for me to actually pay for my food before I left. While I was at the cash register, they amused themselves by talking to each other.

Native #1: "Do you think the police know about these devil computers?"

Native #2: "If they come from California, then the FBI oughta know about 'em."

They escorted me to the door. I tried one last time: "You're really blowing this all out of proportion. A lot of people use this 'kind of computers.' Universities, researchers, businesses. They're actually very useful."

Big, big, *big* mistake. I should have guessed at what came next.

Native: "Does the government use these devil computers?"

Me: "Yes."

Another *big* boo-boo.

Native: "And does the government pay for 'em? With our tax dollars?"

I decided that it was time to jump ship.

Me: "No. Nope. Not at all. Your tax dollars never entered the picture at all. I promise. No sir, not a penny. Our good Christian congressmen would never let something like that happen. Nope. Never. Bye."

Texas. What a country.

In fact, the dæmon tradition goes back quite a way. As recently as 1996, the following message went through the `FreeBSD-chat` mailing list:

To: "Jonathan M. Bresler" <jmb@freefall.freebsd.org>
Cc: obrien@antares.aero.org (Mike O'Brien),
     joerg_wunsch@uriah.heep.sax.de,
     chat@FreeBSD.org, juphoff@tarsier.cv.nrao.edu
Date: Tue, 07 May 1996 16:27:20 -0700
Sender: owner-chat@FreeBSD.org

>   details and gifs PLEASE!

If you insist. :-)

Sherman, set the Wayback Machine for around 1976 or so (see Peter Salus' *A Quarter Century of UNIX* for details), when the first really national UNIX meeting was held in Urbana, Illinois. This would be after the "forty people in a Brooklyn classroom" meeting held by Mel Ferentz (yeah I was at that too) and the more-or-less simultaneous West Coast meeting(s) hosted by SRI, but before the UNIX Users Group was really incorporated as a going concern.

I knew Ken Thompson and Dennis Ritchie would be there. I was living in Chicago at the time, and so was comic artist Phil Foglio, whose star was just beginning to rise. At that time I was a bonded locksmith. Phil's roommate had unexpectedly split town, and he was the only one who knew the combination to the wall safe in their apartment. This is the only apartment I've ever seen that had a wall safe, but it sure did have one, and Phil had some stuff locked in there. I didn't hold out much hope, since safes are far beyond where I was (and am) in my locksmithing sphere of competence, but I figured "no guts no glory" and told him I'd give it a whack. In return, I told him, he could do some T-shirt art for me. He readily agreed.

Wonder of wonders, this safe was vulnerable to the same algorithm that Master locks used to be susceptible to. I opened it in about 15 minutes of manipulation. It was my greatest moment as a locksmith and Phil was overjoyed. I went down to my lab and shot some Polaroid snaps of the PDP-11 system I was running UNIX on at the time, and gave it to Phil with some descriptions of the visual puns I wanted: pipes, demons with forks running along the pipes, a "bit bucket" named */dev/null*, all that.

What Phil came up with is the artwork that graced the first decade's worth of "UNIX T-shirts", which were made by a Ma and Pa operation in a Chicago suburb. They turned out transfer art using a 3M color copier in their basement. Hence, the PDP-11 is reversed (the tape drives are backwards) but since Phil left off the front panel, this was hard to tell. His trademark signature was photo-reversed, but was recopied by the T-shirt people and "re-forwardized", which is why it looks a little funny compared to his real signature.

Dozens and dozens of these shirts were produced. Bell Labs alone accounted for an order of something like 200 for a big picnic. However, only four (4) REAL originals were produced: these have a distinctive red collar and sleeve cuff. One went to Ken, one to Dennis, one to me, and one to my then-wife. I now possess the latter two shirts. Ken and Dennis were presented with their shirts at the Urbana conference.

People ordered these shirts direct from the Chicago couple. Many years later, when I was living in LA, I got a call from Armando Stettner, then at DEC, asking about that now-famous artwork. I told him I hadn't talked to the Illinois T-shirt makers in years. At his request I called them up. They'd folded the operation years ago and were within days of discarding all the old artwork. I requested its return, and duly received it back in the mail. It looked strange, seeing it again in its original form, a mirror image of the shirts with which I and everyone else were now familiar.

I sent the artwork to Armando, who wanted to give it to the Ultrix marketing people. They came out with the Ultrix poster that showed a nice shiny Ultrix machine contrasted with the chewing-gum-and-string PDP-11 UNIX people were familiar with. They still have the artwork, so far as I know.

I no longer recall the exact contents of the letter I sent along with the artwork. I did say that as far as I knew, Phil had no residual rights to the art, since it was a 'work made for hire', though nothing was in writing (and note this was decades before the new copyright law). I do not now recall if I explicitly assigned all rights to DEC. What is certain is that John Lassiter's dæmon, whether knowingly borrowed from the original, or created by parallel evolution, postdates the first horde of UNIX dæmons by at least a decade and probably more. And if Lassiter's dæmon looks a lot like a Phil Foglio creation, there's a reason.

I have never scanned in Phil's artwork; I've hardly ever scanned in anything, so I have no GIFs to show. But I have some very very old UNIX T-shirts in startlingly good condition. Better condition than I am at any rate: I no longer fit into either of them.

Mike O'Brien
creaky antique

Note the date of this message: it's quite recent. Mike has since scanned the original teeshirt, and it may be made available. Remember, you read it here first.

2

Before you install

FreeBSD will run on just about any modern PC. You can skip this chapter and move to Chapter 4, *Quick Installation*, and you'll have a very good chance of success. Nevertheless, it will make things easier if you know the contents of this chapter before you start. If you do run into trouble, this chapter will give you the background information you need to solve the trouble quickly and simply.

Hardware requirements

To run FreeBSD, you will need the following absolute minimum hardware:

- PC with 80386 CPU, or Alpha-based machine with SRM firmware.

- 4 MB memory (Intel) or 24 MB (Alpha?)

- Any display board

- 80 MB free disk space (Intel). Nobody has tried an installation on an Alpha machine with less than 500 MB, though it's certainly possible to reduce this value significantly.

Figure 2-1: Absolute minimum hardware for FreeBSD

When I say *absolute* minimum, I mean it. You can run FreeBSD 3.2 in 4 MB memory, but you will require at least 5 MB in order to install it. You can't do very much with such a minimal system, but for some purposes it might be adequate. For any kind of reasonable response time, you should use at least 8 MB of memory. Before you go to the trouble to even try such a minimal installation, consider the cost of another 4 MB of memory. And you can pick up better machines than this second-hand for $50. Is the hassle worth it?

To get full benefits from FreeBSD, you should be running the X Window system. This uses more memory. Consider 16 MB a usable minimum here, though thanks to FreeBSD's virtual memory system, this is not such a hard limit as it is with some other systems.

The speed of a virtual memory based system such as FreeBSD depends at least as much on memory performance as on processor performance. If you have, say, a 486DX-33 and 8 MB of memory, upgrading memory to 16 MB will probably buy you more performance than upgrading the motherboard to a Pentium 100 and keeping the 8 MB memory. This applies for a usual mix of programs, in particular, programs that don't perform number crunching.

Consider the following the minimum for getting useful work done with FreeBSD and X:

- PC with 80486DX/2-66, or Alpha-based machine

- 16 MB memory (i386) or 32 MB (Alpha).

- SVGA display board with 2 MB memory, 1024x768

- Mouse

- 200 MB free disk space

Figure 2-2: Recommended small FreeBSD and X11 system

Your mileage may vary. During the review phase of this book, one of the reviewers pointed out that he was very happy with his machine, which has a 486-33 processor, 16 MB main memory, and 1 MB memory on his display board. He says that it runs a lot faster than his Pentium 100 at work, which runs Microsoft. If your hardware doesn't measure up to the recommended specification, don't be discouraged: try it out anyway.

Beyond this minimum, FreeBSD supports a large number of other hardware components. FreeBSD is a 32 bit operating system, and it cannot use the 16 bit drivers commonly supplied with PC extension boards. If FreeBSD doesn't know about the board, you probably won't be able to use it.

Compaq/Digital Alpha machines

Since version 3.0, FreeBSD supports computers based on the Compaq (previously Digital) *AXP* processor, commonly called *Alpha*. FreeBSD requires the same *SRM* console firmware as Digital UNIX. It will not work with the ARC firmware used with Microsoft NT. The SRM firmware runs the machine in 64 bit mode, which is required to run FreeBSD, while the *ARC* firmware sets 32 bit mode. If your system is currently running Digital UNIX, then you should be able to use the existing SRM console. You can get firmware updates from *ftp://ftp.digital.com/pub/Digital/Alpha/firmware*. The easiest way to access it is via a web browser at *http://gatekeeper.dec.com/pub/Digital/Alpha/firmware/*. Be careful to transfer in binary mode.

Note that the SRM firmware is board-specific, so take care to choose the correct file that matches your exact system: near enough is not good enough. Unfortunately, some Alpha systems do not support the SRM firmware. You cannot run FreeBSD on these systems.

The SRM console commands differ from one version to another. The commands supported by your version are described in the hardware manual that was shipped with your system. The console `help` command lists all supported console commands. If your system has been set to boot automatically, you must type **Ctrl-C** to interrupt the boot process and get to the SRM console prompt (>>>). If the system is not set to boot automatically, it will display the SRM console prompt after performing system checks.

All SRM console versions support the set and show commands which operate on environment variables that are stored in non-volatile memory. The show command lists all environment variables, including those that are read-only.

Alpha's SRM is picky about which hardware it supports. For example, it recognizes NCR SCSI boards, but it doesn't recognize Adaptec boards. There are reports of some Alphas not booting with particular video boards. The GENERIC kernel configuration (*/usr/src/sys/alpha/conf/GENERIC*) shows what the kernel supports, but that doesn't mean that the SRM supports all the devices. In addition, the SRM support varies from one machine to the next, so there's a danger that what's described here won't work for you.

In the rest of this chapter, we'll look primarily at the i386 architecture. Differences for Alpha include:

- The disk layout for SRM is different from the layout for Microsoft. SRM looks for its bootstrap where Microsoft keeps its partition table. This means that you cannot share a disk between FreeBSD and Microsoft on an Alpha.

- Most SRM-based Alpha machines don't support IDE drives, so you're limited to SCSI.

Laptops

FreeBSD will also run on most laptops; the considerations above apply for laptops as well. The generic kernel does not support all laptops optimally: if you have a laptop, you should check Tatsumi Hosokawa's Mobile Computing page at *http://www.jp.FreeBSD.org/PAO/*.

Drivers

The generic FreeBSD kernel[1] contains support in the form of *drivers* for most common hardware, but some less common drivers have been omitted. If you have a supported product which is not in the generic kernel, you have two options:

- You may be able to use a *Kernel Loadable Module* (*kld*). A kld is a kernel component which can be loaded (and in some cases unloaded) while the kernel is running.

- If no kld exists for your product, you will need to build a special kernel—we'll look at what this entails in Chapter 18, *Configuring the kernel*.

Table 2-3 shows the hardware which the i386 generic kernel supports. New hardware support is being added all the time, so this table can't be definitive. Look in the file */stand/help/hardware.hlp.gz*, from which this table was derived, or, even better, in the configuration file */usr/src/sys/i386/conf/LINT* or */usr/src/sys/alpha/conf/LINT* for authoritative information for your release of FreeBSD.

---

1. The *kernel* is the core program of the operating system, and is resident in memory at all times. To start the operating system, you load the kernel into memory and run it.

Table 2-3. Hardware supported by FreeBSD

Device	Port	IRQ	DRQ	IOMem	Description
fdc0	3f0	6	2		Floppy disk controller
wdc0	1f0	14			IDE/MFM/RLL disk controller
wdc1	170	15			IDE/MFM/RLL disk controller
ncr0					NCR PCI SCSI controller
bt0	330	•	•	•	Buslogic SCSI controller
uha0	330	•	6	•	Ultrastore 14f
aha0	330	•	5	•	Adaptec 154x SCSI controller
ahb0	•	•	•	•	Adaptec 174x SCSI controller
ahc0	•	•	•	•	Adaptec 274x/284x/294x SCSI controller
amd0					Tekram DC-390(T) / AMD 53c974 PCI SCSI
aic0	340	11	•	•	Adaptec 152x/AIC-6360 SCSI controller
nca0	1f88	10	•	•	ProAudioSpectrum cards
sea0	•	5	•	c8000	Seagate ST01/02 8 bit controller
wt0	300	5	1	•	Wangtek and Archive QIC-02/QIC-36
mse0	23c	5			Microsoft Bus Mouse
psm0	60	12			PS/2 Mouse (disabled by default)
mcd0	300	10			Mitsumi CD-ROM
matcd0	230				Matsushita/Panasonic CD-ROM
scd0	230				Sony CD-ROM
sio0	3f8	4			Serial Port 0 (COM1)
sio1	2f8	3			Serial Port 1 (COM2)
lpt0	•	7			Printer Port 0
lpt1	•	•			Printer Port 1
de0					DEC DC21x40 PCI based cards (including 21140 100bT cards)
ed0	280	5	•	d8000	WD & SMC 80xx; Novell NE1000 & NE2000; 3Com 3C503; HP PC Lan+
ed1	300	5	•	d8000	Same as ed0
eg0	310	5	•	•	3Com 3C505
ep0	300	10	•	•	3Com 3C509
ex0	•	•	•		Intel EtherExpress Pro/10 cards
fe0	300	•			Allied-Telesis AT1700, RE2000 and Fujitsu FMV-180 series cards.
fxp0	•	•		•	Intel EtherExpress Pro/100B
ie0	360	7	•	d0000	AT&T StarLAN 10 and EN100; 3Com 3C507; NI5210
ix0	300	10	•	d0000	Intel EtherExpress cards
le0	300	5	•	d0000	Digital Equipment EtherWorks 2 and EtherWorks 3
lnc0	280	10		•	Lance/PCnet cards (Isolan, Novell NE2100, NE32-VL)
vx0	•	•		•	3Com 3c59x / 3c9xx

Device	Port	IRQ	DRQ	IOMem	Description
ze0	300	5		d8000	IBM/National Semiconductor PCMCIA Ethernet Controller
zp0	300	10		d8000	3Com 3c589 Etherlink III PCMCIA Ethernet Controller

The device name in this table is the name by which the device is known to the kernel. It usually corresponds to a name in the */dev* directory, but network interfaces such as Ethernet boards do not have device nodes. See Chapter 13, *File systems* for some other exceptions.

If a field is marked with a bullet (•), the driver is capable of determining the board settings by itself. If the field is empty, this board does not use this particular feature at all. In addition to these controllers, the source distribution contains drivers for a number of other controllers, as shown in the following table. There are a number of reasons for not including these drivers in the generic kernel: they may still be experimental, or they take up too much space in the kernel, or they may conflict with other devices. When configuring a driver for a kernel build, you need to specify the addresses, so I have not included any information here. See the discussion of the *LINT* configuration in Chapter 18, *Configuring the kernel*, page 321, for further details.

Table 2-4. Additional drivers supplied in source

Driver name	Description
ctx	Cortex-I frame grabber
cx	Cronyx/Sigma multiport sync/async
cy	Cyclades high-speed serial driver
el	3Com 3C501
fea	DEV DEFEA EISA FDDI adater
fpa	DEC DEFPA PCI FDDI adapter
gp	National Instruments AT-GPIB and AT-GPIB/TNT board
gsc	Genius GS-4500 hand scanner
gus	Gravis Ultrasound - Ultrasound, Ultrasound 16, Ultrasound MAX
gusxvi	Gravis Ultrasound 16-bit PCM
joy	Joystick
labpc	National Instrument's Lab-PC and Lab-PC+
meteor	Matrox Meteor frame-grabber card
mpu	Roland MPU-401 stand-alone card
mse	Logitech & ATI InPort bus mouse ports
mss	Microsoft Sound System
nic	Dr Neuhaus NICCY 3008, 3009 & 5000 ISDN cards
opl	Yamaha OPL-2 and OPL-3 FM - SB, SB Pro, SB 16, ProAudioSpectrum
pas	ProAudioSpectrum PCM and MIDI
pca	PCM audio (*/dev/audio*) through your PC speaker

Driver name	Description
psm	PS/2 mouse port
rc	RISCom/8 multiport card
sb	SoundBlaster PCM - SoundBlaster, SB Pro, SB16, ProAudioSpectrum
sbmidi	SoundBlaster 16 MIDI interface
sbxvi	SoundBlaster 16
spigot	Creative Labs Video Spigot video-acquisition board
uart	Stand-alone 6850 UART for MIDI
wds	Western Digital WD7000 IDE

Supported hardware—Alpha architecture

FreeBSD/alpha supports the following alpha platforms:

UDB, Multia, AXPpci33, Noname
EB164, PC164, PC164LX, PC164SX
EB64+, Aspen Alpine, etc.
AlphaStation 200, 250, 255, 400
AlphaStation 500, 600
Digital Personal Workstation 433, 500, 600
DEC3000/300 family (netboot only)
DEC3000/[4-9]00 family (netboot only)

You need the SRM console firmware for your platform. In some cases, it is possible to switch between AlphaBIOS (or ARC) firmware and SRM. In others it will be necessary to download new firmware from *ftp.digital.com/pub/DEC/Alpha/firmware*

You need a dedicated disk for FreeBSD/alpha. Currently FreeBSD can't share a disk with another operating system. This disk must be attached to a SCSI controller which is supported by the SRM firmware (currently NCR or SYMBIOS and Qlogic ISP).

The CD-ROM distribution

Walnut Creek CDROM distributes FreeBSD 3.2 on four CD-ROMs:

1. The *Installation Boot CD, packages, X11* CD-ROM. It contains everything you need to install the system itself.

2. The *Live filesystem, CVS Repository, web pages* CD-ROM.

3. The *Packages/ports* CD-ROM.

4. The *Distribution tarballs and packages (overflow)* CD-ROM.

All are mastered in ISO 9660 with Rock Ridge extensions (see page 235 for an explanation of these terms). We'll look at them in the following sections.

CD-ROM 1: Installation

The Installation CD-ROM contains everything you need to install FreeBSD on your system. It supplies two categories of installable software:

- System software is stored as *gzip*ped *tar* archives in the directories *bin, catpages, compat1x, compat20, compat21, des, dict, doc, games, info, manpages* and *proflibs*. To facilitate transport to and installation from floppy, the archives have been divided into chunks of 240,640 bytes. For example, the only required set is in the files *bin/bin.aa* to *bin/bin.cx*.

- The directory *packages/All* contains ported, installable software packages as *gzip*ped *tar* archives. They are designed to be installed directly on a running system, so they have not been divided into chunks. Due to size restrictions on the CD-ROM, this directory does not contain all the packages: some of them are on the fourth CD-ROM.

  packages/All contains well over 1000 packages. To make it easier for you to find your way around them, symbolic links to appropriate packages have been placed in the directories *archivers, astro, audio, benchmarks, cad, chinese, comms, converters, databases, devel, editors, emulators, games, german, graphics, japanese, korean, lang, mail, math, mbone, misc, net, news, perl5, plan9, print, russian, security, shells, sysutils, tcl75, tcl76, tcl80, textproc, tk41, tk42, tk80, vietnamese* and *www*. Don't get the impression that these are different packages—they are really pointers to the packages in *All*. You will find a list of the currently available packages in the file */usr/ports/INDEX*.

Table 2-5 lists the files in the main directory of the installation CD-ROM.

Table 2-5. The installation CD-ROM

File	Contents
00_index.txt	A description of some of the files on the CD-ROM.
ABOUT.TXT	A brief description of FreeBSD.
ERRATA.TXT	A list of last-minute changes. **Read this file. It can save you a lot of headaches**.
HARDWARE.TXT	A list of supported hardware.
INSTALL.TXT	Information about installing FreeBSD.
LAYOUT.TXT	A description of the CD-ROM layout.
README.TXT	The traditional first file to read. It describes how to use the other files.
RELNOTES.TXT	Release notes.
TRANS.TBL	Translation table for Rock Ridge, of no interest to anybody else.
TROUBLE.TXT	Information on what to do if you run into trouble.
UPGRADE.TXT	Notes on upgrading from older versions of FreeBSD.

File	Contents
XF86333	Directory containing the XFree86 3.3.3 distribution. The release number may change in future releases of FreeBSD.
bin	Installation directory: the binary distribution of the system. This is the only required directory for installation. See Chapter 5, *Installing Free-BSD*, for more detail.
book	Information relating to this book, including the complete text in ASCII.
catpages	Pre-formatted man pages. See page 13 for more detail.
cdrom.cfg	Machine-readable file describing the CD-ROM contents for the benefit of Microsoft programs.
cdrom.inf	Machine-readable file describing the CD-ROM contents for the benefit of Microsoft programs.
commerce	Commercial and shareware software for FreeBSD. Some of these packages are demos, others are supplied with restricted licenses. Read the file *README* in each subdirectory for more information.
compat1x	Directory containing libraries to maintain compatibility with version 1.X of FreeBSD.
compat20	Directory containing libraries to maintain compatibility with version 2.0 of FreeBSD.
compat21	Directory containing libraries to maintain compatibility with version 2.1 of FreeBSD.
des	Encryption software. Until recently, this software could be distributed only in the USA and Canada.
dict	Installation directory: dictionaries.
doc	Installation directory: documentation.
filename.txt	A list of all the files on this CD-ROM.
floppies	A directory containing installation floppy disk images.
games	Installation directory: games.
info	Installation directory: GNU info documents.
kernel	The boot kernel.
makeflp.bat	A Microsoft *.BAT* file for copying floppy images to floppy.
manpages	A directory containing the man pages for installation.
packages	A directory containing installable versions of the Ports Collection. See page 112.

File	Contents
ports	The sources for the Ports Collection. See Chapter 8, *The Ports Collection*, page 111.
proflibs	A directory containing profiled libraries, useful for identifying performance problems when programming.
setup.exe	An Microsoft install program for installing from a running Microsoft system.
setup.hlp	Help file for *setup.exe*.
src	A directory containing the system source files.
tools	A directory containing Microsoft tools to prepare for installation.
utils	More Microsoft utilities.
view.exe	An Microsoft based CD-ROM browser program. See page 64.
view.pif	*.PIF* file for *view.exe*.
xperimnt	A number of packages which are under development and were not ready for integration into FreeBSD at the time of release.

CD-ROM 2: Live File System, CVS Repository, web pages

Although the installation CD-ROM contains everything you need to install FreeBSD, the format isn't what you'd like to handle every day. The second CD-ROM in the distribution, the *Live File System* CD-ROM, solves this problem: it contains substantially the same data stored in file system format in much the same way as you would install it on a hard disk. You can access the files directly from this CD-ROM.

The second disk also contains the "CVS Repository". The repository is the master source tree of all source code, including all update information. We'll look at it in more detail in Chapter 19, *Keeping up to date with FreeBSD*, page 365. This disk also contains a snapshot of the Web pages at *www.FreeBSD.org* (directory *www*).

CD-ROMs 3 and 4: The Ports Collection

An important part of FreeBSD is the *Ports Collection*, which comprises over 2000 popular programs. The Ports Collection automates the process of porting software to FreeBSD. A combination of various programming tools already available in the base FreeBSD installation allows you to simply type *make* for a given package. The ports mechanism does the rest, so you need only enough disk space to build the ports you want. We'll look at the Ports Collection in more detail in Chapter 8. The files are spread over 3 CD-ROMs:

- You'll find the *ports*, the instructions for building the packages, on CD-ROM 1.

- The base sources for the Ports Collection fill more than one CD-ROM, even though we were not able to include all sources due to copyright restrictions: some source files are freely distributable on the net, but may not be distributed on CD-ROM. Of the rest, most are on CD-ROM 3, with an overflow into CD-ROM 4.

  Don't worry about the missing sources: if you're connected to the Internet, the Ports Collection will automatically retrieve the sources from an Internet server when you type *make*.

- The *packages*, the precompiled binaries of the ports, are spread between CD-ROM 1, which includes the most popular ones, and CD-ROM 4.

PC hardware

In this section, we'll look at the information you need to understand in order to install FreeBSD on the i386 architecture. In particular, we'll look at the following topics:

- How FreeBSD supports hardware, and what to do if your hardware doesn't correspond to the system's expectations.

- How FreeBSD and other PC operating systems handle disk space, and how to set up your disk for FreeBSD, starting on page 31.

- How to share your disk with another operating system, starting on page 39.

Some of this information also applies to the Alpha architecture. In particular, though, an installation on an Alpha machine is a dedicated installation: you can't share it with other operating systems.

How the system detects hardware

When the system starts, each driver in the kernel examines the system to find any hardware which it might be able to control. This examination is called *probing*. Depending on the driver, the probe may be clever enough to recognize its hardware no matter how it has been set up, or it may expect the hardware to be set up in a specific manner in order to find it. If the driver only looks at specific settings, you have three possibilities:

- You can set the board to match what the driver expects, typically by setting jumpers or using a vendor supplied diagnostic program to set on-board configuration memory.

- You can use *UserConfig* to tell the addresses to the driver when booting the system. UserConfig is a part of the kernel which allows interactive modification of the system configuration at boot time—we'll look at it in more detail in Chapter 5, *Installing FreeBSD*, on page 191.

- You can build a kernel to use the current board parameters.

There are four main parameters that you may need to set for PC controller boards:

1. The *port address* is the address of the first of possibly several control registers which the driver uses to communicate with the board. It is normally specified in hexadecimal, for example 0x320.

   > If you come from a Microsoft background, you might be more comfortable with the notation 320H. The notation 0x320 comes from the C programming language. You'll see a lot of it in UNIX.

   Each board needs its own address or range of addresses. The ISA architecture does not supply many addresses, and one of the most frequent causes of problems when installing a board is that the port addresses overlap with those of another board.

   Beware of boards with a large number of registers. Typical port addresses end in (hexadecimal) 0. Don't rely on being able to take any unoccupied address ending in 0, though: some boards, such as Novell NE2000 compatible Ethernet boards, occupy up to 32 registers—in our example, from 0x320 to 0x33f. Note also that a number of addresses, such as the serial and parallel ports, often end in 8.

2. Boards use an *Interrupt Request*, also referred to as *IRQ*, to get the attention of the driver when a specific event happens. For example, when a serial interface reads a character, it will generate an interrupt to tell the driver to collect the character. Interrupt requests can sometimes be shared, depending on the driver and the hardware. There are even fewer interrupt requests than port addresses: a total of 15, of which a number are reserved by the motherboard. You can usually expect to be able to use IRQs 3, 4, 5, 7, 9, 10, 11, 12, 14 and 15, though some motherboards use IRQ 15 for power saving hardware. IRQ 2 is special: due to the design of the original IBM PC/AT, it is the same thing as IRQ 9. FreeBSD refers to this interrupt as IRQ 9.

3. Some high-speed devices perform *Direct Memory Access*, also known as *DMA*, to transfer data to or from memory without CPU intervention. In order to transfer data, they assert a *DMA Request* (DRQ) and wait for the bus to reply with a *DMA Acknowledge* (DACK). The combination of DRQ and DACK is sometimes called a *DMA Channel*. The ISA architecture supplies 7 DMA channels, numbered 0 to 3 (8 bit) and and 5 to 7 (16 bit). The floppy driver uses DMA channel 2. DMA channels may not be shared.

4. Finally, controllers may have on-board memory which is usually located at addresses between 0xa0000 and 0xefffff. This is sometimes referred to as *I/O memory* or *IOmem*.

Disks

A number of different disks are used on current PCs:

- *ST-506* disks are the oldest. You can tell them by the fact that they have two cables: a *control cable* which usually has connections for two disks, and a thinner *data cable* which is not shared with any other disk. They're just about completely obsolete by now, but FreeBSD still supports them with the *wd* driver. These disks are sometimes called by their modulation format, *Modified Frequency Modulation* or *MFM*. A variant of MFM which offers about 50% more storage is *RLL* or *Run Length Limited* modulation.

- *ESDI* (*Enhanced Small Device Interface*) disks were designed to work around some of the limitations of ST-506 drives. They also use the same cabling as ST-506, but they are not hardware compatible, though most ESDI controllers understand ST-506 commands. They are now also obsolete, but the *wd* driver supports them, too.

- *IDE* (*Integrated Device Electronics*), now frequently called *ATA* (*AT Attachment*), is the current low-cost PC disk interface. The disks (still a maximum of 2) are connected by a single 40-conductor flat cable. From a software viewpoint, they are upwards compatible with the ST-506 drives. Most modern disks are so-called *EIDE* (*Enhanced IDE*) drives. The original IDE disks are were limited by the BIOS standard to a size of 504 MB (1024 * 16 * 63 * 512, or 528,482,304 bytes). EIDE drives exceed this limit, but to do so they play funny games to hide the fact from Microsoft. FreeBSD 3.2 uses a new driver for all IDE disks.

  A problem with older IDE controllers was that they used *programmed I/O* or *PIO* to perform the transfer. In this mode, the CPU is directly involved in the transfer to or from the disk. Older controllers transferred a byte at a time, but more modern controllers can transfer in units of 32 bits. Either way, disk transfers use a large amount of CPU time with programmed I/O, and it's difficult to achieve the transfer rates of modern IDE drives, which can be as high as 10 MB/s. During such transfers, the system appears to be unbearably slow: it "grinds to a halt".

  To solve this problem, modern chipsets offer DMA transfers, which almost completely eliminate CPU overhead. FreeBSD supports DMA with most modern chipsets. If your chipset supports DMA, you should enable it. See page 342 for details of how to do this.

  Another factor influencing IDE performance is the fact that an IDE controller can only perform one transfer at a time. If you have two disks on a controller, and you want to access both, the controller serializes the requests so that a request to one drive completes before the other started. This results in worse performance than on a SCSI chain, which does not have this restriction. If you have two disks and two controllers, it's better to put one disk on each controller.

- *SCSI* is the *Small Computer Systems Interface*. It is used for disks, tapes, CD-ROMs and also other devices such as scanners and printers. The SCSI controller is more correctly called a *host adapter*. SCSI devices are connected by a single flat cable, usually with 50 conductors, which connects a total of 8 devices, including at least one host adapter. A newer standard, Wide SCSI, supports up to 16 devices and has a wider cable. Some SCSI devices have subdevices, for example CD-ROM changers.

  SCSI drives have a reputation for much higher performance than IDE. This is mainly due to the fact that nearly all SCSI host adapters support DMA, whereas in the past IDE controllers usually used programmed I/O. In addition, SCSI host adapters can perform transfers from multiple units at the same time, whereas IDE controllers can only perform one transfer at a time. Typical SCSI drives are still faster than IDE drives, but the difference is nowhere near as large as it used to be.

On the Alpha architecture, only SCSI drives are completely supported. It should be possible to use IDE drives as well once the system is running, but you can't boot from them.

Before you install FreeBSD, you need to decide how you want to use the disk space available to you. If desired, FreeBSD will coexist with other operating systems. In this section, we'll look at the way data is laid out on disk, and what we need to do to create FreeBSD file systems on disk.

PC BIOS and disks

The basics of disk drives are relatively straightforward: data is stored on one or more rotating disks with a magnetic coating similar in function to the coating on an audio tape. Unlike a tape, however, disk heads do not touch the surface: the rotating disk produces an air pressure against the head which keeps it floating very close to the surface. The disk transfers data to and from the disk via (usually) one *read/write head* for each surface. People frequently talk about the number of heads, not the number of surfaces, though strictly speaking this is incorrect: if there are two heads per surface (to speed up access), you're still interested in the number of surfaces, not the number of heads.

While transferring data, the heads are stationary, so data is written on disks in a number of circular *tracks*. Logically, each track is divided into a number of *sectors*, which nowadays almost invariably contain 512 bytes. A single positioning mechanism moves the heads from one track to another, so at any one time all the tracks under the current head position can be accessed without repositioning. This group of tracks is called a *cylinder*.

To access older drives, such as ST-506 (MFM and RLL) drives, you needed to tell the drive which cylinder, head and sector to address. This mode of addressing is thus called *CHS* addressing. Even today, BIOS setup routines give you the option of specifying information about disk drives in terms of the numbers of cylinders, heads and sectors, and some insist on it. In fact, modern disk drives no longer have a fixed number of sectors per track, and they address blocks sequentially, so-called *Logical Block Addressing* or *LBA*. CHS addressing has an additional problem: the ST-506 hardware definition allows up to 1024 cylinders, 16 heads, and 63 sectors, which limits the addressibility of the drive to 504 MB.

SCSI drives are a different matter: the BIOS doesn't know anything about them. They are always addressed as a sequential list of sectors. It's up to the host adapter (or, in the case of dumb host adapters such as the Seagate ST02, the driver software) to interrogate the drive and find out how much space is on it. Typically, the host adapter will have a BIOS which interrogates the drive and finds its dimensions. The values it determines may not be correct: the Microsoft 1 GB address limit (see page 40) might bite you. Check your controller documentation for details.

Logical and physical disk drives

The PC world makes a distinction between *logical disk drives* and *physical disk drives*. Physical disks are easy enough to understand, of course, but the term *logical drive* needs some explanation. It refers to a subdivision of a physical disk to which you can refer as if it were a disk by itself.

Microsoft divides a disk into up to four *partitions*, headed by a *partition table*. FreeBSD uses the term *partition* differently, as we will see, so it refers to Microsoft's partitions as *slices*.

This double usage of the word *partition* is really confusing. In this book, I follow BSD usage, but I will continue to refer to the partition table by that name.

Partitioning offers the flexibility that other operating systems need, so it has been adopted by all operating systems that run on the PC platform. Figure 2-6 shows a disk with all four slices

Master Boot Record
Partition Table
Partition (slice) 1 */dev/da0s1*
Partition (slice) 2 */dev/da0s2*
Partition (slice) 3 */dev/da0s3*
Partition (slice) 4 */dev/da0s4*

Figure 2-6: Partition table

allocated. The *Partition Table* is the most important data structure. It contains information about the size, location and type of the slices (Microsoft partitions). In Microsoft, one of these slices may be designated as *active*: at system startup time, its bootstrap record will be used to start the system.

Although it is not as important as the partition table, the *Master Boot Record* (*MBR*) is located at the very beginning of the disk to make it easier for the system BIOS to find it at boot time. It contains code necessary to find the correct slice from which to boot, so normally you need it only on the first disk in the system. The MBR and the partition table take up the first sector on disk.

Microsoft designates one slice as the *primary Microsoft partition*, the C: drive. Another slice may be designated as an *extended Microsoft partition*, which contains the other "drives" (all together in one slice).

UNIX systems have their own form of partitioning, which predates Microsoft and is not compatible with the Microsoft method. As a result, all versions of PC UNIX which can coexist with Microsoft implement their own partitioning within a single slice (Microsoft partition). BSD systems define up to 8 partitions per slice. They can be used for the following purposes:

- A partition can be a *file system*, a structure in which UNIX stores files.

- It can be used as a *swap partition*. FreeBSD uses virtual memory: the total addressed memory in the system can exceed the size of physical memory, so we need space on disk to store memory pages which don't fit into physical memory.

- The partition may not be within the slice at all: it may refer to other parts of the physical disk. In this case, it will probably overlap other partitions, and you can't use it for file systems or swap space. For obvious reasons, the partitions which represent file systems and swap space (a, b, and d through h) should not overlap.

In order to understand the naming, you need to understand how UNIX treats disks. As we have seen, you can think of a disk as a large number of sequential blocks of data. Looking at it like this doesn't give you a file system—it's more like treating it as a tape. UNIX calls this kind of access *raw* access. You'll also hear the term *character device*.

Normally, of course, you want files on your disk: you don't care where they are, you just want to be able to open them and manipulate them. This involves a whole lot more work than raw devices. The standard term for disks is *block device*. You can recognize block and character devices in an `ls -l` listing by the letters b and c at the beginning of the permissions. For example:

```
$ ls -l /dev/rwd0s1a   /dev/wd0s1a
crw-r-----  1 root   operator    3, 131072 Oct 31 19:59 /dev/rwd0s1a
brw-r-----  1 root   operator    0, 131072 Oct 31 19:59 /dev/wd0s1a
```

Let's look more carefully at how BSD names its partitions:

- Like all other devices, the device entries are stored in the directory */dev*.

- If the partition is raw (character), the name starts with the letter r. If it isn't, there is no prefix.

- Next comes the name of the driver. As we have seen, FreeBSD has drivers for IDE and friends (wd), SCSI disks (da) and floppy disks (fd). With our first SCSI disks, we now have the names */dev/rda* and */dev/da*.

   The abbreviation wd arose because the most popular of the original MFM controllers were made by Western Digital. Others claim, however, that it's an abbreviation for "Winchester Disk". The name da comes from the CAM standard and is short for *direct access*.

- Next comes the unit number, generally a single digit. For example, the first SCSI disk on the system would normally be called */dev/da0*.

   Generally, the numbers are assigned during the boot probes, but you can reserve numbers for SCSI disks if you want. This prevents the absence of a single disk from changing the numbers of all subsequent drives. See page 344 for more details.

   This gives us the names */dev/rda0* and */dev/da0*.

- Next comes the partition information. The so-called *strict slice name* is specified by adding the letter s (for *slice*) and the slice number (1 to 4) to the disk name. BSD systems name partitions by appending the letters a to h to the disk name. Thus, the first partition of the first slice of our disk above (which would typically be a root file system) would be called */dev/rda0s1a* and */dev/da0s1a*. Partition c is an exception: by convention, it represents the whole BSD disk (in this case, the slice in which FreeBSD resides).

Other versions of BSD use a more relaxed terminology for the partition name: they omit the slice information. Instead of calling the root file system */dev/da0s1a*, they refer to it as */dev/da0a*. FreeBSD supports this method as well—it's called *compatibility slice naming*, and it's the form you'll see most frequently.

Table 2-7 gives you an overview of the devices which FreeBSD defines for a single physical disk */dev/da0*:

Table 2-7. Disk partition terminology

Slice name	Usage
/dev/rda0	Whole disk, raw access
/dev/rda0s1	First slice (Microsoft "partition"), raw access
/dev/rda0s1a	First slice (Microsoft "partition"), partition a, raw access
/dev/rda0s1b	First slice (Microsoft "partition"), partition b, raw access
/dev/rda0s1d	First slice (Microsoft "partition"), partition d, raw access
/dev/rda0s1e	First slice (Microsoft "partition"), partition e, raw access
/dev/rda0s1f	First slice (Microsoft "partition"), partition f, raw access
/dev/rda0s1g	First slice (Microsoft "partition"), partition g, raw access
/dev/rda0s1h	First slice (Microsoft "partition"), partition h, raw access
/dev/rda0s2	Second slice (Microsoft "partition"), raw access
/dev/rda0s3	Third slice (Microsoft "partition"), raw access
/dev/rda0s4	Fourth slice (Microsoft "partition"), raw access
/dev/rda0s5	First drive in extended Microsoft partition, raw access
/dev/rda0s6	Second drive in extended Microsoft partition, raw access
/dev/rda0s7	Third drive in extended Microsoft partition, raw access
/dev/rda0a	First partition of BSD slice, usually root file system, raw access
/dev/rda0b	Second partition of BSD slice, usually swap space, raw access
/dev/rda0c	Whole BSD slice, raw access
/dev/rda0d	Additional file system, raw access
/dev/rda0e	*/usr* file system, raw access
/dev/rda0f	Additional file system, raw access
/dev/rda0g	Additional file system, raw access
/dev/rda0h	Additional file system, raw access
/dev/da0s1	First slice (Microsoft "partition")
/dev/da0s1a	First slice (Microsoft "partition"), partition a
/dev/da0s1b	First slice (Microsoft "partition"), partition b
/dev/da0s1d	First slice (Microsoft "partition"), partition d
/dev/da0s1e	First slice (Microsoft "partition"), partition e
/dev/da0s1f	First slice (Microsoft "partition"), partition f
/dev/da0s1g	First slice (Microsoft "partition"), partition g
/dev/da0s1h	First slice (Microsoft "partition"), partition h
/dev/da0s2	Second slice (Microsoft "partition")
/dev/da0s3	Third slice (Microsoft "partition")
/dev/da0s4	Fourth slice (Microsoft "partition")

Slice name	Usage
/dev/da0s5	First drive in extended Microsoft partition
/dev/da0s6	Second drive in extended Microsoft partition
/dev/da0s7	Third drive in extended Microsoft partition
/dev/da0a	First partition of BSD slice, usually root file system
/dev/da0b	Second partition of BSD slice, usually swap space
/dev/da0c	Whole BSD slice
/dev/da0d	Additional file system
/dev/da0e	*/usr* file system
/dev/da0f	Additional file system
/dev/da0g	Additional file system
/dev/da0h	Additional file system

In the interests of space, I haven't included the names of possible FreeBSD partitions in slices 1, 2, and 3.

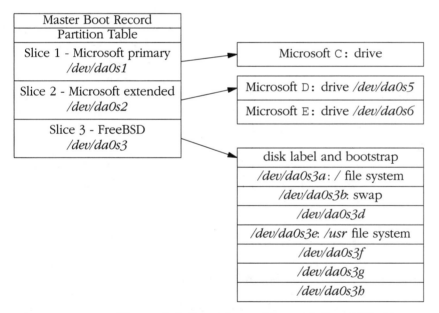

Figure 2-8: Partition table with FreeBSD file system

Figure 2-8 shows a typical layout on a system with a single SCSI disk, shared between Microsoft and FreeBSD. You'll note that partition */dev/da0s3c* is missing from the FreeBSD slice, since it isn't a real partition. Like the Microsoft partition table, the disk label contains information necessary for FreeBSD to manage the FreeBSD slice, such as the location and the lengths of the individual partitions. The bootstrap is needed to load the kernel into memory. If you install the FreeBSD boot manager, it uses the slice which was active at the time of installation, even when booting from other slices. This is not the only way things could have been done, but it makes life easier, since the size of the MBR is limited. If you remove FreeBSD from your system, you will need to either replace the MBR or to create a dummy FreeBSD slice with a bootstrap record only.

> If you need to replace the MBR, and you no longer have FreeBSD installed, you can use the MS-DOS *FDISK* command to do this:

```
C: FDISK /MBR
```

This command doesn't change the partition table: it only writes the Master Boot Record.

Making the file systems

Armed with this knowledge, we can now proceed to make some decisions about how to install our systems. First, we need to answer a number of questions:

* Do we want to share this disk with any other operating system?

* If so, do we have data on this disk which we want to keep?

If you already have another system installed on the disk, it is best to use that system's tools for manipulating the partition table. FreeBSD does not normally have difficulty with partition tables created by other systems, so you can be reasonably sure that the other system will understand what it has left. If the other system is Microsoft, and you have a slice which you don't need, you use the MS-DOS *FDISK* program to free up enough space for you to install FreeBSD. If you don't have a slice to delete, you can use the *FIPS* program to create one—see Chapter 5, *Installing FreeBSD*, page 91.

If for some reason you can't use MS-DOS *FDISK*, for example because you're installing FreeBSD by itself, FreeBSD also supplies a program called *fdisk* which manipulates the partition table. Normally you will invoke it indirectly via the *sysinstall* program—see page 72.

Using a boot manager

If you choose to share your disk between FreeBSD and another operating system, you need to make an additional decision every time you boot the machine: which operating system do you want to run? FreeBSD helps you make this decision with *booteasy*, a so-called *Boot Manager*, which is installed in the Master Boot Record. If you install *booteasy*, it will prompt you for the system to install every time you boot the system, for example:

```
F1  .  .  .  BSD
F2  .  .  .  DOS
F5  .  .  .  Disk 2

Default: F1
```

When you boot the system, it records what slice you booted from, and offers it as a default the next time you boot—in this case, it suggests **F1** for FreeBSD. If you don't respond within 10 seconds, it will accept this default automatically and boot the system accordingly.

If you're only running one system on the disk, the boot manager will still work, but it just holds you up. When you come to specify the choice of MBR, you should specify a standard MBR, which will just boot from the currently active slice. See Chapter 5, *Installing FreeBSD*, page 74, for further details.

Interaction with Microsoft

If you're coming from a Microsoft or a similar operational environment, you might find things strange at first. In particular, you'll probably want to share programs and data between the two systems. You can do this if you have an i386 architecture machine, but not with the Alpha. In the following sections, we'll examine what you can and can't do.

Sharing a disk with Microsoft

If you wish, you can install both Microsoft and FreeBSD on the same disk, subject to space constraints. We will go into great depth about how to do this in Chapter 6, *Shared OS Installation*, page 91.

Using compressed MS-DOS file systems from FreeBSD

If you are using a utility such as *Stacker™* or *DoubleSpace™*, FreeBSD will only be able to use whatever portion of the file system you leave uncompressed. The rest of the file system will show up as one large file with a funny name. Don't let this confuse you: this file is *not* superfluous, it's everything you have.

Your best choice here is to leave one Microsoft partition uncompressed and use it for communications between Microsoft and FreeBSD.

Running Microsoft binaries under FreeBSD

FreeBSD has very limited support for running Microsoft binaries. Work is in progress, but at the moment only two packages are available, both in the Ports Collection:

- *pcemu* runs under the X Window System and emulates an 8088 and enough BIOS services to run MS-DOS text mode applications.

- *WINE* (*Windows Emulator*) can run some Windows applications. It's still more experimental than usable.

Disk size limitations

Disk storage capacity has grown by an order of magnitude in the last few years. As it did so, a number of limits became apparent:

- The first was the BIOS *504 MB limit* on IDE disks, imposed by their similarity with ST-506 disks, and discussed on page 32. Microsoft and other vendors work around this problem in much the same way as FreeBSD: after starting, they load their own driver and disable the BIOS, so they can address disks up to (normally) 8 GB with no problems. The only problem is booting: you must boot from the first 504 MB. If your BIOS has this limitation, you will not be able to boot FreeBSD reliably from a root file system on an IDE if it goes beyond this limit. See below for one solution.

- The next limit was the 1 GB limit, which affected some older SCSI host adapters. Although SCSI drives always use LBA addressing internally, the BIOS needed to simulate CHS addressing for Microsoft. Early BIOSes were limited to 64 heads, 32 sectors and 1024 tracks ($64 \times 32 \times 1024 \times 512 = 1$ GB). This wouldn't be such a problem, except that modern Adaptec controllers offer a 1 GB compatibility option. Don't use it: it's only needed for systems which were installed with the old mapping.

- After that, it's logical that the next limit should come at 2 GB. There are several different problems here. The only one which affects FreeBSD appears to be a bug in some IDE controllers, which don't work beyond this limit. All of these are old, and IDE controllers don't cost anything, so if you are sure you have this problem, you can solve it by replacing the controller. In the process, make sure you get one which supports DMA.

  Other systems, including UNIX System V, have problems with this limit because 2^{31} is the largest number which can be represented in a 32 bit signed integer. FreeBSD does not have this limitation, since file sizes are represented in 64 bit quantities.

- At 4 GB, some IDE controllers have problems because they convert this to a CHS mapping with 256 heads, which doesn't work: the largest number is 255. Again, if you're sure this is the cause of problems you may be having, a new controller can help.

- Finally, at 8 GB, the CHS system runs out of steam. It can't describe more than 1024 cylinders, 255 heads or 63 sectors. Beyond this size, you must use LBA addressing—if your BIOS supports it.

Most of these problems don't affect FreeBSD directly, but FreeBSD uses the system BIOS to load the first bootstrap, so it is bound by the restrictions of the BIOS and the controller. If you have the choice, use LBA addressing. Unfortunately, you can't do so if the disk already contains software which uses CHS addressing.

What do you do if you have an old-style BIOS with the 504 MB limit, a 2 GB IDE disk and you want to allocate 1.3 GB for Microsoft and 700 MB for FreeBSD? Clearly, whichever way round you put the slices, you can't get them both in the first 504 MB. In this case, you should allocate a reasonably sized primary partition for Microsoft, for example 400 MB, then your FreeBSD slice, then a Microsoft extended partition for the remaining 900 MB, as shown in figure 2-9.

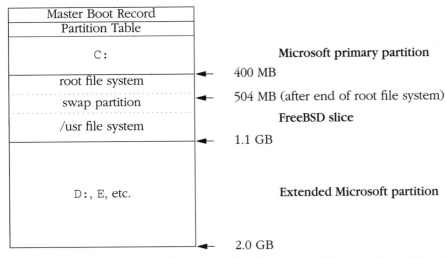

Figure 2-9: Sharing a disk between Microsoft and FreeBSD

Make particularly sure that the *end* of the root partition falls within the first 504 MB. There is no way to ensure that the kernel and bootstrap will be at the beginning of the partition.

Other things to consider are:

- If you have other software already installed on the disk, and you want to keep it, ***do not change the drive geometry***. If you do so, you will no longer be able to run the other software.

- Use LBA addressing if your hardware supports it.

- If you have to use CHS, and you don't have any other software on the drive, use the drive geometry specified on the disk itself or in the manual, if you're lucky enough to get a manual with the disk. Many BIOSes remap the drive geometry in order to get Microsoft to agree to work with the disk, but this can break FreeBSD disk mapping. Check that the partition editor has these values, and change them if necessary.

- If all else fails, install Microsoft in a small slice at the start of the disk. This will create a valid partition table for the drive, and the installation software will understand it. Once you have started the installation process, the Microsoft partition has fulfilled its purpose, and you can delete it again.

3

FreeBSD version 3

FreeBSD version 3.0 was released in September 1998. It represents the biggest change in FreeBSD since the code base was moved to 4.4BSD. A number of new features have been introduced, and upgrading will be a little more complicated than is normally the case. If you're upgrading from release 2 of FreeBSD, you may want to read this chapter before installing.

In this chapter, we'll look at the following new features:

- FreeBSD now supports the Compaq/Digital Equipment *AXP* or *ALPHA* processor. We looked at the supported configurations on page 22, and we'll consider the installation requirements on page 88.

- On the Intel architecture, FreeBSD now supports multiple processors. We'll look at that in the next section.

- A new SCSI driver, *CAM*, has been introduced. This requires some modifications to the kernel configuration, and the device names have changed. We'll look at that on page 44.

- The IDE driver now supports DMA. If your motherboard also supports DMA, you will definitely want to enable it. See page 45 for more details.

- A new console driver has been introduced. Again, this requires some modifications to the kernel configuration. We'll look at it on page 46.

- *Loadable kernel modules*, described on page 384, are being phased out. Support for them is still there, but they are being replaced by *kernel loadable modules* (*kld*s). Does this sound like word play? Well, there's a solid technical background: you can tell the bootstrap to load *kld*s along with the kernel. We'll look at them on page 46.

- A new, more flexible bootstrap (the program that loads the kernel) has been written. The commands are slightly different. We'll look at that on page 47.

- The default object file format has changed from *a.out* to *ELF*. FreeBSD has supported the ELF format for some time, primarily in order to emulate Linux. Now executable FreeBSD binaries also use this format. We'll look at the implications on page 48.

Multiple processor support

FreeBSD version 3 can support most current Intel multiprocessor motherboards. Documentation on SMP support is currently rather scanty, but you can find some information at *http://www.freebsd.org/˜fsmp/SMP/SMP.html*.

The default kernel does not support SMP, so you will need to build a new kernel before you can use more than one processor. To build an SMP kernel, check the comments in the file */sys/i386/conf/LINT*, which contains:

```
# SMP OPTIONS:
#
# SMP enables building of a Symmetric MultiProcessor Kernel.
# APIC_IO enables the use of the IO APIC for Symmetric I/O.
# NCPU sets the number of CPUs, defaults to 2.
# NBUS sets the number of busses, defaults to 4.
# NAPIC sets the number of IO APICs on the motherboard, defaults to 1.
# NINTR sets the total number of INTs provided by the motherboard.
#
# Notes:
#
#  An SMP kernel will ONLY run on an Intel MP spec. qualified motherboard.
#
#  Be sure to disable 'cpu "I386_CPU"' && 'cpu "I486_CPU"' for SMP kernels.
#
#  Check the 'Rogue SMP hardware' section to see if additional options
#   are required by your hardware.
#

# Mandatory:
options         SMP                 # Symmetric MultiProcessor Kernel
options         APIC_IO                 # Symmetric (APIC) I/O

# Optional, these are the defaults plus 1:
options         NCPU=5              # number of CPUs
options         NBUS=5              # number of busses
options         NAPIC=2             # number of IO APICs
options         NINTR=25        # number of INTs
```

See Chapter 18, *Configuring the kernel* for information on how to build a new kernel.

The CAM SCSI driver

FreeBSD 3.0 includes a new SCSI driver, which is based on the ANSI ratified *Common Access Method* or *CAM* specification which defines a software interface for talking to SCSI and ATAPI devices. The FreeBSD driver is not completely CAM compliant, but it follows many of the precepts of CAM. More importantly, it addresses many of the shortcomings of the previous SCSI layer and should provide better performance, reliability, and ease the task of adding support for new controllers.

For most users, the most obvious difference between the old SCSI driver and CAM is the way they named SCSI devices. In the old driver, disks were called *sdn*, and tapes were called *stn*, where *n* was a small positive number. The CAM driver calls disks *dan* (for *direct access*), and tapes are called *san* (for *serial access*). Part of the upgrade procedure will create these new device names, though they are not strictly necessary: the CAM driver uses the same major numbers and the same device encoding scheme for the minor numbers as the old driver did, so */dev/sd0a* and */dev/da0a* are, in fact, the same device. Nevertheless, if you don't create the new device names, you may have some subtle problems.

On the other hand, a number of older SCSI host adaptors are currently not supported. They include:

Tekram DC390 and DC390T controllers, and maybe other boards based on the AMD 53c974 as well.

NCR5380/NCR53400 ("ProAudio Spectrum") SCSI controller.

UltraStor 14F, 24F and 34F SCSI controllers.

Seagate ST01/02 SCSI controllers.

Future Domain 8xx/950 series SCSI controllers.

WD7000 SCSI controller.

Adaptec 1510 series ISA SCSI controllers
Adaptec 152x series ISA SCSI controllers
Adaptec AIC-6260 and AIC-6360 based boards, which includes the AHA-152x and SoundBlaster SCSI boards.

There is work in progress to port the AIC-6260/6360 and UltraStor drivers to the new CAM SCSI framework, but no estimates on when or if they will be completed.

In addition, a new program, *camcontrol*, enables you to administrate the SCSI chain at a more detailed level then previously: for example, it is now possible to add devices to a chain after the system has started. See the man page for more details.

DMA support for IDE disks

Most modern motherboards include IDE (*integrated device electronics*) controllers for up to four disks, and for several years they have supported *direct memory access* or *DMA*, a means of transfer which allows the controller to transfer a complete block of data without CPU intervention. FreeBSD version 2 did not support DMA: a disk transfer required the processor to perform the transfer. DMA brings a very significant performance improvement with it, so if your hardware supports it, you should enable it.

The new console driver

The system console driver, *syscons*, has been rewritten. For most people, there won't be a significant difference. If you're upgrading from FreeBSD version 2, and you have built your own kernel, you'll need to update your kernel configuration file. The following definitions are needed if you are using then *syscons* driver:

```
controller    atkbdc0 at isa? port IO_KBD tty
device        atkbd0  at isa? tty irq 1
#device       psm0    at isa? tty irq 12
device        vga0    at isa? port ? conflicts
device        sc0     at isa? tty

pseudo-device  splash
```

You need `splash` if you intend to use screen savers or splash screen.

If you use *pcvt*, your new configuration will look like this:

```
controller    atkbdc0 at isa? port IO_KBD tty
device        atkbd0  at isa? tty irq 1
#device       psm0    at isa? tty irq 12
device        vt0     at isa? tty
```

The following options for syscons are replaced by new ones:

SC_ALT_SEQACCESS becomesVGA_ALT_SEQACCESS.
SLOW_VGA becomes VGA_SLOW_IOACCESS.

The following flags for syscons are no longer available:

0x08   Force detection of keyboard.
0x10   Old-style (XT) keyboard support.
0x20   Don't reset keyboard.

Instead, use the new *atkbd* flags:

0x01   Don't install the keyboard driver if no keyboard is found. If this flag is not set, always assume a keyboard.
0x02   Don't reset keyboard.
0x04   XT keyboard support.

Kernel loadable modules

Older versions of FreeBSD supplied *Loadable Kernel Modules* or *LKMs*, object files which could be loaded and executed in the kernel while the kernel was running. We discussed them in passing on page 384.

The ELF kernel and the new bootstrap of FreeBSD version 3 allow you to load additional modules at boot time. To do so, however, the format of the modules needed to be changed.

To avoid (too much) confusion, the name changed from *loadable kernel module* to *kernel loadable module (kld)*. FreeBSD still supports LKMs as well, so klds are stored in a different directory and loaded and unloaded by different programs:

Table 3-1. Differences between LKMs and klds

Parameter	LKM	kld
Directory	*/lkm*	*/modules*
Load program	*modload*	*kldload*
Unload program	*modunload*	*kldunload*
List program	*modstat kldstat*	

Some other details have changed as well. *kldload* knows an internal path for finding *kld*s, so you don't need to specify the path. It also assumes that the name of the *kld* ends in *.ko*, and you don't need to specify that either. For example, to load the Linux emulator as an LKM, you entered:

```
# modload /lkm/linux_mod.o
```

To load the *kld*, you enter:

```
# kldload linux
```

The new bootstrap

As we saw above, the *ELF* kernel requires a new bootstrap. We saw how to install it in the upgrade instructions on page 49. There's no change in the way you boot the system normally: you just wait, and it starts. If you want to do special things, though, the details change.

In the following example, we manually load the kernel and a *kld* module at startup.

```
BTX loader 1.00  BTX version is 1.00
BIOS drive A: is disk0
BIOS drive C: is disk1

FreeBSD/i386 bootstrap loader, Revision 0.2  640/64512kB
(grog@bumble.example.org, Sun Jan 31 16:25:12 CST 1999)
/                         this is a "twirling baton"
Hit [Enter] to boot immediately, or any other key for command prompt.
Booting [kernel] in 6 seconds...    this counts down from 10 seconds

Type '?' for a list of commands, 'help' for more detailed help.
disk1s1a:> ?
Available commands:
  reboot              reboot the system
  heap                show heap usage
  bcachestat          get disk block cache stats
  boot                boot a file or loaded kernel
  autoboot            boot automatically after a delay
  help                detailed help
  ?                   list commands
```

```
   show              show variable(s)
   set               set a variable
   unset             unset a variable
   lsdev             list all devices
   include           read commands from a file
   ls                list files
   load              load a kernel or module
   unload            unload all modules
   lsmod             list loaded modules
   pnpscan           scan for PnP devices
disk1s1a:> load kernel               get the kernel into memory
/kernel text=0x14c395 data=0x180d8+0x22ec4 syms=[0x4+0x1e3c0+0x4+0x210f8]
disk1s1a:> load Vinum                and the kld Vinum
/modules/Vinum.ko text=0x1854d data=0x35c+0x9ada8 syms=[0x4+0x13b0+0x4+0xca7]
disk1s1a:> boot -c -s                then start the kernel
/kernel text=0x1b0b72 data=0x1d148+0x1f840 syms=[0x4+0x22570+0x4+0x24809]
/kernel text=0x1b0b72 data=0x1d148+0x1f840 syms=[0x4+0x22570+0x4+0x24809]
Copyright (c) 1992-1999 FreeBSD Inc.
Copyright (c) 1982, 1986, 1989, 1991, 1993
       The Regents of the University of California. All rights reserved.
FreeBSD 3.1-RELEASE #0: Wed Feb  17 13:06:56 CST 1999
(etc)
```

For a complete discussion of the boot sequence, see page 194.

Boot floppies

Computer hardware is changing, and *finally* floppies are going away; instead, modern computers boot from CD-ROM. If yours doesn't, you can still boot from floppy, but in FreeBSD 3.2 the boot image (the data needed to put on the floppy) no longer fits on a single 1.44 MB floppy. The *boot.flp* image still exists, but you will need a 2.88 MB floppy or an LS-120 drive in order to use it. If you still need to boot from a 1.44MB disk, you will need two floppies. Copy *kern.flp* to the first and *msfroot.flp* to the other. Boot from the first floppy (the one containing the *kern.flp* image). After loading the kernel, the system will print the message:

```
Please insert MFS root floppy and press enter:
```

After you replace the floppy and press enter, the boot procedure carries on as before.

The ELF object format

When UNIX was written, the world was simple. The kernel of the Third edition of UNIX, in January 1973, had a little over 7000 lines of code in total. The object format was correspondingly simple: it was named after the name of the output from the assembler, *a.out*.

In the course of time, binaries required additional features, in particular the ability to link to dynamic libraries. UNIX System V introduced a new object file format, *COFF*, but BSD remained with *a.out* and used some rather dirty tricks to link to dynamic libraries. The change to *ELF* enabled a much cleaner interface.

FreeBSD 3.0 uses *ELF* as the default executable format, but the Intel port will still execute *a.out* binaries. The Alpha port does not support *a.out* at all, since it was created at a time where it would not have made sense.

Converting the source tree to ELF

If you build your own FreeBSD versions, things are a little more complicated. Perform the following steps:

- Ensure that you have a suitable release of FreeBSD. It is possible to perform the transition with some version 2 releases of FreeBSD, but it's a moving target, and nobody has checked exactly which versions will work and which will not. One thing is certain: your kernel *must* be able to run ELF binaries, otherwise you'll find yourself unable to run any programs after installing the new software.

  If your kernel does understand ELF (most of the more recent versions do), you have two choices: try it out and hope for the best, or install a basic version of FreeBSD 3.0 and use that to upgrade the rest of the system. In the rest of this section, we'll assume that, one way or another, you have a suitable version of FreeBSD.

- Upgrade your source tree (see Chapter 18, *Configuring the kernel*) to the latest version.

- Build the `aout-to-elf` target:

  ```
  # make aout-to-elf 2>&1 | tee Make.log
  ```

  It's a good idea to save the output to a file so that you can look at it if anything goes wrong. You can also split the build into two parts:

  ```
  # make aout-to-elf-build 2>&1 | tee Make.log      build the system
  # make aout-to-elf-install 2>&1 | tee Make.log    install it
  ```

  During the course of the build, the upgrade procedure will request input several times. On each occasion, you may continue or abort the upgrade by entering **Ctrl-C**.

  At the end, the upgrade procedure creates a file */etc/objformat* with the following content:

  ```
  OBJFORMAT=elf
  ```

  From this point on, all executables will be built in ELF format by default.

    You can still create and execute *a.out* format files if you have a need: build them with

    ```
    $ make -DOBJFORMAT=aout
    ```

- Update the boot blocks. You can boot an old kernel with the new boot blocks; you can't boot the new kernel with the old boot blocks. Do this with:

  ```
  # disklabel -B wd0      for IDE drives
  # disklabel -B da0      for SCSI drives
  ```

- Build a new kernel. That's not as straightforward as it seems: your old kernel configuration file will no longer work. We'll look at it in the next section.

Building a new kernel

The kernel configuration file has changed significantly since FreeBSD version 2. If you are using the GENERIC kernel, you need do nothing: just use the new version of the */usr/src/sys/i386/conf/GENERIC* to build a new kernel. If you have a custom configuration, things are more difficult: You need to make modifications to your old configuration file before you can use it.

One way to make this job easier is to use *diff* to compare your configuration file with the *old* GENERIC configuration file:

```
$ cd /usr/src/sys/i386/conf
$ diff -wu GENERIC MYCONFIG
```

This will give an output something like the following, a so-called *unified context diff*. It's a good idea to print out the diffs, because you'll need to compare them to both the new-style *GENERIC* configuration file and the new-style *LINT* configuration file.

The differences between the files are marked on a per-line basis. Lines starting with @@ refer to the line numbers in the old file and the new file. For example, @@ -21,9 +20,14 @@ means "9 lines from the old file, starting at line 21, compared to 14 lines from the new file, starting at line 20". Lines starting with - are lines present in the old file, but not in the new; lines starting with + are lines present in the new file, but not in the old.

```
--- GENERIC      Sun Feb  7 13:19:54 1999
+++ MYCONFIG     Sun Feb  7 13:19:53 1999
@@ -1,14 +1,13 @@
 #
-# GENERIC -- Generic machine with WD/AHx/NCR/BTx family disks
+# MYCONFIG: Config for bumble.example.org
 #

 machine          "i386"
 cpu          "I386_CPU"
 cpu          "I486_CPU"
 cpu          "I586_CPU"
-cpu          "I686_CPU"
```

Since this config file was written, support for Pentium II class machines was added

```
-ident           GENERIC
-maxusers 32
+ident           MYCONFIG
+maxusers 100
```

Note the increase in MAXUSERS *here. You'll need to keep this.*

```
 options         MATH_EMULATE        #Support for x87 emulation
 options         INET                #InterNETworking
@@ -21,9 +20,14 @@
 options         SCSI_DELAY=15       #Be pessimistic about Joe SCSI device
 options         BOUNCE_BUFFERS      #include support for DMA bounce buffers
 options         UCONSOLE            #Allow users to grab the console
-options         FAILSAFE            #Be conservative
-options         USERCONFIG          #boot -c editor
-options         VISUAL_USERCONFIG   #visual boot -c editor
```

The three options above were added since this config file was written.

```
+options         SYSVSHM              # Include System V shared memory emulation
+options         SYSVSEM              # and the other two ugly sisters
+options         SYSVMSG
+options         USER_LDT             # for wine
+options         KTRACE               # allow kernel tracing
+options         DDB                  # and kernel debugger
+options         DDB_UNATTENDED
+options         BREAK_TO_DEBUGGER
```

The values above are additions made to this specific configuration file. Do they need to be added to the new configuration file? That depends on whether they still exist. A number of options have been eliminated, and others have come into existence. To find out which options still exist, look at */usr/src/sys/i386/conf/LINT*, which contains all the options available. In this case, however, all the options still exist, so we should copy them to the new configuration file.

```
  config          kernel     root on wd0

@@ -36,28 +40,26 @@
  disk      fd1  at fdc0 drive 1
  tape      ft0  at fdc0 drive 2

-options          "CMD640"  # work around CMD640 chip deficiency
-controller       wdc0 at isa? port "IO_WD1" bio irq 14 vector wdintr
+controller       wdc0 at isa? port "IO_WD1" bio irq 14 flags 0x80ff80ff vector wdintr
```

Here we have a modification to the controller parameters for multi-block I/O. You might think that it's sufficient to make a corresponding modification in the new config file, but in fact you'll probably want to enable DMA (see page 45), so you would change this line to:

```
controller wdc0 at isa? port "IO_WD1" bio irq 14 flags 0xa0ffa0ff vector wdintr
```

Continuing,

```
  disk      wd0  at wdc0 drive 0
-disk       wd1  at wdc0 drive 1
+# disk         wd1  at wdc0 drive 1

-controller       wdc1 at isa? port "IO_WD2" bio irq 15 vector wdintr
-disk       wd2  at wdc1 drive 0
-disk       wd3  at wdc1 drive 1
-
-options          ATAPI        #Enable ATAPI support for IDE bus
-options          ATAPI_STATIC    #Don't do it as an LKM
-device           wcd0         #IDE CD-ROM
-device           wfd0         #IDE floppy (LS-120)
+# controller    wdc1 at isa? port "IO_WD2" bio irq 15 vector wdintr
+# disk          wd2  at wdc1 drive 0
+# disk          wd3  at wdc1 drive 1
+
+# options          ATAPI      #Enable ATAPI support for IDE bus
+# device           wcd0       #IDE CD-ROM
```

In the section above, the custom configuration file has commented out the slave disk on the primary IDE controller, and the second IDE controller in its entirety. You'll want to include these changes as well.

```
@@ -73,6 +75,9 @@
 device         cd0    #Only need one of these, the code dynamically grows

+options        SCSIDEBUG
+options        SCSI_REPORT_GEOMETRY
```

Here we have two SCSI options. You'd think that you'd want to copy them, too, but in fact the SCSI_DEBUG option no longer exists. SCSI_REPORT_GEOMETRY does, so you can copy that.

```
-pseudo-device  ppp  1
+pseudo-device  ppp  2
-pseudo-device  vn   1
 pseudo-device  tun  1
-pseudo-device  pty  16
+pseudo-device  pty  64
 pseudo-device  gzip          # Exec gzipped a.out's
+pseudo-device  bpfilter  16  # Berkeley packet filter
+pseudo-device  snoop 4       # snoop around
```

Here we have some modified counts: the custom configuration file includes two *ppp* interfaces instead of one, and 64 *ptys* instead of 16. You'll need to change that in your new file. *vn* wasn't in the custom file; you'll need to add that. In addition, we have 16 *bpfilters* and 4 *snoop* devices.

```
-# KTRACE enables the system-call tracing facility ktrace(2).
-# This adds 4 KB bloat to your kernel, and slightly increases
-# the costs of each syscall.
-options        KTRACE         #kernel tracing
```

Wait a minute, didn't we have KTRACE above? Yes, we did. It was added to the custom file before it was added to *GENERIC*, and they ended up in different places. This doesn't mean that you won't have to add KTRACE after all, since you're going to be using a different *GENERIC* file as a starting point.

```
+# Need a Vnode driver to do a 'make release'
+pseudo-device  vn            # Vnode driver (turns a file into a device)
```

Here we have the opposite scenario: the *vn* driver has also found its way into *GENERIC*, but it was above. Again, this doesn't mean very much.

```
-# This provides support for System V shared memory.
-#
-options        SYSVSHM
+# PS/2
+device         psm0 at isa? port "IO_KBD" conflicts tty irq 12 vector psmintr
```

Finally, we have one of the System V options which we had in the *MYCONFIG* file, but not the other two, and a PS/2 mouse, which will need to be added as well.

At this point, you should have a list of modifications you will need to make:

- Change the name from GENERIC to MYCONFIG (or, more likely, the name of the machine).

- Add the options SYSVSHM, SYSVSEM, SYSVMSG, USER_LDT, KTRACE. DDB, DDB_UNAT-TENDED, and BREAK_TO_DEBUGGER.

- Change the definition of the primary IDE controller to

  ```
  controller wdc0 at isa? port "IO_WD1" bio irq 14 flags 0xa0ffa0ff vector wdintr
  ```

- Comment out the primary slave and the secondary IDE disks, and the secondary IDE controller.

- Add the option SCSI_REPORT_GEOMETRY.

- Increase the number of *ppp* interfaces to 2.

- Increase the number of *pty*s to 64

- Add 16 *bpfilter*s.

- Add 4 *snoop*s.

- Add a *vn* pseudodevice.

- Add the *psm0* device.

The next step is to rename *MYKERNEL*, say to *MYKERNEL.old*, and make a copy of */sys/i386/conf/GENERICupgrade* and call it *MYKERNEL*. Then check if any of these modifications have already been made. It turns out, for example, that KTRACE is in *GENERICupdate*, but *vn* isn't. *psm0* is now also included, so you don't need anything there either, apart from confirming that the definition is the same.

As you can see, this is not easy stuff, and it's easy to make a mistake. If you include an option that no longer exists, for example SCSI_DEBUG, you will get a warning message from *config*. It won't do much harm: the system no longer knows about it, so it will be ignored. In some cases, though, obsolete options have been replaced by new, possibly finer-grained ones. In this case you should check */usr/src/sys/i386/conf/LINT* for comments describing new options.

The rest of the process is as before. See page 361 for more details.

What happened to my libraries?

Old-style *a.out* systems kept dynamic libraries in a number of locations: */usr/lib* contained the system libraries, */usr/lib/compat* contained "compatibility libraries" for older versions of BSD, */usr/local/lib* contained the ports libraries, and */usr/X11R6/lib* contained the X11 libraries.

ELF and *a.out* executables need different libraries, each with their own format, but frequently with the same name. For example, the system now knows the following versions of the standard C library, which is required by every program:

- *libc.a* is a static library used for including the library routines into the program at link time.

- *libc_p.a* is a static library containing profiled versions of the library routines for inclusion into the program at link time.

- *libc_pic.a* is a static library containing position-independent versions of the library routines for inclusion into the program at link time.

- *libc_r.a* is a static library containing reentrant versions of the library routines for inclusion into the program at link time.

- *libc.so* is a symbolic link to the current version of a dynamic library for linking at run time. This link is only used for ELF programs.

- *libc.so.3* is a version of an ELF dynamic library for linking at run time. The number *3* changes with the release.

- *libc.so.3.1* is a version of an *a.out* dynamic library for linking at run time. The number *3.1* changes with the release.

Don't worry if these names don't make much sense to you; unless you're writing programs, all you need to know is that an ELF system uses */usr/lib/libc.so* at run time.

/usr/lib contains a large number of libraries. It would be possible, but messy, to find an alternative arrangement for the name conflicts, and leave the rest of the names unchanged. Instead, the conversion process moves all *a.out* libraries to a subdirectory *aout*, so an *a.out* executable now looks for */usr/lib/aout/libc.so.3.0*. An ELF executable looks for */usr/lib/libc.so.3*.

But how does the system know to look in a different place? It uses a *hints file* generated by the *ldconfig* program. When the system starts, it takes a list of directory names from */etc/rc.conf* and runs *ldconfig* to search the directories for *a.out* libraries and to generate the hints file. In version 2 of FreeBSD, the standard */etc/rc.conf* contained the following definition:

```
ldconfig_paths="/usr/lib/compat /usr/X11R6/lib /usr/local/lib" # search paths
```

In version 3.0, this has changed to:

```
ldconfig_paths="/usr/lib/compat /usr/X11R6/lib /usr/local/lib"
                # shared library search paths
ldconfig_paths_aout="/usr/lib/compat/aout /usr/X11R6/lib/aout /usr/local/lib/aout"
                # a.out shared library search paths
```

Part of the upgrade process changes this entry in */etc/rc.conf*, so there should be no problem with normal libraries. A couple of problems may still occur, however:

- Some programs refer to library names which are symbolic links. The upgrade process doesn't always handle symbolic links correctly, so you may find that the link points to the wrong place. For example, you might have this in a 2.2.7 system */usr/lib/compat*:

```
/usr/lib/compat:
total 1
-r--r--r--  1 root  wheel  8417 Jan 21 18:37 libgnumalloc.so.2.0
-r--r--r--  1 root  wheel  8398 Jan 21 18:37 libresolv.so.2.0
lrwxr-xr-x  1 root  wheel    31 Jan 21 18:36 libtermcap.so.3.0 -> /usr/lib/libtermc
ap.so.2.1
lrwxr-xr-x  1 root  wheel    31 Jan 21 18:36 libtermlib.so.3.0 -> /usr/lib/libterml
ib.so.2.1
-r--r--r--  1 root  wheel  8437 Jan 21 18:37 liby.so.2.0
```

After updating, you could end up with this:

```
/usr/lib/compat/aout:
total 1
-r--r--r--  1 root   wheel   8417 Jan 21 18:37 libgnumalloc.so.2.0
-r--r--r--  1 root   wheel   8398 Jan 21 18:37 libresolv.so.2.0
lrwxr-xr-x  1 root   wheel     31 Jan 21 18:36 libtermcap.so.3.0 -> /usr/lib/libtermc
ap.so.2.1
lrwxr-xr-x  1 root   wheel     31 Jan 21 18:36 libtermlib.so.3.0 -> /usr/lib/libterml
ib.so.2.1
-r--r--r--  1 root   wheel   8437 Jan 21 18:37 liby.so.2.0
```

In other words, the libraries have been moved, but the symbolic links are absolute and still point to the old place. The system doesn't install absolute symbolic links, so it doesn't make any attempt to correct them. You need to fix the problem manually. In this example, we replace the symbolic links with relative symbolic links:

```
# cd /usr/lib/compat/aout
# rm libtermcap.so.3.0
# ln -s libtermcap.so.2.1 libtermcap.so.3.0
# rm libtermlib.so.3.0
# ln -s libtermlib.so.2.1 libtermlib.so.3.0
```

- If you have modified your */etc/rc.conf* significantly, the update may fail, and your *a.out* hints file will still point to the old locations. In this case edit */etc/rc.conf* as shown above.

```
# cd /usr/X11R6/lib
# mkdir aout
# cp -p lib* aout
```

The Ports Collection and ELF

The transition to ELF has had a profound effect on the Ports Collection. The ports are being upgraded to ELF, but it's a big job, and it hasn't been completed yet. You can tell these ports by the entry BROKEN_ELF in the *Makefile*. For example, in */usr/ports/chinese/pine3/Makefile* you may find:

```
BROKEN_ELF=    does not build ELF libs
```

If you try to build this port on an ELF system, you will get the text as an error message:

```
# make install
===>  zh-pine-3.96 is broken for ELF: does not build ELF libs.
```

This doesn't mean you can't build the port: you just need to tell *make* to build it as in *a.out* format:

```
# PORTOBJFORMAT=aout make install
```

Don't count on this working all the time; things are changing, and there will be a few packages which still don't build correctly.

4

Quick Installation

In chapters 5 to 9, we'll go into a lot of detail about how to install the system. Maybe this is too much detail for you. If you're an experienced UNIX user, you should be able to get by with significantly less reading. This chapter presents checklists for some of the more usual kinds of installation. Each of them refer you to the corresponding detailed descriptions in chapters 5 through 9.

On page 59 we'll look at the simplest installation, where FreeBSD is the only system on the disk. Starting on page 60 we'll look at sharing the disk with Microsoft, and on page 60 we'll look at how to install XFree86. You may find it convenient to photocopy these pages and to mark them up as you go along.

Making things easy for yourself

It is probably easier to install FreeBSD than any other PC operating system, including Microsoft products. Well, anyway, most of the time. Some people spend days trying to install FreeBSD, and finally give up. That happens with Microsoft's products as well, but unfortunately it happens more often with FreeBSD.

Now you're probably saying, "That doesn't make sense. First you say it's easier to install, then you say it's more likely to fail. What's the real story?"

As you might expect, the real story is quite involved. In Chapter 2, *Before you install*, I went into some of the background. Before you start, let's look at what you can do to make the installation as easy as possible:

- Use known, established hardware. New hardware products frequently have undocumented problems. You can be sure that they work under Microsoft, because the manufacturer has tested them in that environment. In all probability, he hasn't tested them under any flavour of UNIX, let alone FreeBSD. Usually the problems aren't serious, and the FreeBSD team will solve them pretty quickly, but if you get the hardware before the software is ready, you'll be the guinea pig.

- Perform a standard installation. The easiest way to install FreeBSD is by booting from a floppy disk and installing on an empty hard disk from the CD-ROM. If you proceed as discussed in Chapter 5, *Installing FreeBSD*, you shouldn't have any difficulty.

- If you need to share your hard disk with another operating system, it's easier to install both systems from scratch. If you do already have a Microsoft system on the disk, you can use *FIPS* (see page 91), to make space for it, but this requires more care.

- If you run into trouble, *RTFM*.[1] I've gone to a lot of trouble to anticipate the problems you might encounter, and there's a good chance that you will find something here to help.

- If you do all this, and it still doesn't work, see page 15 for ways of getting external help.

---

1. Hackerspeak for "Read The Manual"—the **F** is usually silent.

FreeBSD alone on the disk

To install FreeBSD from CD-ROM on a disk alone, go through the following steps:

☐ If your BIOS supports direct booting from CD-ROM, boot from CD-ROM. Otherwise,

- Create two boot floppies by copying the images */cdrom/kern.flp* and */cdrom/mfs-root.flp* to 3½" diskettes. Refer to page 65 for more details.

- Insert the CD-ROM in the drive before booting.

- Boot from the *kern.flp* floppy. After loading, insert the *mfsroot.flp* floppy when the system prompts you to do so, then press **Enter**.

    If you have a larger floppy, such as 2.88 MB or LS-120, you can copy the image */cdrom/boot.flp* to it and boot from it. In this case you don't need to change disks.

☐ Select the `Novice` installation, even if you're an experienced UNIX hacker. Refer to page 69.

☐ In the partition editor, delete any existing Microsoft slices, and allocate a single FreeBSD slice which takes up the entire disk. Don't use a true partition entry; you don't need compatibility. Refer to pages 72 and 249.

☐ On exiting from the partition editor, select the *Standard* MBR. Refer to page 74.

☐ In the disk label editor, delete any existing UNIX partitions. If you're not too worried about the exact size of the partitions, select automatically generated disk labels. Refer to page 75.

☐ Alternatively, if you want to specify your file systems yourself, start on the basis of a root file system with 50 MB, a swap partition with 256 MB, and allocate the rest of the space on the disk to the */usr* file system. Refer to page 74.

Note particularly that, if you don't create a */var* file system, as I'm recommending here, you'll need to create a symlink later on.

☐ Choose the distributions you want. Refer to page 79.

☐ Select CD-ROM as installation medium. Refer to page 81.

☐ If you intend to run the X11 windowing system, select the installation now. It's easier than doing it after the system is up and running. Refer to page 121.

☐ Give final confirmation. The system will be installed. Refer to page 83.

☐ After installation, set up at least a user ID for yourself. Refer to page 164.

☐ Do you have a separate */usr* file system and no */var* file system? Then create a directory */usr/var* and make sure that you make */var* point to */usr/var*—see page 87 for further details.

Installing XFree86

As mentioned above, it's much easier to install and configure the XFree86 software during the initial software installation than after you have FreeBSD up and running. If your system is already up and running, however, perform the following steps, which assume the the XFree86 3.3.1 distribution. If you are installing a different distribution, change the name XF86331 accordingly.

☐ Log in as `root`, *cd* to */usr*, and extract all the archives in */cdrom/dists/XF86331* with *tar*. If you're using *sh* or similar, do this with:

```
# cd /usr
# for i in /cdrom/dists/XF86331/X331*.tgz; do
#   tar xzf $i
# done
```

If you're using *csh* or *tcsh*, do it with:

```
% cd /usr
% foreach i (/cdrom/dists/XF86331/X331*.tgz)
%   tar xzf $i
% end
```

☐ Identify the type and memory size of your video board, and the type and serial port name of your mouse.

☐ Select the name of an X server which will work with your video board. Refer to page 123 for further details. Look at the list of servers in table 9-2 on page 123 and create a link between the one you want to use and */usr/X11R6/bin/X*.

☐ Run *xf86config* to create a configuration file. Refer to page 129 for further details.

FreeBSD shared with Microsoft

To install FreeBSD on a disk on which Microsoft is already installed, go through the following steps:

☐ ***Make a backup!*** There's every possibility of erasing your data, and there's absolutely no reason why you should take the risk.

☐ If you have an IDE disk larger than 504 MB, you may run into problems. Refer to page 32 for further details.

If you haven't read the documentation in Chapter 2, consider performing the next couple of steps using *VIEW*, which can show you the on-line documentation and start the programs for you. Refer to page 64 for more information about *VIEW*.

☐ Repartition your disk with *FIPS*. Refer to page 91. You can start *FIPS* directly or via the *VIEW* program.

☐ Insert the CD-ROM in the drive before booting.

☐ Boot the FreeBSD system. If your Microsoft system is configured in a FreeBSD-friendly manner, you can boot directly from Microsoft using the program *INSTALL.BAT* for most CD-ROMs, or *INST_IDE.BAT* for IDE CD-ROM drives. You can also start either of these programs from the *VIEW* program.

☐ If the direct boot doesn't work, it's probably due to your Microsoft configuration. It's not worth trying to reconfigure your Microsoft system to make it work: it's easier to boot from CD-ROM or boot floppy, as described above on page 59 and in more detail on page 65.

☐ Select the `Novice` installation, even if you're an experienced UNIX hacker. Refer to page 69.

☐ In the partition editor, delete *only the second primary Microsoft slice*. The first primary Microsoft partition contains your Microsoft data, and if there is an extended Microsoft partition, it will also contain your Microsoft data. Then create a FreeBSD slice in the space that has been freed. Refer to page 72.

☐ On exiting from the partition editor, select the *BootMgr* MBR. Refer to page 74.

☐ In the disk label editor, select the FreeBSD slice. If you proceeded as above, it should be empty, but if it contains existing UNIX partitions, delete them. If you're not too worried about the exact size of the partitions, select automatically generated disk labels. Refer to page 75.

☐ Before leaving the disk label editor, also select mount points for your DOS partitions if you intend to mount them under FreeBSD. Refer to page 76.

☐ Alternatively, if you want to specify your file systems yourself, start on the basis of a root file system with 50 MB, a swap partition with 256 MB, and allocate the rest of the space on the disk to the */usr* file system. Refer to page 74.

Note particularly that, if you don't create a */var* file system, you'll need to create a symlink later on.

☐ Choose the distributions you want. Refer to page 79.

☐ Select CD-ROM as the installation medium. Refer to page 81.

☐ If you intend to run the X window system, select the installation now. It's much easier than doing it after the system is up and running. Refer to page 121.

☐ Confirm installation. The system will be installed. Refer to page 83.

☐ After installation, set up at least a user ID for yourself. Refer to page 164.

☐ Do you have a separate */usr* file system and no */var* file system? Then create a directory */usr/var* and make sure that you make */var* point to */usr/var*—see page 87 for further details.

5

Installing FreeBSD

So now you're ready to install FreeBSD on your system. In this chapter, we'll look at how to install FreeBSD on a disk by itself. If you run into trouble, I'll refer you back to the page of Chapter 2 which discusses this topic. If you want to install FreeBSD on the same disk as Microsoft or another operating system, move on to Chapter 6, *Shared OS Installation*.

The following discussion relates primarily to installation on the i386 architecture. Support for the AXP ("Alpha") processor is very new, and it will change. The current support is described on page 88.

Installing FreeBSD on the Intel i386 architecture

To install FreeBSD you need the software in a form which the installation software understands. You may also need a boot diskette. The choices you have are, in order of decreasing attractiveness:

- CD-ROM. This is by far the easiest way to install FreeBSD. If your system BIOS supports the *El Torito*[1] CD-ROM boot standard, or you have a running Microsoft system on the machine on which you want to install FreeBSD, you may not even need a boot diskette.

- Over the network. You have the choice of *ftp* or NFS connection. If you're connected to the Internet and you're not in a hurry, you can load directly from one of the distribution sites described in the FreeBSD handbook.

- From a locally mounted disk partition, either FreeBSD (if you have already installed it) or Microsoft.

- From tape in *tar* format. This is slower than CD-ROM, and it requires more space, but once you have the tape, it's just as simple.

- From floppy disk. This is only for masochists or people who really have almost no hardware: depending on the extent of the installation, you will need up to 200 disks, and at least one of them is bound to have an I/O error. And don't forget that a CD-ROM drive

---

1. El Torito is a chain of Tex-Mex restaurants in California and other US states. The story goes that the original concept was hacked out on the back of a serviette one evening after a meal at El Torito.

costs a lot less than 200 floppies.

Booting from CD-ROM

Finally floppy disks are becoming obsolete, and with modern hardware you can perform a FreeBSD installation without even having a floppy drive on your computer: all you need is a CD-ROM drive and a BIOS which understands the *El Torito* standard. If you do, you don't need to do any preparation at all beyond putting the CD-ROM in the drive and setting your BIOS to boot from it. Continue reading on page 68

Preparing a boot floppy

If you can't boot from CD-ROM, you will need two 3½" floppy disks, the *Kernel Disk* and the *MFS Root Disk* to boot the installation programs. The images of these floppies are on the CD-ROM distribution in the files *floppies/kern.flp* and *floppies/mfsroot.flp*. If you have your CD-ROM mounted on a Microsoft system, they will be called *FLOPPIES\KERN.FLP* and *FLOP-PIES\MFSROOT.FLP*. The bootstrap does not recover bad blocks, so the floppy must be 100% readable.

The way you get the boot disk image onto a real floppy depends on the operating system you use. If you are using any flavour of UNIX, just perform something like

```
# dd if=/cdrom/floppies/kern.flp of=/dev/rfd0c bs=36b
```
change the floppy
```
# dd if=/cdrom/floppies/mfsroot.flp of=/dev/rfd0c bs=36b
```

This assumes that your software is on CD-ROM, and that it is mounted on the directory */cdrom*. It also assumes that your floppy drive is called */dev/rfd0c* (this is the FreeBSD name, which is also used by other BSD systems—see page 36 for an overview). If you're using Linux, the device name would be */dev/fd0* or */dev/fd1*.

Some versions of UNIX, particularly older System V variants, may complain about the option `bs=36b`. If this happens, just leave it out. It might take up to 10 minutes to write the floppy, but it will work, and it will make you appreciate FreeBSD all the more.

If you have to create the boot floppy from Microsoft, you have three choices. You can use *VIEW.EXE*, a self-documenting menu-driven utility which is located in the root directory of the CD-ROM, to perform all preparation necessary from Microsoft:

```
C:> E:                    the drive letter of the CD-ROM
E:> VIEW
```

In addition, the CD-ROM distribution includes a program *TOOLS\RAWRITE.EXE* which will copy to floppy. Since the boot floppy image is on *FLOPPIES\BOOT.FLP*, you enter:

```
C:> E:                          the drive letter of the CD-ROM
E:> TOOLS\RAWRITE  FLOPPIES\BOOT.FLP
E:> TOOLS\RAWRITE  FLOPPIES\KERN.FLP
```
change the floppy
```
E:> TOOLS\RAWRITE  FLOPPIES\MFSROOT.FLP
```

This requires just a little more typing, but that's all there is to it. Another alternative is to use the program *MAKEFLP.BAT* supplied with the distribution. This batch file assumes that it is in the parent directory of *TOOLS* and *FLOPPIES* (in our example, the root directory of drive E:). It also formats the floppy before copying the boot disk to it.

Creating floppies for a floppy installation

Installation from floppy disk is definitely the worst choice you have. You will need 14 floppies for the minimum installation, and up to 200 for the complete installation. The chance of one of them being bad is high. Most problems on a floppy install can be traced to bad media, or differences in alignment between the media and the drive in which they are used, so:

> *Before starting, format all floppies in the drive you intend to use, even if they are preformatted.*

The first two floppies you'll need are the Kernel floppy and the MFS Root floppy, which were described in the previous section.

In addition, you will need at minimum as many floppies as it takes to hold all files in the *bin* directory, which contains the binary distribution. The distribution files are split into chunks (currently 52 of them) conveniently sized so that 5 of them will fit on a conventional 5¼" (1.2 MB) floppy, and 6 will fit on a 3½" (1.44 MB) floppy (with a little space left over). For example, the files in the *bin* distribution are:

```
$ ls
00_TRANS.TBL    bin.au      bin.bq      bin.cm      bin.di
CHECKSUM.MD5    bin.av      bin.br      bin.cn      bin.dj
bin.aa          bin.aw      bin.bs      bin.co      bin.dk
bin.ab          bin.ax      bin.bt      bin.cp      bin.dl
bin.ac          bin.ay      bin.bu      bin.cq      bin.dm
bin.ad          bin.az      bin.bv      bin.cr      bin.dn
bin.ae          bin.ba      bin.bw      bin.cs      bin.do
bin.af          bin.bb      bin.bx      bin.ct      bin.dp
bin.ag          bin.bc      bin.by      bin.cu      bin.dq
bin.ah          bin.bd      bin.bz      bin.cv      bin.dr
bin.ai          bin.be      bin.ca      bin.cw      bin.ds
bin.aj          bin.bf      bin.cb      bin.cx      bin.dt
bin.ak          bin.bg      bin.cc      bin.cy      bin.du
bin.al          bin.bh      bin.cd      bin.cz      bin.dv
bin.am          bin.bi      bin.ce      bin.da      bin.dw
bin.an          bin.bj      bin.cf      bin.db      bin.dx
bin.ao          bin.bk      bin.cg      bin.dc      bin.inf
bin.ap          bin.bl      bin.ch      bin.dd      bin.mtree
bin.aq          bin.bm      bin.ci      bin.de      install.sh
bin.ar          bin.bn      bin.cj      bin.df
bin.as          bin.bo      bin.ck      bin.dg
bin.at          bin.bp      bin.cl      bin.dh
```

You'll thus need 9 3½" floppies or 11 5¼" floppies. The floppy set should contain the file *bin.inf* and the ones whose names start with *bin.* followed by two letters. These other files are all 240640 bytes long, except for the final one which is usually shorter. Use the MS-DOS *COPY* program to copy as many files as will fit onto each disk (5 or 6) until you've got all the distributions you want packed up in this fashion. Copy each distribution into subdirectory corresponding to the base name—for example, copy the *bin* distribution to the files *A:\BIN\BIN.INF*, *A:\BIN\BIN.AA* and so on.

Installing via FTP

The fun way to install FreeBSD is via the Internet, but it's not always the best choice. There's a lot of data to transfer, and unless you have a really high-speed, non-overloaded connection to the server, it could take forever. On the other hand, of course, if you have your own private server (like another UNIX machine with the sources on it), and the system on which you want to install FreeBSD doesn't have a CD-ROM drive, these conditions are fulfilled, and this could be for you. Before you decide, though, read about the alternative of NFS installation below: if you don't have an FTP server with the files already installed, it's a lot easier to set up an NFS installation.

There are two FTP installation modes you can use:

- Regular *FTP* mode does not work through most firewalls but will often work best with older *ftp* servers that do not support passive mode. Use this mode if your connection hangs with passive mode.

- If you need to pass through firewalls that do not allow incoming connections, try *passive FTP*.

Whichever mode of installation and whichever remote machine you choose, you need to have access to the remote machine. The easiest and most common way to ensure access is to use anonymous FTP. If you're installing from another FreeBSD machine, read how to install anonymous FTP on page 540. This information is also generally correct for other UNIX systems.

Setting up the ftp server

To set up the ftp server, the system from which you load the software, you must load the software into the public FTP directory. On BSD systems, this will be the home directory of user `ftp`, which in FreeBSD defaults to */usr/ftp*. The name of the directory is the name of the release, which in this example we'll assume to be *3.2-RELEASE*. You can put this directory in a subdirectory of */usr/ftp*, for example */usr/ftp/FreeBSD/3.2-RELEASE*, but the only optional part in this example is the parent directory *FreeBSD*.

This directory has a slightly different structure from the CD-ROM distribution. To set it up, assuming you have your distribution CD-ROM mounted on */cdrom*, and that you are installing in the directory */usr/ftp/FreeBSD/3.2-RELEASE*, perform the following steps:

```
# cd /usr/ftp/FreeBSD/3.2-RELEASE
# mkdir floppies
# cd floppies
# cp /cdrom/floppies/* .            don't omit the . at the end
# cd /cdrom                         the distribution directory on CD-ROM
# tar cf - [b-d]* g* man* po* pr* [s-z]* | (cd /usr/ftp/FreeBSD/3.2-RELEASE; tar xvf -)
```

This copies all the directories of *cdrom* into *usr/ftp/FreeBSD/3.2-RELEASE* except for *packages*, a total of about 180 MB. If you have enough space for the *packages* file as well (about 500 MB more), you can simplify the last line to:

```
# tar cf - . | (cd /usr/ftp/FreeBSD/3.2-RELEASE; tar xvf -)
```

For a minimal installation, you need only the directory *bin*, about 16 MB. To just install *bin* rather than all of the distribution, change the last line of the example above to

```
# mkdir bin
# cp /cdrom/bin/* bin
```

Installing via NFS

If you're installing from a CD-ROM drive on another system in the local network, you will probably find an installation via FTP too complicated for your liking. Installation is a lot easier if the other system supports NFS. Before you start, make sure you have the CD-ROM mounted on the remote machine, and that the remote machine is exporting the file system (in System V terminology, exporting is called *sharing*). When prompted for the name of the directory, specify the name of the directory on which the CD-ROM is mounted. For example, if the CD-ROM is mounted on directory */cdrom* on the system *presto.example.org*, enter **presto.example.org:/cdrom**. That's all there is to it!

> Older versions of FreeBSD stored the distribution on a subdirectory *dists*. Newer versions store it in the root directory of the CD-ROM.

Installing from a Microsoft partition

On the Intel architecture it's also possible to install from a primary Microsoft partition on the first disk. At the moment, it's not possible to install from extended partitions. To prepare for installation from an Microsoft partition, copy the files from the distribution into a directory called *FREEBSD*. For example, to do a minimal installation of FreeBSD from Microsoft using files copied from a CD-ROM mounted on *E:*, you might do something like this:

```
C> MKDIR C:\FREEBSD
C> XCOPY /S E:\BIN C:\FREEBSD\BIN
C> XCOPY /S E:\FLOPPIES C:\FREEBSD\FLOPPIES
```

You need the directory *FLOPPIES* because that's where *sysinstall* looks for the *boot.flp*, the first image in every installation.

The only required directory is *bin.* You can include as many other directories as you want, but be sure to maintain the directory structure. In other words, if you also wanted to install *XF86312* and *manpages*, you would copy them to *C:\FREEBSD\XF86312* and *C:\FREE-BSD\MANPAGES*.

Installing from tape

It's theoretically possible to install FreeBSD from tape, but it probably hasn't been done in the last few years, and it's quite possible that you'll run into trouble. If you're installing from tape, you need a tape written in *tar* format with a block size of 5120 bytes (10 sectors). Don't use *tar*'s default value of 10240 bytes or 20 sectors. Since the install program reads the entire tape onto disk, you will need a **big** disk. As a further restriction, you can install only from the first tape unit in the system.

Installing from a FreeBSD partition

If you already have a copy of the FreeBSD distribution on the disk on which you are installing, you can use this option. Unfortunately, it doesn't work if the partition is on another disk. We're still working on this one—consider it an experimental option.

Booting the install kernel

No matter which installation medium you choose, the first step in installing FreeBSD is to start a minimal version of the operating system. The simplest way is to boot directly from the installation CD-ROM, if your system BIOS supports it. If your system doesn't support this kind of boot, you have the choice of booting directly from CD-ROM floppy or from a running Microsoft system.

In the following sections, we'll look at a real-life installation on a real machine. When you install FreeBSD on your machine, a number of things will be different, depending on the hardware you're running and the way you're installing the software. Nevertheless, you should be able to recognize what is going on.

Booting from CD-ROM

Booting from CD-ROM is mainly a matter of setting up your system BIOS and possibly your SCSI BIOS. Typically, you perform one of the following procedures:

- If you're booting from an IDE CD-ROM, you enter your system BIOS setup routines and set the *Boot sequence* parameter to select CD-ROM booting ahead of hard disk booting, and possibly also ahead of floppy disk booting. A typical sequence might be CDROM,C,A.

- On most machines, if you're booting from a SCSI CD-ROM, you also need a host adapter which supports CD-ROM boot. Set up the system BIOS to boot in the sequence, say, SCSI,A,C. On typical host adapters (such as the Adaptec 2940 series), you set the adapter to enable CD-ROM booting, and set the ID of the boot device to the ID of the CD-ROM drive.

Note that these settings are probably not what you want to use for normal operation. If you leave the settings like this, and there is a bootable CD-ROM in your CD-ROM drive, it always boots from that CD-ROM rather than from the hard disk. After installation, change the parameters back again to boot from hard disk before CD-ROM. See your system documentation for further details.

Booting from floppy

If you are installing from tape or CD-ROM, *put the medium in the drive* before booting. The installation may fail if you boot before inserting the medium.

Boot the system in the normal manner: insert the kernel diskette in */dev/rfd0*, the first floppy drive (which Microsoft calls *A:*), and reset the computer or turn power on. After the PC has gone through its hardware tests, it will boot the FreeBSD install kernel from the floppy.

Installing from a running Microsoft system

If the disk on which you plan to install FreeBSD contains Microsoft, and you're installing from CD-ROM, you can usually boot directly from MS-DOS. This will work whether you plan to overwrite the Microsoft partition, or whether you plan to install to another slice or another disk on the same system. To boot this way, reboot your system in MS-DOS mode, change to the CD-ROM volume (*E:* in this example) and start *INSTALL* or *VIEW*:

```
C> E:          change to CD-ROM
E> cd \        make sure you're in the root directory
E> install     and start the INSTALL program
```

Don't try this from Microsoft Windows—the installation will fail with the message *not enough memory*. The boot will progress in the same way as if you had booted from floppy. The advantage of starting *VIEW* is that you get more documentation: ultimately *VIEW* will start *INSTALL* to boot the system.

INSTALL doesn't always work. It depends on what drivers or TSRs are in your system. There's no reason to try changing your Microsoft configuration to get it to work: it's a lot easier just to boot from floppy, which we looked at on page 64.

The boot process

The boot process itself is very similar to the normal boot process described on page 189. There are a couple of differences:

• At the beginning, you will see the message:

```
/kernel text=0x14c395 data=0x180d8+0x22ec4 syms=[0x4+0x1e3c0+0x4+0x210f8]
Uncompressing kernel...done
Booting the kernel
Copyright (c) 1982, 1986, 1989, 1991, 1993
        The Regents of the University of California.
        All rights reserved.
```

The highlighted line shows that you're loading a compressed kernel, which is necessary when loading from floppy. If the system stops at this point, it probably means that you have memory problems (either not enough memory or defective memory).

- If you're booting from a two-floppy set, the loader will issue the following prompt after loading the kernel:

```
Please insert MFS root floppy and press enter:
```

When you do that, it continues with the probes.

- After the probes (page 194) you always go into the UserConfig menu:

```
Kernel configuration Menu

        Skip kernel configuration and continue with installation
        Start kernel configuration in full-screen visual mode
        Start kernel configuration in CLI mode

Here you have the chance to go into kernel configuration mode, making
any changes which may be necessary to properly adjust the kernel to
match your hardware configuration.

If you are installing FreeBSD for the first time, select Visual Mode
(press Down-Arrow then ENTER).

If you need to do more specialized kernel configuration and are an
experienced FreeBSD user, select CLI mode.

If you are certain that you do not need to configure your kernel
then simply press ENTER or Q now.
```

In order to be able to install the machine, the system must recognize your hardware. But what happens if you want to install via the network and your Ethernet board is set up differently from the way the kernel expects? The driver doesn't notice it, and it won't be until quite some time later that you will find that the installation can't work. That's what *UserConfig* (the kernel configuration editor) is for, and why you get the chance to run it at this point in the installation. See page 191 for an example of how to tell the kernel about your hardware configuration.

If your hardware configuration matches what the generic kernel expects (see page 24), just press **ENTER**. The kernel will continue with the *device probes* (see page 194).

About 30 to 60 seconds after you leave UserConfig, depending on the speed of the machine and the amount of hardware connected to it, the screen will be cleared and you will see the main *sysinstall* menu (in colour, if your system supports it).

Using sysinstall

Figure 5-1 shows the main *sysinstall* menu. *sysinstall* includes on-line help at all stages. Simply press **F1** and you will get appropriate help. Also, if you haven't been here before, the Doc menu gives you a large part of the appropriate information from the handbook.

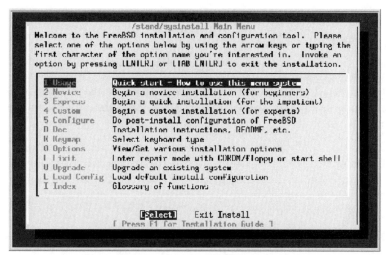

Figure 5-1: Main installation menu

Kinds of installation

To get started, you select one of *Novice*, *Express* or *Custom*. As the names imply, *Novice* installation is intended for people who are new to installing FreeBSD, the *Express* installation is for people in a hurry, and *Custom* installation is for you if you want to specify exactly what is to be done.

There isn't really that much difference between the three forms of installation. In almost every case you will want to perform the same steps:

- Possibly set up options.

- Set up disk partitions, which we'll discuss in the next section.

- Set up file systems and swap space within a FreeBSD slice, which we start on page 74.

- Choose what you want to install, which we discuss on page 79.

- Choose where you want to install it from. We'll look at this on page 81.

- Actually install the software. We'll treat this on page 83.

We looked at disk partitions and file systems on page 33. We'll look at the other points when we get to them.

The Novice and Express installation will take you through these steps in sequence, while the Custom installation will return you to its main menu after each step. It would be confusing to say what happens next after each of the steps, so I won't mention the exact transition each time: it should be obvious what's going on. In practice, you should use the Novice installation, even if you're an experienced UNIX hacker: the term "Novice" applies to the usage of *sysinstall*, not of UNIX.

Creating space on disk

The first step is to set up space for FreeBSD on the disk. We looked at the technical background in Chapter 2, *Before you install*, page 38. In this section, we'll use the term *partition* to refer to a slice or Microsoft partition, since that's the usual terminology, even if it's a little confusing.

Whether or not you need to build or modify a partition table, select *Partition*. The installation routines need to enter this screen in order to read the partition information from the disk. If you like what you see, you can leave again immediately with q (quit), but you must first enter this menu. If you have more than one disk connected to your machine, you will next be asked to choose the drives that you want to use for FreeBSD.

> If you intend to use more than one disk for FreeBSD, you have the choice of setting up all disks now, or setting the others up after the system is up and running. We'll look at the latter option in Chapter 14, *Disks*, on page 243. As you'll see there, it's *much* easier to do it now.

The next screen shows:

```
Disk name:      wd0                          FDISK Partition Editor
BIOS Geometry:  989 cyls/12 heads/35 sectors

      Offset        Size         End      Name     PType    Desc  Subtype    Flags

           0          35          34        -         6   unused       0
          35      414925      414959     wd0s1        2      fat       6      =
      414960         420      415379        -         2   unused       0

The following commands are supported (in upper or lower case):
A = Use Entire Disk    B = Bad Block Scan    C = Create Partition
D = Delete Partition   G = Set BIOS Geometry  S = Set Bootable
U = Undo All Changes   Q = Finish             W = Write Changes

The currently selected partition is displayed in reverse video
Use F1 or ? to get more help, arrow keys to move.
```

Don't use the W *(Write Changes) command here. It's intended for use only once the system is up and running.*

Table 5-2 explains the meanings of the columns in this display. This display shows the current partition table on our Western Digital Caviar 2200 disk drive, one of the smallest disks that you could use to install FreeBSD on. The first partition contains the Master Boot Record, which is exactly one sector long, and the bootstrap, which can be up to 15 sectors long. The partitioning tools use the complete first track: note that the geometry information from BIOS says that it has 35 sectors per track.

In our case, the Microsoft file system uses up the whole disk except for the last track, 420 sectors (210 kB) at the end of the disk. Clearly there's not much left to share. We could shorten the Microsoft partition with *FIPS*—see Chapter 6, *Shared OS Installation*, page 91 if

Table 5-2. fdisk information

Column	description
Offset	the number of the first sector in the partition
Size	the length of the partition in sectors
End	the number of the last sector in the partition
Name	where present, this is the name by which FreeBSD knows the partition. In this example, only the second partition has a name.
Ptype	the partition type. Partition type 6 is the Master Boot Record, which is exactly one track long (note that the header says that this drive has 35 sectors per track). Type 2 is a regular partition.
Subtype Desc	These describe the type of partition numerically and in text. *fat* stands for *File Allocation Table*, which is a central part of the Microsoft disk space allocation strategy. In more general terms, we can say that the first partition is a Microsoft file system.
Flags	can be one or more of the following characters: = The partition is correctly aligned > The partition finishes after cylinder 1024, which can cause problems for Microsoft. A This is the active (bootable) partition. B The partition employs BAD144 bad-spot handling. C This is a FreeBSD compatibility partition. R This partition contains a root file system.

that's what you want to do—but in this example we choose to remove it.

> *Don't forget that if you remove a partition, you lose all the data in it. If the partition contains anything you want to keep, make sure you have a legible backup.*

We remove the partition with the d command. After this, our display looks like:

```
0      415380     415379         -        6    unused        0
```

The next step is to allocate a FreeBSD partition with the C command. We get a menu asking us the size of the partition, with a suggested value of 415380 sectors, the complete size of the disk. We can edit this value if we wish, but in this case it's what we want, so we just press ENTER. Now the display looks like this:

```
   0         35         34        -        6    unused        0
  35     415345     415379    wd0s1       3    freebsd     165  C
```

Although we were offered the complete disk, and we accepted, *fdisk* reserved the complete first track (35 sectors) for the MBR and boot blocks. The new partition uses the rest of the disk, including the last 420 sectors which Microsoft rejected, and it has a partition type 3 (extended partition) and subtype 165 (0xa5), our FreeBSD partition.

All we need to do now is to mark the partition active or bootable, by pressing s. The A flag appears at the end of the partition line:

```
   0         35         34        -        6    unused        0
  35     415345     415379    wd0s1       3    freebsd     165  CA
```

That's all we need to do here: we leave *fdisk* with the q command. Next we are asked what kind of *boot selector* (in other words, *MBR*) we want. We have three choices, as shown in Table 5-3. Since we plan to have only one operating system on this disk, we select Standard. If we were sharing with, say, Microsoft, we could choose *BootMgr* instead.

Table 5-3. MBR choices

Choice	Description
BootMgr	Install the FreeBSD *booteasy* boot manager in the MBR. This will enable you choose which partition to boot every time you start the system.
Standard	Use a standard MBR. You will only be able to boot from the active partition.
None	Don't change the MBR. This is useful if you already have another boot manager installed.

Where we are now

At this point in the installation, we have told *sysinstall* the overall layout of the disk or disks you intend to use for FreeBSD, and whether or how you intend to share them with other operating systems. The next step is to specify how you want to use the FreeBSD partitions.

Specifying disk labels

In the next step we tell the installation program what to put in our FreeBSD partion. We will typically need a root file system, a */usr* file system and swap space—see Chapter 14, *Disks*, page 229, for the reasoning behind the file system layout. When we select *Label*, we get the following screen:

```
                         FreeBSD Disklabel Editor

Disk: wd0   Partition name: wd0s1   Free: 415345 blocks (202MB)


Part    Mount           Size Newfs  Part    Mount           Size Newfs
----    -----           ---- -----  ----    -----           ---- -----


The following commands are valid here (upper or lower case):
C = Create      D = Delete      M = Mount    W = Write
N = Newfs Opts  T = Newfs Toggle  U = Undo    Q = Finish
A = Auto Defaults for all!

The default target will be displayed in reverse video.
Use F1 or ? to get more help, arrow keys to move.
```

In this display, **bold print** indicates the reverse video fields. The highlighted line at the top of the screen is the "cursor", and you can move up and down with the arrow keys.

At this point, we have two choices: decide for ourselves what we want, or let the disk label editor do it for us. Let's look at both ways:

Automatically generated labels

If we enter a, the disk label editor generates everything for us. Even if we don't want to accept them, it's a good idea to look at the suggestions. We get:

```
Part    Mount           Size Newfs  Part    Mount           Size Newfs
----    -----           ---- -----  ----    -----           ---- -----
wd0s1a  /               32MB UFS Y
wd0s1b  <none>          42MB SWAP
wd0s1e  /var            30MB UFS Y
wd0s1f  /usr            97MB UFS Y
```

The disk label editor has given us an additional file system, */var*, which is used to store files which change frequently, such as mail or news. On some systems this might be a good idea, but on this tiny disk it doesn't make any sense. It leaves only 97 MB for */usr*, which is far too little for what we intend to install on this disk.

It's always a potential problem to put more than one file system on a disk: you can end up filling up one file system and having plenty of space on the other. It's almost impossible to change the sizes of the partitions without reinstalling from scratch. In general, the rule of thumb is:

> *Use a /var file system if you know exactly how big it should be. Otherwise place it in the /usr file system.*

In this book, I recommend not to use a */var* file system. We'll see how to fake one on page 87.

For the file systems, the column *Mount* now shows the mount points, and *Newfs* contains the letters UFS for *UNIX File System*, and the letter Y, indicating that we need to create a new file system before we can use it.

Second time through

If you have already started an installation and aborted it for some reason after creating the file systems, things will look a little different when you get here:

```
Part    Mount           Size Newfs  Part    Mount           Size Newfs
----    -----           ---- -----  ----    -----           ---- -----
wd0s1a  <none>          32MB *
wd0s1b  <none>          42MB SWAP
wd0s1e  <none>          30MB *
wd0s1f  <none>          97MB *
```

The label editor has found the partitions, but it doesn't know where to mount the file systems. Before you can use them, you *must* tell the label editor the types and mount points of the UFS partitions. To do this:

- Position the cursor on each of the partitions in turn.

- Press m (Mount). A prompt window will pop up asking you to specify the mount point. Enter the name of the mount point, in this example, first /, then press return. The label editor will enter the name of the mount point under *Mount*, and under *Newfs* it will enter UFS N—it knows that this is a UFS file system, so it will just check its consistency, not overwrite it. Repeat this procedure for */var*, and then */usr*, and you're done. If you are sharing your disk with another system, you can also use this method to specify mount points for your Microsoft file systems. Simply select the Microsoft partition and specify the name of a mount point.

- Unless you are very sure that the file system is valid, and you really want to keep the data in the partitions, press t to specify that the file system should be created. The UFS N will change to UFS Y. If you leave the N there, the commit phase will check the integrity of the file system with *fsck* rather than creating a new one.

Manually generated labels

If we enter c to create a disk partition, the disk label editor prompts us for details of the partition. On this tiny disk, we will use the absolute minimum values which will work. Let's assume that we've decided that, for this disk, we want 20 MB root file system, 32 MB swap and the rest for */usr*. We hit c and get a prompt window asking how much we want, suggesting the whole disk. We replace this with 20m (the trailing m says the the value is in units of megabytes), and get another question asking whether this is a file system or swap space. We choose file system and get a further prompt asking where to mount it. We enter /, and come back to the display, which now shows

```
Part    Mount           Size Newfs  Part    Mount           Size Newfs
----    -----           ---- -----  ----    -----           ---- -----
wd0s1a  /               20MB UFS Y
```

Next we define the swap space. This time we specify 32 MB, and that it should be swap space. Now the display looks like:

```
Part    Mount            Size Newfs  Part    Mount            Size Newfs
----    -----            ---- -----  ----    -----            ---- -----
wd0s1a  /                20MB UFS Y
wd0s1b  <none>           32MB SWAP
```

Finally, we create the */usr* file system. This time we accept the offer of everything available, tell it to mount the file system on */usr*, and end up with:

```
Part    Mount            Size Newfs  Part    Mount            Size Newfs
----    -----            ---- -----  ----    -----            ---- -----
wd0s1a  /                20MB  UFS Y
wd0s1b  <none>           32MB  SWAP
wd0s1e  /usr            150MB  UFS Y
```

That's all we need to do. We enter q to proceed to the next menu.

What size partitions?

In the examples above, we've made severe compromises to get the system on the tiny disk. We've assumed that we can get the root file system in 20 MB, and that 32 MB of swap space is a good value. In fact, most modern disks are an order of magnitude larger than this disk. What do we use?

We've already seen how big to make */usr*: it's the rest of the disk. The root file system is kept separate mainly for reasons of superstition: in the old days, when systems were less reliable, it was a good idea to keep the root file system separate in order to recover a crashed file system. Since it's uncommon to write to the root file system, it's also relatively unlikely that it will be damaged during a crash. Nowadays crashes are very rare, and FreeBSD provides other methods of crash recovery (see page 109), so the separate root file system is not really necessary. In this case it might be a better idea to have only one file system and swap.

If you do have a separate root file system, it doesn't need to be very big, but the size is increasing. A better size would be 30 MB. If you're doing kernel development, you'll probably want to put in a couple of debug kernels at 10 MB apiece, so you could easily justify an 80 MB root file system in such cases.

It's very difficult to predict how much swap space you need. The *automatic* option gave us 42 MB. In the manual example, we chose 32 MB. Maybe you can get by with 16 MB. Maybe you'll need 512 MB. How do you decide?

It's almost impossible to know in advance what your system will require. Here are some considerations:

- Swap space is needed for all pages of virtual memory which contain data that is not locked in memory and which can't be recreated automatically. This is the majority of virtual memory in the system.

- Some people use rules of thumb like "2.5 times the size of physical memory, or 64 MB, whichever is bigger". These rules work only by making assumptions about your workload. If you're using more than 2.5 times as much swap space as physical memory, performance will suffer.

- Known memory hogs are X11 and the GNU C compiler (*gcc*). If you use these, you will probably need more swap space.

- You can add additional swap partitions on other disks. This has the additional advantage of balancing the disk load if your machine swaps a lot.

- About the only ways to change the size of a swap partition are to add another partition or to reinstall the system, so if you're not sure, a little bit more won't do any harm, but too little can really be a problem.

- If your system panics, and memory dumping is enabled, it will write the contents of memory to the swap partition. This will obviously not work if your swap partition is smaller than main memory. Under these circumstances, the system refuses to dump, but it's not impossible that a bug might cause the dump to write beyond the bounds of the swap partition, probably causing irreperable damage to your */usr* partition.

- Even with light memory loads, the virtual memory system slowly pages out data in preparation for a possible sudden demand for memory. This means that it can be more responsive to such requests. As a result, you should have at least as much swap as memory.

A couple of examples might make this clearer:

1. I run *X*, *StarOffice*, *Netscape* and a whole lot of other memory-hungry applications on my old 486 with 16 MB. Sure, it's really slow, especially when changing from one application to another, but it works. Since there's not much memory, it uses a lot of swap.

   To view the current swap usage, use *pstat*. Here's a typical view of this machine's swap space:

   ```
   $ pstat -s
   Device       1024-blocks    Used   Avail Capacity  Type
   /dev/sd0s1b       122880   65148   57668     53%   Interleaved
   ```

2. I run much more stuff on my Pentium with 96 MB of memory. I've got lots of swap space, but what I see is:

   ```
   $ pstat -s
   Device       1024-blocks    Used   Avail Capacity  Type
   /dev/wd0s1b        51200   14416   36720     28%   Interleaved
   /dev/sd0b          66036   14332   51640     22%   Interleaved
   /dev/sd2b         204800   14384  190352      7%   Interleaved
   Total             321844   43132  278712     13%
   ```

It's not so important that the Pentium is using less swap: it's using 0.67 of its memory in swap, whereas the 486 is using 4 times its memory. Look at it from a different point, and it makes more sense: swap makes up for the lack of real memory, so the 486 is using a total of 80 MB of memory, and the Pentium is using 140 MB. In other words, there is a tendency to be able to say "the more main memory you have, the less swap you need".

If, however, you look at it from the point of view of acceptable performance, you will hear things like "you need at least one-third of your virtual memory in real memory". That makes sense from a performance point of view, assuming all processes are relatively active. And, of course, it's another way of saying "take twice as much swap as real memory".

In summary: be generous in allocating swap space. In this example, we have a tiny disk, so we're forced to use a small swap partition. If you have the choice, use more. If you really can't make up your mind, take 256 MB of swap space.

Where we are now

When you get to this point in the installation, you have told *sysinstall* everything it needs to know about the layout of the disk or disks you intend to use for FreeBSD. Next, you tell it what you want to put on the disks.

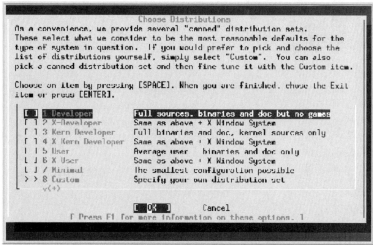

Figure 5-4: Distribution selection menu

Selecting distributions

The next step is to decide what to install. The easiest thing to say, of course, is "everything", but we don't have enough disk space for that. Figure 5-4 shows us the menu we get when we enter *Distributions*. We have a total of 170 MB at our disposal. For this example, we assume that we want to install the X-User distribution. Figure 5-5 shows us the choices offered when we select X-User. Each of these menus goes further. Figure 5-6 shows the *Basic* menu. We select everything from the basic menu, and we also select the X server, but since this machine runs only an ancient Tseng ET4000 display board, we don't need any additional servers. When we've finished, we exit the menu. On the way, we are asked if we want to install the DES software and the Ports Collection. In each case, we decide not to: we can always do it after the system is up and running.

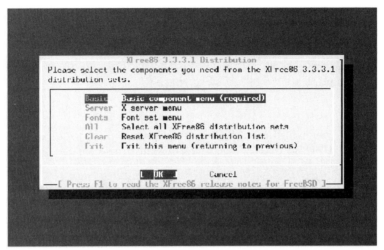

Figure 5-5: X user selection menu

Figure 5-6: X base distribution menu

Where we are now

Now *sysinstall* knows the layout of the disk or disks you intend to use for FreeBSD, and what to put on them. Next, you specify where to get the data from.

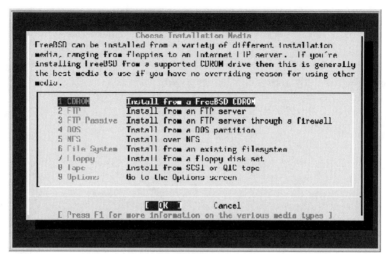

Figure 5-7: Installation medium menu

Selecting the installation medium

The next thing we need to specify is where we will get the data from. Where you go now depends on your installation medium. Figure 5-7 shows the *Media* menu. If you're installing from anything except an FTP server or NFS, you just need to select your medium and then commit the installation, which we look at on page 83.

Installing via FTP

Figure 5-8 shows the menu you get when you select *FTP* or *FTP Passive*. To see the remainder of the sites, use the **PageDown** key. We want to install from *presto*, a system on the local network. *presto* isn't on this list, of course, so we select URL. Another menu appears, asking for an ftp pathname in the URL form `ftp://hostname/pathname`. *hostname* is the name of the system, in this case *presto.example.org*, and *pathname* is the path relative to the anonymous ftp directory, which on FreeBSD systems is usually */usr/ftp*. The install program knows its version number, and it attaches it to the name you supply.

> You can change the version number from the options menu, for example in order to install a snapshot of a newer release of FreeBSD.

In this case, we're installing version 3.2 of FreeBSD, and it's in the directory */pub/Free-BSD/3.2-RELEASE*. *sysinstall* knows the *3.2-RELEASE*, so we enter only *ftp://presto.example.org/pub/FreeBSD*. The next menu asks us to configure our network. This is the same menu which we would normally fill out at the end of the installation—see page 85 for details.

This information will be used to set up the machine after installation, so it pays to fill out this information correctly. You don't have to fill in everything, though: for example, you won't need

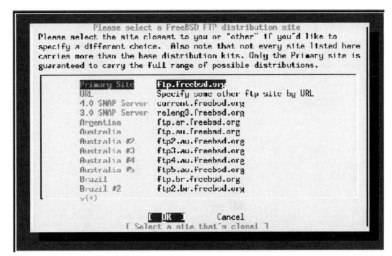

Figure 5-8: Selecting FTP server

a gateway to access *presto* from *freebie*, since they're both on the same local net.

After entering this information, you continue with *Commit* (below).

Installing via NFS

We considered the prerequisites for NFS installation on page 67. All you need to do at this point is to give this information to *sysinstall*, as shown in figure 5-9. After entering this information, *sysinstall* will ask you to configure an interface. This is the same procedure which you would otherwise do after installation—see page 85. After performing this configuration, you continue with *Commit* (below).

Installing from floppy disk

Installation from floppy disk is definitely the worst choice you have. You will need lots of floppies, and the chance of one of them being bad is high. We looked at how to prepare floppies for installation in Chapter 2, *Before you install*, page 65. The installation itself is straightforward enough: select *Floppy* and follow the prompts.

Where we are now

Now *sysinstall* knows everything it needs to install the software. It's just waiting for you to tell it to go ahead.

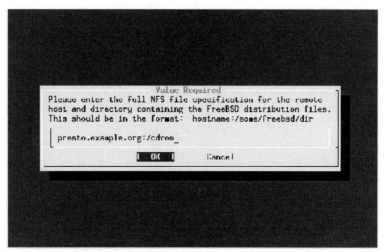

Figure 5-9: Specifying NFS file system

Performing the installation

So far, everything we have done has had no effect on the disk drives. If you change your mind at this point, you can just abort the installation, and the data on your disks will be unchanged.

That changes completely in the next step, which we call *committing* the installation. Now is the big moment. We've set up our partitions, decided what we want to install and from where. Now we do it.

If you are installing with the Custom installation, you need to select *Commit* explicitly. The Novice installation asks you if you want to proceed:

```
Last Chance!  Are you SURE you want continue the installation?

If you're running this on an existing system, we STRONGLY
encourage you to make proper backups before proceeding.
We take no responsibility for lost disk contents!
```

When you answer yes, *sysinstall* does what we've been preparing for:

- It creates the partitions and disk partitions.

- It creates the file system structures in the file system partitions, or it checks them, depending on what you chose in the label editor.

- It mounts the file systems and swap space.

At this point, two other virtual terminals become available. */dev/ttyv1* shows you what's going on behind the scenes. You can switch to it with **ALT-F2**. Right at the beginning you'll see a whole lot of error messages as *sysinstall* tries to initialize every device it can think of. Don't worry about them, they're normal. To get back to the install screen, press **ALT-F1**.

In addition, after *sysinstall* mounts the root file system, it starts an interactive shell on */dev/ttyv3*. You can use it if something goes wrong, or simply to watch what's going on while you're installing. You switch to it with **ALT-F4**.

After reading in all the files, *sysinstall* displays further information messages:

```
Remaking all devices..  Please wait!

Making slice entries

Fixing permissions..
```

And we're done!

Where we are now

When we get here, the software has been installed on the disk, but we still need to customize some information to match our environment. We'll look at this in the following sections.

Network services

Figure 5-10 shows the Network Services Menu. You don't see this menu in the Novice and Express installations: after setting up your network interfaces, *sysinstall* presents you with various items from the Network Services Menu. The Custom installation presents you with the

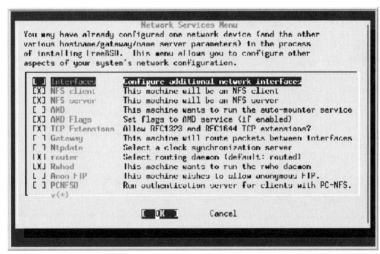

Figure 5-10: Network services menu

menu itself. The first step should always be to set up the network interfaces, so this is where you find yourself if you are performing a Novice or Express installation.

Setting up network interfaces

Figure 5-11 shows the network setup menu. If you installed via FTP or NFS, you will already

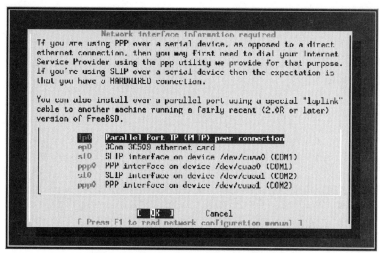

Figure 5-11: Network setup menu

have set up your network interfaces, and *sysinstall* won't ask the questions again. The only real network board on this list is *ep0*, the Ethernet board. The others are standard hardware which can also be used as network interfaces. In our case, we choose the Ethernet board. The next menu asks us to set the internet parameters. Figure 5-12 shows the network configuration menu after filling in the values. You need to specify the local host name and the domain name separately. The names and addresses correspond to the example network that we will look at in Chapter 21, *Networks and the Internet*, on page 400. We have chosen to call this machine *presto*, and the domain is *example.org*. In other words, the full name of the machine is *presto.example.org*. Its IP address is 223.147.37.2. In this configuration, all access to the outside world goes via gw.example.org, which has the IP address 223.147.37.5. The name server is located on the same host, *presto.example.org*. Since the name server isn't running when this information is needed, we specify all addresses in numeric form.

What happens if you don't have a domain name? Well, the simple answer is "go out and get one"—see page 419. But in the meantime, don't fake it. Just leave the fields empty.

As is usual for a class C network, the net mask is 255.255.255.0. You don't need to fill in this information—if you leave this field without filling it in, *sysinstall* will insert it for you. Normally, as in this case, you wouldn't need any additional options to *ifconfig*.

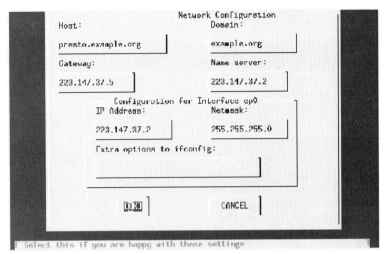

Figure 5-12: Network configuration menu

Other network options

You don't need to specify any of the remaining configuration options during configuration. See the online handbook for further details.

Machine configuration

The final part of the installation deals with optional setup items. You don't need to do any of this right now, but if this is the first time you have installed FreeBSD, you will probably want to at least add a user. If you're like me, you'll also have a couple of favourite programs that you want to install, probably including XFree86. The Express and Novice installations walk you through these points, while figure 5-13 shows you the menu that Custom installation presents.

Rebooting the new system

Finally, it's done. You exit the main menu by selecting Quit. Before you answer the question asking for confirmation, remember to remove the boot diskette—otherwise you'll end up rebooting from the floppy instead. If you have booted from CD-ROM, either remove the CD-ROM, or reset the boot configuration in the BIOS before rebooting.

After that, the system will reboot. The results look much the same as before, but this time, instead of going in to the *sysinstall* menu, it continues to start up the machine and give you a login prompt. We're done!

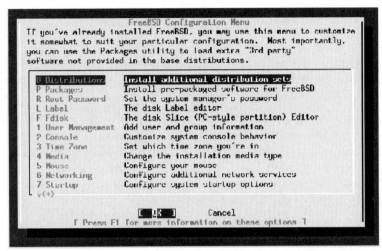

Figure 5-13: Final configuration menu

Where to put */var* and */tmp*

Now the installation is completed, but you may still have some housekeeping to do. Did you include a */var* file system on your disk? In the example, we didn't. If we don't specify anything else, */var* will end up on the root file system, which isn't enormous. If we leave things like that, there's a very good chance that the root file system will fill up. We solve this problem by creating a directory */usr/var* and a symbolic link */var* which points to */usr/var*:

```
# mkdir /usr/var                        create a new directory
# cd /var                               move to the old /var directory
# tar cf - . | (cd /usr/var; tar xf - ) copy its contents
# cd /                                  get out of the directory
# rm -rf /var                           and remove it
# ln -s /usr/var /var                   now link to the new directory
```

After performing these steps, you might see messages like:

```
Jan  9 13:15:00 myname syslogd: /var/run/utmp: no such file or directory
```

syslogd is the System Log dæmon.[1] Don't worry about these messages. If you're intending to restart the system soon, just wait until then and the messages will go away. Otherwise you can restart *syslogd*:

---

1. See page 183 for a description of dæmons.

```
# ps waux | grep syslogd              look for the syslog dæmon
root 152 11.0  1.6    176   476    v0  D+    1:16M   0:00.15 grep syslogd
root  58  0.0  1.1    184   332    ??  Ds    1:13    0:00:57 syslogd
# kill -9 58                          stop the PID of syslogd
# syslogd                             and start it again
```

The PID of the *syslogd* is the second field on the line which ends with just *syslogd*. The first line is the process which is looking for the text `syslogd`. See Chapter 11, *Making friends with FreeBSD*, page 185, for more information on stopping processes.

Programs should not write large files to */tmp*; if a program needs to create a large temporary file, it should create it in */var/tmp*. Unfortunately, the location of the temporary files is not usually in your hands. It would be tempting to also replace */tmp* with a symbolic link to */var/tmp*, but the system handles */tmp* and */var/tmp* slightly differently: after a reboot, it removes all files from */tmp*, but it leaves the files in */var/tmp*. You can solve this problem by creating a directory */usr/tmp* and creating a link to it.

Perform the following steps in single-user mode (see Chapter 11, *Making friends with FreeBSD*, page 201, for a description of single user mode and how to get into it).

```
# mkdir /usr/tmp                      create a new directory
# rm -rf /tmp                         and remove the old /tmp
# ln -s /usr/tmp /tmp                 now link to the new directory
```

Installing FreeBSD on a Compaq AXP (Alpha) system

FreeBSD 3.2 includes support for the AXP (Alpha) processor architecture, but it's not yet of the same standard as for the i386 architecture. The following instructions are preliminary: before following them, read the booklet that came with the CD-ROMs: it's possible that there have been some last-minute changes. If all else fails, you can find the latest installable version of FreeBSD for the alpha at *ftp://ftp.FreeBSD.org/pub/FreeBSD/releases/alpha/* or on a mirror site.

In principle, you perform the same steps to install FreeBSD on the Alpha architecture that you perform for the Intel architecture. See page 22 for some differences.

The easiest type of installation is from CD-ROM. If you have a supported CD-ROM drive and a FreeBSD installation CD for Alpha from Walnut Creek CDROM, you can start the installation by building a set of FreeBSD boot floppy from the files *floppies/kern.flp* and *floppies/mfsroot.flp* as described for the Intel architecture on page 64. Use the CD-ROM marked "Alpha installation". From the SRM console prompt, insert the *kern.flp* floppy and type the following command to start the installation:

```
>>>boot dva0
```

Insert the *mfsroot.flp* floppy when prompted and you will end up at the first screen of the install program. You can then continue as for the Intel architecture on page 68.

To install over the net, fetch the floppy images from the FTP site, boot as above, then proceed as for the Intel architecture.

Once the install procedure has finished, you will be able to start FreeBSD/alpha by typing something like this to the SRM prompt:

```
>>>boot dkc0
```

This instructs the firmware to boot the specified disk. To find the SRM names of disks in your machine, use the show device command:

```
>>>show device
dka0.0.0.4.0            DKA0            TOSHIBA CD-ROM XM-57  3476
dkc0.0.0.1009.0         DKC0                       RZ1BB-BS  0658
dkc100.1.0.1009.0       DKC100          SEAGATE ST34501W     0015
dva0.0.0.0.1            DVA0
ewa0.0.0.3.0            EWA0            00-00-F8-75-6D-01
pkc0.7.0.1009.0         PKC0                   SCSI Bus ID 7 5.27
pqa0.0.0.4.0            PQA0                        PCI EIDE
pqb0.0.1.4.0            PQB0                        PCI EIDE
```

This example comes from a Digital Personal Workstation 433au and shows three disks attached to the machine. The first is a CD-ROM called *dka0* and the other two are disks and are called *dkc0* and *dkc100* respectively.

You can specify which kernel file to load and what boot options to use with the -file and -flags options to boot:

```
>>>boot -file kernel.old -flags s
```

To make FreeBSD/alpha boot automatically, use these commands:

```
>>>set boot_osflags a
>>>set bootdef_dev dkc0
>>>set auto_action BOOT
```

Upgrade installation

As the name implies, upgrade installations are intended to help you upgrade from an earlier version of FreeBSD. This kind of installation is still being developed, and it is possible that all sorts of things can go wrong. If you want to use it, make sure you have backed up your old system before you start, and read carefully the warning messages that appear. If things do go wrong, you can always reinstall and then restore your backups.

Changing configuration

Once your system is up and running, you're bound to find something that you want to change. The online handbook gives more information on this, but it's good to know that you can start *sysinstall* after the system is running: it's called */stand/sysinstall*. For an alternative way to configure additional disks, see Chapter 14, *Disks*, page 243.

Installing additional software

Once your system is up and running, you may find that things you expect are missing. Where's *Emacs*? Where's *bash*? Where's *less*? They're all there, and just about everything else is as well. We'll look at how to install them in Chapter 8, *The Ports Collection*, starting on page 111.

How to uninstall FreeBSD

What, you want to remove FreeBSD? Why would you want to do that?

Seriously, if you decide you want to completely remove FreeBSD from the system, this is no longer a FreeBSD issue, it's an issue of whatever system you use to replace it. For example, on page 72 we saw how to remove a Microsoft partition and replace it with FreeBSD; no Microsoft software was needed to remove it.

6

Shared OS Installation

In the previous chapter, we looked at how to install FreeBSD on a disk by itself. Unfortunately, you might not be able to afford this luxury: you may only have one disk, and you need to use other operating systems as well.

Before you start the installation, read this chapter carefully. It's easy to make a mistake, and one of the most frequent results of mistakes is the total loss of all data on the hard disk.

In this chapter, we'll look at what you need to do to share a disk between FreeBSD and another operating system. In most cases, you will share your disk with a Microsoft platform, but most of this chapter applies to other operating systems as well. You may want to refer to the discussion of Microsoft and FreeBSD disk layouts on page 33. The first question is: is there enough space on the disk for FreeBSD? How much you need depends on what you want to do with FreeBSD, of course, but for the sake of example we'll take 120 MB as a ballpark figure. In the following section, we'll consider what to do if you need to change your partitions. If you already have enough space for a FreeBSD partition (for example, if you have just installed Microsoft specifically for sharing with FreeBSD, and thus have not filled up the disk), continue reading on page 96.

Repartitioning with FIPS

Typically, if you've been running Microsoft on your machine, it will occupy the entire disk. If you need all this space, of course, there's no way to install another operating system as well. Frequently, though, you'll find that you have enough free space in the partition. Unfortunately, that's not where you want it: you want a new partition with this much space. There are a number of ways of getting this space:

- You can reinstall the software. This approach is common in the Microsoft world, but FreeBSD users try to avoid it.

- You can use *FIPS* shrink a Microsoft partition, leaving space for FreeBSD. *FIPS* is a public domain utility, and it is included on the FreeBSD CD-ROM. Unfortunately, it cannot shrink more recent Microsoft file systems.

91

- If you can't use *FIPS*, use a commercial utility like *PartitionMagic*. This is not included on the CD-ROMs, and we won't discuss it further.

In the rest of the section, we'll look at how to shrink a partition with *FIPS*. If you do it with PartitionMagic, the details are different, but the principles are the same. In particular:

Before repartitioning your disk, make a backup. You can shoot yourself in the foot with this method, and the result will almost invariably be loss of data.

If you've been running Microsoft on your system for any length of time, the data in the partition will be spread all around the partition. If you just truncate the partition, you'll lose a lot of data, so you first need to move all the data to the beginning of the partition. Fortunately, MS-DOS 6.x (part of the "Windows" environment) supplies such a tool, called *DEFRAG*. Alternatively, you can use a third-party defragmenter such as the one supplied with the Norton Disk tools. Before proceeding, consider a few gotchas:

- The new Microsoft partition needs to be big enough to hold all the data. If you make it exactly the size of the data, it will effectively be full, and you won't be able to write anything to it.

- The second partition is also a Microsoft partition. To install FreeBSD on it, you need to delete it and create a new FreeBSD partition.

- Most older BIOSes require the root file system in the FreeBSD partition to end before cylinder 1024, otherwise the installation will complete correctly, but you won't be able to boot from it. See the diagram on page 40.

- *FIPS* may result in configuration problems with your Microsoft machine. Since it adds a partition, any automatically assigned partitions which follow will have a different drive letter. In particular, this could mean that your CD-ROM drive will "move". After you delete the second Microsoft partition and change it into a FreeBSD partition, it will "move" back again.

For further information, read the *FIPS* documentation in */cdrom/tools/srcs/fips/fips.doc*. In particular, note these limitations:

- *FIPS* works only with Hard Disk BIOSes that use interrupt 0x13 for low level hard disk access. This is generally not a problem.

- *FIPS* splits only partitions with 16 bit FATs. Older versions of Microsoft use 12 bit FATs, which are too small to be worth splitting.

- *FIPS* splits only Microsoft partitions. The partition table and boot sector must conform to the MS-DOS 3.0+ conventions. This is marked by the system indicator byte in the partition table, which must have the value 4 (16 bit sector number) or 6 (32 bit sector number). In particular, it will *not* split Linux partitions.

- *FIPS* does not yet work on extended Microsoft partitions.

- *FIPS* needs one free partition entry, so it will not work if you already have four partitions.

- *FIPS* will not reduce the original partition to a size of less than 4085 clusters, because this would involve rewriting the 16 bit FAT to a 12 bit FAT.

Repartitioning—an example

In this section, we'll go through the mechanics of repartitioning a disk. We'll start with a Western Digital Caviar 2200 disk, the same one we used for the example on page 69. This time it starts off with a complete MS-DOS 6.21 system.

First, run *CHKDSK* or *SCANDISK* on the partition you want to split. If you have Norton Disk Doctor or something similar, you can use it instead. Make sure no "dead" clusters remain on the disk.

Next, prepare a bootable floppy. When you start *FIPS*, you will be given the opportunity to write backup copies of your root and boot sector to a file on drive *A:*. These will be called *ROOTBOOT.00x*, where *x* represents a digit from 0 to 9. If anything goes wrong while using *FIPS*, you can restore the original configuration by booting from the floppy and running *RESTORRB*.

> If you use *FIPS* more than once (this is normally not necessary, but it might happen), your floppy will contain more than one *ROOTBOOT* file. *RESTORRB* lets you choose which configuration file to restore. The file *RESTORRB.000* contains your original configuration. Try not to confuse the versions.

Before starting *FIPS* you *must* defragment your disk in order to ensure that the space to be used for the new partition is free. This is not as straightforward as it seems:

- Most defragmentation programs don't move the windows swap file. You have to uninstall it (in the *386enhanced* part of the Windows Control Panel) and reinstall it after using *FIPS*.

- Programs like *IMAGE* or *MIRROR* store a hidden system file with a pointer to your mirror files in the last sector of the hard disk. You *must* delete this file before using *FIPS*. It will be recreated the next time you run *MIRROR*. To delete it, in the root directory enter:

```
C> attrib -r -s -h image.idx        for IMAGE
C> attrib -r -s -h mirorsav.fil     for MIRROR
```

Then delete the file.

If *FIPS* does not offer as much disk space for creation of the new partition as you expect, this may mean that:

- You still have too much data in the remaining partition. Consider making the new partition smaller or deleting some of the data. If you delete data, you must run *FIPS* again.

- There are hidden files in the space of the new partition that have not been moved by the defragmentation program. Make sure to which program they belong. If a file is a swap file of some program (for example NDOS) it is possible that it can be safely deleted (and will be recreated automatically later when the need arises). See your manual for details.

If the file belongs to some sort of copy protection, you must uninstall the program to which it belongs and reinstall it after repartitioning.

If you are running early versions of MS-DOS (before 5.0), or another operating system, such as Linux or OS/2, or you are using programs like Stacker, SuperStor, or Doublespace, read the FIPS documentation for other possible problems.

Running FIPS

After defragmenting your Microsoft partition, you can run *FIPS*. In *VIEW*, select *tools*, then *fips*. It's easier to do it from the command line:

```
C> R:                                     change to CD-ROM
R> cd \tools                              make sure you're in the tools directory
R> fips                                   and start the FIPS program
... a lot of copyright information omitted
Press any key                             do what the computer says
Which Drive (1=0x80/2=0x81)?
```

The message *Which Drive* may seem confusing, since it refers to Microsoft internal numbering. Don't worry about it: if you want to partion the first physical drive in the system, (C:), enter 1, otherwise enter 2. Like MS-DOS, *FIPS* handles only two hard disks.

If you start *FIPS* under Windows or DESQview, it will complain and tell you to boot from a floppy disk. It won't stop you from continuing, but it is a Bad Idea to do so.

Next, *FIPS* reads the root sector of the hard disk and displays the partition table:

Part.	bootable	Start Head	Cyl.	Sector	System	End Head	Cyl.	Sector	Start Sector	Number of Sectors	MB
1	yes	0	0	1	06h	11	987	34	0	414960	212
2	no	0	0	0	00h	0	0	0	0	0	0
3	no	0	0	0	00h	0	0	0	0	0	0
4	no	0	0	0	00h	0	0	0	0	0	0

This shows that only first partition is occupied, that it is bootable, and that it occupies the whole disk (212 MB, from Cylinder 0, Head 0, Sector 1 to Cylinder 987, Head 11, Sector 34). Don't worry about the "bootable" flag here—we'll deal with that in the FreeBSD installation. First, *FIPS* does some error checking and then reads and displays the boot sector of the partition:

```
Checking Rootsector ... OK
Press any Key               do what it says
Bytes per sector: 512
Sectors per cluster: 8
Reserved sectors: 1
Number of FATs: 2
Number of rootdirectory entries: 512
Number of sectors (short): 0
Media descriptor byte: f8h
Sectors per FAT: 145
```

```
Sectors per track: 35
Drive heads: 12
Hidden sectors: 63
Number of sectors (long): 414960
Physical drive number: 80h
Signature: 29h
```

After further checking, *FIPS* asks you if you want to make a backup floppy. Enter your formatted floppy in drive *A:* and make the backup. Next, you see:

```
Enter start cylinder for new partition (263 - 987):
Use the cursor keys to choose the cylinder, <enter> to continue
Old partition      Cylinder      New Partition
   53.9 MB           263           148.7 MB
```

Use the **Cursor Left** and **Cursor Right** keys to adjust the cylinder number at which the new partition starts. You can also use the keys **Cursor Up** and **Cursor Down** to change in steps of ten cylinders. *FIPS* updates the bottom line of the display to show the new values selected. Initially, *FIPS* chooses the smallest possible Microsoft partition, so you can only increase the size of the old partition (with the **Cursor Right** key). When you're happy with the sizes, press **Enter** to move on to the next step.

> *Be very sure you're happy before you continue. If you make the first partition too small, there is no way to make it larger again. On the other hand, if you make it too large, you can split it again and then use* fdisk *or MS-DOS* FDISK *to remove the superfluous partitions.*

In this example, we choose the following combination:

```
Old partition      Cylinder      New Partition
   82.0 MB           400           120.6 MB
(pressed Enter
       |        |   Start   |      |      | End     | Start |Number of|
Part.|bootable|Head Cyl. Sector|System|Head Cyl. Sector| Sector |Sectors  |  MB
-----+--------+----------------+------+----------------+--------+---------+----
1    |  yes   |  0    0    1|  06h|  11  399    34|      0|  167965|  53
2    |  no    | 400   0    0|  06h|  11  987    34|      0| 2469600| 120
3    |  no    |  0    0    0|  00h|   0    0     0|      0|       0|   0
4    |  no    |  0    0    0|  00h|   0    0     0|      0|       0|   0

Do you want to continue or reedit the partition table (c/r)? c
```

In order for the partition to be recognized, reboot immediately. Make sure to disable all programs that write to your disk in *CONFIG.SYS* and *AUTOEXEC.BAT* before rebooting. It might be easier to to rename the files or to boot from floppy. Be particularly careful to disable programs like *MIRROR* and *IMAGE*, which might get confused if the partitioning is not to their liking. After rebooting, use *CHKDSK* or Norton Disk Doctor to make sure the first partition is OK. If you don't find any errors, you may now reboot with your normal *CONFIG.SYS* and *AUTOEXEC.BAT*. Start some programs and make sure you can still read your data.

After that, you have two valid Microsoft partitions on your disk. Read the next section to install FreeBSD on the second one.

Installing FreeBSD on a second partition

In this section we'll discuss how to install FreeBSD on the second partition of a hard disk which contains a valid image in the first partition, either because you installed it that way or because you have just used *FIPS* to make it that way. The first step is to boot the FreeBSD as described on page 69. Follow the installation as discussed there until you get to the step *Building a partition table* on page 72.

When you enter the partition editor, you will see something like:

```
Disk name:    wd0                                  FDISK Partition Editor
BIOS Geometry:  989 cyls/12 heads/35 sectors

      Offset      Size        End      Name    PType    Desc  Subtype     Flags

           0        35         34        -        6   unused     0
          35    167965     167999     wd0s1      2      fat      6     =
      168000    246960     414959     wd0s2      2      fat      6     =
      414960       420     415379       -        2   unused     0

The following commands are supported (in upper or lower case):
A = Use Entire Disk     B = Bad Block Scan     C = Create Partition
D = Delete Partition    G = Set BIOS Geometry  S = Set Bootable
U = Undo All Changes    Q = Finish             W = Write Changes

The currently selected partition is displayed in reverse video
Use F1 or ? to get more help, arrow keys to move.
```

This display shows the two Microsoft partitions, *wd0s1* and *wd0s2*. To install FreeBSD, you need to remove one of them. ***Be very careful to remove the correct partition***. It's always the second of the two partitions, in this case *wd0s2*. We remove the partition with the d command. After this, our display looks like:

```
           0        35         34        -        6   unused     0
          35    167965     167999     wd0s1      2      fat      6     =
      168000    247380     415379       -        2   unused     0
```

The next step is to allocate a FreeBSD partition with the C command. The menu asks us the size of the partition, and suggests a value of 247380 sectors, the complete size of the unused area at the end. We can edit this value if we wish, but in this case it's what we want, so we just press ENTER. Now the display looks like this:

```
           0        35         34        -        6   unused     0
          35    167965     167999     wd0s1      2      fat      6     =
      168000    247380     415379     wd0s2      3   freebsd    165     C
```

The new partition uses the rest of the disk, including the last 420 sectors which Microsoft rejected, and it has a partition type 3 (extended partition) and subtype 165 (0xa5), which identifies it as a FreeBSD partition.

All we need to do now is to mark the partition active or bootable, by pressing s. The a flag appears at the end of the partition line:

```
        0         35         34        -          6    unused       0
       35     167965     167999     wd0s1        2       fat        6    =
   168000     247380     415379     wd0s2        3    freebsd     165    CA
```

After this, we select a boot method as described on page 74. Since we have two operating systems on the disk, we select the `BootMgr` option.

At this point, we need to change our terminology. So far, we have been using Microsoft terminology, and we have talked of partitions. FreeBSD calls these same divisions of the disk *slices*. That wouldn't be bad in itself, but it also uses the term *partition* to refer to the contents of the slice. See page 33, for further details.

Our next step is to select FreeBSD partitions within the FreeBSD slice. We have already discussed this on page 74, so we'll look at it more briefly here. As we saw on page 38, we will typically need a root file system, a */usr* file system and swap space. When we select *Label*, we get the following screen:

```
            FreeBSD Disklabel Editor

 Disk: wd0  Partition name: wd0s2   Free: 247380 blocks (120MB)


 Part   Mount          Size Newfs  Part   Mount         Size Newfs
 ----   -----          ---- -----  ----   -----         ---- -----
 wd0s1  <none>         82MB DOS
```

Be careful here. The partition shown in the list is the active Microsoft partion, *not* the FreeBSD partition. At this point, we have two choices: decide for ourselves what we want, or let the disk label editor do it for us. We looked at automatically generated labels on page 75, so we'll just look at the manual generation here. If we enter c to create a disk partition, the disk label editor prompts us for details of the partition. Let's assume that we've decided that, for this disk, we want a 20 MB root file system, 32 MB swap and the rest for */usr*. We hit c and get a prompt window asking how much we want, suggesting the whole disk. We replace this with 20m (the trailing m says the the value is in units of megabytes), and get another question asking whether this is a file system or swap space. We choose `file system` and get a further prompt asking where to mount it. We enter /, and come back to the display, which now shows:

```
 Part   Mount          Size Newfs  Part   Mount         Size Newfs
 ----   -----          ---- -----  ----   -----         ---- -----
 wd0s1  <none>         82MB DOS
 wd0s2a /              20MB UFS Y
```

Next we define the swap space. This time we specify 32 MB, and that it should be swap space. Now the display looks like:

```
 Part   Mount          Size Newfs  Part   Mount         Size Newfs
 ----   -----          ---- -----  ----   -----         ---- -----
 wd0s1  <none>         82MB DOS
 wd0s2a /              20MB UFS Y
 wd0s2b <none>         32MB SWAP
```

Finally, we create the */usr* file system. This time we accept the offer of everything available, and end up with:

```
Part      Mount              Size Newfs  Part    Mount              Size Newfs
----      -----              ---- -----  ----    -----              ---- -----
wd0s1     <none>             82MB DOS
wd0s2a    /                  20MB UFS Y
wd0s2b    <none>             32MB SWAP
wd0s2e    /usr               68MB UFS Y
```

After this point, we can continue at Section *Selecting distributions* on page 79. The rest of the installation is the same as for a dedicated disk.

7

Installation Problems

In Chapter 5, *Installing FreeBSD*, and Chapter 6, *Shared OS Installation*, we saw what *should* happen when you install FreeBSD. Unfortunately, things don't always run smoothly. In this chapter, we'll look at what could go wrong and what to do if it does. In the following section, we'll look at what to do if the installation doesn't work as expected, and on page 109, we'll consider how to recover a crashed system.

If things go wrong

In this section, we'll look at the most common installation problems. Before you start, though, a couple of general recommendations:

- If you can't boot, and if this chapter doesn't help, the most important indication is the point at which the boot failed. It's worth repeating the boot with the -v (verbose) flag: enter it at the `Boot:` prompt:

  ```
  Boot: -v
  ```

  It will give you additional information which might help diagnose the problem.

- If you get the system installed to the point where you can start it, but it doesn't run quite the way you want, *don't reinstall*. In most cases, reinstallation doesn't help. Instead, try to find the cause of the problem—with the aid of the `FreeBSD-questions` mailing list if necessary—and fix the problem.

Most installation problems relate to hardware incompatibilities, either because of inherent problems in the hardware, or because the hardware is not configured in the way the system expects. You have two choices here:

- Modify the kernel's viewpoint to match the hardware. See page 192 for an example of how to do this.

- Modify the hardware to match the kernel's viewpoint. Check your hardware manuals to do this.

Beyond these problems, however, specific hardware or combinations of hardware can cause problems. Check out the file *TROUBLE.TXT* on the first CD-ROM for details of specifics. In the following sections we'll look at the more common cases that it mentions.

Problems with sysinstall

sysinstall is intended to be easy to use, but it is not very tolerant of errors. You may well find that you enter something by mistake and can't get back to where you want to be. In case of doubt, if you haven't yet committed to the install, you can always just reboot.

Problems with CD-ROM installation

If you select to install from CD-ROM, you may get the message:

```
No CD-ROM device found
```

This might even happen if you have booted from CD-ROM! The most common reasons for this problem are:

- You forgot to put the CD-ROM in the drive before you booted. Sorry, this is a current limitation of the boot process. Restart the installation (press **CTRL-ALT-DEL** or the reset button, or power cycle the computer).

- You are using an ATAPI CD-ROM drive which doesn't quite fit the specification. In this case you need help from the FreeBSD developers. Send a message to `FreeBSD-questions@FreeBSD.org` and describe your CD-ROM as accurately as you can.

- You have an old proprietary CD-ROM drive which is not set up the way the generic kernel expects it. See page 24 for details of which hardware is supported. If your CD-ROM is set up differently, you have the choice of setting it to correspond with what the generic kernel expects, or using the configuration manager included in the generic kernel to change the parameters—see page 191.

Install tries to install from floppy

Sometimes when an installation medium fails, *sysinstall* decides to try to get the root file system from floppy. For some reason, you can't cancel this menu. Instead, just let *sysinstall* look for the file system on the floppy. When it doesn't find it, it'll give up by itself.

Can't boot

One of the most terrifying things after installing FreeBSD is if you find that the machine just won't boot. This is particularly bad if you have important data on the disk (either another operating system, or data from a previous installation of FreeBSD).

At this point, seasoned hackers tend to shrug their shoulders and point out that you still have the backup you made before you did do the installation. If you tell them you didn't do a backup, they tend to shrug again and move on to something else.

Still, all is probably not lost. The two most frequent causes of boot failure are:

1. You installed the wrong boot manager, or you wiped it out altogether. This one is harmless. Boot from the floppy disk, but when the prompt appears, enter:

```
Boot: hd()kernel
```

After booting, install the correct bootstrap with `disklabel -B`, and you should be able to boot from hard disk again.

2. Things might continue a bit further: you elect to install *booteasy*, and when you boot you get the Boot Manager prompt, but it just prints F? at the boot menu and won't accept any input. In this case, you may have set the hard disk geometry incorrectly in the Partition editor when you installed FreeBSD. Go back into the partition editor and specify the correct geometry for your hard disk. Unfortunately, you must reinstall FreeBSD from the beginning if this happens.

Can't find correct geometry

If you can't figure out the correct geometry for your machine, and even if you don't want to run Microsoft on your machine, try installing a small Microsoft partition at the beginning of the disk and install FreeBSD after that. The install program will see the Microsoft partition and try to infer the correct geometry from it, which usually works. After the partition editor has accepted the geometry, you can remove the Microsoft partition again. If you are sharing your machine with Microsoft, make sure that the Microsoft partition is before the FreeBSD partition. Remember that, in either case, you may need to locate the FreeBSD root file system completely in the first 1024 cylinders, otherwise you will not be able to boot. See page 32 for further details.

Alternatively, if you don't want to share your disk with any other operating system, select the option to use the entire disk (a in the partition editor). This will leave all geometry considerations aside.

System hangs during boot

A number of problems may lead to the system hanging during the boot process. Here are a couple:

- After installation, you might find that the system hangs after the message:

```
Changing root to /dev/da0a
```

This may happen if your system has a 3com 3c509 Ethernet adapter. The *ep* device driver is sensitive to probes for other devices that also use the same address (by default address 0x300). Reboot the system by power cycling the machine (turning it off and on. Always wait a few seconds between powering off and powering on again). This will probably unwedge the Ethernet board. At the `Boot:` prompt specify the `-c` option to invoke `UserConfig` and use the `disable` command to disable the device probes for all devices at address `0x300` except the `ep0` driver. After this, your machine should boot successfully.

- Sometimes the system appears to hang after the message:

```
fd0: 1.44MB 3.5in
fd1: 1.2MB 5.25in
```

In fact, this usually isn't a hang, just a very long probe for *wdc0*. The probe often takes a long time to complete on certain systems which don't have a WD controller. If your system does have a WD controller, this problem can also happen after the lines:

```
wdc0 at 0x1f0-0x1f7 irq 14 on isa
wdc0: unit 0 (wd0): <WDC AC2200F>
wd0: 202MB (415380 sectors), 989 cyls, 12 heads, 35 S/T, 512 B/S
```

In this case, the driver is looking for a second WD disk controller. Be patient, your system will boot. You can eliminate the problem by using UserConfig to eliminate the device *wdc1*, or by building a custom kernel.

- When booting from floppy, the system might hang after the message:

```
Uncompressing kernel...
```

This is normally an indication that you have a memory problem (not enough memory, faulty cache, or incorrect chipset parameters).

Panic: cannot mount root

If you install FreeBSD on any disk except the first, you might find that the boot proceeds normally, but then dies with the message:

```
changing root device to wd1s1a
panic: cannot mount root
```

This problem comes from the fact that the BIOS uses a different numbering scheme from FreeBSD, and it's difficult to correlate the disk numbers.

In the case where the boot disk is not the first disk in the system, FreeBSD may need help finding it. There are two common situations where you need to tell FreeBSD where the root filesystem is:

1. You have two IDE disks, each configured as the master on their respective IDE busses. You have no disk on the primary slave position (you might have a CD-ROM drive there). FreeBSD is on the second disk. The BIOS sees these as disk 0 and disk 1, while FreeBSD sees them as *wd0* and *wd2*, in other words disk 2. To tell the loader how to find it, stop it before booting and enter:

```
disk1s1a:> boot 1:wd(2,a)kernel
```

If you have a disk on primary master and on slave, the BIOS numbers agree with FreeBSD, so you don't need to do this.

2. If you're booting from a SCSI disk when you have one or more IDE disks in the system, the FreeBSD disk number is lower than the BIOS disk number. If you have two IDE disks as well as the SCSI disk, the SCSI disk is BIOS disk 2, but it's FreeBSD disk number 0, so you would say:

```
disk1s1a:> boot 2:da(0,a)kernel
```

This tells FreeBSD that you want to boot from BIOS disk 2, which is the first SCSI disk in the system. If you only had one IDE disk, you would use `1:` instead.

You don't need to do this every time: once you have determined the correct values to use, put the command exactly as you would have typed it in the file */boot.config*. FreeBSD uses the contents of this file as the default response to the `boot:`prompt.

Can't find Intel EtherExpress board

A couple of problems can prevent recognition of an EtherExpress board:

- You don't have a choice of I/O parameters for the EtherExpress 16. You must set it to be memory mapped at address `0xD0000`, and set the amount of mapped memory to 32K using the Intel-supplied program *softset.exe*.

- The *mcd* driver can mistakenly recognize Intel EtherExpress boards as *mcd* devices. Check the *dmesg* output: if it claims to have an *mcd0* device, disable the *mcd* driver in UserConfig. See page 192 for details of UserConfig.

Can't see 3Com PCMCIA board

There are a couple of possible problems in this area:

- FreeBSD does not support multi-function boards such as the 3C562 ethernet/modem board.

- The 3C589 driver must know the IRQ, I/O port address and IOMem address in order to work. This information is stored in NVRAM on the board. Unfortunately, the only program capable of reading them is the DOS program supplied by 3COM. This program is very finicky about its operating environment, so it's best to run it on a absolutely basic MS-DOS system with no other drivers. Ignore its complaints about CARD-Services not being found: it will continue. If it tells you the board is defective, use other methods to confirm the claim: it sometimes does this even if there's nothing wrong with the board. Note the IRQ, port, and IOMEM values (the latter is called the CIS tuple by 3COM). The first two can be set in the program, the third can only be read. Set these values in your kernel configuration.

No packets are transmitted on PCMCIA network board

Many PCMCIA boards use either 10-Base2 (BNC) or 10-BaseT connectors for connecting to the network. The driver can't auto-select the correct connector, so you must tell it which connector to use with a combination of the *ifconfig* flags link0, link1 and link2. Typically, one of the following commands selects the correct connector:

```
# ifconfig zp0 -link0 link1
# ifconfig zp0 link0 -link1
```

Check the man page for your board for the details: they vary from one board to another. You can set these flags in *sysinstall* by using the Extra options to ifconfig: field in the network setup screen.

Device timeout on *ed* Ethernet boards

You might find that the system finds your *ed* board, but after starting up the system you get device timeout errors. There are two typical reasons for this:

- The Ethernet board may not be correctly attached to the network. If it's not connected, you at least need a terminator.

- Your board is set up for a different IRQ from what the kernel expects. By default, the *ed* driver does not use the "soft" configuration (values entered using EZSETUP in MS-DOS), but it will use the software configuration if you specify ? in the IRQ field of your kernel config file.

If the board is incorrectly configured, either move the jumper on the board to a hard configuration setting (altering the kernel settings if necessary), or specify the IRQ as -1 in UserConfig or ? in your kernel config file. This will tell the kernel to use the soft configuration.

Devices at IRQ 9 don't work

You might find that a board set up to generate IRQ 9 (also known as IRQ 2) doesn't work. It definitely won't work if you define it to be at IRQ 2, but even if you define it to be at IRQ 9, you might have problems. One reason might be that you have a VGA board which generates IRQ 9: some Microsoft programs used to use this feature, though it is now obsolete. Most VGA boards have a jumper to disable generating IRQ 9.

Unfortuntately, this may not be enough. In some cases, you can disable IRQ 9 on the VGA, and the board still won't work: you may have a brain-dead VGA board which doesn't generate any interrupts when you remove the jumper, but it holds the interrupt line anyway and stops any other board from asserting an interrupt.

Kernel doesn't find Matsushita/Panasonic CD-ROM

If you have a Matsushita/Panasonic CD-ROM, and the kernel doesn't recognize it, check that the port address for the *matcd* driver is really correct for your host interface board. Some Microsoft drivers for SoundBlaster report a hardware port address for the CD-ROM interface that is 0x10 lower than it really is.

If you can't figure out the settings by examining the board or documentation, you can restart the system and use UserConfig (see page 191) to change the address to -1. This setting causes the driver to look at a number of I/O ports that various manufacturers use for their Matsushita/Panasonic/Creative CD-ROM interfaces. Once the driver locates the address, you should run UserConfig again and specify the correct address. Leaving the parameter port set to -1 increases the amount of time that it takes the system to boot, and this could interfere with other devices.

FreeBSD 3.2 supports only the double-speed Matsushita CR-562 and CR-563. The Matsushita/Panasonic CR-522, Matsushita/Panasonic CR-523 and TEAC CD55a drives are currently not supported—the command sets for these drives are not compatible with the double-speed CR-562 and CR-563 drives. You can recognize the single-speed CR-522 and CR-523 drives by their use of a CD caddy.

Can't install from tape

If you try to install from tape you might get messages like:

```
sa0(aha0:1:0) NOT READY csi 40,0,0,0
```

This is typically what happens if you forget to put the tape in the tape drive before booting from floppy. Put the tape in the drive, reboot and try again.

Can't detect SCSI boards on HP Netserver

There is a known problem detecting the on-board AIC-7xxx host adapter on an EISA HP Netserver. The EISA on-board SCSI controller in the HP Netserver machines occupies EISA slot 11, so all the "true" EISA slots are in front of it. Unfortunately, the address space for EISA slots 10 and higher collides with the address space assigned to PCI, and FreeBSD's auto-configuration currently cannot handle this situation very well.

For the time being, the best you can do is to pretend there is no address range clash by increasing the value of kernel option EISA_SLOTS to a value of 12. To do this, boot with the -c option into UserConfig and type:

```
eisa 12
quit
```

Later, you can compile a custom kernel with the option line

```
options    EISA_SLOTS=12
```

Can't install on Panasonic AL-N1 or Rios Chandler

For some reason, these machines have problems with newer versions of FreeBSD, so you could have this problem even if you have been running an older version of FreeBSD. Specifically, they don't like the new `i586_copyout` and `i586_copyin` functions. To disable this, boot the installation boot floppy and enter UserConfig and type the following at it:

```
flags npx0 1
quit
```

Then proceed normally to boot. This will be saved into your kernel, so you only need to do it once.

Problems with the CMD640 IDE controller

This controller is broken: it can't handle commands on both channels simultaneously. The driver should recognize this problem and work around it, so the only situation where you can run into problems is if you're upgrading from an older version of FreeBSD. In this case, build a custom kernel with the line

```
options    "CMD640"
```

Can't find the floppy on Compaq Aero notebook

Compaq does not store information about the floppy drive in the CMOS RAM of an Aero notebook, so the FreeBSD floppy driver assumes there is no drive configured. To fix this, use UserConfig to set the Flags value of the fdc0 device to 0x1, or build a kernel with this flag set (see page 341 for details). This tells the driver of the existence of the first floppy drive (as a 1.44 MB drive) and doesn't probe the CMOS at all.

Read errors on Intel AL440LX based systems

The AL44LX is also called *Atlanta*. When booting from hard disk the first time, you may find that it stops with a "Read Error" message. There appears to be a bug in the BIOS on at least some of these boards. This bug causes the FreeBSD boot loader to think that it is booting from a floppy disk. This is only a problem if you are not using the BootEasy boot manager. Slice the disk in "compatible" mode and install BootEasy during the FreeBSD installation to avoid the bug, or upgrade the BIOS (see Intel's website for details).

Can't recognize Dell DSA on Poweredge XE

By default, FreeBSD does not recognize Dell's proprietary DSA (Dell SCSI Array) RAID controller on the Dell Poweredge XE. To fix this, use the EISA configuration utility to configure the DSA for Adaptec 1540 emulation. After that FreeBSD detects the DSA as an Adaptec 1540 SCSI controller, with irq 11 and port 0x340. In emulation mode the system will use the DSA RAID disks, but you cannot use DSA specific features such as watching RAID health.

Can't use the AMD PCnet-FAST Ethernet board

These boards are fitted to machines such as the IBM Netfinity 5xxx or 7xxx series. The *lnc* driver is currently faulty, and will often not work correctly with the PCnet-FAST and PCnet-FAST+. At the moment, there is no known solution: you'll have to install a different board.

Can't operate IBM EtherJet board

Sometimes the *fxp* driver correctly detects an IBM EtherJet PCI board, but the lights on the board don't come on and it doesn't connect to the network. We don't understand why this happens, and IBM hasn't been able to explain it either. The board is a standard Intel EtherExpress Pro/100 with an IBM label on it, and these boards normally work just fine. You may see these symptoms only in some IBM Netfinity servers. The only current solution is to install a different Ethernet adapter.

IBM Netfinity 3500 freezes during network installation

There is an unidentified problem with the onboard Ethernet board in these machines. It may be related to the SMP features of the system being misconfigured. You will have to install another Ethernet adapter, and avoid attempting to configure the onboard adapter at any time.

TEAC CD-220E (rev 1.0D) IDE CD-ROM hangs the system

There are apparently firmware problems with the TEAC CD-220E. Fixes may be forthcoming, but at the moment it's best to use a different drive.

Root file system fills up

You might find that the installation completes successfully, and you get your system up and running, but almost before you know it, the root file system fills up. It could be, of course, that you just haven't made it big enough—FreeBSD root file systems have got bigger over the years. In the first edition of this book I recommended 32 MB "to be on the safe side". Nowadays 50 MB looks good, and it wouldn't do any harm to use 80 MB.

On the other hand, maybe you already have an 80 MB root file system, and it still fills up. In this case, you should check where you have put your */tmp* and */var* file systems. See page 87 for further information.

Panic

Sometimes the system gets into so much trouble that it can't continue. It should notice this situation and stop more or less gracefully: you might see a message like

```
panic: free vnode isn't

Syncing disks 14 13 9 5 5 5 5 5 5 5 giving up

dumping to dev 20001 offset 0
dump 15 14 13 12 11 10 9 8 7 6 5 4 3 2 1 0 succeeded
Automatic reboot in 15 seconds - press a key on the console to abort
Reboooting...
```

Just because the system has panicked doesn't mean that you should panic too. It's a sorry fact of life that software contains bugs. Many commercial systems just crash when they hit a bug, and you never know why, or they print a message like General protection error, which doesn't tell you very much either. When a UNIX system panics, it tells you why—in this case here, the reason is *free vnode isn't*. You may not be any the wiser for a message like this (it tells you that the file system handling has got confused about the current state of storage on a disk), but other people might. In particular, if you *do* get a panic and you want to ask, say, the FreeBSD hackers, please don't just say "My system panicked, what do I do?" The answer—if you get one—will be "What was the panic string?"

After panicking, the system tries to write file system buffers back to disk so that they don't get lost. This is not always possible, as we see on the second line of this example. It started off with 14 buffers to write, but it only managed to write 9 of them, possibly because it was confused about the state of the disk. This can mean that you will have difficulties after rebooting, but it might also mean that the system was wrong in its assumptions about the number of buffers needed to be written.

In addition to telling you the cause of the panic, FreeBSD will optionally copy the current contents of memory to the swap file for post-mortem analysis. This is called *dumping* the system, and is shown on the next two lines. In order to enable dumping, you need to specify where the dump should be written. In */etc/defaults/rc.conf*, you will find:

```
dumpdev="NO"           # Device name to crashdump to (if enabled).
```

To enable dumping, put something like this in */etc/rc.conf*:

```
dumpdev=/dev/wd0s1b
```

If you don't already have a file */etc/rc.conf*, just create it. Make sure that the name of the dumpdev corresponds to a swap partition with at least as much space as your total memory. You can use *pstat* to check this:

```
# pstat -s
Device          1024-blocks      Used   Avail Capacity  Type
/dev/wd0s1b          51200      50108    1028    98%     Interleaved
/dev/da0b            66036      51356   14616    78%     Interleaved
/dev/da2b           204800      51220  153516    25%     Interleaved
Total               321844     152684  169160    47%
```

As long as this machine doesn't have more than about 192 MB of memory, it will be possible to take a dump on */dev/da2b*.

In addition, ensure you have a directory */var/crash*. After rebooting, the system first checks the integrity of the file systems, then it checks for the presence of a dump. If it finds one, it copies the dump and the current kernel to */var/crash*.

It's always worth enabling dumping, assuming your swap space is at least as large as your memory. You can analyze the dumps with *kgdb*—see the online handbook for more details.

To get the best results from a dump analysis, you need a *debug kernel*. This kernel is in fact identical to a normal kernel, but it includes a lot of information that can be used for dump analysis. See page 361 for details of how to build a debug kernel. Since you never know when you might run into a problem, it's highly recommended to use a debug kernel at all times.

Fixing a broken installation

A really massive crash may damage your system to such an extent that you need to reinstall the whole system. For example, if you overwrite your hard disk from start to finish, you don't have any other choice. In many cases, though, the damage is serious but repairable. The problem is, you can't start the system to fix the problems. In this case, you have two possibilities:

- Boot from the second CD-ROM (*Live Filesystem*). It will be mounted as the root file system.

- Boot from the *Fixit* floppy. The Fixit floppy is in the distribution in the same directory as the boot diskette, *floppies*. Just copy *floppies/fixit.flp* to a disk in the same way as described for boot diskettes in page 64. To use the fixit floppy, first boot with the boot diskette and select "Fixit floppy" from the main menu. The fixit floppy will be mounted under the root MFS as */mnt2*.

In either case, the hard disks aren't mounted: you might want to do repair work on them before any other access.

Use this option only if you have a good understanding of the system installation process. Depending on the damage, you may or may not be successful. If you have a recent backup of your system, it might be faster to perform a complete installation than to try to fix what's left, and after a re-installation you can be more confident that the system is correctly installed.

8

The Ports Collection

The Internet is full of free software which is normally distributed in source form. That's the problem: the way from the source archive that you get free from the Internet to the finished, installed, running program on your machine—normally called *porting*—can be a long and frustrating one. See my book *Porting UNIX Software* for more details of the porting process.

In order to get a software package up and running on your system, you need to go through most of these steps:

1. Get the source files on your machine. They are usually contained in an *archive*, a file containing a number of other files. Archives used for the ports collection are generally *gzipped tar* files, packed with *tar* and compressed with *gzip*, but other formats are also possible. Whatever the format, you'll typically use *ftp* to get them to your machine.

2. Unpack the archive into a *source tree*, using *gunzip* and *tar*.

3. *Configure* the package. Most packages include shell scripts to do this. Configuration performs a threefold adaptation of the package:

   1. It adapts it to the system hardware.

   2. It adapts it to the software environment you're running (in this case, FreeBSD).

   3. It adapts it to your personal preferences.

4. *Build* the package. For most packages, this involves compiling the source files and creating executables.

5. *Installing* the package. This involves mainly copying the executables, configuration files and documentation created by a *build* to the correct place in the directory hierarchy.

6. *Configuring* the installed software. This is similar in concept to package configuration, except that it occurs in the run-time environment. The package configuration may perform all the necessary configuration for you.

These are a lot of steps, and you'll often find they're laid through a minefield: one false move, and everything blows up. To make porting and installing software easier, the FreeBSD team created a framework called the *Ports Collection*. In addition, the CD-ROM edition of FreeBSD includes a large number of pre-built packages which just need to be installed.

In this chapter, we'll consider the following points as they relate to the FreeBSD ports collection:

- How to install a pre-compiled package. We'll look at this in the next section.

- What the ports tree is, and how to compile and install ("build") a package. We'll look at this on page 112.

- How to create and submit a new port, on page 116

How to install a package

In FreeBSD parlance, a package is simply a special archive which contains the files (usually executable binary files) which are installed when you build and install a port. Compared to the full-blown port, packages are much faster to install—most take less than a minute. On the other hand, they don't give you the choice of configuration that the complete port does. The first and third CD-ROMs of the distribution each contain a directory *packages* with a total of nearly 1000 pre-compiled software packages, totalling about 1 GB after compression. Alternatively, you can find FreeBSD packages on many servers on the Internet—check the online handbook for some places to look.

To help maintain an overview, both ports and packages are divided into categories. They are stored in directories named after the category. See the file */usr/ports/INDEX* for a list. For example, *emacs* under *editors* is in the file *packages/editors/emacs-20.3.tgz*. To install it, you simply enter:

```
# pkg_add /cdrom/packages/editors/emacs-20.3.tgz
```

Alternatively, you can install packages from the */stand/sysinstall* Final Configuration Menu. We saw this menu on page in figure 5-13 on page 86. When you start *sysinstall* from the command line, you get to this menu by selecting Index, and then selecting Configure.

Building a port

The FreeBSD project uses the term *port* to describe the additional files needed to adapt a package to build under FreeBSD. It does *not* include the code itself, though many code archives are on the third and fourth CD-ROMs in the directory */ports/distfiles*.

Before you get started with the ports, you need to install the port information on your system. The location is fixed: they must be installed in */usr/ports*. This directory tree is frequently called the *Ports Tree*. There are a number of ways to install them.

Installing ports during system installation

The simplest way to install the Ports Collection is when you install the system. You can install it with the base system if you select the Custom distribution and include the ports collection.

Install ports from the first CD-ROM

The file *ports/ports.tgz* on the first CD-ROM is a *tar* archive containing all the ports. If you didn't install it during system installation, use the following method to install the complete collection (about 40 MB). Make sure your CD-ROM is mounted (in this example on */cdrom*), and enter:

```
# cd /usr
# tar xzvf /cdrom/ports/ports.tgz
```

If you only want to extract a single package, say *inn*, which is in the category *news*, enter:

```
# cd /usr
# tar xzvf /cdrom/ports/ports.tgz   ports/news/inn
```

Installing ports from the ports CD-ROM

Alternatively, you can install the files from the ports CD-ROM. This is not much of an advantage for installation, but you may find it convenient to browse through the source trees in the directory *ports* on the CD-ROM. Let's assume you have found a directory */ports/graphics/hpscan* on the CD-ROM, and it is your current working directory. You can move the data across with the following:

```
# cd /cdrom/ports/graphics
# mkdir -p /usr/ports/graphics
# tar cf - . | (cd /usr/ports/graphics; tar xvf -)
```

Ports via FTP

Of course, maybe you've just heard about this great new port of *xmbase-grok*, and you want to get hold of it as soon as possible. It's brand new, so it's obviously not on your CD-ROM.

All ports are kept in subdirectories of the URL *ftp://ftp.FreeBSD.org/pub/FreeBSD*. The directory *ftp://ftp.FreeBSD.org/pub/FreeBSD/ports/ports* contains ports for FreeBSD-CURRENT (see Chapter 19, *Keeping up to date with FreeBSD*, page 365). The other directories are named after the release. For example, for FreeBSD-3.2, you would select *ftp://ftp.FreeBSD.org/pub/Free-BSD/ports/ports-3.2*. To get this one, you might perform the following steps:

```
# ftp ftp.freebsd.org
Connected to wcarchive.cdrom.com.
220 wcarchive.cdrom.com FTP server (Version DG-3.1.27 Wed Dec 2 01:29:08 PST 1998) ready.
331 Guest login ok, send your complete e-mail address as password.
...lots of blurb omitted
ftp> cd /pub/FreeBSD/ports/ports-3.2/databases
250 CWD command successful.
ftp> ls -ltr
200 PORT command successful.
150 Opening ASCII mode data connection for /bin/ls.
total 36
drwxrwxr-x  2 2035   ftp-Free   512 Apr  9  1996 pkg
drwxrwxr-x  5 2035   ftp-Free   512 Dec 12  1996 typhoon
drwxrwxr-x  4 2035   ftp-Free   512 Jan 28  1997 gdbm
drwxr-xr-x  4 2035   ftp-Free   512 Jun 13 15:13 db
drwxr-xr-x  4 2035   ftp-Free   512 Jun 24 15:15 p5-DBD-Pg
drwxrwxr-x  5 2035   ftp-Free   512 Jun 24 15:15 p5-Pg
drwxr-xr-x  5 2035   ftp-Free   512 Jun 24 15:15 p5-Mysql
drwxrwxr-x  4 2035   ftp-Free   512 Jun 27 01:48 p5-DBI
drwxr-xr-x  4 2035   ftp-Free   512 Jul  2 15:20 p5-DBD-mysql
drwxrwxr-x  6 2035   ftp-Free   512 Jul 14 15:20 msql
drwxrwxr-x  4 2035   ftp-Free   512 Jul 15 15:27 p5-Msql
drwxrwxr-x  6 2035   ftp-Free   512 Jul 17 15:24 postgresql
drwxr-xr-x  6 2035   ftp-Free   512 Jul 18 03:19 mysql
drwxrwxr-x  6 2035   ftp-Free   512 Aug 27 03:21 gnats
drwxr-xr-x  5 root   ftp-Free   512 Aug 30 15:18 xmbase-grok
-rw-rw-r--  1 2035   ftp-Free   442 Sep  2 15:30 Makefile
drwxr-xr-x  5 root   ftp-Free   512 Sep  2 15:31 xmysql
drwxr-xr-x  4 root   ftp-Free   512 Sep  2 15:31 xmysqladmin
226 Transfer complete.
ftp> get xmbase-grok.tar.gz
local: xmbase-grok.tar.gz remote: xmbase-grok.tar.gz
200 PORT command successful.
150 Opening BINARY mode data connection for /usr/bin/tar.
226 Transfer complete.
2390 bytes received in 1.37 seconds (1.71 KB/s)
```

Since *xmbase-grok* is a directory, you tell *ftp* to automatically *tar* and *gzip* the directory and return you a file *xmbase-grok.tar.gz*. Not all ftp servers support tarring and gzipping, since gzipping in particular takes up a lot of CPU time.

Next, you unpack it in your */usr/ports/databases* directory:

```
# cd /usr/ports/databases/
# tar xzvf /home/Book/FreeBSD/xmbase-grok.tar.gz
xmbase-grok/
xmbase-grok/files/
xmbase-grok/files/md5
xmbase-grok/pkg/
xmbase-grok/pkg/COMMENT
xmbase-grok/pkg/DESCR
xmbase-grok/pkg/PLIST
xmbase-grok/Makefile
xmbase-grok/patches/
xmbase-grok/patches/patch-aa
xmbase-grok/patches/patch-ab
xmbase-grok/patches/patch-ac
```

What's in that port?

One problem with the Ports Collection is the sheer number. It can be difficult just to find out what they're supposed to do. If you build all the ports, you'll be busy for weeks, and there's no way you could read all the documentation in one lifetime. Where can you get an overview? Here are some suggestions:

- You can print the index with the following commands:

  ```
  # cd /usr/ports
  # make print-index | lpr
  ```

- You can search for a specific keyword with the `search` target. For example, to find ports related to *Emacs*, you might enter:

  ```
  # cd /usr/ports
  # make search key=Emacs
  ```

- You can build a series of *html* pages like this:

  ```
  # cd /usr/ports
  # make readmes
  ```

  You can then browse them at the URL *file:/usr/ports/README.html*.

- You can find a printable version in the files */cdrom/book/docs*:

Table 8-1. Ports overview

File	Content
packages-by-category.ps	Packages sorted by category, in PostScript
packages-by-category.txt	Packages sorted by category, in ASCII
packages.ps	Packages sorted alphabetically, in PostScript
packages.txt	Packages sorted alphabetically, in ASCII

Ports via CVSup

If you're using *CVSup* to keep up to date with the source tree, you have the option of including the ports tree */usr/ports* in the trees you maintain. See page 368 for more details.

Getting the source archive

You'll see from the above example that there are not many files in the port. Most of the files required to build the software are in the original source code archive, but you don't have it yet!

Well, that's not a problem. Part of the function of the ports collection is to go out on the Net and get them for you. This is completely automatic: you just type `make`, and the build process gets the source archive for you and builds it. Of course, you must be connected to the Internet for this to work.

In any case, are you sure you don't have the sources? Maybe you do. As we saw, most of them are on the third and fourth CD-ROM, in the directory */cdrom/ports/distfiles*. The ports collection Makefiles look for them in this directory (another good reason to mount your CD-ROM on */cdrom*) and also in */usr/ports/distfiles*.

If you mount your CD-ROM elsewhere (maybe because you have more than one CD-ROM drive, and so you have to mount the CD-ROM on, say, */cd4*), the Makefiles will not find the distribution files and will try to load the files from the Internet. One way to solve this problem is to create a symbolic link from */cd4/ports/distfiles* to */usr/ports/distfiles*. The trouble with this approach is that you will then no longer be able to load new distribution files into */usr/ports/distfiles*, since it will be on CD-ROM. Instead, do:

```
# cd /cd4/ports/distfiles
# mkdir -p /usr/ports/distfiles          make sure you have a distfiles directory
# for i in *; do
>   ln -s /cd4/ports/distfiles/$i /usr/ports/distfiles/$i
> done
```

If you're using *csh* or *tcsh*, enter:

```
# cd /cd4/ports/distfiles
# mkdir -p /usr/ports/distfiles          make sure you have a distfiles directory
# foreach i (*)
?   ln -s /cd4/ports/distfiles/$i /usr/ports/distfiles/$i
? end
```

This creates a symbolic link to each of the distribution files, but if the file for a specific port isn't there, the ports collection can fetch it and store it in the directory.

Building the port

Once you have the skeleton files for the port, the rest is simple. Just enter:

```
# cd /usr/ports/databases/xmbase-grok
# make
# make install
```

It's a good idea to perform the *make* step first: *make install* does not always build the package.

Port dependencies

Sometimes, it's not enough to build a single port. Many ports depend on other ports. If you have the complete, up-to-date ports tree installed on your system, the Ports Collection will take care of this for you: it will check if the other port is installed, and if it isn't, it will install it for you. For example, *tkdesk* depends on *tk*. *tk* depends on *tcl*. If you don't have any of them installed, and you try to build *tkdesk*, it will recursively install *tk* and *tcl* for you.

Things get a little more complicated if your tree isn't complete, or if you have updated specific packages. For example, the latest version of *tkdesk* depends on *tk* version 4.1. Older versions depended on version 3.6. If you update the directory */usr/ports/x11/tkdesk*, but not */usr/ports/x11/tk*, the build will probably fail.

There are two possible solutions to this problem:

- Keep the tree up to date with *CVSup* or *ctm* (see Chapter 19, *Keeping up to date with FreeBSD*).

- Check the dependencies, and update them manually.

To check the dependencies, look at the *Makefile*. For example, the current version of */usr/ports/x11/tkdesk/Makefile* contains:

```
# New ports collection makefile for: tkdesk
# Version required:     1.0b2
# Date created:         30 Jul 1996
# Whom:                 shanee@rabbit.augusta.de
#
# $Id: Makefile,v 1.4 1997/04/20 13:19:59 wosch Exp $
#

DISTNAME=   tkdesk-1.0b3
PKGNAME=    tkdesk-1.0b3
CATEGORIES=     misc x11 tk41
MASTER_SITES=   http://sun1.rrzn-user.uni-hannover.de/~zzhibol/tkdesk/

MAINTAINER=     nox@jelal.hb.north.de

LIB_DEPENDS=    tk41\.1\.:${PORTSDIR}/x11/tk41          look at this line

post-patch:
    -rm ${WRKSRC}/tcldesk/*.orig ${WRKSRC}/tcldesk/*/*.orig

.include <bsd.port.mk>
```

The definition `LIB_DEPENDS` tells you the dependencies. In this case, it will first look for the libraries */usr/lib/libtk41.so.1.0* or */usr/local/lib/libtk41.so.1.0*. If it finds them, it will be satisfied. Otherwise it will build the port at */usr/ports/x11/tk41*. The *make* variable `PORTSDIR` represents the name of the top-level ports directory, currently `/usr/ports`.

Getting common software

A lot of software doesn't need to be ported. For example, if you want *Netscape*, you can just download it from *ftp.netscape.com*. In fact, you have a choice of three different versions of *Netscape*: you can take the native FreeBSD version, the BSD/OS version or the Linux version.

That's where the trouble starts. Which one do you use? How do you install it? Netscape's installation procedures are getting better, but they still leave something to be desired.

The answer's simple: take the port! Although Netscape comes only in binary form, the port handles getting the correct version and installing it for you. Another advantage to using a port instead of installing the package manually is that the port installs the software as a FreeBSD package, which makes it much easier to remove the software later.

This method can be used to install some other software as well, for example *StarOffice*. The moral is simple: always check the ports collection before getting a software package from the net.

Maintaining ports

Once you install a port, you might consider that to be the end of the story. That's seldom the case. For example:

- One day, you might find your disk fills up, so you go looking for old stuff you don't use any more. How do you know whether it's part of a port or not?

- You might need to replace a port by a newer version. How do you do it?

Controlling installed ports

We've already seen the program *pkg_add* when installing pre-compiled packages. There are a number of other *pkg_* programs which can help you maintain installed ports, whether they have been installed by *pkg_add* or by *make install* from the Ports Collection:

- *pkg_info* will tell you which ports are installed. For example,

```
$  pkg_info -I -a | sort -f | less
a2ps-A4-4.9.7          Formats an ascii file for printing on a postscript printer.
aalib-1.2              An ascii art library
acroread-3.01          View, distribute and print PDF documents.
afm-1.0                Adobe Font Metrics.
apache-1.2.4           The extremely popular Apache http server.  Very fast, very c
apache-1.2b10          The extremely popular Apache http server.  Very fast, very c
... etc
elm-2.4ME+22           ELM Mail User Agent
elm-2.4ME+32           ELM Mail User Agent
... etc
```

  The option -a tells *pkg_list* to list all packages; otherwise you should specify a package name. The option -I specifies that the list should be a one-line "Index" description; otherwise you get a multi-line description of the package.

  By default, *pkg_info* lists the packages in the order in which they were installed, which is not normally of great interest. By piping into the command *sort -f*, we get it in alphabetical order. The -f flags tells *sort* to *fold* upper case into the same sort order as lower case; otherwise all packages with names starting with a capital letter would come first. Finally, *less* allows us to page through what could be a very long list.

  Note the advantage of sorting in this example: it seems we have two versions of *apache* and two versions of *elm* installed, probably not what we intended. If it had been unsorted, it would be difficult to discover this fact.

- You can *remove* a package with *pkg_delete*. You need to be root to do this. For example, the list above shows two versions of the *elm* mail user agent. To remove the older one, we enter:

```
# pkg_delete elm-2.4ME+22
File '/usr/local/man/man1/answer.1' doesn't really exist.
Unable to completely remove file '/usr/local/man/man1/answer.1'
File '/usr/local/man/man1/checkalias.1' doesn't really exist.
Unable to completely remove file '/usr/local/man/man1/checkalias.1'
... etc
Couldn't entirely delete package (perhaps the packing list is
incorrectly specified?)
```

In this case, it looks as if somebody has tried to remove the files before, so *pkg_delete* couldn't do so.

Another problem with *pkg_delete* is that it might delete files of the same name which have been replaced by newer packages. After performing this operation, we try:

```
$ elm
bash: elm: command not found
```

Oops! We tried to delete the old version, but we deleted at least part of the new version. Now we need to install it again.

The moral of this story is that things aren't as simple as they might be. When you install a new version of a package, you may want to test it before you commit to using it all the time. You can't just go and delete the old version. One possibility would be to install the new package, and try it out. When you've finished testing, delete *both* packages and re-install the one you want to keep.

Keeping track of updates

The best way to find out about updates is to subscribe to the FreeBSD-ports mailing list. That way, you will get notification every time something changes. If you're tracking the ports tree, you'll also get the updates to the ports tree automatically. Otherwise you will have to download the port. In either case, to update your installed port, just repeat the build.

Submitting a new port

The ports collection is constantly growing. Hardly a day goes by without a new port being added to the list. Maybe you want to submit the next one?

It's beyond the scope of this book to give you all the details of how to go about submitting a port. Check in the online handbook for the details, which might change from time to time. Basically, however, the sequence is:

- Read the instructions *before* starting the port. There are many ways to port a package—there could even be more than one correct way to port it. If you port it in the wrong way, the ports team will be unable to accept it, and fixing the problem can easily be as difficult as doing the port was in the first place.

- Write a top-level *Makefile* for the port, including information on the master sites from which the package may be downloaded, the name and category of the package, and the name of the maintainer (you).

- Perform the port.

- Submit it.

9

Setting up X11

FreeBSD 3.2 comes with XFree86 version 3.3.3.1, a port of X11R6 that supports several versions of Intel-based UNIX. This chapter describes how to set up your XFree86 server. It is based on material supplied with the FreeBSD release, specifically the files *README.FreeBSD* and *README.Config* in the directory */usr/X11R6/lib/X11/doc*. If you find any discrepancy, the material in those files will be more up-to-date than this description. In addition, the file */usr/X11R6/lib/X11/doc/RELNOTES* contains OS-independent information about the 3.3.3 release.

X uses a lot of memory. In order to run X, your system should have an absolute minimum of 8 MB of memory, but performance will be painful with so little memory. A more practical minimum is 16 MB, and you can improve performance by adding much more memory. If you use X intensively, you will continue seeing performance improvement by increasing to as much as 128 MB of RAM.

For the impatient

There's lots of useful information in the rest of this chapter, but maybe you're not interested in information right now. You just want to get your X server up and running. However, be warned:

> *An incorrect installation can burn out your monitor or your video board.*

Read page 142 for further details.

However, if you know you're in spec, and you have a standard Super VGA board and a good multifrequency monitor, then you can probably get things up and running without reading this chapter. Read the section on X installation in Chapter 4, *Quick Installation*, page 60. If things don't work, come back here and read on.

Installing XFree86

The easiest way to install XFree86 is with the *sysinstall* program, either when you're installing the system, or later by starting the program */stand/sysinstall*. See Chapter 5, *Installing FreeBSD*, page 79, for details of how to install the software. In the rest of this chapter, we'll look at what makes up the distribution, and on page 129 we'll look at how to configure X once it has been installed.

The XFree86 distribution

XFree86 is distributed as a bewildering number of archives in the directory */cdrom/XF86333*. In the following section, we'll take a look at what you should install. Don't worry too much, though: if you can't decide what to pick and you have 200MB of disk space free, it's safe to unpack everything.

At a minimum you need to unpack the archives in the following table and at least one server that matches your VGA board. You'll need 10Mb for the minimum required run-time binaries only, and between 1.7 and 3 MB for the server.

Table 9-1. Required components of XFree86

Archive	Description
X333bin.tgz	All the executable X client applications and shared librariess
X333fnts.tgz	The misc and 75 dpi fonts
X333lib.tgz	Data files and libraries needed at runtime
X3331upd.tgz	Update number 1 to the XFree86 release.

The file *X3331upd.tgz* updates XFree86 from the base release (3.3.3) to release 3.3.3.1. Each incremental update includes the contents of any previously released updates (in this case there are none). You must extract these updates after extracting the base release, since they contain replacements for files in the other archives. The archives on the FreeBSD 3.2 CD-ROM include update 1 of XFree86 3.3.3. They are not the same as the XFree86 3.3.3 archives on *ftp://ftp.XFree86.org/*.

The X Server

In addition to the archives above, you need at least one server, which will take up about 3 MB of disk. The choice depends primarily on what kind of display board you have. The default server name is */usr/X11R6/bin/X*, and it is a link to a specific server binary */usr/X11R6/bin/XF86_xxxx*. You'll find the server archives for the standard PC architecture in */cdrom/XF86333/Servers*, and the servers for the Japanese PC98 architecture in */cdrom/XF86333/PC98-Servers*:

Table 9-2. XFree86 servers for standard PC architecture

Archive	Description
X3338514.tgz	8-bit colour for IBM 8514 and true compatibles.
X333AGX.tgz	8 and 16-bit colour for AGX and XGA boards.
X333I128.tgz	8 and 16-bit colour for I128 boards.
X333Ma32.tgz	8 and 16-bit colour for ATI Mach32 boards.
X333Ma64.tgz	8, 16 and 32-bit colour for ATI Mach64 boards.
X333Ma8.tgz	8-bit colour for ATI Mach8 boards.
X333Mono.tgz	1-bit monochrome for VGA, Super-VGA, Hercules, and others.
X333P9K.tgz	8, 16, and 32-bit colour for Weitek P9000 boards (Diamond Viper).
X333S3.tgz	8, 16 and 32-bit colour for S3 boards.
X333S3V.tgz	8 and 16-bit colour for S3 ViRGE boards.
X333SVGA.tgz	>=8-bit colour for Super-VGA cards.
X333VG16.tgz	4-bit colour for VGA and Super-VGA cards
X333W32.tgz	8-bit colour for ET4000/W32, /W32i, /W32p and ET6000 cards.

Table 9-3. XFree86 servers for Japanese PC98 architecture

Archive	Description
X3339GAN.tgz	8-bit colour for PC98 GA-98NB/WAP boards
X3339GA9.tgz	8, 16 and 32-bit colour for PC98 S3 GA-968 boards
X3339480.tgz	8-bit colour for PC98 PEGC
X3339NKV.tgz	8-bit colour for PC98 NEC-CIRRUS/EPSON NKV/NKV2 boards
X3339WBS.tgz	8-bit colour for PC98 WAB-S boards
X3339WEP.tgz	8-bit colour for PC98 WAB-EP boards
X3339WSN.tgz	8-bit colour for PC98 WSN-A2F boards
X3339EGC.tgz	4-bit colour for PC98 EGC
X3339TGU.tgz	8 and 16-bit colour for PC98 Trident Cyber9320/9680 boards
X3339NS3.tgz	8 and 16-bit colour for PC98 NEC S3 boards
X3339SPW.tgz	8 and 16-bit colour for PC98 S3 PW/PCSKB boards
X3339LPW.tgz	8 and 16-bit colour for PC98 S3 PW/LB boards

Each of these servers includes a manual page which contains details of supported chipsets and server-specific configuration options.

A number of archives are provided for X programmers:

Table 9-4. XFree86 programmer's files

Archive	Description
X333prog.tgz	config, *lib*.a* and **.h* files needed for compiling clients.
X333ctrb.tgz	Contributed sources.
X333lk98.tgz	The "link kit" for building servers, Japanese PC98 version.
X333lkit.tgz	The "link kit" for building servers, normal architecture version.
X333src-1.tgz	Part 1 of the complete sources
X333src-2.tgz	Part 2 of the complete sources
X333src-3.tgz	Part 3 of the complete sources

You'll need *X333prog.tgz* if you intend to install ports of X software.

Finally, XFree86 includes a number of optional parts:

Table 9-5. XFree86 documentation

Archive	Description
X333doc.tgz	READMEs
X333jdoc.tgz	READMEs in Japanese
X333ps.tgz	READMEs in PostScript
X333html.tgz	READMEs in HTML
X333man.tgz	man pages

Table 9-6. XFree86 setup programs

Archive	Description
X333cfg.tgz	Customizable *xinit* and *xdm* runtime configuration files.
X333set.tgz	The *XF86Setup* utility, a graphical version of the *xf86config* utility that we will look at on page 129.
X333jset.tgz	The *XF86Setup* utility, Japanese version, for the normal PC architecture.

XF86Setup is a graphical mode setup program for XFree86, and you may prefer it to the standard setup program *xf86config*. You don't need any special archives for *xf86config*: it's included in *X333bin.tgz*.

The first time you install, you will need *X333cfg.tgz* to create your initial configuration files.

Don't use it when upgrading: it overwrites your configuration files.

Table 9-7. Additional fonts

Archive	Description
X333f100.tgz	100dpi fonts
X333fscl.tgz	Speedo and Type1 fonts
X333fnon.tgz	Japanese, Chinese and other non-english fonts
X333fcyr.tgz	Cyrillic fonts

Unlike the X servers described above, the archives for the following servers are all in the main directory */cdrom/disk/XF86333*:

Table 9-8. Miscellaneous servers

Archive	Description
X333fsrv.tgz	The font server
X333nest.tgz	A nested server running as a client window on another display.
X333prt.tgz	The X print server.
X333vfb.tgz	The Virtual Framebuffer X server, which renders into memory or an *mmap*ped file.

Earlier versions of FreeBSD also supplied a separate *xdm* archive due to export restrictions on the encryption software included in *xdm*. FreeBSD 3.2 handles encryption in shared libraries now, so that *xdm* no longer contains *DES*, and has been included in the standard archives.

In addition, earlier versions of XFree86 included the archives *X333pex.tgz*, with software for 3D applications, and *X333lbx.tgz*, the low bandwidth X proxy server and libraries. The files in these archives are now included in the appropriate places in the other archives. You no longer need to install them explicitly.

Installing XFree86 manually

If you don't use *sysinstall* to install X, you need to perform a number of steps:

- First, create the directories and unpack the required archives.

- Choose and install an X server.

- Install any updates.

- Set up the environment to be able to access X.

- Find a virtual terminal in which to run X.

- Configure X for your hardware.

This sounds like a lot of work, but if you approach it methodically, it's not too bad. In the rest of the chapter, we'll look at each step in turn.

Unpacking the archives

You must unpack the archives as `root`, since a number of the executables are set-user-id (they run as `root` even when started by other users). If you unpack the server as an ordinary user, it may abort when you try to run it. You must also use a `umask` value of `022` (permissions `rwxr-xr-x`), because the X server requires special permissions. See page 227 for an explanation of *umask*.

```
$ su
Password:
# umask 022
```

If you don't have enough space in the */usr* file system, create a directory on another partition and symlink it to */usr*. For example, if you have a file system */home* with adequate space, you could do:

```
# cd /home
# mkdir X11R6
# ln -s /home/X11R6 /usr/X11R6
```

Next, decide which archives you want to install. For a minimal installation, choose */cdrom/XF86333/X333bin.tgz*, */cdrom/XF86333/X333fnts.tgz*, */cdrom/XF86333/X333lib.tgz*, */cdrom/XF86333/X333cfg.tgz*, and finally any updates, in this case */cdrom/XF86333/X3331upd.tgz*. If you have already configured X for your hardware, omit */cdrom/XF86333/X333cfg.tgz*.

If you are using sh, unpack like this:

```
# mkdir -p /usr/X11R6
# cd /usr/X11R6
# for i in bin fnts lib cfg 1upd; do
#   tar xzf /cdrom/XF86333/X333$i.tgz
# done
```

If you are using csh, enter:

```
% mkdir -p /usr/X11R6
% cd /usr/X11R6
% foreach i (bin fnts lib cfg 1upd)
?   tar xzf /cdrom/XF86333/X333$i.tgz
? end
```

If you're installing update archives, it's very important that the last name in the list is the abbreviation of the name of the update (*1upd*): this update archive contains replacements for files in the other archives. This also makes it complicated if you want to install everything: you can't just write */cdrom/XF86333/X333*.tgz*, since that would install the update (*1upd*) before most of the other archives. Instead, you need to spell it out:

```
# mkdir -p /usr/X11R6
# cd /usr/X11R6
# for i in 9set bin cfg contrib doc f100 fcyr fnon fnts fscl fsrv \
>           html jdoc jset lib lkit man nest prog prt ps set \
>           src-1 vfb 1upd; do
#    tar xzf /cdrom/XF86333/X333$i.tgz
# done
```

If you are using csh, enter:

```
% mkdir -p /usr/X11R6
% cd /usr/X11R6
% foreach i (9set bin cfg contrib doc f100 fcyr fnon fnts fscl fsrv \
             html jdoc jset lib lkit man nest prog prt ps set \
             src-1 vfb 1upd; do
?    tar xzf /cdrom/XF86333/X333$i.tgz
? end
```

As with the minimal install, make sure that the abbreviation for the update archive *1upd* comes last.

The prompts during the command (# and >, or %, nothing and ?) are typical. Depending on your shell, you may get other prompts.

Installing the server

Choose a server archive corresponding to your VGA board. If table 9-2 on page 123 doesn't give you enough information, check the server man pages, */usr/X11R6/man/man1/XF86_**, which list the VGA chip sets supported by each server. For example, if you have an ET4000 based board you will use the XF86_SVGA server. In this case you would enter:

```
# cd /usr/X11R6
# tar xzf /cdrom/XF86333/Server/X333SVGA.tgz    substitute your server name here
```

If you are using csh, enter:

```
% cd /usr/X11R6
% tar xzf /cdrom/XF86333/Server/X333SVGA.tgz    substitute your server name here
```

Setting up the environment

Next, you may wish to create a symbolic link */usr/X11/bin/X* that points to the server that matches your video board. In this example, it's the *XF86_SVGA* server:

```
# cd /usr/X11R6/bin          change to bin directory
# rm X                       remove the current server
# ln -s XF86_SVGA X          and create a link to the new server
```

X needs this symbolic link in order to be able to work correctly, but you have the option of setting it when you run *xf86config*—see below.

Next, check that the directory */usr/X11R6/bin* is in the default path for *sh* in */etc/profile* and for *csh* in */etc/csh.login*, and add it if it is not. It's best to do this with an editor, but if you want to take a short cut, you can enter:

```
# echo 'set path = ($path /usr/X11R6/bin)' >>/etc/csh.login
# echo 'PATH=$PATH:/usr/X11R6/bin' >>/etc/profile
```

Alternatively, make sure everybody who uses X puts */usr/X11R6/bin* in their shell's PATH variable.

Next, invoke *ldconfig* to put the shared libraries in *ld.so*'s cache:

```
# ldconfig -m /usr/X11R6/lib
```

You can omit invoking *ldconfig* if you plan to reboot before using X.

> You don't need to uncompress the font files, but if you do, you must run *mkfontdir* in the corresponding font directory; otherwise your server will abort with the message "could not open default font 'fixed'".

Assigning a virtual terminal to X

Next, make sure you have a spare virtual console which is running a *getty*. First check how many virtual consoles you have:

```
# dmesg | grep virtual
sc0: VGA color <16 virtual consoles, flags=0x0>
```

Then check */etc/ttys* to make sure there is at least one virtual terminal (*ttyvxx* device) which doesn't have a *getty* enabled. Look for the keyword off:

```
# grep ttyv /etc/ttys
ttyv0   "/usr/libexec/getty Pc"  cons25  on secure
ttyv1   "/usr/libexec/getty Pc"  cons25  on secure
ttyv2   "/usr/libexec/getty Pc"  cons25  on secure
ttyv3   "/usr/libexec/getty Pc"  cons25  off secure
```

In this case, */dev/ttyv3* is available, if your kernel has least 4 VTs. If not, either disable a getty in */etc/ttys* by changing on to off, or build another kernel with more virtual terminals—see Chapter 18, *Configuring the kernel*, page 339, for details of how to set the kernel parameter MAXCONS.

Configuring X for Your Hardware

After installing the X software, you will need to customize the file */usr/X11R6/lib/X11/XF86Config*, which tells the X server about your hardware and how you want to run it.

> The format of *XF86Config* has changed since version 2 of XFree86. If you are upgrading from version 2, use the *reconfig* utility to perform a partial translation of the old *XConfig* file to the new format. You'll still need to make some changes manually.
>
> ```
> # reconfig < Xconfig > XF86Config
> ```
>
> The man page *XF86Config(5)* and the file */usr/X11R6/lib/X11/XF86Config.eg* will help you complete the changes.

In order to set up *XF86Config*, you'll need the following hardware information:

- Your mouse type, the bit rate if it's a serial mouse, and the name of the device to which it is connected. This will typically be */dev/ttyd0* or */dev/ttyd1* for a serial mouse, */dev/psm0* for a PS/2 mouse, or */dev/mse0* for a bus mouse.

- The type of the video board and the amount of display memory. If it's a no-name board, establish what VGA chip set it uses.

- The parameters of your monitor: vertical and horizontal frequency.

Identifying the hardware

How do you decide what your hardware is? The manufacturer *should* tell you, but very often the information you get about your display board and monitor is pitiful: "Super VGA board with 76 Hz refresh rate and 16,777,216 colours". This tells you the maximum pixel depth (24 bits: the number of colours is $2^{(\text{pixel depth})}$), but it doesn't tell you *anything* else about the display board. As we'll see in Chapter 10, *XFree86 configuration in depth*, the real parameters you need to know are the maximum horizontal frequency, the dot clock range, the chip set and the amount of display memory.

You could be unlucky trying to get some of this information, but you can get some with the *SuperProbe* program. It should always be able to tell you the chip set and the amount of memory on board.

> *Occasionally SuperProbe can crash your system. Make sure you are not doing anything important when you run it.*

Running *SuperProbe* looks like this:

```
# SuperProbe
(warnings and acknowledgements omitted)
First video: Super-VGA
        Chipset: Tseng ET4000 (Port Probed)
        Memory:  1024 Kbytes
        RAMDAC:  Generic 8-bit pseudo-color DAC
                 (with 6-bit wide lookup tables (or in 6-bit mode))
```

SuperProbe is very finicky about running at all, and you'll often get messages like:

```
SuperProbe: Cannot be run while an X server is running
SuperProbe: If an X server is not running, unset $DISPLAY and try again
SuperProbe: Cannot open video
```

In other words, even if no X server is running, *SuperProbe* won't work if you have the environment variable DISPLAY set. How do you unset it? With Bourne-style shells, you enter:

```
# unset DISPLAY
```

In the C shell, you enter:

```
% unsetenv DISPLAY
```

Running xf86config

The easy way to create your configuration file is with one of the utilities *xf86config* (note the lower case name) or *XF86Setup*. Both leads you through the configuration step by step. *xf86config* runs in character mode, while *XF86Setup* runs in a graphical mode. *XF86Setup* can have problems with unusual hardware, so I personally prefer *xf86config*.

You can also use *sysinstall*, but this doesn't change much: *sysinstall* just starts *xf86config* for you, and it's easier to start it directly. In this section, we'll use an example to illustrate *xf86config* configuration: we're installing X for an ancient Diamond SpeedStar with 1 MB of display memory, a Logitech MouseMan mouse, and an ADI MicroScan 5AP monitor. The mouse is connected to the system via the first serial port, */dev/ttyd0*.

To run *xf86config*, type in the name. If */usr/X11R6/bin* is included in your PATH environment variable (see page 178), you just need to type *xf86config*:

```
# /usr/X11R6/bin/xf86config
This program will create a basic XF86Config file, based on menu selections you
make.

The XF86Config file usually resides in /usr/X11R6/lib/X11 or /etc. A sample
XF86Config file is supplied with XFree86; it is configured for a standard
VGA card and monitor with 640x480 resolution. This program will ask for a
pathname when it is ready to write the file.

You can either take the sample XF86Config as a base and edit it for your
configuration, or let this program produce a base XF86Config file for your
configuration and fine-tune it. Refer to /usr/X11R6/lib/X11/doc/README.Config
for a detailed overview of the configuration process.

For accelerated servers (including accelerated drivers in the SVGA server),
there are many chipset and card-specific options and settings. This program
does not know about these. On some configurations some of these settings must
be specified. Refer to the server man pages and chipset-specific READMEs.

Before continuing with this program, make sure you know the chipset and
amount of video memory on your video card. SuperProbe can help with this.
It is also helpful if you know what server you want to run.

Press enter to continue, or ctrl-c to abort. ENTER

First specify a mouse protocol type. Choose one from the following list:
```

```
1.  Microsoft compatible (2-button protocol)
2.  Mouse Systems (3-button protocol)
3.  Bus Mouse
4.  PS/2 Mouse
5.  Logitech Mouse (serial, old type, Logitech protocol)
6.  Logitech MouseMan (Microsoft compatible)
7.  MM Series
8.  MM HitTablet
9.  Microsoft IntelliMouse

If you have a two-button mouse, it is most likely of type 1, and if you have
a three-button mouse, it can probably support both protocol 1 and 2. There are
two main varieties of the latter type: mice with a switch to select the
protocol, and mice that default to 1 and require a button to be held at
boot-time to select protocol 2. Some mice can be convinced to do 2 by sending
a special sequence to the serial port (see the ClearDTR/ClearRTS options).

Enter a protocol number: 6            Logitech MouseMan

You have selected a Logitech MouseMan type mouse. You might want to enable
ChordMiddle which could cause the third button to work.

Please answer the following question with either 'y' or 'n'.
Do you want to enable ChordMiddle? n
```

You definitely want to enable the third button on your mouse, since many X clients use it. With a genuine Logitech mouse, however, you don't need to enable ChordMiddle in order to use the button. If you find that the third button doesn't work when you start X, you can enable ChordMiddle by editing the configuration file—it's much easier and less error-prone than rerunning *XF86Setup*. See page 149 for details of how to edit the configuration file.

Continuing,

```
If your mouse has only two buttons, it is recommended that you enable
Emulate3Buttons.

Please answer the following question with either 'y' or 'n'.
Do you want to enable Emulate3Buttons? n

Now give the full device name that the mouse is connected to, for example
/dev/tty00. Just pressing enter will use the default, /dev/mouse.

Mouse device: /dev/ttyd1
```

Be very careful about this entry: you must specify the correct name for the device to which the mouse is connected. *xf86config* is not specific to FreeBSD, and the suggested example is just plain wrong for FreeBSD. Use the names */dev/ttyd0* through */dev/ttyd3* for serial mice, */dev/psm0* for PS/2 mice or */dev/mse0* for a bus mouse. See page 149 for more details.

Continuing, we see:

```
Beginning with XFree86 3.1.2D, you can use the new X11R6.1 XKEYBOARD
extension to manage the keyboard layout. If you answer 'n' to the following
question, the server will use the old method, and you have to adjust
your keyboard layout with xmodmap.

Please answer the following question with either 'y' or 'n'.
Do you want to use XKB? y
```

The following dialogue will allow you to select from a list of already
preconfigured keymaps. If you don't find a suitable keymap in the list,
the program will try to combine a keymap from additional information you
are asked then. Such a keymap is by default untested and may require
manual tuning. Please report success or required changes for such a
keymap to XFREE86@XFREE86.ORG for addition to the list of preconfigured
keymaps in the future.

Press enter to continue, or ctrl-c to abort.

List of preconfigured keymaps:

```
 1   Standard 101-key, US encoding
 2   Microsoft Natural, US encoding
 3   KeyTronic FlexPro, US encoding
 4   Standard 101-key, US encoding with ISO9995-3 extensions
 5   Standard 101-key, German encoding
 6   Standard 101-key, French encoding
 7   Standard 101-key, Thai encoding
 8   Standard 101-key, Swiss/German encoding
 9   Standard 101-key, Swiss/French encoding
10   None of the above
```

Enter a number to choose the keymap.

1   *Choose the standard US keyboard*

Now we want to set the specifications of the monitor. The two critical
parameters are the vertical refresh rate, which is the rate at which the
the whole screen is refreshed, and most importantly the horizontal sync rate,
which is the rate at which scanlines are displayed.

The valid range for horizontal sync and vertical sync should be documented
in the manual of your monitor. If in doubt, check the monitor database
/usr/X11R6/lib/X11/doc/Monitors to see if your monitor is there.

Press enter to continue, or ctrl-c to abort. **ENTER**
You must indicate the horizontal sync range of your monitor. You can either
select one of the predefined ranges below that correspond to industry-
standard monitor types, or give a specific range.

It is VERY IMPORTANT that you do not specify a monitor type with a horizontal
sync range that is beyond the capabilities of your monitor. If in doubt,
choose a conservative setting.

```
     hsync in kHz; monitor type with characteristic modes
 1   31.5; Standard VGA, 640x480 @@ 60 Hz
 2   31.5 - 35.1; Super VGA, 800x600 @@ 56 Hz
 3   31.5, 35.5; 8514 Compatible, 1024x768 @@ 87 Hz interlaced (no 800x600)
 4   31.5, 35.15, 35.5; Super VGA, 1024x768 @@ 87 Hz interlaced, 800x600 @@ 56 Hz
 5   31.5 - 37.9; Extended Super VGA, 800x600 @@ 60 Hz, 640x480 @@ 72 Hz
 6   31.5 - 48.5; Non-Interlaced SVGA, 1024x768 @@ 60 Hz, 800x600 @@ 72 Hz
 7   31.5 - 57.0; High Frequency SVGA, 1024x768 @@ 70 Hz
 8   31.5 - 64.3; Monitor that can do 1280x1024 @@ 60 Hz
 9   31.5 - 79.0; Monitor that can do 1280x1024 @@ 74 Hz
10   31.5 - 82.0; Monitor that can do 1280x1024 @@ 76 Hz
11   Enter your own horizontal sync range
```

Enter your choice (1-11):

See Chapter 10, *XFree86 configuration in depth*, page 142, for an explanation of the warnings.

Unfortunately, our monitor isn't mentioned in the file */usr/X11R6/lib/X11/doc/Monitors*, but by
chance the manual does specify the frequency range in the Technical Data section: the
horizontal frequency range is from 30 to 64 kHz, and the vertical frequency range is from 50 to

100 Hz. The horizontal frequency range is almost exactly covered by choice 8, but that setting threatens to go 0.3 kHz higher in frequency than the technical data state. Do you want to risk it? Probably there won't be a problem, since it's unlikely that the monitor will die at such a small deviation from the specs, and it's also unlikely that your *XF86Config* will actually generate a horizontal frequency between 64.0 and 64.3 kHz. However, there's no need to take even this slight risk. Just specify the real values:

```
Enter your choice (1-11): 11

Please enter the horizontal sync range of your monitor, in the format used
in the table of monitor types above. You can either specify one or more
continuous ranges (e.g. 15-25, 30-50), or one or more fixed sync frequencies.

Horizontal sync range: 30-64
```

Next, we select the vertical frequency range:

```
You must indicate the vertical sync range of your monitor. You can either
select one of the predefined ranges below that correspond to industry-
standard monitor types, or give a specific range. For interlaced modes,
the number that counts is the high one (e.g. 87 Hz rather than 43 Hz).

 1   50-70
 2   50-90
 3   50-100
 4   40-150
 5   Enter your own vertical sync range

Enter your choice: 3                      this time, exactly the range of the monitor
```

The next step is to specify identification strings. You can think out names if you want, but unless you're juggling a lot of different hardware, you can let *xf86config* do it for you:

```
You must now enter a few identification/description strings, namely an
identifier, a vendor name, and a model name. Just pressing enter will fill
in default names.

The strings are free-form, spaces are allowed.
Enter an identifier for your monitor definition: ENTER
Enter the vendor name of your monitor:   ENTER
Enter the model name of your monitor:   ENTER
```

Next comes the choice of the video board. We have an elderly Diamond SpeedStar Plus with an ET4000 chip, and unknown Ramdac and Clock Chip. Let's see how we fare:

```
Now we must configure video card specific settings. At this point you can
choose to make a selection out of a database of video card definitions.
Because there can be variation in Ramdacs and clock generators even
between cards of the same model, it is not sensible to blindly copy
the settings (e.g. a Device section). For this reason, after you make a
selection, you will still be asked about the components of the card, with
the settings from the chosen database entry presented as a strong hint.

The database entries include information about the chipset, what server to
run, the Ramdac and ClockChip, and comments that will be included in the
Device section. However, a lot of definitions only hint about what server
to run (based on the chipset the card uses) and are untested.
```

If you can't find your card in the database, there's nothing to worry about. You should only choose a database entry that is exactly the same model as your card; choosing one that looks similar is just a bad idea (e.g. a GemStone Snail 64 may be as different from a GemStone Snail 64+ in terms of hardware as can be).

Do you want to look at the card database? **y**

```
 0  2 the Max MAXColor S3 Trio64V+          S3 Trio64V+
 1  928Movie                                S3 928
 2  AGX (generic)                           AGX-014/15/16
 3  ALG-5434(E)                             CL-GD5434
 4  ASUS 3Dexplorer                         RIVA128
 5  ASUS PCI-AV264CT                         ATI-Mach64
 6  ASUS PCI-V264CT                          ATI-Mach64
 7  ASUS Video Magic PCI V864               S3 864
 8  ASUS Video Magic PCI VT64               S3 Trio64
 9  AT25                                     Alliance AT3D
10  AT3D                                     Alliance AT3D
11  ATI 3D Pro Turbo                         ATI-Mach64
12  ATI 3D Xpression                         ATI-Mach64
13  ATI 3D Xpression+ PC2TV                  ATI-Mach64
14  ATI 8514 Ultra (no VGA)                  ATI-Mach8
15  ATI All-in-Wonder                        ATI-Mach64
16  ATI Graphics Pro Turbo                   ATI-Mach64
17  ATI Graphics Pro Turbo 1600              ATI-Mach64
```

Enter a number to choose the corresponding card definition.
Press enter for the next page, q to continue configuration.
ENTER

Dozens of board definitions come in alphabetic order. Finally we see:

```
108  DSV3325                                 S3 ViRGE
109  DSV3326                                 S3 Trio64V+
110  DataExpert DSV3325                      S3 ViRGE
111  DataExpert DSV3365                      S3 Trio64V+
112  Dell S3 805                             S3 801/805
113  Dell onboard ET4000                     ET4000
114  Diamond Edge 3D                         nv1
115  Diamond Multimedia Stealth 3D 2000      S3 ViRGE
116  Diamond Multimedia Stealth 3D 2000 PRO  S3 ViRGE/DX
117  Diamond SpeedStar (Plus)                ET4000
118  Diamond SpeedStar 24                    ET4000
119  Diamond SpeedStar 24X (not fully supported)  WD90C31
120  Diamond SpeedStar 64                    CL-GD5434
121  Diamond SpeedStar HiColor               ET4000
122  Diamond SpeedStar Pro (not SE)          CL-GD5426/28
123  Diamond SpeedStar Pro 1100              CL-GD5420/2/4/6/8/9
124  Diamond SpeedStar Pro SE (CL-GD5430/5434)  CL-GD5430/5434
125  Diamond SpeedStar64 Graphics 2000/2200  CL-GD5434
```

Enter a number to choose the corresponding card definition.
Press enter for the next page, q to continue configuration.

117

Your selected card definition:

```
Identifier: Diamond SpeedStar (Plus)
Chipset:    ET4000
Server:     XF86_SVGA
```

Press enter to continue, or ctrl-c to abort.**ENTER**

Now you must determine which server to run. Refer to the manpages and other

documentation. The following servers are available (they may not all be
installed on your system):

1   The XF86_Mono server. This a monochrome server that should work on any
    VGA-compatible card, in 640x480 (more on some SVGA chipsets).
2   The XF86_VGA16 server. This is a 16-color VGA server that should work on
    any VGA-compatible card.
3   The XF86_SVGA server. This is a 256 color SVGA server that supports
    a number of SVGA chipsets. On some chipsets it is accelerated or
    supports higher color depths.
4   The accelerated servers. These include XF86_S3, XF86_Mach32, XF86_Mach8,
    XF86_8514, XF86_P9000, XF86_AGX, XF86_W32, XF86_Mach64, XF86_I128 and
    XF86_S3V.

These four server types correspond to the four different "Screen" sections in
XF86Config (vga2, vga16, svga, accel).

5   Choose the server from the card definition, XF86_SVGA.

Which one of these screen types do you intend to run by default (1-5)?

The system already chose *XF86_SVGA* for us. Do we want to change? We would need a good
reason. In this case, we don't have a reason, so we'll keep the server from the card definition:

Which one of these screen types do you intend to run by default (1-5)? **5**

The server to run is selected by changing the symbolic link 'X'. For example,
the SVGA server.

Please answer the following question with either 'y' or 'n'.
Do you want me to set the symbolic link? **y**

All the programs that start X (*xinit*, *startx* and *xdm*) start a program */usr/X11R6/bin/X*. This
symbolic link makes */usr/X11R6/bin/X* point to your X server. If you don't have a link, you
won't be able to start X.

Now you must give information about your video card. This will be used for
the "Device" section of your video card in XF86Config.

You must indicate how much video memory you have. It is probably a good
idea to use the same approximate amount as that detected by the server you
intend to use. If you encounter problems that are due to the used server
not supporting the amount memory you have (e.g. ATI Mach64 is limited to
1024K with the SVGA server), specify the maximum amount supported by the
server.

How much video memory do you have on your video card:

1   256K
2   512K
3   1024K
4   2048K
5   4096K
6   Other

Enter your choice: **3**

You must now enter a few identification/description strings, namely an
identifier, a vendor name, and a model name. Just pressing enter will fill
in default names (possibly from a card definition).

Your card definition is Diamond SpeedStar (Plus).

The strings are free-form, spaces are allowed.
Enter an identifier for your video card definition: **ENTER**
You can simply press enter here if you have a generic card, or want to
describe your card with one string.
Enter the vendor name of your video card: **ENTER**
Enter the model (board) name of your video card: **ENTER**

Especially for accelerated servers, Ramdac, Dacspeed and ClockChip settings
or special options may be required in the Device section.

The RAMDAC setting only applies to the S3, AGX, W32 servers, and some
drivers in the SVGA servers. Some RAMDAC's are auto-detected by the server.
The detection of a RAMDAC is forced by using a Ramdac "identifier" line in
the Device section. The identifiers are shown at the right of the following
table of RAMDAC types:

```
 1  AT&T 20C490 (S3 and AGX servers, ARK driver)          att20c490
 2  AT&T 20C498/21C498/22C498 (S3, autodetected)          att20c498
 3  AT&T 20C409/20C499 (S3, autodetected)                 att20c409
 4  AT&T 20C505 (S3)                                       att20c505
 5  BrookTree BT481 (AGX)                                  bt481
 6  BrookTree BT482 (AGX)                                  bt482
 7  BrookTree BT485/9485 (S3)                              bt485
 8  Sierra SC15025 (S3, AGX)                               sc15025
 9  S3 GenDAC (86C708) (autodetected)                      s3gendac
10  S3 SDAC (86C716) (autodetected)                        s3_sdac
11  STG-1700 (S3, autodetected)                            stg1700
12  STG-1703 (S3, autodetected)                            stg1703
```

Enter a number to choose the corresponding RAMDAC.
Press enter for the next page, q to quit without selection of a RAMDAC.

q   *We don't need this*

A Clockchip line in the Device section forces the detection of a
programmable clock device. With a clockchip enabled, any required
clock can be programmed without requiring probing of clocks or a
Clocks line. Most cards don't have a programmable clock chip.
Choose from the following list:

```
 1  Chrontel 8391                                          ch8391
 2  ICD2061A and compatibles (ICS9161A, DCS2824)           icd2061a
 3  ICS2595                                                ics2595
 4  ICS5342 (similar to SDAC, but not completely compatible)  ics5342
 5  ICS5341                                                ics5341
 6  S3 GenDAC (86C708) and ICS5300 (autodetected)          s3gendac
 7  S3 SDAC (86C716)                                       s3_sdac
 8  STG 1703 (autodetected)                                stg1703
 9  Sierra SC11412                                         sc11412
10  TI 3025 (autodetected)                                 ti3025
11  TI 3026 (autodetected)                                 ti3026
12  IBM RGB 51x/52x (autodetected)                         ibm_rgb5xx
```

Just press enter if you don't want a Clockchip setting.
What Clockchip setting do you want (1-12)? **ENTER**

For most configurations, a Clocks line is useful since it prevents the slow
and nasty sounding clock probing at server start-up. Probed clocks are
displayed at server startup, along with other server and hardware
configuration info. You can save this information in a file by running
imprecise; some clocks may be slightly too high (varies per run).

At this point I can run X -probeonly, and try to extract the clock information
from the output. It is recommended that you do this yourself and add a clocks
line (note that the list of clocks may be split over multiple Clocks lines) to

```
your Device section afterwards. Be aware that a clocks line is not
appropriate for drivers that have a fixed set of clocks and don't probe by
default (e.g. Cirrus). Also, for the P9000 server you must simply specify
clocks line that matches the modes you want to use.  For the S3 server with
a programmable clock chip you need a 'ClockChip' line and no Clocks line.

You must be root to be able to run X -probeonly now.

Do you want me to run 'X -probeonly' now?
```

This last question is worth thinking about. You should run *X -probeonly* at some point, but it requires some extra work. We'll take the recommendation and try it later.

```
Do you want me to run 'X -probeonly' now? n

For each depth, a list of modes (resolutions) is defined. The default
resolution that the server will start-up with will be the first listed
mode that can be supported by the monitor and card.
Currently it is set to:

"640x480" "800x600" "1024x768" for 8bpp
"640x480" "800x600" for 16bpp
"640x480" for 24bpp
"640x400" for 32bpp

Note that 16, 24 and 32bpp are only supported on a few configurations.
Modes that cannot be supported due to monitor or clock constraints will
be automatically skipped by the server.

1  Change the modes for 8pp (256 colors)
2  Change the modes for 16bpp (32K/64K colors)
3  Change the modes for 24bpp (24-bit color, packed pixel)
4  Change the modes for 32bpp (24-bit color)
5  The modes are OK, continue.

Enter your choice: 5 accept the defaults

You can have a virtual screen (desktop), which is screen area that is larger
than the physical screen and which is panned by moving the mouse to the edge
of the screen. If you don't want virtual desktop at a certain resolution,
you cannot have modes listed that are larger. Each color depth can have a
differently-sized virtual screen

Please answer the following question with either 'y' or 'n'.
Do you want a virtual screen that is larger than the physical screen? n
```

It's difficult to decide whether you want a virtual screen larger than the physical screen. I find it extremely disturbing, so I suggest you answer **n**. You might find it useful, especially if your highest resolution is small.

Now the configuration is complete, and *sysinstall* just need to write the configuration file:

```
I am going to write the XF86Config file now. Make sure you don't accidently
overwrite a previously configured one.

Shall I write it to /etc/XF86Config? y

File has been written. Take a look at it before running 'startx'. Note that
the XF86Config file must be in one of the directories searched by the server
(e.g. /usr/X11R6/lib/X11) in order to be used. Within the server press
ctrl, alt and '+' simultaneously to cycle video resolutions. Pressing ctrl,
```

```
alt and backspace simultaneously immediately exits the server (use if
the monitor doesn't sync for a particular mode).
```

```
For further configuration, refer to /usr/X11R6/lib/X11/doc/README.Config.
```

Once you have completed this configuration, you are ready to start X. We'll look at how to do that in Chapter 17, *Setting up your FreeBSD desktop*. If you run into trouble, or if you're interested in the background, read Chapter 10, *XFree86 configuration in depth*.

10

XFree86 configuration in depth

In most cases, the information in Chapter 9, *Setting up X11*, should be enough to get X up and running. If it doesn't work for some reason, or if you're a masochist, or if you just want to understand the procedure better, this chapter should be able to help.

In the next section, we'll look at the technical background, and on page 147 we'll look at setting up the *XF86Config* file.

X configuration: the theory

Setting up your *XF86Config* file normally takes a few minutes, but sometimes you can run into problems which make grown men cry. In the rest of this chapter, we'll look at the technical background:

- How display boards and monitors work.

- How to set up XFree86 to work with your hardware.

- How to tune your hardware for maximum display performance.

- How to fry your monitor.

I mean the last point seriously: conventional wisdom says that you can't damage hardware with a programming mistake, but in this case, you can, and people do it from time to time. When you've read the section on how monitors work, you'll understand, but *please* don't start tuning until you understand the dangers involved.

How TVs and monitors work

You don't have to be a computer expert to see the similarity between monitors and TVs: current monitor technology is derived from TV technology, and most older display boards have modes which can use TVs instead of monitors. Those of us who were on the microcomputer scene 15 to 20 years ago will remember the joy of getting a computer display on a portable TV, a "glass tty" connected by a serial line running at 300 or 1200 bps.

There are at least two ways to create pictures on a cathode ray tube: one is derived from oscilloscopes, where each individual character is scanned by the electron beam, rather like writing in the sand with your finger. Some early terminals used this technology, but it has been obsolete for at least 20 years.

TVs and monitors display the picture by scanning lines across the screen. Like in a book, the first line starts at the top left of the screen and goes to the top right. Each successive line starts slightly below the previous line. This continues until the screen is full. Like in a book, the lines don't have to be full: the picture is formed by altering the intensity of the electron beam as it scans the lines.

To perform this scan, the TV has two *deflection units*: one scans from left to right, and the other scans, much more slowly, from top to bottom. Not surprisingly, these units are called the *horizontal* and *vertical* deflection units. You may also encounter the terms *line* and *frame* deflection.

The tube can only move the electron beam at a finite speed. When the electron beam reaches the right hand side of the screen, it needs to be deflected back again. This part of the scan is called the *horizontal flyback*, and it is not used for displaying picture data. The actual time that the hardware requires for the flyback depends on the monitor, but it is in the order of 5% to 10% of the total line scan time. Similarly, when the vertical deflection reaches the bottom of the screen, it performs a *vertical flyback*, which is also not used for display purposes. Figure 10-1 shows the resultant pattern.

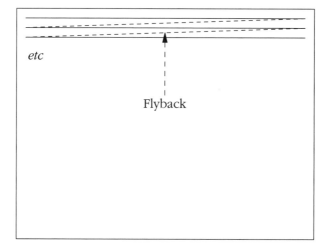

Figure 10-1: Scanning pattern on the monitor

It's not enough to just deflect, of course: somehow you need to ensure that the scanning is synchronized with the incoming signal, so that the scan is at the top of the screen when the picture information for the top of the screen arrives. You've seen what happens when this doesn't happen: the picture runs up and down the screen (incorrect vertical synchronization) or tears away from the left of the screen (incorrect horizontal synchronization). Synchronization is achieved by including synchronization pulses in the horizontal and vertical flyback periods. They have a voltage level outside the normal picture data range in order to ensure that they are recognized as synchronization pulses.

As if that wasn't enough, the video amplifier, the part of the TV which alters the intensity of the spot as it travels across the screen, needs time to ensure that the flyback is invisible, so there are brief pauses between the end of the line and the start of the sync pulse, and again between the end of the sync pulse and the beginning of the data. This process is called *blanking*, and the delays are called the *front porch* (before the sync pulse) and the *back porch* (after the sync pulse). Figure 10-2 depicts a complete scan line.

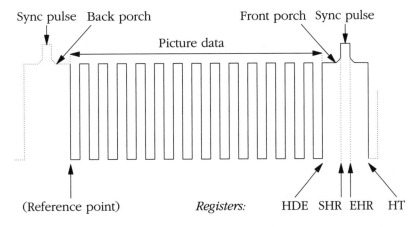

Figure 10-2: Scan line and register values

The register information at the bottom of the picture refers to the video controller registers. We'll look at how to interpret them on page 143.

That, in a nutshell, is how horizontal deflection works. Vertical deflection works in almost the same way, just slower, with one minor exception. This basic display mechanism was developed for TVs in the 1930s, at a time when terms like high-tech (or even electronics) hadn't even been invented, and even today we're stuck with the low data rates that they decided upon in those days. Depending on the country, TVs display only 25 or 30 frames (pages of display) per second. This caused an unpleasant flicker in the display. This flicker was avoided with a trick called *interlacing*: instead of displaying the frame in one vertical scan, the odd and even lines are displayed in two alternating half frames, which increases the apparent frame frequency to 50 or 60 Hz.

How monitors differ from TVs

So how do we apply this to computer displays? Let's look at the US standard NTSC system—the international PAL and SECAM systems are almost identical except for the number of lines and a minor difference in the vertical frequency. NTSC specifies 525 lines, but that includes the vertical flyback time, and in fact only about 480 lines are visible. The aspect ratio of a normal TV is 4:3, in other words the screen is one-third wider than it is high, so if we want square pixels,[1] we need to have one-third more pixels per line. This means that we can display 640 pixels per line on 480 lines.[2] This resolution is normally abbreviated to "640x480". PAL and SECAM have lower vertical frequencies, which allows a nominal 625 lines, of which about 580 are displayed. Either way, these values have two huge disadvantages: first, the resolution is barely acceptable for modern graphics displays, and secondly they are interlaced displays. Older PC display hardware, such as the CGA and some EGA modes, was capable of generating these signal frequencies, but VGAs can no longer do it. This is a pity, in some ways: I'd like to have an X display on my TV in the lounge room, but my last EGA died a couple of years ago.

The first problem is interlace: it works reasonably for TVs, but it's a pain for computer displays—there's still more flicker than a real 50 Hz or 60 Hz display. Modern display boards can still run in interlace mode, but don't even think about doing so unless you're forced to—the resultant picture looks out of focus and is very tiring to read.

The second problem is the resolution: nowadays, 1024x768 is a normal enough resolution, but I'm writing this on a display with 1280x1024, and many modern boards display 1600x1200. On the other hand, even 60 Hz refresh rate is barely adequate: read any marketing literature and you'll discover that 72 Hz is the point at which flicker suddenly disappears. To get high-resolution, high refresh rate displays, you need some very high internal frequencies—we'll see how high further down.

How to fry your monitor

Remember that a monitor is just a glorified TV? Well, one of the design constraints of real TVs is that they have only a single horizontal frequency and only a single vertical frequency. This simplifies the hardware design considerably: the horizontal deflection uses a tuned circuit to create both the deflection frequency and the high voltage required to run the tube. This circuit is comprised of a transformer (the *line transformer*) and a condenser. Run a line transformer even fractionally off its intended frequency and it will run much less efficiently and use more current, which gets converted to heat. If you run a conventional monitor off spec for any length of time, it will burn out the line transformer.

You don't have to roll your own X configuration to burn out the monitor: ten years ago, the standard display boards were CGAs and HDAs,[3] and they had different line frequencies and thus required different monitors. Unfortunately, they both used the same data connector. If you connected an HDA (18.43 kHz line frequency) to a CGA monitor (15.75 kHz, the NTSC line

---

1. A square pixel is one with the same height and width. They don't have to be that way, but it makes graphics software much simpler.
2. Does this look familiar? Now you know why.
3. Color Graphics Adapter and Hercules Display Adapter.

frequency), you could expect smoke signals within a few minutes.

Modern PC monitors no longer use line transformers, and there are few of them which can't handle at least a range of line frequencies, but this doesn't mean you can't damage them—you'll just burn out something else, frequently the power supply. In addition, just because the monitor displays correctly doesn't mean that it is running in spec. I have a rather elderly Eizo 9500 (called Nanao in the US) which has three frequency ranges: (exactly) 31.5 kHz, 48 to 50 kHz, or 64 to 78 kHz. In fact, it will display at any frequency between 48 and 78 kHz, but if it were run at 57 kHz for any length of time, I would be in for a hefty repair bill. The moral of the story:

> *Never run your monitor out of spec. If your display is screwed up, there's a good chance that the frequencies are out, so turn off the monitor.*

Monitors aren't the only thing that you can burn out, of course. If you try hard, you can also burn out chips on some display boards by running them at frequencies which are out of spec. In practice, though, this doesn't happen nearly as often.

Another difference between TVs and monitors is the kind of signal they take. A real TV includes a receiver, of course, so you have an antenna connection, but modern TVs also have connections for inputs from VCRs, which are usually an audio signal and a video signal. The video signal consists of five important parts: the *red* signal, the *green* signal, the *blue* signal, and the horizontal and vertical sync pulses. This kind of signal is called *composite video*. By contrast, most modern monitors separate these signals onto separate signal lines, and older boards, such as the EGA, even used several lines per colour. Unfortunately, there is no complete agreement about how these signals should work: the polarity of the sync pulses varies from one board to the next, and some boards cheat and supply the sync pulses on the green signal line. This is mainly of historical interest, but occasionally you'll come across a real bargain 20" monitor which only has 3 signal connections, and you may not be able to get it to work—this could be one of the reasons.

The CRT controller

The display controller, usually called a CRT (Cathode Ray Tube) controller, is the part of the display board which creates the signals we've just been talking about. Early display controllers were designed to produce signals that were compatible with TVs: they had to produce a signal with sync pulses, front and back porches, and picture data in between. Modern display controllers can do a lot more, but the principles remain the same.

The first part of the display controller creates the framework we're looking for: the horizontal and vertical sync pulses, blanking and picture information, which is represented as a series of points or *dots*. To count, we need a pulse source, which also determines the duration of individual dots, so it is normally called a *dot clock*. For reasons lost in history, CRT controllers start counting at the top left of the display, and not at the vertical sync pulse, which is the real beginning of the display. To define a line to the horizontal deflection, we need to set four CRTC registers to tell it—see the diagram on page 141:

- The *Horizontal Display End* register (HDE) specifies how many dots we want on each line. After the CRTC has counted this many pixels, it stops outputting picture data to the display.

- The *Start Horizontal Retrace* register (SHR) specifies how many dot clock pulses occur before the sync pulse starts. The difference between the contents of this register and the contents of the HDE register defines the length of the front porch.

- The *End Horizontal Retrace* register (EHR) defines the end of the sync pulse. The width of the sync pulse is the difference between the contents of this register and the SHR register.

- The *Horizontal Total* register (HT) defines the total number of dot clocks per line. The width of the back porch is the difference between the contents of this register and the EHR register.

In addition, the *Start Horizontal Blanking* and *End Horizontal Blanking* registers (SHB and EHB) define when the video signals are turned off and on. The server sets these registers automatically, so we don't need to look at them in more detail.

The control of the vertical deflection is similar. In this case, the registers are *Vertical Display End* (VDE), *Start Vertical Retrace* (SVR), *End Vertical Retrace* (EVR), *Vertical Total* (VT), *Start Vertical Blanking* (SVB), and *End Vertical Blanking* (EVB). The values in these registers are counted in lines.

VGA hardware evolved out of older 8 bit character-based display hardware, which counted lines in characters, not dot clocks. As a result, all of these registers are 8 bits wide. This is adequate for character displays, but it's a problem when counting dots: the maximum value you can set in any of these registers is 255. The designers of the VGA resorted to a number of nasty kludges to get around this problem: the horizontal registers count in groups of 8 dot clocks, so they can represent up to 2048 dot clocks. The vertical registers overflow into an overflow register. Even so, the standard VGA can't count beyond 1024 lines. Super VGAs vary in how they handle this problem, but typically they add additional overflow bits. To give you an idea of how clean the VGA design is, consider the way the real Vertical Total (total number of lines on the display) is defined on a standard VGA. It's a 10 bit quantity, but the first 8 bits are in the VT register, the 9th bit is in bit 0 of the overflow register, and the 10th bit is in bit 5 of the overflow register.

The XF86Config mode line

One of the steps in setting up XFree86 is to define these register values. Fortunately, you don't have to worry about which bits to set in the overflow register: the mode lines count in dots, and it's up to the server to convert the dot count into something that the display board can understand. A typical Mode line looks like:

```
Modeline "640x480a" 28 640 680 728 776 480 480 482 494
```

These ten values are required. In addition, you may specify modifiers at the end of the line. The values are:

- A label for the resolution line. This must be enclosed in quotation marks, and is used to refer to the line from other parts of the *XF86Config* file. Traditionally, the label represents the resolution of the display mode, but it doesn't have to. In this example, the resolution really is 640x480, but the a at the end of the label is a clue that it's an alternative value.

- The clock frequency, 28 MHz in this example.

- The Horizontal Display End, which goes into the HDE register. This value and all that follow are specified in dots. The server mangles them as the display board requires and puts them in the corresponding CRTC register.

- The Start Horizontal Retrace (SHR) value.

- The End Horizontal Retrace (EHR) value.

- The Horizontal Total (HT) value.

- The Vertical Display End (VDE) value. This value and the three following are specified in lines.

- The Start Vertical Retrace (SVR) value.

- The End Vertical Retrace (EVR) value.

- The Vertical Total (VT) value.

This is pretty dry stuff. To make it easier to understand, let's look at how we would set a typical VGA display with 640x480 pixels. Sure, you can find values for this setup in any release of XFree86, but that doesn't mean that they're the optimum for *your system*. We want a non-flicker display, which we'll take to mean a vertical frequency of at least 72 Hz, and of course we don't want interlace. Our multiscan monitor can handle any horizontal frequency between 15 and 40 kHz: since we want the least flicker, we'll aim for 40 kHz.

First, we need to create our lines. They contain 640 pixels, two porches and a sync pulse. The only value we really know for sure is the number of pixels. How long should the porches and the sync pulses be? If you have a good monitor with good documentation, it should tell you, but most monitor manufacturers don't seem to believe in good documentation. When they do document the values, they vary significantly from monitor to monitor, and even from mode to mode: they're not as critical as they look. For example, here are some typical values from my NEC 5D handbook:

Horizontal sync pulse: 1 to 4 µs, front porch 0.18 to 2.1 µs, back porch 1.25 to 3.56 µs.

As we'll see, the proof of these timing parameters is in the display. If the display looks good, the parameters are OK. I don't know of any way to damage the monitor purely by modifying these parameters, but there are other good reasons to stick to this range. As a rule of thumb, if you set each of the three values to 2 µs to start with, you won't go too far wrong. Alternatively, you could start with the NTSC standard values: the standard specifies that the horizontal sync pulse lasts for 4.2 to 5.1 µs, the front porch must be at least 1.27 µs. NTSC doesn't define the length of the back porch—instead it defines the total line blanking, which lasts for 8.06 to 10.3 µs. For our purposes, we can consider the back porch to be the length of the total blanking minus the lengths of the front porch and the sync pulse. If you take values somewhere in the middle of the ranges, you get a front porch of 1.4 µs, a sync pulse of 4.5 µs, and total blanking 9 µs, which implies a back porch of 9 - 1.4 - 4.5 = 3.1 µs.

For our example, let's stick to 2 µs per value. We have a horizontal frequency of 40 kHz, or 25 µs per line. After taking off our 6 µs for flyback control, we have only 19 µs left for the display data. In order to get 640 pixels in this time, we need one pixel every 19 ÷ 640 µs, or about 30 ns. This corresponds to a frequency of 33.6 MHz. This is our desired dot clock.

The next question is: do we have a dot clock of this frequency? Maybe. This should be in your display board documentation, but I'll take a bet that it's not. Never mind, the XFree86 server is clever enough to figure this out for itself. At the moment, let's assume that you do have a dot clock of 33 MHz.

> If you don't have a suitable clock, you'll have to take the next lower clock frequency that you do have: you can't go any higher, since this example assumes the highest possible horizontal frequency.

You now need to calculate four register values to define the horizontal lines:

- The first value is the Horizontal Display End, the number of pixels on a line. We know this one: it's 640.

- You calculate SHR by adding the number of dot clocks that elapse during the front porch to the value of HDE. Recall that we decided on a front porch of 2 µs. In this time, a 33 MHz clock will count 66 cycles. So we add 66, right? Wrong. Remember that the VGA registers count in increments of 8 pixels, so we need to round the width of the front porch to a multiple of 8. In this case, we round it to 64, so we set SHR to 640 + 64 = 704.

- The next value we need is EHR, which is SHR plus the width of the horizontal retrace, again 64 dot clocks, so we set that to 704 + 64 = 768.

- The final horizontal value is HT. Again, we add the front porch—64 dot clocks—to EHR and get 768 + 64 = 832.

At this point, our vestigial mode line looks like:

```
Modeline "640x480"   28   640 704 768 832
```

Next, we need another four values to define the vertical scan. Again, of the four values we need, we only know the number of lines. How many lines do we use for the porches and the vertical sync? As we've seen, NTSC uses about 45 lines for the three combined, but modern monitors can get by with much less. Again referring to the Multisync manual, we get a front porch of betwwen 0.014 and 1.2 ms, a sync pulse of between 0.06 and 0.113 ms, and a back porch of between 0.54 and 1.88 ms. But how many lines is that?

To figure that out, we need to know our *real* horizontal frequency. We were aiming at 40 kHz, but we made a couple of tradeoffs along the way. The real horizontal frequency is the dot clock divided by the horizontal total, in this case 33 MHz ÷ 832, which gives us 39.66 kHz—not too bad. At that frequency, a line lasts 1÷39660 seconds, or just over 25 µs, so our front porch can range between ½ and 48 lines, our sync pulse between 2 and 5 lines, and the back porch between 10 and 75 lines. Do these timings make any sense? No, they don't—they're just values which the monitor can accept.

To get the highest refresh rate, we can go for the lowest value in each case. It's difficult to specify a value of ½, so we'll take a single line front porch. We'll take two lines of sync pulse and 10 lines of back porch. This gives us:

- VDE is 480.

- SVR is 481.

- EVR is 483.

- VT is 493.

Now our mode line is complete:

```
Modeline "640x480" 28   640 704 768 832   480 481 483 493
```

Now we can calculate our vertical frequency, which is the horizontal frequency divided by the Vertical Total, or 39.66 ÷ 493 kHz, which is 80.4 Hz—that's not bad either. By comparison, if you use the standard entry in *XF86config*, you will get a horizontal frequency of 31.5 kHz and a vertical frequency of only 60 Hz.

If you know the technical details of your monitor and display board, it really is that simple. This method doesn't require much thought, and it creates results which work.

XF86Config

The *XF86Config* file contains several sections; these procedures will lead you through filling out each part. There is a sample *XF86Config* file in */usr/X11R6/lib/X11/XF86Config.eg*. You can copy this to */usr/X11R6/lib/X11/XF86Config*, and edit that file to your specific configuration. In the following examples, we'll look at the relevant sections of *XF86Config* and discuss what might need changing. Refer to the man page *XF86Config(5)* as you fill in your *XF86Config* file. Table 10-3, overleaf, gives you an overview of the sections in *XF86Config*. Note that the X server treats lines beginning with # as comments. You'll see many definitions with a # in front of them in the following examples. You activate the definition by removing the #.

Normally, you'll set up your *XF86Config* when you run the *xf86config* program (note the difference in character case; in UNIX, *XF86Config* and *xf86config* are two different file names). We looked at that in Chapter 9, *Setting up X11*, on page 129. The following discussion will apply equally well to the *XF86Config* file that you generate by this procedure.

Table 10-3. XF86Config sections

Section	Description
Files	Sets the default font and RGB paths—see page 148.
Server Flags	Sets a few general server options. Refer to the server manual page for more information about them.
Keyboard	Sets up keyboard devices, and sets a few optional parameters—see page 149
Pointer	Sets up the pointer devices, and sets a few optional parameters—see page 149
Monitor	Describes your monitor to the server—see page 153
Device	Describes your video hardware to the server—see page 150
Screen	Describes how to use the monitor and video hardware—see page 155

The Files section

The *Files* section of the *XF86Config* file contains the path to the RGB database file, which should never need to be changed, and the default font path. You may want to add more font paths: the FontPath lines in your *XF86Config* are concatenated to form a search path. Ensure that each directory listed exists and is a valid font directory.

The standard *Files* section looks like:

```
Section "Files"

# The location of the RGB database.  Note, this is the name of the
# file minus the extension (like ".txt" or ".db").  There is normally
# no need to change the default.

    RgbPath     "/usr/X11R6/lib/X11/rgb"

# Multiple FontPath entries are allowed (which are concatenated together),
# as well as specifying multiple comma-separated entries in one FontPath
# command (or a combination of both methods)

    FontPath    "/usr/X11R6/lib/X11/fonts/misc/"
#   FontPath    "/usr/X11R6/lib/X11/fonts/Type1/"
#   FontPath    "/usr/X11R6/lib/X11/fonts/Speedo/"
#   FontPath    "/usr/X11R6/lib/X11/fonts/75dpi/"
#   FontPath    "/usr/X11R6/lib/X11/fonts/100dpi/"

EndSection
```

Sometimes the server complains about:

```
Can't open default font 'fixed'
```

This is almost certainly the result of an invalid entry in your font path. Try running *mkfontdir* in each directory if you are certain that each one is correct. The *XF86Config* man page describes other parameters that may be in this section of the file.

The Keyboard section

The *Keyboard* section specifies the keyboard protocol, the repeat rate, and the default mapping of some of the modifier keys:

```
Section "Keyboard"

    Protocol    "Standard"

# when using XQUEUE, comment out the above line, and uncomment the
# following line

#    Protocol    "Xqueue"

    AutoRepeat  500 5

# Let the server do the NumLock processing.  This should only be required
# when using pre-R6 clients
#    ServerNumLock

# Specifiy which keyboard LEDs can be user-controlled (eg, with xset(1))
#    Xleds       1 2 3

# To set the LeftAlt to Meta, RightAlt key to ModeShift,
# RightCtl key to Compose, and ScrollLock key to ModeLock:

#    LeftAlt     Meta
#    RightAlt    ModeShift
#    RightCtl    Compose
#    ScrollLock  ModeLock

EndSection
```

About the only thing you're likely to want to change are the definitions of the modifier keys for non-English keyboards. See the *XF86Config(5)* man page for details.

The Pointer section

The *Pointer* section specifies the pointer protocol and device, which is almost always a mouse.

```
Section "Pointer"

    Protocol    "Microsoft"
    Device "/dev/com1"

# When using XQUEUE, comment out the above two lines, and uncomment
# the following line.

#    Protocol    "Xqueue"

# Baudrate and SampleRate are only for some Logitech mice

#    BaudRate    9600
```

```
#       SampleRate 150

# Emulate3Buttons is an option for 2-button Microsoft mice
# Emulate3Timeout is the timeout in milliseconds (default is 50ms)

#       Emulate3Buttons
#       Emulate3Timeout 50

# ChordMiddle is an option for some 3-button Logitech mice

#       ChordMiddle

EndSection
```

These values are defaults, and many are either incorrect for FreeBSD (for example the device name */dev/com1*) or do not apply at all (for example Xqueue). If you are configuring manually, select one Protocol and one Device entry from the following selection. If you must use a two-button mouse, uncomment the keyword Emulate3Buttons—in this mode, pressing both mouse buttons simultaneously within Emulate3Timeout milliseconds causes the server to report a middle button press.

```
Section "Pointer"

    Protocol    "Microsoft"     for Microsoft protocol mice
    Protocol    "MouseMan"      for Logitech mice
    Protocol    "PS/2"          for a PS/2 mouse
    Protocol    "Busmouse"      for a bus mouse

    Device "/dev/ttyd0"         for a mouse on the first serial port
    Device "/dev/ttyd1"         for a mouse on the second serial port
    Device "/dev/ttyd2"         for a mouse on the third serial port
    Device "/dev/ttyd3"         for a mouse on the fourth serial port
    Device "/dev/psm0"          for a PS/2 mouse
    Device "/dev/mse0"          for a bus mouse

    Emulate3Buttons             only for a two-button mouse

EndSection
```

You'll notice that the protocol name does not always match the manufacturer's name. In particular, the *Logitech* protocol only applies to older Logitech mice. The newer ones use either the MouseMan or Microsoft protocols. Nearly all modern serial mice run one of these two protocols, and most run both.

If you are using a bus mouse or a PS/2 mouse, make sure that the device driver is included in the kernel. The GENERIC kernel contains drivers for both mice, but the PS/2 driver is disabled. Use UserConfig (see page 191) to enable it.

The Device section

The *Device* section describes the video hardware. You can specify multiple device sections, each section describing a single graphics board. Here are some typical examples:

```
# Any number of graphics device sections may be present

Section "Device"
    Identifier  "Generic VGA"
    VendorName  "Unknown"
    BoardName   "Unknown"
    Chipset     "generic"
#   VideoRam    256
#   Clocks      25.2 28.3
EndSection

Section "Device"
    # SVGA server auto-detected chipset
    Identifier  "Generic SVGA"
    VendorName  "Unknown"
    BoardName   "Unknown"
EndSection

# Section "Device"
#   Identifier "Any Trident TVGA 9000"
#   VendorName "Trident"
#   BoardName  "TVGA 9000"
#   Chipset    "tvga9000"
#   VideoRam   512
#   Clocks     25 28 45 36 57 65 50 40 25 28 0 45 72 77 80 75
# EndSection

# Section "Device"
#   Identifier "Actix GE32+ 2MB"
#   VendorName "Actix"
#   BoardName  "GE32+"
#   Ramdac     "ATT20C490"
#   Dacspeed   110
#   Option     "dac_8_bit"
#   Clocks      25.0  28.0  40.0   0.0  50.0  77.0  36.0  45.0
#   Clocks     130.0 120.0  80.0  31.0 110.0  65.0  75.0  94.0
# EndSection
```

Be sure to read the server manual pages and the chipset-specific *README* files for any non-generic information that may apply to your setup.

To create a *Device* section you need to collect the data for your hardware, and make some configuration decisions. The hardware data you need is:

- Chipset

- Amount of video memory

- Dot-clocks available or clock chip used (if programmable)

- Ramdac type (for some servers)

The server can usually determine this information on its own, but it is best to fully specify things in the *XF86Config* file, so that no mistakes are made. The *Chipset* is one of the keyword strings for a configured driver—you can display it with

```
$ X -showconfig
XFree86 Version 3.3.3.1 / X Window System
(protocol Version 11, revision 0, vendor release 6300)
Release Date: December 29 1998
        If the server is older than 6-12 months, or if your card is newer
        than the above date, look for a newer version before reporting
        problems.  (see http://www.XFree86.Org/FAQ)
Operating System: FreeBSD 3.0-CURRENT i386 [ELF]
Configured drivers:
  SVGA: server for SVGA graphics adaptors (Patchlevel 0):
      NV1, STG2000, RIVA128, RIVATNT, ET4000, ET4000W32, ET4000W32i,
      ET4000W32i_rev_b, ET4000W32i_rev_c, ET4000W32p, ET4000W32p_rev_a,
      ET4000W32p_rev_b, ET4000W32p_rev_c, ET4000W32p_rev_d, ET6000, ET6100,
      et3000, pvga1, wd90c00, wd90c10, wd90c30, wd90c24, wd90c31, wd90c33,
      gvga, ati, sis86c201, sis86c202, sis86c205, sis86c215, sis86c225,
      sis5597, sis5598, sis6326, tvga8200lx, tvga8800cs, tvga8900b,
      tvga8900c, tvga8900cl, tvga8900d, tvga9000, tvga9000i, tvga9100b,
      tvga9200cxr, tgui9400cxi, tgui9420, tgui9420dgi, tgui9430dgi,
      tgui9440agi, cyber9320, tgui9660, tgui9680, tgui9682, tgui9685,
      cyber9382, cyber9385, cyber9388, cyber9397, cyber9520, 3dimage975,
      3dimage985, clgd5420, clgd5422, clgd5424, clgd5426, clgd5428,
      clgd5429, clgd5430, clgd5434, clgd5436, clgd5446, clgd5480, clgd5462,
      clgd5464, clgd5465, clgd6205, clgd6215, clgd6225, clgd6235, clgd7541,
      clgd7542, clgd7543, clgd7548, clgd7555, clgd7556, ncr77c22, ncr77c22e,
      cpq_avga, mga2064w, mga1064sg, mga2164w, mga2164w AGP, mgag200,
      mgag100, oti067, oti077, oti087, oti037c, al2101, ali2228, ali2301,
      ali2302, ali2308, ali2401, cl6410, cl6412, cl6420, cl6440, video7,
      ark1000vl, ark1000pv, ark2000pv, ark2000mt, mx, realtek, s3_virge,
      AP6422, AT24, AT3D, s3_svga, NM2070, NM2090, NM2093, NM2097, NM2160,
      NM2200, ct65520, ct65525, ct65530, ct65535, ct65540, ct65545, ct65546,
      ct65548, ct65550, ct65554, ct65555, ct68554, ct69000, ct64200,
      ct64300, mediagx, V1000, V2x00, p9100, spc8110, generic
```

Note that the operating system is reported as FreeBSD 3.0-CURRENT. This is the release of FreeBSD under which the server was built, not necessarily the release for which it was intended. In particular, it does not mean that it is out of date, or that you have accidentally installed the wrong version.

Only some of the accelerated servers currently have chipset drivers. The amount of memory is specified in KBytes, so you specify 1 MB of memory as 1024.

The dot-clocks are the trickiest part of board configuration. Fortunately a large database of collected dot-clocks is available. You can find a list of Device entries for some graphics boards in the file */usr/X11R6/lib/X11/doc/Devices*. If you find one for your board, you can start with that. Also, the first part of the file */usr/X11R6/lib/X11/doc/modeDB.txt* lists information for a myriad of SVGA boards. For accelerated boards, you can also look in the file */usr/X11R6/lib/X11/doc/AccelCards*. If you find your board, copy the numbers from the database to the Clocks line in your *XF86Config* file, exactly as they appear in the database, without sorting, and leaving any duplicates. Note that some of the newer accelerated boards use a programmable clock generator, in which case a ClockChip line is used in your *XF86Config* file to identify the type of clock generator. For example, for a #9 GXe board you would specify

```
ClockChip "icd2061a"
```

If you can't find a listing for your board, you can attempt to have the server detect them. Run the command:

```
$ X -probeonly >/tmp/out 2>&1    for sh, ksh, bash, or zsh
% X -probeonly >&/tmp/out        for csh or tcsh
```

Be sure that the *XF86Config* file does not contain a Clocks line at this point. Running this will cause your monitor to freak out for a couple of seconds, as the server cycles through the clocks rapidly. It should not damage your monitor, but some newer monitors may shut themselves off because things may go out of spec. Anyhow, when this gets done, look in the file */tmp/out* for the detected dot-clocks. Copy these to the Clocks line in your *XF86Config* file, exactly as they appear in */tmp/out*. Don't sort them or rearrange them in any way.

Your board may have a programmable clock generator. A symptom of this will be a printout of only 2 or 3 clock values, with the rest all zeros. If you run into this, and your board is not listed in the databases, contact the XFree86 team for help, or post a message to comp.windows.x.i386unix.

Some servers (S3 and AGX) require you to identify the type and speed of the RAMDAC your board uses in order to get the most out of the hardware. This is done by adding entries Ramdac and DacSpec. For details of the supported RAMDACs, refer to the appropriate server manual page. Previous versions of XFree86 specified the RAMDAC type with an Option flag.

You may need to specify some option flags for your hardware. The server manual pages will describe these options, and the chipset-specific *README* files will tell you if any are required for your board.

Configuring the Monitor and its Modes

Configuring monitor modes can be a trying experience because of the lack of standardization in monitor hardware. The XFree86 project has attempted to simplify this by collecting databases of specific monitor information, and assembling a set of generic modes that should get pretty much any monitor up and functional. For all the gory details of mode generation and tuning, refer to the file */usr/X11R6/lib/X11/doc/VideoModes.doc*.

The Monitor section

The monitor specs and video modes are described in the *Monitor* sections in the *XF86Config* file:

```
# Any number of monitor sections may be present

Section "Monitor"

    Identifier  "Generic Monitor"
    VendorName  "Unknown"
    ModelName   "Unknown"
```

```
# HorizSync is in kHz unless units are specified.
# HorizSync may be a comma separated list of discrete values, or a
# comma separated list of ranges of values.
# NOTE: THE VALUES HERE ARE EXAMPLES ONLY.  REFER TO YOUR MONITOR'S
# USER MANUAL FOR THE CORRECT NUMBERS.

    HorizSync    31.5  # typical for a single frequency fixed-sync monitor

#    HorizSync 30-64        # multisync
#    HorizSync 31.5, 35.2   # multiple fixed sync frequencies
#    HorizSync 15-25, 30-50 # multiple ranges of sync frequencies

# VertRefresh is in Hz unless units are specified.
# VertRefresh may be a comma separated list of discrete values, or a
# comma separated list of ranges of values.
# NOTE: THE VALUES HERE ARE EXAMPLES ONLY.  REFER TO YOUR MONITOR'S
# USER MANUAL FOR THE CORRECT NUMBERS.

    VertRefresh 60  # typical for a single frequency fixed-sync monitor

#    VertRefresh    50-100        # multisync
#    VertRefresh    60, 65        # multiple fixed sync frequencies
#    VertRefresh    40-50, 80-100 # multiple ranges of sync frequencies

# Modes can be specified in two formats.  A compact one-line format, or
# a multi-line format.

# A generic VGA 640x480 mode (hsync = 31.5kHz, refresh = 60Hz)
# These two are equivalent

#    ModeLine "640x480" 25.175 640 664 760 800 480 491 493 525

    Mode "640x480"
        DotClock    25.175
        HTimings    640 664 760 800
        VTimings    480 491 493 525
    EndMode

# These two are equivalent

#    ModeLine "1024x768i" 45 1024 1048 1208 1264 768 776 784 817 Interlace

#    Mode "1024x768i"
#        DotClock    45
#        HTimings    1024 1048 1208 1264
#        VTimings    768 776 784 817
#        Flags       "Interlace"
#    EndMode

EndSection
```

To create a Monitor section, you need to know your monitor's specifications, in particular its video bandwidth and what range of horizontal sync and vertical sync rates it supports. If you can't find this information in the monitor's user manual, check the file */usr/X11R6/lib/X11/doc/Monitors* to see if it has an entry for your monitor. The *XF86Config* man page describes how to enter this information into the Monitor section.

Next, you need to provide a set of video modes that are suitable for the monitor. The first step is to check in the *Monitors* and *modeDB.txt* files to see if there is a listing of modes for your specific monitor. If there is, copy those modes to the Monitor section of your *XF86Config* file. Verify that there is a clock listed on the Clocks line in your *XF86Config* that matches the dot clock in the 2nd parameter of each mode line; delete any mode line that does not have a matching clock on your board. If you still have modes left, you are in good shape.

If you don't find any specific modes, or need more modes for the resolutions you want to use, refer to the Generic Video Modes listing in the file */usr/X11R6/lib/X11/doc/README.Config*. Match the mode specification against your monitor's specifications; pick the highest-refresh mode that is within specs, and make sure you have a matching dot-clock on your Clocks line. Try the VESA modes before any corresponding alternate mode setting. Copy the mode specification to the Monitor section of your *XF86Config* file. Note that these modes are likely not optimal; they may not be sized perfectly, or may not be correctly centered. But they should get you up and running. If you want to tune the mode to your monitor, you can read the section *Fixing Problems with the Image* in *VideoModes.doc*.

A note before you are done. If the same mode name occurs more than once in the Monitor section of the *XF86Config* file, the server will use the first mode with a matching clock. It is generally considered a bad idea to have more than one mode with the same name in your *XF86Config* file.

The Screen section

Once you have given a description of your monitor and graphics hardware you need to specify how they are to be used by the servers. This is the purpose of the *Screen* sections in the *XF86Config* file:

```
# The colour SVGA server
Section "Screen"
    Driver "svga"
    Device "Generic SVGA"
    Monitor      "Generic Monitor"
    Subsection "Display"
        Depth         8
        Modes         "640x480"
        ViewPort      0 0
        Virtual       800 600
    EndSubsection
EndSection

# The 16-colour VGA server
Section "Screen"
    Driver "vga16"
    Device "Generic VGA"
    Monitor      "Generic Monitor"
    Subsection "Display"
        Modes         "640x480"
        ViewPort      0 0
        Virtual       800 600
    EndSubsection
EndSection

# The Mono server
Section "Screen"
    Driver "vga2"
    Device "Generic VGA"
    Monitor      "Generic Monitor"
    Subsection "Display"
        Modes         "640x480"
        ViewPort      0 0
        Virtual       800 600
    EndSubsection
```

```
EndSection

# The accelerated servers (S3, Mach32, Mach8, 8514, P9000, AGX, W32)
# Section "Screen"
#      Driver    "accel"
#      Device    "Actix GE32+ 2MB"
#      Monitor   "Generic Monitor"
#      Subsection   "Display"
#         Depth     8
#         Modes     "640x480"
#         ViewPort   0 0
#         Virtual        1280 1024
#      EndSubsection
#      SubSection "Display"
#         Depth     16
#         Weight         565
#         Modes     "640x480"
#         ViewPort   0 0
#         Virtual        1024 768
#      EndSubsection
# EndSection
```

Supply a Screen section for each of the server driver types you will be using. The driver types are SVGA (*XF86_SVGA*), VGA16 (*XF86_VGA16*), VGA2 (*XF86_Mono*), MONO (*XF86_Mono*, *XF86_VGA16*), and ACCEL (*XF86_S3*, *XF86_Mach32*, *XF86_Mach8*, *XF86_Mach64*, *XF86_8514*, *XF86_P9000*, *XF86_AGX*, and *XF86_W32*). Each Screen section specifies which Monitor description and Device description are to be used.

The Screen sections include one or more *Display* subsections. One Display subsection may be provided for each pixel depth (the number of bits per pixel) that the server supports. In the Display subsection you can specify the size of the virtual screen the server will use. The virtual screen allows you to have a *root window* larger than can be displayed on your monitor. For example, you can have an 800x600 display, but a 1280x1024 virtual size. Use the keyword Virtual to specify this size. Note that many of the new accelerated servers use non-displayed memory for caching. It is not desirable to use all of your memory for virtual display, as this leaves none for caching, and this can cost as much as 30-40% of your server performance.

The last thing you specify in Display subsection are the display modes, the physical display resolutions that the server will use. The name is arbitrary, but must match something in the appropriate *Monitor* section. By convention, these names are the display resolution (for example 1024x768), but this is not a requirement. You can list as many as desired; the first is the initial display resolution, and you can cycle through the list with **Ctrl-Alt-Keypad+** or **Ctrl-Alt-Keypad-** hotkey sequences.

11

Making friends with FreeBSD

So now you have installed FreeBSD, and it successfully boots from the hard disk. Your first encounter with FreeBSD can be rather puzzling. Sure, you didn't expect to see the same things you know from Microsoft platforms, but you might not have expected what you see either:

```
FreeBSD (freebie.example.org) (ttyv0)

 login:
```

Where do you go from here? This chapter tells you.

FreeBSD is a very powerful operating system, but power doesn't come without a certain complexity. As a result, that some mundane operations can seem more difficult than they need be. There isn't space in this book to explain everything there is about working with FreeBSD, but in the following few chapters I'd like to make the transition easier for people who have prior experience with Microsoft platforms or with other flavours of UNIX. You can find a lot more information about these topics in *UNIX for the Impatient*, by Paul W. Abrahams and Bruce R. Larson, *UNIX Power Tools*, by Jerry Peek, Tim O'Reilly, and Mike Loukides, and *UNIX System Administration Handbook*, by Evi Nemeth, Garth Snyder, Scott Seebass, and Trent R. Hein. See Appendix C, *Bibliography*, for more information.

If you've come from Microsoft, you will notice a large number of differences between UNIX and Microsoft, but in fact the two systems have more in common than meets the eye. Indeed, back in the mid-80s, one of the stated goals of MS-DOS 2.0 was to make it more UNIX-like. You be the judge of how successful that attempt was, but in the following sections you'll notice some similarities. You'll find a comparison of the more common MS-DOS and UNIX commands in Appendix B, *Command equivalents*.

In this chapter, we'll look at FreeBSD from the perspective of a newcomer with no UNIX background. If you *do* have a UNIX background, you may still find it interesting. Specifically, we'll consider:

- Your primary interface with FreeBSD is via the *shell*. This looks rather like the command-line interface to Microsoft's MS-DOS, but there are a number of differences which aren't immediately obvious. We'll look at them in the next section.

- UNIX is a multi-user operating system. This means that you have to tell the system who you are before you can access it. On page 162 we'll look at how to define users.

- Once you have defined a user, you need to log in to the system and tell it what to do. We'll look at that on page 164.

- Not all users are created equal. In particular, the system administration login `root` has power over all other users. We'll look at this topic on page 167.

- UNIX implements multi-tasking via a mechanism called *processes*. We'll look at them on page 181.

- Timekeeping is extremely important in a networking system. If your system has the wrong time, it can cause all sorts of strange effects. On page 186 we'll look at how to ensure that your system is running the correct time.

- Other aspects of FreeBSD are so extensive that we'll dedicate separate chapters to them. We'll look at them in Chapter 12, *Starting and stopping the system*, Chapter 13, *File systems*, Chapter 14, *Disks*, and Chapter 15, *Tapes, backups and floppy disks*. In particular, on page 239 we'll see how to access multiple "terminals" or windows.

Differences from other environments

At first sight, UNIX can look really arcane. People often get really frustrated when working with the shell: it just doesn't seem to do what you want, and there's no good reason.

Well, of course there's always a good reason, but they are often so non-obvious that even experienced programmers find it hard to believe. Here are some of the most popular, seen from a Microsoft perspective:

Upper and lower case names

UNIX file names are *case-sensitive*: the names *FOO*, *Foo* and *foo* are three different names. This may seem silly at first, but any alternative is going to make things slower (the system must internally upshift or downshift the names), and it means that the names must be associated with a specific character set. How do you upshift the German name *Blödsinn*? What if the same characters appear in a Chinese name? Do they still shift the same? In fact, all characters are legal in a UNIX file name, with one exception: / is a separator which indicates a directory, and you can't use it in a file name. Still, there are some characters you should avoid: spaces are a pain, as we'll see below, and binary 0s (the ASCII *NUL* character) can confuse a lot of programs. It's almost impossible to get a binary 0 into a file name anyway, since the character is used to represent the end of a string in the C programming language.

This isn't the problem it used to be: web browsers have made UNIX file names more popular with *Uniform Resource Locators* or *URLs*. We'll look at them on page 563.

File names and extensions

The Microsoft naming convention (name, period and extension) is similar to that of UNIX. UNIX also uses extensions to represent specific kinds of files. The difference is that these extensions (and their lengths) are implemented by convention, not by the file system. In Microsoft, the period between the name and the extension is a typographical feature which only exists at the display level: it's not part of the name. In UNIX, the period is part of the name, and names like *foo.bar.bazzot* are perfectly valid file names. The system doesn't assign any particular meaning to file name extensions; instead, it looks for *magic numbers*, specific values in specific places in the file.

Globbing characters

Most systems have a method of representing groups of filenames and other names, usually by using special characters for representing an abstraction. The most common in UNIX are the characters *, ? and the square brackets []. UNIX calls these characters *globbing characters*. The Microsoft usage comes from UNIX, but the underlying file name representation makes for big differences. Table 11-1 gives some examples.

Name	Microsoft meaning	UNIX meaning
CONFIG.*	All files with the name *CONFIG*, no matter what their extension.	All files whose name starts with *CONFIG.*, no matter what the rest is. Note that the name includes a period at the end.
CONFIG.BA?	All files with the name *CONFIG* and an extension which starts with *BA*, no matter what the last character.	All files which start with *CONFIG.BA* and have one more character in their name.
*	Depending on the Microsoft version, all files without an extension, or all files.	All files.
.	All files with an extension.	All files which have a period after the beginning of their name.
foo[127]	In older versions, invalid. In newer versions with long file name support, the file with the name *foo[127]*.	*foo1*, *foo2* and *foo7*.

Figure 11-1: Globbing examples

Shell parameters

When you invoke a program with the shell, it first *parses* the input line before passing it to the program: it turns the line into a number of parameters (called *arguments* in the C programming language). Normally the parameters are separated by *white space*, either a space or a tab character. If you write a program or script *foo*, and invoke it like this:

```
$ foo and a lot more
```

the program will receive five arguments, numbered 0 to 4:

Argument	Value
0	foo
1	and
2	a
3	lot
4	more

What happens if you want to pass a name with a space? For example, you might want to look for the text "`Mail rejected`" in a log file. We have a program for looking for text, called *grep*. The syntax is:

```
grep expression files
```

Argument 1 is the expression; all additional arguments are the names of files to search. We could write

```
$ grep Mail rejected /var/log/maillog
```

but that would try to look for the text `Mail` in the files *rejected* (probably causing an error message that the file did not exist) and */var/log/maillog* (where just about every line contains the text `Mail`). That's not what we want. Instead, we do pretty much what I wrote above:

```
$ grep "Mail rejected" /var/log/maillog
```

In other words, if we put quote characters `""` around a group of words, the shell will interpret them as a single parameter. The parameter that is passed to *grep* is `Mail rejected`, not `"Mail rejected"`.

This behaviour of the shell is a very good reason not to use file names with spaces in them. It's perfectly legitimate to embed spaces into UNIX file names, but it's a pain to use.

It's even more interesting to see what happens when you pass a globbing character to a program, for example:

```
$ cc -o foo *.c
```

This invocation compiles all C source files (*.c) and creates a program *foo*. If you do this with Microsoft, the C compiler gets four parameters, and it has to find the C source files itself. In UNIX, the shell expands the text *.c and replaces it with the names of the source files. If there are thirty source files in the directory, it will pass a total of 33 parameters to the compiler.

Fields which can contain spaces

The solution to the "Mail rejected" problem isn't ideal, but it works well enough as long as you don't have to do it all the time. In many cases, though, particularly in configuration files, you do have to do it relatively often. As a result, a number of system configuration files use a colon (:) as a delimiter. This looks very confusing at first, but it turns out not to be as bad as the alternatives. We'll see some examples in the password file on page 163, in the login class file on page 168, and in the PATH environment variable on page 178.

Slashes: backward and forward

Some of the most confusing characters in computers are / and \. UNIX uses / to delimit directories: for example, */etc/fstab* starts from the *root directory* (/), and represents the directory *etc* inside this directory, and the file *fstab* within that directory. The backslash \ is called an *escape character* it has a number of different purposes:

- You can put it in front of another special character to say "don't interpret this character in any special way". For example, we've seen that the shell interprets a space character as the end of a parameter. In the previous example we changed Mail rejected to "Mail rejected" to stop the shell from interpreting it. We could also have written it like this: Mail\ rejected.

  A more common use for this *quoting* is to tell the shell to ignore the end of a line. If a command line in a shell script gets too long, you might like to split it up into several lines; but the shell sees the end of a line as a go-ahead to perform the command. You can stop it from doing so by putting a backslash *immediately* before the end of the line:

  ```
  $ grep \
    "Mail rejected" \
    /var/log/maillog
  ```

  Don't put any spaces between the \ and the end of the line; otherwise the shell will interpret the first space as a parameter by itself, and then it will interpret the end of line as the end of the command.

- In the C programming language, the backslash is used to represent several *control characters*. For example, \n means "new line". This usage appears in many other places as well.

- Using \ as an escape character causes problems: how do we put a \ character on a line? The answer: quote it. Write \\ when you mean \. This causes particular problems when interfacing with Microsoft—see page 588 for an example.

There are many more such surprises in store; take a look at *UNIX Power Tools* for a good overview.

Tab characters

We've seen that the shell treats white space, either spaces or tab characters, as the same. Unfortunately, some other programs do not. *make*, *sendmail* and *syslogd* make a distinction between the two kinds of characters, and they all require tabs (not spaces) in certain places. This is a *real* nuisance, since hardly any editor makes a distinction between them.

Carriage control characters

In the olden days, the standard computer terminal was a Teletype, a kind of computer-controlled electric typewriter. When it got to the end of a line, it required two mechanical operations to move to the beginning of the next line: the *Carriage Return* control character told it to move the carriage back to the beginning of the line, and the *Line Feed* character told it to move to the next line.

Generations of computer systems emulated this behaviour by putting both characters at the end of each text line. This makes it more difficult to recognize the end of line, it uses up more storage space, and normally it doesn't buy you much. The implementors of UNIX decided instead to use a single character, which it calls the *Newline* character. For some reason, they chose the line feed to represent newline, though the character generated by **Enter** is a carriage return. As we saw above, the C programming language represents it as \n.

This causes problems transferring data between FreeBSD and Microsoft, and also when printing to printers which still expect both characters. We'll look at the file transfer issues on page 290, and the printer issues on page 295.

Users and groups

Probably the biggest difference between traditional Microsoft platforms and FreeBSD also takes the longest to appreciate: FreeBSD is a multi-user, multi-tasking system. This means that many people can use the system at once, and each of them can do several things at the same time. You may think "why would I want to do that?". Once you've got used to this idea, though, you'll never be satisfied with Microsoft again, even if you were in the first place. If you use the X window system, you'll find that all windows can be active at the same time—you don't have to select them. You can monitor some activity in the background in another window while writing a letter, testing a program, or playing a game.

In order to access a FreeBSD system, you must be registered as a *user*. The registration defines a number of parameters:

- A *user name*, also often called *user ID*. This is a name which you use to identify yourself to the system.

- A *password*, a security device to ensure that other people don't abuse your user ID. In order to log in, you need to specify both your user ID and the correct password. When you type in the password, nothing appears on the screen, so that people looking over your shoulder can't read it.

  It may seem strange to go to such security measures on a system which you alone use, but if you connect to the Internet, even via PPP or SLIP, other people can at least theoretically access your system while you are connected. If you don't connect to the Internet, you can get away without a password, but you can't get away without a user ID.

- A *shell*, a program which reads in your commands and executes them. MS-DOS uses the program *COMMAND.COM* to perform this function. UNIX has a large choice of shells: the traditional UNIX shells are the Bourne shell *sh* and the C shell *csh*, but FreeBSD also supplies *bash*, *tcsh*, *zsh* and others. The UNIX shells are orders of magnitude more powerful than *COMMAND.COM*—see *UNIX Power Tools* for a good discussion. I personally use the *bash* shell.

- A *home directory*. Since the system can have multiple users, each one needs a separate directory in which to store his private files. Typically, users have a directory */home/username*, where **username** is the name they use to log in. When you log in to the system, the shell sets the current directory to your home directory. In it, you can do what you want, and normally it is protected from access by other users. Many shells, including the *bash* used in these examples, use the special notation ~ (tilde) to represent the name of the home directory.

- A *group* number. UNIX collects users into *groups* who have specific access permissions. When you add a user, you need to make him a member of a specific group, which is entered in the password information. Your group number indirectly helps determine what you are allowed to do in the system. As we'll see on page 224, your user and group determine what access you have to the system. You can belong to more than one group.

  Group numbers generally have names associated with them. The group names and numbers are stored in the file */etc/group*. In addition, this file may contain userids of users who belong to another group, but who are allowed to belong to this group as well.

  If you find the concept of groups confusing, don't worry about them. You can get by quite happily without using them at all. You'll just see references to them when we come to discuss file permissions. For further information, look at the man page for *group(5)*.

In addition to "real" users, who represent people, the system has a number of pseudo-users who represent tasks performed by the system. Don't remove them, or you could run into problems.

The list of users is kept in the file */etc/passwd*. In older UNIX systems, this was the only file used to store user information, and the passwords were also stored here in encrypted form. Nowadays processors are much faster, and it's too easy to crack a password. As a result, FreeBSD keeps the real information in a file called */etc/master.passwd*, and for performance reasons it also makes it available in database form in */etc/pwd.db* and */etc/spwd.db*. */etc/passwd* remains for compatibility reasons: some programs access it directly to get information about the environment in which they are running.

By default, there are no real users on a freshly installed system. Optionally, *sysinstall* will do it for you, but there's no particular reason to do it during system installation. In the next section, we'll look at two ways to add and modify users.

Choosing a user name

So what user name do you choose? User names are usually related to your real name and can be up to 8 characters long. By convention, they are in all lower case, even when they represent real names. Typical ways to form a user name are:

- First name. In my personal case, this would be greg.

- Last name (lehey).

- First name and initial of last name (gregl).

- Inital of first name, and last name (glehey).

- Initials (gfl).

- Nickname (for example, grog).

I choose the last possibility, as we will see in the following discussion.

Adding users

There are two ways to add users. One is the program *adduser*:

```
# adduser
Use option ''-verbose'' if you want see more warnings & questions
or try to repair bugs.

Enter username [a-z0-9]: yana
Enter full name []: Yana Lehey
Enter shell bash csh date no sh [bash]:      accept the default
Uid [1000]:                                  accept the default
Enter login class: default []:               accept the default
Login group yana [yana]: home
Login group is ''home''. Invite yana into other groups: no
[no]: wheel                                  in order to use su
Enter password []:                           no echo
Enter password again []:                     no echo

Name:   yana
Password: ****
Fullname: Yana Lehey
Uid:    1000
Gid:    1001 (home)
Class:
Groups:       home wheel
HOME:   /home/yana
Shell:        /bin/bash
OK? (y/n) [y]:                               accept the default
Added user ''yana''
Add another user? (y/n) [y]: n
```

An alternative way of adding or removing users is with the *vipw* program. This is a more typical UNIX-hackish approach: *vipw* starts your favourite editor and allows you to edit the contents of the file */etc/master.passwd*. After you have finished, it checks the contents and rebuilds the password database. Figure 11-2 shows an example.

```
root::0:0::0:0:Charlie &:/root:/bin/csh
toor:*:0:0::0:0:Bourne-again Superuser:/root:
daemon:*:1:1::0:0:Owner of many system processes:/root:/nonexistent
operator:*:2:20::0:0:System &:/usr/guest/operator:/bin/csh
bin:*:3:7::0:0:Binaries Commands and Source,,:/:/nonexistent
games:*:7:13::0:0:Games pseudo-user:/usr/games:/nonexistent
news:*:8:8::0:0:News Subsystem:/:/nonexistent
man:*:9:9::0:0:Mister Man Pages:/usr/share/man:/nonexistent
uucp:*:66:66::0:0:UUCP pseudo-user:/var/spool/uucppublic:/usr/libexec/uucp/uucic
o
xten:*:67:67::0:0:X-10 daemon:/usr/local/xten:/nonexistent
nobody:*:65534:65534::0:0:Unprivileged user:/nonexistent:/nonexistent
yvonne:$1$BaTr5OfB$yZpEOkpCnAORfc4eItisK/:1005:1001::0:0:Yvonne Lehey, Echunga,
+61-8-8388-8250:/home/yvonne:/bin/bash
yana:xCOict4JpfFqc:1006:1001::0:0:Yana Lehey, Echunga, +61-8-8388-8250:/home/yan
a:/bin/bash
grog:$1$6C.je$xhvXgPBUdkruwLXlxst.Gt.:1004:1000::0:0:Greg Lehey,Echunga SA,+61-8-
8388-8286,+61-8-8388-8250:/home/grog:/bin/bash
norm::1021:1001::0:0:Norman Lehey, Beach of Passionate Love, +60-9-774-5023:/hom
e/norm:/bin/bash

~
~
~
```

Figure 11-2: *vipw* display

You're probably wondering why would you ever want to do things this way, and you might find it funny that most experienced UNIX administrators prefer it. The reason is that you get more of an overview than with a peephole approach that graphical environments give you, but of course you need to understand the format better. It's less confusing once you know that each line represents a single user, that the lines are divided into *fields* (which may be empty), and that each field is separated from the next by a colon (:). Table 11-3 describes the fields you see on the line on which the cursor is positioned. You can read more about the format of */etc/master.passwd* in the man page for *passwd* for further details.

We'll see a valid use of this approach on page 462: if you want to make a second user almost the same as the first, it's easier to use an editor than type in all the parameters again.

Table 11-3. */etc/master.passwd* format

Field	Meaning
yvonne	User name
(gibberish)	Encrypted password. When adding a new user, leave this field empty and add it later with the *passwd* program.
1005	User number
1000	Group number
(empty)	Login class. We'll look at this below. This field is not included in */etc/passwd*.
0	Password change time. If non-0, it is the time in seconds after which the password must be changed. This field is not included in */etc/passwd*.
0	Account expiration time. If non-0, it is the time in seconds after which the user expires. This field is not included in */etc/passwd*.
Yvonne Lehey, Echunga, +61-8-8388-8250	The so-called *gecos* field, which describes the user. This field is used by a number of programs, in particular mail readers, to extract the real name of the user.
/home/yvonne	The name of the home directory.
/bin/bash	The shell to be started when the user logs in.

Adding or changing passwords

If your system has any connection with the outside world, it's a good idea to change your password from time to time. Do this with the *passwd* program. The input doesn't look very interesting:

```
$ passwd
Changing local password for yana.
Old password:               doesn't echo
New password:               doesn't echo
Retype new password:        doesn't echo
passwd: rebuilding the database...
passwd: done
```

You have to enter the old password to make sure that some passer-by doesn't change it for you while you're away from your monitor, and you have to enter the new password twice to make sure that you don't mistype and lock yourself out of your account. If this does happen anyway, you can log in as root and change the password: root doesn't have to enter the old password, and it can change anybody's password. For example:

```
# passwd
Changing local password for yana.
New password:                       doesn't echo
Retype new password:                doesn't echo
passwd: rebuilding the database...
passwd: done
```

In this case, you specify the name of the user for whom you change the password.

If you are changing the *root* password, be careful: it's easy enough to lock yourself out of the system if you mess things up, which could happen if, for example, you mistyped the password twice in the same way (don't laugh, it happens). If you're running X, open another window and use *su* to become *root*. If you're running in character mode, select another virtual terminal and log in as *root* there. Only when you're sure you can still access *root* should you log out.

If you *do* manage to lose the `root` password, all may not be lost. Reboot the machine to single user mode (see page 201), and enter:

```
# mount -u /                        mount root file system read/write
# mount /usr /                      mount /usr file system (if separate)
# passwd root                       change the password for root
Enter new password:
Enter password again:
# ^D                                enter ctrl-D to continue with startup
```

If you have a separate */usr* file system (the normal case), you need to mount it as well, since the *passwd* program is in the directory */usr/bin*. Note that you should explicitly state the name `root`: in single user mode, the system doesn't have the concept of user IDs.

The super user

FreeBSD has a number of privileged users for various administration functions. Some are just present to be the owners of particular files, while others, such as `daemon` and `uucp`, exist to run particular programs. One user stands above all others, however: `root` may do just about anything. The kernel gives `root` special privileges, and you need to become `root` in order to perform a number of functions, including adding other users. Make sure `root` has a password if there is any chance that other people can access your system (this is a must if you have any kind of dialup access). Apart from that, `root` is a user like any other, but to quote the man page *su(1)*,

> *By default (unless the prompt is reset by a startup file) the super-user prompt is set to #*
> *to remind one of its awesome power.*

Becoming super user

Frequently when you're logged in normally, you want to do something which requires you to be `root`. You can log out and log in again as `root`, of course, but there's an easier way:

```
$ su                                    become super user
Password:                               as usual, it doesn't echo
#                                       root prompt
```

In order to be able to use *su*, you must be a member of the group `wheel`. Normally you do this when you add the user, but otherwise just put the name of the user at the end of the line in */etc/group*:

```
wheel:*:0:root,grog                     add the text in bold face
```

> BSD treats *su* somewhat differently from System V. First, you need to be a member of the group `wheel`, and secondly BSD gives you more of the super-user environment than System V. See the man page for further information.

Login classes

In UNIX tradition, `root` has been the owner of the universe. In a large installation, this is rather primitive, and the 4.3BSD Net/2 release introduced a new concept, *login classes*, which determine session accounting, resource limits and user environment settings. Various programs in the system use the database described in */etc/login.conf* to set up a user's login environment and to enforce policy, accounting and administrative restrictions. The login class database also provides the means by which users are able to be authenticated to the system and the types of authentication available.

When creating a user, you may optionally enter a class name, which should match an entry in */etc/login.conf*—see page 165 for more details. If you don't, the system uses the entry `default` for a non-root user. For the root user, the system uses the entry `root` if it is present, and `default` otherwise.

The structure of the login configuration database is relatively extensive. It describes a number of parameters, many of which can have two values: a *current* value and a *maximum* value. On login, the system sets the values to the `-cur` (current) value, but the user may, at his option, increase the value to the `-max` (maximum) value. We'll look at the `default` entry for an example.

```
# Example defaults
# These settings are used by login(1) by default for classless users
# Note that entries like "cputime" set both "cputime-cur" and "cputime-max"

default:\
        :cputime=infinity:\
        :datasize-cur=64M:\
        :stacksize-cur=64M:\
        :memorylocked-cur=10M:\
        :memoryuse-cur=100M:\
        :filesize=infinity:\
        :coredumpsize=infinity:\
        :maxproc-cur=64:\
        :openfiles-cur=64:\
        :priority=0:\
        :requirehome@:\
        :umask=022:\
        :tc=auth-defaults:
```

As in the password file, the fields are delimited by colons (:). In this example, though, lines are *continued* by placing a backslash (\) at the end of each line except the last. This usage is common in UNIX. Unlike Microsoft usage, a backslash is never used to represent a directory.

This entry defines the following parameters:

- Processes may use as much CPU time as they want. If you change this, you can stop processes which use more than a specific amount of CPU time.

- The current maximum sizes of the user data segment and the stack are set to 64 MB. The entry doesn't define maximum values for these parameters.

- The user may lock a maximum of 10 MB of memory per process.

- The total memory use per process may not exceed 100 MB.

- There is no limit on the size of data files or core dump files that the user may create.

- The user may have up to 64 processes.

- Each process may have up to 64 open files. For some programs, this could be a limitation.

- The user *need not* have a home directory in order to log in. The @ symbol specifies that the preceding symbol (`requirehome`) should be undefined. As a result, the system does not require the home directory.

- By default, the *umask* is set to 022. See page 227 for more details of *umask*.

- The system uses the default authentication scheme for this user.

See the man page *login.conf(5)* for further details.

Referring to other classes

If you want to create a new class, you don't have to start from scratch. You can derive the defaults from a different class. For example, if you have one user on the system who uses a lot of memory, you might create a class like this:

```
glutton:\
    :tc=default:\
    :memoryuse-cur=infinity:
```

The property `tc` refers to the `default` class. A good example of this is the `xuser` class, designed for the needs of X11 users:

```
xuser:\
    :manpath=/usr/share/man /usr/X11R6/man /usr/local/man:\
    :cputime=4h:\
    :datasize=12M:\
    :stacksize=4M:\
    :filesize=8M:\
    :memoryuse=16M:\
    :openfiles=32:\
    :maxproc=48:\
    :tc=standard:
```

In this example, you'll notice also that the class definition defines a default for the environment variable MANPATH.

Using login classes

Login classes are a relatively recent addition to FreeBSD. There are a couple of things to note about their use:

- At the time of writing, not all parameters are implemented.

- The data is stored in the file database format for faster access. After modifying the file */etc/login.conf*, be sure to run the following command to update the database:

```
# cap_mkdb /etc/login.conf
```

Using the shell

So now we have a user ID, and we can get beyond the prompt on page 157. When you log in, you start your *shell*. As we saw on page 163, the shell takes your input as commands and ensures that they are executed. To log in, you type in your user ID, and when asked, your password:

```
login: grog
Password:                        password doesn't show on the screen
Last login: Sun Dec 21 18:56:11 on ttyv0
Copyright (c) 1980, 1983, 1986, 1988, 1989, 1991, 1993, 1994
    The Regents of the University of California.  All rights reserved.

FreeBSD 2.2.5 (FREEBIE) #14: Tue Jan  2 06:56:46 MET 1998

Welcome to FreeBSD!

You have mail.
erase ^H, kill ^U, intr ^C, status ^T
Niklaus Wirth has lamented that, whereas Europeans pronounce his name
correctly (Ni-klows Virt), Americans invariably mangle it into
(Nick-les Worth).  Which is to say that Europeans call him by name, but
Americans call him by value.
=== grog@freebie(/dev/ttyv0) ~ 1 ->
```

There's a lot of stuff here, and it's worth looking at it in more detail:

- The program that asks you to log in is called *getty*. It reads in your user ID and starts a program called *login* and passes the user ID to it.

- *login* asks for the password and checks your user ID.

- If the user ID and password are correct, *login* starts your designated shell.

- While starting up, the shell looks at a number of files. See the man page for your particular shell for details of what they are for. In this case, though, we can see the results: one file contains the time you last logged in, another one contains the *Message of the day* (*/etc/motd*), and a third one contains your mail. The shell prints out the message of the day unaltered—in this case, it contains information about the name of the kernel and a welcome message. The shell also prints information on last login time and whether you have mail.

- The line "erase ^H, kill ^U, intr ^C, status ^T" looks strange. It's telling you the current editing control characters. We'll look at these on page 171.

- It changes the current directory to your *home directory*.

- Then it runs the *fortune* program, which prints out a random quotation from a database of "fortune cookies". In this case, we get a message about Niklaus Wirth, the inventor of the Pascal programming language.

- Finally, the last line is a prompt, the information that tells you that the shell is ready for input.

It's worth looking at the prompt in more detail, since it illustrates a number of things about the UNIX environment. By default, *sh* and friends prompt with a $, and *csh* and friends prompt with a %. In the same way that you can change the MS-DOS command prompt away from C:\> to, say, show the current directory, you can change it to just about anything you want with the UNIX shells. You don't have to like my particular version, but it's worth understanding what it's trying to say.

The first part, ===, is just to make it easier to find in a large list on an X display. An *xterm* window (a terminal emulator which runs under X11) on a high resolution X display can contain up to 90 lines, and searching for command prompts can be non-trivial.

Next, grog@freebie is my user ID and the name of system on which I am working, in the RFC 822 format used for mail IDs. Multiple systems and multiple users can all be present on a single X display. This way, I can figure out which user I am and what system I am running on.

/dev/ttyv0 is the name of the current controlling terminal. This can sometimes be useful.

~ is the name of the home directory. Most shells, but not all of them, support this symbolism.

1 is the prompt number. Each time you enter a command, it is associated with this number, and the prompt number is incremented. One way to re-execute the command is to enter !!1 (two exclamation marks and the number of the command). We'll look at more comfortable ones in the next section.

Command line editing

Typing is a pain. If you're anything like me, you're continually making mistakes, and you may spend more time correcting typing errors than doing the typing in the first place. It's particularly frustrating when you enter something like:

```
$ groff -rex=7.5 -r$$ -rL -rW -rN2 -mpic tmac.M unixerf.mm
troff: fatal error: can't open 'unixerf.mm': No such file or directory
```

This command *should* create the PostScript version of this chapter, but unfortunately I messed up the name of the chapter: it should have been *unixref.mm*, and I typed *unixerf.mm*.

Yes, I know this looks terrible. UNIX isn't all like this, but sometimes this kind of notation has its advantages: it offers a flexibility that you can't get any other way. In addition, it's relatively easy to generate this kind of command line automatically: the command I really use to format this chapter is make unixref.

It would be particularly frustrating if I had to type the whole command in again. UNIX offers a number of ways to make life easier. The most obvious one is so obvious that you tend to take it for granted: the **Backspace** key erases the last character you entered. Well, most of the time. What if you're running on a machine without a **Backspace** key? You won't have that problem with a PC, of course, but a lot of workstations have a **DEL** key instead of a **Backspace** key. UNIX lets you specify what key to use to erase the last character entered. By default, the erase character really is **DEL**, but the shell startup changes it and prints out a message saying what it has done:

```
erase ^H, kill ^U, intr ^C, status ^T
```

in the example above. ^H (CTRL-H) is an alternative representation for **Backspace**.

The three other functions kill, intr, and status perform similar editing functions. kill erases the whole line, and intr stops a running program.

> More correctly, intr sends a *signal* called SIGINTR to the process. This normally causes a program to stop.

You'll notice that it is set to **Ctrl-C**, so its function is very similar to that of the MS-DOS **Break** key. status is an oddball function: it doesn't change the input, it just displays a statistics message. *bash* doesn't in fact use it: it has a better use for **Ctrl-T**.

In fact, these control characters are just a few of a large number of control characters that you can set. Table 11-4 gives an overview.

Table 11-4. Terminal control characters

Name	Default	Function
CR	\r	Go to beginning of line. Normally, this also terminates input (in other words, it returns the complete line to the program, which then acts on the input).
NL	\n	End line. Normally, this also terminates input.
INTR	CTRL-C	Generate an SIGINT signal. This normally causes the process to terminate.
QUIT	CTRL-|	Generate a SIGQUIT signal. This normally causes the process to terminate.
ERASE	DEL	Erase last character. FreeBSD sets this to **Backspace** on login, but under some unusual circumstances you will find it still set to **DEL**.
KILL	CTRL-U	Erase current input line.

Name	Default	Function
EOF	CTRL-D	Return end-of-file indication. Most programs stop when they receive an EOF.
EOL		Alternate end-of-line character. This is not normally used, and by default it is disabled.
EOL2		Alternate end-of-line character. Also seldom used.
START	CTRL-Q	Resume output after stop. See the next entry.
STOP	CTRL-S	Stop output. Use this to examine text which is scrolling faster than you can read.
SUSP	CTRL-Z	Suspend process. This key generates a SIGTSTP signal when typed. This normally causes a program to be suspended. To restart, use the *fg* command.
DSUSP	CTRL-Y	Delayed suspend. Generate a SIGTSTP signal when the character is read. Otherwise, this is the same as SUSP.
REPRINT	CTRL-R	Redisplay all characters in the input queue (in other words, characters that have been input but not yet read by any process). The term "print" recalls the days of harcopy terminals. Many shells disable this function.
DISCARD	CTRL-O	Discard all terminal output until another DISCARD character arrives, more input is typed or the program clears the condition.
WERASE	CTRL-W	Erase the preceding word.
LNEXT	CTRL-V	Interpret next character literally. Many shells disable this function.
STATUS	\377	Send a SIGINFO signal to the foreground process group. If NOKERNINFO is not set, the kernel also prints a status message on the terminal.

To set these characters, use the *stty* program. For example, if you're used to erasing the complete input line with **Ctrl-X**, and specifying an end-of-file condition with **Ctrl-Z**, you could enter:

```
$ stty susp \377 kill ^X eof ^Z
```

You need to set SUSP to something else first, because by default it is Ctrl-Z, so the system wouldn't know which function to perform if you press ^Z

> The combination \377 is the character octal 377 (this notation comes from the C language, and its origin is lost in the mists of time, back in the days when UNIX ran on PDP-11s). This character is the "null" character which turns off the corresponding function. System V uses the character \0 for the same purpose.

In this particular case, ^X really does mean the letter ^ followed by the letter X, and not **CTRL-**

X, the single character created by holding down the **Control** character and pressing **X** at the same time.

Command history and other editing functions

The editing characters we looked at above are provided by the terminal driver, which is part of the kernel, so they are available to all processes. They all have the limitation that they only work on the line you're currently typing. Once you've pressed **Enter**, there's nothing they can do any more.

Nowadays, most shells supply a *command history* function and additional functionality for editing it. We'll take a brief look at these features here—for more details, see the man pages for your shell.

Table 11-5. Command line editing—*Emacs* mode

Key	Function
Ctrl-A	Move to the beginning of the line
LeftArrow	Move to previous character on line
Ctrl-B	Move to previous character on line (alternative)
Ctrl-D	Delete the character under the cursor. Be careful with this character: it's also the End-of-file character, so if you enter it on an empty line, it stops your shell and logs you out.
Ctrl-E	Move to the end of the line
RightArrow	Move to next character on line
Ctrl-F	Move to next character on line (alternative)
Ctrl-K	Erase the rest of the line
Ctrl-L	Erase screen contents
DownArrow	Move to next input line
Ctrl-N	Move to next input line (alternative)
UpArrow	Move to previous input line
Ctrl-P	Move to previous input line (alternative)
Ctrl-R	Incremental search backward for text
Ctrl-S	Incremental search for text forward
Ctrl-T	Transpose the character under the cursor with the character before the cursor
Ctrl-U	Erase the current line
Ctrl-Y	Insert previously erased with **Ctrl-K** or **Alt-D**
Ctrl-_	Undo the last command
Alt-C	Capitalize the following word
Alt-D	Delete the following word
Alt-F	Move forward one word
Alt-L	Convert the following word to lower case
Alt-T	Transpose the word before the cursor with the one after it
Alt-U	Convert the following word to upper case

Shell command line editing has been through a number of evolutionary phases. The original Bourne shell supplied no command line editing at all, though the version supplied with FreeBSD gives you many of the editing features of more modern shells. Still, it's unlikely that you'll want to use the Bourne shell as your shell: *bash*, *ksh*, and *zsh* are all compatible with the Bourne shell, but they also supply better command line editing.

The next phase of command line editing was introduced with the C shell, *csh*. By modern standards, it's also rather pitiful. It's described in the *csh* man page if you really want to know. About the only part that is still useful is the ability to repeat a previous command with the ! ! construct. Modern shells supply command line editing which resembles the editors *vi* or *Emacs*. In *bash*, *sh*, *ksh*, and *zsh* you can make the choice by entering

```
$ set -o emacs          for Emacs-style editing
$ set -o vi             for vi-style editing
```

In *tcsh*, the corresponding commands are:

```
% bind emacs
% bind vi
```

Normally you put one of these commands in your startup file.

Table 11-6. Command line editing—*vi* mode

Key	Function
ˆ	Move to the beginning of the line
h	Move to previous character on line
x	Delete the character under the cursor
$	Move to the end of the line
l	Move to next character on line
D	Erase the rest of the line
Ctrl-L	Erase screen contents
j	Move to next input line
k	Move to previous input line
K	Search for text backward
J	Search for text forward
u	Undo the last command
w	Move forward one word
i	Change to insert mode

In *Emacs* mode, you enter the commands simply by typing them in. In *vi* mode, you have to press **ESC** first. Table 11-5 shows an overview of the more typical Emacs-style commands in *bash*, and Table 11-6 shows the commands for *tcsh* in *vi* mode. Many other shells supply similar functionality.

File name completion

As we have seen, UNIX file names can be much longer than traditional Microsoft names, and it becomes a problem to type them correctly. To address this problem, newer shells provide *file name completion*. In *Emacs* mode, you typically type in part of the name, then press the **Tab** key. The shell checks which file names begin with the characters you typed. If there is only one, it puts in the missing characters for you. If there are none, it beeps (rings the "terminal bell"). If there are more than one, it puts in as many letters as are common to all the file names, and then beeps. For example, if I have a directory *documentation* in my home directory, I might enter:

```
=== grog@freebie (/dev/ttyp4) ~ 14 -> cd documentation/
=== grog@freebie (/dev/ttyp4) ~/documentation 15 -> ls
freebsd.faq  freebsd.fbc  freeware
=== grog@freebie (/dev/ttyp4) ~/documentation 16 -> emacs freebeepbsd.fbeepaq
```

Remember that my input is in **fixed bold** font, and the shell's output is in `fixed` font. On the first line, I entered the characters `cd doc` followed by a **Tab** character, and the shell completed with the text `umentation/`. On the last line, I entered the characters `emacs f` and a **Tab**. In this case, the shell determined that there was more than one file which started like this, so it added the letters `ree` and rang the bell. I entered the letter `b` and pressed **Tab** again, and the shell added the letters `sd.f` and beeped again. Finally, I added the letters `aq` to complete the file name *freebsd.faq*.

Command line completion in *vi* mode is similar: instead of pressing **Tab**, you press **ESC** twice.

Environment variables

The UNIX programming model includes a concept called *environment variables*. This rather unusual sounding name is simply a handy method of passing relatively long-lived information of a general nature from one program to another. It's easier to demonstrate the use than to describe. Table 11-7 takes a look at some typical environment variables. To set environment variables from Bourne-style shells, enter

```
$ TERM=xterm export TERM
```

This sets the value of the `TERM` variable to `xterm`. If you want, you can also set it at the beginning of a command line:

```
$ TERM=xterm-color mutt
```

This starts the *mutt* mail reader (see page 546) with *xterm*'s colour features enabled.

For *csh* and *tcsh*, set environment variables with:

```
% setenv TERM xterm
```

To start a process with these variables, enter:

```
% env xterm-color mutt
```

Table 11-7. Common environment variables

Name	Purpose
BLOCKSIZE	The size of blocks which programs like *df* count. The default is 512 bytes, but it's often more convenient to use 1024.
COLUMNS	The number of columns on the current display. This variable should not be used, since the number of columns is defined in the *termcap* description for terminals with a fixed display size, and the software should be able to ask the others, such as *xterm*, for their size. Unfortunately, other systems frequently have difficulties in this area, and COLUMNS can help.
DISPLAY	When running X, the name of the X server. For a local system, this is typically unix:0. For remote systems, it's in the form *system-name*:*server-number*.*screen-number*. For the system *bumble.example.org*, you would probably write bumble.example.org:0.
EDITOR	The name of your favourite editor. Various programs that start editors look at this variable to know which editor to start.
HOME	The name of your home directory.
LANG	The *locale* which you use. This should be the name of a directory in */usr/share/locale*.
LINES	See COLUMNS above. This second variable defines the number of lines on the screen.
MAIL	Some programs use this variable to find your incoming mail file.
MANPATH	A list of path names, separated by colons (:), which specifies where the *man* program should look for man pages. A typical string might be /usr/share/man:/usr/local/man, and specifies that there are man pages in each of the directories */usr/share/man* and */usr/local/man*.
NTAPE	The name of the non-rewinding tape device. See page 282 for more details.
PATH	A list of path names, separated by colons (:), which specifies where the shell should look for executable programs if you specify just the program name.
PS1	In Bourne-style shells, this is the prompt string. It's usually set to **$**, but can be changed. See page 171 for a discussion of a possible prompt for *bash*.
PS2	In Bourne-style shells, this is the prompt string for continuation lines. It's usually set to **>**.

Name	Purpose
SHELL	The name of the shell. You can use this for starting a new copy.
TAPE	The name of the rewinding tape device. See page 282 for more details.
TERM	The type of terminal emulation you are using. This is very important: there is no other way for an application to know what the terminal is, and if you set it to the wrong value, full-screen programs will behave incorrectly.
TZ	Time zone. This is the name of a file in */usr/share/zoneinfo* which describes the local time zone. See the section on timekeeping on page 186 for more details.

Note particularly the PATH variable. One of the most popular questions in the FreeBSD-questions mailing list is "I have compiled a program, and I can see it in my directory, but when I try to run it, I get the message command not found". This is usually because the current directory is not in the PATH.

> It's good practice *not* to have your current directory or your home directory in the PATH: if you do, you can be subject to security attacks.

You should set your PATH variable to point to the most common executable directories. Add something like this to your *.profile* file (for Bourne-style shells):

```
PATH=/usr/bin:/usr/local/bin:/usr/sbin:/bin:/sbin:/usr/X11R6/bin
export PATH
```

Alternatively, for *csh*-style shells, put this in your *.cshrc*:

```
set path = (/usr/bin /usr/local/bin /usr/sbin /bin /sbin /usr/X11R6/bin)
```

This specifies to look for executable programs in the sequence */usr/bin*, */usr/local/bin*, */usr/sbin*, */bin*, */sbin* and */usr/X11R6/bin*. This variable is of great importance: one of the leading problems that beginners have is to have an incorrect PATH variable.

Shell startup files

As we saw above, there are a lot of ways to customize your shell. It would be inconvenient to have to set them every time, so all shells provide a means to set them automatically when you log in. Nearly every shell has its own startup file. Table 11-8 gives an overview.

The format of these files is like a shell script—in other words, straight shell commands. Figure 11-9 shows a typical *.bashrc* file to set the environment variables we discussed.

Table 11-8. Shell startup files

Shell	*startup file*
bash	*.profile*, then *.bashrc*
csh	*.login* on login, always *.cshrc*
sh	*.profile*
tcsh	*.login* on login, always *.tcshc, .cshrc if .tcshrc not found*

```
umask 022
BLOCKSIZE=1024  # for df
CVSROOT=/src/ncvs
EDITOR=/opt/bin/emacs;export EDITOR
LANG=en_AU.ISO8859-1 export LANG
MANPATH=/usr/share/man:/usr/local/man
MOZILLA_HOME=/usr/local/netscape export MOZILLA_HOME
PAGER=less export PAGER
PATH=/usr/bin:/usr/local/bin:/usr/sbin:/bin:/sbin:/usr/X11R6/bin
PS1="=== \u@\h ('tty') \w \# -> "
PS2="\u@\h \w \! ++ "
SHELL=/bin/bash export SHELL
TAPE=/dev/nrst0 export TAPE     # note non-rewinding as standard
if [ "$TERM" = "" ]; then
  TERM=xterm
fi
if [ "$DISPLAY" = "" ]; then
  DISPLAY=unix:0;export DISPLAY
fi
/usr/games/fortune          # print a fortune cookie
```

Figure 11-9: Minimal *.bashrc* **file**

It would be tedious for every user to put settings in their private initialization files, so the shells also read a system-wide default file. For the Bourne shell family, it is */etc/profile*, while the C shell family has three files: */etc/csh.login* to be executed on login, */etc/csh.cshrc* to be executed when a new shell is started after you log in, and */etc/csh.logout* to be executed when you stop a shell. The start files are executed before the corresponding individual files.

In addition, login classes (page 168) offer another method of setting environment variables at a global level.

Changing your shell

The FreeBSD installation gives `root` a C shell, *csh*. This is the traditional Berkeley shell, but it has a number of disadvantages: command line editing is very primitive, and the script language is significantly different from that of the Bourne shell, which is the *de facto* standard for shell scripts: if you stay with the C shell, you may still need to understand the Bourne shell. The latest version of the Bourne shell *sh* also includes some command line editing. See page 175 for details of how to enable it.

You can get better command line editing with *tcsh*, in the Ports Collection. You can get both better command line editing and Bourne shell syntax with *bash*, also in the Ports Collection.

If you have `root` access, you can use *vipw* to change your shell, but there's a more general way: use *chsh* (*Change Shell*). Simply run the program. It starts your favourite editor (as defined by the EDITOR environment variable). Here's an example before:

```
#Changing user database information for velte.
Shell: /bin/csh
Full Name: Jack Velte
Location:
Office Phone:
Home Phone:
```

You can change anything after the colons. For example, you might change this to:

```
#Changing user database information for velte.
Shell: /usr/local/bin/bash
Full Name: Jack Velte
Location: On the road
Office Phone: +1-408-555-1999
Home Phone:
```

chsh checks and updates the password files when you save the modifications and exit the editor. The next time you log in, you get the new shell. *chsh* tries to ensure you don't make any mistakes—for example, it won't let you enter the name of a shell which isn't mentioned in the file */etc/shells*—but it's a *very* good idea to check the shell before logging out. You can try this with *su*, which you normally use to become super user:

```
bumble# su velte
Password:
su-2.00$                    note the new prompt
```

There are a couple of problems in using *tcsh* or *bash* as a root shell:

- The shell for `root` *must* be on the root file system, otherwise will not work in single user mode. Unfortunately, most ports of shells put the shell in the directory */usr/local/bin*, which is almost never on the root file system.

- Most shells are *dynamically linked*: they rely on library routines in files such as */usr/lib/libc.a*. These files are not available in single user mode, so the shells won't work. You can solve this problem by creating *statically linked* versions of the shell, but this requires programming experience beyond the scope of this book.

If you can get hold of a statically linked version, perform the following steps to install it:

- Copy the shell to */bin*, for example:

  ```
  # cp /usr/local/bin/bash /bin
  ```

- Add the name of the shell to */etc/shells*, in this example the line in **bold print**:

```
# List of acceptable shells for chpass(1).
# Ftpd will not allow users to connect who are not using
# one of these shells.
/bin/sh
/bin/csh
/bin/bash
```

Processes

As we have seen, UNIX is a multi-user, multi-tasking operating system. In particular, you can run a specific program more than once. We use the term *process* to refer to a particular instance of a running program. Each process is given a *process ID*, more frequently referred to as *PID*, a number between 0 and 29999 which uniquely identifies it. There are many things that you might like to know about the processes which are currently running, such as:

- How many processes are running?

- Who is running the processes?

- Why is the system so slow?

- Which process is blocking my access to the modem?

Your primary tool for investigating process behaviour is the *ps* (*process status*) command. It has a large number of command options, and it can tell you a whole lot of things which you will only understand when you have investigated how the kernel works, but it can be very useful for a number of things. Here are some typical uses:

What processes do I have running?

After starting a large number of processes in a number of windows under X, you probably can't remember what is still running. Maybe processes that you thought had stopped are still running. To display a brief summary of the processes you have running, use the *ps* command with no options:

```
$ ps
  PID  TT  STAT      TIME COMMAND
  187  p0  Is+    0:01.02 -bash (bash)
  188  p1  Ss     0:00.62 -bash (bash)
  453  p1  R+     0:00.03 ps
```

This display shows the following information:

- The *PID* of the process.

- *TT* is short for *teletype*, and shows the last few letters of the name of the *controlling terminal*, the terminal on which the process is running. In this example, the terminals are */dev/ttyp0* and */dev/ttyp1*.

- *STAT* shows the current process status. It's involved and requires a certain amount of understanding of how the kernel runs in order to interpret it—see the man page for *ps* for more details.

181

- *TIME* is the CPU time that the process has used in minutes, seconds and hundredths of a second. Note that many other UNIX systems, particularly System V, only show this field to the nearest second.

- *COMMAND* is normally the command you entered, but don't rely on this. In the next section, you'll see that *sendmail* has changed its *COMMAND* field to tell you what it is doing. You'll notice that the command on the last line is the *ps* which performs the listing. Due to some complicated timing problems in the kernel, this process may or may not appear in the listing.

What processes are running?

There are many more processes in the system than the list above shows. To show them all, use the a option to *ps*. To show dæmons as well (see the next section for a definition of *dæmon*), use the x option. To show much more detail, use the u or l options. For example,

```
$ ps waux
USER      PID  %CPU %MEM   VSZ   RSS  TT  STAT  STARTED      TIME COMMAND
grog      510   0.0  0.9   448   272  p1  R+     2:49PM  0:00.02 ps -waux
root        1   0.0  0.6   324   180  ??  Is    10:10AM  0:00.15 /sbin/init --
root        2   0.0  0.1     0    12  ??  DL    10:10AM  0:00.00 (pagedaemon)
root        3   0.0  0.1     0    12  ??  DL    10:10AM  0:00.00 (vmdaemon)
root        4   0.0  0.1     0    12  ??  DL    10:10AM  0:08.61 (update)
root       23   0.0  0.3   196    72  ??  Is    10:10AM  0:00.02 adjkerntz -i
root       49   0.0  0.4   220   116  ??- I      9:11AM  0:00.10 mount -a -t nfs
root       71   0.0  1.1   188   340  ??  Ss     9:11AM  0:00.78 syslogd
daemon     76   0.0  0.9   176   272  ??  Is     9:11AM  0:00.03 portmap
root       81   0.0  0.9   160   280  ??  Is     9:11AM  0:00.84 rwhod
root       85   0.0  0.6   408   176  ??  Is     9:11AM  0:00.03 mountd
root       87   0.0  0.4   232   104  ??  Is     9:11AM  0:00.03 nfsd: master (nfsd)
root       90   0.0  0.2   224    56  ??  I      9:11AM  0:00.02 nfsd: server (nfsd)
root       91   0.0  0.2   224    56  ??  I      9:11AM  0:00.00 nfsd: server (nfsd)
root       92   0.0  0.2   224    56  ??  I      9:11AM  0:00.00 nfsd: server (nfsd)
root       93   0.0  0.2   224    56  ??  I      9:11AM  0:00.00 nfsd: server (nfsd)
root       98   0.0  1.0   192   300  ??  Is     9:11AM  0:00.54 inetd
root      105   0.0  1.1   236   340  ??  Is     9:11AM  0:01.19 cron
root      107   0.0  1.1   192   320  ??  Is     9:11AM  0:00.07 lpd
root      110   0.0  1.3   484   376  ??  Is     9:11AM  0:00.16 sendmail: accepting connecti
root      150   0.0  1.8   156   536  v0  Is+    9:11AM  0:00.06 /usr/libexec/getty Pc ttyv0
root      151   0.0  1.8   156   536  v1  Is+    9:11AM  0:00.06 /usr/libexec/getty Pc ttyv1
root      152   0.0  1.8   156   536  v2  Is+    9:11AM  0:00.06 /usr/libexec/getty Pc ttyv2
root      153   0.0  1.8   156   536  v3  Is+    9:11AM  0:00.05 /usr/libexec/getty Pc ttyv3
root      154   0.0  1.8   156   536  v4  Is+    9:11AM  0:00.07 /usr/libexec/getty Pc ttyv4
root      155   0.0  1.8   156   536  v5  Is+    9:11AM  0:00.06 /usr/libexec/getty Pc ttyv5
root      156   0.0  1.8   156   536  v6  Is+    9:11AM  0:00.05 /usr/libexec/getty Pc ttyv6
root      160   0.0  1.8   176   556  ??  I      9:11AM  0:00.08 /usr/libexec/yagetty 38400
root      163   0.0  0.6   284   168  ??  I      9:12AM  0:01.55 nfs radio.example.org /C
root      173   0.0  1.8   168   540  ??  Is     9:29AM  0:00.11 rshd
root      174   0.0  5.7   540  1728  ??  I      9:29AM  0:03.04 xterm
root      180   0.0  1.8   168   544  ??  Is     9:29AM  0:00.21 rshd
root      181   0.1  6.0   540  1820  ??  S      9:29AM  0:06.12 xterm
grog      187   0.0  1.7   808   520  p0  Is     9:30AM  0:01.10 -bash (bash)
grog      188   0.0  1.9   768   568  p1  Ss     9:30AM  0:00.75 -bash (bash)
root      462   0.0  2.0   752   600  p0  I+     2:35PM  0:00.78 su (bash)
root        0   0.0  0.0     0     0  ??  DLs    -        0:00.00 (swapper)
```

We've seen a number of these fields already. The others are:

- *USER* is the *real user ID* of the process, the user ID of the person who started it.

- *%CPU* is an approximate count of the proportion of CPU time that the process has been using in the last few seconds. This is the column to examine if things suddenly get slow.

- *%MEM* is an approximate indication of the amount of physical memory that the process is using.

- *VSZ* (*virtual size*) is the number of 4096 byte pages of virtual memory that the process is using.

- *RSS* (*resident segment size*) is the number of 4096 byte pages of physical memory currently in use.

- *STARTED* is the time or date when the process was started.

In addition, a surprising number of processes don't have a controlling terminal. They are *dæmons*, and we'll look at them in the next section.

top

Another tool for investigating system performance is *top*, which shows a number of performance criteria, including the status of the processes which are using the most resources. Start it with the number of processes you want displayed, for example:

```
$ top 4
last pid: 10887;  load averages:  0.27,  0.43,  0.32                   14:18:05
109 processes: 6 running, 96 sleeping, 7 zombie
CPU states:  3.5% user,   0.0% nice,   5.0% system,   0.0% interrupt, 91.5% idle
Mem: 6456K Active, 53M Inact, 21M Wired, 11M Cache, 8341K Buf, 588K Free
Swap: 314M Total, 97M Used, 218M Free, 31% Inuse

  PID USERNAME PRI NICE   SIZE    RES STATE    TIME   WCPU     CPU COMMAND
15027 grog       2    0 38788K 16000K select  52:34  2.02%   2.02% X
22478 grog       2    0  6232K  3160K select   3:44  0.72%   0.72% emacs
10887 grog      28    0   920K   692K RUN      0:00  0.70%   0.65% top
15058 grog       2    0   484K   456K select   0:09  0.11%   0.11% fvwm2
```

See the man page *top(1)* for more details.

Dæmons

A significant part of the work in a FreeBSD system is performed by *dæmons*. A dæmon is not just the friendly little guy on the cover of this book—it's a process which goes around in the background and does routine work such as sending mail (*sendmail*), accepting or denying Internet access (*inetd*), or starting jobs at particular times (*cron*).

> To quote the *Shorter Oxford English Dictionary*: **Demon** Also **dæmon**. ME [In form, and in sense I, a. L. *dæmon* (med. L. *demon*)...] 1. Gr. Myth. (= δαιμων): A being of a nature intermediate between that of gods and men; an inferior divinity, spirit (including the souls of deceased persons). Often written *dæmon* for distinction. 1569.

You can recognize dæmons in a *ps waux* listing by the fact that they don't have a controlling terminal. Each dæmon has a man page which describes what it does.

183

Normally, dæmons are started when the system is booted and run until the system is stopped. If you stop one by accident, you could be in trouble. For example, *init* is responsible for starting other processes. If you kill it, you effectively kill the system, so, unlike traditional UNIX systems, FreeBSD does not allow *init* to be killed.

cron

One of the more useful dæmons is *cron*, named after Father Time. *cron* performs functions at specific times. For example, by default the system runs the script */etc/daily* every day at 2:00 am, the script */etc/weekly* every Saturday at 3:30 am, and the script */etc/monthly* on the first day of every month at 5:30 am.

To tell *cron* to perform a function at a particular time, you need a file called a *crontab*. The system keeps the real *crontab* where you can't get at it, but you can keep a copy. It's a good idea to call it *crontab* as well.

Let's look at the format of the default system *crontab*, located in */etc/crontab*:

```
# /etc/crontab - root's crontab for FreeBSD
#
# $Id: crontab,v 1.10 1995/05/27 01:55:21 ache Exp $
# From: Id: crontab,v 1.6 1993/05/31 02:03:57 cgd Exp
#
SHELL=/bin/sh
PATH=/etc:/bin:/sbin:/usr/bin:/usr/sbin
HOME=/var/log
#
#minute hour    mday monthwday who   command
#
*/5  *    *    *    *    root /usr/libexec/atrun
#
# rotate log files every hour, if necessary
#0   *    *    *    *    root /usr/bin/newsyslog
#
# do daily/weekly/monthly maintenance
0    2    *    *    *    root /etc/daily 2>&1 | sendmail root
30   3    *    *    6    root /etc/weekly 2>&1 | sendmail root
30   5    1    *    *    root /etc/monthly 2>&1 | sendmail root
#
# time zone change adjustment for wall cmos clock,
# does nothing, if you have UTC cmos clock.
# See adjkerntz(8) for details.
1,31 0-4  *    *    *    root /sbin/adjkerntz -a
```

As usual, lines starting with # are comments. The others have seven fields. The first five fields specify the minute, the hour, the day of the month, the month, and the day of the week on which an action should be performed. The character * means "every". Thus, 0 2 * * * (for */etc/daily*) means "0 minutes, 2 o'clock (on the 24 hour clock), every day of the month, every month, every weekday".

Field number six is special: it only exists in */etc/crontab*, and it specifies the user as which the operation should be performed. When you write your own *crontab* file, don't use this field.

The remaining fields define the operation to be performed. *cron* doesn't read your shell initialization files. In particular, this can mean that it won't find programs you expect it to find. It's a good idea to put in explicit PATH definitions, or specify an absolute pathname for the

184

program, as is done in this example. *cron* mails the output to you, so you should check root's mail from time to time.

To install or list a *crontab*, use the *crontab* program:

```
$ crontab crontab              install a crontab
$ crontab -l                   list the contents of an installed crontab
# DO NOT EDIT THIS FILE - edit the master and reinstall.
# (crontab installed on Wed Jan  1 15:15:10 1997)
# (Cron version -- $Id: crontab.c,v 1.7 1996/12/17 00:55:12 pst Exp $)
0 0 * * * /home/grog/Scripts/rotate-log
```

Stopping processes

Sometimes you may find that you want to stop a currently running process. There are a number of ways to do this, but the easiest are:

- If the process is running on a terminal, and it's accepting input, hitting the *EOF* key (usually **CTRL-D**) will often do it.

- If *EOF* doesn't do it, try the *INTR* key (usually **Ctrl-C**).

- If the process is ignoring *INTR*, or if it is not associated with a terminal, use the *kill* command. For example, to find who is using all the CPU time, use *ps* and look at the %CPU field:

```
# ps waux
USER     PID %CPU %MEM   VSZ  RSS  TT  STAT STARTED      TIME COMMAND
root     105 97.3  1.1   236  340  ??  Is    9:11AM 137:14.29 cron
(other processes omitted)
```

Here, *cron* is using 97% of the CPU time, and has accumulated over 2 hours of CPU time since this morning. It's obviously sick, and we should put it out of its misery. To stop it, enter:

```
# kill 105
```

This command sends a signal called SIGTERM (terminate) to the process. This signal gives the process time to tidy up before exiting, so you should always try to use it first. The 105 is *cron*'s PID, which we got from the *ps* command.

If the process doesn't go away within a few seconds, it's probably ignoring SIGTERM. In this case, you can use the ultimate weapon:

```
# kill -9 105
```

The -9 is the number of SIGKILL, a signal that cannot be caught or ignored. You can find a list of the signals and their numeric values in */usr/include/sys/signal.h*, which is part of the software development package.

Timekeeping

FreeBSD is a networking system, so keeping the correct time is more important than on a standalone system. Apart from the obvious problem of keeping the same time as other local systems, it's also important to keep time with systems in other time zones.

Internally, FreeBSD keeps the time as the number of seconds since the *epoch*, the beginning of recorded history: 00:00:00 UTC, 1 January 1970. *UTC* is the international base time zone, and means *Universal Coordinated Time*, despite the initials. It corresponds very closely, but not exactly, to Greenwich Mean Time (GMT), the local time in England in the winter. It would be inconvenient to keep all dates in UTC, so the system understands the concept of *Time Zones*. For example, in Walnut Creek, CA, the time zone in the winter is called *PST* (*Pacific Standard Time*), and in the summer it is *PDT* (*Pacific Daylight Time*). FreeBSD stores information about the local time zone in a file called *etc/localtime*. Normally, *sysinstall* installs the correct data in this file, but if you got it wrong, or if you move time zones, you can do it yourself easily enough by running the *tzsetup* program.

The `TZ` environment variable

An alternate means of describing the time zone is to set the environment variable `TZ`, which we looked at on page 176. This looks like the way that System V does it, but that's not quite accurate. System V doesn't have the time zone definition files in *usr/share/zoneinfo*, so the `TZ` variable tells it information about the time zone. For example, the value of `TZ` for Berlin, Germany is `MEZ1MSZ2` in System V, but `Germany/Berlin` in FreeBSD.

Keeping the correct time

If you're connected to the Internet on a reasonably regular basis, there are a number of programs which can help you synchronize your time via the *ntp* service.

A number of systems around the world supply time information via the `ntp` service. The first thing you need to do is to find one near you. One place to look is at *http://www.eecis.udel.edu/˜mills/ntp/servers.html*.

Your choice of program depends on the nature of your connection to the Internet. If you're connected full time, you'll probably prefer *xntpd*, which keeps the system synchronized. Otherwise you can use *ntpdate*, which you can run as you feel like it.

xntpd

xntpd performs periodic queries to keep the system synchronized with a time server. There are many ways to run it—see the man page *xntpd(8)*. In most cases, you can set up one system on the network to connect to an external time reference, and the other systems on the same Ethernet can get the time information from the first system.

To get the time from an external source and broadcast it to the other systems on the network, create a file *etc/ntp.conf* with a content like this:

```
server      203.21.37.18    # ns.saard.net
driftfile /etc/ntp.drift
broadcast 223.147.37.255
```

The first line defines the server. It's important to get one near you: network delays can significantly impair the accuracy of the results. *xntpd* uses the file */etc/ntp.drift* to record information about the (in)accuracy of the local system's clock. You only need the final line if you have other systems on the network which wait for a broadcast message. It specifies the broadcast address for the network and also tells *xntpd* to broadcast on this address

After setting up this file, you just need to start *xntpd*:

```
# xntpd
```

To ensure that *xntpd* gets started every time you reboot, ensure that you have the the following lines in */etc/rc.conf*:

```
xntpd_enable="YES"          # Run xntpd Network Time Protocol (or NO).
xntpd_flags=""              # Flags to xntpd (if enabled).
```

If */etc/rc.conf* doesn't exist, create it.

The comment on the first line is misleading: the value of xntpd_enable must be YES. You don't need any flags. You put exactly the same text in the */etc/rc.conf* on the other machines, and simply omit the file */etc/ntp.conf*. This causes *xntpd* on these machines to monitor broadcast messages.

ntpdate

If you only infrequently connect to the Internet, *xntpd* may become discouraged and not keep good time. In this case, it's better to use *ntpdate*. Simply run it when you want to set the time:

```
# ntpdate server
```

You can't use both *ntpdate* and *xntpd*: they both use the same port.

12

Starting and stopping the system

Before you can run FreeBSD, you need to start it up. That's normally pretty straightforward: you turn the machine on, a lot of things scroll off the screen, and about a minute later you have a `login:` prompt on the screen. Nevertheless, there are a number of items of interest on the way. In particular, the boot process tells you a lot of information about the system hardware configuration. This can be of use when upgrading the system, or if you have problems.

It's not so obvious that you need to adhere to a procedure when shutting down the system. We'll look at the hows and whys on page 220.

Starting the system

When you power up the system, or when you reboot, a number of actions occur before the system is up and running:

- First, the system firmware[1] performs tests which check that the machine is working correctly and determines the hardware configuration. This *Power On Self Test* or *POST* has nothing to do with FreeBSD.

- Next, the BIOS loads the first of three *bootstraps* from the first sector on the hard disk. This bootstrap may or may not be part of the FreeBSD system. It's up to this bootstrap to decide which operating system to boot. Typically it will load the FreeBSD bootstrap from the second sector on disk.

- The FreeBSD bootstrap first loads the second-level bootstrap, *BTX*, from the next 15 sectors on disk and executes it. This bootstrap prints out the message:

---

1. The firmware is called *BIOS* (*Basic Input/Output System*) on the i386 architecture, or *SRM* on the Alpha architecture. We'll refer to it as BIOS in the rest of this section.

189

```
BTX loader 1.00  BTX version is 1.00
BIOS drive A: is disk0
BIOS drive C: is disk1
```

- The second-level boot locates the third-level bootstrap, called *loader*, and loads it into memory. *loader*, which is new with FreeBSD 3.1, is an intelligent bootstrap component which allows preloading of multiple kernel components. See the man page *loader(8)* for more information. *loader* locates the kernel, by default the file */kernel* on the root file system, and loads it into memory. It prints the `Boot:` prompt at this point so that you can influence this choice—see the man page *boot(8)* for more details of what you can enter at this prompt.

- The kernel switches the machine into 32-bit mode (on Intel) or 64-bit mode (on Alpha) and disables the system BIOS. It then performs its own tests to look for hardware it knows about. It's quite verbose about this, and prints messages about both the hardware it finds and the hardware it doesn't find. This operation is called *probing*. It's normal to have more "didn't find" messages than "found" messages. You'll see an example of these messages on pages 190 to 199.

- After the probe, the kernel starts two processes, numbered 0 and 1. Process 0 is the *swapper* and is responsible for emergency clearing of memory when the standard virtual memory algorithms aren't fast enough.

- Process 1 is called *init*. As the name suggests, it is responsible for starting up the system and dæmons. When coming up in the default multi-user mode, it spawns a shell to execute the shell script */etc/rc*.

- */etc/rc* first reads in the description files */etc/defaults/rc.conf*, which contains defaults for a number of configuration variables, and */etc/rc.conf*, which contains your modifications to the defaults. It then proceeds to perform the steps necessary to bring up the system, first starting virtual disk drivers, mounting swap space and checking the file system integrity if necessary.

- When */etc/rc* exits, *init* reads the file */etc/ttys* and starts processes as determined there. It spends the rest of its life looking after these processes.

Boot messages

As the bootstrap loaders load, you will see something like:

```
/                                        this is a "twirling baton"
BTX loader 1.00  BTX version is 1.00
BIOS drive A: is disk0
BIOS drive C: is disk1
```

These messages are printed by *BTX*. If you're loading from disk, the / character at the end of the previous line keeps changing through -, \, and | before going back to / again, giving the impression that the character is rotating. This display, called a *twirling baton*, is your indication that the system hasn't crashed and burned.

190

Next, *loader* prints its prompt:

```
FreeBSD/i386 bootstrap loader, Revision 0.5  640/64512kB
(jkh@time.cdrom.com, Sun Jul 24 16:25:12 CST 1999)
```

If you do nothing, or if you press **Enter**, it will load the kernel. Once the kernel has been loaded, it will take control of the machine. Messages from the kernel are in high-intensity text (brighter than normal). This is the only time you will normally see them, but sometimes you'll see them during normal machine operation. The boot messages look like:

```
/kernel text=0x14c395 data=0x180d8+0x22ec4 syms=[0x4+0x1e3c0+0x4+0x210f8]
Booting the kernel
Copyright (c) 1982, 1986, 1989, 1991, 1993
     The Regents of the University of California.
     All rights reserved.

FreeBSD 3.0 #0: Wed Jan 28 14:43:28  1998
   jkh@westhill.cdrom.com:/usr/src/sys/compile/GENERIC
```

The first line tells you how large the kernel is. Unless you run into problems, which are unlikely at this point, this information is of little interest. If you *do* have problems, the most important information is the date of compilation and the pathname of the kernel on the last two lines of this example. Please include this information if you report a problem.

Next, you see:

```
Please insert MFS root floppy and press enter:
```

When you insert the MFS root floppy and press **Enter**, you see more twirling batons, then the UserConfig screen appears.

UserConfig: Modifying the boot configuration

After the kernel has been loaded, the following screen will appear:

```
Kernel configuration Menu

     Skip kernel configuration and continue with installation
     Start kernel configuration in full-screen visual mode
     Start kernel configuration in CLI mode

Here you have the chance to go into kernel configuration mode, making
any changes which may be necessary to properly adjust the kernel to
match your hardware configuration.

If you are installing FreeBSD for the first time, select Visual Mode
(press Down-Arrow then ENTER).

If you need to do more specialized kernel configuration and are an
experienced FreeBSD user, select CLI mode.

If you are certain that you do not need to configure your kernel
then simply press ENTER or Q now.
```

If your hardware configuration matches what the generic kernel expects (see page 24), just press **ENTER**. The kernel will continue with the *device probes*, which we discuss on page 194.

If you do need to change the configuration, press the **down arrow** key to choose the kernel configuration in full-screen mode, then press **ENTER**. This starts *UserConfig*, a part of the kernel which can be activated at boot time to change the system's idea of device configuration. It presents you with a full-screen menu:

```
---Active Drivers--------------------------25 Conflicts------Dev---IRQ--Port--
  Storage : (Collapsed)
  Network : (Collapsed)
  Communications : (Collapsed)
  Input : (Collapsed)
  Multimedia :
  Miscellaneous :


---Inactive Drivers---------------------------------------------Dev-------------
  Storage : (Collapsed)
  Network : (Collapsed)
  Communications : (Collapsed)
  Input : (Collapsed)
  Multimedia :
  Miscellaneous :
```

Note the word `Conflicts` at the top of the screen. This is a warning, not an error. We'll see on page 194 that the drivers look for hardware in a number of configurations. Not all of these configurations can coexist, but there will not be a problem unless you install hardware that can't coexist.

The word (`Collapsed`) doesn't mean that your hardware has given up the ghost—it means that the information about the corresponding hardware, which is usually a large number of devices, has been omitted. You can expand it by placing the cursor on the appropriate line and pressing **Enter**. A bar cursor stretches across the line `Storage  (Collapsed)`. You can move it up and down with the arrow keys. In our example, we have a NE2000 compatible Ethernet board, but its I/O registers start at address `0x320`, it is set up for IRQ 9, and we want to change the kernel configuration to recognize it. We move the bar down to the line `Network` and press **Enter**. The display changes to:

```
---Active Drivers-----------------------25 Conflicts------Dev---IRQ--Port--
  Storage : (Collapsed)
  Network :
NE1000,NE2000,3C503,WD/SMC80xx Ethernet adapters         conf    ed0    5    0x280
NE1000,NE2000,3C503,WD/SMC80xx Ethernet adapters         conf    ed1    5    0x300
3C509 Ethernet adapter                                   conf    ep0    10   0x300
Fujitsu MD86960A/MB869685A Ethernet adapters             conf    fe0    5    0x240
Intel EtherExpress Ethernet adapter                      conf    ix0    10   0x300
DEC Etherworks 2 and 3 Ethernet adapters                 conf    le0    5    0x300
---Inactive Drivers----------------------------------------Dev-------------
  Storage : (Collapsed)
  Network : (Collapsed)
  Communications : (Collapsed)
  Input : (Collapsed)
  Multimedia :
  Miscellaneous :
```

The highlighted `conf` means that the current configuration could conflict with another device:

the I/O address, IRQ or memory address will also be probed by another driver. This is only a problem if you really have two boards with the same configuration; otherwise you can ignore this warning. In this case, by chance our Novell NE2000 board is already highlighted, so all we need to do is to press **Enter** again to edit the configuration. The configuration is copied to individual fields at the bottom of the screen, so we now see:

```
---Active Drivers--------------------------25 Conflicts------Dev---IRQ--Port--
  Storage : (Collapsed)
  Network :
NE1000,NE2000,3C503,WD/SMC80xx Ethernet adapters          conf   ed0   5    0x280
NE1000,NE2000,3C503,WD/SMC80xx Ethernet adapters          conf   ed1   5    0x300
3C509 Ethernet adapter                                    conf   ep0   10   0x300
Fujitsu MD86960A/MB869685A Ethernet adapters              conf   fe0   5    0x240
Intel EtherExpress Ethernet adapter                       conf   ix0   10   0x300
DEC Etherworks 2 and 3 Ethernet adapters                  conf   le0   5    0x300
---Inactive Drivers---------------------------------------Dev-------------
  Storage : (Collapsed)
  Network : (Collapsed)
  Communications : (Collapsed)
  Input : (Collapsed)
  Multimedia :
  Miscellaneous :
-------------------------------------------------------------------------------
  Port address : 0x280     Memory address : 0xd8000   Conflict allowed
  IRQ number   : 5
  Flags        : 0
-------------------------------------------------------------------------------
```

The port address is in reverse video, which means that we can edit it. We type in 0x320 and press **Tab** to get to the IRQ field, where we enter 9. Then we press **Enter** to leave the edit mode, and q to leave the configuration editor. Booting continues as normal, but this time the system finds our Ethernet board.

This is only an example, of course. It's easier to play around with the editor than to describe it. Don't worry about damaging anything on disk, since at this point it's just you and the computer, and the computer doesn't yet know about any peripherals.

> *Due to the nature of PC hardware, IRQ 2 and IRQ 9 are the same thing. Never specify IRQ 2 to UserConfig: use IRQ 9 instead. If you use IRQ 2, the driver will not work correctly.*

Starting UserConfig from hard disk

When you boot from hard disk, the selection menu does not appear, since this would be a nuisance: normally you will not want to change your configuration once it is installed. If you need to do so, however, make sure that UserConfig is included in your kernel (see Chapter 18, *Configuring the kernel*, page 332). To activate UserConfig on boot, wait until you see:

```
BTX loader 1.00  BTX version is 1.00
BIOS drive A: is disk0
BIOS drive C: is disk1

FreeBSD/i386 bootstrap loader, Revision 0.2  640/64512kB
(grog@bumble.example.org, Sun Jan 31 16:25:12 CST 1999)
```

```
/                              this is a "twirling baton"
Hit [Enter] to boot immediately, or any other key for command prompt.
Booting [kernel] in 6 seconds...   this counts down from 10 seconds
```

Normally, you just wait until the countdown reaches 0, or press **Enter**, and the bootstrap will continue and load the kernel. You have a number of options, however—see the man page *boot(8)* for a complete discussion. To interrupt the boot process, press the space bar (most keys will do, but the space bar is easiest to remember). You will get:

```
Type '?' for a list of commands, 'help' for more detailed help.
disk1s1a:>
```

To start UserConfig, enter:

```
disk1s1a:> boot -c
Copyright (c) 1992-1999 The FreeBSD Project.
Copyright (c) 1982, 1986, 1989, 1991, 1993
     The Regents of the University of California. All rights reserved.
FreeBSD 3.1-RELEASE #0: Wed Feb 17 13:06:56 CST 1999
     grog@daemon.lemis.com:/usr/src/sys/compile/GENERIC
Timecounter "i8254"  frequency 1193182 Hz
Timecounter "TSC"    frequency 132968074 Hz
CPU: Pentium/P54C (132.97-MHz 586-class CPU)
   Origin = "GenuineIntel"   Id = 0x52c   Stepping=12
   Features=0x1bf<FPU,VME,DE,PSE,TSC,MSR,MCE,CX8>
real memory  = 67108864 (65536K bytes)
FreeBSD Kernel Configuration Utility - Version 1.2
 Type "help" for help or "visual" to go to the visual
 configuration interface (requires MGA/VGA display or
 serial terminal capable of displaying ANSI graphics).
config> v                        go into visual mode
```

You can type `help` for help, as the prompt suggests, but just about the only thing you need is the visual configuration interface.

Probing the hardware

When you continue from the UserConfig selection menu, an incredible amount of information will scroll off the screen. Once the boot is complete, you can go back and examine text that has scrolled off the top of the screen: press **ScrollLock**. The cursor will disappear, and you can use the **PageUp** and **PageDown** keys to scroll up to 3 previous screenfuls. To exit this mode, press **ScrollLock** again. We'll go through this output in some detail over the next few pages.

Once it has finished loading, the kernel calls all configured drivers to examine the hardware configuration of the machine on which it is running. This is called *probing* for the devices. If you have time to follow it, it's a good idea to confirm that it's correct. It's not that important unless something goes wrong, and then it *won't* scroll off the screen. We see something like:

```
Copyright (c) 1992-1999 FreeBSD Inc.
Copyright (c) 1982, 1986, 1989, 1991, 1993
     The Regents of the University of California. All rights reserved.
FreeBSD 3.2-RELEASE #1733: Wed May 12 10:47:53 CST 1999
   grog@presto.example.org:/usr/src/sys/compile/PRESTO
Timecounter "i8254"  frequency 1193182 Hz
Timecounter "TSC"    frequency 132955161 Hz
```

```
CPU: Pentium/P54C (132.96-MHz 586-class CPU)
  Origin = "GenuineIntel"  Id = 0x52c  Stepping=12
  Features=0x1bf<FPU,VME,DE,PSE,TSC,MSR,MCE,CX8>
```

The lines above identify the CPU: it's an original Pentium (internal code P54C), and it runs at 133 MHz.

```
real memory  = 67108864 (65536K bytes)
avail memory = 62017536 (60564K bytes)
Preloaded elf kernel "kernel" at 0xf0337000.
```

The real memory is the size of RAM. Some systems reserve 1 kB of RAM in real mode, but this should not have any effect on the value of real memory. Available memory is the memory available to users after the kernel has been loaded and initialized. The load address of the kernel is not of much interest unless you have specific problems.

Sometimes the kernel will report only 16 MB even on larger systems. This is due to BIOS incompatibilities, and occurs surprisingly often on big-name machines. To fix it, build a custom kernel which specifies the memory size explicitly—see the description of the MAXMEM parameter on page 338.

Next we look for the other chips on the motherboard:

```
Probing for devices on PCI bus 0:
chip0: <Intel 82437FX PCI cache memory controller> rev 0x01 on pci0.0.0
chip1: <Intel 82371FB PCI to ISA bridge> rev 0x02 on pci0.7.0
ide_pci0: <Intel PIIX Bus-master IDE controller> rev 0x02 on pci0.7.1
```

This is an Intel 82437 FX chipset. We continue to look at the hardware connected to the motherboard, some of which is in fact implemented in the FX chipset:

```
ahc0: <Adaptec 2940 Ultra SCSI adapter> rev 0x00 int a irq 14 on pci0.17.0
ahc0: aic7880 Wide Channel A, SCSI Id=7, 16/255 SCBs
```

As the first line states, this is a SCSI host adapter using PCI interrupt A, IRQ 14, and its PCI slot number is 17.

```
Probing for devices on the ISA bus:
sc0 on isa                                  this is the system console
sc0: VGA color <16 virtual consoles, flags=0x0>
ed0 not found at 0x280                       ed0 is a possible Ethernet board
ed1 not found at 0x300                       and ed1 is another one at a different address
atkbdc0 at 0x60-0x6f on motherboard
atkbd0 irq 1 on isa
sio0 at 0x3f8-0x3ff irq 4 flags 0x0 on isa  the first serial port
sio0: type 16550A                            it's a buffered UART
sio1 at 0x2f8-0x2ff irq 3 on isa            the second serial port
sio1: type 16550A
sio2 not found at 0x3e8                       no more serial I/O ports
sio3 not found at 0x2e8
```

Recall from page 24 that UNIX devices start counting from 0, whereas Microsoft starts counting from 1. Devices *sio0* through *sio3* are known as *COM1:* through *COM4:* in the Microsoft world.

```
psm0 not found                                  no PS/2 mouse
mse0 not found at 0x23c                          and no Microsoft mouse
fdc0 at 0x3f0-0x3f7 irq 6 drq 2 on isa           Floppy controller
fdc0: FIFO enabled, 8 bytes threshold
fd0: 1.44MB 3.5in                                one 3½" drive
wdc0 at 0x1f0-0x1f7 irq 14 flags 0xa0ffa0ff on isa   first IDE controller
wdc0: unit 0 (wd0): <ST51270A>, DMA, 32-bit, multi-block-32    Seagate ST51270A
wd0: 1223MB (2504880 sectors), 2485 cyls, 16 heads, 63 S/T, 512 B/S
wdc1 at 0x170-0x177 irq 15 flags 0xa0ffa0ff on isa   second IDE controller
wdc1: unit 0 (wd2): <IBM-DHEA-36480>, DMA, 32-bit, multi-block-16
wd2: 6197MB (12692736 sectors), 12592 cyls, 16 heads, 63 S/T, 512 B/S
wdc1: unit 1 (wd3): <IBM-DHEA-38451>, DMA, 32-bit, multi-block-16
wd3: 8063MB (16514064 sectors), 16383 cyls, 16 heads, 63 S/T, 512 B/S
```

This system has only one floppy drive, but three IDE drives on two controllers. The controllers both run in DMA mode. The flags value (0xa0ffa0ff) gives more detail about how the controller runs. See page 341 for more details of the flags.

In this case, both IDE controllers have disks connected, and the boot proceeds relatively quickly. If one of the controllers has no disks connected, things are different: before the disk driver gives up, it waits for quite a long time, about 30 seconds. Don't despair, the system probably hasn't crashed and burned, the driver just wants to be *really* sure that there is no disk there. If this wait gets on your nerves, you can rebuild the kernel with a shorter wait. See page 342 for further information.

The disk driver reads the information about the disk drives directly from the drive. This is a relatively new feature of IDE drives. ST506 drives did not supply this information, and many BIOSes do not read the drive. Instead, they store information about the drive configuration in their CMOS memory. If the stored values don't match the real parameters, you may have difficulty booting. Since FreeBSD doesn't use the BIOS after booting, it might work fine with a system, but if you also have Microsoft or another operating system on the disk, it may not work. In this case, compare the values above with those stored in CMOS memory.

Next, more SCSI drivers check for their boards:

```
bt_isa_probe: Probe failed for card at 0x330
bt0 not found at 0x330
aha0 at 0x330-0x333 irq 12 drq 6 on isa
aha0: AHA-1542 64 head BIOS FW Rev. 0.5 (ID=41) SCSI Host Adapter, SCSI ID 7, 16 CCBs
aha1 not found at 0x334
```

Here we have found another SCSI host adapter, this time an Adaptec 1542. The SCSI driver can read the DMA channel number and the IRQ value, but it hasn't checked the bus speed, since this can cause some controllers to crash. There is no particular sequence in booting, and in this example the two host adapters were found at significantly different times.

Next, a number of other drivers probe:

```
wt0 not found at 0x300
mcd0 not found at 0x300
matcdc0 not found at 0x230
scd0 not found at 0x230
ppc0 at 0x378 irq 7 flags 0x40 on isa
ppc0: SMC-like chipset (ECP/EPP/PS2/NIBBLE) in COMPATIBLE mode
lpt0: <generic printer> on ppbus 0
```

```
lpt0: Interrupt-driven port
ppi0: <generic parallel i/o> on ppbus 0
plip0: <PLIP network interface> on ppbus 0
lpt0: <generic printer> on ppbus 0
lpt0: Interrupt-driven port
```

The only thing found here is the parallel port. Since FreeBSD 3.1, this port is under control of the *ppbus* driver, and the printer is a subdevice.

Continuing,

```
1 3C5x9 board(s) on ISA found at 0x250
ep0 at 0x250-0x25f irq 10 on isa
ep0: aui/utp/bnc[*BNC*] address 00:a0:24:37:0c:bd
```

Here the *ep* driver has found a 3Com 3C509 Ethernet board. In addition to I/O address and IRQ, it displays the Ethernet address (00:a0:24:37:0c:bd) and the information that this board, which has multiple interfaces, is using the BNC interface.

```
vga0 at 0x3b0-0x3df maddr 0xa0000 msize 131072 on isa
npx0 flags 0x1 on motherboard
npx0: INT 16 interface
sb_reset_dsp failed
sb0 not found at 0x220
Intel Pentium detected, installing workaround for F00F bug
```

Here the VGA display driver reports the board that it found. The value `msize` is for text mode only. Modern display boards have several megabytes of memory, but that will not show.

The SoundBlaster driver reports a failure (`sb_reset_dsp failed`) before deciding that there is no SoundBlaster board present. This occurs relatively frequently and is no cause for concern unless you really do have a SoundBlaster board installed.

The *F00F bug* refers to a bug in the original Pentium chipset whereby programs can hang the CPU by executing an invalid instruction with the code 0xf00f. The workaround prevents this bug from having any effect, but it slows down the machine a little. This bug only affects the original Pentium, not the Pentium Pro, Pentium II or Pentium III. If you don't have an original Pentium, you can improve performance fractionally by using the configuration option NO_F00F_HACK. See page 336 for more details.

```
Waiting 3 seconds for SCSI devices to settle
```

At this point, most of the probes are finished. The SCSI drivers reset the SCSI busses and wait 3 seconds for the devices to complete their reset. This kernel has been modified to wait only 3 seconds: by default the value is 15 seconds. See the description of the parameter SCSI_DELAY on page 345 details of how to change this value.

So far, the kernel has been running entirely in memory. Now it mounts the root file system:

```
changing root device to da0s1e
```

In previous versions of FreeBSD, this was the last message you would see from the kernel. The disks would already have been located, and there would be no more highlighted messages. This is also the case if you have an IDE-only system. The CAM driver, however, delays device probes until they are needed, so next you see:

```
da1 at ahc0 bus 0 target 2 lun 0
da1: <CDC 94181-15 0293> Fixed Direct Access SCSI-CCS device
da1: 3.300MB/s transfers
da1: 573MB (1173930 512 byte sectors: 64H 32S/T 573C)
da2 at ahc0 bus 0 target 3 lun 0
da2: <CDC 94181-15 0293> Fixed Direct Access SCSI-CCS device
da2: 3.300MB/s transfers
da2: 573MB (1173930 512 byte sectors: 64H 32S/T 573C)
da3 at ahc0 bus 0 target 4 lun 0
da3: <CDC 94181-15 0293> Fixed Direct Access SCSI-CCS device
da3: 3.300MB/s transfers
da3: 573MB (1173930 512 byte sectors: 64H 32S/T 573C)
da4 at ahc0 bus 0 target 5 lun 0
da4: <CDC 94181-15 0293> Fixed Direct Access SCSI-CCS device
da4: 3.300MB/s transfers
da4: 573MB (1173930 512 byte sectors: 64H 32S/T 573C)
sa0 at aha0 bus 0 target 3 lun 0
sa0: <EXABYTE EXB-8505SMBANSH2 0793> Removable Sequential Access SCSI-2 device
sa0: 5.000MB/s transfers (5.000MHz, offset 11)
sa1 at aha0 bus 0 target 4 lun 0
sa1: <ARCHIVE Python 28849-XXX 4.CM> Removable Sequential Access SCSI-2 device
sa1: 5.000MB/s transfers (5.000MHz, offset 15)
sa2 at aha0 bus 0 target 5 lun 0
sa2: <TANDBERG TDC 3800 -03:> Removable Sequential Access SCSI-CCS device
sa2: 3.300MB/s transfers
pass4 at aha0 bus 0 target 4 lun 1
pass4: <ARCHIVE Python 28849-XXX 4.CM> Removable Changer SCSI-2 device
pass4: 5.000MB/s transfers (5.000MHz, offset 15)
da5 at aha0 bus 0 target 2 lun 0
da5: <CONNER CFP4207S  4.28GB 2847> Fixed Direct Access SCSI-2 device
da5: 3.300MB/s transfers, Tagged Queueing Enabled
da5: 4096MB (8388608 512 byte sectors: 64H 32S/T 4096C)
cd0 at aha0 bus 0 target 6 lun 0
cd0: <NRC MBR-7 110> Removable CD-ROM SCSI-2 device
cd0: 3.300MB/s transfers
cd0: cd present [322265 x 2048 byte records]
da0 at aha0 bus 0 target 0 lun 0
da0: <IBM DORS-32160 WA0A> Fixed Direct Access SCSI-2 device
da0: 10.000MB/s transfers (10.000MHz, offset 15), Tagged Queueing Enabled
da0: 2063MB (4226725 512 byte sectors: 64H 32S/T 2063C)
```

There are a number of things to note here:

- The SCSI subsystem includes a total of six disk drives, three tape drives and a CD-ROM.

- The first SCSI disk drive gets the ID *da1*, not *da0*. *da0* is there, but it comes at the very end. This indicates that the drive has been "wired down" (see page 344), because it is the system disk. This is the only way to put a system disk on the second SCSI controller in this configuration.

- The probes also find a device *pass4* at aha target 4, *LUN* (*logical unit*) 1. This is the same target as *sa1*, which is on LUN 0, and it represents the changer device.

198

At this point, the kernel has finished probing, and it transfers control to the shell script */etc/rc*. From this point on the display is in normal intensity. */etc/rc* first reads the configuration information in */etc/defaults/rc.conf* and */etc/rc.conf* (see page 203). After that, it starts *ccd* and *vinum* if requested:

```
vinum: loaded
vinum: reading configuration from /dev/da2h
vinum: updating configuration from /dev/da3h
vinum: updating configuration from /dev/da4h
vinum: updating configuration from /dev/da1h
```

Next, it checks the consistency of the file systems. Normally you'll see messages like this for each file system in */etc/fstab*:

```
/dev/rda0s1a: FILESYSTEM CLEAN; SKIPPING CHECKS
/dev/rda0s1a: clean, 6311 free (367 frags, 743 blocks, 0.9% fragmentation)
/dev/rda0s1e: FILESYSTEM CLEAN; SKIPPING CHECKS
/dev/rda0s1e: clean, 1577 files, 31178 used, 7813 free (629 frags, 898 blocks, 1.6% fr
agmentation)
```

If your system has crashed, however, either due to a software or hardware problem, or because it was not shut down correctly, you'll see something like:

```
WARNING: / was not properly dismounted
/dev/rda0s1a: 6311 free (367 frags, 743 blocks, 0.9% fragmentation)
```

Next, */etc/rc* invokes the first of three network start invocations. This one initializes the interfaces, sets the routes and starts the firewall if necessary:

```
Doing initial network setup: hostname.
ep0: flags=8843<UP,BROADCAST,RUNNING,SIMPLEX,MULTICAST> mtu 1500
        inet 223.147.37.2 netmask 0xffffff00 broadcast 223.147.37.255
        ether 00:a0:24:37:0c:bd
lo0: flags=8049<UP,LOOPBACK,RUNNING,MULTICAST> mtu 16384
        inet 127.0.0.1 netmask 0xff000000

add net default: gateway 223.147.37.5
Additional routing options:.
routing daemons:.
```

In this example, there were no additional routing options, and no routing dæmons. The messages accordingly have nothing between the characters : and .. You'll see this relatively frequently.

Next, */etc/rc* mounts the network file systems, cleans up */var/run/* and then starts *syslogd* unless you have disabled it:

```
Mounting NFS file systems.
Additional daemons: syslogd.
```

Then it checks if we have a core dump. If so, it will try to save it to */var/crash*.

```
checking for core dump...savecore: no core dump
```

This may fail if there isn't enough space in */var/crash*. If the dump does fail, you can clean up and save the dump later, as long as you haven't used enough swap space to overwrite the dump.

Next comes the second pass of the network startup, which starts our choice of *named, ntpdate, xntpd, timed, portmap, ypserv, rpc.ypxfrd, rpc.yppasswdd, ypbind, ypset, keyserv* and *rpc.ypupdated*:

```
Doing additional network setup: named xntpd portmap.
starting.  named 8.1.2 Sun May 9 13:04:13 CST 1999  grog@freebie.example.org:/usr/ob
j/usr.sbin/named
master zone "example.org" (IN) loaded (serial 1997010902)
master zone "37.147.223.in-addr.arpa" (IN) loaded (serial 1996110801)
listening on [192.109.197.149].53 (ep0)
listening on [127.0.0.1].53 (lo0)
Forwarding source address is [0.0.0.0].1063
Ready to answer queries.
```

With the exception of the first line, all the messages come from *named*. They may come in the middle of the first line, rather than waiting for the end of the line.

Next, */etc/rc* enables quotas if asked, and then runs the third network pass, which starts our choice of *mountd, nfsd, rpc.lockd, rpc.statd, nfsiod, amd, rwhod* and *kerberos*:

```
Starting final network daemons: mountd nfsd rpc.statd nfsiod rwhod.
```

Now we're almost done. */etc/rc* rebuilds a couple of internal databases (for use by the *ps* command and some others), then it sets the default paths for *ldconfig*:

```
setting ELF ldconfig path: /usr/lib /usr/lib/compat /usr/X11R6/lib /usr/local/lib
setting a.out ldconfig path: /usr/lib/aout /usr/lib/compat/aout /usr/X11R6/lib/aout /
usr/local/lib/aout
```

Next, it starts your choice of *inetd, cron, printer, sendmail* and *usbd*:

```
starting standard daemons: inetd cron sendmail.
```

The last thing that */etc/rc* does is to check for other startup files. These could be in the files specified in the variable `local_startup`, or in the file */etc/rc.local*. In our case, there are none, so all we see is:

```
Local package initialization:.
```

Finally, we're done. */etc/rc* stops, and *init* proecesses */etc/ttys*, which starts *getty* processes on specified terminals. On the console, we see:

```
Wed May 12 13:52:00 CST 1999

FreeBSD (freebie.example.org) (ttyv0)

login:
```

At this point, we're at the beginning of Chapter 11, *Making friends with FreeBSD* (page 157).

Single user mode

Sometimes it's inconvenient that multiple users can access the system. For example, if you're repartitioning a disk, you don't want other people walking all over the disk while you're doing so. Even if you're the only user on the system, dæmons may be doing things in the background. In order to avoid this problem, you can stop the boot process before most of the dæmons have been started and enter *single user mode*. To do this, specify the -s flag at boot time:

```
Boot: -s
```

As soon as the device probes have been completed, the system startup will be interrupted, and you will be prompted for a shell. Always choose *sh*: some other shells, notably *bash*, get confused in single user mode. Only the root file system will be accessible, and it will be mounted read-only. The reason for this is that the file system may be damaged and require repair before you can write to it. If you do need to write to the root file system, you should first check the consistency of the file system with *fsck*. For example,

```
npx0 on motherboard
npx0: INT 16 interface                          end of the probes (high intensity display)
Enter pathname of shell or RETURN for sh:  hit RETURN
erase ^H, kill ^U, intr ^C
# fsck -y /dev/rwd0a                             check the integrity of the root file system
** /dev/rwd0a
** Last Mounted on /
** Root file system
** Phase 1 - Check Blocks and Sizes
** Phase 2 - Check Pathnames
** Phase 3 - Check Connectivity
** Phase 4 - Check Reference Counts
** Phase 5 - Check Cyl groups
1064 files, 8190 used, 6913 free (61 frags, 1713 blocks, 0.4% fragmentation)
# mount -u /                                     remount root file system read/write
# mount /usr                                     mount any other file systems you need
```

To leave single user mode and enter multi user mode, just enter **CTRL-D**:

```
# ^D
Skipping file system checks...
(the rest of the boot sequence)
```

System V has the concept of *run levels*, which are controlled by *init*. Single user mode corresponds to run level S, and multi user mode corresponds to run level 3. There is nothing to correspond to the other System V run levels, in particular run level 2, which starts a System V system without networking. Networking is such an integral part of FreeBSD that this is just not practicable. You also can't enter single user mode with the System V command *init S*. If you try, you get:

```
# init S
init: already running
```

You can enter single user mode from a running FreeBSD system with the *shutdown* command, which we'll look at in the next section. Unfortunately, *shutdown* leaves some dæmons running and file systems mounted, so it's preferable to enter by rebooting, as shown above.

Password protecting single-user mode

If you run a secure environment, you could be concerned about the fact that you can start up in single-user mode without entering a password. That's the default—normally, if somebody can access your system console, a password is no longer much use, and it can be a nuisance—but you can change it. Find this entry in */etc/ttys*, and change the word secure to insecure:

```
# If you want to be asked for password, change "secure" to "insecure" here
console   none                    unknown   off insecure
```

FreeBSD configuration files

One of the outstanding things about UNIX is that all system configuration information is stored in text files, usually in the directory */etc*. Some people think that this method seems primitive by comparison with a flashy GUI configuration editor, but it has significant advantages. In particular, you see *exactly* what the program reads. WIth a GUI editor, the real configuration is usually stored in a format which you can't read, and even when you can, it's undocumented. Also, you can see more of the configuration at a time: a GUI editor usually presents you with only small parts of the configuration, and it's difficult to see the relationships.

In the Microsoft world, one of the most common methods of problem resolution is to reinstall the system. This is a declaration of bankruptcy: it takes forever, you're liable to cause other problems on the way, and you never find out what the problem was. If your FreeBSD system doesn't do what you expect, ***don't reinstall the system***. Take a look at the configuration files, and there's a good chance that you'll find the problem there.

The vast majority of configuration files are the same across all versions of UNIX. This appendix touches on them briefly, but you can get in-depth information in books such as the *UNIX System Administration Handbook*, by Evi Nemeth, Garth Snyder, Scott Seebass, and Trent R. Hein. In all cases, you can get more information from section 5 of the man pages.

In this section, we'll first look at */etc/defaults/rc.conf* and */etc/rc.conf*. On page 212 we'll look at the other non-network configuration files, and on page 217 we'll look at the files related to network configuration.

/etc/rc.conf

/etc/rc.conf is the main system configuration file, and in this format it is unique to FreeBSD. In older versions of FreeBSD, this file was called */etc/sysconfig*—only the name has changed.

/etc/rc.conf is intended to be the one file which defines the configuration of your system—that is to say, what the system needs to do when it starts up. It's not quite that simple, but nearly all site-dependent information is stored here. We'll walk through the version that was current at the time of writing. The files will change as time goes on, but most of the information will remain relevant.

/etc/rc.conf is completely your work. When you install the system, there is no such file: you have to create it. What you will find is a file */etc/defaults/rc.conf*, which contains default values for everything in */etc/rc.conf*. Why do it this way? In fact, previous versions of FreeBSD supplied the file */etc/rc.conf* and you had to edit it. The problems arrived when you upgraded: which variables were the old defaults, and which ones had you changed? It was quite difficult to decide. As a result, FreeBSD 3.2 has the defaults in one file. You shouldn't change this file: if you want to override the default, put the new value in */etc/rc.conf*. Then, when you upgrade, you can keep your old */etc/rc.conf*, and you only need to change it if new features have been introduced and you want to change them.

Let's walk through */etc/defaults/rc.conf*. As we do, we'll build up our */etc/rc.conf*. To avoid too much confusion, I show the text which goes into */etc/rc.conf* in **constant width bold**, whereas the text in */etc/defaults/rc.conf* is in constant width.

```
#!/bin/sh
#

# This is rc.conf - a file full of useful variables that you can set
# to change the default startup behavior of your system.  You should
# not edit this file!  Put any overrides into one of the ${rc_conf_files}
# instead and you will be able to update these defaults later without
# spamming your local configuration information.
#
# All arguments must be in double or single quotes.
#
#     $Id: rc.conf,v 1.1.2.4 1999/05/03 08:13:55 grog Exp $

##############################################################
### Important initial Boot-time options  ####################
##############################################################
swapfile="NO"                  # Set to name of swapfile if aux swapfile desired.
```

You only need to set swapfile if you want an additional swap file. We will see an example of this on page 264.

```
apm_enable="NO"                # Set to YES if you want APM enabled.
pccard_enable="NO"             # Set to YES if you want to configure PCCARD devices.
pccard_mem="DEFAULT"           # If pccard_enable=YES, this is card memory address.
pccard_ifconfig="NO"           # Specialized pccard ethernet configuration (or NO).
```

The four preceding parameters apply to notebooks only. We don't discuss them in this book.

```
local_startup="/usr/local/etc/rc.d /usr/X11R6/etc/rc.d"  # startup script dirs.
```

This is a list of directories which are searched for startup scripts. If you come from a System V background, you would expect to find these scripts in the directories such as */etc/rc2.d.*

```
local_periodic="/usr/local/etc/periodic /usr/X11R6/etc/periodic" # periodic script dirs
```

local_periodic is a list of directories to search for scripts to be run by *cron.* Currently it is not used.

```
rc_conf_files="/etc/rc.conf /etc/rc.conf.local"
```

rc_conf_files is a list of files to read after this file. You'll recognize */etc/rc.conf,* which we discussed above. */etc/rc.conf.local* is an idea that hasn't completely died, but there's a good chance that it will. You'd be best off not to use it until you're sure it's going to stay.

For obvious reasons, this is one entry in */etc/defaults/rc.conf* which you can't override in */etc/rc.conf.*

```
###############################################################
###   Network configuration sub-section  ######################
###############################################################

### Basic network options: ###
hostname="myname.my.domain"     # Set this!
```

hostname is the fully qualified name of the host. You should always override it in */etc/rc.conf.* See page 404 for more details. In */etc/rc.conf,* we'll put:

```
hostname="presto.example.org"   # Set this!
```

Continuing in */etc/defaults/rc.conf,*

```
nisdomainname="NO"              # Set to NIS domain if using NIS (or NO).
```

If you're using Sun's NIS, set this. We don't discuss NIS in this book.

```
firewall_enable="NO"            # Set to YES to enable firewall functionality
firewall_script="/etc/rc.firewall" # Which script to run to set up the firewall
firewall_type="UNKNOWN"         # Firewall type (see /etc/rc.firewall)
firewall_quiet="NO"             # Set to YES to suppress rule display
```

Parameters for the *ipfw* firewall. See page 502, where we set the following flags in */etc/rc.conf*:

```
firewall_enable="YES"           # Set to YES to enable firewall functionality
firewall_type="client"          # Firewall type (see /etc/rc.firewall)
```

```
natd_program="/sbin/natd"    # path to natd, if you want a different one.
natd_enable="NO"             # Enable natd (if firewall_enable == YES).
natd_interface="fxp0"        # Public interface or IPaddress to use.
natd_flags=""                # Additional flags for natd.
```

Parameters for *natd*. See page 507 for more details. In the example there, we'll add these lines to */etc/rc.conf*:

```
natd_enable="YES"            # Enable natd (if firewall_enable == YES).
natd_interface="tun0"        # Public interface or IPaddress to use.
```

Continuing with */etc/defaults/rc.conf*,

```
tcp_extensions="NO"          # Disallow RFC1323 extensions (or YES).
```

We don't discuss these extensions in this book. Leave this variable set to NO unless you have problems.

```
network_interfaces="lo0"     # List of network interfaces (lo0 is loopback).
ifconfig_lo0="inet 127.0.0.1" # default loopback device configuration.
#ifconfig_lo0_alias0="inet 127.0.0.254 netmask 0xffffffff" # Sample alias entry.
```

This is one area that you must change if you have any network interfaces at all. On page 404, we come up with the following entries in */etc/rc.conf*:

```
network_interfaces="ed0 lo0"   # List of network interfaces (lo0 is loopback).
ifconfig_ed0="inet 223.147.37.2 netmask 255.255.255.0"
ifconfig_lo0="inet 127.0.0.1"  # default loopback device configuration.
```

Continuing with */etc/defaults/rc.conf*,

```
# If you have any sppp(4) interfaces above, you might also want to set
# the following parameters.  Refer to spppcontrol(8) for their meaning.
sppp_interfaces=""           # List of sppp interfaces.
#sppp_interfaces="isp0"      # example: sppp over ISDN
#spppconfig_isp0="authproto=chap myauthname=foo myauthsecret='top secret' hisauthname
=some-gw hisauthsecret='another secret'"
```

These are parameters for the *sppp* implementation for *ISDN4BSD*, which we won't discuss here.

```
### Network daemon (miscellaneous) & NFS options: ###
syslogd_enable="YES"         # Run syslog daemon (or NO).
syslogd_flags=""             # Flags to syslogd (if enabled).
```

You should always run syslogd unless you have a very good reason not to. `syslogd_flags` is normally empty, as in this example.

```
inetd_enable="YES"           # Run the network daemon dispatcher (or NO).
inetd_flags=""               # Optional flags to inetd (always enabled).
```

We will look at *inetd* on page 393. Normally you will want to keep it enabled, and you won't need any flags for it.

```
named_enable="NO"               # Run named, the DNS server (or NO).
named_program="named"           # path to named, if you want a different one.
named_flags=""                  # Flags for named
#named_flags="-u bind -g bind"  # Flags for named
```

These parameters specify whether we should run the name server, and what flags we should use if we do. See page 480 for more details. Previous versions of *named* required a flag to specify the location of the configuration file, but the location FreeBSD uses has now become the standard, so we no longer need to specify any flags. All we put in */etc/rc.conf* is:

```
named_enable="YES"              # Run named, the DNS server (or NO).
```

Continuing with */etc/defaults/rc.conf*,

```
kerberos_server_enable="NO"     # Run a kerberos master server (or NO).
kadmind_server_enable="NO"      # Run kadmind (or NO) -- do not run non
                                # a slave kerberos server
kerberos_stash=""               # Is the kerberos master key stashed?
```

Set these if you want to run Kerberos. We don't discuss Kerberos in this book.

```
rwhod_enable="NO"               # Run the rwho daemon (or NO).
rwhod_flags=""                  # Flags for rwhod
```

Set this if you want to run the *rwhod* dæmon, which broadcasts information about the system load.

```
amd_enable="NO"                 # Run amd service with $amd_flags (or NO).
amd_flags="-a /net -c 1800 -k i386 -d my.domain -l syslog /host /etc/amd.map"
amd_map_program="NO"            # Can be set to "ypcat -k amd.master"
```

Enable the automounter. We don't discuss the automounter in this book.

```
nfs_client_enable="NO"          # This host is an NFS client (or NO).
nfs_client_flags="-n 4"         # Flags to nfsiod (if enabled).
nfs_access_cache="2"            # Client cache timeout in seconds
nfs_server_enable="NO"          # This host is an NFS server (or NO).
nfs_server_flags="-u -t -n 4"   # Flags to nfsd (if enabled).
mountd_flags="-r"               # Flags to mountd (if NFS server enabled).
nfs_reserved_port_only="NO"     # Provide NFS only on secure port (or NO).
rpc_lockd_enable="NO"           # Run NFS rpc.lockd (*broken!*) if nfs_server.
rpc_statd_enable="YES"          # Run NFS rpc.statd if nfs_server (or NO).
portmap_enable="YES"            # Run the portmapper service (or NO).
portmap_program="/usr/sbin/portmap" # path to portmap, if you want a different one.
portmap_flags=""                # Flags to portmap (if enabled).
rpc_ypupdated_enable="NO"       # Run if NIS master and SecureRPC (or NO).
```

Flags for NFS. See page 523. There we set the following values in */etc/rc.conf*:

```
nfs_client_enable="YES"         # This host is an NFS client (or NO).
nfs_server_enable="YES"         # This host is an NFS server (or NO).
```

```
keyserv_enable="NO"            # Run the SecureRPC keyserver (or NO).
keyserv_flags=""               # Flags to keyserv (if enabled).
rarpd_enable="NO"              # Run rarpd (or NO).
rarpd_flags=""                 # Flags to rarpd.
xtend_enable="NO"              # Run the X-10 power controller daemon.
xtend_flags=""                 # Flags to xtend (if enabled).
```

These entries refer to the Secure RPC key server, *rarpd* and the X-10 dæmon. We don't discuss any of them in this book. See the man pages *keyserv(8)*, *rarpd(8)* and *xtend(8)* respectively.

```
### Network Time Services options: ###
timed_enable="NO"              # Run the time daemon (or NO).
timed_flags=""                 # Flags to timed (if enabled).
ntpdate_enable="NO"            # Run the ntpdate to sync time (or NO).
ntpdate_program="ntpdate"      # path to ntpdate, if you want a different one.
ntpdate_flags=""               # Flags to ntpdate (if enabled).
xntpd_enable="NO"              # Run xntpd Network Time Protocol (or NO).
xntpd_program="xntpd"          # path to xntpd, if you want a different one.
xntpd_flags="-p /var/run/xntpd.pid" # Flags to xntpd (if enabled).
```

timed, *ntpdate* and *xntpd* are three different ways of synchronizing your machine with the current date and time. See page 186 for more information. There we put the following values into */etc/rc.conf*:

```
xntpd_enable="YES"             # Run xntpd Network Time Protocol (or NO).
xntpd_flags=""                 # Flags to xntpd (if enabled).
```

Continuing with */etc/defaults/rc.conf*,

```
# Network Information Services (NIS) options: ###
nis_client_enable="NO"         # We're an NIS client (or NO)
nis_client_flags=""            # Flags to ypbind (if enabled).
nis_ypset_enable="NO"          # Run ypset at boot time (or NO).
nis_ypset_flags=""             # Flags to ypset (if enabled).
nis_server_enable="NO"         # We're an NIS server (or NO)
nis_server_flags=""            # Flags to ypserv (if enabled).
nis_ypxfrd_enable="NO"         # Run rpc.ypxfrd at boot time (or NO).
nis_ypxfrd_flags=""            # Flags to rpc.ypxfrd (if enabled).
nis_yppasswdd_enable="NO"      # Run rpc.yppasswdd at boot time (or NO).
nis_yppasswdd_flags=""         # Flags to rpc.yppasswdd (if enabled).
```

More parameters for configuring NIS. As mentioned above, this book does not deal with NIS.

```
### Network routing options: ###
defaultrouter="NO"             # Set to default gateway (or NO).
static_routes=""               # Set to static route list (or leave empty).
gateway_enable="NO"            # Set to YES if this host will be a gateway.
```

Here's another area that we need to change if we're using any kind of a network. On page 408 we set the following values in */etc/rc.conf*:

```
defaultrouter="223.147.37.5"    # Set to default gateway (or NO).
static_routes=""                # Set to static route list (or leave empty).
```

Continuing with */etc/defaults/rc.conf,*

```
router_enable="NO"              # Set to YES to enable a routing daemon.
router="routed"                 # Name of routing daemon to use if enabled.
router_flags="-q"               # Flags for routing daemon.
mrouted_enable="NO"             # Do multicast routing (see /etc/mrouted.conf).
mrouted_flags=""                # Flags for multicast routing daemon.
```

These parameters relate to the routing dæmons *routed* and *mrouted*. In the configurations we considered, you don't need them.

```
ipxgateway_enable="NO"          # Set to YES to enable IPX routing.
ipxrouted_enable="NO"           # Set to YES to run the IPX routing daemon.
ipxrouted_flags=""              # Flags for IPX routing daemon.
```

IPX is a Novell proprietary networking protocol which is designed to be similar to IP. FreeBSD supplies the dæmon *IPXrouted* (note the capitalization) which handles IPX routing tables. See the man page *IPXrouted(8)* for further details.

```
arpproxy_all=""                 # replaces obsolete kernel option ARP_PROXYALL.
forward_sourceroute="NO"        # do source routing (only if gateway_enable is set to "YES")
accept_sourceroute="NO"         # accept source routed packets to us
```

Various IP options.

```
### ATM interface options: ###
atm_enable="NO"                 # Configure ATM interfaces (or NO).
#atm_netif_hea0="atm 1"         # Network interfaces for physical interface.
#atm_sigmgr_hea0="uni31"        # Signalling manager for physical interface.
#atm_prefix_hea0="ILMI"         # NSAP prefix (UNI interfaces only) (or ILMI).
#atm_macaddr_hea0="NO"          # Override physical MAC address (or NO).
# ATMARP server address (or local).
#atm_arpserver_atm0="0x47.0005.80.999999.9999.9999.9999.999999999999.00"
#atm_scsparp_atm0="NO"          # Run SCSP/ATMARP on network interface (or NO).
atm_pvcs=""                     # Set to PVC list (or leave empty).
atm_arps=""                     # Set to permanent ARP list (or leave empty).

### ISDN interface options: ###
isdn_enable="NO"                # Enable the ISDN subsystem (or NO).
isdn_fsdev="/dev/ttyv4"         # Output device for fullscreen mode (or NO for daemon mode).
isdn_flags="-dn -d0x1f9"        # Flags for isdnd
isdn_trace="NO"                 # Enable the ISDN trace subsystem (or NO).
isdn_traceflags="-f /var/tmp/isdntrace0"  # Flags for isdntrace
```

Parameters for ATM and ISDN, which this book doesn't discuss.

```
### Miscellaneous network options: ###
icmp_bmcastecho="NO"            # respond to broadcast ping packets
```

This parameter relates to the so-called *smurf* "denial of service" attack: according to the RFCs, a machine should respond to a ping to its broadcast address. But what happens if somebody pings a remote network's broadcast address across the Internet, as fast as he can? Each system on the remote network will reply, completely overloading the Internet interface. Yes, this is silly, but there are silly people out there. If you leave this parameter as it is, your system will not be vulnerable. See *http://www.cert.org/advisories/CA-98.01.smurf.html* for more details.

```
############################################################
###   System console options   ############################
############################################################
keymap="NO"                     # keymap in /usr/share/syscons/keymaps/* (or NO).
keyrate="NO"                    # keyboard rate to: slow, normal, fast (or NO).
keybell="NO"                    # bell to duration.pitch or normal or visual (or NO).
keychange="NO"                  # function keys default values (or NO).
cursor="NO"                     # cursor type {normal|blink|destructive} (or NO).
scrnmap="NO"                    # screen map in /usr/share/syscons/scrnmaps/* (or NO).
font8x16="NO"                   # font 8x16 from /usr/share/syscons/fonts/* (or NO).
font8x14="NO"                   # font 8x14 from /usr/share/syscons/fonts/* (or NO).
font8x8="NO"                    # font 8x8 from /usr/share/syscons/fonts/* (or NO).
blanktime="300"                 # blank time (in seconds) or "NO" to turn it off.
saver="NO"                      # screen saver: Uses /modules/${saver}_saver.ko
```

These parameters describe the use of alternate keyboard mappings when using the standard character-based terminals only. See the files in */usr/share/syscons/keymaps* for key map files, and */usr/share/syscons/fonts* for alternate fonts. These parameters have no effect on the X-based displays that this book assumes.

```
moused_enable="NO"              # Run the mouse daemon.
moused_type="auto"             # See man page for rc.conf(5) for available settings.
moused_port="/dev/cuaa0"       # Set to your mouse port.
moused_flags=""                 # Any additional flags to moused.
allscreens_flags=""             # Set this vidcontrol mode for all virtual screens
```

Parameters for *moused*, a mouse driver for the character-based terminals, and global flags for virtual screens.

```
############################################################
###   Miscellaneous administrative options   ##############
############################################################
cron_enable="YES"               # Run the periodic job daemon.
```

Run *cron*, the dæmon responsible for running things at specific times. See page 184 for a description of *cron*. You should leave this enabled unless you have a good reason not to.

```
lpd_enable="YES"                # Run the line printer daemon
lpd_program="/usr/sbin/lpd"     # path to lpd, if you want a different one.
lpd_flags=""                    # Flags to lpd (if enabled).
```

See page 293 for a discussion of printing. There's no particular reason to change these defaults.

```
usbd_enable="NO"                # Run the usbd daemon.
usbd_flags=""                   # Flags to usbd (if enabled).
```

Support for the *Universal Serial Bus* or *USB* is relatively new, and it is liable to change. Consider this an experimental option at the moment. See the man pages *usbd(8)* and *usb(4)* for more information.

```
sendmail_enable="YES"          # Run the sendmail daemon (or NO).
sendmail_flags="-bd -q30m"     # -bd is pretty mandatory
```

See page 555 for a discussion of *sendmail*. There's normally no need to change these values.

```
dumpdev="NO"                   # Device name to crashdump to (if enabled).
```

This parameter specifies how to take dumps when the system panics. See page 108 for details, where we set the following value in */etc/rc.conf*:

dumpdev=/dev/wd0s1b

Continuing with */etc/defaults/rc.conf,*

```
enable_quotas="NO"             # turn on quotas on startup (or NO).
check_quotas="NO"              # Check quotas on startup (or NO).
accounting_enable="NO"         # Turn on process accounting (or NO).
ibcs2_enable="NO"              # Ibcs2 (SCO) emulation loaded at startup (or NO).
linux_enable="NO"              # Linux emulation loaded at startup (or NO).
```

We don't discuss quotas or accounting in this book. We will look at the parameters ibcs2_enable on page 385 and linux_enable on page 384.

```
rand_irqs="NO"                 # Stir the entropy pool (or NO).
```

rand_irqs is used by the *random number devices, /dev/random* and */dev/urandom*. These devices gather environmental noise from device drivers and return good random numbers, suitable for cryptographic use. These numbers are also good for seeding TCP sequence numbers, and other places where it is desirable to have numbers which are not only random, but hard to predict by an attacker.

```
clear_tmp_enable="NO"          # Clear /tmp at startup.
```

In the old days, the startup sequence automatically deleted everything in the file system */tmp*. Sometimes this wasn't desirable, so now it's your choice. Change this value to YES if you want the old behaviour.

```
ldconfig_paths="/usr/lib/compat /usr/X11R6/lib /usr/local/lib"
               # shared library search paths
ldconfig_paths_aout="/usr/lib/compat/aout /usr/X11R6/lib/aout /usr/local/lib/aout"
               # a.out shared library search paths
```

These two variables are lists of the directories which are searched to find *ELF* and *a.out* dynamic libraries, respectively. See page 53 for more details. You would normally not remove anything from these lists, but you might want to add something.

```
kern_securelevel_enable="NO"      # kernel security level (see init(8)),
kern_securelevel="-1"             # range: -1..3 ; '-1' is the most insecure
update_motd="YES"                 # update version info in /etc/motd (or NO)
```

The kernel runs with four different levels of security. Any superuser process can raise the security level, but only init can lower it. The security levels are:

-1. Permanently insecure mode: always run the system in level 0 mode. This is the default initial value.

0. Insecure mode: the immutable and append-only flags may be turned off. All devices may be read or written subject to their permissions.

1. Secure mode: the system immutable and system append-only flags may not be turned off. Disks for mounted filesystems, */dev/mem* and */dev/kmem* may not be opened for writing.

2. Highly secure mode. This is the same as secure mode with the addition that disks may not be opened for writing (except by *mount(2)*), whether or not they are mounted. This level precludes tampering with filesystems by unmounting them, but it also prevents running *newfs(8)* while the system is multi-user.

3. Network secure mode. This is the same as highly secure mode with the addition that IP packet filter rules (see page 502) can not be changed and dummynet configuration can not be adjusted. We don't discuss dummynet in this book.

To set the secure level to anything except -1, set the variable `kern_securelevel` to the value you want, and set `kern_securelevel_enable` to YES.

```
start_vinum=""          # set to YES to start vinum
vinum_drives=""         # put in names of disks containing vinum drives
                        # to start vinum on only specific disks.
```

We will look at *Vinum* on page 266. There we put the following text into */etc/rc.conf* in order to start it on booting:

```
start_vinum="YES"       # set to YES to start vinum
```

Our /etc/rc.conf

To summarize the changes from the defaults, our */etc/rc.conf* should now contain the following entries:

```
hostname="presto.example.org"
firewall_enable="YES"           # Set to YES to enable firewall functionality
firewall_type="client"          # Firewall type (see /etc/rc.firewall)
natd_enable="YES"               # Enable natd (if firewall_enable == YES).
natd_interface="tun0"           # Public interface or IPaddress to use.
named_enable="YES"              # Run named, the DNS server (or NO).
nfs_client_enable="YES"         # This host is an NFS client (or NO).
nfs_server_enable="YES"         # This host is an NFS server (or NO).
xntpd_enable="YES"              # Run xntpd Network Time Protocol (or NO).
xntpd_flags=""                  # Flags to xntpd (if enabled).
dumpdev=/dev/wd0s1b             # Device name to crashdump to (if enabled).
```

```
start_vinum="YES"              # set to YES to start vinum
```

Other configuration files

This section handles the non-network configuration files in alphabetical order. See page 217 for a description of network configuration files.

/etc/aliases

/etc/aliases is used by *sendmail* to describe mail aliases. See page 557 for more details.

/etc/csh.cshrc, /etc/csh.login, /etc/csh.logout

These are default initialization files for *csh*. See the man page *csh(1)* for more details.

/etc/crontab

/etc/crontab describes the jobs to be performed by *cron* on behalf of the system. See page 184 for more details.

/etc/disktab

/etc/disktab contains descriptions of disk geometries for *disklabel*. See page 258 for further details.

/etc/fstab

/etc/fstab contains a list of file systems known to the system. The script */etc/rc* starts *mount* twice during system startup first to mount the local file systems, and later to mount the NFS file system. *mount* will mount all file systems unless they are explicitly excluded.

Here's a typical */etc/fstab*, from host *freebie.example.org*:

```
/dev/wd0a              /           ufs      rw            1 1
/dev/wd0s1b            none        swap     sw            0 0
/dev/wd0s1e            /usr        ufs      rw            2 2
/dev/sd0b              none        swap     sw            0 0
/dev/sd0h              /src        ufs      rw            2 2
/dev/sd1h              /home       ufs      rw            2 2
/dev/sd2b              none        swap     sw            0 0
/dev/sd2e              /S          ufs      rw,noauto     2 2
/dev/sd3a              /mod        ufs      rw,noauto     0 0
# /dev/sd1e            /src        ufs      rw,noauto     0 0
proc                   /proc       procfs   rw            0 0
# /dev/mcd0a           /cdrom      cd9660   ro,noauto     0 0
/dev/cd0a              /cdrom/1    cd9660   ro,noauto     0 0
/dev/cd1a              /cdrom/2    cd9660   ro,noauto     0 0
/dev/cd2a              /cdrom/3    cd9660   ro,noauto     0 0
/dev/cd3a              /cdrom/4    cd9660   ro,noauto     0 0
/dev/cd4a              /cdrom/5    cd9660   ro,noauto     0 0
/dev/cd5a              /cdrom/6    cd9660   ro,noauto     0 0
/dev/cd6a              /cdrom/7    cd9660   ro,noauto     0 0
/dev/cd7a              /cdrom/8    cd9660   ro,noauto     0 0
presto:/               /presto     nfs      soft,rw,noauto 0 0
```

```
presto:/usr            /presto/usr     nfs     soft,rw,noauto 0 0
# presto:/var          /presto/var     nfs     soft,rw,noauto 0 0
presto:/home           /presto/home    nfs     soft,rw,noauto 0 0
bumble:/               /bumble         nfs     soft,rw,noauto 0 0
bumble:/usr            /bumble/usr     nfs     soft,rw,noauto 0 0
wait:/C                /C              nfs     soft,rw,noauto 0 0
wait:/                 /wait           nfs     soft,rw,noauto,tcp 0 0
```

This information has the following meaning:

- The first column contains either the name of a device (for swap, *ufs* and *cd9660* file systems), the name of a file system (for NFS file systems), or `proc` for the *proc* file system.

- The lines beginning with # are *commented out*: *mount* ignores them completely.

- The second column is either a mount point or the keyword `none` in the case of a partition which is not mounted, such as swap.

- The third column is the kind of file system (or `swap`).

- The fourth column are flags relating to the particular file system being mounted. Some of the more common are:

Table 12-1. Mount flags

Flag	Purpose
ro	Mount read-only
rw	Mount read/write
sw	Mount as swap
noauto	Don't mount automatically
soft	For an NFS mount, fail if the request times out. If you don't specify this option, NFS will keep retrying for ever.
tcp	For NFS only, mount with TCP transport rather than the standard UDP transport. This feature is supported almost only by BSD systems—check whether the other end offers TCP transport.

For NFS mount flags, see Chapter 30, *The Network File System*, page 525.

Why are there so many entries with the `noauto` keyword? If you don't bother to mount them, why bother to mention them?

If file system has an entry in */etc/fstab*, *mount* is clever enough to get all the information it needs from this file. You just need to specify the name of the mount point or the name of the special device (for *ufs* and *cd9660*) or the remote file system (for NFS). This is particularly useful for *cd9660*. Without an entry in */etc/fstab*, you would have to write:

```
# mount -t cd9660 -o ro /dev/cd0a /cdrom
```

With the entry, you can simplify this to:

```
# mount /cdrom
```

/etc/gettytab

/etc/gettytab describes profiles for *getty*. You probably don't need it; check the man page (on your system, but not in this book) if you're interested.

/etc/group

/etc/group defines the groups known to the system. See page 163 for more details.

/etc/login.conf

/etc/login.conf describes user parameters set at login time. See page 168 for more details.

/etc/manpath.config

/etc/manpath.config is a configuration file for *man*. You don't usually need to change this file.

/etc/master.passwd

/etc/master.passwd is the real password file. We looked at it on page 163.

/etc/motd

/etc/motd (*message of the day*) is a file which is printed out at login. See page 170 for an example.

/etc/passwd

/etc/passwd is the old-style password file. It is now present only for programs which expect to read it. See page 163 for more details.

/etc/printcap

/etc/printcap describes the printers connected to a system. See page 294 for more details.

/etc/profile

/etc/profile is a default startup file for Bourne-style shells. See page 178 for more details.

/etc/pwd.db

/etc/pwd.db is a machine-readable form of the user database with the passwords removed. We looked at it on page 163.

/etc/rc

/etc/rc is the main script which starts up the system. It uses the other files whose names start with */etc/rc* to perform specific initialization. See page 190 for more details.

/etc/rc.i386

/etc/rc.i386 is used to initialize features specific to the Intel 386 architecture, such as SCO and Linux emulation. You don't normally need to look at or change this file.

/etc/rc.local

/etc/rc.local is the configuration file which you use to include specific commands which are not catered for in */etc/rc.conf*. We've seen a few examples in the book; check the index for more information.

/etc/rc.pccard

/etc/rc.pccard sets up laptops using the PCCARD bus. We don't discuss this in this book.

/etc/rc.serial

/etc/rc.serial sets default values for serial devices. We don't discuss this in this book.

/etc/sendmail.cf

/etc/sendmail.cf is the main configuration file for *sendmail*. We will look at it on page 555.

/etc/shells

/etc/shells is a list of valid shells, used by *ftp* and some other programs. See page 541 for more details.

/etc/spwd.db

/etc/spwd.db is a machine-readable form of the user database with the passwords intact. We looked at it on page 163.

/etc/syslog.conf

/etc/syslog.conf is the configuration file for *syslogd*. We will look at it on page 541.

/etc/termcap

/etc/termcap (*terminal capabilities*) describes terminal control sequences. By default, programs use the value of the TERM environment variable to look up the terminal capabilities in this database. See page 176 for more details.

/etc/ttys

/etc/ttys is a file which describes terminals and pseudo-terminals to *init*. We've looked at it in a number of places: check the index.

Here's an excerpt from the default */etc/ttys*:

```
# This entry needed for asking password when init goes to single-user mode
# If you want to be asked for password, change "secure" to "insecure" here
console    none                        unknown    off secure
```

The system console. This is not a real terminal: it can be moved from one device to another. By default, it corresponds to */dev/ttyv0* (the next entry).

```
ttyv0 "/usr/libexec/getty Pc"         cons25     on  secure
```

This is the first virtual terminal, the one which you get automatically at boot time. To change to the others, press **Alt-F***x*, where *x* is between 1 and 16. This will give you one of the others:

```
# Virtual terminals
ttyv1 "/usr/libexec/getty Pc"         cons25     on secure
ttyv2 "/usr/libexec/getty Pc"         cons25     on secure
ttyv3 "/usr/libexec/getty Pc"         cons25     off secure
```

The default kernel supports four virtual terminals. See page 339 for details of how to configure more. As we saw on page 128, you need to keep one off if you want to run X.

```
# Serial terminals
ttyd0 "/usr/libexec/getty std.9600"   unknown    off secure
ttyd1 "/usr/libexec/getty std.9600"   unknown    off secure
ttyd2 "/usr/libexec/getty std.9600"   unknown    off secure
ttyd3 "/usr/libexec/getty std.9600"   unknown    off secure
```

These are the serial ports on your machine. It doesn't matter if it contains names which correspond to non-existent hardware, such as */dev/ttyd3*, as long as you don't try to enable them.

```
# Pseudo terminals
ttyp0    none              network
ttyp1    none              network
```

There's a whole list of these. The purpose here is to tell network programs the properties of the terminal: in particular, they're not secure, which means that you're not allowed to log in on them as root.

/etc/periodic/

The directory */etc/periodic* contains three directories used by *cron* at regular intervals: *daily*, *weekly* and *monthly*. The directories contain a number of files for performing specific tasks. For example, */etc/periodic/daily* contains the following files:

```
-rwxr-xr-x  1 grog   example    321 Apr  6 18:25 100.clean-disks
-rwxr-xr-x  1 grog   example    651 Apr  6 18:25 110.clean-tmps
-rwxr-xr-x  1 grog   example    231 Apr  6 18:25 120.clean-preserve
-rwxr-xr-x  1 grog   example    223 Aug 18  1997 130.clean-msgs
-rwxr-xr-x  1 grog   example    217 Apr  6 18:25 140.clean-rwho
-rwxr-xr-x  1 grog   example   1059 May 25  1998 200.backup-passwd
-rwxr-xr-x  1 grog   example    499 Aug 17  1997 210.backup-aliases
-rwxr-xr-x  1 grog   example    322 Aug 18  1997 220.backup-distfile
-rwxr-xr-x  1 grog   example    458 Aug 18  1997 300.calendar
-rwxr-xr-x  1 grog   example    410 Aug 18  1997 310.accounting
-rwxr-xr-x  1 grog   example    186 Aug 18  1997 320.rdist
-rwxr-xr-x  1 grog   example    253 Aug 17  1997 330.news
-rwxr-xr-x  1 grog   example    321 Jan  2 07:37 340.uucp
-rwxr-xr-x  1 grog   example    184 Aug 17  1997 400.status-disks
-rwxr-xr-x  1 grog   example    182 Aug 18  1997 410.status-uucp
-rwxr-xr-x  1 grog   example    179 Aug 18  1997 420.status-network
-rwxr-xr-x  1 grog   example    284 Oct  6  1998 430.status-rwho
-rwxr-xr-x  1 grog   example    425 Apr 18  1998 440.status-mailq
-rwxr-xr-x  1 grog   example    261 Aug 18  1997 450.status-security
-rwxr-xr-x  1 grog   example    432 Feb  9  1998 460.status-mail-rejects
-rwxr-xr-x  1 grog   example    288 Aug 17  1997 999.local
```

The files are executed in the order of their names, so the names consist of two parts: a number indicating the sequence, and a name indicating the function. This method is new with FreeBSD version 3. In older versions of FreeBSD, these functions were performed by files with the names */etc/daily*, */etc/weekly* and */etc/monthly*. See page 184 for more details of *cron*.

Network configuration files

This section describes the network configuration files in alphabetical order. The main script for starting the network is */etc/rc.network*, which in earlier BSD versions, including FreeBSD, was called */etc/network*. You normally don't change this file: it reads all the necessary definitions from */etc/rc.conf*, and that's the file you should change.

/etc/exports

/etc/exports is a list of file systems which should be NFS exported. We will look at it on page 527. See also the man page *exports(5)*.

/etc/rc.firewall

/etc/rc.firewall is used to initialize the packet filtering firewall *ipfw*. See page 502 for further details.

/etc/ftpusers

/etc/ftpusers is a list of users who are *not* allowed to connect to this system using *ftp*.

/etc/host.conf

/etc/host.conf describes the order in which to perform name resolution. We have three choices: BIND, */etc/hosts*, and NIS. The file simply specifies which of these options should be used, and in which order:

```
# $Id: host.conf,v 1.2 1993/11/07 01:02:57 wollman Exp $
# Default is to use the nameserver first
bind
# If that doesn't work, then try the /etc/hosts file
hosts
# If you have YP/NIS configured, uncomment the next line
# nis
```

/etc/hosts

For a small network, especially if you're not permanently connected to the Internet, you have the option of placing the addresses of the systems you want to talk to in a file called */etc/hosts*. This file is simply a list of IP addresses and host names, for example:

```
# Local network host addresses
#
# loopback address for all systems
127.1 loopback local localhost

###### domain example.com.
#
223.147.37.1    freebie freebie.example.org       # FreeBSD 3.0
223.147.37.2    presto.example.org presto         # 66 MHz 486 (BSD UNIX)
223.147.37.3    bumble bumble.example.org         # 33 MHz 486 (UNIX SVR3.2)
223.147.37.4    wait wait.example.org             # 33 MHz 486 (DOS)
223.147.37.129 solo solo.example.org      lxn     # LXN
223.147.37.132 dinosaur dinosaur.example.org      # 25 MHz 386 running DOS
223.147.37.133 andante andante.example.org        # Toshiba laptop - 16 MHz 386SX
223.147.37.135 onlyyou onlyyou.example.org        # Consensys Destiny machine
223.147.37.136 zaphod zaphod.example.org          # 2-headed X machine
```

Obviously, you need to set up this file yourself, and you need it on every machine on the network. As you can see, a system can have more than one name: just put as many names as you want behind the IP address. This method is hard to maintain: a better alternative is the Domain Name Service, which we discuss in Chapter 27.

/etc/hosts.equiv

/etc/hosts.equiv is a list of hosts whose users may use *rsh* to access this system without supplying a password. We'll look at it on page 534.

/etc/hosts.lpd

/etc/hosts.lpd is a list of hosts which can use the *lpd* spooler on this system.

/etc/inetd.conf

/etc/inetd.conf is the configuration file for *inetd*, the Internet dæmon. It dates back to the original implementation of TCP/IP in 4.2BSD, and the format is the same for all versions of UNIX. We have looked at various modifications to this file throughout the network part of the book. See the index (`inetd.conf`) and the man page *inetd.conf(5)* for further details.

/etc/namedb/named.conf

/etc/named/named.conf is the main configuration file for *named*, the Domain Name Service dæmon. We will look at it in Chapter 27, *The Domain Name Service.* Previous versions of *named* used a different form of configuration file which was stored in */etc/named.boot*.

/etc/networks

/etc/networks is a list of networks in the Internet. Although this sounds like a good idea, it is almost useless: if you connect to the Internet, you should use a name server, which supplants this file.

/etc/protocols

/etc/protocols is a list of known protocols which run on the IP layer. This file should be seen and not changed.

/etc/rc.network

/etc/rc.network is the main script which starts up the network. You shouldn't need to change this file.

/etc/services

/etc/services, a list of the IP services which this system supports. Like */etc/protocols*, you should not change this file.

Obsolete configuration files

/etc/sysconfig

/etc/sysconfig was a file which contained all the site-specific configuration definitions. Its name has been changed to */etc/rc.conf*.

/etc/netstart

/etc/netstart was a script called by */etc/rc* to start up the network. Its name has now been changed to */etc/rc.network*. FreeBSD still includes a file */etc/netstart*, but its only purpose is to start the network in single-user mode.

Shutting down the system

FreeBSD uses a number of sophisticated techniques to achieve its high performance. In particular, when you write data to a disk, the system doesn't put it on the disk immediately: it waits for more data to arrive, which improves performance dramatically, since it reduces the number of disk accesses by up to several orders of magnitude.

The result of turning power off before the data is written is equally dramatic. You may just lose the data, but if the data is information on a change in file system structure, your file system will be broken. To check for this, the system runs a program called *fsck* (File System Check) at startup. *fsck* can repair minor damage, but it's obviously a better idea to avoid damage by ensuring that the system is shut down in an orderly way.

> *Never stop your machine by just turning off the power. The results could be devastating.*

The correct way to shut a system down is with the *shutdown* command. To quote the man page *shutdown(8)*:

> Shutdown provides an automated shutdown procedure for super-users to nicely notify users when the system is shutting down, saving them from system administrators, hackers, and gurus, who would otherwise not bother with such niceties.

This command has a number of useful options:

- Use the -r option to reboot the computer. You sometimes need to do this, for example after installing a new kernel.

- Use the -h option to stop the machine. This is the normal case, but it isn't the default.

- Without an option, shutdown attempts to put the machine in single user mode. This doesn't always work as well as booting in single user mode.

- Shutdown takes a time parameter which tells it when to actually perform the shutdown. This is useful in a multi-user environment, but normally you'll want to shutdown now, so *shutdown* understands the keyword now.

In the normal case, where you want to stop the machine right now so you can turn the power off, you would type:

```
# shutdown -h now
Feb  4 12:38:36 freebie shutdown: halt by grog:
Feb  4 12:38:39 freebie syslogd: exiting on signal 15

syncing disks... done

The operating system has halted.
Please press any key to reboot.
```

Be sure to wait for this message before you turn off the power.

Rebooting

To reboot the machine, enter

```
# shutdown -r now        or
# reboot                 or
CTRL-ALT-DEL
```

13

File systems

One of the most far-reaching concepts of the UNIX operating system was its *file system*, the way in which it stores data. Although most other operating systems have copied it since then, including Microsoft's platforms, none have come close to the elegance with which it is implemented. In this chapter, we'll look at what that means to you.

File systems

Both UNIX and Microsoft environments store disk data in *files*, which in turn are placed in *directories*. A file may be a directory: that is, it may contain other files.

File names

The differences between UNIX and Microsoft start with *file names*. Traditional Microsoft file names are rigid: a file name consists of eight characters, possibly followed by a period and another three characters (the so-called *file name extension*). There are significant restrictions on which characters may be used to form a file name, and upper and lower case letters have the same meaning (internally, Microsoft converts the names to UPPER CASE). Directory members are selected with a backslash (\), which conflicts with other meanings in the C programming language—see page 161 for more details.

By comparison, UNIX file names are much more flexible. They may contain any character except a slash (/), which is used to indicate a directory component, and they may be up to 255 characters long.

> In some older versions of UNIX and early versions of Linux, file names were restricted to 14 characters.

Upper and lower case letters have different meanings, so in UNIX the names *foo*, *FOO*, and *Foo* are three different names.

Permissions

Since a UNIX system may potentially be used by many people, it includes a method of protecting data from access by unauthorized persons. Every file has three items of information associated with it which describes who can access it in what manner:

- The *file owner*, the user ID of the person who owns the file.

- The *file group*, the group ID of the group which "owns" the file.

- A list of what the owner, the group and other people can do with the file. The possible actions are reading, writing or executing.

For example, you might have a program which accesses private data, and you want to be sure that only you may execute it. You do this by setting the permissions so that only the owner may execute it. Or you might have a text document in development, and you want to be sure that you are the only person who can change it. On the other hand, the people who work with you have a need to be able to refer to the document. You set the permissions so that only the owner may write it, that the owner and group may read it, and, since it's not ready for publication yet, you don't allow anybody else to access it.

Traditionally, the permissions are represented by three groups of rwx: r stands for *read* permission, w stands for *write* permission, and x stands for *execute* permission. The three groups represent the permissions for the owner, the group and others respectively. If the permission is not granted, it is represented by a hyphen (-). Thus, the permissions for the program I discussed above would be r-x------ (I can read and execute the program, and nobody else can do anything with it). The permissions for the draft document would be rw-r----- (I can read and write, the group can read, and others can't access it).

Typical FreeBSD file access permissions are rwxr-xr-x for programs and rw-r--r-- for other system files. In some cases, however, you'll find that other permissions are *required*. For example, the file ˜/.rhosts, which is used by some network programs for user validation, may contain the user's password in legible form. To help ensure that other people don't read it, the network programs will refuse to read it unless its permissions are rw-------. The vast majority of system problems in UNIX can be traced to incorrect permissions, so you should pay particular attention to them.

Apart from these access permissions, executables can also have two bits set to specify the access permissions of the process when it is run. If the *setuid* (*set user ID*) bit is set, the process will always run as if it had been started by its owner. If the *setgid* (*set group* ID) bit is set, it will run as if it had been started by its group. This is frequently used to start system programs which need to access resources which the user may not access directly. We'll see an example of this with the *ps* command on page 227. *ls* represents the *setuid* bit by setting the third letter of the permissions string to s instead of x; similarly, it represents the *setgid* bit by setting the sixth letter of the permissions string to s instead of x.

In addition to this access information, the permissions contain a character which describes what kind of file it represents. The first letter may be a - (hyphen), which designates a regular file, the letter d for directory, or the letters b or c for a device node. We'll look at device nodes in

Chapter 14, *Disks*, page 231. There are also a number of other letters which are less used. See the man page *ls(1)* for a full list.

To list files and show the permissions, use the *ls* command with the -1 option:

```
$ ls -l
total 2429
-rw-rw-r--   1 grog    wheel        28204 Jan  4 14:17 %backup%~
drwxrwxr-x   3 grog    wheel          512 Oct 11 15:26 2.1.0-951005-SNAP
drwx------   4 grog    wheel          512 Nov 25 17:23 Mail
-rw-rw-r--   1 grog    wheel          149 Dec  4 14:18 Makefile
-rw-rw-r--   1 grog    wheel          108 Dec  4 12:36 Makefile.bak
-rw-rw-r--   1 grog    wheel          108 Dec  4 12:36 Makefile~
-rw-rw-r--   1 grog    wheel            0 Dec  4 12:36 depend
-rw-rw-r--   1 root    wheel      1474560 Dec 14 17:03 deppert.floppy
-rwxr-xr-x   1 grog    wheel          100 Dec 19 15:24 doio
-rwxrwxr-x   1 grog    wheel          204 Dec 19 15:25 doiovm
-rwxrwxr-x   1 grog    wheel          204 Dec 19 15:16 doiovm~
-rwxr-xr-x   1 grog    wheel          115 Dec 26 08:42 dovm
-rwxr-xr-x   1 grog    wheel          114 Dec 19 15:30 dovm~
drwxr-xr-x   2 grog    wheel          512 Oct 16  1994 emacs
drwxrwxrwx   2 grog    wheel          512 Jan  3 14:07 letters
```

This format shows the following information:

- First, the permissions, which we've already looked at.

- Then, the *link count*. This is the number of hard links to the file. For a regular file, this is normally 1, but directories have at least 2. We'll look at links on page 228.

- Next come the names of the owner and the group, and the size of the file in bytes. You'll notice that the file *deppert.floppy* belongs to root. This was probably an accident, and it could lead to problems. Incidentally, looking at the name of the file and its size, it's fairly obvious that this is an *image* of a 3½" floppy, that is to say, a literal copy of the complete floppy.

- The date is normally the date that the file was last modified. With the -u option to *ls*, you can list the last time the file was accessed.

- Finally comes the name of the file. As you can see from this example, the names can be quite varied.

A couple of the permissions are of interest. The directories all have the x (execute) permission bit set. This is necessary in order to be able to access the files in the directory—that's the way the term *execute* is defined for a directory. If I reset the execute permission, I can still list the names of the files, but I can't access them.

I am the only person who can access the directory *Mail*. This is the normal permission for a mail directory.

Changing file permissions and owners

Often enough, you may want to change file permissions or owners. UNIX supplies three programs to do this:

- To change the file owner, use *chown*. For example, to change the ownership of the file *deppert.floppy*, which in the list above belongs to root, root would enter:

  ```
  # chown grog deppert.floppy
  ```

  Note that this operation must be performed by root.

- To change the file group, use *chgrp*, which works in the same way as *chown*. To change the group ownership to *lemis*, you would enter:

  ```
  # chgrp lemis deppert.floppy
  ```

  chown can also change both the owner and the group. Instead of the two previous examples, you could enter:

  ```
  # chown grog.lemis deppert.floppy
  ```

  This would change the owner to grog, as before, and also change the group to lemis.

- To change the permissions, use the *chmod* program. *chmod* has a number of different formats, but unfortunately the 9-character representation isn't one of them. Read the man page *chmod(1)* for the full story, but you can achieve just about anything you want with one of the formats shown in table 13-1:

Table 13-1. chmod permission codes

Specification	Effect
go-w	Deny write permission to group and others
=rw,+X	Set the read and write permissions to the usual defaults, but retain any execute permissions that are currently set
+X	Make a directory or file searchable/executable by everyone if it is already searchable/executable by anyone
u=rwx,go=rx	Make a file readable/executable by everyone and writable by the owner only
go=	Clear all mode bits for group and others
g=u-w	Set the group bits equal to the user bits, but clear the group write bit

Permissions for new files

None of this tells us what the permissions for new files are going to be. The wrong choice could be disastrous. For example, if files were automatically created with the permissions rwxrwxrwx, anybody could access them in any way. On the other hand, creating them with r-------- could result in a lot of work setting them to what you really want them to be. UNIX solves this problem with a thing called *umask* (*User mask*). This is a default non-permission: it specifies which permission bits *not* to allow.

As if this weren't confusing enough, it's specified in the octal number system, in which the valid digits are 0 to 7. Each octal digit represents 3 bits. By contrast, the more common hexadecimal system uses 16 digits, 0 to 9 and a to f. The original versions of UNIX ran on machines which used the octal number system, and since the permissions come in threes, it made sense to leave the *umask* value in octal.

An example: by default, you want to create files which anybody can read, but only you can write. You set the mask to 022. This corresponds to the binary bit pattern 000010010.

> The leading 0 is needed to specify that the number is in octal, not to make up three digits. If you want to set the permissions so that by default nobody can read, you'd set it to 0222. Some shells automatically assume that the number is octal, so you *may* be able to omit the 0, but it's not good practice.

The permissions are allowed where the corresponding bit is 0:

```
rwxrwxrwx        Possible permissions
000010010        umask
rwxr-xr-x        resultant permissions
```

By default, files are created without the x bits, whereas directories are created with the allowed x bits, so with this *umask*, a file would be created with the permissions rw-r--r--.

umask is a shell command. To set it, just enter:

```
$ umask 022
```

It's preferable to set this in your shell initialization file—see page 178 for further details.

Beware of creating a too restrictive umask. For example, you will get into a lot of trouble with a umask like 377, which creates files which you can only read, and which nobody else can access. If you disallow the x (executable) bit, you will not be able to access directories you create, and you won't be able to run programs you compile.

Making a program executable

File permissions enable one problem that occurs so often that it's worth drawing attention to it. Many operating systems require that an executable program have a special naming convention, such as *COMMAND.COM* or *FOO.BAT*, which in MS-DOS denotes a specific kind of binary executable and a script file, respectively. In UNIX, you don't need a special suffix in order to be able to execute a program, but it must have the x bit set. Sometimes this bit gets reset (turned off), for example if you copy it across the net with *ftp*. The result looks like this:

```
$ ps
bash: ps: Permission denied
$ ls -l /bin/ps
-r--r--r--  1 bin  kmem   163840 May  6 06:02 /bin/ps
$ su                                 you need to be super user to set ps permission
Password:                            password doesn't echo
# chmod +x /bin/ps                   make it executable
# ps                                 now it works
  PID  TT  STAT       TIME COMMAND
  226  p2  S       0:00.56 su (bash)
  239  p2  R+      0:00.02 ps
  146  v1  Is+     0:00.06 /usr/libexec/getty Pc ttyv1
  147  v2  Is+     0:00.05 /usr/libexec/getty Pc ttyv2
# ^D                                 exit su
$ ps
ps: /dev/mem: Permission denied      hey! it's stopped working
```

Huh? It only worked under *su*, and stopped working when I became a mere mortal again? What's going on here?

There's a second problem with privileged programs like *ps*: they need to be able to access special files, in this case */dev/mem*, a special file which addresses the system memory. In order to do this, we need to set the *setuid* bit, s. To do this, we become superuser again:

```
$ su                                 you need to be super user to set ps permission
Password:                            password doesn't echo
# chmod g+s /bin/ps                  set the setgid bit
# ls -l /bin/ps                      see what it looks like
-r-xr-sr-x  1 bin  kmem   163840 May  6 06:02 /bin/ps
# ^D                                 exit su
$ ps                                 now it still works
  PID  TT  STAT       TIME COMMAND
  226  p2  S       0:00.56 su (bash)
  239  p2  R+      0:00.02 ps
  146  v1  Is+     0:00.06 /usr/libexec/getty Pc ttyv1
  147  v2  Is+     0:00.05 /usr/libexec/getty Pc ttyv2
```

In this example, the permissions in the final result really are the correct permissions for *ps*. It's impossible to go through the permissions for every standard program. If you suspect that you have the permissions set incorrectly, use the permissions of the files on the Live Filesystem CD-ROM as a guideline.

Links

Files may have more than one name. There are two methods: one, called a *link*, or sometimes *hard link*, really gives the same file two different names. There is a requirement that files be on the same file system as the directory, so this method restricts the names to the same file system.

Alternatively, *symbolic links*, sometimes called *soft links*, are not restricted to the same file system (not even to the same system!), and they refer to another file name, not to the file itself. The difference is most evident if you delete a file: if the file has been hard linked, the other names still exist and you can access the file by them. If you delete a file name which has a symbolic link pointing to it, the file will go away and the symbolic link will not be able to find it any more.

It's not easy to decide which kind of link to use—see *UNIX Power Tools* for more details.

Directory structure

Although Microsoft platforms have a hierarchical directory structure, there is little standardization of the directory names: it's difficult to know where a particular program or data file might
be. UNIX systems have a standard directory hierarchy, though every vendor loves to change it
just a little bit to ensure that they're not absolutely compatible. In the course of its evolution,
UNIX has changed its directory structure several times. Still, it's much better than the almost
complete lack of standardization in the Microsoft world. The most recent, and probably most
far-reaching changes, occurred with System V.4 and 4.4BSD, both of which made almost
identical changes.

Nearly every version of UNIX prefers to have at least two file systems, / (the *root file system*)
and */usr*, even if they only have a single disk. This arrangement is more reliable than a single
file system: it's possible for a file system to crash so badly that it can't be mounted any more,
and you need to read in a tape backup, or use programs like *fsck* or *fsdb* to piece them
together. If you have only one file system, you may need to completely reinstall the system
under these circumstances. If, however, you have a small root file system with only enough on
it to get the machine running in single user mode, you can subsequently recover the */usr* file
system relatively easily. If you also almost never write to your root file system, the chances of
damaging it are remote.

For these reasons, BSD systems like to have as small a root file system as possible. They store
much of the data that System V stores in its root file system in */usr*. You should never need a
root file system with more than 40 MB, and I get by quite happily with 30 MB.

One problem with this method is the */tmp* file system, which is normally located on the root
file system. As its name implies, it is used to store temporary files. This creates two problems
for this method:

- If you create temporary files, you want to write to them, and we don't want to write to the
  root file system if we can avoid it.

- The files may become large and fill up the file system.

The standard solution for these problems is to relocate the */tmp* file system to a different
directory, say */usr/tmp*, and create a symbolic link from */usr/tmp* to */tmp*—see page 87 for more
details. Table 13-2 gives an overview of the standard FreeBSD directories.

Table 13-2. FreeBSD directory hierarchy

Directory Name	Usage
/	Root file system. Contains the kernel, the bootstrap, and mount points for other file systems. It should not contain anything else.
/bin	Executable programs of general use which are needed at system start-up time. The name was originally an abbreviation for *binary*, but many of the files in here are shell scripts.
/cdrom	A mount point for CD-ROM drives
/compat	A directory containing code for emulated systems, such as Linux.
/dev	Directory of device nodes. The name is an abbreviation for *devices*. We'll look at the contents of this directory in more detail on page 237.
/etc	Files used at system startup. Unlike System V, */etc* does not contain kernel build files, which are not needed at system startup. Unlike earlier UNIX versions, it also does not contain executables—they have been moved to */sbin*.
/mnt	A mount point for floppies and other temporary file systems
/modules	Directory containing *kernel loadable modules*, parts of the kernel which can be started at run time.
/proc	The *process file system*. This directory contains pseudo-files which refer to the virtual memory of currently active processes.
/root	The home directory of the user `root`. In traditional UNIX file systems, `root`'s home directory was /, but this is messy.
/sbin	System executables needed at system startup time. These are typically system administration files that used to be stored in */etc*.
/stand	Directory with *standalone* programs. In fact, most of the programs are the same file, */stand/sysinstall*, which we discussed in great detail in Chapter 5, *Installing FreeBSD*.
/usr	The "second file system". See the discussion above.
/usr/X11R6	The X11 windowing system
/usr/X11R6/bin	Executable X11 programs
/usr/X11R6/include	Header files for X11 programming
/usr/X11R6/lib	Library files for X11
/usr/X11R6/man	Man pages for X11

Directory Name	Usage
/usr/bin	Standard executable programs that are not needed at system start. Most programs you use will be stored here.
/usr/games	Games
/usr/include	Header files for programmers
/usr/lib	Library files for programmers. FreeBSD does not have a directory */lib*.
/usr/libexec	Executable files which are not started directly by the user, for example the phases of the C compiler (which are started by */usr/bin/gcc*) or the *getty* program, which is started by *init*.
/usr/local	Additional programs which are not part of the operating system. It parallels the */usr* directory in having subdirectories *bin*, *include*, *lib*, *man*, *sbin*, and *share*. This is where you can put programs which you get from other sources.
/usr/sbin	System administration programs which are not needed at system start-up.
/usr/share	Miscellaneous read-only files, mainly informative. Subdirectories include *doc*, the FreeBSD documentation, *games*, *info*, the GNU *info* documentation, *locale*, internationization information, and *man*, the man pages.
/var	A file system for data which changes frequently, such as mail, news, and log files. If */var* is not a separate file system, you should create a directory on another file system and symlink */var* to it—see page 87).
/var/log	Directory with system log files
/var/mail	Incoming mail for users on this system
/var/spool	Spool data, such as data waiting to be printed (*/var/spool/lpd*), */var/spool/mqueue* (outgoing mail), UUCP data (*/var/spool/uucp*), and */var/spool/ftp* (anonymous FTP).
/var/tmp	Temporary files. See the discussion above.

FreeBSD devices

Like all traditional UNIX systems, FreeBSD refers to devices by a *major number* and a *minor number*. The major number is in fact an index into a list of drivers, and the minor number is a number which the driver uses to distinguish the individual device and how it should treat it. FreeBSD also distinguishes between *block devices*, on which you can store a file system, and *character devices*, which do not. Block devices have a corresponding raw device which is used for some purposes, such as file system consistency checks. You can see this information in an *ls -l* listing:

```
$ ls -l /dev/rfd0 /dev/rft0 /dev/ft0 /dev/fd0
brw-r-----  9 root   operator   2,   0 Nov 12 13:32 /dev/fd0
brw-r-----  2 root   operator   2,  32 Nov 12 13:33 /dev/ft0
crw-r-----  9 root   operator   9,   0 Nov 12 13:32 /dev/rfd0
crw-r-----  2 root   operator   9,  32 Oct 31 19:59 /dev/rft0
```

The letter at the beginning of the permissions shows that */dev/fd0* and */dev/ft0* are block devices, and */dev/rfd0* and */dev/rft0* are character devices. The major number of the character devices is 9, and the major number of the block devices is 2. In each case, they are separated from the minor number by a comma.

If you find a strange device which isn't listed here, you might get an idea from the company it keeps: here, for example, we know that */dev/fd0* is a floppy disk, and since the same driver also handles */dev/ft0*, it's reasonable to assume that it has something to do with a floppy disk. In fact, */dev/ft0* is the *floppy tape* driver, which handles tape drives connected to the floppy disk controller.

Long minor numbers

Traditionally, major and minor numbers are stored in the same machine word. Originally, the word was 16 bits long, and the major and minor numbers were each 8 bit quantities, which limited their maximum values to 255. Then System V.4 increased the word size to 32 bits, and gave 14 bits to the major numbers and 18 bits to the minor numbers, giving maximum values of 16383 and 262143 respectively. 4.4BSD also introduced 32 bit device numbers, but left the major number in the same place, and left it 8 bits long. The minor number takes up the rest of the word, and is thus 24 bits long with a hole in the middle.

Here's a overview:

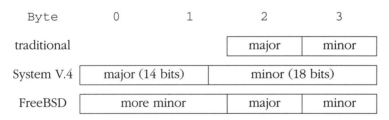

Figure 13-3: Major and minor numbers

FreeBSD uses the high-order minor for very special devices, such as control ports for disks. Normally, you'll never see them, but if you *do* find a minor number in the millions, it's not a bug, it's a feature.

Creating new device nodes

Just because the system supports a device doesn't mean that it automatically has a name. The name is an entry in the */dev* directory, and needs to be added manually. If you boot a different kernel, you may have a mismatch between your */dev* directory and your kernel—either you have names for devices which aren't included in the kernel, or you don't have names for devices which are included in the kernel. In addition, some devices don't have device nodes, for example Ethernet interfaces: they are treated differently by the *ifconfig* program.

As a result, you may have to create device nodes in order to access the devices. For example, the system supports any combination of SCSI devices on a controller, up to seven of them, but by default only one tape and four disks are configured. If you add a second tape drive or a fifth SCSI disk, you will need to add device nodes to be able to talk to them. You can do this the hard way or the easy way. The hard way uses the *mknod* command (see the man page *mknod(8)*). The easy way uses the script */dev/MAKEDEV*. For example, by default FreeBSD only supplies definitions for four SCSI disks. If you add a fifth SCSI disk, enter:

```
# cd /dev
# ./MAKEDEV da4                    create the device
# ./MAKEDEV da4s0a                 create the slice entries too
```

MAKEDEV assumes that you are in the */dev* directory, as indicated in this example.

The names that *MAKEDEV* chooses aren't the most intuitive. You may have difficulty deciding how to tell it to build the devices you want. Here's an overview:

Table 13-4. Parameters for *MAKEDEV*

Parameter	Function
all	Make all known devices, with a standard number of units. Beware of this option: it first removes any device nodes in */dev*.
std	Makes "standard" devices
local	Configuration specific devices
mach-4	Devices for Mach's XFree86 distribution. See *http://www.cs.hut.fi/lites.html* for more info on LITES.
wt*	QIC-02 interfaced cartridge tape. Don't use this for SCSI tape.
sa*	SCSI tape drives.
ft*	QIC-40/QIC-80 cartridge tapes interfaced via the floppy disk controller.
wd*	ST506, IDE, ESDI, RLL and similar disk drives.
fd*	Floppy disk drives, both 3½" and 5¼"
da*	SCSI disks
cd*	SCSI CD-ROM drives
mcd*	Mitsumi CD-ROM drives
scd*	Sony CD-ROM drives
matcd*	Matsushita and Panasonic CD-ROM drives
wcd*	IDE (ATAPI) CD-ROM drives

Parameter	Function
vn*	"vnode" virtual disks.
od*	Optical disks
vty*	Virtual console devices for *syscons* and *pcvt*
mse*	Logitech and ATI Inport bus mouse
psm*	PS/2 mouse
sysmouse	Mousesystems mouse emulator for *syscons*
refclock-*	Serial ports used by *xntpd* parse refclocks.
tty*	General purpose serial ports
cua*	Dialout serial ports
ttyA*	Specialix SI/XIO dialin ports
cuaA*	Specialix SI/XIO dialout ports
ttyD*	Digiboard - 16 dialin ports
cuaD*	Digiboard - 16 dialout ports
pty*	Set of 32 master and slave pseudo terminals
vty*	Virtual terminals using *syscons* and *pcvt* console drivers.
lpt*	Standard parallel printer.
uk*	"unknown" SCSI device (supports ioctl calls only).
worm*	WORM driver.
pt*	SCSI processor type (scanners, for example)
PC-CARD	PC-CARD (previously called PCMCIA) support
card*	PC-CARD slots
apm	Advanced Power Management BIOS
bpf*	Berkeley packet filter
speaker	PC speaker
tw*	xten power controller
snd*	various sound cards
pcaudio	PCM audio driver
socksys	iBCS2 socket system driver
vat	VAT compatibility audio driver (requires snd*)
gsc	Genius GS-4500 hand scanner
joy	PC joystick
tun*	Tunneling IP device
snp*	tty snoop devices
spigot	Video Spigot video acquisition card
ctx*	Cortex-I video acquisition card
meteor*	Matrox Meteor video acquisition card (PCI)
bktr*	Bt848 based video acquisition card (PCI)
qcam*	Connectix QuickCam™ parallel port camera
isdn*	ISDN devices
labpc*	National Instrument's Lab-PC and LAB-PC+

Parameter	Function
`perfmon`	CPU performance-monitoring counters
`pci`	PCI configuration-space access from user mode

The asterisk (*) after some names indicates that you should specify the number of devices to create. Be careful here: the number of devices is not the number of the last device. If you specify, say, `tty8`, *MAKEDEV* will create the devices */dev/tty0* to */dev/tty7*: it will not create a */dev/tty8*.

Also be careful of `./MAKEDEV all`: it first removes existing entries. If this happens to you, you can remake them again with a more specific application, such as in the example above.

File system types

FreeBSD supports a number of file system types. The most important are:

- *ufs* is the *UNIX File System*. All native disk files are of this type.

- *cd9660* is the ISO 9660 CD-ROM format with the so-called *Rock Ridge Extensions* which enable UNIX-like file names to be used. Use this file system type for all CD-ROMs, even if they don't have the Rock Ridge Extensions.

- *nfs* is the *Network File System*, a means of sharing file systems across a network. We'll look at it in Chapter 30, *The Network File System*.

- You can access Microsoft files with the *msdos* and *ntfs* file systems. See the man page *mount_msdos(8)* and page *mount_ntfs(8) for further details*.

Mounting file systems

Microsoft platforms identify partitions by letters which are assigned at boot time. There is no obvious relation between the partitions, and you have little control over the way the system assigns them. By contrast, all UNIX partitions have a specific relation to the *root file system*, which is called simply */.* This flexibility has one problem: you have the choice of where in the overall file system structure you put your individual file systems. You specify the location with the *mount* command. For example, you would typically mount a CD-ROM in the directory */cdrom*, but if you have three CD-ROM drives attached to your SCSI controller, you might prefer to mount them in the directories */cd0*, */cd1*, and */cd2*.[1] In order to mount a file system, you need to specify the device to be mounted, where it is to be mounted, and the type of file system (unless it is ufs). The *mount point*, (the directory where it is to be mounted) must already exist. To mount your second CD-ROM on */cd1*, you would enter:

---

1. This numbering is in keeping with the UNIX tradition of numbering starting from 0. There's nothing to stop you choosing some other name, of course.

```
# mkdir /cd1                        only if it doesn't exist
# mount -t cd9660 -o ro /dev/cd1a /cd1
```

When the system boots, it calls the startup script */etc/rc*, which amongst other things automatically mounts the file systems. All you need to do is to supply the information: what is to be mounted, and where? This is in the file */etc/fstab*. If you come from a System V environment, you'll notice significant difference in format—see the man page *fstab(5)* for the full story. A typical */etc/fstab* might look like:

```
/dev/wd0a       /               ufs       rw 1 1  root file system
/dev/wd0s1b     none            swap      sw 0 0  swap
/dev/wd0s1e     /usr            ufs       rw 2 2  /usr file system
/dev/sd1e       /src            ufs       rw 2 2  additional file system
proc            /proc           procfs    rw 0 0  proc pseudo-file system
/dev/cd0a       /cdrom          cd9660    ro 0 0  CD-ROM
presto:/        /presto/root    nfs       rw 0 0  NFS file systems on other systems
presto:/usr     /presto/usr     nfs       rw 0 0
presto:/home    /presto/home    nfs       rw 0 0
presto:/S       /S              nfs       rw 0 0
radio:/C        /C              nfs       rw 0 0
```

The format of the file is reasonably intelligible:

- The first column gives the name of the device (if it's a real file system), or the name of the remote file system for NFS mounts.

- The second column specifies the mount point.

- The third column specifies the type of file system. Local file systems on hard disk are always *ufs*, and file systems on CD-ROM are *cd9660*. Remote file systems are always *nfs*. Specify swap partitions with *swap*, and the *proc* file system with *proc*.

- The fourth column contains rw for file systems which can be read or written, ro for file systems (like CD-ROM) which can only be written, and sw for swap partitions.

- The fifth and sixth columns are used by the *dump* and fsck programs. You won't normally need to change them. Enter 1 for a root file system, 2 for other ufs file systems, and 0 for everything else.

Unmounting file systems

When you mount a file system, the system assumes it is going to stay there, and in the interests of efficiency it delays writing data back to the file system. This is the same effect we discussed on page 220. As a result, if you want to stop using a file system, you need to tell the system about it. You do this with the *umount* command. Note the spelling—there's no **n** in the command name.

You need to do this even with read-only media such as CD-ROMs: the system assumes it can access the data from a mounted file system, and it gets quite unhappy if it can't. Where possible, it locks removable media so that you can't remove them from the device until you unmount them.

Using *umount* is straightforward: just tell it what to unmount, either the device name or the

236

directory name. For example, to unmount the CD-ROM we mounted in the example above, you could enter one of these commands:

```
# umount /dev/cd1a
# umount /cd1
```

Before unmounting a file system, *umount* checks that nobody is using it. If somebody is using it, it will refuse to unmount it with a message like umount: /cd1: Device busy. This message often occurs because you have changed your directory to a directory on the file system you want to remove. For example (which also shows the usefulness of having directory names in the prompt):

```
=== root@freebie (/dev/ttyp2) /cd1 16 -> umount /cd1
umount: /cd1: Device busy
=== root@freebie (/dev/ttyp2) /cd1 17 -> cd
=== root@freebie (/dev/ttyp2) ~ 18 -> umount /cd1
=== root@freebie (/dev/ttyp2) ~ 19 ->
```

Overview of FreeBSD devices

Every UNIX system has its own peculiarities when it comes to device names and usage. Even if you're used to UNIX, you'll find the following table useful.

Table 13-5. FreeBSD device names

Device	Description
bpf0	Berkeley packet filter—see the description of bpfilter on page 355
cd0a	First SCSI CD-ROM drive
ch0	SCSI CD-ROM changer (juke box)
console	System console, the device which receives console messages. Initially it is /dev/ttyv0, but it can be changed
cuaa0	First serial port in callout mode
cuaia0	First serial port in callout mode, initial state. Note the letter i for *initial*.
cuala0	First serial port in callout mode, lock state. Note the letter l for *lock*.
da0	First SCSI disk drive, block device. See Chapter 2, *Before you install*, page 36, for a complete list of disk drive names.
drum	System paging device (i.e. swap partition). The name reminds of the days when the system really did page to a magnetic drum.
ersa0	First SCSI tape drive, eject on close mode
fd	File descriptor pseudo-devices: a directory containing pseudo-devices which, when opened, return a duplicate of the file descriptor with the same number. For example, if you open */dev/fd/0*, you will get another handle on your *stdin* stream (file descriptor 0).

Device	Description
fd0	The first floppy disk drive, accessed as a file system
fd0.1200	The first floppy disk drive, accessed as a 5¼" drive file system (1200 kB)
fd0.1440	The first floppy disk drive, accessed as a 3½" drive file system (1440 kB)
fd0a	The first floppy disk drive, accessed as a file system. Floppy disks are not partitioned in the same way as hard disks, and the names *fd0a, fd0b, fd0c, fd0d, fd0e, fd0f, fd0g,* and *fd0h* all refer to the same device.
ft0	"Floppy tape": A device for QIC-40 and QIC-80 tape devices. These devices are not fully supported as tape drives—see the man page on the system for more details.
kmem	Kernel virtual memory pseudo-device
lpctl0	Control port of first parallel printer
lpt0	First parallel printer
matcd0a	Matsushita CD-ROM
matcd0la	Matsushita CD-ROM with tray locking: the CD-ROM cannot be removed from the drive until it is unmounted
mcd0a	Mitsumi CD-ROM
mem	Physical virtual memory pseudo-device
mse0	Bus mouse
nrsa0	First SCSI tape drive, no-rewind mode
nrwt0	First QIC-36 tape drive, no-rewind mode
null	The "bit bucket". Write data to this device if you never want to see it again.
ptyp0	First master pseudo-terminal. Master pseudo-terminals are named *ptyp0* through *ptypv, ptyq0* through *ptyqv, ptyr0* through *ptyrv, ptys0* through *ptysv, ptyP0* through *ptyPv, ptyQ0* through *ptyQv, ptyR0* through *ptyRv* and *ptyS0* through *ptySv.*
rcd0a	First SCSI CD-ROM drive, raw access
rch0.ctl	SCSI CD-ROM changer (juke box)
rda0	First SCSI disk drive, raw mode. See Chapter 2, *Before you install*, page 36, for a complete list of disk drive names.
rfd0	The first floppy disk drive, raw mode
rft0	"Floppy tape", raw mode
rmatcd0a	Matsushita CD-ROM, raw mode
rmatcd0la	Matsushita CD-ROM with tray locking, raw mode
rmcd0c	Mitsumi CD-ROM, raw mode for playing audio
rsa0	First SCSI tape drive, rewind on close mode

Device	Description
rscd0c	Sony CD-ROM with proprietary interface, raw mode for playing audio
rwd0	First IDE or similar disk drive, raw mode. See Chapter 2, *Before you install*, page 36, for a complete list of disk drive names.
rwt0	First QIC-36 tape drive, rewind mode
scd0a	Sony CD-ROM with proprietary interface
speaker	PC speaker device
tty	Current controlling terminal
ttyd0	First serial port in callin mode
ttyid0	First serial port in callin mode, initial state
ttyld0	First serial port in callin mode, lock state
ttyp0	First slave pseudo-terminal. Slave pseudo-terminals are named *ttyp0* through *ttypv*, *ttyq0* through *ttyqv*, *ttyr0* through *ttyrv*, *ttys0* through *ttysv*, *ttyP0* through *ttyPv*, *ttyQ0* through *ttyQv*, *ttyR0* through *ttyRv* and *ttyS0* through *ttySv*. Some processes, such as *xterm*, only look at *ttyp0* through *ttysv*.
ttyv0	First virtual tty. This is the display with which the system starts. Up to 10 virtual ttys can be activated by adding the appropriate *getty* information in the file */etc/ttys*. See Chapter 24, *Serial communications and modems*, page 437, for further details.
tw0	TW-523 power line interface driver
ttyv0	Console virtual terminals
wd0	First IDE or similar disk drive, block device. See Chapter 2, *Before you install*, page 36, for a complete list of disk drive names.
zero	Dummy device which always returns the value 0 when read

You'll note a number of different modes associated with the serial ports. See Chapter 24, *Serial communications and modems*, page 427, for more details.

Virtual terminals

As we have seen, UNIX is a multitasking operating system, but a PC generally only has one screen. FreeBSD solves this problem with *virtual terminals*. When in text mode, you can change between up to 16 different screens with the combination of the **Alt** key and a function key. The devices are named */dev/ttyv0* through */dev/ttyv15*, and correspond to the keystrokes **Alt-F1** through **Alt-F16**. By default, three virtual terminals are active: */dev/ttyv0* through */dev/ttyv2*. The system console is the virtual terminal */dev/ttyv0*, and that's what you see when you boot the machine. To activate additional virtual terminals, edit the file */etc/ttys*. There you will find:

```
ttyv0 "/usr/libexec/getty Pc"          cons25    on  secure
ttyv1 "/usr/libexec/getty Pc"          cons25    on  secure
ttyv2 "/usr/libexec/getty Pc"          cons25    on  secure
ttyv3 "/usr/libexec/getty Pc"          cons25    off secure
```

The keywords on and off refer to the state of the terminal: to enable one, set its state to on. To enable extra virtual terminals, add a line with the corresponding terminal name, in the range */dev/ttyv4* to */dev/ttyv15*.

In addition, you may need to create the device nodes if they don't already exist. By default, the system contains four virtual terminal devices in the */dev* directory. If you use more than this number, you must create them, either with *MAKEDEV* (see page 233), or with *mknod* (see page *mknod(8)*). When calculating how many devices you need, note that if you intend to run X11, you need a terminal device without a *getty* for the X server. For example, if you have enabled */dev/ttyv3*, */dev/ttyv4*, and */dev/ttyv5*, and you also want to run X, you will need a total of 7 virtual terminals (*/dev/ttyv0* through */dev/ttyv6*). With *MAKEDEV*, you specify how many virtual terminals you need:

```
# cd /dev
# ./MAKEDEV vty7              make 7 vtys
```

Alternatively, you can do this with *mknod*:

```
# cd /dev
# ls -1 ttyv0
crw-------  1 root  wheel  12,   0 Nov 28 10:25 ttyv0
# mknod ttyv3 c 12 3
# mknod ttyv4 c 12 4
# mknod ttyv5 c 12 5
# mknod ttyv6 c 12 6
```

In this example, you list the entry for */dev/ttyv0* in order to check the *major device number* of the virtual terminals (that's the 12, in this example; it may change from one release to another). You need to specify this number to *mknod*. For more details about major and minor device numbers, see page 231.

After you have edited */etc/ttys*, and possibly created the device nodes, you need to tell the system to re-read it in order to start the terminals. Do this as root with this command:

```
# kill -1 1
```

Process 1 is *init*—see page 190 for more details.

Pseudo-terminals

In addition to virtual terminals, FreeBSD offers an additional class of terminals called *pseudo-terminals*. They come in pairs: a *master device*, also called a *pty* (pronounced *pity*) is used only by processes which use the interface, and has a name like */dev/ptyp0*. The *slave device* looks like a terminal, and has a name like */dev/ttyp0*. Any process can open it without any special knowledge of the interface. These terminals are used for network connections such as *xterm*, *telnet* and *rlogin*. You don't need a *getty* for pseudo-terminals.

You need one pseudo-terminal for each terminal-like connection, for example for an *xterm*. It's quite easy to run out of them; if you do, you can configure more—see page 354. In addition, generate the device nodes. For example, to generate a second set of 32 pseudo-terminals, enter:

```
# cd /dev
# ./MAKEDEV pty1
```

You can generate up to 256 pseudo-terminals. They are named *ttyp0* through *ttypv*, *ttyq0* through *ttyqv*, *ttyr0* through *ttyrv*, *ttys0* through *ttysv*, *ttyP0* through *ttyPv*, *ttyQ0* through *ttyQv*, *ttyR0* through *ttyRv* and *ttyS0* through *ttySv*. To create each set of 32 terminals, use the number of the set: the first set is `pty0`, and the eighth set is `pty7`. Note that some processes, such as *xterm*, only look at *ttyp0* through *ttysv*.

14

Disks

One of the most important parts of running any computer system is handling data on disk. We have already looked at UNIX file handling in Chapter 13, *File systems*. In this chapter, we'll look at two ways to add another disk to your system.

Adding a hard disk

When you installed FreeBSD, you created file systems on a first hard disk. At the same time you had the option of creating file systems on other disks on the system. As I said at the time, it's a good thing to do it then, because it's *much* easier that way. Unfortunately, that's not always possible: you might decide that you need more disk space, and so you buy a new hard disk. In this section, we'll look at how to set it up to work under FreeBSD.

The real problem with adding a second disk is that the "easy-to-use" programs to set them up are not always 100% reliable, and you may need to do everything by hand. It is possible to use *sysinstall* to do the job, but there are a few nasty rough corners that you might run up against. In this section we'll look at *sysinstall*, and on page 252 we'll see how to do it manually if *sysinstall* won't cooperate.

We've been through all the details of disk layout and slices and partitions in Chapter 2, *Before you install*, so I won't repeat them here. Basically, to add a new disk to the system, you need to:

- Possibly, format the disk. More and more, modern disks come pre-formatted, and you will only need to format them if there are defects on the disk, or if it's ancient.

- If you want to share with other operating systems, create a Microsoft style partition table on the disk. We looked at the concepts on page 72.

- Define a FreeBSD slice (which Microsoft calls a "partition").

- Define the partitions in the FreeBSD slice.

- Tell the system about the file systems and where to mount them.

- Create the file systems.

These are exactly the same operations as we performed in Chapter 5, *Installing FreeBSD*.

Disk hardware installation

Before you can do anything with the disk, you have to install it in the system. To do this, you shut down the system and turn the power off. If the disk is IDE, and you already have an IDE disk on the controller, you need to set the second disk as "slave" drive. *And* you may have to set the first disk as "master" drive: if you only have one drive, you don't set any jumpers, but if you have two drives, some disks require you to set jumpers on both disks. If you don't do this, the system will appear to hang during the power-on self test, and will finally report some kind of disk error.

Adding a SCSI disk is more complicated. Up to 8 SCSI devices can be connected to most systems (newer SCSI variants allow 16), but this number includes the host adapter. Typically, your first SCSI disk will have the SCSI ID 0, and the host adapter will have the SCSI ID 7. Traditionally, the IDs 4, 5, and 6 are reserved for tape and CD-ROM drives, and the IDs 0 to 3 are reserved for disks, though FreeBSD doesn't impose any restrictions on what goes where.

Whatever kind of disk you're adding, look at the boot messages, which you can retrieve with the *dmesg* command. For example, if you're planning to add a SCSI device, you might see:

```
ahc0: <Adaptec 2940 SCSI adapter> rev 0x03 int a irq 11 on pci0.9.0
ahc0: aic7870 Single Channel A, SCSI Id=7, 16/255 SCBs
further down...
Waiting 3 seconds for SCSI devices to settle
sa0 at ahc0 bus 0 target 3 lun 0
sa0: <EXABYTE EXB-8505SMBANSH2 0793> Removable Sequential Access SCSI-2 device
sa0: 5.000MB/s transfers (5.000MHz, offset 11)
sa1 at ahc0 bus 0 target 4 lun 0
sa1: <ARCHIVE Python 28849-XXX 4.CM> Removable Sequential Access SCSI-2 device
sa1: 5.000MB/s transfers (5.000MHz, offset 15)
sa2 at ahc0 bus 0 target 5 lun 0
sa2: <TANDBERG TDC 3800 -03:> Removable Sequential Access SCSI-CCS device
sa2: 3.300MB/s transfers
pass4 at ahc0 bus 0 target 4 lun 1
pass4: <ARCHIVE Python 28849-XXX 4.CM> Removable Changer SCSI-2 device
pass4: 5.000MB/s transfers (5.000MHz, offset 15)
da0 at ahc0 bus 0 target 2 lun 0
da0: <CONNER CFP4207S  4.28GB 2847> Fixed Direct Access SCSI-2 device
da0: 3.300MB/s transfers, Tagged Queueing Enabled
da0: 4096MB (8388608 512 byte sectors: 64H 32S/T 4096C)
cd0 at ahc0 bus 0 target 6 lun 0
cd0: <NRC MBR-7 110> Removable CD-ROM SCSI-2 device
cd0: 3.300MB/s transfers
cd0: cd present [322265 x 2048 byte records]
changing root device to wd0s1a
```

This output shows three tape drives (*sa0*, *sa1* and *sa2*), a CD-ROM drive (*cd0*), a tape changer (*pass4*), and also a disk drive *da0* on target 2.

Installing an external SCSI device

External SCSI devices are connected together by cables. Each device has two connectors: one goes towards the host adapter, and the other towards the next device. This method is called *daisy chaining*. At the end of the chain, the spare connector is usually plugged with a *terminator*, a set of resistors designed to keep noise off the bus. Some devices have internal terminators, however. When installing an external device, you will have to do one of the following:

- If you are installing a first external device (one connected via the cable connector on the backplane of the host adapter), you will have to ensure that the device provides termination. Assuming you already have an internal device, you will also have to stop the host adapter from providing termination. Modern SCSI host adapters can decide whether they need to terminate or not, but older host adapters have resistor packs. In the latter case, remove these resistor packs.

- If you are adding an additional external device, you have two choices: you can remove a cable in the middle of the daisy chain and plug it into your new device. You then connect a new cable from your device to the device from which you removed the original cable.

- Alternatively, you can add the device at the end of the chain. Remove the terminator or turn off the termination, and plug your cable into the spare socket. Insert the terminator in your device (or turn termination on).

Installing an internal SCSI device

Installing an internal SCSI device is much the same as installing an external device. Instead of daisy chains, you have a flat band cable with a number of connectors. Find one which suits you, and plug it into the device. Again, you need to think about termination:

- If you are installing the device at the end of the chain, it should have termination enabled. You should also remove the terminators from the device that was previously at the end of the chain.

- If you are installing the device in the middle of the chain, make sure it does not have termination enabled.

In this case, we'll install a CDC 94181 drive in the existing SCSI chain. We could be in for a surprise: the device ID we get for the new drive depends on what is currently on the chain. For example, we might have a chain with a single drive on it:

```
da0 at ahc0 bus 0 target 2 lun 0
da0: <CONNER CFP4207S  4.28GB 2847> Fixed Direct Access SCSI-2 device
da0: 3.300MB/s transfers, Tagged Queueing Enabled
da0: 4096MB (8388608 512 byte sectors: 64H 32S/T 4096C)
```

This drive on target 2. If we put our new drive on target 0 and reboot, we see:

```
da0 at ahc0 bus 0 target 0 lun 0
da0: <CDC 94181-15 0293> Fixed Direct Access SCSI-CCS device
da0: 3.300MB/s transfers
da0: 573MB (1173930 512 byte sectors: 64H 32S/T 573C)
da1 at ahc0 bus 0 target 2 lun 0
da1: <CONNER CFP4207S  4.28GB 2847> Fixed Direct Access SCSI-2 device
da1: 3.300MB/s transfers, Tagged Queueing Enabled
da1: 4096MB (8388608 512 byte sectors: 64H 32S/T 4096C)
```

Since the target ID of the new disk is lower than the target ID of the old disk, the system recognizes the new disk as *da0*, and our previous *da0* has become *da1*.

This change of disk ID can be a problem. You'll have to edit */etc/fstab* in order to be able to mount any file systems which are on the disk. Alternatively, you can wire down the device names—see page 344 for more details. The alternative is to change the SCSI IDs. We do that, and the CDC drive becomes *da1*:

```
da0 at ahc0 bus 0 target 0 lun 0
da0: <CONNER CFP4207S  4.28GB 2847> Fixed Direct Access SCSI-2 device
da0: 3.300MB/s transfers, Tagged Queueing Enabled
da0: 4096MB (8388608 512 byte sectors: 64H 32S/T 4096C)
da1 at ahc0 bus 0 target 2 lun 0
da1: <CDC 94181-15 0293> Fixed Direct Access SCSI-CCS device
da1: 3.300MB/s transfers
da1: 573MB (1173930 512 byte sectors: 64H 32S/T 573C)
```

Formatting the disk

Formatting is the process of rewriting every sector on the disk with a specific data pattern, one that the electronics find most difficult to reproduce: if they can read this pattern, they can read anything. Microsoft calls this a *low-level format*. Obviously it destroys any existing data, so

If you have anything you want to keep, back it up before formatting.

Most modern disks don't need formatting unless they're damaged. In particular, formatting will not help if you're having configuration problems, if you can't get PPP to work, or you're running out of disk space.[1]

If you do need to format a SCSI disk, use *camcontrol*. *camcontrol* is a control program for SCSI devices, and it includes a lot of useful functions which you can read about in the man page. To format a disk, use the following syntax:

```
# camcontrol format da0
```

At the time of writing, the *format* subcommand of *camcontrol* has not been implemented. If it doesn't work for you, you can go back to basics and issue the raw SCSI format command with this invocation:

---

1. Well, it *will* solve the disk space problem, but not in the manner you probably desire.

```
# camcontrol cmd -n da -u 0 -v -t 7200 -c "4 0 0 0 0 0"
```

Note that here you specify the name of the disk as the type (da) and the unit number (-u 0).
If you wanted to format */dev/da9*, you would use the option -u 9.

The other parameters are:

- -v: be verbose.

- -t 7200: time out after two hours (7200 seconds). On a very large disk, you may find that
  two hours is not enough to format it. In this case, you'll need to increase this value.

  If the format finishes very quickly—in about 5 minutes—there's a good chance that it is
  faking the FORMAT UNIT command. It doesn't support it, so it just goes away and returns
  in a few minutes having done nothing.

- -c "4 0 0 0 0 0" is the SCSI "FORMAT UNIT" command. The disk goes away and
  formats itself.

> *Remember that low level formatting a disk destroys all data on the
> disk. Before using the command, make sure that you need to do so:
> there are relatively few cases that call for low-level formatting a disk.
> About the only reasons are if you want to change the physical sector
> size of the disk, or if you are getting "medium format corrupted"
> errors from the disk in response to read and write requests.*

FreeBSD can format only floppies and SCSI disks. If you find you have to format an IDE disk,
you'll have to use the format utility in your system BIOS. Fortunately, you almost never need to
reformat a disk.

Using sysinstall

If you can, use *sysinstall* to partition your disk. Looking at the *dmesg* output for our CDC
94181 SCSI disk, we see:

```
da1 at ahc0 bus 0 target 2 lun 0
da1: <CDC 94181-15 0293> Fixed Direct Access SCSI-CCS device
da1: 3.300MB/s transfers
da1: 573MB (1173930 512 byte sectors: 64H 32S/T 573C)
```

We start *sysinstall* with:

```
# /stand/sysinstall
```

You will see the standard installation screen (see Chapter 5, *Installing FreeBSD*, page 70).
Select Index, then Partition, and you will see the following screen:

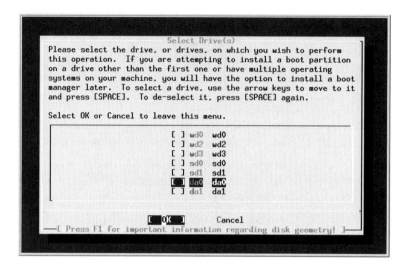

Don't be put off by the drive names sd0 and sd1. These are the old names for the SCSI drives da0 and da1. Currently, *sysinstall* shows both the old and the new names.

In this case, we want to partition */dev/da1*, so we position the cursor on da0 (as shown) and press **Space** (not **Enter**; that would just take us back to the previous menu). At this point you may see a warning message that the drive geometry is incorrect. If you do, it's probably a bug: we saw in the *dmesg* output that the probes had no trouble with the geometry, and geometry is not of great importance for a SCSI drive anyway: you only need it if you want to boot from the drive. If you get this message, you press **Enter** to continue.

Next, we see:

```
Disk name:     da1                                    FDISK Partition Editor
DISK Geometry: 9782 cyls/10 heads/12 sectors = 1173840 sectors

   Offset      Size       End    Name PType      Desc  Subtype     Flags

        0        12        11      -      6    unused        0
       12   1173828   1173839   da1s1      3   freebsd      165     C
  1173840        90   1173929      -      6    unused        0




The following commands are supported (in upper or lower case):

A = Use Entire Disk     B = Bad Block Scan      C = Create Slice
D = Delete Slice        G = Set Drive Geometry  S = Set Bootable
T = Change Type         U = Undo All Changes    W = Write Changes


Use F1 or ? to get more help, arrow keys to select.
```

Here we see that the disk currently contains three partitions:

- The first starts at offset 0, and has a length of 12. This is *not* unused, no matter what the description says. It's the partition table, padded to the length of a "track".

- The next partition takes up the bulk of the drive and is the current FreeBSD partition.

- Finally, we have 90 sectors left over as a result of the partitioning scheme. Sometimes this can be much larger—I have seen values as high as 35 MB. This is the price we pay for compatibility with Microsoft partitioning.

We're using this disk for FreeBSD only, and we don't want to waste even this much space, so we'll select the option "use whole disk for FreeBSD", the so-called "dangerously dedicated" mode. This term comes partially from superstition and partially because some BIOSes expect to find a partition table on the first sector of a disk, and they can't access the disk if they don't find one. If your BIOS has this bug, you'll find this one out pretty quickly when you try to boot. If it doesn't fail on the first boot, it won't fail.

To use the whole disk, we first delete the current partition: we press the cursor down key until it highlights the FreeBSD partition. Then we press **d**, and the three partitions are joined into one, marked unused.

The next step is to create a new partition using the entire disk. We press a, and get the following message:

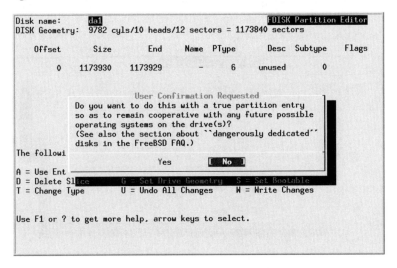

We've already decided to use the whole disk, so we move the cursor right to No, as shown in the figure, and press **Enter**. Then we press q to exit the partition editor, get back to the function index, and select Label. We see:

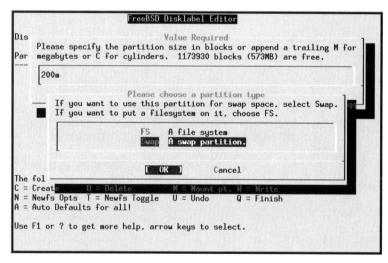

We want to create two partitions: first, a swap partition of 200 Megabytes, and then a file system taking up the rest of the disk. We press C, and are shown a submenu offering us all 1173930 blocks on the disk. We erase that and enter 200m, which represents 200 Megabytes. Then we press **Enter**, and another submenu appears, asking us what kind of slice it is. We move the cursor down to select A swap partition:

Next, we press c again to create a new partition. This time, we accept the offer of the rest of the space on the disk, 764330 sectors, we select A file system, and we are presented with yet another menu asking for the name of the file system. We enter the name, which happens to be /S:

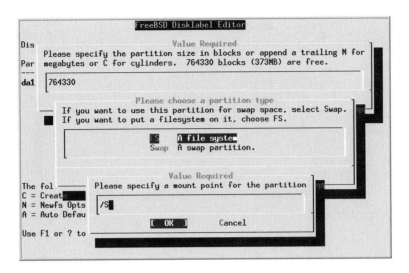

After pressing **Enter**, we see:

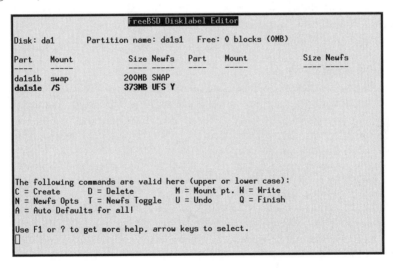

Finally, we press W to tell the disk label editor to perform the function. We get an additional warning screen:

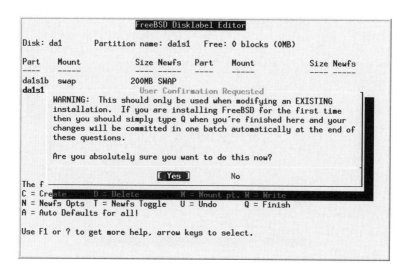

Since we're doing this on-line, that's OK. We select `Yes`, and *sysinstall* creates the file system and mounts both it and the swap partition. This can take quite a while. Don't try to do anything with the drive until it's finished.

Doing it the hard way

Unfortunately, sometimes you may not be able to use the *sysinstall* method. That leaves us with the old way to add disks. The only difference is that this time, we need to use different tools. In the following sections, we'll look at what we have to do to install an old CDC SCSI drive, even older than the one in the previous section.

Creating a partition table

We looked at how to format the disk on page 246. The next step is to create a Microsoft style partition table on the disk. We looked at the concepts on page 72, but this time we use different tools. As in Microsoft, the partitioning program is called *fdisk*, and the man page is on page 621. In the following discussion, you'll find a pocket calculator useful.

Depending on what was on the disk before, *fdisk* could get sufficiently confused to not work correctly. If you don't format the disk, it's a good idea to overwrite the beginning of the disk with *dd*:

```
# dd if=/dev/zero of=/dev/rda1 count=100
100+0 records in
100+0 records out
51200 bytes transferred in 1 secs (51200 bytes/sec)
```

Next, we look at what's on the disk. This doesn't seem to make much sense, since we have just overwritten the contents, but *fdisk* will tell us one thing of importance: the disk geometry.

We'll need this later on.

```
# fdisk /dev/rda1
****** Working on device /dev/rda1 ******
parameters extracted from in-core disklabel are:
cylinders=967 heads=9 sectors/track=35 (315 blks/cyl)

parameters to be used for BIOS calculations are:
cylinders=967 heads=9 sectors/track=35 (315 blks/cyl)

fdisk: Invalid fdisk partition table found
Warning: BIOS sector numbering starts with sector 1
Information from DOS bootblock is:
The data for partition 0 is:
<UNUSED>
The data for partition 1 is:
<UNUSED>
The data for partition 2 is:
<UNUSED>
The data for partition 3 is:
sysid 165,(FreeBSD/NetBSD/386BSD)
    start 1, size 304604 (148 Meg), flag 80
        beg: cyl 0/ sector 2/ head 0;
        end: cyl 967/ sector 1/ head 0
```

You'll notice that *fdisk* has decided to put a FreeBSD partition in partition 3. That's not what we want in this case: we want a Microsoft partition as well. This is a small disk by modern standards, only 150 MB, so we'll assign 100 MB to FreeBSD, and leave 50 MB for Microsoft. Our resulting partition table should look like:

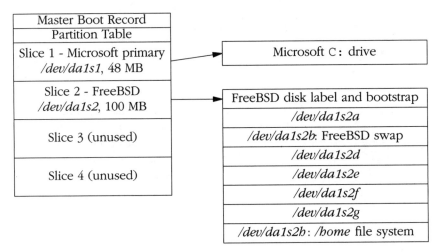

Figure 14-1: Partition table on second FreeBSD disk

The Master Boot Record and the Partition Table take up the first sector of the disk, and the rest can be divided between the partitions. It's easy to make a mistake in specifying the parameters, and *fdisk* performs as good as no checking. You can easily create a partition table that has absolutely no relationship with reality, so it's a good idea to calculate them in advance. For each partition, we need to know three things:

- The *partition type*, which *fdisk* calls *sysid*. This is a number describing what the partition is used for. FreeBSD partitions have partition type 165, and modern (release 4 and later) Microsoft partitions have type 6.

- The *start sector*, the first sector in the partition.

- The *end sector* for the partition.

In addition, we need to decide which partition is the *active* partition, the partition from which we want to boot. In this case, it doesn't make any difference, since we won't be booting from the disk, but it's always a good idea to set it anyway.

We specify the partitions we don't want by giving them a type, start sector and end sector of 0. As we have seen, our disk has 304605 sectors, numbered 0 to 304604. Partitions should start and end on a cylinder boundary. We want the FreeBSD partitions to be about 100 MB, or 204,800 sectors, which leaves 99,806 sectors for the Microsoft partition. We know the geometry from the *fdisk* output above: `cylinders=967 heads=9 sectors/track=35 (315 blks/cyl)`. So our 204,800 sectors would take up 204800 / 315, or 650.1587302 cylinders. Since we want to use this disk primarily for FreeBSD, we'll round this value up to 651 cylinders, or 205,065 sectors. This leaves 316 cylinders, less the first sector on the disk, for Microsoft, a total of (316 * 315) - 1 or 99,539 sectors. Our resulting information is:

Table 14-2. sample *fdisk* parameters

Partition number	Partition type	Start sector	Size
1	6	1	99539
2	165	304604	205065
3	0	0	
4	0	0	

If you're unlucky, *fdisk* will give you a completely different idea of the disk geometry from what *scsiformat* did. Possibly you can decide by examination which program is wrong, or maybe you can look at the *dmesg* output for a tie-breaker. In all cases I have seen, it has been *fdisk* that returned the incorrect information, and only when the disk did not have a valid partition table. For example, this happened with a disk formatted for BSD/OS:

```
# scsiformat da1
MICROP
2112-15MQ1094802
HQ48

Mode data length:  35
Medium type:  0
Device Specific Parameter:  0
Block descriptor length:  8
Density code:  0
Number of blocks:  2051615
Reserved:  0
Block length:  512
PS:  1
Reserved:  0
```

254

```
Page code:  4
Page length:  22
Number of Cylinders:  1760
Number of Heads:  15
Starting Cylinder-Write Precompensation:  0
Starting Cylinder-Reduced Write Current:  0
Drive Step Rate:  0
Landing Zone Cylinder:  0
Reserved:  0
RPL:  0
Rotational Offset:  0
Reserved:  0
Medium Rotation Rate:  5400
Reserved:  0
Reserved:  0
# fdisk da1
****** Working on device /dev/rda1 ******
parameters extracted from in-core disklabel are:
cylinders=160 heads=256 sectors/track=50 (12800 blks/cyl)

 Figures below won't work with BIOS for partitions not in cyl 1
parameters to be used for BIOS calculations are:
cylinders=160 heads=256 sectors/track=50 (12800 blks/cyl)

Warning: BIOS sector numbering starts with sector 1
Information from DOS bootblock is:
The data for partition 0 is:
sysid 255,(BBT (Bad Blocks Table))
    start 1023744, size 2108293151 (1029440 Meg), flag 0
        beg: cyl 768/ sector 15/ head 147;
        end: cyl 0/ sector 0/ head 255
The data for partition 1 is:
sysid 101,(Novell Netware 3.xx)
    start 1646292846, size 1814062195 (885772 Meg), flag 0
        beg: cyl 356/ sector 50/ head 0;
        end: cyl 256/ sector 50/ head 114
The data for partition 2 is:
sysid 0,(unused)
    start 0, size 0 (0 Meg), flag 61
        beg: cyl 364/ sector 37/ head 98;
        end: cyl 0/ sector 0/ head 0
The data for partition 3 is:
<UNUSED>
```

Looking at the output from *dmesg*, we see:

```
(aha0:1:0): "MICROP 2112-15MQ1094802 HQ48" type 0 fixed SCSI 2
da1(aha0:1:0): Direct-Access 1001MB (2051615 512 byte sectors)
da1(aha0:1:0): with 1760 cyls, 15 heads, and an average 77 sectors/track
```

In this case, then, you should use the parameters 1760 cylinders, 15 heads, and 77 sectors per track. What's less obvious here is the number of cylinders: fdisk doesn't have an opinion, and *scsiformat* and *dmesg* decided it has 2,051,615 sectors. Unfortunately, if you calculate the number according to the formula *cylinders × heads × sectors*, you'll come up with a different result: in this case 1760 × 15 × 77 = 2,032,800. How come? The disks report the total number of sectors, including spare tracks and such, but you can't use them all. The 2,032,800 is the correct number, and if you try to specify 2,051,615 to *disklabel*, it will spit out lots of messages about partitions which go beyond the end of the disk.

Next we run *fdisk* in earnest by specifying the -i option. During this time, you will see messages on the console:

```
da1: invalid primary partition table: no magic
```

The message *no magic* doesn't mean that *fdisk* is out of purple smoke. It refers to the fact that it didn't find the so-called *magic number*, which identifies the partition table. Since we don't have a partition table yet, this message isn't surprising. It's also completely harmless.

fdisk prompts interactively:

```
# fdisk -i /dev/rda1
******* Working on device /dev/rda1 *******
parameters extracted from in-core disklabel are:
cylinders=967 heads=9 sectors/track=35 (315 blks/cyl)

parameters to be used for BIOS calculations are:
cylinders=967 heads=9 sectors/track=35 (315 blks/cyl)

Do you want to change our idea of what BIOS thinks ? [n] Enter pressed
fdisk: Invalid fdisk partition table found
Warning: BIOS sector numbering starts with sector 1
Information from DOS bootblock is:
The data for partition 0 is:
<UNUSED>
Do you want to change it? [n] y
Supply a decimal value for "sysid" [0] 6
Supply a decimal value for "start" [0] 1
Supply a decimal value for "size" [0] 99539
Explicitly specifiy beg/end address ? [n] Enter pressed
sysid 6,(Primary 'big' DOS (> 32MB))
    start 1, size 99539 (48 Meg), flag 0
        beg: cyl 0/ sector 2/ head 0;
        end: cyl 315/ sector 35/ head 8
Are we happy with this entry? [n] y
The data for partition 1 is:
<UNUSED>
Do you want to change it? [n] y
Supply a decimal value for "sysid" [0] 165
Supply a decimal value for "start" [0] 99540
Supply a decimal value for "size" [0] 205065
Explicitly specifiy beg/end address ? [n] Enter pressed
sysid 165,(FreeBSD/NetBSD/386BSD)
    start 99540, size 205065 (100 Meg), flag 0
        beg: cyl 316/ sector 1/ head 0;
        end: cyl 966/ sector 35/ head 8
Are we happy with this entry? [n] y
The data for partition 2 is:
<UNUSED>
Do you want to change it? [n] Enter pressed
The data for partition 3 is:
sysid 165,(FreeBSD/NetBSD/386BSD)
    start 1, size 304604 (148 Meg), flag 80
        beg: cyl 0/ sector 2/ head 0;
        end: cyl 967/ sector 1/ head 0
Do you want to change it? [n] y

The static data for the DOS partition 3 has been reinitialized to:
sysid 165,(FreeBSD/NetBSD/386BSD)
    start 1, size 304604 (148 Meg), flag 80
        beg: cyl 0/ sector 2/ head 0;
        end: cyl 967/ sector 1/ head 0
Supply a decimal value for "sysid" [165] 0
Supply a decimal value for "start" [1] 0
Supply a decimal value for "size" [304604] 0
Explicitly specifiy beg/end address ? [n] Enter pressed
sysid 0,(unused)
```

```
        start 0, size 0 (0 Meg), flag 80
            beg: cyl 0/ sector 0/ head 0;
            end: cyl 0/ sector 0/ head 0
Are we happy with this entry? [n] y
Do you want to change the active partition? [n] y
Supply a decimal value for "active partition" [3] 1
Are you happy with this choice [n] y

We haven't changed the partition table yet.  This is your last chance.
parameters extracted from in-core disklabel are:
cylinders=967 heads=9 sectors/track=35 (315 blks/cyl)

parameters to be used for BIOS calculations are:
cylinders=967 heads=9 sectors/track=35 (315 blks/cyl)

Information from DOS bootblock is:
0: sysid 6,(Primary 'big' DOS (> 32MB))
        start 1, size 99539 (48 Meg), flag 0
            beg: cyl 0/ sector 2/ head 0;
            end: cyl 315/ sector 35/ head 8
1: sysid 165,(FreeBSD/NetBSD/386BSD)
        start 99540, size 205065 (100 Meg), flag 80
            beg: cyl 316/ sector 1/ head 0;
            end: cyl 966/ sector 35/ head 8
2: <UNUSED>
3: <UNUSED>
Should we write new partition table? [n] y
```

By default, *fdisk* creates a FreeBSD partition in slice 3. Even though we didn't have any space left, it created a partition there. You don't need to delete it if you don't want to, but since it overlaps the other partitions, it would probably confuse Microsoft utilities, so it's a good idea.

Labelling the disk

Once we have a valid Microsoft partition table, we need to pay more attention to our FreeBSD slice (slice 1, or Microsoft partition 2). It'll make life easier here to remember a few things:

- From now on, we're just looking at the slice, which we can think of as a logical disk. Names like *disk label* really refer to the slice, but since many standard terms use the word *disk*, we'll continue to use them.

- All offsets are relative to the beginning of the slice, not the beginning of the disk. Sizes also refer to the slice and not the disk.

- Depending on the operation, we may need to take the raw disk (*/dev/rda1c*) or the block device (*/dev/da1c*). Sometimes the programs can recover if you specify the wrong device, but sometimes they produce some really strange error messages instead.

The first thing we need is the disk label, which supplies information about the disk geometry and the layout of the file systems. These are two different things, of course: the overall disk geometry is determined by the kind of disk, but you have decided (with *fdisk*) what part of the disk represents the FreeBSD slice, and you also need to define what file systems you want. As we saw in Chapter 5, *Installing FreeBSD*, page 74, a typical first disk will contain a root file system, swap space and a */usr* file system. On other disks, this arrangement may be different. The arguments in favour of a small root file system are less powerful on other disks. On the other hand, you may want to add swap on other disks: firstly, it's possible that you are a bit low on swap, and secondly, spreading swap over other disks can improve performance if you are low on memory. In our example, let's add 20 MB of swap and make the rest of the slice a */home* file system. In addition, we need to define the c partition, which represents the whole disk. Traditionally, data disks use the h partition and not the a partition, so we'll stick to that tradition, though there's nothing to stop you from using the a partition if you prefer. For each partition, we need to know the start offset, the size and the file system type. In summary, the FreeBSD slice we want to create looks like:

FreeBSD disk label and bootstrap
/dev/da1a (empty)
/dev/da1s2b: FreeBSD swap, 20 MB
/dev/da1s2d (empty)
/dev/da1s2e (empty)
/dev/da1s2f (empty)
/dev/da1s2g (empty)
/dev/da1s2h: */home* file system, 80 MB

Figure 14-3: FreeBSD slice on second disk

Disklabel

The program which writes the disk label is called (wait for it) *disklabel*. You can tell it the geometry and file system layout information in two different ways: you can find or create an entry in */etc/disktab*, or you can create your own prototype file. We'll look at both ways in the following sections.

/etc/disktab

You can label the disk with a command like

```
# disklabel -w -r da1 disktype
```

disktype is a label in the file */etc/disktab*, which contains definitions of disk geometry for a number of known disks. There's a good chance that your disk won't be in it, though. An entry in *disktab* looks like:

```
fuji2266|Fujitsu M2266S: \
    :ty=winchester:dt=SCSI:se#512:nt#15:ns#85:nc#1658:rm#3600:\
    :pc#2113950:oc#0: \
    :ph#2107704:oh#0:bh#4096:fh#512:th=4.2BSD:
```

The format of this file is derived from *termcap*, and it's a bit tough at first sight. In fact, there isn't too much you need to understand. The first name, up to the | symbol, is the *label*. This is the name you specify to *disklabel*, so you don't want to make it too long. The next name, up to the :, is a more verbose description of the disk. After the colon come specifications consisting of a property name, followed by either a = symbol and a string value, or a # symbol and a numeric value. See the man page *disktab(5)* for further details. The values that interest us are:

Table 14-4. disktab values

Name	Meaning
ty	Type of disk. **winchester** specifies a non-removable hard disk.
dt	Type of controller, in this case SCSI
se	Number of bytes per sector. For current FreeBSD systems, this must be 512
nt	Number of tracks per cylinder, in this case 15.
ns	Number of sectors per track, in this case 85.
nc	Number of cylinders, in this case 1658.
rm	Rotational speed of the disk, by default 3600. This is not absolutely essential.
b*x*	The size of ufs file system blocks in partition *x*, where *x* is a partition letter from a to h. See the discussion of partitions in Chapter 2, *Before you install*, page 36, for more information.
o*x*	Offset (starting sector) of partition *x*, where *x* is a partition letter from a to h. See the discussion of partitions in Chapter 2, *Before you install*, page 36, for more information.
p*x*	Size in sectors of partition *x*.
b*x*	The size of ufs file system blocks in partition *x*.
f*x*	The size of ufs file system fragments in partition *x*.
t*x*	The type of the partition. This can be 4.2BSD (for ufs; the name is historical) or swap for a swap partition.

We won't look at the block and fragment sizes in this discussion. See the man page for *newfs* on page 703 for further details.

There's no definition in */etc/disktab* for our CDC 94161-9 disk, of course, so we'll have to write one. We need the following information on the disk geometry, all of which we can find in the printout from *fdisk*:

- The number of tracks or heads (nt), 9.

- The number of cylinders (nc). Well, that should be 967, but don't forget that we're looking at the slice, not the disk, and our slice only has 651 cylinders, so that's what we say.

- The number of sectors per track (ns), 35.

- The total number of sectors in the partition. Calculate the number from the formula *cylinders × heads × sectors*, even if you are using the whole disk: the output from *dmesg* or *scsiformat* is not correct here.

OK, let's roll up our sleeves. The swap partition comes directly after the bootstrap and the disk label, each of which take up 1 sector, so the swap partition starts at offset 2. It's 20 MB

259

(20,971,520 bytes or 40,960 sectors), but it would be nice to have it end on a cylinder boundary, so we'll divide by the number of sectors per cylinder. 40,960 / 315 = 130.031746 cylinders, so we'll call it 130 cylinders or 40,950 sectors. Since we don't start on a cylinder boundary (the bootstrap and disk label come first), we subtract their length (2) and end up with 40,948 sectors, so the definitions for swap (partition b) are: start (ob) is 2, size (pb) is 40948, and type (tb) is swap.

Next we look at the */home* file system. It starts immediately after the swap partition (offset 40950), and takes up the rest of the space on the partition, so the size is 205065 (the length of the partition) - 40950 (the length of the bootstrap, disk label, and swap space) = 164115 sectors. The type (tb) is 4.2BSD.

Finally, we define partition c. That's easy: the start (oc) is the 0, and the size (pc) is the size of the FreeBSD partition, 205065, and the type isn't defined, so we don't have a td parameter.

Putting all this together, we get:

```
cdc94161|CDC 94161-9: \
    :ty=winchester:dt=SCSI:se#512:nt#9:ns#35:nc#651:rm#3600:\
    :ob#2:pb#40948:tb=swap:\
    :oc#0:pc#205065:\
    :oh#40950:ph#164115:tb=4.2BSD:
```

Finally, we can label the disk:

```
# disklabel -w -r /dev/da1c cdc94161
```

When you do this, expect a kernel message (in high-intensity display) saying "**Cannot find disk label**". Since there isn't any label, it can't be found. This is another harmless chicken and egg problem.

Disk prototype file

Alternatively, you can create a *disk prototype file* just for this disk. This has the advantage that most of the work is done for you. Start by entering:

```
# disklabel /dev/rda1 >diskproto          write info to file diskproto
Warning, revolutions/minute 0
boot block size 0
super block size 0
# cat diskproto                           look at what we got
# /dev/rda1:
type: unknown
disk:
label:
flags:
bytes/sector: 512
sectors/track: 35
tracks/cylinder: 9
sectors/cylinder: 315
cylinders: 967
sectors/unit: 304605
rpm: 0
interleave: 0
trackskew: 0
```

```
cylinderskew: 0
headswitch: 0              # milliseconds
track-to-track seek: 0  # milliseconds
drivedata: 0

3 partitions:
#        size   offset     fstype   [fsize bsize bps/cpg]
  c:   304605        0     unused        0     0          # (Cyl.    0 - 966)
```

We have to change a number of things in this file:

- The values for `interleave` (the number of physical sectors between logical sectors; don't worry if you don't understand this) and `prm` (the number of rotations of the disk platter per minute) are both 0, which is invalid. FreeBSD doesn't use these values, but it still refuses to label the disk unless you enter some plausible value. We set `interleave` to 1 and `rpm` to 3600, which used to be a standard value for disks.

- In addition, although our partition table says that the FreeBSD slice only has 651 cylinders, the value here shows the complete disk. We need to change this value to 651.

- The `type` field says `unknown`. We change it to `SCSI`.

- For documentation purposes, we set the `disk` field to `cdc94161`, and the `label` field to FreeBSD. *disklabel* doesn't care what's in these fields, but it copies them to disk.

- In addition, we need to add the definitions of the file system layout. We'll look at that in the rest of this section.

The last part of the prototype file describes the partitions. In this case, we have three lines: the number of partitions, a comment describing the format, and a definition of the c partition. The disk prototype file here ignores the partition table completely: it claims that partition c takes up the whole disk. We need to fix that, and we need to add information about slices b and h.

Since we are using partition h, we need to change the information `3 partitions` at the bottom of the file to `8 partitions` so that *disklabel* will be able to create partition h.

We'll use the same sizes as in the previous example: We'll put the swap partition first. Remembering that we specify our offsets relative to the start of the FreeBSD slice, so the swap partition has offset 2, immediately after the boot sector and the disk label. It's 20 MB (20,971,520 bytes or 40,960 sectors), but want it to finish at the end of a cylinder, so we divide by the number of sectors per cylinder. 40,960 / 315 = 130.031746 cylinders, so we'll call it 130 cylinders, which corresponds to 40,950 sectors. Since we don't start on a cylinder boundary (the bootstrap and disk label come first), we subtract their length (2) and end up with 40,948 sectors, so the definitions for swap (partition b) are: size is 40948, offset is 2, and type is `swap`.

Next we look at the */home* file system. It starts immediately after the swap partition (sector 40950 relative to the beginning of the slice), and takes up the rest of the space on the partition, so the size is 205065 (the length of the partition) - 40950 (the length of the swap space) = 164115 sectors. Accordingly, the definitions for */home* are: size 164430, offset 49050, and *fstype* `4.2BSD`.

Finally, we define partition c. That's easy: the start is 0, and the size is the size of the FreeBSD partition, 205380. We leave *fstype* as unused.

With an editor, we make these changes to *diskproto*. The result looks like:

```
# /dev/rda1c:
type: SCSI
disk: cdc94161
label: FreeBSD
flags:
bytes/sector: 512
sectors/track: 35
tracks/cylinder: 9
sectors/cylinder: 315
cylinders: 651
sectors/unit: 205065
rpm: 3600
interleave: 1
trackskew: 0
cylinderskew: 0
headswitch: 0           # milliseconds
track-to-track seek: 0  # milliseconds
drivedata: 0

8 partitions:
#        size    offset     fstype  [fsize bsize bps/cpg]
    b:   40948        2       swap                        # (Cyl.    0*- 129*)
    c:  205065        0     unused       0     0          # (Cyl.    0 - 650)
    h:  164115    40950     unused       0     0          # (Cyl.  130 - 650)
```

Finally, we label the disk:

```
# disklabel -R -r da1 diskproto
```

Checking the results

Whichever way we label the disk, it's a good idea to check that it really did the job. Along with some strange error messages, *disklabel* occasionally forgets to tell you that it didn't do anything—for example, if the partition table was defective. We can list the label with *disklabel -r*:

```
# disklabel -r da1
# /dev/rda1c:
type: SCSI
disk: cdc94161
label: FreeBSD
flags:
bytes/sector: 512
sectors/track: 35
tracks/cylinder: 9
sectors/cylinder: 315
cylinders: 651
sectors/unit: 205065
rpm: 3600
interleave: 1
trackskew: 0
cylinderskew: 0
headswitch: 0           # milliseconds
track-to-track seek: 0  # milliseconds
drivedata: 0

8 partitions:
```

```
#         size    offset    fstype    [fsize bsize bps/cpg]
  b:     40948         2      swap                            # (Cyl.    0*- 129*)
  c:    205065         0    unused         0      0           # (Cyl.    0 - 650)
  h:    164115     40950    unused         0      0           # (Cyl.  130 - 650)
```

Things that can go wrong

To get *disklabel* to do what you want, you really must stick to every tiny detail here. If you don't, you can expect a number of strange error messages. Here are some that you could encounter.

- `No disk label on disk` is straightforward enough. You tried to use *disklabel* to look at the label before you had a label to look at. This happens when you use */dev/da1* instead of */dev/rda1*.

- `Label magic number or checksum is wrong!` tells you that *disklabel* thinks it has a label, but it's invalid. This could be the result of an incorrect previous attempt to label the disk. It can be difficult to get rid of an incorrect label. The best thing to do is to repartition the disk with the label in a different position, and then copy */dev/zero* to where the label used to be. Then you can repartition again the way you want to have it.

- `Open partition would move or shrink` probably means that you have specified incorrect values in your slice definitions. Check particularly that the c partition corresponds with the definition in the partition table.

- `write: Read-only file system` means that you are trying to do something invalid with a valid disk label. FreeBSD write protects the disk label, which is why you get this message.

- When labelling via */etc/disktab*, you might get the message `cdc94161: unknown disk type`. This could mean that you forgot to terminate the last line in the file—add a blank line after just to be sure.

- In addition, you might get kernel messages like `fixlabel: raw partition size > slice size` or `fixlabel: raw partitions offset != slice offset`, whose meanings should be obvious.

Creating the file systems

Now that we have a valid label, the next thing we need to do is to create the file systems. In this case, there's only one file system, on */dev/da1h*. Mercifully, this is easier:

```
# newfs /dev/rda1h
Warning: 3822 sector(s) in last cylinder unallocated
/dev/rda1h:     164114 sectors in 41 cylinders of 1 tracks, 4096 sectors
        80.1MB in 3 cyl groups (16 c/g, 32.00MB/g, 7680 i/g)
super-block backups (for fsck -b #) at:
 32, 65568, 131104,
```

Well, that warning doesn't look nice. It looks as if we've lost nearly 2 MB of space on a very small disk. In fact, this message is the wrong way round: there are 3822 sectors not available for the last cylinder group, in other words, it only has 274 sectors. This isn't really a problem, since they can be used anyway. If you want to be tidy, you can can go back and change the division between swap and file system if we want: we *subtract* 274 sectors from partition h, which gives us the new *disktab* entry:

```
cdc94161|CDC 94161-9: \
    :ty=winchester:dt=SCSI:se#512:nt#9:ns#35:nc#651:rm#3600:\
    :ob#2:pb#41222:tb=swap:\
    :oc#0:pc#205065:\
    :oh#41224:ph#163841:tb=4.2BSD:
```

or the diskproto entry

```
#       size    offset    fstype    [fsize bsize bps/cpg]
   b:   41222        2      swap                          # (Cyl.    0*- 130*)
   c:  205065        0    unused       0     0            # (Cyl.    0 - 650)
   h:  163841    41224    unused       0     0            # (Cyl.  130*- 650*)
```

You can then go back and re-label the disk. This time, you see:

```
# newfs /dev/rda1h
/dev/rda1h:     163840 sectors in 40 cylinders of 1 tracks, 4096 sectors
        80.0MB in 3 cyl groups (16 c/g, 32.00MB/g, 7680 i/g)
super-block backups (for fsck -b #) at:
 32, 65568, 131104,
```

As you can see, the partition has become smaller, but at least the error message is gone.

Editing disk labels

If you already have a disk label, and you just want to change it, as in the example in the previous section, you have an alternative method: you can start *disklabel* in *edit* mode by entering

```
# disklabel -e da1
```

In edit mode, *disklabel* creates a diskproto entry and edits it with your favourite editor (if you have set the environment variable EDITOR) or *vi* otherwise. When you leave the editor, it writes the label back to the disk. If you use this method, be sure to remove your *diskproto* file, since it will be out of date.

Mounting the file systems

Finally the job is done. Well, almost. You still need to mount the file system, and to tell the system that it has more swap. But that's not much of a problem:

```
# mkdir /home          make sure we have a directory to mount on
# mount /dev/da1h /home  and mount it
# swapon /dev/da1b
# df                   show free capacity and mounted file systems
Filesystem    1024-blocks     Used    Avail Capacity  Mounted on
/dev/wd0a           19966    17426      944     95%    /
/dev/wd0s1e       1162062   955758   113340     89%    /usr
procfs                  4        4        0    100%    /proc
```

264

```
presto:/           15823      6734      8297    45%   /presto/root
presto:/usr       912271    824927     41730    95%   /presto/usr
presto:/home     1905583   1193721    521303    70%   /presto/home
presto:/S        4065286   3339635    563039    86%   /S
/dev/da1h          79270         1     72928     0%   /home
```

This looks fine, but when you reboot the system, */home* will be gone. To ensure that it gets mounted every time, you need to add the following line to */etc/fstab*:

```
/dev/da1h                /home     ufs   rw    0 0
```

This will cause *da1h* to be mounted at system startup time—see the description of *mount* on page 235, and the man page on page 696.

Recovering from disk data errors

Modern hard disks are a miracle in evolution. Today you can buy a 16 GB hard disk for well under $500, and it will fit in your shirt pocket. 30 years ago, a typical disk was the size of a washing machine and stored 20 MB. You would need 800 of them to store 16 GB.

At the same time, reliability has gone up, but disks are still relatively unreliable devices. You can achieve maximum reliability by keeping them cool, but sooner or later you are going to run into some kind of problem. One kind is due to surface irregularities: the disk can't read a specific part of the surface.

Modern disks make provisions for recovering from such errors by allocating an alternate sector for the data. IDE drives do this automatically, but with SCSI drives you have the option of enabling or disabling reallocation. Usually it is turned on when you buy them, but occasionally it is not. When installing a new disk, you should check that the parameters *ARRE* (*Auto Read Reallocation Enable*) and *AWRE* (*Auto Write Reallocation Enable*) are turned on. For example, to check and set the values for disk *da1*, you would enter:

```
# scsi -f /dev/rda1c -m 1 -e -P 3
```

This command will start up your favourite editor (either the one specified in the EDITOR environment variable, or *vi* by default) with the following data:

```
AWRE (Auto Write Reallocation Enbld):  0
ARRE (Auto Read Reallocation Enbld):  1
TB (Transfer Block):  0
PER (Post Error):  0
DTE (Disable Transfer on Error):  0
DCR (Disable Correction):  0
Read Retry Count:  1
Correction Span:  0
Write Retry Count:  1
```

The values for AWRE and ARRE should both be 1. If they aren't, as in this case, where AWRE is 0, change the data with the editor, write it back, and exit. The *scsi* program will write the data back to the disk and enable the option.

Virtual disks: the Vinum Volume Manager

No matter what disks you have, there will always be limitations:

- They can be too small.

- They can be too slow.

- They can be too unreliable.

Vinum is a so-called *Volume Manager*, a virtual disk driver that addresses these three problems. Let's look at them in more detail. Various solutions to these problems have been proposed and implemented:

Disks are too small

The *ufs* file system can theoretically span more than a petabyte (2^{50} or 10^{15} bytes) of storage, but no current disk drive comes close to this size. Often you'll find you want a file system that is bigger than the disks you have available. Admittedly, this problem is not as acute as it was ten years ago, but it still exists. Some systems have solve this by creating an abstract device which stores its data on a number of disks.

Access bottlenecks

Modern systems frequently need to access data in a highly concurrent manner. For example, *ftp.FreeBSD.org* maintains up to 5,000 concurrent *FTP* sessions and has a 100 Mbit/s connection to the outside world, corresponding to about 12 MB/s.

Current disk drives can transfer data sequentially at up to 30 MB/s, but this value is of little importance in an environment where many independent processes access a drive, where they may achieve only a fraction of these values. In such cases it's more interesting to view the problem from the viewpoint of the disk subsystem: the important parameter is the load that a transfer places on the subsystem, in other words the time for which a transfer occupies the drives involved in the transfer.

In any disk transfer, the drive must first position the heads, wait for the first sector to pass under the read head, and then perform the transfer. These actions can be considered to be atomic: it doesn't make any sense to interrupt them.

Consider a typical transfer of about 10 kB: the current generation of high-performance disks can position the heads in an average of 6 ms. The fastest drives spin at 10,000 rpm, so the average rotational latency (half a revolution) is 3 ms. At 30 MB/s, the transfer itself takes about 350 µs, almost nothing compared to the positioning time. In such a case, the effective transfer rate drops to a little over 1 MB/s and is clearly highly dependent on the transfer size.

The traditional and obvious solution to this bottleneck is "more spindles": rather than using one large disk, it uses several smaller disks with the same aggregate storage space. Each disk is capable of positioning and transferring independently, so the effective throughput increases by a factor close to the number of disks used.

The exact throughput improvement is, of course, smaller than the number of disks involved: although each drive is capable of transferring in parallel, there is no way to ensure that the requests are evenly distributed across the drives. Inevitably the load on one drive will be higher than on another.

The evenness of the load on the disks is strongly dependent on the way the data is shared across the drives. In the following discussion, it's convenient to think of the disk storage as a large number of data sectors which are addressable by number, rather like the pages in a book. The most obvious method is to divide the virtual disk into groups of consecutive sectors the size of the individual physical disks and store them in this manner, rather like taking a large book and tearing it into smaller sections. This method is called *concatenation* and has the advantage that the disks do not need to have any specific size relationships. It works well when the access to the virtual disk is spread evenly about its address space. When access is concentrated on a smaller area, the improvement is less marked. Figure 14-5 illustrates the sequence in which storage units are allocated in a concatenated organization.

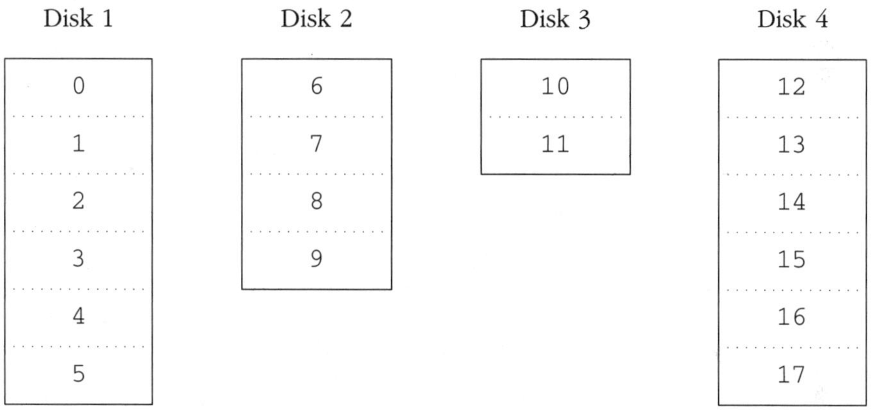

Figure 14-5: Concatenated organization

An alternative mapping is to divide the address space into smaller, even-sized components and store them sequentially on different devices. For example, the first 256 sectors may be stored on the first disk, the next 256 sectors on the next disk and so on. After filling the last disk, the process repeats until the disks are full. This mapping is called *striping* or RAID-0,[1] though the latter term is somewhat misleading: it provides no redundancy. Striping requires somewhat more effort to locate the data, and it can cause additional I/O load where a transfer is spread over multiple disks, but it can also provide a more constant load across the disks. Figure 14-6 illustrates the sequence in which storage units are allocated in a striped organization.

---

1. *RAID* stands for *Redundant Array of Inexpensive Disks* and offers various forms of fault tolerance.

Disk 1	Disk 2	Disk 3	Disk 4
0	1	2	3
4	5	6	7
8	9	10	11
12	13	14	15
16	17	18	19
20	21	22	23

Figure 14-6: Striped organization

Data integrity

The final problem with current disks is that they are unreliable. Although disk drive reliability has increased tremendously over the last few years, they are still the most likely core component of a server to fail. When they do, the results can be catastrophic: replacing a failed disk drive and restoring data to it can take days.

The traditional way to approach this problem has been *mirroring*, keeping two copies of the data on different physical hardware. Since the advent of the RAID levels, this technique has also been called *RAID level 1* or *RAID-1*. Any write to the volume writes to both locations; a read can be satisfied from either, so if one drive fails, the data is still available on the other drive.

Mirroring has two problems:

- The price. It requires twice as much disk storage as a non-redundant solution.

- The performance impact. Writes must be performed to both drives, so they take up twice the bandwidth of a non-mirrored volume. Reads do not suffer from a performance penalty: it even looks as if they are faster.

Vinum objects

In order to address these problems, vinum implements a four-level hierarchy of objects:

- The most visible object is the virtual disk, called a *volume*. Volumes have essentially the same properties as a UNIX disk drive, though there are some minor differences. They have no size limitations.

- Volumes are composed of *plexes*, each of which represent the total address space of a volume. This level in the hierarchy thus provides redundancy.

- Since Vinum exists within the UNIX disk storage framework, it would be possible to use UNIX partitions as the building block for multi-disk plexes, but in fact this turns out to be too inflexible: UNIX disks can have only a limited number of partitions. Instead, Vinum subdivides a single UNIX partition (the *drive*) into contiguous areas called *subdisks*, which it uses as building blocks for plexes.

- Subdisks reside on Vinum *drives*, currently UNIX partitions. Vinum drives can contain any number of subdisks. With the exception of a small area at the beginning of the drive, which is used for storing configuration and state information, the entire drive is available for data storage.

The following sections describe the way these objects provide the functionality required of Vinum.

Volume size considerations

Plexes can include multiple subdisks spread over all drives in the Vinum configuration. As a result, the size of an individual drive does not limit the size of a plex, and thus of a volume.

Redundant data storage

Vinum implements mirroring by attaching multiple plexes to a volume. Each plex is a representation of the data in a volume. A volume may contain between one and eight plexes.

Although a plex represents the complete data of a volume, it is possible for parts of the representation to be physically missing, either by design (by not defining a subdisk for parts of the plex) or by accident (as a result of the failure of a drive). As long as at least one plex can provide the data for the complete address range of the volume, the volume is fully functional.

Performance issues

Vinum implements both concatenation and striping at the plex level:

- A *concatenated plex* uses the address space of each subdisk in turn.

- A *striped plex* stripes the data across each subdisk. The subdisks must all have the same size, and there must be at least two subdisks in order to distinguish it from a concatenated plex.

Which plex organization?

The version of Vinum supplied with FreeBSD 3.2 implements two kinds of plex:

- Concatenated plexes are the most flexible: they can contain any number of subdisks, and the subdisks may be of different length. The plex may be extended by adding additional subdisks. They require less CPU time than striped plexes, though the difference in CPU overhead is not measurable. On the other hand, they are most susceptible to hot spots, where one disk is very active and others are idle.

• The greatest advantage of striped (RAID-0) plexes is that they reduce hot spots: by choosing an optimum sized stripe (about 256 kB), you can even out the load on the component drives. The disadvantages of this approach are (fractionally) more complex code and restrictions on subdisks: they must be all the same size, and extending a plex by adding new subdisks is so complicated that Vinum currently does not implement it. Vinum imposes an additional, trivial restriction: a striped plex must have at least two subdisks, since otherwise it is indistinguishable from a concatenated plex.

Table 14-7 summarizes the advantages and disadvantages of each plex organization.

Plex type	Minimum subdisks	can add subdisks	must be equal size	application
concatenated	1	yes	no	Large data storage with maximum placement flexibility and moderate performance.
striped	2	no	yes	High performance in combination with highly concurrent access.

Figure 14-7: Vinum plex organizations

Some examples

Vinum maintains a *configuration database* which describes the objects known to an individual system. Initially, the user creates the configuration database from one or more configuration files with the aid of the *vinum(8)* utility program. Vinum stores a copy of its configuration database on each disk slice (which Vinum calls a *device*) under its control. This database is updated on each state change, so that a restart accurately restores the state of each Vinum object.

The configuration file

The configuration file describes individual Vinum objects. The definition of a simple volume might be:

```
drive a device /dev/da3h
volume myvol
  plex org concat
    sd length 512m drive a
```

This file describes four Vinum objects:

- The `drive` line describes a disk partition (*drive*) and its location relative to the underlying hardware. It is given the symbolic name *a*. This separation of the symbolic names from the device names allows disks to be moved from one location to another without confusion.

- The `volume` line describes a volume. The only required attribute is the name, in this case `myvol`.

- The `plex` line defines a plex. The only required parameter is the organization, in this case `concat`. No name is necessary: the system automatically generates a name from the volume name by adding the suffix `.px`, where *x* is the number of the plex in the volume. Thus this plex will be called *myvol.p0*.

- The `sd` line describes a subdisk. The minimum specifications are the name of a drive on which to store it, and the length of the subdisk. As with plexes, no name is necessary: the system automatically assigns names derived from the plex name by adding the suffix `.sx`, where *x* is the number of the subdisk in the plex. Thus Vinum gives this subdisk the name *myvol.p0.s0*

After processing this file, *vinum(8)* produces the following output:

```
vinum -> create config1
Configuration summary

Drives:        1 (4 configured)
Volumes:       1 (4 configured)
Plexes:        1 (8 configured)
Subdisks:      1 (16 configured)

D a                    State: up        Device /dev/da3h       Avail: 2061/2573 MB (80%)

V myvol                State: up        Plexes:      1 Size:       512 MB

P myvol.p0        C State: up        Subdisks:    1 Size:       512 MB

S myvol.p0.s0          State: up        PO:      0  B Size:       512 MB
```

This output shows the brief listing format of *vinum(8)*. It is represented graphically in Figure 14-8.

This figure, and the ones which follow, represent a volume, which contains the plexes, which in turn contain the subdisks. In this trivial example, the volume contains one plex, and the plex contains one subdisk.

This particular volume has no specific advantage over a conventional disk partition. It contains a single plex, so it is not redundant. The plex contains a single subdisk, so there is no difference in storage allocation from a conventional disk partition. The following sections illustrate various more interesting configuration methods.

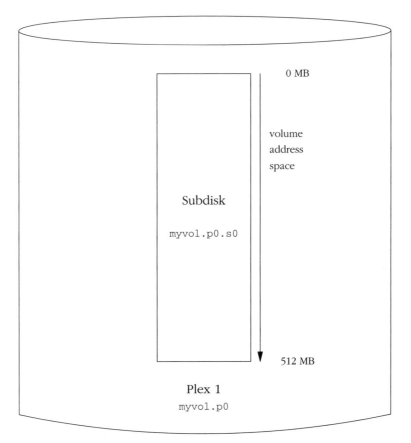

Figure 14-8: A simple Vinum volume

Increased resilience: mirroring

The resilience of a volume can be increased by mirroring. When laying out a mirrored volume, it is important to ensure that the subdisks of each plex are on different drives, so that a drive failure will not take down both plexes. The following configuration mirrors a volume:

```
drive b device /dev/da4h
volume mirror
  plex org concat
    sd length 512m drive a
  plex org concat
    sd length 512m drive b
```

In this example, it was not necessary to specify a definition of drive *a* again, since Vinum keeps track of all objects in its configuration database. After processing this definition, the configuration looks like:

```
Drives:         2 (4 configured)
Volumes:        2 (4 configured)
Plexes:         3 (8 configured)
Subdisks:       3 (16 configured)

D a                    State: up        Device /dev/da3h      Avail: 1549/2573 MB (60%)
D b                    State: up        Device /dev/da4h      Avail: 2061/2573 MB (80%)

V myvol                State: up        Plexes:       1 Size:      512 MB
V mirror               State: up        Plexes:       2 Size:      512 MB

P myvol.p0      C State: up        Subdisks:     1 Size:      512 MB
P mirror.p0     C State: up        Subdisks:     1 Size:      512 MB
P mirror.p1     C State: initializing   Subdisks:    1 Size:        512 MB

S myvol.p0.s0          State: up        PO:       0  B Size:      512 MB
S mirror.p0.s0         State: up        PO:       0  B Size:      512 MB
S mirror.p1.s0         State: empty     PO:       0  B Size:      512 MB
```

Figure 14-9 shows the structure graphically.

In this example, each plex contains the full 512 MB of address space. As in the previous example, each plex contains only a single subdisk.

Optimizing performance

The mirrored volume in the previous example is more resistant to failure than an unmirrored volume, but its performance is less: each write to the volume requires a write to both drives, using up a greater proportion of the total disk bandwidth. Performance considerations demand a different approach: instead of mirroring, the data is striped across as many disk drives as possible. The following configuration shows a volume with a plex striped across four disk drives:

```
drive c device /dev/da5h
drive d device /dev/da6h
volume stripe
  plex org striped 512k
    sd length 128m drive a
    sd length 128m drive b
    sd length 128m drive c
    sd length 128m drive d
```

As before, it is not necessary to define the drives which are already known to Vinum. After processing this definition, the configuration looks like:

```
Drives:         4 (4 configured)
Volumes:        3 (4 configured)
Plexes:         4 (8 configured)
Subdisks:       7 (16 configured)

D a                    State: up        Device /dev/da3h      Avail: 1421/2573 MB (55%)
D b                    State: up        Device /dev/da4h      Avail: 1933/2573 MB (75%)
D c                    State: up        Device /dev/da5h      Avail: 2445/2573 MB (95%)
D d                    State: up        Device /dev/da6h      Avail: 2445/2573 MB (95%)

V myvol                State: up        Plexes:       1 Size:      512 MB
V mirror               State: up        Plexes:       2 Size:      512 MB
V striped              State: up        Plexes:       1 Size:      512 MB
```

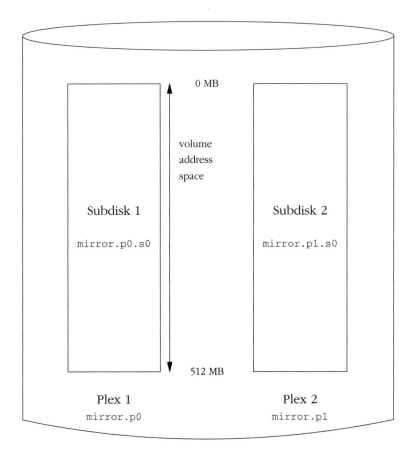

Figure 14-9: A mirrored Vinum volume

```
P myvol.p0          C State: up         Subdisks:     1 Size:         512 MB
P mirror.p0         C State: up         Subdisks:     1 Size:         512 MB
P mirror.p1         C State: initializing   Subdisks:     1 Size:        512 MB
P striped.p1          State: up         Subdisks:     1 Size:         512 MB

S myvol.p0.s0         State: up         PO:       0  B Size:         512 MB
S mirror.p0.s0        State: up         PO:       0  B Size:         512 MB
S mirror.p1.s0        State: empty      PO:       0  B Size:         512 MB
S striped.p0.s0       State: up         PO:       0  B Size:         128 MB
S striped.p0.s1       State: up         PO:     512 kB Size:         128 MB
S striped.p0.s2       State: up         PO:    1024 kB Size:         128 MB
S striped.p0.s3       State: up         PO:    1536 kB Size:         128 MB
```

This volume is represented in Figure 14-10. The darkness of the stripes indicates the position within the plex address space: the lightest stripes come first, the darkest last.

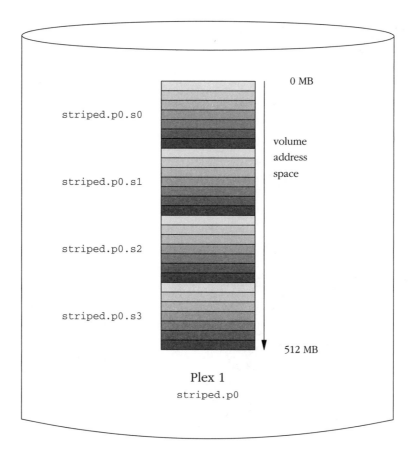

striped.p0.s0

striped.p0.s1

striped.p0.s2

striped.p0.s3

0 MB

volume
address
space

512 MB

Plex 1
striped.p0

Figure 14-10: A striped Vinum volume

Resilience and performance

With sufficient hardware, it is possible to build volumes which show both increased resilience and increased performance compared to standard UNIX partitions. A typical configuration file might be:

```
volume raid10
  plex org striped 512k
    sd length 102480k drive a
    sd length 102480k drive b
    sd length 102480k drive c
    sd length 102480k drive d
    sd length 102480k drive e
  plex org striped 512k
    sd length 102480k drive c
    sd length 102480k drive d
    sd length 102480k drive e
    sd length 102480k drive a
    sd length 102480k drive b
```

The subdisks of the second plex are offset by two drives from those of the first plex: this helps ensure that writes do not go to the same subdisks even if a transfer goes over two drives.

Figure 14-11 represents the structure of this volume.

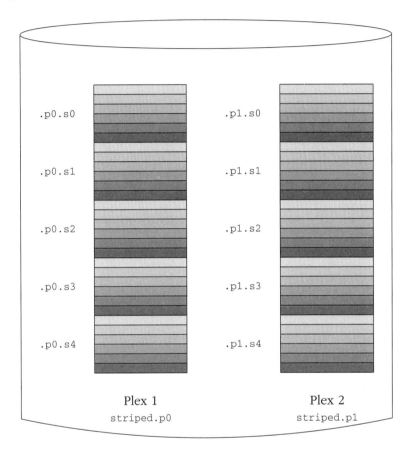

Figure 14-11: A mirrored, striped Vinum volume

Object naming

As described above, Vinum assigns default names to plexes and subdisks, although they may be overridden. Overriding the default names is not recommended: experience with the VERITAS® volume manager, which allows arbitrary naming of objects, has shown that this flexibility does not bring a significant advantage, and it can cause confusion.

Names may contain any non-blank character, but it is recommended to restrict them to letters, digits and the underscore characters. The names of volumes, plexes and subdisks may be up to

64 characters long, and the names of drives may up to 32 characters long.

Vinum objects are assigned device nodes in the hierarchy */dev/vinum*. The configuration shown above would cause Vinum to create the following device nodes:

- The control devices */dev/vinum/control* and */dev/vinum/controld*, which are used by *vinum(8)* and the Vinum dæmon respectively.

- Block and character device entries for each volume. These are the main devices used by Vinum. The block device names are the name of the volume, while the character device names follow the BSD tradition of prepending the letter r to the name. Thus the configuration above would include the block devices */dev/vinum/myvol*, */dev/vinum/mirror*, */dev/vinum/striped*, */dev/vinum/raid5* and */dev/vinum/raid10*, and the character devices */dev/vinum/rmyvol*, */dev/vinum/rmirror*, */dev/vinum/rstriped*, */dev/vinum/rraid5* and */dev/vinum/rraid10*. There is obviously a problem here: it is possible to have two volumes called *r* and *rr*, but there will be a conflict creating the device node */dev/vinum/rr*: is it a character device for volume *r* or a block device for volume *rr*? Currently Vinum does not address this conflict: the first-defined volume will get the name.

- A directory */dev/vinum/drive* with entries for each drive. These entries are in fact symbolic links to the corresponding disk nodes.

- A directory */dev/vinum/volume* with entries for each volume. It contains subdirectories for each plex, which in turn contain subdirectories for their component subdisks.

- The directories */dev/vinum/plex* and */dev/vinum/sd*, */dev/vinum/rsd*, which contain block device nodes for each plex and block and character device nodes respectively for subdisk.

For example, consider the following configuration file:

```
drive drive1 device /dev/sd1h
drive drive2 device /dev/sd2h
drive drive3 device /dev/sd3h
drive drive4 device /dev/sd4h
volume s64 setupstate
 plex org striped 64k
   sd length 100m drive drive1
   sd length 100m drive drive2
   sd length 100m drive drive3
   sd length 100m drive drive4
```

After processing this file, *vinum(8)* creates the following structure in */dev/vinum*:

```
brwx------  1 root  wheel  25, 0x40000001 Apr 13 16:46 Control
brwx------  1 root  wheel  25, 0x40000002 Apr 13 16:46 control
brwx------  1 root  wheel  25, 0x40000000 Apr 13 16:46 controld
drwxr-xr-x  2 root  wheel      512 Apr 13 16:46 drive
drwxr-xr-x  2 root  wheel      512 Apr 13 16:46 plex
crwxr-xr--  1 root  wheel  91,    2 Apr 13 16:46 rs64
drwxr-xr-x  2 root  wheel      512 Apr 13 16:46 rsd
drwxr-xr-x  2 root  wheel      512 Apr 13 16:46 rvol
brwxr-xr--  1 root  wheel  25,    2 Apr 13 16:46 s64
drwxr-xr-x  2 root  wheel      512 Apr 13 16:46 sd
drwxr-xr-x  3 root  wheel      512 Apr 13 16:46 vol

/dev/vinum/drive:
```

```
total 0
lrwxr-xr-x  1 root   wheel    9 Apr 13 16:46 drive1 -> /dev/sd1h
lrwxr-xr-x  1 root   wheel    9 Apr 13 16:46 drive2 -> /dev/sd2h
lrwxr-xr-x  1 root   wheel    9 Apr 13 16:46 drive3 -> /dev/sd3h
lrwxr-xr-x  1 root   wheel    9 Apr 13 16:46 drive4 -> /dev/sd4h

/dev/vinum/plex:
total 0
brwxr-xr--  1 root   wheel   25, 0x10000002 Apr 13 16:46 s64.p0

/dev/vinum/rsd:
total 0
crwxr-xr--  1 root   wheel   91, 0x20000002 Apr 13 16:46 s64.p0.s0
crwxr-xr--  1 root   wheel   91, 0x20100002 Apr 13 16:46 s64.p0.s1
crwxr-xr--  1 root   wheel   91, 0x20200002 Apr 13 16:46 s64.p0.s2
crwxr-xr--  1 root   wheel   91, 0x20300002 Apr 13 16:46 s64.p0.s3

/dev/vinum/rvol:
total 0
crwxr-xr--  1 root   wheel   91,    2 Apr 13 16:46 s64

/dev/vinum/sd:
total 0
brwxr-xr--  1 root   wheel   25, 0x20000002 Apr 13 16:46 s64.p0.s0
brwxr-xr--  1 root   wheel   25, 0x20100002 Apr 13 16:46 s64.p0.s1
brwxr-xr--  1 root   wheel   25, 0x20200002 Apr 13 16:46 s64.p0.s2
brwxr-xr--  1 root   wheel   25, 0x20300002 Apr 13 16:46 s64.p0.s3

/dev/vinum/vol:
total 1
brwxr-xr--  1 root   wheel   25,    2 Apr 13 16:46 s64
drwxr-xr-x  3 root   wheel       512 Apr 13 16:46 s64.plex

/dev/vinum/vol/s64.plex:
total 1
brwxr-xr--  1 root   wheel   25, 0x10000002 Apr 13 16:46 s64.p0
drwxr-xr-x  2 root   wheel       512 Apr 13 16:46 s64.p0.sd

/dev/vinum/vol/s64.plex/s64.p0.sd:
total 0
brwxr-xr--  1 root   wheel   25, 0x20000002 Apr 13 16:46 s64.p0.s0
brwxr-xr--  1 root   wheel   25, 0x20100002 Apr 13 16:46 s64.p0.s1
brwxr-xr--  1 root   wheel   25, 0x20200002 Apr 13 16:46 s64.p0.s2
brwxr-xr--  1 root   wheel   25, 0x20300002 Apr 13 16:46 s64.p0.s3
```

Although it is recommended that plexes and subdisks should not be allocated specific names, Vinum drives must be named. This makes it possible to move a drive to a different location and still recognize it automatically. Drive names may be up to 32 characters long.

Creating file systems

Volumes appear to the system to be identical to disks, with one exception. Unlike UNIX drives, Vinum does not partition volumes, which thus do not contain a partition table. This has required modification to some disk utilities, notably *newfs*, which previously tried to interpret the last letter of a Vinum volume name as a partition identifier. For example, a disk drive may have a name like */dev/wd0a* or */dev/da2b*. These names represent the first partition (a) on the first (0) IDE disk (wd) and the eight partition (h) on the third (2) SCSI disk (da) respectively. By contrast, a Vinum volume might be called */dev/vinum/concat*, a name which has no relationship with a partition name.

Normally, *newfs(8)* interprets the name of the disk and complains if it cannot understand it. For example:

```
# newfs /dev/vinum/concat
newfs: /dev/vinum/concat: can't figure out file system partition
```

In order to create a file system on this volume, use the -v option to *newfs(8)*:

```
# newfs -v /dev/vinum/concat
```

Configuring Vinum

The GENERIC kernel does not contain Vinum. It's possible to build a special kernel which includes Vinum, but this is not recommended. The standard way to start Vinum is as a *kld* (see page 363 for more details). You don't even need to use *kldload* for Vinum: when you start *vinum(8)*, it checks whether the module has been loaded, and if it isn't, it loads it automatically.

Startup

Vinum stores configuration information on the disk slices in essentially the same form as in the configuration files. When reading from the configuration database, Vinum recognizes a number of keywords which are not allowed in the configuration files. For example, a disk configuration might contain the following text:

```
volume myvol state up
volume bigraid state down
plex name myvol.p0 state up org concat vol myvol
plex name myvol.p1 state up org concat vol myvol
plex name myvol.p2 state init org striped 512b vol myvol
plex name bigraid.p0 state initializing org raid5 512b vol bigraid
sd name myvol.p0.s0 drive a plex myvol.p0 state up len 1048576b driveoffset 265b plexo
ffset 0b
sd name myvol.p0.s1 drive b plex myvol.p0 state up len 1048576b driveoffset 265b plexo
ffset 1048576b
sd name myvol.p1.s0 drive c plex myvol.p1 state up len 1048576b driveoffset 265b plexo
ffset 0b
sd name myvol.p1.s1 drive d plex myvol.p1 state up len 1048576b driveoffset 265b plexo
ffset 1048576b
sd name myvol.p2.s0 drive a plex myvol.p2 state init len 524288b driveoffset 1048841b
plexoffset 0b
sd name myvol.p2.s1 drive b plex myvol.p2 state init len 524288b driveoffset 1048841b
plexoffset 524288b
sd name myvol.p2.s2 drive c plex myvol.p2 state init len 524288b driveoffset 1048841b
plexoffset 1048576b
sd name myvol.p2.s3 drive d plex myvol.p2 state init len 524288b driveoffset 1048841b
plexoffset 1572864b
sd name bigraid.p0.s0 drive a plex bigraid.p0 state initializing len 4194304b driveoff
set 1573129b plexoffset 0b
sd name bigraid.p0.s1 drive b plex bigraid.p0 state initializing len 4194304b driveoff
set 1573129b plexoffset 4194304b
sd name bigraid.p0.s2 drive c plex bigraid.p0 state initializing len 4194304b driveoff
set 1573129b plexoffset 8388608b
```

```
sd name bigraid.p0.s3 drive d plex bigraid.p0 state initializing len 4194304b driveoff
set 1573129b plexoffset 12582912b
sd name bigraid.p0.s4 drive e plex bigraid.p0 state initializing len 4194304b driveoff
set 1573129b plexoffset 16777216b
```

The obvious differences here are the presence of explicit location information and naming (both of which are also allowed, but discouraged, for use by the user) and the information on the states (which are not available to the user). Vinum does not store information about drives in the configuration information: it finds the drives by scanning the configured disk drives for partitions with a Vinum label. This enables Vinum to identify drives correctly even if they have been assigned different UNIX drive IDs.

Automatic startup

In order to start Vinum automatically when you boot the system, ensure that you have the following line in your */etc/rc.conf*:

```
start_vinum="YES"          # set to YES to start vinum
```

If you don't have a file */etc/rc.conf*, create one with this content. This will cause the system to load the Vinum kld at startup, and to start any objects mentioned in the configuration. This is done before mounting file systems, so it's possible to automatically *fsck* and mount file systems on Vinum volumes.

When you start Vinum with the `vinum start` command, Vinum reads the configuration database from one of the Vinum drives. Under normal circumstances, each drive contains an identical copy of the configuration database, so it does not matter which drive is read. After a crash, however, Vinum must determine which drive was updated most recently and read the configuration from this drive. It then updates the configuration if necessary from progressively older drives.

## 15

Tapes, backups and floppy disks

In the last chapter, we looked at hard disks. In this chapter, we'll consider how to guard against data loss, and how to transfer data from one location to another. These are functions that UNIX traditionally performs with tapes, and we'll look at them in the next sections. Because FreeBSD runs on PCs, however, you can't completely escape floppy disks, though it would be an excellent idea. We'll look at floppies on page 285.

Backing up your data

No matter how reliable your system, you are never completely protected against loss of data. The most common reasons are hardware failure and human error. By comparison, it's *very* seldom that a software error causes data loss, but this, too, can happen.

UNIX talks about *archives*, which are copies of disk data in a form suitable for writing on a serial medium such as tape. You can, however, write them to disk files as well, and that's what people do when they want to move a source tree from one system to another. You'll also hear the term *tarball* for an archive made by the *tar* program, which we will discuss below.

What backup medium?

Traditionally, PCs use floppy disks as a removable storage medium. We'll look at floppies below, but you can sum the section up in one statement:

Don't use floppy disks.

Floppy disks are particularly unsuited as a backup medium for modern computers. Consider a typical system with a 2 GB hard disk. Storing 2 GB of data on floppies requires about 1,500 floppies, which, at $0.30 each, would cost you $450. Copying the data to a floppy takes about 50 seconds per floppy, so the raw backup time would be about 21 hours, plus the time it takes you to change the floppies, which could easily take another 3 or more hours. During this time you have to sit by the computer playing disk jockey, a total of three days' work during which you could hardly do anything else. When you try to read in the data again, there's a virtual certainty that one of the floppies will have a data error, especially if you read them with a different drive.

By contrast, a QIC-525 tape cartridge will store 500 MB of data for about $20. The media for the same operation would cost $80, and it will take about 6 hours, during which you just need to change the tapes three times. A single DDS or Exabyte cassette stores several gigabytes and costs about $6. The backup time for 2 GB is about 90 minutes, and the operation can be performed completely unattended.

You can currently get a number of relatively cheap tape drives which can connect to your floppy controller. Don't buy them. FreeBSD does have some kind of support for them, but it's rudimentary, and the drives themselves are unreliable and slow. There's no point in making a backup if you can't read the data in again when you need it.

Tape devices

FreeBSD tape devices have names like */dev/nrsa0* (see page 238). Each letter has a significance:

- n means *non-rewinding*. When the process which accesses the tape closes it, the tape remains at the same position. This is inconvenient if you want to remove the tape (before which you should rewind it), but it's the only way if you want to handle multiple archives on the tape. The name of the corresponding *rewind device* has no n (for example, the rewind device corresponding to */dev/nrsa0* is */dev/rsa0*). A rewind device rewinds the tape when it is closed.

- r stands for *raw*, in other words a character device. Modern tape devices are always raw.

- sa stands for *serial access*, and is always SCSI. You can also have a QIC-02 interface tape, which would be called */dev/rwst0*.

- 0 is the *unit number*. If you have more than one tape, the next will be called */dev/nrsa1*, and so on.

Backup software

FreeBSD does not require special "backup software". The base operating system supplies all the programs you need. The tape driver is part of the kernel, and the system includes a number of backup programs. The most popular are:

- *tar*, the *tape archiver*, has been around longer than anybody can remember. It is particularly useful for data exchange, since everybody has it. There are even versions of *tar* for Microsoft platforms. It's also an adequate backup program.

- *cpio* is an alternative backup program. About its only advantage over *tar* is that it can read *cpio* format archives.

- *pax* is another alternative backup program. It has the advantage that it can also read and write *tar* and *cpio* archives.

- *dump* is geared more towards backups than towards archiving. It can maintain multiple levels of backup, each of which backs up only those files which have changed since the last backup of the next higher (numerically lower) level. It is less suited towards data exchange, since its formats are very specific to BSD.

- *amanda*, in the Ports Collection, is another popular backup program.

Backup strategies are frequently the subject of religious wars. I personally find that *tar* does everything I want, but you'll find plenty of people who will recommend *dump* or *amanda* instead. In the following section, we'll look at the basics of using *tar*. See the man page *dump(8)* for more information on *dump*.

tar

tar, the *tape archiver*, performs the following functions:

- Creating an *archive*, which can be a serial device such as a tape, or a disk file, from the contents of a number of directories.

- Extracting files from an archive.

- Listing the contents of an archive.

tar does not compress the data. The resulting archive is slightly larger than the sum of the files which it contains, since it also contains a certain amount of header information. You can, however, use the *gzip* program to compress a *tar* archive, and *tar* will invoke it for you automatically. The resultant archives are typically 80% smaller than the constituent files.

Creating a *tar* archive

Create an archive with the c option. Unlike most UNIX programs, *tar* does not require a hyphen (-) in front of the options. For example, to save your complete kernel source tree, you could write:

```
# tar cvf source-archive.tar /usr/src/sys
tar: Removing leading / from absolute path names in the archive.
usr/src/sys/
usr/src/sys/CVS/
usr/src/sys/CVS/Root
usr/src/sys/CVS/Repository
usr/src/sys/CVS/Entries
usr/src/sys/compile/
usr/src/sys/compile/CVS/
(etc)
```

The parameters have the following meaning:

- cvf are the options. c stands for *create* an archive, v specifies *verbose* operation (in this case, this causes *tar* to produce the list of files being archived), and f specifies that the next parameter is the name of the archive file.

- `source-archive.tar` is the name of the archive. In this case, it's a disk file.

- `/usr/src/sys` is the name of the directory to archive. *tar* archives all files in the directory, including most devices. For historical reasons, *tar* can't back up devices with minor numbers greater than 65536, and changing the format would make it incompatible with other systems.

The message on the first line (`Removing leading / ...`) indicates that, although the directory name was specified as `/usr/src/sys`, *tar* treats it as *usr/src/sys*. This makes it possible to restore the files into another directory at a later time.

You can back up to tape in exactly the same way:

```
# tar cvf /dev/nrsa0 /usr/src/sys
```

There is a simpler way, however: if you don't specify a file name, *tar* looks for the environment variable TAPE. If it finds it, it interprets it as the name of the tape drive. You can make things a lot easier by setting the following line in the configuration file for your shell (*.profile* for *sh*, *.bashrc* for *bash*, *.login* for *csh* and *tcsh*):

```
TAPE=/dev/nrsa0 export TAPE        for sh and bash
setenv TAPE /dev/nrsa0             for csh and tcsh
```

After this, the previous example simplifies to:

```
# tar cv /usr/src/sys
```

Listing an archive

To list an archive, use the option `t`:

```
# tar t                                from tape
usr/src/sys/
usr/src/sys/CVS/
usr/src/sys/CVS/Root
usr/src/sys/CVS/Repository
usr/src/sys/CVS/Entries
usr/src/sys/compile/
usr/src/sys/compile/CVS/
usr/src/sys/compile/CVS/Root
(etc)
# tar tvf source-archive.tar          from disk
drwxrwxrwx root/bin          0 Oct 25 15:07 1997 usr/src/sys/
drwxrwxrwx root/bin          0 Oct 25 15:08 1997 usr/src/sys/CVS/
-rw-rw-rw- root/wheel        9 Sep 30 23:13 1996 usr/src/sys/CVS/Root
-rw-rw-rw- root/wheel       17 Sep 30 23:13 1996 usr/src/sys/CVS/Repository
-rw-rw-rw- root/bin        346 Oct 25 15:08 1997 usr/src/sys/CVS/Entries
drwxrwxrwx root/bin          0 Oct 27 17:11 1997 usr/src/sys/compile/
drwxrwxrwx root/bin          0 Jul 30 10:52 1997 usr/src/sys/compile/CVS/
(etc)
```

This example shows the use of the `v` (*verbose*) option with `t`. If you don't use it, *tar* displays only the names of the files (first example, from tape). If you do use it, *tar* also displays the permissions, ownerships, sizes and last modification date in a form reminiscent of *ls -l* (second example, which is from the disk file *source-archive.tar*).

Extracting files

To extract a file from the archive, use the x option:

```
# tar xv usr/src/sys/Makefile            from tape
usr/src/sys/Makefile                     confirms that the file was extracted
```

As with the c option, if you don't use the v option, *tar* will not list any file names. If you omit the names of the files to extract, *tar* will extract the complete archive.

Compressed archives

You can use the *gzip* program in combination with *tar* by specifying the z option. For example, to create the archive *source-archive.tar.gz* in compressed format, write:

```
# tar czf source-archive.tar.gz /usr/src/sys
```

You *must* specify the z option when listing or extracting compressed archives, and you must not do so when listing or extracting non-compressed archives. Otherwise you will get messages like:

```
# tar tzvf source-archive.tar

gzip: stdin: not in gzip format
tar: child returned status 1
# tar tvf source-archive.tar.gz
tar: only read 2302 bytes from archive source-archive.tar.gz
```

Using floppy disks under FreeBSD

I don't like floppy disks. UNIX doesn't like floppy disks. Probably you don't like floppy disks either, but we occasionally have to live with them.

FreeBSD requires floppy disks for one thing only: for initially booting the system. This is only because this is still the only way to boot most PC which don't have an operating system on disk. We've already seen that they're unsuitable for archival data storage and data transfer. For this purpose, FreeBSD uses tapes and CD-ROMs, which are much more reliable, and for the data volumes involved in modern computers, they're cheaper and faster.

So why use floppies? The only good reasons are:

- You have a floppy drive. You may not have a tape drive. Before you go out and buy all those floppies, though, consider that it might be cheaper to buy a tape drive and some tapes instead.

- You need to exchange data with people using Microsoft platforms, or with people who don't have the same kind of tape as you do.

In the following sections, we'll look at how to handle floppies under FreeBSD, with particular regard to coexisting with Microsoft. Here's an overview:

- Always format floppies before using them on your system for the first time, even if they've been formatted before. We'll look at that in the next section.

- Just occasionally, you need to create a UNIX file system on floppy. We'll look at that on page 286.

- When exchanging with Microsoft users, you need to create a Microsoft file system. We'll look at that on page 288.

- When exchanging with other UNIX users, whether FreeBSD or not, use *tar* or *cpio*. We'll look at how to do that on page 288.

Formatting a floppy

Even if you buy preformatted floppies, it's a good idea to reformat them. Track alignment can vary significifantly between individual floppy drives, and the result can be that your drive doesn't write quite on top of the pre-written tracks. I have seen read failure rates as high as 2% on pre-formatted floppies: in other words, after writing 100 floppies with valuable data, the chances are that two of them will have read errors. You can reduce this problem by reformatting the floppy in the drive in which it is to be written, but you can't eliminate it.

On Microsoft platforms, you format floppies with the *FORMAT* program, which performs two different functions when invoked on floppies: it performs both a *low-level* format, which re-writes the physical sector information, and then it performs a *high-level* format, which writes the information necessary for Microsoft platforms to use it as a file system. UNIX calls the second operation creating a file system. It's not always necessary to have a file system on the diskette—in fact, as we'll see, it can be a disadvantage. In addition, FreeBSD offers different kinds of file system, so it performs the two functions with different programs. In this section, we'll look at *fdformat*, which performs the low-level format. We'll look at how to create a *ufs* or Microsoft file system in the next section.

To format the first floppy drive, */dev/rfd0*, you would enter:

```
$ fdformat /dev/rfd0
Format 1440K floppy '/dev/rfd0'? (y/n): y
Processing ------------------------------------
```

Each of the hyphen characters (-) represent two tracks. As the format proceeds, they change individually to an **F** (Format) and then to **V** (Verify) in turn, so at the end the line reads

```
Processing VVVVVVVVVVVVVVVVVVVVVVVVVVVVVVVVVVVVV done.
```

File systems on floppy

It's possible to use floppies as file systems under FreeBSD. You can create a *ufs* file system on a floppy just like on a hard disk. This is not necessarily a good idea: the *ufs* file system is designed for performance, not maximum capacity. By default, it doesn't use the last 8% of disk space, and it includes a lot of structure information which further reduces the space available on the disk. Here's an example of creating a file system, mounting it on the directory */A*, and listing the remaining space available on an empty 3½" floppy. We use the *disktab* approach to

labelling the disk, as we saw on page 258. */etc/disktab* does have labels for floppy disks: use
`fd1440` for a 3½" 1.44 MB floppy, and `fd1200` for a 5¼" 1.2 MB floppy:

```
# disklabel -w -r /dev/rfd0 fd1440    label the floppy
# disklabel -r /dev/rfd0              and list the information
# /dev/rfd0:
type: unknown
disk: fd1440
label:
flags:
bytes/sector: 512
sectors/track: 18
tracks/cylinder: 2
sectors/cylinder: 36
cylinders: 80
sectors/unit: 2880
rpm: 300
interleave: 1
trackskew: 0
cylinderskew: 0
headswitch: 0          # milliseconds
track-to-track seek: 0  # milliseconds
drivedata: 0

3 partitions:
#       size    offset    fstype    [fsize bsize bps/cpg]
  a:    2880        0     unused     512   4096        # (Cyl.    0 - 79)
  b:    2880        0     unused     512   4096        # (Cyl.    0 - 79)
  c:    2880        0     unused     512   4096        # (Cyl.    0 - 79)
# newfs /dev/rfd0                     create a new file system
Warning: Block size restricts cylinders per group to 6.
Warning: 1216 sector(s) in last cylinder unallocated
/dev/rfd0.1440: 2880 sectors in 1 cylinders of 1 tracks, 4096 sectors
        1.4MB in 1 cyl groups (6 c/g, 12.00MB/g, 736 i/g)
super-block backups (for fsck -b #) at:
 32,
# mount /dev/fd0 /A                    mount the floppy on /A
# df /A                               display the space available
Filesystem   1024-blocks    Used    Avail Capacity  Mounted on
/dev/fd0           1319        0     1213      0%     /mnt
```

Let's look at this in a little more detail:

- The first invocation of *disklabel*, with the `-w` option, writes a disk label to the floppy, which supplies enough information for *newfs* to create a *ufs* file system on it.

- The second invocation of *disklabel*, just with the `-r` option, lists the information written by the first invocation. This isn't necessary for creating the file system, but it helps to check that the disk is labelled correctly.

- *newfs* creates the *ufs* file system on the floppy.

- We have already seen *mount* on page 235. In this case, we use it to mount the floppy on the file system */A*.

- The *df* program shows the maximum and available space on a file system. By default, *df* displays usage in blocks of 512 bytes, an inconvenient size. In this example, the environment variable `BLOCKSIZE` was set to 1024 to display the usage in 1 kB (1024 byte) blocks. See page 176 for more details of environment variables.

The output of *df* looks terrible! Our floppy only has 1213 kB left for normal user data, even though there is nothing on it and even *df* claims that it can really store 1319 kB. This is because *ufs* keeps a default of 8% of the space free for performance reasons. You can change this, however, with *tunefs*, the file system tune program:[1]

```
# umount /A                          first unmount the floppy
# tunefs -m 0 /dev/rfd0              and change the minimum free to 0
tunefs: minimum percentage of free space changes from 8% to 0%
tunefs: should optimize for space with minfree < 8%
# mount /dev/fd0 /A                  mount the file system again
# df /A                             and take another look
Filesystem   1024-blocks     Used     Avail Capacity  Mounted on
/dev/fd0            1319        0      1319     0%      /A
```

Still, this is a far cry from the claimed data storage of a Microsoft disk. In fact, Microsoft disks can't store the full 1.4 MB either, since it also needs space for storing directories and allocation tables. The moral of the story: only use file systems on floppy if you don't have any alternative.

Microsoft file systems

To create an MS-DOS file system, use the *mkdosfs* command:

```
$ mkdosfs -f 1440 /dev/rfd0
```

The specification `-f 1440` tells *mkdosfs* that this is a 1.4 MB floppy. Alternatively, you can use the *mformat* command:

```
$ mformat A:
```

You can specify the number of tracks with the `-t` option, and the number of sectors with the `-s` option. To explicitly specify a floppy with 80 tracks and 18 sectors (a standard 3½" 1.44 MB floppy), you could enter:

```
$ mformat -t 80 -s 18 A:
```

mformat is one of the *mtools* that we will look at in the next section.

Other uses of floppies

Well, you could take the disks out of the cover and use them as a kind of frisbee. But there is one other useful thing you can do with floppies: as an archive medium, they don't need a file system on them. They just need to be low-level formatted. For example, to write the contents of the current directory onto a floppy, you could enter:

---

1. To quote the man page: *You can tune a file system, but you can't tune a fish.*

```
$ tar cvfM /dev/rfd0 .
./
.xfmrc
.x6530modkey
.uwmrc
.twmrc
.rnsoft
.rnlast
.rhosts~
.rhosts
...etc
Prepare volume #2 for /dev/rfd0 and hit return:
```

Since we are writing to the floppy as a character device, the name is */dev/rfd0*—as with tapes, the r stands for the *raw* device. Note also the solitary dot (.) at the end of the command line. That's the name of the current directory, and that's what you're backing up. Note also the option M, which is short for --multi-volume. There's a very good chance that you'll run out of space on a floppy, and this option says that you have a sufficient supply of floppies to perform the complete backup.

To extract the data again, use *tar* with the x option:

```
$ tar xvfM /dev/rfd0
./
.xfmrc
.x6530modkey
.uwmrc
...etc
```

See the man page *tar(1)* for other things you can do with *tar*.

Accessing Microsoft floppies

Of course, most of the time you get data on a floppy, it's not in *tar* format: it has a Microsoft file system on it. We've already seen the Microsoft file system type on page 235, but that's a bit of overkill if you just want to copy files from floppy. In this case, use the *mtools* package. *mtools* is an implementation of the MS-DOS commands *ATTRIB, CD, COPY, DEL, DIR, FORMAT, LABEL, MD, RD, READ, REN,* and *TYPE* under UNIX. To avoid confusion with existing utilities, the UNIX versions of these commands start with the letter m. They are also written in lower case. For example, to list the contents of a floppy and copy one of the files to the current (FreeBSD) directory, you might enter:

```
$ mdir                           list the current directory on A:
 Volume in drive A is MESSED OS
 Directory for A:/

IO       SYS       33430    4-09-91    5:00a
MSDOS    SYS       37394    4-09-91    5:00a
COMMAND  COM       47845   12-23-92    5:22p
NFS               <DIR>    12-24-92   11:03a
DOSEDIT  COM        1728   10-07-83    7:40a
CONFIG   SYS         792   10-07-94    7:31p
AUTOEXEC BAT         191   12-24-92   11:10a
MOUSE             <DIR>    12-24-92   11:09a
     12 File(s)      82944 bytes free
$ mcd nfs                        Change to directory A:\NFS
```

```
$ mdir                              and list the directory
 Volume in drive A is MESSED OS
 Directory for A:/NFS

 .                    <DIR>     12-24-92   11:03a
 ..                   <DIR>     12-24-92   11:03a
 HOSTS                 5985     10-07-94    7:34p
 NETWORK   BAT          103     12-24-92   12:28p
 DRIVES    BAT           98     11-07-94    5:24p
 ...and many more
       51 File(s)      82944 bytes free
$ mtype drives.bat                  type the contents of DRIVES.BAT
net use c: presto:/usr/dos
c:
cd \nfs
# net use f: porsche:/dos
# net use g: porsche:/usr
$ mcopy a:hosts .                   copy A:HOSTS to local UNIX directory
Copying HOSTS
$ ls -l hosts                       and list it
-rw-rw-rw-   1 root      wheel        5985 Jan 28 18:04 hosts
```

You must specify the drive letter to mcopy, since it uses this indication to decide whether the file name is a UNIX file name or a Microsoft file name. You can copy files from FreeBSD to the floppy as well, of course.

A word of warning. UNIX uses a different text data format from Microsoft: in UNIX, lines end with a single character, called **Newline**, and represented by the characters \n in the C programming language. It corresponds to the ASCII character **Line Feed** (represented by ^J). Microsoft uses two characters, a **Carriage Return** (^M) followed by a **Line Feed**. This unfortunate difference causes a number of unexpected compatibility problems, since both characters are usually invisible on the screen.

In FreeBSD, you won't normally have many problems. Occasionally a program will complain about non-printable characters in an input line. Some, like *Emacs*, will show them. For example, our last file, *drives.bat*, would show as:

```
net use c: presto:/usr/dos^M
c:^M
cd \nfs^M
# net use f: porsche:/dos^M
# net use g: porsche:/usr^M
```

This may seem relatively harmless, but it confuses some programs, including the C compiler and pagers like *more*, which may react in confusing ways. You can remove them with the -t option of *mcopy*:

```
$ mcopy -t a:drives.bat .
```

Transferring files in the other direction is more likely to cause problems. For example, you might edit this file under FreeBSD and then copy it back to the diskette. The results depend on the editor, but assuming we changed all occurrences of the word porsche to freedom, and then copied the file back to the diskette, Microsoft might then find:

```
C:> type drives.bat
net use c: presto:/usr/dos
                            c:
                          cd \nfs
                               # net use f: freedom:/dos
                                              # net use g: freedom:/usr
```

This is a typical result of removing the **Carriage Return** characters. The -t option to *mcopy* can help here, too. If you use it when copying *to* a Microsoft file system, it will reinsert the **Carriage Return** characters.

16

Printers

In this chapter, we'll look at some aspects of using printers with FreeBSD. FreeBSD users do not access printers directly. Instead, a series of processes, collectively called the *spooler*, manage print data. One process, *lpr*, writes user print data to disk, and another, *lpd*, copies the print data to the printers. This method enables processes to write print data even if the printers are busy and ensures optimum printer availability.

In this section, we'll look briefly at what you need to do to set up printers. For more details, look in the online handbook section on printing, from which this section is derived.

lpd is the central spooler process. It is responsible for a number of things:

- It controls access to attached printers and printers attached to other hosts on the network.

- It enables users to submit files to be printed. These submissions are known as jobs.

- It prevents multiple users from accessing a printer at the same time by maintaining a queue for each printer.

- It can print header pages, also known as banner or burst pages, so users can easily find jobs they have printed in a stack of printouts.

- It takes care of communications parameters for printers connected on serial ports.

- It can send jobs over the network to another spooler on another host.

- It can run special filters to format jobs to be printed for various printer languages or printer capabilities.

- It can account for printer usage.

Through a configuration file, and by providing the special filter programs, you can enable the spooler to do all or some subset of the above for a great variety of printer hardware.

This may sound like overkill if you are the only user on the system. It *is* possible to access the printer directly, but it's not a good idea:

- The spooler prints jobs in the background. You don't have to wait for data to be copied to the printer.

- The spooler can conveniently run a job to be printed through filters to add headers or convert special formats (such as PostScript) into a format the printer will understand.

- Most programs that provide a print feature expect to talk to the spooler on your system.

Printer configuration

Nowadays, most printers are connected by the *parallel port*. Parallel ports enable faster communication with the printer, up to about 100,000 bytes per second, while serial printers seldom transmit more than 1,920 characters per second.

> Older UNIX systems frequently used serial printers, but they are no longer in common use. Look at the handbook article for specifies of serial printers.

More modern printers may also have an Ethernet interface, which enables them to connect to several machines at once.

It's pretty straightforward to connect a parallel printer: plug in the cable between the printer and the computer. You don't need any adjustments. If you have more than one parallel interface, of course, you'll have to decide which one to use. Parallel printer devices are called */dev/lptn*, where *n* is the number, starting with 0. See table 13-5 on page 237 for further details.

You don't need to do anything special to configure the line printer driver *lpt*: it's in the kernel by default. Of course, if you have previously removed it, you'll have to replace it. See page 341 for more details.

Testing the printer

When you have connected and powered on the printer, run the manufacture's test if one is supplied. Typically there's a function which produces a printout describing the printer's features. After that, check the communication between the computer and the printer.

```
# lptest > /dev/lpt0
```

This will not produce any output with a pure PostScript printer, but you should see some reaction on the status display. See the description in the online handbook for testing PostScript printers.

Configuring */etc/printcap*

The next step is to configure the central configuration file, */etc/printcap*. This file is not the easiest to read, but after a while you'll get used to it. Here are some typical entries:

```
lp|lj|ps|local LaserJet 6MP printer:\
    :lp=/dev/lpt0:sd=/var/spool/output/lpd:lf=/var/log/lpd-errs:sh:mx#0:\
    :if=/usr/local/libexec/lpfilter:

rlp|sample remote printer:\
    :rm=freebie:sd=/var/spool/output/freebie:lf=/var/log/lpd-errs:
```

Let's look at this in detail:

- All fields are delimited by a colon (:).

- Continuation lines require a backslash character (\). Note particularly that you require a colon at the end of a continued line, and another at the beginning of the following line.

- The first line of each entry specifies a number of names separated by vertical bar symbols |. By tradition, the last name is a more verbose description.

- The following fields have an identification followed by an optional delimiter. If the field takes a string parameter, the delimiter is =, and if it takes a numeric value, the delimiter is #.

- The first entry defines a local printer, called lp, lj, ps and local LaserJet 6MP printer. Why so many names? lp is the default, so you should have it somewhere. lj is frequently used to talk to printers which understand HP's LaserJet language (now PCL), and ps might be used to talk to a printer which understands PostScript. The final name is more of a description.

- The entry lp tells the spooler the name of the physical device to which the printer is connected. Remote printers don't have physical devices.

- sd tells the spooler the directory in which to store jobs awaiting printing. You must check that this directory exists.

- lf specifies the name of a file into which to log errors.

- sh is a flag telling *lpd* to omit a header page. If you don't have that, every job will be preceded by a descriptor page. In a small environment, this doesn't make sense, and is just a waste of paper.

- The parameter mx tells *lpd* the maximum size of a spool job in kilobytes. If the job is larger than this value, *lpd* refuses to print it. In our case, we don't want to limit the size. We do this by setting mx to 0.

- if tells *lpd* to apply a *filter* to the job before printing. We'll look at this below.

- In the remote printer entry, rm tells *lpd* the name of the system to which to send the data. This could be a fully qualified domain name, of course.

Spooler filters

Probably the least intelligible entry in the previous configuration file was the if entry. It specifies the name of an *input filter*, a program through which *lpd* passes the complete print data before printing.

What does it do that for? There can be a number of reasons. Maybe you have data in a format which isn't fit to print. For example, it might be PostScript, and your printer might not understand PostScript. Or it could be the other way around: your printer understands *only* PostScript, and the input isn't PostScript.

There's a more likely reason to require a filter, though: most printers still emulate the old teletypes, so they require a carriage return character (**Ctrl-M** or **^M**) to start at the beginning of the line, and a new line character (**Ctrl-J** or **^J**) to advance to the next line. UNIX uses only **^J**, so if you copy data to it, you're liable to see a staircase effect. For example, *ps* may tell you:

```
$ ps
  PID  TT  STAT      TIME COMMAND
 2252  p1  Ss      0:01.35 /bin/bash
 2287  p1  IW      0:04.77 e /etc/printcap
 2346  p1  R+      0:00.05 ps
```

When you try to print it, however, you get:

```
  PID  TT  STAT      TIME COMMAND
                           2252  p1  Ss      0:01.35 /bin/bash
                                                      2287  p1  IW      0
```

The rest of the page is empty: you've gone off the right margin.

There are a number of ways to solve this problem:

- You may be able to configure your printer to interpret **Ctrl-J** as both **newline** and **return**, and to ignore **Ctrl-M**. Check your printer handbook.

- You may be able to issue a control sequence to your printer to tell it to interpret **Ctrl-J** as both new line and return to the beginning of the line, and to ignore **Ctrl-M**. For example, HP LaserJets and compatibles will do this if you send them the control sequence **ESC**&k2G.

- You can write an *input filter* which transforms the print job into a form which the printer understands. We'll look at this option below.

There are a couple of options for the print filter. One of them, taken from the online handbook, sends out a LaserJet control sequence before every job. Put the following shell script in */usr/local/libexec/lpfilter*:

```
#!/bin/sh
printf "\033&k2G" && cat && printf "\f" && exit 0
exit 2
```

Figure 16-1: Simple print filter

This approach does not work well with some printers, such as my HP LaserJet 6MP, which can print both PostScript and LaserJet (natural) formats at random. They do this by recognizing the text at the beginning of the job. This particular filter confuses them by sending a LaserJet command code, so the printer prints the PostScript as if it were plain text. The source file */book/scripts/lpfilter.c* contains a filter which replaces all **Ctrl-Js** with **Ctrl-J Ctrl-M**. Compile this program and store the executable in */usr/local/libexec/lpfilter*.

```
# cc /book/scripts/lpfilter.c -o /usr/local/libexec/lpfilter
```

That's all you normally need to do to set up your printers. Next, you should test them.

Starting the spooler

As we saw above, the line printer dæmon *lpd* is responsible for printing spooled jobs. By default it isn't started at boot time. If you're `root`, you can start it by name:

```
# lpd
```

Normally, however, you will want it to be started automatically when the system starts up. You do this by setting the variable `lpd_enable` in */etc/rc.conf*:

```
lpd_enable="YES"            # Run the line printer daemon
```

See page 203 for more details of */etc/rc.conf*.

Another line in */etc/rc.conf* refers to the line printer dæmon:

```
lpd_flags=""               # Flags to lpd (if enabled).
```

You don't normally need to change this line. See the man page for *lpd* for details of the flags.

Testing the spooler

To test the spooler, you can run the *lptest* program again. This time, however, instead of sending it directly to the printer, you send it to the spooler:

```
$ lptest 20 5 | lpr
```

The results should look like:

```
!"#$%&'()*+,-./01234
"#$%&'()*+,-./012345
#$%&'()*+,-./0123456
$%&'()*+,-./01234567
%&'()*+,-./012345678
```

Troubleshooting

Here's a list of the most common problems and how to solve them:

Table 16-2. Common printer problems

Problem	Cause
The printer prints, but the last page doesn't appear. The status shows that the printer still has data in the buffer. After several minutes, the last page may appear.	Your output data is not ejecting the last page. The printer is configured to either wait for an explicit eject request (the ASCII *Form feed* character, **Ctrl-L**) or to eject after a certain period of time. You have a choice as to what you do about this. Usually you can configure the printer, or you could get the print filter to print a form feed character at the end of the job. Figure 16-1 already does this—that's the `printf "\f"`.
The lines wander off to the right edge of the paper and are never seen again.	This is the *staircase effect* that we saw on page 296. See there for a couple of solutions.
Individual characters or whole sections of text are missing.	This problem occurs almost only on serial printers. It's a result of incorrect handshaking—see page 430 and the online handbook for more details.
The output was completely unintelligible random characters.	On a serial printer, if the characters appear slowly, and there's a predominance of the characters {	} ~, this probably means that you have set up the communication parameters incorrectly. Check the online handbook for a solution. Make sure you don't confuse this problem with the following one.
The text was legible, but it bore no relationship to what you wanted to print.	One possibility is that you are sending PostScript output to your printer. Look at the example on page 300 to check if it is PostScript. If it is, your printer is not interpreting it correctly, either because it doesn't understand PostScript, or because it has been confused (see the discussion on page 296 for one reason). We'll look at PostScript in more detail on page 300.

Problem	Cause
The display on the printer shows that data are arriving, but the printer doesn't print anything.	You might be sending normal text to a PostScript printer which doesn't understand normal text. In this case, too, you will need a filter to convert the text to PostScript—the opposite of the previous problem. Alternatively, your printer port may not be interrupting correctly. This will not stop the printer from printing, but it can take up to 20 minutes to print a page. You can fix this by issuing the following command, which puts the printer /dev/lpt0 into polled mode: `# lptcontrol -p`
You get the message `lpr: cannot create /var/spool/output/freebie/.seq`	You have forgotten to create the spool directory /var/spool/output/freebie.

Using the spooler

Using the spooler is relatively simple. Instead of outputting data directly to the printer, you *pipe* it to the spooler *lpr* command. For example, here is the same print command, first printing directly to the printer, and secondly via the spooler:

```
# ps waux > /dev/lpt0
# ps waux | lpr
```

The spooler creates a *job* from this data. You can look at the current print queue with the *lpq* program:

```
$ lpq
waiting for lp to become ready (offline ?)
Rank   Owner     Job  Files                    Total Size
1st    grog      313  (standard input)         9151 bytes
2nd    grog      30   (standard input)         3319 bytes
3rd    yvonne    31   (standard input)         3395 bytes
4th    root      0    (standard input)         2611 bytes
```

The first line is a warning that *lpd* can't currently print. You should take it seriously. In this example, the printer was deliberately turned off so that the queue did not change from one example to the next.

Normally, the job numbers increase sequentially: this particular example came from three different machines. You can get more detail with the `-l` option:

```
$ lpq -l
waiting for lp to become ready (offline ?)

grog: 1st                                [job 313freebie.example.org]
         (standard input)                9151 bytes

grog: 2nd                                [job 030presto.example.org]
         (standard input)                3319 bytes

yvonne: 3rd                              [job 031presto.example.org]
         (standard input)                3395 bytes

root: 4th                                [job 000bumble.example.org]
         (standard input)                2611 bytes
```

Removing print jobs

Sometimes you may want to delete spool output without printing it. You don't need to do this because of a printer configuration error: just turn the printer off, fix the configuration error, and turn the printer on again. The job should then be printed correctly. But if you discover that the print job itself contains garbage, you can remove it with the *lprm* program. First, though, you need to know the job number. Assuming the list we have above, we might want to remove job 30:

```
# lprm 30
dfA030presto.example.org dequeued
cfA030presto.example.org dequeued
# lpq
waiting for lp to become ready (offline ?)
Rank   Owner    Job  Files                    Total Size
1st    grog     313  (standard input)         9151 bytes
2nd    yvonne   31   (standard input)         3395 bytes
3rd    root     0    (standard input)         2611 bytes
```

If the printer is offline, it may take some time for the *lprm* to complete.

PostScript

We've encountered the term *PostScript* several times already. It's a powerful *Page Description Language*. With it, you can transmit detailed documents such as this book electronically and print them out in exactly the same form elsewhere. PostScript is a very popular format on the World-Wide Web, and browsers like Netscape usually print in PostScript format.

Most other document formats describe special print features with *escape sequences*, special commands which start with a special character. For example, the HP LaserJet and PCL formats use the ASCII **ESC** character (0x1b) to indicate the beginning of an escape sequence. PostScript uses the opposite approach: unless defined otherwise, the contents of a PostScript file are commands, and the printable data is enclosed in parentheses. PostScript documents start with something like:

```
%!PS-Adobe-3.0
%%Creator: groff version 1.10
%%CreationDate: Fri Oct 31 18:36:45 1997
%%DocumentNeededResources: font Symbol
%%+ font Courier
%%+ font Times-Roman
%%DocumentSuppliedResources: file images/vipw.ps
%%Pages: 32
%%PageOrder: Ascend
%%Orientation: Portrait
%%EndComments
%%BeginProlog
```

This is the *prologue* (the beginning) of the PostScript output for this chapter. The *prologue* of such a program can be several hundred kilobytes long if it includes embedded fonts or images. A more typical size is about 500 lines.

You can do a number of things with PostScript:

- You can look at it with *ghostscript* or *ghostview*, both of which are in the Ports Collection.

- Many printers understand PostScript and print it directly. You should know this, since it's an expensive option, but in case of doubt check your printer manual.

- If your printer doesn't understand PostScript, you can print with the aid of ghostscript.

Installing *ghostscript* and *ghostview*

ghostview is an interface to *ghostscript*, so you need to install it in any case. Older versions supplied the fonts separately, but you no longer need to worry about that: they're now part of the package.

Install the packages by first checking the names on the CD-ROM:

```
# cd /cdrom/packages/All
# ls gh*
ghostscript-2.6.2.tgz ghostscript-3.53.tgz  ghostscript-4.03.tgz  ghostview-1.5.tgz
# pkg_add ghostscript-4.03.tgz ghostview-1.5.tgz
```

Viewing with *ghostview*

To view a file with *ghostview*, simply start it:

```
$ ghostview &
```

You will get a blank display, but you can open a file window by pressing o, after which you can select files and display them. Figure 16-3 shows the display of a draft version of this page with an overlaid open window at the top left. The *selFile* window contains a field at the top into which you can type the name of a file. Alternatively, the three columns below, with scroll bars, allow you to browse the current directory and the parent and grandparent directories. The interface looks relatively primitive, but it works.

The window below shows the text of the previous page (roughly) on the right hand side. with drag scroll bars operated by the middle button. At top left are five oval menu buttons which

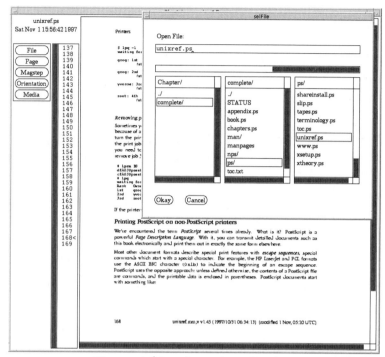

Figure 16-3: *ghostview* **display**

you can select with the left mouse button. Note particularly the `Magstep` button, which sets the size of the display.

The column to the right of these buttons is a list of page numbers. You can select a page number with the middle mouse button. You can also get an enlargement display of the text area around the mouse cursor by pressing the left button. Press the area marked `Dismiss` to remove the enlargement.

Printing with *ghostscript*

If your printer doesn't support PostScript, you can still print some semblance of the intended text with the help of *ghostscript*. The results are very acceptable with laser and inkjet printers, less so with matrix printers, even 24 pin versions.

To print on your particular printer, you first need to find a *driver* for it in *ghostscript*. In this context, the term *driver* means some code inside *ghostscript* which converts the data into something that the printer can print. Unfortunately, the man page doesn't help much. To find out which driver it supports, start *ghostscript* and enter the following in the text window, ignoring the display window that it opens:

```
$ gs                                    that's the name of the ghostscript program
Aladdin Ghostscript 5.03 (1997-8-8)
Copyright (C) 1997 Aladdin Enterprises, Menlo Park, CA.  All rights reserved.
This software comes with NO WARRANTY: see the file PUBLIC for details.
GS>devicenames ==                       list device names
[/tiff24nc /ppm /pcxgray /cgm8 /sgirgb /pnm /mgr8 /bmp16m /psmono /pgnm /mgrgray8 /bmp
16 /png256 /pgm /mgrgray2 /bitcmyk /pnggray /pbm /miff24 /bit /nullpage /pkmraw /pcx24
b /jpeg /pdfwrite /tifflzw /ppmraw /pcx16 /cgm24 /tiff12nc /pnmraw /pcxmono /cgmmono /
psgray /pgnmraw /mgr4 /bmp256 /png16m /pgmraw /mgrgray4 /bmpmono /png16 /pbmraw /mgrmo
no /bitrgb /pngmono /pcxcmyk /jpeggray /pswrite /tiffpack /pkm /pcx256 /cif /t4693d8 /
paintjet /ljet3d /iwlq /declj250 /appledmp /tiffg32d /t4693d2 /oki182 /ljet2p /iwhi /c
dj850 /sxlcrt /tiffcrle /st800 /necp6 /ln03 /ibmpro /cdj500 /x11gray2 /faxg32d /r4081
/lp8000 /lbp8 /eps9high /cdjcolor /x11alpha /dfaxlow /pxlmono /lj5gray /la75 /epson /c
cr /xes /pjxl /ljetplus /la50 /djet500c /bjc600 /tek4696 /pj /ljet4 /jetp3852 /deskjet
 /bj10e /tiffg4 /t4693d4 /okiibm /ljet3 /iwlo /cp50 /ap3250 /tiffg3 /stcolor /oce9050
/lj250 /imagen /cdj550 /x11mono /faxg4 /sj48 /m8510 /lips3 /epsonc /cdjmono /x11cmyk /
faxg3 /pxlcolor /lp2563 /la75plus /eps9mid /cdeskjet /x11 /dfaxhigh /pjxl300 /lj5mono
/la70 /dnj650c /bjc800 /uniprint /pjetxl /lj4dith /laserjet /djet500 /bj200 /epswrite]
GS>^D                                   exit
```

Unfortunately, it's very difficult to decide which of these drivers does what without looking at the source code, or at least the *Makefile*, so it's comforting to know that the most common non-PostScript printer, the Hewlett-Packard LaserJet series, uses the driver prefix `ljet`. Modern versions will all run with `ljet4`; if you run into trouble, try one of the older ones. In particular, the original LaserJet requires the driver `ljet`.

The following one-line script will print PostScript documents to the spooler. It is present on the CD-ROM as */book/scripts/gsp*.

```
#!/bin/sh
gs -dNOPAUSE -q -sDEVICE=ljet4 -sOutputFile=\|lpr -- $*
```

Note that the output to the printer is binary data, so a filter of the kind shown in */book/scripts/lpfilter.c* will destroy the format and produce nonsensical output. This shouldn't be a problem, since that filter is intended specifically for PostScript printers, which don't need *ghostscript*.

17

Setting up your FreeBSD desktop

So far, we've looked at FreeBSD from a system administration viewpoint. You didn't install FreeBSD in order to perform system administration: you want to do some work with it.

Nowadays, every computer system has the concept of a *desktop*, a surface on the glass of your monitor on which you do your work. For years, UNIX users have worked with a single 80x25 character mode display. Users of Microsoft Windows considered this old-fashioned in the extreme, but in fact the flexibility of the UNIX system made this quite a good way to work.

Still, there's no doubt of the advantage of a system which offers the possibility of performing multiple operations at once, and this is one of the declared advantages of UNIX. But you normally need a terminal to interact with each task. Under UNIX, the best way to do this is with the X window system.

FreeBSD comes with over a thousand ported software packets. One user described putting them together as trying to do a jigsaw puzzle without the picture on the box.

In fact, it's even worse than that: you can imagine your own picture. Depending on your imagination and your luck, the results can be good, bad, or unusable. In this chapter, I describe a framework for how to work with FreeBSD. Not surprisingly, this closely resembles the environment in which I work, and it may not be to everybody's taste. It will, however, give you a usable start from which you can diverge when you have the time, the inclination and the understanding.

The hardware

The desktop I describe will run on almost any hardware. That doesn't mean that all hardware is equal, of course. Here are some considerations:

The display board and monitor

X enables you to do a lot more in parallel than other windowing environments. As a result, screen real estate is at a premium. Use as big a monitor as you can afford, and as high a resolution as your monitor can handle. You should be able to display a resolution of 1600x1200 on a good 21" monitor, 1280x1024 on an average 21" monitor, and 1024x768 on a 17" monitor. If you're using a 14" monitor, you will have to compromise: it's difficult to use 1024x768 on a monitor of this size, but any lower resolution is just too low for reasonable use. I use 1024x768 when I have to use a 14" monitor.

The keyboard

Keyboards have not changed much since the function keys were moved to the top of the keyboard, where you have to search for them. It's obvious that keyboard layouts are dictated by people who can't touch-type. In my opinion, this applies particularly to the so-called "ergonomic" keyboards, which require a lot of learning to use correctly, and don't seem to give anything in return. Your mileage may vary, but bear in mind that FreeBSD places more emphasis on the keyboard and less on the mouse than other systems.

The mouse

PC mice originally had three buttons. To be different, Microsoft introduced a two-button mouse, and to make it work anyway, they require the use of *double-click* to execute many standard functions. In my opinion, more arm injuries are caused by double-clicking mice than anything else I know. Ask anybody with *CTS*[1] what they think about double-clicking. X generally does not require a double-click.

Get the best mouse you can. Prefer a short, light switch. It *must* have three buttons. Accept no substitutes. Three-button mice are usually cheaper than the Microsoft mice, so there's no financial incentive to buy a Microsoft mouse. Even if you want to use Microsoft with your computer as well, you should choose a three-button mouse. Logitech makes some nice mice which are supplied with drivers for Microsoft products which can optionally simulate a double-click with a press on the middle button.

Running X

There are a number of ways to start X:

- You can run the programs *startx* or *xinit* from a shell prompt. They will start X directly.

- If you don't want to even see a character mode display, you can run *xdm*, a *display manager* which makes your PC look like an X terminal: it presents you with a login screen that runs under X. This requires some configuration, which we'll look at in the next section.

---

1. *Carpal tunnel syndrome*, an inflammation of the forearm caused by repetitive strain.

Configuring *xdm*

To enable *xdm*,

1. Add the following line (in **bold face**) to */etc/rc.local*:

```
# put your local stuff here
echo " xdm"; /usr/X11R6/bin/xdm

echo '.'
```

2. Add a line to the *xdm* configuration file */usr/X11R6/lib/X11/xdm/Xservers*:

```
:0 local /usr/X11R6/bin/X :0 vt03      you can add more options here
```

This will start an *xdm* login window on */dev/ttyv3* when you start the system. You must ensure that */dev/ttyv3* is disabled in */etc/ttys*. See page 128 for more details.

You can also test the display manager manually by logging in as root on the console and typing:

```
$ xdm -nodaemon &
```

Yet another way to start the display manager automatically when the system boots is to add a line in */etc/ttys* to start it on one of the unoccupied virtual terminals. This is a very dangerous method: if you make a mess of your X configuration, you may no longer be able to access the system.

Running *xinit*

Running *xinit* or *startx* is simpler: after logging in, you just run the program.

startx and *xinit* both output messages to their standard output, which is the virtual terminal on which you started it. Sometimes they produce copious output. If you're having trouble getting X running, you might like to redirect the output to a file:

```
$ startx 2>&1 > /tmp/startx.log
```

Stopping X

X stops automatically when the *.xinitrc* script finishes. For this reason, you should not include an ampersand (&) after the last program you start—we'll look at this in more detail when we look at the sample *.xinitrc* below. Of course, this isn't the easiest way to stop X: you have to know which process was started last, and then you have to stop it. There's an easier way: press the key combination **CTRL-ALT-Backspace**, which is deliberately chosen to resemble the key combination **CTRL-ALT-Delete** used to reboot the machine. **CTRL-ALT-Backspace** will stop X and return you to the virtual terminal in which you started it.

Changing screen resolution

When you set up your *XF86Config* file, you may have specified more than one resolution. For example, on page 137 we selected the resolutions 640x480, 800x600 and 1024x768 pixels when running at 8 bits per pixel (bpp). When you start X, it will automatically select the first resolution, in this case 640x480. You can change to the previous resolution (the one to the left in the list) by pressing the **CTRL-ALT-Keypad -** key, and to the following resolution (the one to the right in the list) with **CTRL-ALT-Keypad +**. *Keypad +* and *Keypad -* refer to the + and - symbols on the numeric keypad at the right of the keyboard; you can't use the + and - symbols on the main keyboard for this purpose. The lists wrap around: in our example, if your current resolution is 640x480, and you press **CTRL-ALT-Keypad -**, the display will change to 1024x768. It's a very good idea to keep the default resolution at 640x480 until you have debugged your *XF86Config* parameters: 640x480 almost always works, so if your display is messed up, you can just switch back to a known good display with a single keystroke.

Selecting pixel depth

On page 137 we also saw that you can configure most display boards to display a different pixel depth (a different number of bits per pixel, which translates to a different number of colours). When you start X, however, it defaults to 8 bits per pixel (256 colours). In order to start it with a different number, specify the number of planes. For example, to start with 16 bits per pixel (65,536 colours), enter:

```
$ startx -- -bpp 16
```

This will normally limit the maximum resolution available.

Customizing X

startx and *xinit* both look for a file called *.xinitrc* when they start up. This file typically contains commands for starting up X clients such as terminal windows and a window manager If you don't have this file, you will get a single *xterm* window without a frame, as in figure 17-1.

Here you have a single *xterm* window in the top left corner. You can't move it, you have no menus. To make life worth living, you need at least a *window manager*, a program which controls other windows on the display. If you start X from *xdm*, you will get the *twm* window manager and a default environment. *twm* is a pretty basic window manager. In this example, I use *fvwm2*, which has more features than *twm*.

A large number of window managers are available for X11. I prefer a relatively sober looking manager, but there are many more with other features. You can get a good overview at *http://www.plig.org/xwinman/*. If you like Microsoft's "Windows 95" environment, you might prefer *fvwm95*, which is similar. Before you do, however, consider the advantages of other window managers: Microsoft's environment does not scale well.

You can start a window manager from a shell prompt, but it's easier to put the invocation in the

Figure 17-1: Vanilla X display

.xinitrc file. A simple *.xinitrc* might be:

```
xhost presto bumble gw                                             allow access from other hosts
xrdb -load .Xdefaults                                             load default settings
xmodmap -e 'keysym Alt_L = Meta_L Meta_L'                          remap keys for Emacs
xterm -s -sl 256 -sb -ls -j -rw -geometry 100x55 &                start xterm left
xterm -s -sl 256 -sb -ls -j -rw -geometry 100x55-0+0 &            and right
xearth &                                                          start a root background
emacs -name "grog emacs"  -geometry 100x55-0+0 -font 6x13&        and biff at the bottom
xbiff -geometry +450-0 -fg green -bg black&
fvwm2                                                             start fvwm
```

This file performs the following functions:

- The *xhost* line allows connections from all systems in the Internet. In the interests of security, you will probably want to limit the systems to your local network. Check the man page *xhost(1)* for how to do this.

- The *xrdb* line loads your local preferences. See the man page *X(1)* for more details.

- The *xmodmap* invocation sets the **Alt** key to perform the **Meta** function for *Emacs*. If this doesn't say anything to you, don't worry. You'll see more of it when you get to know *Emacs*.

  The two *xterm* lines start two *xterm*s, one on the left of the screen, one on the right. The geometry keyword determines this: they have 55 lines of 100 characters each, suitable for a standard 1024x768 display. If your display is larger, you can expand the size of these windows to advantage.

- The invocation of *xearth* starts a program which updates the *root window*[1] with a current view of the world. In Microsoft circles, this might be called a *screen saver*.

- *Emacs* takes a relatively long time to start, so it's a good idea to start one when you start X, and leave it running.

- *xbiff* is a little program which shows a picture of a US-style mailbox. When mail arrives, it changes colour, beeps, and raises the flag.

- Finally, we start the window manager, *fvwm2*. As noted above, we don't specify an ampersand (&) at the end of this command, so that the *.xinitrc* script does not complete. If you stop the window manager, however, the script will complete, and the X session will stop. We'll look at what we can do with *fvwm2* in more detail below.

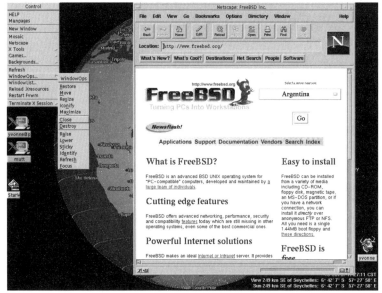

Figure 17-2: Typical X display with *fvwm2*

You'll find this *.xinitrc* file on the installation CD-ROM */book/scripts/.xinitrc*. On page 315 we'll see how to install this and the other files I describe in this chapter.

Now, when you start X, you will be given a somewhat better looking screen. After opening a *Netscape* window and iconifying it and one of the *xterm* windows, it might look like figure 17-2. Here we see a Netscape window on the right and four icons:

- On the left are two *xterm* icons. The first has the name (yvonne@presto: it has been truncated to fit the box) and a small picture. The second has the name mutt, indicating that it is running the *mutt* mail reader.

---

1. The root window is the background on which the other windows are displayed,.

- Underneath the *xterm* icons is a *StarWriter* icon. The name of this icon has been truncated to fit.

- On the right is an *Emacs* icon, the figure of a gnu. The name yvonne is the name of the user, not the program.

You'll notice that some of the names in the icons have been truncated. This is because the names can get *very* long. The text on a *Netscape* icon is the name on the title, which can be over 100 characters long. If this text were in the icon, it would take up half the width of the screen. *fvwm2* makes a compromise: the text expands to full size when you run the mouse cursor over the icon.

In addition, we can see a couple of nested menus. We'll look at them later.

Navigating the desktop

If you're used to Microsoft Windows, X may seem strange to you at first. On the one hand, you can recognize parallels, but on the other hand there are enormous differences. One of the most obvious things is the layout of the screen. The Microsoft desktop is not really suited to a large number of objects on the screen. As I write this, I have a total of 28 windows open on the screens—this does not scale well with Microsoft.

One similarity is that you can *iconify* windows: when you don't need them, you can reduce them to a small symbol, as we saw in Figure 17-2. One of the consequences of this is that you may want smaller icons. Do you really need a picture of a terminal for each of 10 different *xterm*s? Maybe just the bar beneath would do. It's your choice, but you have the choice.

You'll also notice that the windows have much more text in them than in a Microsoft environment. This is not simply primitive: you can do more things with text. Compared to Microsoft, an X environment uses the keyboard more and the mouse less. When you do use the mouse, you'll find that there are many more ways to use it. Although an X mouse should have at least three buttons,[1] many operations require the keyboard as well. In addition, the function of the mouse depends on where the cursor is positioned at the time. We'll look at that in the next section.

Mouse menus

fvwm and X distinguish several places on the screen:

- The *root window* is the "background", the window that is left behind when all the other ones are closed or iconified. You can't use it for much, you can't iconify it, and you can't put it on top of other window. Typically you'll display some pattern or picture on it. In figure 17-2 we display a map of the world on it.

---

1. X supports up to 5 mouse buttons. No, I've never seen a mouse with more than three buttons.

- We've already seen an *icon*: it's a small symbol or picture representing a window which is not currently being displayed.

- A *window* is a unit of display. You might think of a window as equal to a process, but this isn't correct. For example, *Netscape* and *Emacs* frequently display more than one window at a time.

- Windows typically have a *frame*, which contains a number of elements:

- The *title* is at the top of the window, and typically contains a text identifying the window and possibly some *buttons* which provide mouse functions.

- *fvwm* treats the *sides* of the frame separately from the corners. We'll see the difference in the tables below.

- Finally, an *fvwm* frame may have up to 10 buttons, which *fvwm* numbers 0 to 9.

You can see the typical *fvwm* border in example 17-2. The most important part is the title bar:

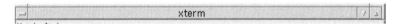

There are a total of three fields, called *buttons*, on the title bar: one on the left and two on the right. If you position the mouse cursor on the left button and press any any mouse button, you will get a menu:

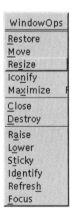

Figure 17-3: Window Operations Menu

This looks familiar to Microsoft users, but in time, you will find that this menu is less useful that it appears, since you can perform most functions without a menu.

There are two buttons on the right of the title bar. The left-hand button is the *iconify* button. If you click here with any mouse button, the window will be *iconified*: it will disappear and be replaced by a small symbol or *icon*, such as the ones on the left and bottom of figure 17-2. Iconification frees up screen area, but it doesn't stop or suspend process execution. If you want to stop a program, you should either exit the application or close the window. It's preferable to exit, since the application is more likely to perform its housekeeping before stopping.

The right-hand button is the *maximize* button. If you click here with any mouse button, the window will be expanded to fill the screen. If you click again, the window will be returned to its former size and position.

Pressing mouse buttons elsewhere performs other functions. For example, when you move the mouse cursor to one of the corners, it changes shape to a corner with an arrow. This cursor shape indicates that you can extend the window in that direction by keeping the mouse button down and dragging the border.

In most windows, the mouse keys will produce an application-specific menu. By convention, however, combinations of the mouse key and the **Alt** key are interpreted by the window manager even when the cursor is in a window. For example, with the sample *.fvwm2rc*, **Alt-Mouse2** (the **Alt** key and the middle mouse button) iconifies the window.

In the next few sections, we'll look at all the mouse functions:

Mouse key functions on the root window

On the root window, the mouse keys are used only to produce menus. Table 17-4 gives an overview.

Table 17-4. Mouse key functions on the root window

Mouse Key	Keyboard	Function
1		Produce a menu of *xterm*s for the left side of the screen. This is the menu *LeftHosts*.
2		Produce a menu of other applications, the menu *Applications*
3		Produce a menu of *xterm*s for the right side of the screen. This is the menu *RightHosts*.
1	Shift	Produce the *Control* menu. This menu includes various control functions. This is the left-hand of the menus displayed in figure 17-2.
2	Shift	Display a list of the active windows. Selecting a window will deiconify it if necessary and bring it to the top of the screen (in other words, no other window will cover it).
3	Shift	Bring up the "Window operations" menu on page 312.

It's desirable for some menus to be independent of the position on the screen. That way, you don't have to look carefully before selecting them. To ensure that they don't clash with anything else, select all of them with the key combination **Shift-Alt**:

Table 17-5. Position-independent mouse key functions

Mouse Key	Keyboard	Function
1	Shift-Alt	Produce the *Control* menu. This menu includes various control functions. This is the left-hand of the menus displayed in figure 17-2.
2	Shift-Alt	Display the *Applications* menu.
3	Shift-Alt	Move the current window. This doesn't work on the root window.

Use of colour

You'll find that your X display doesn't look as brightly coloured as, say, a Microsoft desktop. In particular, *xterm* is monochrome black on pale. If you want *xterm* to display in colour, you need two things:

1. Change the TERM environment variable from xterm to xterm-color. This enables the control sequences which *xterm* uses to display in colour.

2. You need applications which display in colour. The *mutt* mail reader will do this—see Chapter 32, *Electronic Mail*, page 546, for further details. So will some programs in the Ports Collection, such as *colorls*, a version of *ls* which displays different kinds of files in different colors when you supply it the -G option.

Network windowing

FreeBSD is an operating system which is designed to run in a networked environment, so it should come as no surprise that you a system can create windows on a display on a different system. To avoid confusion, it's a good idea to look at some terminology before we continue:

- An *X Server* is the display manager, so it runs on the machine with the display. Theoretically there can be multiple X servers on one machine, though I've never seen this implemented.

- A *screen* is one of possibly many display board and monitor combinations controlled by a specific X server. Some X servers, notably the server from Xi Graphics, do support multiple screens.

- An *X Client* is a program which uses an X Server to display its data. The prototypical example is *xterm*.

A special notation exists to address X servers and screens:

System name **:** *server number* **.** *screen number*

When looking at X client-server interaction, remember that the server is the software component that manages the display. This means that you're always sitting at the server, not at the client. For example, if you want to start an *xterm* client on *freebie* and display it on *presto*, you'll be sitting at *presto*. To do this, you could type in, on *presto*,

```
$ rsh freebie xterm -ls -display presto:0 &
```

The flag -ls tells *xterm* that this is a *login shell*, which causes it to read in the startup files. It might work without this flag, but there's a good chance that some environment variables, such as PATH, may not be set.

In practice, the *xterms* menus in the window manager will perform this function for you when you select the appropriate menu item. For this to work, you'll need to have remote access enabled via the `~/.rhosts` file (see Chapter 31, *Basic network access*, page 533). In addition, you'll need to tell the X server to allow the connection. You do this with the *xhost* command, specifying the names of the systems which have access:

```
$ xhost freebie presto bumble wait gw
```

This will enable access from all the systems on our reference network, including the one on which it is run. You don't need to include your own system, which is enabled by default, but if you do, you can use the same script on all systems on the network.

Installing the sample desktop

You'll find all the files described in this chapter on the first CD-ROM (Installation CD-ROM) in the directory */book*. Remember that you must mount the CD-ROM before you can access the files—see page 235 for further details. The individual scripts are in the directory */book/scripts*, but you'll probably find it easier to install them with the script *install-desktop*:

```
# /cdrom/book/scripts/install-desktop
```

The sample desktop uses a number of packages from the Ports Collection. Look at the file */book/scripts/install-desktop* for more details.

The shell

One of the big differences between X and Microsoft environments is that X has not gone overboard and eliminated typing. You will find that you still spend a considerable amount of time with the old-style shell. You don't have to: UNIX always gives you the choice, but most users find that once you have relatively complicated things to to, it is easier to tell the system what they want rather than to wade through lots of menus.

We looked at the *bash* shell in Chapter 11, *Making friends with FreeBSD*, page 163. When you start up an *xterm*, you will automatically have a *bash* shell running.

The *Emacs* editor

Another divergence of concept between UNIX and Microsoft environments is that UNIX gives you a choice of editors in just about anything you do. Microsoft products frequently try to redefine the whole environment, so if you change mailers, you may also have to change the editor you use to write mail. This has a profound effect on the way you work. In particular, the Microsoft way makes it uninteresting to write a really good editor, since you can't use it all the time.

You may have heard of the *vi* editor, about which people speak with a mixture of admiration, awe and horror. *vi* is one of the oldest parts of BSD. It is a very powerful editor, but nobody would say that it is easy to learn. There are two reasons to use *vi*:

1. If you're already an experienced *vi* hacker, you probably won't want to change.

2. If you do a lot of work on different UNIX systems, you can rely on *vi* being there. There's no other editor about which you can say the same.

If, on the other hand, you don't know *vi*, and you only work on systems whose software you can control, you probably shouldn't use *vi*. *Emacs* is much easier to learn, and it is more powerful than *vi*.

> I'm sticking my neck out here. Holy wars have been fought about the differences between *vi* and *Emacs*, and they continue to be fought. To quote version 4.0 of Eric Raymond's *The New Hackers' Dictionary*:
>
> **holy wars** */n./ [from {Usenet}, but may predate it] /n./ {flame war}s over {religious issues}. The paper by Danny Cohen that popularized the terms {big-endian} and {little-endian} in connection with the LSB-first/MSB-first controversy was entitled "On Holy Wars and a Plea for Peace". Other perennial Holy Wars have included {EMACS} vs. {vi}, my personal computer vs. everyone else's personal computer, {{ITS}} vs. {{Unix}}, {{Unix}} vs. {VMS}, {BSD} Unix vs. {USG Unix}, {C} vs. {{Pascal}}, {C} vs. FORTRAN, etc., ad nauseam. The characteristic that distinguishes holy wars from normal technical disputes is that in a holy war most of the participants spend their time trying to pass off personal value choices and cultural attachments as objective technical evaluations. See also {theology}.*
>
> **:EMACS:** */ee'maks/ /n./ [from Editing MACroS] The ne plus ultra of hacker editors, a programmable text editor with an entire LISP system inside it. It was originally written by Richard Stallman in {TECO} under {{ITS}} at the MIT AI lab; AI Memo 554 described it as "an advanced, self-documenting, customizable, extensible real-time display editor". It has since been reimplemented any number of times, by various hackers, and versions exist that run under most major operating systems. Perhaps the most widely used version, also written by Stallman and now called "{GNU} EMACS" or {GNUMACS}, runs principally under Unix. It includes facilities to run compilation subprocesses and send and receive mail; many hackers spend up to 80% of their {tube time} inside it. Other variants include {GOSMACS}, CCA EMACS, UniPress EMACS, Montgomery EMACS, jove, epsilon, and MicroEMACS.*
>
> *Some EMACS versions running under window managers iconify as an overflowing kitchen sink, perhaps to suggest the one feature the editor does not (yet) include. Indeed, some hackers find EMACS too {heavyweight} and {baroque} for their taste, and expand the name as 'Escape Meta Alt Control Shift' to spoof its heavy reliance on keystrokes decorated with {bucky bits}. Other spoof expansions include 'Eight Megabytes And Constantly Swapping', 'Eventually 'malloc()'s All Computer Storage', and 'EMACS Makes A Computer Slow' (see {{recursive acronym}}). See also {vi}.*

When running under X, *Emacs* displays its own window (*vi* always uses an *xterm*). As a result, if you start *Emacs* from an *xterm*, you should use the & character to start it in the background:

```
$ emacs &
```

The resulting display looks like:

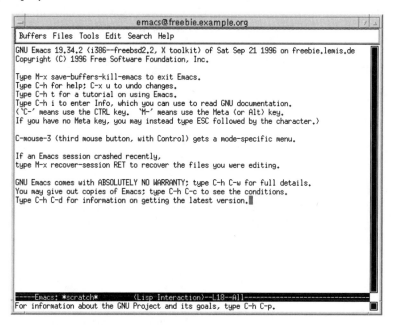

As you can see, the first thing that *Emacs* offers you is a tutorial. You should take it. You'll also notice the menu bars at the top. Although they look primitive compared to graphics toolbars, they offer all the functionality of graphics-oriented menus. In addition, they will tell you the keystrokes which you can use to invoke the same functions. Here's an example of the *Files* menu:

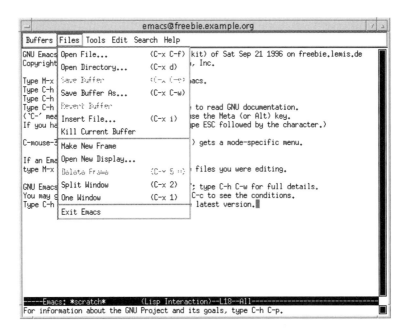

18

Configuring the kernel

So far, everything we've done has been with the standard GENERIC kernel distributed with FreeBSD. But we've seen that the GENERIC kernel has its limitations, and you may find advantages in a custom kernel:

- As we saw in Chapter 2, *Before you install*, GENERIC doesn't support everything that FreeBSD knows about. For example, if you want to install a Yoyodyne frobulator, you'll need to install special support for it.

  > In fact, the developer working on the Yoyodyne has defected to the Free Software Foundation. See the appendix to the GNU General Public License, reprinted in Appendix D, *License agreements*, for further details.

- It will take less time to boot because it does not have to spend time probing for hardware which you do not have.

- A custom kernel often uses less memory, which is important because the kernel is the one system component which must always be present in memory, so unused code ties up memory which would otherwise be available to the virtual memory system. On a system with limited RAM, you can save some memory by building a custom kernel. Don't overestimate the savings: a minimal kernel might save 500 kB over the GENERIC kernel supplied with the system.

- Finally, there are several kernel options which you can tune to fit your needs.

If you just need to add device support, you may be able to load a *Kernel Loadable Module*, or *kld*. In all other cases you'll need to build a new kernel. See page 363 for more information on klds.

FreeBSD is distributed in source, and building a kernel primarily involves compiling the source files needed for the kernel. To build a kernel, you perform the following steps:

- Install the system source, if you haven't already done so.

- Define your kernel configuration in a *kernel configuration file*. This file defines parameters to use during the build process. We'll look at how to do this starting on page 321.

- Create the configuration directory with the program *config*. We'll discuss this on page 361.

- Run *make depend* to create the dependency information for the kernel build.

- Run *make* to build the kernel. We'll look at this step on page 362.

- Install the kernel, which we'll discuss on page 362.

Configuring I/O devices

A lot of the configuration file relates to the I/O devices that you may connect to your machine. Recall from Chapter 2, *Before you install*, that in the most cases you will need to specify some of IRQ, DMA channel, board memory, and I/O addresses for the devices you configure. Note particularly that the config file will not handle references to IRQ 2 correctly: you *must* specify them as IRQ 9. See page 31 for further details.

The kernel build directory

The kernel sources are kept in the directory */usr/src/sys*. The symbolic link */sys* also points to this directory. There are a number of subdirectories of */usr/src/sys* which represent different parts of the kernel, but for our purposes, the most important are the architecture dependent directories *i386/conf* (for the i386 architecture) or *alpha/conf* (for the Alpha architecture), where you edit your custom kernel configuration, and *compile*, where you build your kernel. Notice the logical organization of the directory tree: each supported device, file system, and option has its own subdirectory. In the rest of this chapter, we'll look at the i386 architecture. Most of this applies to the Alpha architecture as well, but there are differences not covered here. See */usr/src/sys/alpha/conf/LINT* for more information.

If your system doesn't have the directory */usr/src/sys*, then the kernel source has not been installed. The sources are on the first CD-ROM in the directory */src*. To install from the CD-ROM, perform the following steps:

```
# mkdir -p /usr/src/sys
# ln -s /usr/src/sys /sys
# cd /
# cat /cdrom/src/ssys.[a-d]* | tar xzvf -
```

The symbolic link */sys* for */usr/src/sys* is not strictly necessary, but it's a good idea: some software uses it, and otherwise you may end up with two different copies of the sources.

Next, move to the directory *i386/conf* and copy the *GENERIC* configuration file to the name you want to give your kernel. For example:

```
# cd /usr/src/sys/i386/conf
# cp GENERIC FREEBIE
```

Traditionally, this name is in all capital letters and, if you are maintaining multiple FreeBSD machines with different hardware, it's a good idea to name it after your machine's hostname. In this example we call it *FREEBIE*.

Now, edit *FREEBIE* with your favorite text editor. Change the comment lines at the top to reflect your configuration or the changes you've made to differentiate it from *GENERIC*:

```
#
# FREEBIE -- My personal configuration file
#
# For more information read the handbook part System Administration ->
# Configuring the FreeBSD Kernel -> The Configuration File.
# The handbook is available in /usr/share/doc/handbook or online as
# latest version from the FreeBSD World Wide Web server
# <URL:http://www.FreeBSD.ORG/>
#
# An exhaustive list of options and more detailed explanations of the
# device lines is present in the ./LINT configuration file. If you are
# in doubt as to the purpose or necessity of a line, check first in LINT.
#
#       $Id: FREEBIE,v 1.101 1997/10/31 22:10:02 jseger Exp $
machine         "i386"
cpu             "I386_CPU"
cpu             "I486_CPU"
cpu             "I586_CPU"
cpu             "I686_CPU"
ident           FREEBIE
maxusers        10
```

If you've build a kernel under SunOS or some other BSD operating system, much of this file will be very familiar to you. If you're coming from some other operating system such as MS-DOS, on the other hand, the *GENERIC* configuration file might seem overwhelming to you, so follow the descriptions in the following section slowly and carefully.

The configuration file

The directory */sys/i386/conf* contains a number of configuration files:

GENERIC   General-purpose configuration file
LINT   Complete configuration file with copious comments. This file is intended for regression testing and documentation, not for building kernels, which would be far too bloated.
PCCARD   A configuration file for laptops which use PCCARD controllers.
SMP-GENERIC   A generic configuration file for symmetrical multiprocessor machines.

The general format of a configuration file is quite simple. Each line contains a keyword and one or more arguments. For simplicity, most lines only contain one argument. Anything following a # is considered a comment and ignored. Keywords which contain numbers used as text must be enclosed in quotation marks.

One of the results of this simplicity is that you can put in options which have absolutely no effect. For example, you could add a line like this:

```
options          APPLE_MAC_COMPATIBILITY
```

You can build a kernel with this option. It will make no difference whatsoever. Now it's unlikely that you'll think up a non-existent option like this, but it's much more possible that you'll misspell a valid option, especially finger-twisters like SYSVSHM, with the result that you don't compile in the option you wanted. The *config* program warns if you use unknown options, so take these warnings seriously.

The following sections describe the keywords not in the order they are listed in *LINT*: instead, related keywords have been grouped together in a single section (such as Networking), but in *LINT* they might be scattered throughout the file. Following this overview we'll look at some of the more important ones. You can find more information from the comments in the *LINT* file. Here's an overview in alphabetical order. The keywords without a page number are not discussed in more detail.

Table 18-1. Configuration file keywords

Keyword	Page	Purpose
adv0	346	AdvanSys narrow SCSI host adaptor
adw0	346	Second Generation AdvanSys controllers including the ADV940UW.
aha0	346	Adaptec 154x SCSI host adapters
ahb0	346	Adaptec 174x SCSI host adapters
ahc0	346	Adaptec 274X and 284X adapters
AHC_ALLOW_MEMIO		enable memory mapped I/O on Adaptec 274X and 284X adapters
alpha	330	Define the alpha architecture
alpm0		Acer Aladdin-IV/V/Pro2 Power Management Unit
APIC_IO	335	enable the use of the IO APIC for Symmetric I/O
apm0	360	Laptop Advanced Power Management
ar0	352	Arnet SYNC/570i hdlc sync 2/4 port V.35/X.21 serial driver (requires sppp)
asc0	360	GI1904-based hand scanners, e.g. the Trust Amiscan Grey
atkbd0	338	The keyboard controller. It controls the keyboard and the PS/2 mouse.
atkbdc0	338	
ATKBD_DFLT_KEYMAP		specify the built-in keymap
atm		generic ATM functions
ATM_CORE	357	core ATM protocol family
ATM_IP	357	IP over ATM support
ATM_SIGPVC	357	SIGPVC signalling manager

Keyword	Page	Purpose
ATM_SPANS	357	SPANS signalling manager
ATM_UNI	357	UNI signalling manager
AUTO_EOI_1	337	Enable the automatic EOI feature for the master 8259A interrupt controller
AVM_A1		AVM A1 or AVM Fritz!Card ISDN adaptor
AVM_A1_PCMCIA		AVM A1 or AVM Fritz!Card ISDN adaptor, PCMCIA
ax0	352	PCI fast ethernet adapters based on the ASIX Electronics AX88140A chip, including the Alfa Inc. GFC2204.
bktr0	360	Bt848 capture boards (http://www.free-bsd.org/~fsmp/HomeAuto/Bt848.html)
BOOTP		Use BOOTP to obtain IP address/hostname
BOOTP_COMPAT		Workaround for broken bootp daemons.
BOOTP_NFSROOT		NFS mount root filesystem using BOOTP info
BOOTP_NFSV3		Use NFS v3 to NFS mount root
BOOTP_WIRED_TO		Use interface fxp0 for BOOTP
bpfilter	355	Berkeley packet filter
BREAK_TO_DEBUGGER	334	A BREAK on a comconsole goes to *ddb*
BRIDGE	351	Enable bridging between ethernet boards.
bt0	346	Most Buslogic SCSI host adapters
card0	337	PCMCIA slot controller.
ccd	346	Concatenated disk driver
cd0	344	SCSI CD-ROMs
CD9660	349	ISO 9660 filesystem
CD9660_ROOT	349	CD-ROM usable as root device
CD9660_ROOTDELAY		Timeout on mounting CD-ROM root
ch0	344	SCSI media changers
CODA	349	CODA filesystem.
COMPAT_43	331	Implement system calls compatible with 4.3BSD
COM_ESP	340	code for Hayes ESP
COM_MULTIPORT	340	code for some serial boards with shared IRQs
config	331	Define kernel parameters
CONSPEED	340	Default speed for serial console
cpu	330	Specify the CPU chip (not the hardware)
CPU_UPGRADE_HW_CACHE		
CRTX_S0_P		
cs0	352	IBM Etherjet and other Crystal Semi CS89x0-based Ethernet adapters.
css0	357	Crystal Sound System (CSS 423x PnP).
ctx0	360	Cortex-I frame grabber
cx0	352	Cronyx/Sigma multiport sync/async (with Cisco or PPP framing)

Keyword	Page	Purpose
cy0	360	Cyclades serial driver
CYRIX_CACHE_REALLY_WORKS	335	Enables CPU cache on Cyrix 486 CPUs without cache flush at hold state, and write-back CPU cache on early-revision Cyrix 6x86
CYRIX_CACHE_WORKS	335	Enable CPU cache on Cyrix 486 CPUs with cache flush at hold state.
CY_PCI_FASTINTR		Use with cy_pci unless irq is shared
da0	344	SCSI direct access devices (aka disks)
DDB	334	Enable the kernel debugger
DDB_UNATTENDED	334	Dont drop into DDB for a panic
de0	352	Digital Equipment DC21040 Ethernet adapter
DEVFS		Device filesystem
DFLDSIZ		Soft maximum data size
dgb0	360	Digiboard PC/Xi and PC/Xe series driver (ALPHA QUALITY!)
dgm0	360	
DIAGNOSTIC	334	Enable extra sanity checking of internal structures
disc	354	Discard device—discard all packets
DONTPROBE_1284		Avoid boot detection of PnP parallel devices
dpt0		Support for DPT RAID controllers.
DRN_NGO		Dr. Neuhaus Niccy Go@ ISDN board
DUMMYNET	351	Enable the "dummynet" bandwidth limiter
DYNALINK		Dynalink IS64PH ISDN board
ed0	352	Western Digital and SMC 80xx; Novell NE1000 and NE2000; 3Com 3C503
eisa0	337	EISA bus
EISA_SLOTS	337	Number of EISA slots to probe
el0	352	3Com 3C501
ELSA_QS1ISA		ELSA QuickStep 1000pro ISA ISDN board
ELSA_QS1PCI	356	ELSA QuickStep 1000pro PCI ISDN board
en0	352	Efficient Networks (ENI) ENI-155 PCI midway cards and Adaptec 155Mbps PCI ATM cards (ANA-59x0)
ENABLE_ALART		
ep0	352	3Com 3C509
ether	355	Generic Ethernet support
ex0	352	Intel EtherExpress Pro/10 and other i82595-based Ethernet adapters
EXPORTMFS	348	Allow MFS filesystems to be exported via NFS.
EXT2FS		Linux ext2fs file system.
EXTRA_SIO	340	number of extra sio ports to allocate

Keyword	Page	Purpose
FAILSAFE	331	Be particularly conservative in various parts of the kernel and choose functionality over speed (on the widest variety of systems).
FAT_CURSOR	339	start with block cursor
fd0	341	Floppy disk
fdc0	341	Floppy disk controller
FDC_DEBUG		Enable floppy debugging
FDC_YE		
fddi	354	Generic FDDI support
FDESC	349	File descriptor filesystem
fe0	352	Fujitsu MB86960A/MB86965A Ethernet
fea0	352	DEC DEFEA EISA FDDI adapter
FFS	348	Fast filesystem
FFS_ROOT	348	FFS usable as root device
fpa0	352	Digital DEFPA PCI FDDI adapter
fxp0	352	Intel EtherExpress Pro/100B PCI Fast Ethernet adapters
GDB_REMOTE_CHAT	334	Use *gdb* protocol for remote debugging
gp0	360	National Instruments AT-GPIB and AT-GPIB/TNT board
GPL_MATH_EMULATE	331	Alternate x87 math emulation
gsc0	360	Genius GS-4500 hand scanner.
gus0	357	Gravis Ultrasound - Ultrasound, Ultrasound 16, Ultrasound MAX
gzip	359	Exec gzipped *a.out*s
hea0	357	Efficient ENI-155p ATM PCI
hfa0	357	FORE PCA-200E ATM PCI
HW_WDOG		
i386	330	Define the i386 architecture
I386_CPU	330	Intel i386 processor
I486_CPU	330	Intel i486 processor
i4b		ISDN subsystem
I586_CPU	330	Intel Pentium processor
I686_CPU	330	Intel Pentium Pro and Pentium 2 processors
IBCS2		SCO UNIX binary emulation.
ic0		Philips i2c bus support.
ident	330	Identify the kernel configuration
IDE_DELAY	342	Specify probe delay for IDE devices
ie0	352	AT&T StarLAN 10 and EN100; 3Com 3C507; unknown NI5210
iicbus0		Philips i2c bus support.

Keyword	Page	Purpose
INCLUDE_CONFIG_FILE	332	Store this configuration file into the kernel binary itself
INET	351	Internet communications protocols
intpm0		
INTRO_USERCONFIG		imply -c and show intro screen
INVARIANTS	334	Enable extra sanity checking of internal structures.
IPDIVERT	351	Divert sockets
IPFILTER	351	kernel ipfilter support
IPFIREWALL	350	Firewall
IPSTEALTH		support for stealth forwarding
IPX		Include IPX/SPX communications protocols
IPXIP		Include IPX in IP encapsulation
isa0	337	ISA bus
joy0	360	joystick
KERNFS	349	Kernel filesystem
KTRACE	334	Enable kernel tracing
labpc0	360	National Instruments Lab-PC and Lab-PC+
le0	352	Digital Equipment EtherWorks 2 and EtherWorks 3 (DEPCA, DE100, DE101, DE200, DE201, DE202, DE203, DE204, DE205, DE422)
lnc0	352	Lance/PCnet cards (Isolan, Novell NE2100, NE32-VL)
LOCKF_DEBUG		
loop	355	Network loopback device support
lpt0	341	Printer port
LPT_DEBUG		Printer driver debug
matcd0	360	Matsushita/Panasonic CD-ROM
MATH_EMULATE	331	Support for x87 emulation
MAXCONS	339	Number of virtual consoles for *syscons*
MAXDSIZ		Maximum data size
MAXMEM	338	Specify explicit memory size
maxusers	331	Set kernel parameters based on the number of expected users. This parameter *doesn't limit the number of users*
mcd0	360	Mitsumi CD-ROM
MD5	333	Include an MD5 encryption routine in the kernel
meteor0	360	Matrox Meteor video capture board
meteor0	360	PCI video capture board
MFS	348	Memory File System
MFS_ROOT	348	MFS root file system
mpu0	357	Roland MPU-401 stand-alone card
MROUTING	350	Multicast routing

Keyword	Page	Purpose
MSDOSFS	349	MS DOS File System
mse0	340	Logitech and ATI InPort bus mouse ports
MSGBUF_SIZE	332	Set size of kernel internal message buffer.
mss0	357	Microsoft Sound System
mx0	352	Fast ethernet adapters based on the Macronix 98713, 987615 ans 98725 series chips.
NAPIC	335	Set number of IO APICs on SMP
NATM		Native ATM
NBUS	335	Set number of busses on SMP
NCPU	335	Set number of CPUs on SMP
ncr0	346	NCR 53C810 and 53C825 SCSI host adapters
NDGBPORTS		Defaults to 16*NDGB
NETATALK	350	Appletalk communications protocols
NFS	348	Network File System
NINTR	335	Set number of INTs on SMP
npx0	337	Numeric Processing eXtension driver, for machines with math co-processor
NSFBUFS		Number of virtual buffers to map file VM pages for sendfile(2).
NSWAPDEV	349	Allow this many swap-devices.
NTFS		Microsoft NT File System
NULLFS	349	NULL filesystem
opl0	357	Yamaha OPL-2 and OPL-3 FM - SB, SB Pro, SB 16, ProAudioSpectrum
P1003_1B		Set 1993 POSIX real time extensions.
pas0	357	ProAudioSpectrum PCM and MIDI
pass0	344	CAM passthrough driver
pca0	357	PCM audio through your PC speaker
pcf0		Philips PCF8584 ISA-bus controller.
pci0	337	PCI bus
pcic0		PCCARD/PCMCIA slots
pcm0	357	PCM audio through various sound cards.
PERFMON	335	Include driver for Pentium/Pentium Pro performance counters
PERIPH_1284		Makes your computer act as a IEEE1284
plip0	341	Parallel IP interface.
PMAP_SHPGPERPROC		The number of PV entries per process.
pn0	352	Fast ethernet adapters based on the Lite-On 82c168 and 82c169 PNIC chips, including the LinkSys LNE100TX, the NetGear FA310TX rev. D1 and the Matrox FastNIC 10/100.
pnp0		Enable PnP support in the kernel

327

Keyword	Page	Purpose
PORTAL	349	Portal filesystem
POWERFAIL_NMI		Don't panic on laptop power fail
ppbus0	341	Parallel port bus support
ppc0	341	ISA-bus parallel port interfaces.
ppi0	341	Parallel port general-purpose I/O
ppp	355	Kernel PPP support
PROCFS	349	Process filesystem
psm0	338	PS/2 mouse interface.
pt0	344	SCSI processor type
pty	354	Pseudo ttys
QUOTA	350	enable disk quotas
rc0	360	RISCom/8 multiport card
rdp0	353	RealTek RTL 8002-based pocket ethernet adapters.
rp0	360	Comtrol Rocketport(ISA) - single card
sa0	344	SCSI tapes
sb0	358	SoundBlaster PCM - SoundBlaster, SB Pro, SB16, ProAudioSpectrum
sbmidi0	358	SoundBlaster 16 MIDI interface
sbxvi0	358	SoundBlaster 16
sc0	339	The default *syscons* console driver
scd0	360	Sony CD-ROM
sctarg0	344	SCSI target
SHOW_BUSYBUFS		List buffers that prevent root unmount
si0	360	Specialix SI/XIO 4-32 port terminal multiplexor
SIMPLELOCK_DEBUG		
sio0	340	Serial I/O port
sl	355	Serial Line IP
smb0		System Management Bus support.
SMP	335	Symmetric Multiprocessor Kernel
snd0	358	Voxware sound support code
snp	360	Snoop device
speaker	359	Play IBM BASIC-style noises out your speaker
spigot0	360	The Creative Labs Video Spigot video-acquisition board
splash	338	Splash screen at start up.
sppp	354	Generic Synchronous PPP
sr0	353	RISCom/N2 hdlc sync 1/2 port V.35/X.21 serial driver (requires sppp)
sscape0	358	Ensoniq Soundscape MIDI interface
STD8X16FONT		*syscons*: compile font in
stl0	360	Stallion EasyIO and EasyConnection 8/32 (cd1400 based)

Keyword	Page	Purpose
stli0	360	Stallion EasyConnection 8/64, ONboard, Brumby (intelligent)
SYSVMSG	333	Support for System V message queues
SYSVSEM	333	Support for System V semaphores
SYSVSHM	333	Support for System V shared memory
TCP_COMPAT_42	350	emulate 4.2BSD TCP bugs
tun	355	Tunnel driver, used mainly for User PPP.
TUNE_1542	345	Enable automatic ISA bus speed selection for Adaptec 1542 boards
tw0	360	TW-523 power line interface for use with X-10 home control products
tx0	353	SMC 9432TX based Ethernet boards.
uart0	358	stand-alone 6850 UART for MIDI
UCONSOLE	334	Allow ordinary users to take the console
ugen0		Generic USB interface
UMAPFS	349	UID map filesystem
ums0		USB mouse.
UNION	349	Union filesystem
usb0		Base USB support
USERCONFIG	332	Include *UserConfig* editor
USER_LDT	332	allow user-level control of i386 LDT
vcoda		coda minicache <-> venus comm.
VESA		Support for VESA video modes
vga0		VGA driver
vinum	346	Vinum volume manager
VISUAL_USERCONFIG	331	With USERCONFIG: enable visual editor
VM86	333	Allow processes to switch to VM86 mode
vn	359	Vnode driver (turns a file into a device)
VP0_DEBUG		ZIP/ZIP+ debug
vpo0	341	Parallel port Iomega Zip Drive
vr0	353	Fast ethernet adapters based on the VIA Technologies VT3043 'Rhine I' and VT86C100A 'Rhine II' chips, including the D-Link DFE530TX.
vt0	339	pcvt vt220 compatible console driver
vx0	353	3Com 3C590 and 3C595
wb0	353	Fast ethernet adapters based on the Winbond W89C840F chip.
wd0	341	IDE disk
wdc0	341	IDE disk controller
wfd0	343	IDE floppy interface.
wl0	353	Lucent Wavelan (ISA card only).
WLCACHE	354	Enable the RISCom/N2 signal-strength cache

Keyword	Page	Purpose
wst0	343	IDE tape driver
xl0	353	3Com 3c900, 3c905 and 3c905B (Fast) Etherlink XL cards and integrated controllers.
xrpu0		HOT1 Xilinx 6200 board.
XSERVER	339	support for running an X server.
ze0	353	IBM/National Semiconductor PCMCIA ethernet controller.
zp0	353	3Com PCMCIA Etherlink III

Naming the kernel

Every kernel you build requires the keywords `machine`, `cpu`, and `ident`. For example,

```
machine      "i386"          For i386 architecture
machine      "alpha"         For alpha architecture
cpu          "I386_CPU"
cpu          "I486_CPU"
cpu          "I586_CPU"
cpu          "I686_CPU"
ident        FREEBIE
```

machine

The keyword `machine` describes the machine architecture for which the kernel is to be built. Currently it should be `i386` for the Intel architecture, and `alpha` for the AXP architecture. Don't confuse this with the processor: for example, the `i386` architecture refers to the Intel 80386 and all its successors, including lookalikes made by AMD, Cyrix and IBM.

cpu *cpu_type*

`cpu` describes which CPU chip is to be supported by this kernel. For the `i386` architecture, the possible values are `I386_CPU`, `I486_CPU`, `I586_CPU` and `I686_CPU`, and you can specify any combination of these values. For a custom kernel, it is best to specify only the cpu you have. If, for example, you have an Intel Pentium, use `I586_CPU` for *cpu_type*.

ident *machine_name*

`ident` specifies a name used to identify the kernel. In the file *GENERIC* it is `GENERIC`. Change this to whatever you named your kernel, in this example, FREEBIE. The value you put in `ident` will print when you boot up the kernel, so it's useful to give a kernel a different name if you want to keep it separate from your usual kernel (if you want to build an experimental kernel, for example). As with `machine` and `cpu`, enclose your kernel's name in quotation marks if it contains any numbers.

Since this name is passed to the C compiler as a variable, don't use names like DEBUG, or something that could be confused with another machine or CPU name, like vax.

maxusers *number*

This value sets the size of a number of important system tables. It is intended to be roughly equal to the number of simultaneous users you expect to have on your machine. However, even if you are the only person to use the machine, you shouldn't set `maxusers` lower than the default value 32, especially if you're using X or compiling software. The reason is that the most important table set by `maxusers` is the maximum number of processes, which is set to `20 + 16 * maxusers`, so if you set `maxusers` to one, then you can only have 36 simultaneous processes, including the 18 or so that the system starts up at boot time, and the 15 or so you will probably create when you start X. Even a simple task like reading a man page can start up nine processes to filter, decompress, and view it. Setting `maxusers` to 32 will allow you to have up to 532 simultaneous processes, which is normally ample. If, however, you see the dreaded *proc table full* error when trying to start another program, or are running a server with a large number of simultaneous users (like Walnut Creek CDROM's FTP site *wcarchive.cdrom.com*), you can always increase this number and rebuild.

> `maxusers` does *not* limit the number of users which can log into your machine. It simply sets various table sizes to reasonable values considering the maximum number of users you will likely have on your system and how many processes each of them will be running. One keyword which *does* limit the number of simultaneous *remote* logins is `pseudo-device pty`.

config *kernel_name*

This line specifies the location and name of the kernel. Traditionally the BSD kernel is called *vmunix*, but for copyright reasons FreeBSD calls it *kernel*. A number of system utilities rely on this name, so don't change it. The second part of the line specifies the disk and partition where the root file system and kernel can be found. Typically this will be `wd0` for systems with non-SCSI drives, or `sd0` for systems with SCSI drives.

> The name *vmunix* came into usage at Berkeley with the first versions of UNIX with support for virtual memory. UNIX System V still calls the kernel *unix*, and you can often use this to distinguish between a BSD and a System V system.

Kernel options

```
makeoptions     DEBUG=-g                  # Build kernel with gdb(1) debug symbols
options         MATH_EMULATE              # Support for x87 emulation
options         GPL_MATH_EMULATE          # Support for x87 emulation via new math emulator
options         "COMPAT_43"               # Compatible with BSD 4.3 [KEEP THIS!]
options         UCONSOLE                  # Allow users to grab the console
options         FAILSAFE                  # Be conservative
options         USERCONFIG                # boot -c editor
options         VISUAL_USERCONFIG         # visual boot -c editor
options         INCLUDE_CONFIG_FILE       # Include this file in kernel
options         USER_LDT                  # allow user-level control of i386 ldt
options         "MSGBUF_SIZE=40960"
```

These lines provide global kernel options. In the GENERIC configuration file you'll also find file system options here; we'll look at them on page 348.

makeoptions

makeoptions specifies options to be processed by *config*. Use the -g option to create a *debug kernel* unless you're seriously short of space; it doesn't run any more slowly, but it gives you the chance of analysing dumps if you have any problems with the system.

MATH_EMULATE and GPL_MATH_EMULATE

This line allows the kernel to simulate a math coprocessor if your computer does not have one (386 or 486SX). If you have a Pentium, a 486DX, or a 386 or 486SX with a separate 387 or 487 chip, you can comment this line out.

> The normal math coprocessor emulation routines that come with FreeBSD are *not* very accurate. If you do not have a math coprocessor, and you need the best accuracy, I recommend that you change this option to GPL_MATH_EMULATE to use the GNU math support, which is better, but which is not included by default for licensing reasons.

COMPAT_43

Compatibility with 4.3BSD. Leave this in: some programs will act strangely if you comment this out.

USERCONFIG and VISUAL_USERCONFIG

These options enable the *UserConfig* configuration editor that we looked at on page 191. USERCONFIG enables the base editor, and you need VISUAL_USERCONFIG to enable the full-screen editor as well.

INCLUDE_CONFIG_FILE

INCLUDE_CONFIG_FILE allows you to actually store this configuration file into the kernel binary itself. You can extract it later (into a file *MYKERNEL*) with:

```
$ strings -n 3 /kernel | grep ^___ | sed -e 's/^___//' > MYKERNEL
```

USER_LDT

USER_LDT allows user processes to manipulate their *local descriptor table*. This is required for some Linux programs, in particular *WINE*.

MSGBUF_SIZE

MSGBUF_SIZE is the size of the kernel message buffer. You read this buffer with *dmesg(8)*. If you write a lot of kernel messages (for example, as a result of verbose booting) you may need to increase this value. Make sure you keep it a multiple of the virtual memory page size, currently 4096 bytes.

System V compatibility

```
options          SYSVSHM
options          SYSVSEM
options          SYSVMSG
```

These options provide support for some UNIX System V features:

SYSVSHM

This option provides for System V shared memory. The most common use of this is the XSHM extension in X, which many graphics-intensive programs (such as the movie player *XAnim*, and Linux *DOOM*) will automatically take advantage of for extra speed. If you use X, you'll definitely want to include this.

SYSVSEM

Support for System V semaphores. Less commonly used but only adds a few hundred bytes to the kernel.

SYSVMSG

Support for System V messages. Again, this option only adds a few hundred bytes to the kernel.

> Use the *ipcs* command to find processes using these facilities.

```
options          "MD5"
options          "VM86"
```

MD5

MD5 includes a MD5 routine in the kernel, for various authentication and privacy uses.

VM86

VM86 allows processes to switch to *vm86* mode, as well as enabling direct user-mode access to the I/O port space. This option is necessary for the *doscmd* emulator to run and the VESA modes in syscons to be available.

```
options          DDB
options          BREAK_TO_DEBUGGER
options          DDB_UNATTENDED        # Don't drop into DDB for a panic
options          GDB_REMOTE_CHAT       # Use gdb remote debugging protocol
options          KTRACE
options          DIAGNOSTIC
options          UCONSOLE              # Allow users to grab the console
options          INVARIANTS
options          INVARIANT_SUPPORT
options          PERFMON
```

These options provide support for various debugging features.

DDB

Specify DDB to include the kernel debugger, *ddb*. If you set this option, you might also want to set the BREAK_TO_DEBUGGER option,

BREAK_TO_DEBUGGER

Use the option BREAK_TO_DEBUGGER if you have installed the kernel debugger and you have the system console on a serial line—see page 340).

DDB_UNATTENDED

If you have a panic on a system with *ddb*, it will not reboot automatically. Instead, it will enter *ddb* and give you a chance to examine the remains of the system before rebooting. This can be a disadvantage on systems which run unattended: after a panic, they would wait until somebody comes past before rebooting. Use the DDB_UNATTENDED option to cause a system with *ddb* to reboot automatically on panic.

GDB_REMOTE_CHAT

ddb supports remote debugging from another FreeBSD machine via a serial connection. See the online handbook for more details. To use this feature, set the option GDB_REMOTE_CHAT.

KTRACE

Set KTRACE if you want to use the system call trace program *ktrace*.

DIAGNOSTIC

A number of source files use the DIAGNOSTIC option to enable extra sanity checking of internal structures. This support is not enabled by default because of the extra time it would take to check for these conditions, which can only occur as a result of programming errors.

UCONSOLE

UCONSOLE allows users to grab the console. This is useful if you're running X:, you can create a console xterm by typing **xterm -C**, which will display any *write*, *talk*, and other messages you receive, as well as any console messages sent by the kernel.

INVARIANTS and INVARIANT_SUPPORT

INVARIANTS is used in a number of source files to enable extra sanity checking of internal structures. This support is not enabled by default because of the extra time it would take to check for these conditions, which can only occur as a result of programming errors.

INVARIANT_SUPPORT option compiles in support for verifying some of the internal structures. It is a prerequisite for INVARIANTS. The intent is that you can set INVARIANTS for single source files (by changing the source file or specifying it on the command line) if you have INVARIANT_SUPPORT enabled.

PERFMON

`PERFMON` causes the driver for Pentium/Pentium Pro performance counters to be compiled. See *perfmon(4)* for more information.

Multiple processors

FreeBSD 3.2 supports most modern multiprocessor systems with i386 architecture. The `GENERIC` kernel does not support them by default: set the following options:

```
# To make an SMP kernel, the next two are needed
options SMP                     # Symmetric MultiProcessor Kernel
options APIC_IO                 # Symmetric (APIC) I/O
# Optionally these may need tweaked, (defaults shown):
options NCPU=2                  # number of CPUs
options NBUS=4                  # number of busses
options NAPIC=1                 # number of IO APICs
options NINTR=24                # number of INTs
```

An SMP kernel will only run on a motherboard which adheres to the Intel MP specification. Be sure to disable the `cpu "I386_CPU"` and `cpu "I486_CPU"` options for SMP kernels. Note also that currently only genuine Intel processors will run in SMP mode; at the time of writing, processors by AMD and Cyrix do not support multiprocessor operation, though the AMD K7 will support it.

At the time of writing, no SMP hardware is known on which FreeBSD will not run. Before buying a board, though, check the *Rogue SMP hardware* section in */usr/src/sys/i386/conf/LINT*. Note that the MP tables of most of the current generation MP motherboards do not properly support bridged PCI cards.

CPU options

A number of options exist for specific processors:

```
options            "CPU_BLUELIGHTNING_FPU_OP_CACHE"
options            "CPU_BLUELIGHTNING_3X"
options            "CPU_BTB_EN"
options            "CPU_DIRECT_MAPPED_CACHE"
options            "CPU_DISABLE_5X86_LSSER"
options            "CPU_FASTER_5X86_FPU"
options            "CPU_I486_ON_386"
options            "CPU_IORT"
options            "CPU_LOOP_EN"
options            "CPU_RSTK_EN"
options            "CPU_SUSP_HLT"
options            "CPU_WT_ALLOC"
options            "CYRIX_CACHE_WORKS"
options            "CYRIX_CACHE_REALLY_WORKS"
options "NO_F00F_HACK"
```

`CPU_BLUELIGHTNING_FPU_OP_CACHE` enables FPU operand cache on IBM *BlueLightning* CPU. It works only with Cyrix FPU. Don't use this option with an Intel FPU.

`CPU_BLUELIGHTNING_3X` enables triple-clock mode on IBM Blue Lightning CPU if CPU supports it. The default is double-clock mode on BlueLightning CPU box.

CPU_DIRECT_MAPPED_CACHE sets the L1 cache of Cyrix 486DLC CPU in direct mapped mode. The default is 2-way set associative mode.

CPU_CYRIX_NO_LOCK enables weak locking for the entire address space of Cyrix 6x86 and 6x86MX CPUs. If this option is not set and FAILSAFE is defined, the NO_LOCK bit of register CCR1 is cleared.[1]

CPU_DISABLE_5X86_LSSER disables load store serialize (in other words, it enables reorder). Don't use this option if you use memory mapped I/O devices.

CPU_FASTER_5X86_FPU enables a faster FPU exception handler.

CPU_I486_ON_386 enables CPU cache on i486 based CPU upgrade products for i386 machines.

CPU_SUSP_HLT enables suspend on the HALT instruction. If this option is set, CPU enters suspend mode following execution of HALT instruction.

CPU_WT_ALLOC enables write allocation on Cyrix 6x86/6x86MX and AMD K5/K6/K6-2 cpus.

CYRIX_CACHE_WORKS enables CPU cache on Cyrix 486 CPUs with cache flush at hold state.

CYRIX_CACHE_REALLY_WORKS enables CPU cache on Cyrix 486 CPUs without cache flush at hold state, and write-back CPU cache on Cyrix 6x86 chips with revision levels below 2.7. It has no effect on Cyrix 6x86 chips with revision levels of 2.7 or above.

NO_F00F_HACK disables the hack that prevents Pentiums (and only original Pentiums, not including Pentium Pro and Pentium II) from locking up when a LOCK CMPXCHG8B instruction is executed. Include this option for all kernels that won't run on a Pentium.

NO_MEMORY_HOLE is an optimisation for systems with AMD K6 processors which indicates that the 15-16MB range is not being occupied by an ISA memory hole.

Basic controllers and devices

These sections describe the basic disk, tape, and CD-ROM controllers supported by FreeBSD. We'll look at SCSI host adapters on page 343, and network boards on page 352.

```
controller      isa0
controller      eisa0
controller      pci0
controller      card0

device          npx0 at isa? port "IO_NPX" irq 13

options         "AUTO_EOI_1"
options         "AUTO_EOI_2"
options         "MAXMEM=(96*1024)"        # 96 MB memory
options         "EISA_SLOTS=12"
```

---

1. This option may cause failures for software that requires locked cycles in order to operate correctly.

controller isa0

All PC's supported by FreeBSD have one of these, including motherboards with EISA and PCI support. FreeBSD 3.2 does not support the IBM PS/2 (Micro Channel Architecture).

controller eisa0

Specify `eisa0` in addition to `isa0` if you have an EISA motherboard. It provides auto-detection and configuration support for all devices on the EISA bus.

controller pci0

Specify `pci0` in addition to `isa0` if you have a PCI motherboard. This enables auto-detection of PCI boards and gatewaying from the PCI to the ISA bus.

EISA_SLOTS

By default, only 10 EISA slots are probed, since the slot numbers above clash with the configuration address space of the PCI subsystem, and the EISA probe is not very smart about this. This is sufficient for most machines, but in particular the HP NetServer LC series comes with an onboard AIC7770 dual-channel SCSI controller on EISA slot 11, which the `GENERIC` kernel will not find. Build a kernel with options "EISA_SLOTS=12" for this machine.

card0

Specify `card0` in addition to `isa0` if you have a PCMCIA bus controller (laptop).

device npx0

`npx0` is the interface to the math (floating point) coprocessor. This entry is required whether your CPU has a math coprocessor or not. If you don't have a coprocessor, make sure that you also define the option `MATH_EMULATE` (page 332).

AUTO_EOI_1

`AUTO_EOI_1` enables the "automatic EOI" feature for the master 8259A interrupt controller. This saves about 0.7 to 1.25 μsec for each interrupt, but it breaks suspend/resume on some portables.

AUTO_EOI_2

`AUTO_EOI_2` enables the "automatic EOI" feature for the slave 8259A interrupt controller. This saves about 0.7 to 1.25 μsec usec for each interrupt. Automatic EOI is documented not to work for the slave with the original i8259A, but it works for some clones and some integrated versions.

MAXMEM

MAXMEM specifies the amount of RAM on the machine; if this is not specified, FreeBSD will first read the amount of memory from the CMOS RAM. Some BIOSes don't report the amount of RAM correctly, so if FreeBSD reports a different amount of RAM from what is actually installed, use MAXMEM to tell it the true value.

Keyboard, console, bus mouse, and X server

The most basic peripherals on a PC are the keyboard and display. FreeBSD offers a choice of two different console drivers. We'll also look at the PS/2 mouse here, since it is used together with the keyboard. See page 339 for other kinds of mouse.

```
controller      atkbdc0 at isa? port IO_KBD tty                    keyboard controller
device          atkbd0  at isa? tty irq 1 flags 0                  keyboard
# 'flags' for atkbd:
#       0x01    Force detection of keyboard, else we always assume a keyboard
#       0x02    Don't reset keyboard, useful for some newer ThinkPads
#       0x04    Old-style (XT) keyboard support, useful for older ThinkPads

device          psm0    at isa? tty irq 12                         PS/2 mouse
device          vga0    at isa? port ? conflicts                   VGA display
pseudo-device   splash                                            splash screen
# syscons is the default console driver, resembling an SCO console
device          sc0     at isa? tty
options         MAXCONS=16              # number of virtual consoles
# Enable this and PCVT_FREEBSD for pcvt vt220 compatible console driver
# device        vt0     at isa? tty
# options       XSERVER                # support for X server
# options       FAT_CURSOR             # start with block cursor
# If you have a ThinkPAD, uncomment this along with the rest of the PCVT lines
# options       PCVT_SCANSET=2         # IBM keyboards are non-std

#
'flags' for sc0:
        0x01    Use a 'visual' bell
        0x02    Use a 'blink' cursor
        0x04    Use a 'underline' cursor
        0x06    Use a 'blinking underline' (destructive) cursor
#       0x40    Make the bell quiet if it is rung in the backgroud vty.
```

atkbdc0 and atkbd0

These devices define the keyboard. You never need to change them, except possibly for the flags, but you should check that they exist: older versions of FreeBSD did not define them.

psm0

Use this device if your mouse plugs into the PS/2 mouse port. Note the options for notebooks. Try them if you run into problems after a power-management suspend.

splash

splash is a pseudo-device which allows the system to display a so-called *splash screen*, an arbitrary bitmap image file as welcome banner on the screen when the system is booting. This image will remain on the screen during kernel initialization process until the "Login" prompt appears on the screen or until a screen saver is loaded and initialized. The image will also disappear if you hit any key, although this may not work immediately if the kernel is still probing devices. This device is also used for screen savers.

sc0

sc0 is the default console driver. It resembles the console of SCO UNIX, and includes support for colour. Since most full-screen programs access the console through a terminal database library like *termcap*, it should not matter much whether you use this or vt0, the VT220 compatible console driver. When you log in, set your TERM variable to scoansi if full-screen programs have trouble running under this console. The following options can be used with the *sc0* driver:

vt0

vt0 is the driver name for *pcvt*, a VT220-compatible console driver which is backwards compatible to VT100 and VT102. It works well on some laptops which have hardware incompatibilities with sc0. This driver might also prove useful when connecting to a large number of different machines over the network, where the *termcap* or *terminfo* entries for the sc0 device are often not available—vt100 should be available on virtually any platform. When using this driver, set your TERM variable to vt100 or vt220.

MAXCONS

Both drivers support multiple virtual consoles. By pressing **ALT** and a function key, you can switch between them. MAXCONS is maximum number of virtual consoles. Due to restrictions in the number of function keys, this can be no more than 16.

XSERVER

This includes code required to run the XFree86 X Server. You only need this if you're using both the pcvt console driver and X, so it is normally commented out.

FAT_CURSOR

By default, *pcvt* displays a block cursor. If you don't like it, comment out this line. You can also change the cursor with the *cursor* program if you're using the pcvt VT220 driver.

Serial and parallel ports

Almost every PC has two serial ports and a parallel port. Nowadays they are usually integrated on the motherboard. Nowadays most mice are connected via a serial port or the PS/2 port, but some still use a separate board, the so-called *bus mice*. We looked at PS/2 mice on page 338. We'll look at the others here.

```
device          mse0 at isa? port 0x23c tty irq 5
device          sio0 at isa? port "IO_COM1" tty flags 0x10 irq 4

#
# 'flags' for serial drivers that support consoles (only for sio now):
#     0x10 enable console support for this unit.  The other console flags
#          are ignored unless this is set.  Enabling console support does
#          not make the unit the preferred console - boot with -h or set
```

```
#           the 0x20 flag for that.  Currently, at most one unit can have
#           console support; the first one (in config file order) with
#           this flag set is preferred.  Setting this flag for sio0 gives
#           the old behaviour.
#      0x20 force this unit to be the console (unless there is another
#           higher priority console).  This replaces the COMCONSOLE option.
#      0x40 reserve this unit for low level console operations.  Do not
#           access the device in any normal way.
#
# PnP 'flags' (set via userconfig using pnp x flags y)
#      0x1  disable probing of this device.  Used to prevent your modem
#           from being attached as a PnP modem.
#

options         CONSPEED=9600        # default speed for serial console (default 9600)

options         COM_ESP              # code for Hayes ESP
options         COM_MULTIPORT        # code for some cards with shared IRQs
options         "EXTRA_SIO=2"        # number of extra sio ports to allocate

# Other flags for sio that aren't documented in the man page.
#      0x20000   enable hardware RTS/CTS and larger FIFOs.  Only works for
#                ST16650A-compatible UARTs.
```

COMCONSOLE

Setting serial port flag 0x20 specifies that you would prefer to have the system console on a serial line. This replaces the old COMCONSOLE option.

mse0

Use this device if you have a Logitech or ATI InPort bus mouse board.

sio0

sio0 through *sio3* are the four serial ports referred to as *COM1* through *COM4* in the MS-DOS world. By default, *sio0* and *sio2* both use IRQ 4, and *sio1* and *sio3* both use IRQ 3. Due to the brain-damaged design of the standard serial board, each serial port requires a unique IRQ, so the default IRQs for *sio2* and *sio3* cannot be used: you will have to select a different IRQ.

> So how can MS-DOS use them? It's hard to believe, but MS-DOS doesn't use the interrupt. Other software can use them, as long as both interrupts aren't enabled at the same time. This is clearly an impossible restriction for a multitasking operating system.

More modern multiport boards don't have this problem. If you have a multiport serial board, check the manual page for *sio* for more information on the proper values for these lines. Some video boards (notably those based on S3 chips) use IO addresses of the form 0x*2e8, and since many cheap serial boards do not fully decode the 16-bit IO address space, they clash with these boards, making the sio3 port practically unavailable.

See Chapter 24, *Serial communications and modems*, for more details on serial ports.

Parallel-port bus

```
controller ppbus0
controller vpo0  at ppbus?
device        lpt0  at ppbus?
device        plip0 at ppbus?
device        ppi0  at ppbus?
device        pps0  at ppbus?
device        lpbb0 at ppbus?
device        ppc0  at isa? disable port? tty irq 7
```

Once upon a time, a parallel port was used only for printing. Nowadays, it is used for a lot of different things, and since version 3.0 FreeBSD has a new driver called *ppbus*. The following devices are supported:

vpo   Iomega Zip Drive. This requires SCSI disk support (*scbus* and *da*). You'll get best performance with ports in EPP 1.9 mode.

lpt   Parallel Printer. The old driver, which is now deprecated, is called *olpt*.

plip   Parallel network interface.

ppi   General-purpose I/O ("Geek Port")

pps   Pulse per second Timing Interface.

lpbb   Philips official parallel port I2C bit-banging interface

Disk controllers

controller fdc0

```
controller fdc0 at isa? port "IO_FD1" bio irq 6 drq 2
disk        fd0       at fdc0 drive 0
disk        fd1       at fdc0 drive 1
```

fd0 is the first floppy drive (A: in MS-DOS parlance), and fd1 is the second drive (B:). Comment out any lines corresponding to devices you do not have.

The ft0 driver for QIC-80 tape drives attached to the floppy controller was never reliable (nor were the drives), and it is no longer supported.

controller wdc0

First IDE controller
```
controller wdc0 at isa? port "IO_WD1" bio irq 14
disk        wd0   at wdc0 drive 0
disk        wd1   at wdc0 drive 1
```

Second IDE controller
```
controller wdc1 at isa? port "IO_WD2" bio irq 15
disk        wd2   at wdc1 drive 0
disk        wd3   at wdc1 drive 1
```

Third IDE controller
```
# controller    wdc2 at isa? port "0" bio irq ? flags 0xa0ffa0ff
```

```
# disk        wd4   at wdc2 drive 0
# disk        wd5   at wdc2 drive 1

options       "CMD640"       # Enable work around for CMD640 h/w bug
options       ATAPI          # Enable ATAPI support for IDE bus
options       ATAPI_STATIC   # Don't do it as an LKM
options       IDE_DELAY=8000 # Be optimistic about Joe IDE device

device        acd0           ATAPI (IDE) CD-ROM
device        wfd0           ATAPI floppy
device        wst0           ATAPI tape units
```

wdc0 is the primary IDE controller, and *wd0* and *wd1* are the master and slave hard drive, respectively. *wdc1* is a secondary IDE controller where you might have a third or fourth hard drive, or an IDE CD-ROM. Comment out the lines which do not apply. If you have only a SCSI hard drive, you can comment out all six lines.

A number of flags and options apply to *wdc0*:

- The *flags* fields are used to enable the multi-sector I/O and the 32 bit I/O modes. You can use them either in the controller definition or in the individual disk definitions. If you want to use them during boot configuration, specify them in the controller definition.

  16 flag bits are provided for each drive. The first 16 flag bits refer to drive 1, and the second 16 bits refer to drive 0. In each set of flags,

  - Bit 15 (0x8000) specifies to probe for 32 bit transfers.

  - Bit 14 (0x4000) enables waking powered-down laptop drives.

  - Bit 13 (0x2000) allows probing for PCI IDE DMA controllers.

  - Bit 12 (0x1000) enables LBA (logical block addressing mode). If this bit is not set, the driver accesses the disk in CHS (cylinder/head/sector) mode. See page 33 for a discussion of LBA.

  - The low 8 bits specify the maximum number of sectors per transfer. The special case 0xff represents the maximum transfer size which the drive can handle.

  See the man page *wd(4)* for more details.

  Thus, we can break down the example value 0xff8004 (the full 32 bits are 0x00ff8004) into 0x00ff for drive 1 (use the maximum transfer size) and 0x8004 for drive 0 (allow probing for 32 bit support, and use a transfer size of 4 sectors). We use CHS addressing for this drive.

- The option CMD640 enables serializing access to primary and secondary channel of the CMD640B IDE chip if the chip is probed by the PCI system. This works around a bug in this particular chip.

- The option ATAPI enables support for the ATAPI-compatible IDE devices *acd0*, *wfd0* and *wst0*.

- If you specify ATAPI_STATIC in addition to ATAPI, the kernel will not allow ATAPI support as an LKM (loadable kernel module).

It's particularly important to use DMA if you possibly can: programmed I/O (PIO, the alternative to DMA) is an order of magnitude slower. See page 32 for more details.

controller wdc2

Most modern machines have two IDE controllers on the motherboard. You can add additional plug-in boards. The example *wdc2* shows how to do this: you specify dummy port and irq numbers, and the kernel will fill the values in during the probes.

controller acd0

acd0 provides ATAPI (IDE) CD-ROM support. This controller requires options ATAPI.

device wfd0

wfd0 controls floppy drives on IDE interfaces. You don't need it for normal floppy drives.

device wst0

Wangtek and Archive QIC-02/QIC-36 tape drive support.

SCSI devices

FreeBSD 3.2 includes a new SCSI driver based on the ANSI ratified *Common Access Method* or *CAM* specification which defines a software interface for talking to SCSI and ATAPI devices. The FreeBSD driver is not completely CAM compliant, but it follows many of the precepts of CAM. More importantly, it addresses many of the shortcomings of the previous SCSI layer and should provide better performance, reliability, and ease the task of adding support for new controllers.

For most users, the most obvious difference between the old SCSI driver and CAM is the way they named SCSI devices. In the old driver, disks were called *sdn*, and tapes were called *stn*, where *n* was a small positive number. The CAM driver calls disks *dan* (for *direct access*), and tapes are called *san* (for *serial access*). Part of the upgrade procedure will create these new device names, though they are not strictly necessary: the CAM driver uses the same major numbers and the same device encoding scheme for the minor numbers as the old driver did, so */dev/sd0a* and */dev/da0a* are, in fact, the same device. Nevertheless, if you don't create the new device names, you may have some subtle problems.

The SCSI subsystem consists of the base SCSI code, a number of high-level SCSI device 'type' drivers, and the low-level host-adapter device drivers.

SCSI units

CAM supports the following kinds of SCSI device:

```
controller scbus0                    #base SCSI code
device          ch0                  #SCSI media changers
device          da0                  #SCSI direct access devices (aka disks)
device          sa0                  #SCSI tapes
device          cd0                  #SCSI CD-ROMs
# device    od0                      #SCSI optical disk
device          pass0                #CAM passthrough driver
device          pt0 at scbus?        # SCSI processor type
device          sctarg0 at scbus?    # SCSI target
```

The number 0 in the above entries is slightly misleading: all these devices are automatically configured as they are found, regardless of how many of them there are, and which target IDs they have.

Defining names for specific targets

By default, FreeBSD assigns SCSI unit numbers in the order in which it finds the devices on the SCSI bus. This means that if you remove or add a disk drive, you may have to rewrite your */etc/fstab* file. To avoid this problem, you can *wire down* your SCSI devices so that a given bus, target, and unit (*LUN*) always come on line as the same device unit.

The unit assignment begins with the first non-wired down unit for a device type. Units that are not specified are treated as if specified as LUN 0. For example, if you wire a disk as sd3 then the first non-wired disk will be assigned sd4.

The syntax for wiring down devices is:

```
controller scbus0 at ahc0         # Single bus device
controller scbus1 at ahc1 bus 0 # Single bus device
controller scbus3 at ahc2 bus 0 # Twin bus device
controller scbus2 at ahc2 bus 1 # Twin bus device
disk        da0 at scbus0 target 0 unit 0
disk        da1 at scbus3 target 1
disk        da2 at scbus2 target 3
tape        sa1 at scbus1 target 6
device      cd0 at scbus?
```

Units that are not specified are treated as if specified as LUN 0.

SCSI options

A number of options allow you to modify the behaviour of the SCSI subsystem. Most of them are for debugging purposes, and are not discussed here. The ones that might be of interest are:

```
options          SCSI_REPORT_GEOMETRY
options          SCSI_DELAY=8000 # Be pessimistic about Joe SCSI device

options          "CHANGER_MIN_BUSY_SECONDS=2"
options          "CHANGER_MAX_BUSY_SECONDS=10"

Options for the CAM sequential access driver:
SA_SPACE_TIMEOUT: Timeout for space operations, in minutes
SA_REWIND_TIMEOUT: Timeout for rewind operations, in minutes
SA_ERASE_TIMEOUT: Timeout for erase operations, in minutes
options          "SA_SPACE_TIMEOUT=(60)"
options          "SA_REWIND_TIMEOUT=(2*60)"
options          "SA_ERASE_TIMEOUT=(4*60)"
```

```
options          "TUNE_1542"
```

SCSI_REPORT_GEOMETRY

Use SCSI_REPORT_GEOMETRY to always report disk geometry at boot up instead of only when booting verbosely. This shows in the last line of the following excerpt from *dmesg*:

```
da0: <Quantum XP34300W L915> Fixed Direct Access SCSI-2 device
da0: 20.000MB/s transfers (10.000MHz, offset 15, 16bit), Tagged Queueing Enabled
da0: 4303MB (8813920 512 byte sectors: 255H 63S/T 548C)
```

SCSI_DELAY

SCSI_DELAY is the number of *milliseconds* to wait after resetting the SCSI bus. Some devices spend a considerable period of times performing internal checks when after a bus reset. This is most evident when probing. This value used to be in seconds: be careful when upgrading.

Changer parameters

A number of SCSI devices, such as CD-ROMs and tapes, can use changers, devices which automatically load a number of media into a single drive. This can be a performance problem: the change operation is much slower than the I/O operations. If you change too often, you will get poor performance. If you wait too long before changing, you will also get poor performance. CAM attempts to control this with two build parameters: CHANGER_MIN_BUSY_SECONDS (default 2 seconds) is the guaranteed minimum time that a changer will wait before changing the medium. CHANGER_MAX_BUSY_SECONDS (default 10 seconds) is the maximum time that a changer will wait before changing the medium if a request is outstanding for another logical unit. Note that these values are far too low for tape units, where they should be set to between 100 and 500 seconds.

You don't need to rebuild the kernel to set these values: instead, you can change them with *sysctl(8)* by setting the variables kern.cam.cd.changer.min_busy_seconds and kern.cam.cd.changer.max_busy_seconds:

```
# sysctl kern.cam.cd.changer
kern.cam.cd.changer.min_busy_seconds: 2
kern.cam.cd.changer.max_busy_seconds: 10
# sysctl -w kern.cam.cd.changer.min_busy_seconds=6
kern.cam.cd.changer.min_busy_seconds: 2 -> 6
```

TUNE_1542

TUNE_1542 enables the automatic ISA bus speed selection for the Adaptec 1542 boards. It doesn't work for all boards, so use it with caution.

SCSI host adapters

FreeBSD 3.2 supports the following SCSI host adapters:

Device	Description
adv	All Narrow SCSI bus AdvanSys controllers.
adw	Second Generation AdvanSys controllers including the ADV940UW.
aha	Adaptec 154x
ahb	Adaptec 174X adapter.
ahc	Adaptec 274x/284x/294x, 29/3940(U)(W) and motherboard based AIC7870/AIC7880 adapters.
bt	Most Buslogic controllers isp#T{ Qlogic ISP 1020, 1040 and 1040B PCI SCSI host adapters, as well as the Qlogic ISP 2100 FC/AL Host Adapter.
ncr	NCR 53C810 and 53C825 self-contained SCSI host adapters.

For example, to configure an Adaptec 2940 host adapter, you might enter the following line in the configuration file:

```
controller ahc0
```

Virtual disks

```
pseudo-device   ccd   4        Concatenated disk driver
pseudo-device   vinum          Vinum volume manager
options   VINUMDEBUG           enable Vinum debugging hooks
```

FreeBSD supplies two kinds of virtual disks:

- *ccd* is the old *Concatenated disk* driver, which provides concatenation, mirroring and striping.

- *Vinum* is a new volume manager with greatly increased functionality. See page 266 for more details.

  The *vinum* pseudo-device is included for completeness' sake. You should use the *kld* instead.

  Note that the VINUMDEBUG option must match the CFLAGS specification in */usr/src/sbin/vinum/Makefile*. If this file defines VINUMDEBUG, your kernel must also define it. If this file does not define VINUMDEBUG, your kernel must also not define it. If you mix these components, *vinum(8)* will not be able to control the kernel module.

DPT SmartRAID controllers

The *dpt* driver provides support for DPT hardware RAID controllers (see *http://www.dpt.com/* for more details). The DPT controllers are commonly re-licensed under other brand-names - some controllers by Olivetti, Dec, HP, AT&T, SNI, AST, Alphatronic, NEC and Compaq are actually DPT controllers.

```
controller      dpt0

options DPT_VERIFY_HINTR
options DPT_RESTRICTED_FREELIST
options DPT_FREELIST_IS_STACK
options DPT_TIMEOUT_FACTOR=4
options    DPT_INTR_DELAY=200        # Some motherboards need that
options DPT_LOST_IRQ
options DPT_RESET_HBA
```

DPT_VERIFY_HINTR

`DPT_VERIFY_HINTR` performs some strict hardware interrupts testing. Use this only if you suspect PCI bus corruption problems

DPT_RESTRICTED_FREELIST

`DPT_RESTRICTED_FREELIST` restricts the number of queue slots to exactly what the DPT can hold at one time. This growth will NOT shrink. Normally, the freelist used by the DPT for queue will grow to accomodate increased use.

DPT_FREELIST_IS_STACK

Enable `DPT_FREELIST_IS_STACK` for optimal CPU cache utilization. Otherwise, the transaction queue is a LIFO. This option does not appear to make any difference to performance.

DPT_TIMEOUT_FACTOR

Use `DPT_TIMEOUT_FACTOR` to compute the excessive amount of time to wait when timing out with `DPT_HANDLE_TIMEOUTS`.

DPT_LOST_IRQ

Enable `DPT_LOST_IRQ` to try, once per second, to catch any interrupt that got lost. This option seems to help in some cases where the DPT firmware appears not to be compatible with the motherboard.

DPT_RESET_HBA

Use `DPT_RESET_HBA` to make the *reset* command actually reset the controller instead of fudging it. Only enable this if you are 100% certain you need it.

DPT_SHUTDOWN_SLEEP

Set `DPT_SHUTDOWN_SLEEP` to reset the controller if a request take more than this number of seconds. Do NOT enable this unless you are really certain you need it. Don't set this value to less than 300s (5 minutes).

File system options

These options specify which file systems the kernel will support. You must include at least support for the device you boot from.

```
options        FFS                        # Berkeley Fast Filesystem
options        FFS_ROOT                   # FFS usable as root device [keep this!]
options        NFS                        # Network Filesystem
options        NFS_ROOT                   # NFS usable as root device, "NFS" req'ed
options        MFS                        # Memory Filesystem
options        MFS_ROOT                   # MFS usable as root device, "MFS" req'ed
options        MFS_ROOT_SIZE=10
options        EXPORTMFS
```

FFS

FFS (*Fast File System*) is the original name of the *UNIX File System* or *ufs*. Use it (and FFS_ROOT) if you're running a normal system with the root file system on local disk.

NFS

Network File system. You can comment this out if you don't plan to mount partitions from a UNIX file server over Ethernet.

MFS

MFS is the *Memory-mapped file system*, basically a RAM disk for fast storage of temporary files. It's useful if you have a lot of swap space that you want to take advantage of, or if your system doesn't have any disks at all. A perfect use of an MFS partition is on the */tmp* directory, since many programs store temporary data here. To mount an MFS RAM disk on */tmp*, add the following line to */etc/fstab* and then reboot or type **mount /tmp**:

```
/dev/wd1s2b    /tmp mfs rw 0 0
```

Replace the */dev/wd1s2b* with the name of your swap partition, which will be listed in your */etc/fstab* as follows:

```
/dev/wd1s2b none swap sw 0 0
```

MFS_ROOT_SIZE specifies the size of an MFS root filesystem in kilobytes. EXPORT_NFS Allows MFS filesystems to be exported via NFS.

You can include other commonly-used file systems in the kernel, but many are also available as *kld*s. If this is the case, you can comment out support for them, and they will be dynamically loaded from the *kld* directory */modules* the first time you mount a partition of that type. Here's a list of the currently defined file systems. Many are experimental, so we won't talk about them all. In particular, *NULL, PORTAL, UMAP* and *UNION* filesystems are known to be buggy, and will panic your system if you attempt to do anything with them. They are included in *LINT* as an incentive for some enterprising soul to sit down and fix them.

```
options          "CD9660"          # ISO 9660 Filesystem
options          "CD9660_ROOT"     # CD-ROM usable as root. "CD9660" req'ed
options          NQNFS             # Enable NQNFS lease checking
options          FDESC             # File descriptor file system
options          KERNFS            # Kernel file system
options          LFS               # Log file system
options          MFS               # Memory File System
options          MSDOSFS           # MS DOS File System
options          NTFS              # NT File System
options          NULLFS            # NULL file system
options          PORTAL            # Portal file system
options          PROCFS            # Process file system
options          UMAPFS            # UID map file system
options          UNION             # Union file system
options          CODA              # CODA file system
options          SUIDDIR
options          QUOTA
```

MSDOSFS

MS-DOS File system. You only need this if you plan to mount a MS-DOS formatted hard drive partition at boot time—otherwise you can safely comment this out. It will be automatically loaded the first time you mount a MS-DOS partition, as described above. Also, the *mtools* package (in the ports collection) allows you to access MS-DOS floppies without having to mount and unmount them, and does not require MSDOSFS.

CD9660

ISO 9660 file system for CD-ROMs. Comment it out if you do not have a CD-ROM drive or only mount data CD's occasionally (since it will be dynamically loaded the first time you mount a data CD). Audio CD's do not need this file system.

PROCFS

Process file system. This is a pseudo file system mounted on */proc*, which gives access to various information relating to currently active processes. It allows programs like *ps* to give you more information on what processes are running. Consider it mandatory: *ps* and some other programs won't work without it.

NSWAPDEV

NSWAPDEV defines the number of swap devices that the kernel will support. Typical systems only have one swap device, and the default of 20 is so far beyond anything you're likely to need that there's no need to change it.

SUIDDIR

If you are running a machine as a fileserver for PC and MAC users using SAMBA or Netatalk, consider setting this option and keeping user directories on a file system that is mounted with the suiddir option. This gives new files the same ownership as the directory (similiar to group). It's a security hole if you let these users run programs, so confine it to file servers, but it'll save you lots of headaches in those cases. Directories owned by root are excepted, and the execution permission bits are cleared. The suid bit must be set on the directory as well; see *chmod(1)*. PC owners can't see or set ownerships so they keep getting their toes trodden on.

This saves you all the support calls as the filesystem it's used on will act as they expect: "It's my directory, so it must be my file".

QUOTA

Enable disk quotas. If you have a public access system, and do not want users to be able to overflow the */home* partition, you can establish disk quotas for each user. This code is a little buggy, so do not enable it unless you have to. View the manual page for *quota* to learn more about disk quotas.

Networking

The Internet grew up with BSD, so it's not surprising that FreeBSD places a *big* emphasis on networking. Even if you do not have a network board, you still need minimal network support: many programs require at least loopback networking (making network connections within your PC). Here's the complete network configuration section—we'll look at the more important entries below. Some of the support is seriously buggy: to quote *LINT: Source code for the NS (Xerox Network Service) is provided for amusement value.*

```
options         INET                        # InterNETworking

options         "TCP_COMPAT_42"             # emulate 4.2BSD TCP bugs
options         MROUTING                    # Multicast routing
options         IPFIREWALL                  # firewall
options         IPFIREWALL_VERBOSE          # print information about
                                            # dropped packets
options         IPFIREWALL_FORWARD          #enable transparent proxy support
options         "IPFIREWALL_VERBOSE_LIMIT=100" #limit verbosity
options         IPFIREWALL_DEFAULT_TO_ACCEPT #allow everything by default
options         IPDIVERT                    #divert sockets
options         IPFILTER                    #kernel ipfilter support
options         IPFILTER_LOG                #ipfilter logging
# options  IPFILTER_LKM                     #kernel support for ip_fil.o LKM
options         "ICMP_BANDLIM"
options    DUMMYNET
options    BRIDGE
options         NETATALK                    #Appletalk communications protocols
```

TCP_COMPAT_42

TCP_COMPAT_42 causes the TCP code to emulate certain bugs present in 4.2BSD. Don't use this unless you have a 4.2BSD machine and TCP connections fail.

MROUTING

MROUTING enables the kernel multicast packet forwarder, which works with mrouted(8).

IPFIREWALL

IPFIREWALL enables support for IP firewall construction, in conjunction with the *ipfw* program. IPFIREWALL_VERBOSE sends logged packets to the system logger. IPFIRE-WALL_VERBOSE_LIMIT limits the number of times a matching entry can be logged.

Warning: IPFIREWALL defaults to a policy of deny ip from any to any. If you do not add other rules during startup to allow access, ***You will lock yourself out***. It's a good idea to set firewall=open in */etc/rc.conf* when you first enable this feature Then you can refine the firewall rules in */etc/rc.firewall* after you've verified that the new kernel feature works properly.

IPFIREWALL_DEFAULT_TO_ACCEPT

IPFIREWALL_DEFAULT_TO_ACCEPT causes the default rule (at boot) to allow everything. Use with care, if a cracker can crash your firewall machine, they can get to your protected machines. However, if you are using it as an as-needed filter for specific problems as they arise, then this may be for you. Changing the default to allow means that you won't get stuck if the kernel and */sbin/ipfw* binary get out of sync.

IPDIVERT

IPDIVERT enables the divert IP sockets, used by *ipfw divert*.

IPFILTER

IPFILTER enables Darren Reed's ipfilter package.

IPFILTER_LOG

IPFILTER_LOG enables ipfilter's logging.

IPFILTER_LKM

IPFILTER_LKM enables LKM support for an ipfilter module.

ICMP_BANDLIM

ICMP_BANDLIM enables icmp error response bandwidth limiting. You typically want this option as it will help protect the machine from denial-of-service packet attacks.

DUMMYNET

DUMMYNET enables the *dummynet* bandwidth limiter. You need IPFIREWALL as well. See the *dummynet(4)* manpage for more information.

BRIDGE

BRIDGE enables bridging between ethernet cards. You can use IPFIREWALL and DUMMYNET together with bridging.

INET

Define networking support. You don't really have any choice: FreeBSD is a network operating system, and this entry must be present.

IPFIREWALL

`IPFIREWALL` and friends implement the IP firewall packet filter. See page 350 for more information.

Network interfaces

The next lines enable support for network boards. If you do not have a network board, you can comment out all of these lines. Otherwise, you'll want to leave in support for your particular board:

Table 18-2. Supported network interfaces

Interface name	Description
ar	Arnet SYNC/570i HDLC sync 2/4 port V.35/X.21 serial driver (requires sppp)
ax	PCI fast Ethernet adapters based on the ASIX Electronics AX88140A chip, including the Alfa Inc. GFC2204.
cs	IBM Etherjet and other Crystal Semi CS89x0-based adapters
cx	Cronyx/Sigma multiport sync/async (with Cisco or PPP framing).
de	Digital Equipment DC21040 self-contained Ethernet adapter.
ed	Western Digital and SMC 80xx; Novell NE1000 and NE2000; 3Com 3C503
el	3Com 3C501
en	Efficient Networks (ENI) ENI-155 PCI midway ATM boards, and the Adaptec 155Mbps PCI ATM boards (ANA-59x0).
ep	3Com 3C509 (buggy)
ex	Intel EtherExpress Pro/10 and other i82595-based adapters
fe	Fujitsu MB86960A/MB86965A Ethernet
fea	DEC DEFEA EISA FDDI adapter.
fpa	Digital DEFPA PCI FDDI adapter. `pseudo-device fddi` is also needed.
fxp	Intel EtherExpress Pro/100B PCI Fast Ethernet adapters.
ie	AT&T StarLAN 10 and EN100; 3Com 3C507; unknown NI5210; Intel EtherExpress
le	Digital Equipment EtherWorks 2 and EtherWorks 3 (DEPCA, DE100, DE101, DE200, DE201, DE202, DE203, DE204, DE205, DE422)
lnc	Lance/PCnet boards (Isolan, Novell NE2100, NE32-VL, AMD Am7990 & Am79C960)
mx	Fast Ethernet adapters based on the Macronix 98713, 987615 ans 98725 series chips.

Interface name	Description
pn	Fast Ethernet adapters based on the Lite-On 82c168 and 82c169 PNIC chips, including the LinkSys LNE100TX, the NetGear FA310TX rev. D1 and the Matrox FastNIC 10/100.
rdp	RealTek RTL 8002-based pocket Ethernet adapters
rl	PCI fast Ethernet adapters based on the RealTek 8129/8139 chipset. Note that the RealTek driver defaults to useing programmed I/O to do register accesses because memory mapped mode seems to cause severe lockups on SMP hardware. This driver also supports the Accton EN1207D 'Cheetah' adapter, which uses a chip called the MPX 5030/5038, which is either a RealTek in disguise or a RealTek workalike.
sr	RISCom/N2 hdlc sync 1/2 port V.35/X.21 serial driver (requires sppp)
ti	PCI gigabit Ethernet NICs based on the Alteon Networks Tigon 1 and Tigon 2 chipsets. This includes the Alteon AceNIC, the 3Com 3c985, the Netgear GA620 and others. Note that you will probably want to bump up NBMCLUSTERS a lot to use this driver.
tl	the Texas Instruments TNETE100 series 'ThunderLAN' boards and integrated Ethernet controllers. This includes several Compaq Netelligent 10/100 boards and the built-in Ethernet controllers in several Compaq Prosignia, Proliant and Deskpro systems. It also supports several Olicom 10Mbps and 10/100 boards.
tx	SMC 9432TX boards.
vr	fast Ethernet adapters based on the VIA Technologies VT3043 'Rhine I' and VT86C100A 'Rhine II' chips, including the D-Link DFE530TX.
vx	3Com 3C590 and 3C595 early support
wb	Fast Ethernet adapters based on the Winbond W89C840F chip. This is not the same as the Winbond W89C940F, which is an NE2000 clone.
wl	Lucent Wavelan (ISA board only).
xl	3Com 3c900, 3c905 and 3c905B (Fast) Etherlink XL boards and integrated controllers. This includes the integrated 3c905B-TX chips in certain Dell Optiplex and Dell Precision desktop machines and the integrated 3c905-TX chips in Dell Latitude laptop docking stations.
ze	IBM/National Semiconductor PCMCIA Ethernet controller.
zp	3Com PCMCIA Etherlink III. It does not require shared memory for send/receive operation, but it needs 'iomem' to read/write the attribute memory)

The entries include a number of other undocumented drivers. The complete list is:

```
device ar0 at isa? port 0x300 net irq 10 iomem 0xd0000
device cs0 at isa? port 0x300 net irq ?
device cx0 at isa? port 0x240 net irq 15 drq 7
device ed0 at isa? port 0x280 net irq 5 iomem 0xd8000
device el0 at isa? port 0x300 net irq 9
device ep0 at isa? port 0x300 net irq 10
device ex0 at isa? port? net irq?
device fe0 at isa? port 0x300 net irq ?
device ie0 at isa? port 0x300 net irq 5 iomem 0xd0000
device ie1 at isa? port 0x360 net irq 7 iomem 0xd0000
device le0 at isa? port 0x300 net irq 5 iomem 0xd0000
device lnc0 at isa? port 0x280 net irq 10 drq 0
device rdp0 at isa? port 0x378 net irq 7 flags 2
device sr0 at isa? port 0x300 net irq 5 iomem 0xd0000
options        WLCACHE       # enables the signal-strength cache
options        WLDEBUG       # enables verbose debugging output
device wl0 at isa? port 0x300 net irq ?
We can (bogusly) include both the dedicated PCCARD drivers and the generic
support when COMPILING_LINT.
device ze0 at isa? port 0x300 net irq 5 iomem 0xd8000
device zp0 at isa? port 0x300 net irq 10 iomem 0xd8000
```

For example, to configure a 3Com 3C509 interface, you might enter the following line in the configuration file:

```
device ep0 at isa? port 0x300 net irq 10
```

If you have more than one network board, don't change the sequence of the entries in the configuration file: the kernel probes for the boards in this sequence, and the probe routines can interfere with each other.

Network pseudo-devices

In addition to real devices, FreeBSD defines a number of *pseudo-devices* which behave to the user as if they were real devices, but which have no hardware behind them. The following pseudo-devices are related to networking; we'll look at the rest on page 359.

```
pseudo-device    pty      16    # Pseudo-ttys
pseudo-device    ether          # Generic Ethernet
pseudo-device    fddi           # Generic FDDI
pseudo-device    sppp           # Generic Synchronous PPP
pseudo-device    loop           # Network loopback device
pseudo-device    bpfilter 4     # Berkeley packet filter
pseudo-device    disc           # Discard device
pseudo-device    tun      1     # Tunnel driver (user process ppp(8))
pseudo-device    sl       2     # Serial Line IP
pseudo-device    ppp      2     # Point-to-point protocol
options PPP_BSDCOMP             # PPP BSD-compress support
options PPP_DEFLATE             # PPP zlib/deflate/gzip support
options PPP_FILTER             # enable bpf filtering (needs bpfilter)
```

pseudo-device pty

pty is a *pseudo-tty* or simulated login port. It's used by incoming *telnet* and *rlogin* sessions, *xterm*, and some other applications. The *number* indicates the number of ptys to create. If you need a total of more than the GENERIC default of 16 simultaneous xterm windows and remote logins, you can increase this number accordingly, up to a maximum of 64.

pseudo-device ether

`ether` provides generic Ethernet protocol code for Ethernet boards.

pseudo-device loop

`loop` is the generic loopback device for TCP/IP. If you telnet or FTP to `localhost` (`127.0.0.1`) it will come back at you through this pseudo-device. You must specify this option.

pseudo-device bpfilter

The *Berkeley Packet Filter* (*bpf*) allows you to capture packets crossing a network interface to disk or to examine them with the *tcpdump* program. Note that this capability represents a significant compromise of network security. The *number* after bpfilter is the number of concurrent processes that can use the facility. Not all network interfaces support bpf.

In order to use the Berkeley Packet Filter, you must also create the device nodes */dev/bpf0* to */dev/bpf3* (if you're using the default number 4). Currently, *MAKEDEV* doesn't help much—you need to create each device separately:

```
# cd /dev
# ./MAKEDEV bpf0
# ./MAKEDEV bpf1
# ./MAKEDEV bpf2
# ./MAKEDEV bpf3
```

pseudo-device sl

`sl` is for SLIP (Serial Line Internet Protocol) support. This has been almost entirely supplanted by PPP, which is easier to set up, better suited for modem-to-modem connections, as well as more powerful. The *number* after `sl` specifies how many simultaneous SLIP sessions to support. See page 468 for more information on setting up SLIP.

pseudo-device tun

`tun` is the *tunnel driver* used by the user-mode PPP software. See page 447 for more details. The number after `tun` specifies the number of simultaneous PPP sessions to support.

pseudo-device ppp

`ppp` is for kernel-mode PPP (Point-to-Point Protocol) support for dial-up Internet connections. See page 454 for a detailed description. *number* specifies how many simultaneous PPP connections to support.

ISDN support

Pn config-i4b FreeBSD 3.2 includes the *i4b* package, which is short for *ISDN4BSD*. Currently it supports only the ETSI Basic Rate Interface protocol specified in ITUT recommendations I.430, Q.921 and Q.931. In Europe this is sometimes known as as DSS1, and in Germany as "Euro-ISDN".

i4b allows you to make IP network connections by using either IP packets sent in raw HDLC frames on the B channel or by using synchronous PPP. For telephony, *i4b* can answer incoming phone calls like an answering machine.

```
pseudo-device    "i4bq921"          Q.921 (layer 2): i4b passive board D channel handling
pseudo-device    "i4bq931"          Q.931 (layer 3): i4b passive board D channel handling
pseudo-device    "i4b"              layer 4: common passive and active board handling
pseudo-device    "i4btrc"      4    userland driver to do ISDN tracing (for passive boards only)
pseudo-device    "i4bctl"           userland driver to control the whole thing
pseudo-device    "i4brbch" 4        userland driver for access to raw B channel
pseudo-device    "i4btel"      2    userland driver for telephony
pseudo-device    "i4bipr"      4    network driver for IP over raw HDLC ISDN
options          IPR_VJ             enable VJ header compression detection for ipr i/f
pseudo-device    "i4bisppp" 4       network driver for sync PPP over ISDN

options          "TEL_S0_16_3"      sample option (see table below)
device           isic0 at isa? port ? iomem 0xd0000 net irq 5 flags 1        ISDN board

device tina0 at isa? port 0x260 net irq 10 Stollmann Tina-dd control device
```

The ISDN board configuration is unusual in the fact that, with the exception of the Stollmann Tina-dd, the device name is always *isic0*. You select the device not by device name, but by an option which specifies the name, such as the `TEL_S0_16_3` in the example above. Depending on the board, you must also set some of the values for `port`, `iomem`, `irq` and `flags`. Table 18-3 shows which values you need:

Table 18-3. Supported ISDN boards

Board	option	Port	iomem	irq	flags
AVM A1, AVM Fritz!Card	AVM_A1	0x340		5	4
AVM PCMCIA Fritz!Card	AVM_A1_PCMCIA	0x340		5	10
Creatix ISDN-S0 P&P	CRTX_S0_P	?		?	
Dr. Neuhaus Niccy Go@	DRN_NGO	?		?	
Dynalink IS64PH	DYNALINK	?		?	
ELSA QuickStep 1000pro ISA	ELSA_QS1ISA	?		?	
ELSA QuickStep 1000pro PCI	ELSA_QS1PCI				
ITK ix1 Micro	ITKIX1	0x398		10	18
Sedlbauer Win Speed	SEDLBAUER	?		?	
Teles S0/16, Creatix ISDN-S0, Niccy 1016	TEL_S0_16	0xd80	0xd0000	5	2
Teles S0/16.3 PnP	TEL_S0_16_3_P	?		?	
Teles S0/16.3	TEL_S0_16_3	0xd80		5	3
Teles S0/8, Niccy 1008	TEL_S0_8		0xd0000	5	1
US Robotics Sportster ISDN TA internal	USR_STI	0x268		5	7

356

ATM support

FreeBSD includes the *HARP* implementation of ATM (*Asynchronous Transfer Mode*). Here are the configuration entries:

```
options     ATM_CORE        core ATM protocol family
options     ATM_IP          IP over ATM support
options     ATM_SIGPVC      SIGPVC signalling manager
options     ATM_SPANS       SPANS signalling manager
options     ATM_UNI         UNI signalling manager
device      hea0            Efficient ENI-155p ATM PCI
device      hfa0            FORE PCA-200E ATM PCI
```

`ATM_CORE` includes the base ATM functionality code. This must be included for ATM support.

`ATM_IP` includes support for running IP over ATM.

At least one (and usually only one) of the following signalling managers must be included:

- `ATM_SIGPVC` includes support for the PVC-only signalling manager *sigpvc*.

- `ATM_SPANS` includes support for the 'spans' signalling manager, which runs the FORE Systems's proprietary SPANS signalling protocol.

- `ATM_UNI` includes support for the *uni30* and *uni31* signalling managers, which run the ATM Forum UNI 3.x signalling protocols.

All signalling managers include PVC support.

The *hea* driver provides support for the Efficient Networks, Inc. ENI-155p ATM PCI Adapter.

The *hfa* driver provides support for the FORE Systems, Inc. PCA-200E ATM PCI Adapter.

Sound boards

Table 18-3 shows the sound boards that FreeBSD supports.

Device	Description
css	Crystal Sound System (CSS 423x PnP)
gus	Gravis Ultrasound - Ultrasound, Ultrasound 16, Ultrasound MAX
gusxvi	Gravis Ultrasound 16-bit PCM (do not use)
mpu	Roland MPU-401 stand-alone card
mss	Microsoft Sound System
opl	Yamaha OPL-2 and OPL-3 FM - SB, SB Pro, SB 16, ProAudioSpectrum
pas	ProAudioSpectrum PCM and MIDI
pca	PCM audio through your PC speaker.

Device	Description
pcm	PCM audio through various sound cards. This has support for a large number of new audio cards, based on CS423x, OPTi931, Yamaha OPL-SAx, and also for SB16, GusPnP. For more information about this driver and supported cards, see the man page *pcm(4)* and */sys/i386/isa/snd/CARDS*.
	The device flags tell the device a bit more info about the device than the PnP interface supplies: flag bits 2:0 define the secondary DMA channel number, bit 4 is set if the board uses two dma channels, and bits 15:8 define the board type and override autodetection. Leave it this field zero at the moment.
sb	SoundBlaster PCM - SoundBlaster, SB Pro, SB16, ProAudioSpectrum
sbmidi	SoundBlaster 16 MIDI interface
sbxvi	SoundBlaster 16
snd	Voxware sound support code
sscape	Ensoniq Soundscape MIDI interface
sscape_mss	Ensoniq Soundscape PCM (requires sscape)
uart	stand-alone 6850 UART for MIDI

```
controller snd0
device pas0      at isa? port 0x388 irq 10 drq 6
device sb0       at isa? port 0x220 irq 5 drq 1
device sbxvi0    at isa? drq 5
device sbmidi0   at isa? port 0x330
device awe0      at isa? port 0x620
device gus0 at isa? port 0x220 irq 12 drq 1
device mss0 at isa? port 0x530 irq 10 drq 1
device css0      at isa? port 0x534 irq 5 drq 1 flags 0x08
device sscape0   at isa? port 0x330 irq 9 drq 0
device trix0     at isa? port 0x330 irq 6 drq 0
device sscape_mss0  at isa? port 0x534 irq 5 drq 1
device opl0      at isa? port 0x388
device mpu0      at isa? port 0x330 irq 6 drq 0
device uart0 at isa? port 0x330 irq 5

device pcm0 at isa? port ? tty irq 10 drq 1 flags 0x0
```

There are three basic way to configure a sound device:

- If you are outputting to the PC speaker with the *pca* driver, that's all you need.

- Alternatively, use the *snd0* controller and one of the devices listed below it.

- The third choice is the *pcm0* driver. If you use this driver, don't define *snd0*.

Other points to be noted about sounds boards are:

- The addresses specified in the device entries are also hard-coded in *i386/isa/sound/sound_config.h*. If you change the values in the configuration, you must also change the values in the include file.

- If you have a GUS-MAX card and want to use the CS4231 codec on the card the drqs for the gus max must be 8 bit (1, 2, or 3).

- If you would like to use the full duplex option on the gus, then define flags to be the "read dma channel".

Pseudo-devices

Pseudo-device drivers are parts of the kernel that act like device drivers but do not correspond to any actual hardware in the machine. See page 354 for a discussion of network-related pseudo-devices.

```
pseudo-device    speaker            # Play IBM BASIC-style noises out your speaker
pseudo-device    log                # Kernel syslog interface (/dev/klog)
pseudo-device    gzip               # Exec gzipped binaries
pseudo-device    vn                 # Vnode driver (turns a file into a device)
pseudo-device    snp       3        # Snoop device - to look at pty/vty/etc..
```

pseudo-device speaker

```
pseudo-device speaker
```

Supports IBM BASIC-style noises through the PC speaker. Some fun programs which use this are */usr/sbin/spkrtest*, which is a shell script that plays some simple songs, and */usr/games/piano* which lets you play songs using the keyboard as a simple piano (this file only exists if you've installed the *games* package). Also, the excellent text role-playing game NetHack (in the ports collection) can be configured to use this device to play songs when you play musical instruments in the game.

See also the device pca0 on page 357.

pseudo-device log

log is used for logging of kernel error messages. Mandatory.

pseudo-device gzip

gzip allows you to run FreeBSD programs that have been compressed with *gzip*. This is useful when you need to compress FreeBSD programs to fit on a boot floppy.

pseudo-device vn

Vnode driver. Allows a file to be treated as a device after being set up with the *vnconfig* command. This driver can be useful for manipulating floppy disk images and using a file as a swap device (e.g. an MS Windows swap file). You also need this driver if you want to build a FreeBSD release, which you might want to do to get a boot floppy. This book doesn't discuss the release process in any more detail. For the final word on this subject, look at */usr/src/release/Makefile*. Building a FreeBSD release is still an 'expert level' job.

pseudo-device snp

Snoop device. This pseudo-device allows one terminal session to watch another using the *watch* command. Note that implementation of this capability has important security and privacy implications. The *number* after snp is the total number of simultaneous snoop sessions.

Miscellaneous devices

This section describes some miscellaneous hardware devices supported by FreeBSD. None of these definitions are included in the GENERIC kernel: you'll have to enter them manually or copy them from the LINT kernel.

Table 18-4. Miscellaneous drivers

Device	Description
apm	Laptop Advanced Power Management/
asc	GI1904-based hand scanners, e.g. the Trust Amiscan Grey
bktr	Brooktree bt848/848a/849/878/879 family video capture and TV Tuner board. See *http://www.freebsd.org/~fsmp/HomeAuto/Bt848.html* for further details.
ctx	Cortex-I frame grabber.
cy	Cyclades serial driver.
dgb	Digiboard PC/Xi and PC/Xe series driver.
dgm	Digiboard PC/Xem driver.
gp	National Instruments AT-GPIB and AT-GPIB/TNT board
gsc	Genius GS-4500 hand scanner.
joy	Joystick.
labpc	National Instrument's Lab-PC and Lab-PC+
matcd	Matsushita/Panasonic CD-ROM.
mcd	Mitsumi CD-ROM.
meteor	Matrox Meteor video capture board.
rc	RISCom/8 multiport card
rp	Comtrol Rocketport(ISA) - single card.
scd	Sony CD-ROM.
si	Specialix SI/XIO 4-32 port terminal multiplexor.
spigot	Creative Labs Video Spigot video-acquisition board.
stl	Stallion EasyIO and EasyConnection 8/32 (cd1400 based)
stli	Stallion EasyConnection 8/64, ONboard, Brumby (intelligent)
tw	TW-523 power line interface for use with X-10 home control products

The CD-ROM drives mentioned here are the old drives with the proprietary interfaces. Modern CD-ROM drives are either SCSI or IDE.

The corresponding entries are:

```
device          mcd0    at isa? port 0x300 bio irq 10
# for the Sony CDU31/33A CDROM
device          scd0    at isa? port 0x230 bio
# for the SoundBlaster 16 multicd - up to 4 devices
controller      matcd0  at isa? port 0x230 bio
device          ctx0    at isa? port 0x230 iomem 0xd0000
device          spigot0 at isa? port 0xad6 irq 15 iomem 0xee000
device          qcam0   at isa? port "IO_LPT3" tty
device          apm0    at isa?
options         APM_BROKEN_STATCLOCK
device          gp0     at isa? port 0x2c0 tty
device          gsc0    at isa? port "IO_GSC1" tty drq 3
device          joy0    at isa? port "IO_GAME"
device          cy0     at isa? tty irq 10 iomem 0xd4000 iosiz 0x2000
device          dgb0    at isa? port 0x220 iomem 0xfc0000 iosiz ? tty
device          labpc0  at isa? port 0x260 tty irq 5
device          rc0     at isa? port 0x220 tty irq 12
# the port and irq for tw0 are fictitious
device          tw0     at isa? port 0x380 tty irq 11
device          si0     at isa? iomem 0xd0000 tty irq 12
device          asc0    at isa? port IO_ASC1 tty drq 3 irq 10
device          bqu0    at isa? port 0x150
device          stl0    at isa? port 0x2a0 tty irq 10
device          stli0   at isa? port 0x2a0 tty iomem 0xcc000 flags 23 iosiz 0x1000
```

Building and installing the new kernel

After editing the configuration file, you create the build environment with *config*. In the directory */usr/src/sys/i386/conf*, you enter:

```
# /usr/sbin/config -g FREEBIE
Kernel build directory is ../../compile/FREEBIE
```

The -g flag tells *config* to generate symbolic information for the kernel. If you run into trouble with the kernel, this information will help you analyse the cause; see page 108 for further details.

It's possible to get error messages when running *config* if you have made a mistake in the config file. If the *config* command fails when you give it your kernel description, you've probably made a simple error somewhere. Fortunately, *config* will print the line number that it had trouble with, so you can quickly find it with an editor. For example:

```
config: line 17: syntax error
```

One possibility is that you have mistyped a keyword. Compare it to the entry in the GENERIC or LINT kernel definitions.

You'll need about 30 MB of free space on */usr/src* in order to build a kernel. If you're really tight on space, you can reduce this value significantly by omitting the -g option, but if you have problems with the system at some later stage, it will be much more difficult to find what is causing them.

Building the kernel

Next, change to the build directory and build the kernel:

```
# cd ../../compile/FREEBIE
# make
```

This procedure can take some time, up to an hour on a slow machine. It's also possible to have errors here, and unfortunately they are usually *not* self-explanatory. If the *make* command fails, it usually signals an error in your kernel description which is not obvious enough for *config* to catch it. Again, look over your configuration, and if you still cannot resolve the problem, send mail to questions@FreeBSD.ORG with your kernel configuration, and it should be diagnosed very quickly. A description of how to interpret these errors is in the works, but at the moment this is still deep magic.

Finally, install the new kernel:

```
# make install
```

This renames the current kernel to */kernel.old* and copies the new kernel to the root directory as */kernel.* Next, shutdown the system and reboot load the new kernel:

```
# shutdown -r now
```

If the new kernel does not boot, or fails to recognize your devices, don't panic. Reset the machine, and when the boot prompt appears, boot the old kernel:

```
Boot: boot kernel.old
```

When reconfiguring a kernel, it is always a good idea to keep on hand a kernel that is known to work. Since *kernel.old* gets overwritten every time you install a new kernel, I also keep a kernel called *kernel.save.*

After booting with a good kernel you can check over your configuration file and try to build it again. One helpful resource is the */var/log/messages* file which records, among other things, all of the kernel messages from every successful boot. Also, the *dmesg* command will print the kernel messages from the current boot.

If you are having trouble building a kernel, make sure to keep a GENERIC, or some other kernel that is known to work on hand as a different name that will not get erased on the next build. Don't rely on *kernel.old* because the kernel installation process overwrites *kernel.old* every time. Also, as soon as possible, move the working kernel to the proper location. The proper command to "unlock" the kernel file that *make* installs (in order to move another kernel back permanently) is:

```
# chflags noschg /kernel
```

And, if you want to "lock" your new kernel (or any file for that matter) into place so that it cannot be moved or tampered with:

```
# chflags schg /kernel
```

Making device nodes

If you've added any new devices to your kernel, you may have to add device nodes to your */dev* directory before you can use them. See page 233 for further details.

Kernel loadable modules

As we saw at the beginning of the chapter, you may not have to build a new kernel to implement the functionality you want. Instead, just load it into the running kernel with a *Kernel Loadable Module* (*kld*). The directory */modules* contains a number of klds. To load them, use *kldload*. For example, if you wanted to load SCO UNIX compatibility, you would enter:

```
# kldload ibcs2
```

This loads the module */modules/ibcs2.ko*. Note that you don't need to specify the directory name, nor the *.ko* extension.

To find what modules are loaded, use *kldstat*:

```
# kldstat
Id Refs Address    Size    Name
 1    5 0xc0100000 1d08b0  kernel
 2    2 0xc120d000 a000    ibcs2.ko
 3    1 0xc121b000 3000    ibcs2_coff.ko
 5    1 0xc1771000 e000    linux.ko
 6    1 0xc177f000 bf000   vinum.ko
```

You can also unload some klds, but not all of them. Use *kldunload* for this purpose:

```
# kldunload -n vinum
```

19

Keeping up to date with FreeBSD

It's convenient to get FreeBSD on CD-ROM, but that isn't the only way it is distributed. The CD-ROMs are probably the cheapest way to get a base distribution. Unfortunately, they're not the most up-to-date. In this chapter we'll look at alternative sources of FreeBSD sources.

The FreeBSD project keeps a single master source tree, called a *repository*, which is maintained by the *Concurrent Versions System*, or *cvs*. You'll find it on the second CD-ROM of the set in the directory *CVSROOT*. The repository contains all versions of FreeBSD back to the last release from the Computer Sciences Research Group of the University of California at Berkeley, 4.4BSD-Lite. Each of these versions is called a *branch*. There are three main branches of interest, which we'll look at in the following sections.

FreeBSD releases

One of the problems understanding releases is that they're a moving target. At any one time, three basic "latest" versions of FreeBSD are available:

FreeBSD-RELEASE

FreeBSD-RELEASE is the latest version of FreeBSD which has been released for general use. It contains as many new features as are consistent with stability. It has been through extensive testing. You can get it on CD-ROM. FreeBSD-RELEASEs are given a release number which uniquely identifies them, such as 2.2.5. There are two or three releases a year.

FreeBSD-STABLE

FreeBSD-STABLE is a version of FreeBSD-RELEASE to which all possible bug fixes have been applied, in order to make it as stable as possible. Fixes are made several times a week. The development cycle is independent of FreeBSD-RELEASE, so at some times it may be based on an older release of FreeBSD than the current FreeBSD-RELEASE, and it may be missing some features of the current FreeBSD-RELEASE. For example, the current FreeBSD-RELEASE might be 2.2.5, but FreeBSD-STABLE will be based on FreeBSD-RELEASE 2.2.2. At other times it may be based on the same release as FreeBSD-RELEASE, in which case it will have all the features and fewer bugs.

Due to the frequent updates, FreeBSD-STABLE is not currently available on CD-ROM, and there are no plans to do so.

FreeBSD-CURRENT

FreeBSD-CURRENT is the very latest version of FreeBSD, still under development. All new development work is done on this branch of the tree. FreeBSD-CURRENT is an ever-changing snapshot of the working sources for FreeBSD, including work in progress, experimental changes and transitional mechanisms that may or may not be present in the next official release of the software. Many users compile almost daily from FreeBSD-CURRENT sources, but there times when the sources are uncompilable. The problems are always resolved, but others can take their place. On occasion, keeping up with FreeBSD-CURRENT can be a full-time business. If you use -CURRENT, you should be prepared to spend a lot of time keeping the system running. The following extract from the RCS log file for */usr/src/Makefile* should give you a feel for the situation:

> *revision 1.152*
> *Hooboy!*
>
> *Did I ever spam this file good with that last commit. Despite 3 reviewers, we still managed to revoke the eBones fixes, TCL 8.0 support, libvgl and a host of other new things from this file in the process of parallelizing the Makefile. DOH! I think we need more pointy hats - this particular incident is worthy of a small children's birthday party's worth of pointy hats. ;-)*
>
> *I certainly intend to take more care with the processing of aged diffs in the future, even if it does mean reading through 20K's worth of them. I might also be a bit more careful about asking for more up-to-date changes before looking at them. ;)*

So why use -CURRENT? The main reasons are:

- You yourself might be working on some part of the source tree. Keeping "current" is an absolute requirement.

- You may be an active tester, which imples that you're willing to spend time working through problems in order to ensure that FreeBSD-CURRENT remains as sane as possible. You may also wish to make topical suggestions on changes and the general direction of FreeBSD.

- You may just want to keep an eye on things and use the current sources for reference purposes.

People occasionally have other reasons for wanting to use FreeBSD-CURRENT. The following are *not* good reasons:

- They see it as a way to be the first on the block with great new FreeBSD features. This is not a good reason, because there's no reason to believe that the features will stay, and there is good reason to believe that they will be unstable.

- They see it as a quick way of getting bug fixes. In fact, it's a way of *testing* bug fixes. Bug fixes will be retrofitted into the -STABLE branch as soon as they have been properly tested.

- They see it as the newest officially supported release of FreeBSD. This is incorrect: FreeBSD-CURRENT is *not* officially supported. The support is provided by the users.

Snapshots

FreeBSD-CURRENT *is* available on CD-ROM from Walnut Creek. Several times a year, at irregular intervals when the tree is relatively stable, the core team makes a *snapshot* of the repository and the -CURRENT source tree. This is a possible alternative to on-line updates if you don't want the absolute latest version of the system.

The repository

The *repository* is the home of all FreeBSD releases. As we have seen, it is maintained by *CVS*, which is a system built on top of the *Revision Control System*, or *RCS*.

The repository is a duplicate of the source tree with copies of each file in the source tree. It modifies the names by appending the suffix *,v*: for example, *main.c* in the source tree becomes *main.c,v* in the repository. These files contain a copy of the most recent version of the file, along with a lot of information about how to create older versions of the source from the current version. Each version has an identification which is either in two parts (for example, version 1.3), or in four parts (for example, version 1.2.1.4). The two-part versions are said to be on the *trunk* of the tree, whereas the four-part versions are on *branches*. In FreeBSD, the trunk is the -CURRENT version.

In addition to the numeric identifiers, each of which relates only to a single file, RCS allows you to attach *symbolic names* to specific revisions. FreeBSD uses these to indicate the revisions corresponding to a particular release. For example, in the directory */usr/src/sys/kern*, version 1.13 of *kern_clock.c*, version 1.12 of *kern_fork.c* and version 1.21.4.1 of *kern_exec.c* participate in `RELENG_2_1_0_RELEASE`. For more details of *RCS*, see the man page.

If you're a serious developer, there are a number of advantages to keeping a copy of the repository. If you're a casual user, it's probably overkill.

Getting updates from the net

There are a number of possibilities to keep up with the daily modifications to the source tree. The first question is: how much space do you want to invest in keeping the sources? Table 19-1 shows the space required by different parts of the sources.

Table 19-1. Approximate source tree sizes

Component	Size (MB)
Repository *src/sys*	53
Repository *src*	330
Repository *ports*	36
Source tree */usr/src/sys*	65
Source tree */usr/src*	225
Source tree */usr/ports*	200
Object tree *src*	160

The size of */usr/src/sys* includes the files involved in a single kernel build. This changes the size of */usr/src* as well, of course. Similarly, the size of */usr/ports* includes a few ports. It will, of course, grow extremely large (several gigabytes) if you start porting all available packages.

If you're maintaining multiple source trees (say, for different versions), you still only need one copy of the repository.

How to get the updates

You also have the choice of how to get the updates. If you have a reasonably good connection to the Internet, use *CVSup* to update your repository. Otherwise, you may find *CTM* more useful. We'll look at both in the following sections.

CVSup

CVSup is a software package which distributes updates to the repository. You can run the client at regular intervals—for example, with *cron* (see page 184) to update your repository.

To get started with *CVSup*, you need the following:

- A source tree or repository. This is not absolutely necessary, but the initial setup will be much faster if you do it this way.

- A copy of the *cvsup* program. Install this with *pkg_add* from the CD-ROM (currently */cdrom/packages/All/cvsup-15.2.tgz*; the suffix may change in future releases).

- A *cvsupfile*, a command file for *cvsup*. We'll look at this below.

- A *mirror site* from which you can load the software. We'll discuss this below as well.

The *cvsupfile* contains a description of the packages you want to download. You can find all the details in the online handbook, but the following example shows a reasonably normal file:

```
*default release=cvs
*default host=cvsup2.freebsd.org
*default base=/src/cvsup
*default prefix=/src/ncvs
*default delete
*default use-rel-suffix
*default compress
src-all
ports-all
doc-all
```

The lines starting with `*default` specify default values; the lines which do not are collections which you want to track. This file answers these implicit questions:

- Which files do you want to receive? These are the names of the *collections* in the last five lines: all of the sources, all of the ports, and all of the documentation.

- Which versions of them do you want? By default, you get updates to the repository. If you want a specific version, you can write:

  `*default tag=`*version*

  version is one of the tags we saw on page 365, or `.` (a period) to represent the -CURRENT version.

  Alternatively, you might ask for a version as of a specific date. For example:

  `*default date=97.09.13.12.20`

  This would specify that you want *the version* as it was on 13 September 1997 at 12:20. In this case, *version* defaults to `..`.

- Where do you want to get them from? Two parameters answer this question: `host=cvsup2.freebsd.org` specifies the name of the host from which to load the files, and `release=cvs` specifies to use the *cvs* release. The *release* option is obsolescent, but it's a good idea to leave it in there until it is officially removed.

- Where do you want to put them on your own machine? This question is answered by the line `*default prefix=/src/ncvs`. Since we're tracking the repository in this example, this is the name of the repository. If we were tracking a particular release, we would use `*default prefix=/usr`. Since the collections are called *doc*, *ports* and *src*, we refer to the parent directory in each case.

- Where do you want to put your status files? This question is answered by the line `*default base=/src/cvsup`.

In addition, the file contains three other lines. `*default delete` means that *cvsup* may delete files where necessary. Otherwise you run the risk of accumulating obsolete files. `*default compress` enables compression of the data transmitted, and `*default use-rel-suffix` specifies how *cvsup* should handle list files. It's not well-documented, but it's necessary. Don't worry about it.

Which CVSup server?

In this example, we've chosen one of the backup US servers, *cvsup2.FreeBSD.org*. In practice, this may not be the best choice. A large number of servers are spread around the world, and you should choose the one topographically closest to you. This isn't the same thing as being geographically closest—I live in Adelaide, South Australia, and some ISPs in the same city are further away on the net than many systems in California. Look in the appendix *Obtaining FreeBSD* in the online handbook for an up-to-date list.

Running *cvsup*

The handbook recommends running *cvsup* via a GUI interface. I don't. *cvsup* is a typical candidate for a *cron* job. I rebuild the -CURRENT tree every Thursday morning at 2:40 am. To do so, I have the following entry in */root/crontab*:

```
# Get the latest and greatest FreeBSD stuff, only on Thursdays
40 2 * * 4 ./extract-updates
```

The file */root/extract-updates* contains, amongst other things,

```
cvsup -g -L2 /src/cvsup/cvs-cvsupfile
```

/src/cvsup/cvs-cvsupfile is the name of the *cvsupfile* we looked at above. The other parameters to *cvsup* specify *not* to use the GUI (-g), and -L2 specifies to produce moderate detail about the actions being performed.

Other possible cvsupfiles

The example *cvsupfile* above is useful if you're maintaining a copy of the repository. If you just want to maintain a copy of the sources of one version, say 2.2.5, use the following file instead:

```
*default tag=RELENG_2_2_5_RELEASE
*default release=cvs
*default host=cvsup2.freebsd.org
*default base=/usr                    for /usr/doc, /usr/ports, /usr/src
*default prefix=/src/ncvs
*default delete
*default use-rel-suffix
*default compress
src-all
ports-all
doc-all
```

One collection causes special problems: *cvs-crypto* contains cryptographic software. Until recently, exporting this software from the USA was subject to strict export restrictions, and it's not clear that these restrictions might not be reimposed. To be on the safe side, don't load them from a US site if you are located outside the USA. It *is* legal to import them into the USA, but once you have done so, you may not be allowed to re-export them. If you are in the USA, or if you are loading from *cvsup.internat.freebsd.org*, you can also add the following line to the end of either *cvsupfile*:

```
cvs-crypto
```

Otherwise create a second *cvsupfile* to load from *cvsup.internat.freebsd.org*: each *cvsupfile* file may refer to only one host. Write:

```
*default tag=RELENG_2_2_5_RELEASE
*default release=cvs
*default host=cvsup.internat.freebsd.org    the international security mirror
*default base=/usr                          for /usr/doc, /usr/ports, /usr/src
*default prefix=/src/ncvs
*default delete
*default use-rel-suffix
*default compress
cvs-crypto
```

CTM

If your Internet connection isn't good enough for *CVSup*, *CTM* might be for you. *CTM* distributes updates by mail. To get started, do the following:

- Send mail to `majordomo@FreeBSD.org` with an empty subject and a body containing the lines

  ```
  subscribe ctm-announce@FreeBSD.org
  subscribe ctm-src-cur@FreeBSD.org
  ```

  `ctm-src-cur` is the list on which *CTM* distributes the deltas for -CURRENT. There are a number of other mailing lists, but their purpose is not well documented.

- Make sure you have the programs *ctm* and *ctm_rmail*. They're part of the FreeBSD distribution, and should be in */usr/sbin*.

- Get a source tree. Unlike *CVSup*, this is *not* optional. You can get one in the form of a *base delta* from *ftp://ftp.FreeBSD.org/pub/FreeBSD/CTM*. In this directory you will find a number of choices: *cvs-cur*, *ports-cur* and *src-cur* are the -CURRENT directories, and *src-2.1*, *src-2.2* etc. are the release directories. In any of these you will find file names like:

  ```
  -r--r--r--  1 root  wheel  37754436 Aug  9 11:22 src-cur.0400xEmpty.gz
  -r--r--r--  1 root  wheel      8740 Aug 10 02:45 src-cur.0401.gz
  -r--r--r--  1 root  wheel     12552 Aug 11 02:46 src-cur.0402.gz
  -r--r--r--  1 root  wheel     13353 Aug 11 18:45 src-cur.0403.gz
  -r--r--r--  1 root  wheel      3538 Aug 12 10:39 src-cur.0404.gz
  -r--r--r--  1 root  wheel     10973 Aug 13 02:46 src-cur.0405.gz
  -r--r--r--  1 root  wheel      8556 Aug 13 18:40 src-cur.0406.gz
  ```

  As you can see from its size, the first of these files, *src-cur.0400xEmpty.gz*, is a *base delta*. The remaining files represent updates, called *deltas* in *CTM* terminology. Get the newest of the base deltas, since you need to apply all subsequent deltas to it.

- Decide on two directories:

1. A directory in which to store the deltas. Make sure you have plenty of space here. For the sake of example, call it */src/ctm/0400*. It's a good idea, but not essential, to keep multiple directories, each with 100 deltas. Every time the number increments by 100, create a new directory. For example, the next directory could be */src/ctm/0500*. This speeds up the operation of *ctm*.

2. A directory where you're going to maintain the tree. This is the same consideration as for *CVSup*: if you're maintaining a repository, it should have a name like */src/ncvs*. Otherwise it will be */usr/doc*, */usr/ports* or */usr/src*.

Now you're ready to go. To extract your deltas, do:

```
# cd /usr/src
# ctm -v -v /src/ctm/0400/*
Warning: .ctm_status not found.
Working on </src/ctm/0400/src-2.2.0400xEmpty.gz>
Expecting Global MD5 <557c6f7601490a32d89114361beebdca>
Reference Global MD5 <557c6f7601490a32d89114361beebdca>
> FM .ctm_status
> FM COPYRIGHT
> FM Makefile
> FM README
> DM bin
> FM bin/Makefile
> FM bin/Makefile.inc
> DM bin/cat
> FM bin/cat/Makefile
... etc
> FM usr.sbin/zic/zic.c
All done ok
Working on </src/ctm/0400/src-2.2.0401.gz>
Expecting Global MD5 <690bc0bbe90d846566f2af1dcd7cc25c>
Reference Global MD5 <690bc0bbe90d846566f2af1dcd7cc25c>
> FS .ctm_status
> FN usr.bin/tip/tip/cmds.c
... etc
> FN usr.sbin/sendmail/cf/cf/hub.mc
All done ok
Working on </src/ctm/0400/src-2.2.0402.gz>
Expecting Global MD5 <0941d8a04d828eef3ba3bbc0bd400d89>
Reference Global MD5 <0941d8a04d828eef3ba3bbc0bd400d89>
> FS .ctm_status
> FN sbin/shutdown/shutdown.c
... etc
> FN usr.sbin/lpr/lpd/lpd.c
All done ok
Exit(0)
```

The first time round, this will extract your base delta and then all other deltas you might have collected. *ctm* notes the last delta it extracts, so next time it will start with the next higher number. This is the reason why it's a good idea to keep separate directories for each 100 deltas, so that *ctm* doesn't have to examine all the deltas to find out which need to be applied.

Getting deltas by mail

When you receive deltas by mail, you will first need to convert them into the format used by *ctm*. *ctm_rmail* performs this job. First, save the messages into a folder, say *ctm*, then enter:

```
# cd /src/ctm/0400
# ctm_rmail -p ~/Mail/ctm -d .
```

This assumes you are using a standard mailer which keeps its folders in the subdirectory *Mail* of your home directory (*˜/Mail*).

ctm_rmail will extract the files no matter what sequence they are in—they will seldom be in the correct sequence. Often you will find that a large delta is split into multiple parts, and that only some of them have arrive at any particular occasion. This does not confuse *ctm_rmail* either: when they have all arrived, it will create a correct delta.

Getting deltas with *ftp*

As we saw above on page 371, you can also get deltas with *ftp*. You may need to do this, for example, if a mail message gets lost. Proceed as described above.

Creating the source tree

If you're tracking the repository, you're not finished yet. Once you have an up-to-date repository, the next step is to create a source tree. By default, the source tree is called */usr/src*, though it's very common for */usr/src* to be a symbolic link to a source tree on a different file system. You create the tree with *cvs*.

Before you check anything out with *cvs*, you need to know:

1. What do you want to check out? You specify this by the name of a directory (for example, *src/sys*), or with the keyword `world`. Note that there are three top-level directories: *doc*, *ports* and *src*.

2. Which version do you want to check out? By default, you get the latest version, which is FreeBSD-CURRENT. If you want a different version, you need to specify its *tag*.

3. Possibly, the date of the last update that you want to be included in the checkout. If you specify this date, *cvs* ignores any more recent updates. This option is often useful when somebody discovers a recently introduced bug in -CURRENT: you check out the modules as they were before the bug was introduced. You specify the date with the `-D` option, for example `-D "10 December 1997"`.

The tags

FreeBSD releases contain two, three or four numbers separated by periods. Each number represents a progressively smaller increment in the functionality of the release. The first number is the base release of FreeBSD. The number is incremented only when significant functionality is added to the system. For example, release 1 of FreeBSD was based on the Net/2 tapes from Berkeley, which were a heavily modified 4.3BSD. Release 2 bases on 4.4BSD. Release 3 includes significant new development, particularly in the areas of file system and memory management.

The second number represents a less significant, but still important difference in the functionality, and the third number represents a minor release. The fourth number is only used when a significant bug requires re-release of an otherwise unchanged release.

Tags for released versions of FreeBSD follow the release numbers. For release $x.y.z$ you would look for the tag RELENG_x_y_z_RELEASE. For example, to get the current state of the FreeBSD 2.2.5 source tree, you would look for the tag RELENG_2_2_5_RELEASE.

Some tags diverge from this scheme. In particular, CSRG and bsd_44_lite both refer to the original 4.4BSD sources from Berkeley. If you feel like it, you can extract this source tree as well.

To find out what tags are available, do:

```
# cd $CVSROOT/src
# cvs log Makefile | less

RCS file: /src/cvs/src/Makefile,v
Working file: Makefile
head: 1.155
branch:
locks: strict
access list:
symbolic names:
        RELENG_2_2_5_RELEASE: 1.109.2.19
        RELENG_2_2_2_RELEASE: 1.109.2.4
        RELENG_2_2_1_RELEASE: 1.109.2.2
        RELENG_2_2_0_RELEASE: 1.109.2.2
        RELENG_2_1_7_RELEASE: 1.57.4.19
        RELENG_2_1_6_1_RELEASE: 1.57.4.19
        RELENG_2_1_6_RELEASE: 1.57.4.19
        RELENG_2_2: 1.109.0.2
        RELENG_2_2_BP: 1.109
        RELENG_2_1_5_RELEASE: 1.57.4.17
        RELENG_2_1_0_RELEASE: 1.57.4.8
        RELENG_2_1_0: 1.57.0.4
        RELENG_2_1_0_BP: 1.57
        RELENG_2_0_5_RELEASE: 1.57
        RELENG_2_0_5: 1.57.0.2
        RELENG_2_0_5_BP: 1.57
        RELENG_2_0_5_ALPHA: 1.56
        RELEASE_2_0: 1.30
        BETA_2_0: 1.30
        ALPHA_2_0: 1.29.0.2
        bsd_44_lite: 1.1.1.1
        CSRG: 1.1.1
keyword substitution: kv
total revisions: 179;    selected revisions: 179
description:
```

cvs expects to find the name of its repository in the environment variable CVSROOT, and it won't work if you don't put it there. The repository contains three directories:

- *CVSROOT* contains files used by CVS. It is not part of the source tree.

- *ports* contains the Ports Collection

- *src* contains the system sources.

The directories *ports* and *src* correspond to the directories */usr/ports* and */usr/src* for a particular release. To extract the *src* tree of the most up-to-date version of FreeBSD-CURRENT, do the following:

```
# cd /usr
# cvs co src 2>&1 | tee /var/tmp/co.log
```

To check out any other version, say, everything for release 2.2.2, you would enter

```
# cd /usr
# cvs co -r RELENG_2_2_2_RELEASE world 2>&1 | tee /var/tmp/co.log
```

If you need to check out an older version, for example if there are problems with the most recent version of -CURRENT, you could enter:

```
# cvs co  -D "10 December 1997" src/sys
```

This command checks out the kernel sources as of 10 December 1997. During checkout, *cvs* creates a subdirectory *CVS* in each directory. *CVS* contains four files. We'll look at typical values when checking out the version of the directory */usr/src/usr.bin/du* for release 2.2.2, from the repository at */src/ncvs*:

- *Entries* contains a list of the files being maintained in the parent directory, along with their current versions. In our example, it would contain:

  ```
  /Makefile/1.1.1.1/Fri May 27 12:31:05 1994/TRELENG_2_2_2_RELEASE
  /du.1/1.6/Wed Oct 23 06:53:55 1996/TRELENG_2_2_2_RELEASE
  /du.c/1.6/Wed Oct 23 06:53:57 1996/TRELENG_2_2_2_RELEASE
  ```

  Note that *cvs* prepends a T to the version name.

- *Repository* contains the name of the directory in the repository which contains the repository for this directory. This corresponds to *$CVSROOT/directory*. In our example, it would contain /src/ncvs/src/usr.bin/du.

- *Root* contains the name of the root of the repository. In our example, it would contain /src/ncvs/src/usr.bin/du.

- *Tag* contains the *version tag* of the source tree. This is the RCS tag prefixed by a T. In this case, it is TRELENG_2_2_2_RELEASE.

cvs co produces a lot of output—at least one line for each directory, and one line for each file it checks out. Here's part of a typical output:

```
U src/usr.sbin/mrouted/rsrr_var.h
U src/usr.sbin/mrouted/vif.c
U src/usr.sbin/mrouted/vif.h
cvs checkout: Updating src/usr.sbin/mrouted/common
U src/usr.sbin/mrouted/common/Makefile
cvs checkout: Updating src/usr.sbin/mrouted/map-mbone
U src/usr.sbin/mrouted/map-mbone/Makefile
cvs checkout: Updating src/usr.sbin/mrouted/mrinfo
U src/usr.sbin/mrouted/mrinfo/Makefile
cvs checkout: Updating src/usr.sbin/mrouted/mrouted
U src/usr.sbin/mrouted/mrouted/Makefile
cvs checkout: Updating src/usr.sbin/mrouted/mtrace
U src/usr.sbin/mrouted/mtrace/Makefile
cvs checkout: Updating src/usr.sbin/mrouted/testrsrr
U src/usr.sbin/mrouted/testrsrr/Makefile
U src/usr.sbin/mrouted/testrsrr/testrsrr.c
```

The flag U at the beginning of the line stands *update*, but it can also mean that the file was checked out of the repository, as in this case. Other important flags are ?, which means that *cvs* found the file in the directory, but it doesn't know it, M, which means that the file in your working directory has been modified since checkout, so *cvs* doesn't change it, and C, which implies a *conflict*: *cvs* found that the file was modified and was unable to merge the changes.

> *After checkout, check the log file for conflicts. For each conflict, you must check the files manually and possibly recover the contents.*

See the man page *cvs(1)* for more details.

Updating an existing tree

Once you have checked out a tree, the ground rules change a little. Next time you do a checkout, files may also need to be deleted. Apart from that, there isn't much difference between checkout and updating. To update the */usr/src* directory after updating the repository, do:

```
# cd /usr/src
# cvs update -P -d
```

Note that this time we can start in */usr/src*: since we now have the *CVS/* subdirectories in place, *cvs* knows what to do without being given any more information.

Making a new world

The next step after making the source tree is to build all the software. This is relatively simple for you, but depending on the speed of the machine, it may keep the computer busy for up to a day:

```
# cd /usr/src
# make world
```

This operation performs a number functions, which can be influenced by variables you pass to *make*. Without any variables, *make world* performs the following steps:

- It removes the old build directories and creates new ones. You can skip this step by setting the NOCLEAN variable.

- It rebuilds and installs *make*, the C compiler and the libraries.

- It builds the rest of the system, with the exception of the kernel.

- It installs everything. You can omit this stage by building the *buildworld* target instead of *world*.

Table 19-2. Targets for top-level *Makefile*

Target	Purpose
buildworld	rebuild everything, including glue to help do upgrades.
installworld	install everything built by buildworld
world	perform buildworld and installworld
update	update your source tree
most	build user commands, no libraries or include files
installmost	install user commands, but not libraries or include files
reinstall	If you have a build server, you can NFS mount the source and object directories and do a make reinstall on the *client* to install new binaries from the most recent build on the server.

It does this by building a number of subtargets. Occasionally, you might find it useful to build them individually. Table 19-2 gives an overview of the more useful targets to the top-level *Makefile*, and table 19-3 gives an overview of the more common variables for make world and make buildworld. Note that make world doesn't rebuild the kernel. This doesn't mean that it's optional: you need to keep some programs, for example *ps*, in step with the kernel. make world builds *ps*, but it doesn't build the kernel.

The good news is: building the kernel for -CURRENT is just the same as it always is. See Chapter 18, *Configuring the kernel*, for more details. There is one possible problem that is specific to -CURRENT: if you try to build a kernel without first performing a make world, you might find that the kernel fails to link with lots of undefined references. One possible reason for this would be that the *config* program is out of synchronization with the kernel modules. Before you try anything else, rebuild *config*:

Table 19-3. Variables for *make world*

Variable	Function
ALLLANG	build documentation for all languages, where available. See *share/doc/Makefile* for more details.
CLOBBER	remove */usr/include*.
MAKE_EBONES	build eBones (KerberosIV)
NOCLEAN	Do not clean out the old build tree. This can save on build time, but may introduce subtle problems. You'll probably want to use this if your *make world* dies in mid-build.
NOCLEANDIR	run `make clean` instead of `make cleandir`
NOCRYPT	don't build crypt versions
NOGAMES	Don't rebuild the games.
NOINFO	don't make or install info files
NOLIBC_R	don't build *libc_r*.
NOLKM	don't build loadable kernel modules
NOOBJDIR	don't run `make obj`
NOPROFILE	Don't build the profiling libraries. If you're not doing any development involving profiling, this can save a considerable amount of time and space. If you don't know what profiling libraries are, you don't want them.
NOSECURE	Don't build the export-restricted modules. If you haven't downloaded the source for these, then you won't want to try to build them. This is a good option to use if you are not in the USA.
NOSHARE	Don't rebuild */usr/share*. This can save some time, and if */usr/share* (which contains manpages, data files and examples) hasn't changed much, it won't cause you any trouble.

```
# cd /usr/src/usr.sbin/config
# make depend all install clean
```

You need to *make clean* at the end since this method will store the object files in non-standard locations.

Putting it all together

There are a number of steps in updating a repository and building a new version of the operating system. Make just a small mistake, and things won't work. On the other hand, none of the steps are complicated. This is obviously a job for a computer.

The following script is designed to be run by *cron*. It first updates the repository with *CVSup*, then it updates the source tree with *cvs*, and finally it builds a new version of the system and the kernel. If you schedule this script to start late at night on a fast machine, it should all be done by the following morning.

```
echo ====== 'date': Getting CVSUP updates
cvsup -g -L2 /src/cvsup/cvs-cvsupfile            get the updates
cvsup -g -L2 /src/cvsup/secure-cvsupfile         security comes from a different site
echo ====== 'date': Updating /usr/src
echo cd /usr/src
cd /usr/src
cvs update -P -d                                 update the source tree
echo ====== 'date': Rebuilding TAGS
cd /usr/src/sys
rm -f TAGS                                        rebuild TAGS file for Emacs
find . -follow -name "*.[csh]" | xargs etags -a
echo ====== 'date': Rebuilding CURRENT
echo cd /usr/src
cd /usr/src
make world                                        rebuild everything
echo ====== 'date': Rebuilding FREEBIE kernel
cd /usr/src/sys/compile
mv FREEBIE/version .                              save the version number
cd /usr/src/sys/i386/conf
config -g FREEBIE                                 reconfigure the kernel with debugging
echo cd /usr/src/sys/compile/FREEBIE
cd /usr/src/sys/compile/FREEBIE
cp ../version .                                   restore the version number
make -k                                           and make everything we can
if [ $? -ne 0 ]; then                             failed, give up
   echo ====== 'date': '***' Build failed
   exit 1
fi
chflags noschg /kernel
mv /kernel /kernel.yesterday                      save the old kernel
rm -f kernel.gdb
if [ -f /var/crash/kernel.gdb ]; then
   mv /var/crash/kernel.gdb /var/crash/kernel.gdb.old   save any old /var/crash/kernel.gdb
fi
cp -p kernel kernel.gdb                           rename kernel to debug version
ln -s kernel.gdb /var/crash/kernel.gdb           and link to the current version
strip -d kernel                                   strip the kernel we're going to run
cp kernel /kernel                                 and move it to the root directory
echo ====== 'date': Build completed
if [ $? -eq 0 ]; then
   echo ====== 'date': FREEBIE kernel build completed
else
   echo '******' 'date': FREEBIE kernel build failed
fi
```

You can, of course, use *make install* to install the kernel, but it will install the full debug kernel in the root file system. Apart from the fact that it will fill up the file system—currently the debug kernel is about 10 MB in size, it will also fill up memory.

Living with FreeBSD-CURRENT

Keeping up with FreeBSD-CURRENT requires work on your part. You should be on the `FreeBSD-current` mailing list. To join, send mail to `majordomo@FreeBSD.org` with the single line text (not subject):

```
subscribe FreeBSD-current
```

If the mail ID that you want to add to the list is different from the ID you're sending from, put the ID at the end of the line. This will require manual intervention to confirm that the user really wants to be on the list, so it can take longer. It's always better to send the mail from the ID at which you want to receive the mail.

ps doesn't work any more!

One of the more common problems that people see after building a new -CURRENT kernel looks like this:

```
$ ps
ps: proc size mismatch (15800 total, 656 chunks)
```

This is a sure indication that your *ps* program or the *kvm* library no longer match your kernel. To solve this problem, do the following:

```
# cd /usr/src/lib/libkvm
# make all install clean
# cd /usr/src/bin/ps
# make all install clean
```

The reason for the target `clean` is that such a build will place the objects in the source directory, and not in the object directory. If you don't make `clean` now, a subsequent build will not replace them.

Build kernels with debug symbols

FreeBSD-CURRENT is not as stable as the released versions. To prepare yourself for possible problems, you should build kernels which include debug symbols. The resultant kernel is about 10 MB in size, but it will make debugging with *ddb* (the kernel debugger) or *gdb* much easier. Even if you don't intend to do this yourself, the information will be of great use to anybody you may call in to help.

We looked at how to build a debug kernel on page 361. If you're running -CURRENT, you might prefer to install the complete debug kernel. Do this with:

```
# make install.debug
```

instead of the usual target `install`.

Solving problems in FreeBSD-CURRENT

You *will* run into problems with FreeBSD-CURRENT. When it happens, please first read the mailing list and possibly the mail archives (see *http://www.FreeBSD.ORG/search.html* for a search engine) and see if the problem has been reported. If it hasn't, try to investigate the problem yourself. Then send mail to `FreeBSD-current` describing the problem and what you have done to solve it.

If you experience a panic, please don't just send a message to `FreeBSD-current` saying "My kernel panics when I type *foo*". Remember that you're asking somebody to use their spare time to look at the problem. Make it easy for them. Go through this procedure:

1. Update to the absolutely latest sources, unless emails have been warning against this.

2. Remove all loadable kernel modules (the contents of the directory */lkm/**).

3. If you have any local patches, back them out.

4. Recompile, from scratch, your kernel with *ddb* and with complete symbols (see above). If possible, don't strip your kernel before booting. An unstripped kernel will take up about 8 MB more memory than a stripped one, so this is not possible with very small memory systems.

   It's still important to build the debug kernel if you do have a small memory. You'll have to strip the version you boot, but you can still use the debug version with *gdb* to debug a panic dump.

5. Report all details from the panic. At an absolute minimum, give all information from `show reg` and `trace`.

6. Try to dump the system.

If you don't do at least this, there isn't much chance that a mail message to `FreeBSD-current` will have much effect.

Problems with CVS

Occasionally, you'll run into problems updating your source tree. Here are some possibilities:

Can't find directory

Occasionally *cvs* will crash during an update with a message like:

```
cvs update: Updating games/sail
U games/sail/externs.h
cvs update: Updating games/snake
cvs update: Updating games/snake/snake
U games/snake/snake/snake.c
cvs update: Updating games/snake/snscore
cvs update: Updating games/tetris
cvs [update aborted]: cannot open directory /src/cvs/src/games/tetris: No such file or
  directory
```

> This particular incident occurred after the owner of the name *Tetris* required FreeBSD to remove the game then called *tetris* from the sources.

The problem here is that the file */usr/src/games/CVS/Entries* still contained a reference to the directory, so *cvs* failed. One way to fix this problem is to manually edit the file *CVS/Entries*, but it's easier to remove the *CVS* directory and start again:

```
# cd /usr/src/games
# rm -rf CVS              remove the CVS information
# cd ..                   go to the parent directory
# cvs co games 2>&1 | tee /var/tmp/co.log   and check the games directory out again
```

20

Emulating other operating systems

A large number of operating systems run on Intel hardware, and there is a lot of software which is available for these other operating systems, but not for FreeBSD. As a result, FreeBSD can *emulate* many other systems to a point where applications written for these systems will run under FreeBSD. You'll find all the emulators in the Ports Collection in the directory */usr/ports/emulators*. This directory also contains a number of emulators for less well known systems.

In a number of cases, the emulation support is in an experimental stage. Here's an overview:

- FreeBSD will run most BSD/OS programs with no problems. The exceptions are mainly ELF binaries, which were introduced with BSD/OS 3.0, and some old BSD/386 1.x binaries, which will also no longer run under BSD/OS 2.x or 3.x: they contain calls to the function lockf(2), which was changed for 4.4BSD. Work is in progress on BSDI ELF support: check the errata if you need this feature.

- FreeBSD will also run most NetBSD and OpenBSD executables, though not many people do this: it's safer to recompile them under FreeBSD. As a result, there is a chance you'll run into a bug nobody knows about.

- FreeBSD can run *Linux* executables in both *a.out* and *ELF* object formats with the aid of the *linux kld* (*loadable kernel module*). We'll look at how to use it in the next section.

- FreeBSD can run SCO COFF executables with the aid of the *ibcs2 kld*. This support is a little patchy: although the executables will run, you may run into problems caused by differences in the directory structure between SCO and FreeBSD. We'll look at it on page 385.

- A *Microsoft Windows* emulator is available. We'll look at it on page 386.

- Two MS-DOS emulators are available. Consider them both experimental.

Emulating Linux

Linux is a UNIX-like operating system which in many ways is very similar to FreeBSD. It is not based on UNIX, however: it was written from scratch by Linus Torvalds, a Helsinki student. As a result, some of the interfaces are different from those of FreeBSD. The Linux compatibility package handles these differences, and most Linux software will run on FreeBSD. Most of the exceptions use specific drivers which don't run on FreeBSD, though there is a considerable effort to minimize even this category.

To install the Linux emulator, you must:

- Run the Linux emulator kld, *linux*.

- Install the compatibility libraries.

Running the Linux emulator

Running the emulator is straightforward: just type in its name, which, not surprisingly, is *linux*:

```
# linux
#
```

You don't interact directly with the emulator module: it's just there to supply kernel functionality, so you get a new prompt immediately when you start it.

If you use Linux emulation, it's a good idea to enable the *linux* kld in */etc/rc.conf*:

```
linux_enable="YES"   # Linux emulation loaded at startup (or NO).
```

This will cause it to be started every time you boot the system; it won't start it immediately.

Since *linux* is an kld, it won't show up in a *ps* listing. To check whether it is loaded, use *kldstat*:

```
$ kldstat
Id Refs Address    Size     Name
 1    5 0xc0100000 1d08b0   kernel
 2    2 0xc120d000 a000     ibcs2.ko
 3    1 0xc121b000 3000     ibcs2_coff.ko
 5    1 0xc1771000 e000     linux.ko
```

This listing shows that the SCO UNIX emulation (*ibcs2*) has also been loaded.

Installing the Linux libraries

In addition to the kld, Linux emulation requires compatibility libraries. You can find them on the installation CD-ROM as *packages/emulators/linux_lib-2.4.tgz*, or in the Ports Collection as */usr/src/ports/emulators/linux_lib*. To install from the installation CD-ROM, enter

```
# pkg_add /cdrom/packages/emulators/linux_lib-2.4.tgz
```

To build the latest version of the library, do

```
# cd /usr/src/ports/emulators/linux_lib
# FORCE_PKG_REGISTER=yes make all install
```

The FORCE_PKG_REGISTER=yes enables you to install the library even if an older version is currently installed.

The Linux emulator and programs are located in the directory hierarchy */usr/compat/linux/*. You won't normally need to access them directly, but if you get a Linux program which includes libraries destined for */lib*, you will need to manually place them in */usr/compat/linux/lib*. Be *very* careful not to replace any files in the */usr/lib/* hierarchy with Linux libraries; this would make it impossible to run programs which depend on them, and it's frequently very difficult to recover from such problems. Note that FreeBSD does not have a directory */lib*, so the danger is relatively minor.

Problems executing Linux binaries

One of the problems with the ELF format used by more recent Linux binaries is that they usually contain no information to identify them as Linux binaries. They might equally well be BSD/OS or UnixWare binaries. That's normally not a problem, unless there are library conflicts: the system can't decide which shared library to use. If you have this kind of binary, you must *brand* the executable using the program *brandelf*. For example, to brand the *StarOffice* program *swriter3*, you would enter:

```
# brandelf -t linux /usr/local/StarOffice-3.1/linux-x86/bin/swriter3
```

SCO UNIX emulation

SCO UNIX, also known as *SCO OpenDesktop* and *SCO Open Server*, is based on UNIX version System V.3.2. This particular version of UNIX was current about 7 years ago, and uses a binary format called *COFF* (*Common Object File Format*). COFF is now considered obsolescent, and SCO is moving to ELF.

Like Linux support, SCO support for FreeBSD is supplied as a loadable kernel module. It's not called *sco*, though, since a number of older System V.3.2 systems, including Interactive UNIX, also support the *ibcs2*[1] standard. As a result, the kld is called *ibcs2*.

Run ibcs2 support like Linux support: start it manually, or modify */etc/rc.conf* to start it automatically at bootup:

---

1. *ibcs2* stands for *Intel Binary Compatibility System 2*.

```
ibcs2_enable="YES"  # Ibcs2 (SCO) emulation loaded at startup (or NO).
```

One problem with SCO emulation are the SCO shared libraries. These are required to execute many SCO executables, and they're not supplied with the emulator. They *are* supplied with SCO's operating systems. Check the SCO license to determine whether you are allowed to use them on FreeBSD. You may also be eligible for a free SCO license—see *http://www.sco.com/offers/index.htm* for further details.

Emulating Microsoft Windows

The *wine* project has been working for some time to provide an emulation of Microsofts *Windows* range of execution environments. It's part of the Ports Collection.

21

Networks and the Internet

In this part of the book we'll look at the fastest-growing part of the industry: *Networks*, and in particular the latest network buzzword, the *Internet*.

The industry has seen many different kinds of network software:

- Years ago, the *CCITT* started a group of recommendations for individual protocols. The CCITT is now called the ITU-T, and its data communications recommendations have not been wildly successful. The best known is probably recommendation *X.25*, which still has a large following in some parts of the world. An X.25 package was available for FreeBSD, but it died for lack of love. If you need it, you'll need to invest a lot of work to get it running.

- IBM introduced their *Systems Network Architecture*, *SNA*, decades ago. It's still going strong in IBM shops. FreeBSD has minimal support for it in the Token Ring package being developed in FreeBSD-CURRENT.

- Early UNIX machines had a primitive kind of networking called *UUCP*, for *UNIX to UNIX Copy*. It ran over dialup phone lines or dedicated serial connections. System V still calls this system *Basic Networking Utilities*, or *BNU*. Despite its primitiveness, and despite the Internet, there are still some applications where UUCP makes sense. We'll look at it in Chapter 26, *UUCP and SLIP*.

- The *Internet Protocols* were developed by the US *Defense Advanced Research Projects Agency* (*DARPA*) for its *ARPANET* network. The software was originally developed in 1982 at the University of California at Berkeley and integrated into their 4.2BSD operating system—the granddaddy of FreeBSD. After the introduction of IP, the ARPANET gradually changed its name to *Internet*.

  The Internet Protocol is usually abbreviated to *IP*. People often refer to it as *TCP/IP*, which stands for *Transmission Control Protocol/Internet Protocol*. In fact, TCP is just one of many other protocols which run on top of IP. In this book, I will refer to the IP protocol, but of course FreeBSD includes TCP and all the other standard protocols. The IP implementation supplied with FreeBSD is the most mature technology you can find anywhere, at any price.

In this part of the book, we'll look only at the Internet Protocols. Thanks to its background,

FreeBSD is a particularly powerful contender in this area, and we'll go into a lot of detail about how to set up and operate networks and network services. In the chapters following, we'll look at:

- How to set up the system as a network client, which we'll look at in the next section.

- How to set up local network connections in Chapter 22, *Configuring the local network*.

- How to select an Internet Service Provider in Chapter 23, *Connecting to the Internet*.

- How to use the hardware in Chapter 24, *Serial communications and modems*.

- How to use PPP in Chapter 25, *Configuring PPP*.

- How to use SLIP and UUCP in Chapter 26, *UUCP and SLIP*.

- How to set up domain name services in Chapter 27, *The Domain Name Service*.

- How to protect yourself from crackers in Chapter 28, *Firewalls and IP aliasing*.

- How to solve network problems in Chapter 29, *Network debugging*.

- How to set up NFS in Chapter 30, *The Network File System*.

- How to use the basic Internet services in Chapter 31, *Basic network access*.

- How to set up electronic mail in Chapter 32, *Electronic Mail*.

- How to use the Web, including setting up Web servers, in Chapter 33, *The World-Wide Web*.

- How to send faxes in Chapter 34, *HylaFAX*.

- How to Interface with Microsoft based networking products in Chapter 35, *Connecting to non-IP networks*.

In the rest of this chapter, we'll look at the theoretical background of the Internet Protocols and Ethernet.

You can set up networking without understanding any of it, as long as you and your hardware don't make any mistakes. This is the approach most commercial systems take. It's rather like crossing a lake on a set of stepping stones, blindfolded. In this book, I take a different approach: in the following discussion, you'll be inside with the action, not on the outside looking in through a window. It might seem unusual at first, but once you get used to it, you'll find it much less frustrating.

Network layering

One of the problems with networks is that they can be looked at from a number of different levels. End-users of PCs access the *World-Wide Web* (*WWW*), and often enough they call it the *Internet*, which is just plain wrong. At the other end of the scale is the *Link Layer*, the viewpoint you'll take when you first create a connection to another machine.

Years ago, the International Standards Organization came up with the idea of a seven-layered model of networks, often called the *OSI reference model*. Why *OSI* and not *ISO*? *OSI* stands for *Open Systems Interconnect*. Since its introduction, it has become clear that it doesn't map very well to modern networks. W. Richard Stevens presents a better layering in *TCP/IP Illustrated*, Volume 1, page 6, shown here in Figure 21-1.

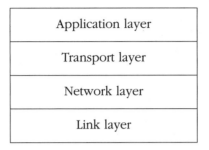

Application layer
Transport layer
Network layer
Link layer

Figure 21-1: Four-layer network model

We'll look at these layers from the bottom up:

* The *Link layer* is responsible for the lowest level of communication, between machines which are physically connected. The most common kinds of connection are *Ethernet* and telephone lines. This is the only layer associated with hardware.

* The *Network layer* is responsible for communication between machines which are not physically connected. In order for this to function, the data must pass through other machines which are not directly interested in the data. This function is called *routing*. We'll look at how it works in Chapter 22, *Configuring the local network*.

* The *Transport Layer* is responsible for communication between any two processes, regardless of the machines on which they run.

* The *Application Layer* defines the format used by specific applications, such as email or the Web.

The link layer

The *link layer* is responsible for getting packets between two systems which are connected to each other. The most trivial case is a point-to-point network, a physical connection where any data sent down the line will arrive at the other end. More generally, though, multiple systems are connected to the network, as in an Ethernet. This causes a problem: how does each system know what is intended for it?

IP solves this problem by including a *packet header* in each IP packet. Consider the header something like the information you write on the outside of a letter envelope: address to send to, return address, delivery instructions. In the case of IP, the addresses are 32-bit digits which are conventionally represented in *dotted decimal* notation: the value of each byte is converted into decimal. The four values are written separated by dots. Thus the hexadecimal address

`0xdf932501` would normally be represented as `223.147.37.1`.

> UNIX uses the notation `0x` in a number to represent a hexadecimal number. The usage comes from the C
> programming language.

As we will see in Chapter 29, *Network debugging*, it makes debugging much easier if we understand the structure of the datagrams, so I'll show some of the more common ones in this chapter. Figure 21-2 shows the structure of an IP header.

0					31

	Version	IP Header length	Type of service	Total length in bytes	
0	Version	IP Header length	Type of service	Total length in bytes	
4	identification			flags	fragment offset
8	Time to live		Protocol	Header Checksum	
12	Source IP address				
16	Destination IP address				

Figure 21-2: IP Header

We'll only look at some of these fields; for the rest, see *TCP/IP Illustrated*, Volume 1.

- The *Version* field specifies the current version of IP. This is currently 4. A newer standard is *IPv6*, version number 6, which is currently in an early implementation stage. IPv6 headers are very different from those shown here.

- The *time to live* field specifies how many hops the packet may survive. Each time it is passed to another system, this value is decremented. If it reaches 0, the packet is discarded. This prevents packets from circulating in the net for ever as the result of a routing loop.

- The *protocol* specifies the kind of the packet. The most common protocols are TCP and UDP, which we'll look at in the section on the network layer.

- Finally come the *source address*, the address of the sender, and the *destination address*, the address of the recipient.

The network layer

The main purpose of the network layer is to ensure that packets get delivered to the correct recipient when it is not directly connected to the sender. This function is usually called *routing*.

Imagine routing to be similar to a postal system: if you want to send a letter to somebody you don't see often, you put the letter in a letter box. The people or machines who handle the letter look at the address and either deliver it personally or forward it to somebody else who is closer to the recipient, until finally somebody delivers it.

Have you ever received a letter which has been posted months ago? Did you wonder where they hid it all that time? Chances are it's been sent round in circles a couple of times. That's what can happen in the Internet if the routing information is incorrect, and that's why all packets have a *time to live* field. If it can't deliver a packet, the Internet Protocol simply drops (forgets about) it. You may find parallels to physical mail here, too.

It's not usually acceptable to lose data. We'll see how we avoid doing so in the next section.

The transport layer

The *transport layer* is responsible for end-to-end communication. The IP address just identifies the interface to which the data is sent. What happens when it gets there? There could be a large number of processes using the link. The IP header doesn't contain sufficient information to deliver messages to specific users within a system, so two additional protocols have been implemented to handle the details of communications between "end users".[1] These end users connect to the network via *ports*, or communication end points, within individual machines.

TCP

The *Transmission Control Protocol*, or *TCP*, is a so-called *reliable protocol*: it ensures that data gets to its destination, and if it doesn't, it sends another copy. If it can't get through after a large number of tries (14 tries and nearly 10 minutes), it gives up, but it doesn't pretend the data got through. In order to perform this service, TCP is also *connection oriented*: before you can send data with TCP, you must establish a connection, which is conceptually similar to opening a file.

In order to implement this protocol, TCP packets include a *TCP header* after the IP header, as shown in figure 21-3. This figure ignores the possible options which follow the IP header. The offset of the TCP header, shown here as 20, is really specified by the value of the IP Header length field in the first byte of the packet. Since this is only a 4 bit field, it is counted in words of 32 bits: for a 20 byte header, it will have the value 5. A number of fields are of interest when debugging network connections:

- The *sequence number* is the byte offset of the last byte that has been sent to the other side.

- The *acknowledgement number* is the byte offset of the last byte that has received from the other side.

- The *window size* is the number of bytes that can be sent before an acknowledgement is required.

These three values are used to ensure efficient and reliable transmission of data. For each connection, TCP maintains a copy of the highest acknowledgement number received from the other side and a copy of all data which the other side has not acknowledged receiving. It will not send more than *window size* bytes of data beyond this value. If it does not receive an acknowledgement of transmitted data within a predetermined time, usually one second, it will send all the unacknowledged data again and again at increasingly large intervals. If it can't

---

1. In practice, these end users are processes.

0   31

	Version	IP Header length	Type of service		Total length in bytes	
0	Version	IP Header length	Type of service		Total length in bytes	
4	identification			flags	fragment offset	
8	Time to live		Protocol		Header Checksum	
12	Source IP address					
16	Destination IP address					
20	source port			destination port		
24	sequence number					
28	acknowledgement number					
32	TCP Header length	reserved	flags		window size	
36	TCP checksum			urgent pointer		

Figure 21-3: TCP Header with IP header

transmit the data after about ten minutes, it will give up and close the connection.

UDP

The *User Datagram Protocol*, or *UDP*, is different: it's an *unreliable protocol*. It sends data out and never cares whether it gets to its destination or not. So why do we use it if it's unreliable? It's faster, and thus cheaper. Consider it a junk mail delivery agent: who cares if you get this week's AOL junk CD-ROM or not? There will be another one in next week's mail. Since it doesn't need to reply, UDP is connectionless: you can just send a message off with UDP without worrying about establishing a connection first. For example, the *rwhod* dæmon broadcasts summary information about a system on the LAN every few minutes. In the unlikely event that a message gets lost, it's not serious: another one will come soon.

Port assignment and Internet services

A *port* is simply a 16 bit number which is assigned to specific processes and which represents the source and destination end points of a specific connection. A process can either request to be connected to a specific port, or the system will assign him one which is not in use.

RFC 1700 defines a number of *well-known ports* which are used to request specific services from a machine. On a UNIX machine, these are provided by dæmons which *listen* on this port

0   31

	Version	IP Header length	Type of service	Total length in bytes	
0	Version	IP Header length	Type of service	Total length in bytes	
4	identification			flags	fragment offset
8	Time to live		Protocol	Header Checksum	
12	Source IP address				
16	Destination IP address				
20	source port			destination port	
24	sequence number			checksum	

Figure 21-4: UDP Header with IP header

number—in other words, when a message comes in on this port number, the IP software will pass it to them, and they process it. These ports are defined in the file */etc/services*. Here's an excerpt:

```
# Network services, Internet style
#
# WELL KNOWN PORT NUMBERS
#
ftp             21/tcp          #File Transfer [Control]
telnet          23/tcp
smtp            25/tcp          mail            #Simple Mail Transfer
smtp            25/udp          mail            #Simple Mail Transfer
domain          53/tcp          #Domain Name Server
domain          53/udp          #Domain Name Server
```

This file has a relatively simple format: the first column is a service name, and the second column contains the port number and the name of the service (either `tcp` or `udp`). Optionally, alternative names for the service may follow. In this example, `smtp` may also be called `mail`.

When the system starts up, specific dæmons may be started. For example, if you're running mail, you may start up *sendmail* as a dæmon. Any mail requests coming in on port 25 (`smtp`) will then be routed to *sendmail* for processing.

The Internet dæmon

If you look at */etc/services*, you'll find that there are over 800 services available, most of which are only supported on a small number of machines. Nevertheless, it's not always the best idea to start up a dæmon for every possible service you may want to offer. IP supplies an alternative: *inetd*, the *Internet dæmon*, sometimes called a *superserver*, will listen on multiple ports. When a request arrives on a specific port, *inetd* will start a dæmon specific to the port.

For example, FreeBSD supports anonymous ftp, but most people don't receive enough requests to warrant having the FTP dæmon, *ftpd*, running all the time. Instead, *inetd* will start an *ftpd* when a request comes in on port 21.

At startup, *inetd* reads a configuration file */etc/inetd.conf* to determine which ports to monitor and what to do when a message comes in. Here's an excerpt:

```
#
# Internet server configuration database
#
#     @(#)inetd.conf  5.4 (Berkeley) 6/30/90
#
ftp   stream     tcp  nowait    root /usr/libexec/ftpd      ftpd -l
telnet     stream    tcp  nowait    root /usr/libexec/telnetd telnetd
shellstream    tcp  nowait    root /usr/libexec/rshd     rshd
loginstream    tcp  nowait    root /usr/libexec/rlogind rlogind
#execstream    tcp  nowait    root /usr/libexec/rexecd  rexecd
#uucpd      stream    tcp  nowait    root /usr/libexec/uucpd    uucpd
nntp stream     tcp  nowait    usenet    /usr/local/bin/nntpd nntpd
```

This file has the following format:

- The first column is the service on which *inetd* should listen. If it starts with a # sign, *inetd* ignores it. You'll note in this example that the services exec and uucpd have been commented out. Unless you run the dæmon independently of *inetd*, a request for one of these services will be rejected with the message

  ```
  Unable to connect to remote host: Connection refused
  ```

- The next three columns determine the nature of the connection, the protocol to use, and whether *inetd* should wait for the process to complete before listening for new connections.

- The next column specifies the user as which the function should be performed. Be careful here: for example, the service nntp is intended to be run as user usenet, but there is no user usenet on this system. The nntp service supports *NNTP*, the *Network News Transfer Protocol*.

- The next column is the full pathname of the program (almost always a dæmon) to start when a message comes in. Alternatively, it might be the keyword internal, which specifies that *inetd* should perform the function itself.

- All remaining columns are the parameters to be passed to the dæmon.

Kinds of network connection

The most obvious thing about your network connection is what it looks like. It will usually involve some kind of cable going out of your computer,[1] but there the similarity ends. FreeBSD supports most modern network interfaces:

---

1. Maybe it won't. For example, you might use wireless Ethernet, which broadcasts in the microwave radio spectrum.

- The most popular choice for *Local Area Networks* is *Ethernet*, which transfers data between a number of computers at speeds of 10 Mb/s, 100 Mb/s or 1000 Mb/s (1 Gb/s). We'll look at it in the following section.

- *FDDI* stands for *Fiber Distributed Data Interface*, and was originally run over glass fibres. In contrast to Ethernet, it ran at 100 Mb/s instead of 10 Mb/s. Nowadays Ethernet runs at 100 Mb/s as well, and FDDI runs over copper wire, so the biggest difference is the protocol. FreeBSD does support FDDI, but we won't look at it here.

- *Token Ring* is yet another variety of LAN, introduced by IBM. It has never been very popular in the UNIX world, and FreeBSD 3.2 doesn't support it. There is some support in FreeBSD-CURRENT, but it's still under development.

- Probably the most common connection to a *Wide-Area Network* is via a telephone with a modem. Modems have the advantage that you can also use them for non-IP connections such as UUCP (see Chapter 26, *UUCP and SLIP*) and direct dialin (see page 437). If you use them to connect to the Internet, you'll probably use either the *Serial Line Internet Protocol*, *SLIP*, which we discuss on page 468, or the *Point to Point Protocol*, *PPP*, which we look at on page 439. If you have the choice, you should use PPP, which is a more modern and flexible protocol.

- In some areas, *Integrated Services Digital Networks* (*ISDN*) are an attractive alternative to modems. They are much faster than modems, both in call setup time and in data transmission capability, and they are also much more reliable. FreeBSD includes the *ISDN4BSD* package, which was developed in Germany and allows the direct connection of low-cost German ISDN boards to FreeBSD.

- If you have a large Internet requirement, you may find it suitable to connect to the Internet via a *Leased Line*, a telephone line which is permanently connected. This is a relatively expensive option, of course, and we won't discuss it here, particularly as the options vary greatly from country to country and from region to region.

The decision on which WAN connection you use depends primarily on the system you are connecting to, in many cases an *Internet Service Provider* or *ISP*. We'll look at ISPs in Chapter 23, *Connecting to the Internet*. Most ISPs support IP connections via PPP or SLIP, and an increasing number are supporting ISDN. Other things being equal, you should prefer ISDN to PPP and PPP to SLIP.

> Many ISPs which supply ISDN require you to use PPP over the ISDN line. There is nothing in the standard which requires you to do so, however, and it degrades performance somewhat. Still, PPP over ISDN is preferable to PPP over an analogue telephone line.

Ethernet

In the early 1970s, the Xerox Company chartered a group of researchers at its Palo Alto Research Center (*PARC*) to brainstorm the *Office of the Future*. This innovative group created the mouse, the window interface metaphor and an integrated, object oriented programming environment called *Smalltalk*. In addition, a young MIT engineer in the group named Bob

Metcalfe came up with the concept which is the basis of modern local area networking, the *Ethernet*. The Ethernet protocol is a low-level broadcast packet-delivery system which employed the revolutionary idea that it was easier to re-send packets which didn't arrive than it was to make sure all packets arrived. There are other network hardware systems out there, IBM's Token Ring architecture and Fiber Channel, for example, but by far the most popular is the Ethernet system in its various hardware incarnations. Ethernet is by far the most common local area network medium. There are three types:

1. Originally, Ethernet ran at 10 Mb/s over thick coaxial cable, usually bright yellow in colour. This kind of Ethernet is often referred to as *thick Ethernet*, also called *10B5*, and the line interface is called *AUI*. You may also hear the term *yellow string* (for tying computers together), though this term is not limited to thick Ethernet. Thick Ethernet is now practically obsolete: it is expensive, difficult to lay, and relatively unreliable.

2. As the name suggests, *thin Ethernet* is thin coaxial cable, and otherwise quite like thick Ethernet. It is significantly cheaper (thus the term *Cheapernet*), and the only disadvantage over thick Ethernet is that the cables can't be quite as long. The cable is called *RG58*, and the cable connectors are called *BNC*. Both terms are frequently used to refer to this kind of connection, as is *10 Base 2*.

3. Modern Ethernets tend to run over telephone cable, though it is usually called *10BaseT* or *UTP*, for *Unshielded Twisted Pair*. *Twisted pair* means that each pair of wires are twisted to minimize external electrical influence—after all, the frequencies on a 100 Mb/s Ethernet are way up in the UHF range. In fact, telephone cable is not twisted, and 10 Mb/s Ethernets run just fine on it. 100Mb/s Ethernet requires the twisted cable due to the higher rate. Unlike coaxial connections, where all machines are connected to a single cable, UTP connects individual machines to a *hub*, a box which distributes the signals.

Compared to coaxial Ethernet, UTP cables are much cheaper, and they are more reliable. If you damage or disconnect a coaxial cable, the whole network goes down. If you damage a UTP cable, you only lose the one machine connected to it. On the down side, UTP requires hubs, which cost money, though the price is rapidly decreasing. UTP systems employ a star architecture rather than the string of coaxial stations with terminators. You can connect many hubs together simply by reversing the connections at one end of a hub-to-hub link. In addition, UTP is the only cost-effective medium currently available that will support the new 100Base-T protocol. Upgrading to 100 Megabit Ethernet is as simple as replacing the hubs and the Ethernet boards.

How Ethernet works

A large number of systems can be connected to a single Ethernet. Each system has a 48 bit address, the so-called *Ethernet Address*. Ethernet addresses are usually written in bytes separated by colons (:), for example 0:a0:24:37:0d:2b. All data sent over the Ethernet contains two addresses: the Ethernet address of the sender and the Ethernet address of the receiver. Normally, each system responds only to messages sent to it or to a special broadcast address.

You'll also frequently hear the term *MAC address*. *MAC* stands for *Media (sic) Access Control* and thus means the address used to access the network. For Ethernets I prefer to use the more exact term *Ethernet address*.

The fact that multiple machines are on the same network gives rise to a problem: obviously only one system can transmit at any one time, or the data will be garbled. But how do you synchronize the systems? The answer is simple, but possibly surprising: trial and error. Before any system transmits, it checks that the net is idle—in the Ethernet specification, this is called *Carrier Sense*. Unfortunately, this isn't enough: two systems might start sending at the same time. To solve this problem, while it sends, each system checks that it can still recognize what it is sending. If it can't, it assumes that another system has started sending at the same time— this is called a *collision*. When a collision occurs, both systems stop sending, wait a random amount of time, and try again. You'll see this method referred to as *CSMA/CD* (*Carrier Sense Multiple Access/Collision Detect*).

Transmitting Internet data across an Ethernet has another problem. Ethernet evolved independently of the Internet standards. As a result, Ethernets can carry different kinds of traffic. In particular, Microsoft uses a protocol called *NetBIOS*, and Novell uses a protocol called *IPX*. In addition, Internet addresses are only 32 bits, and it would be impossible to map them to Ethernet addresses even if they were the same length. The result? You guessed it, another header. Figure 21-5 shows an Ethernet packet carrying an IP datagram.

Finding Ethernet addresses

So we send messages to Ethernet interfaces by setting the correct Ethernet address in the header. But how do we find the Ethernet address? All our IP packets use IP addresses. And it's not a good solution to just statically assign Ethernet addresses to IP addresses: first, there would be problems if an interface board or an IP address was changed, and secondly multiple boards can have the same IP address.

The chosen solution is the *Address Resolution Protocol*, usually called *ARP*. ARP sends out a message on the Ethernet broadcast address saying effectively "who has IP address `223.147.37.1`? Tell me your Ethernet address". Since the message is sent on the broadcast address, each system on the net will receive it. In each machine, the ARP protocol will check the specified IP address with the IP address of the interface which received the packet. If they match, the machine replies with the message "I am IP `223.147.37.1`, my Ethernet address is `00:a0:24:37:0d:2b`"

Ethernet terminators

Coaxial Ethernet requires 50 Ω resistors at each end of the cable in order to transmit signals correctly. If you leave these out, you won't get degraded performance: the network Will Not Work at all.

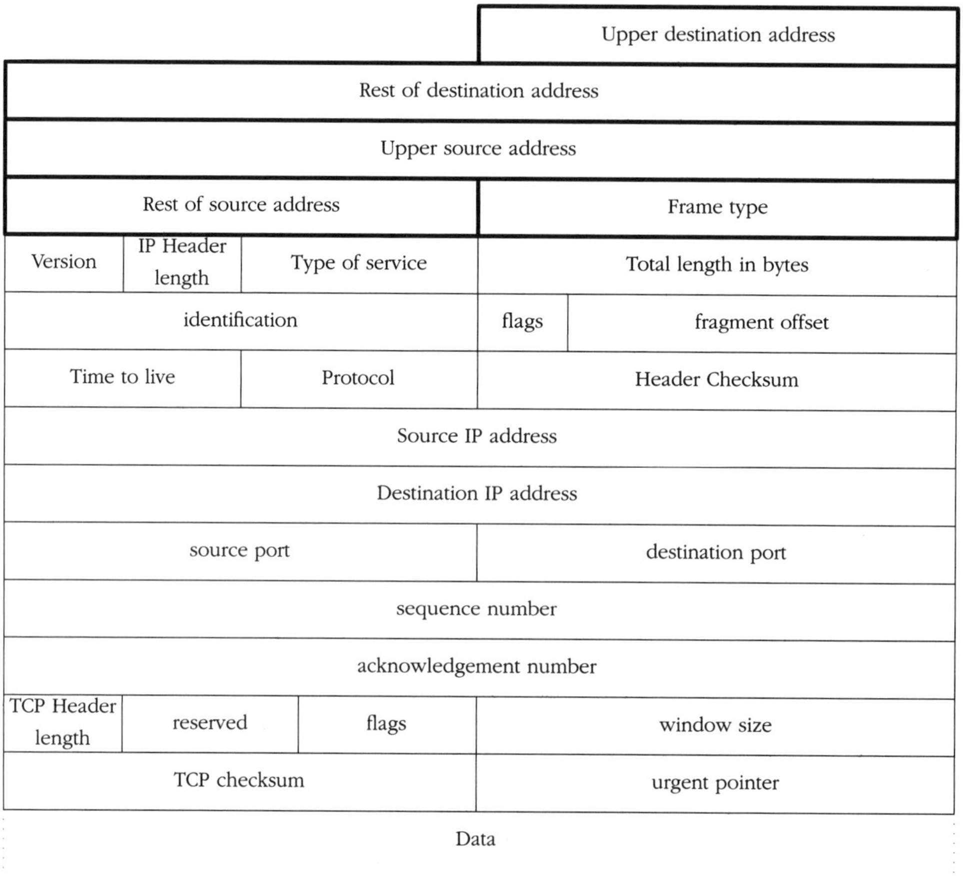

			Upper destination address	
Rest of destination address				
Upper source address				
Rest of source address			Frame type	
Version	IP Header length	Type of service	Total length in bytes	
identification			flags	fragment offset
Time to live		Protocol	Header Checksum	
Source IP address				
Destination IP address				
source port			destination port	
sequence number				
acknowledgement number				
TCP Header length	reserved	flags	window size	
TCP checksum			urgent pointer	
Data				

Figure 21-5: Ethernet frame with TCP datagram

What systems are on that Ethernet?

Since multiple systems can be accessed via an Ethernet, there must be some means for a system to determine which other systems are present on the network. There might be a lot of them, several hundred for example. You could keep a list, but the system has to determine the interface for every single packet, and a list that long would slow things down. The preferred method is to specify a *range* of IP addresses which can be reached via a specific interface. Since the computer works in binary, one of the easiest functions to perform is a *logical and*. As a result, you specify the range by a *netmask*: the system considers all addresses in which a specific set of bits have a particular value to be reachable via the interface. The specific set of bits is called the *interface address*.

For example, let's look forward to the reference network on page 400 and consider the local network, which has the network address 223.147.37.0 and the netmask 255.255.255.0.

The value 255 means that every bit in the byte is set. The logical *and* function says "if a specific bit is set in both operands, then set the result bit to 1; otherwise set it to 0". Figure 21-5 shows how the system creates a network address from the IP address 223.147.37.5 and the net mask 255.255.255.0.

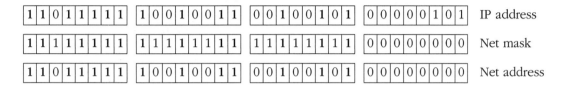

The result is the same as the IP address for the first three bytes, but the last byte is 0: 223.147.37.0.

This may seem unnecessarily complicated. An easier way to look at it is to say that the *1* bits of the net mask describe which part of the address is the network part, and the *0* bits describe which part represents hosts on the network.

Address classes

When the Internet Protocols were first introduced, they included the concept of a default netmask. These categories of address were called *address classes*. They've been updated recently—see RFC 1375 for details. Here's an overview:

Table 21-6. Address classes

Class	Address range	Net mask	Network address bits	Host address bits	Number of systems
A	0-127	255.0.0.0	8	24	16777216
B	128-191	255.255.0.0	16	16	65536
C	192-207	255.255.255.0	24	8	256
F	208-215	255.255.255.240	28	4	16
G	216-219	*(reserved)*			
H	220-221	255.255.255.248	29	3	8
K	222-223	255.255.255.254	31	1	2
D	224-239	*(multicast)*			
E	240-255	*(reserved)*			

This method is no longer used for specifying net masks, though the software will still default to these values, but it is used for allocating networks. In addition you will frequently hear the term *Class C network* to refer to a network with 256 addresses in the range 192-223. This usage goes back to before RFC 1375.

The reference network

One of the problems in talking about networks is that there are so many different kinds of network connection. To simplify things, this book bases on one of the most frequent environments: a number of computers connected together by an Ethernet LAN with a single gateway to the Internet. Figure 21-7 shows the layout of the network to which we will refer in the rest of this book.

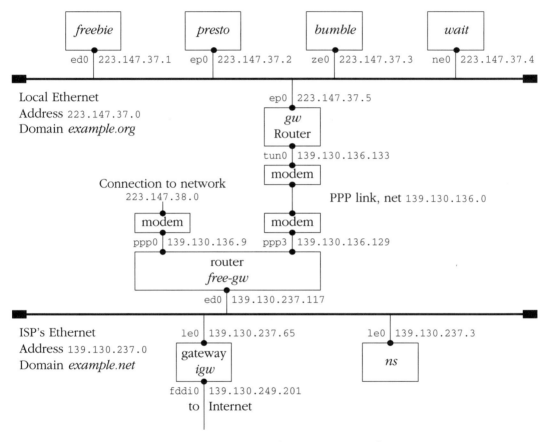

Figure 21-7: Reference network

This figure contains a lot of information, which we will examine in detail in the course of the text:

- The boxes in the top row represent the systems in the local network `example.org`: *freebie*, *presto*, *bumble*, and *wait*.

- The line underneath is the local Ethernet. The address is 223.147.37.0. It has a full 256 addresses ("Class C"), so the network mask is 255.255.255.0.

- The machines on this Ethernet belong to the domain *example.org*. Thus, the full name of *bumble* is *bumble.example.org.*—we'll look at these names in Chapter 27, *The Domain Name Service*.

- The connections from the systems to the Ethernet are identified by two values: on the left is the *interface name*, and on the right the address associated with the interface name.

- Further down the diagram is the router, gw. It has two interfaces: ep0 interfaces to the Ethernet, and tun0 interfaces to the PPP line to the ISP. Each interface has a different addresses.

- The lower half of the diagram shows part of the ISP's network. He, too, has an Ethernet, and his router looks very much like our own. On the other hand, he interfaces to a third network via the machine *igw*. To judge by the name of the interface, it is a *FDDI* connection—see page 395 for more details.

- The ISP runs a name server on the machine ns, address 139.130.237.3.

- The ends of the Ethernets are thickened. This represents the *terminators* required at the end of a coaxial Ethernet. We talked about them on page 397.

22

Configuring the local network

In Chapter 21, we looked at the basic concepts surrounding BSD networking. In this chapter and the following two, we'll look at what we need to do to configure a network, first manually, then automatically. Configuring serial line communications such as *PPP* and *SLIP* is still a whole lot more difficult than configuring an Ethernet, and they require more prerequisites, so we'll dedicate Chapter 25, *Configuring PPP*, and Chapter 26, *UUCP and SLIP*, to them.

In this chapter, we'll first look at *example.org* in the reference network on page 400, since it's the easiest to set up. After that, we'll look at what additional information is needed to configure machines on *example.net*.

Network configuration with *sysinstall*

To configure a network, you must describe its configuration to the system. Normally *sysinstall* will do this for you.

The system initialization routines that we discussed on page 189 include a significant portion which sets up the network environment. In addition, the system contains a number of standard IP configuration files which define your system's view of the network. On page 84 we saw how to set up the network with *sysinstall*. If you didn't configure the network when you installed your system, you can still do it now. Perform the following steps:

- Log in as `root` and start */stand/sysinstall*.

- Select the `Index`, then `Networking Services`, then `Interfaces` (press **Space** to select `Interfaces`). You will see the same menu as in figure 5-9 on page 84.

- Continue as described on page 84. *sysinstall* will present you with the question

```
Running multi-user, assume that the network is already configured?
```

Select No, and you will be given the menu shown on page 85. Proceed as described there.

sysinstall configures the system by making entries in a number of files in the directory */etc*. When the system starts, the startup scripts use this information to configure the network. You can also issue these commands during normal system operation in order to modify the configuration. We'll look at them next.

Manual network configuration

Usually FreeBSD will configure your network automatically when it boots. To do so, it uses the configuration files in */etc*. So why do it manually? There are several reasons:

- It makes it easier to create and maintain the configuration files if you know what's going on behind the scenes.

- It makes it easier to modify something "on the fly".

- With this information, you can edit the configuration files directly rather than use the menu interface, which saves a lot of time.

> We spend a lot of time discussing this point on the FreeBSD-chat mailing list. One thing's for sure: neither method of configuration is perfect. Both menu-based and text-file-based configuration schemes offer you ample opportunity to shoot yourself in the foot. But at the moment, the configuration file system is easier to check *if you understand what's going on*. That's the reason for the rest of this chapter.

In this section, we'll look at the manual way to do things first, and then we'll see how to put it in the configuration files so that it gets done automatically next time. You can find a summary of the configuration files and their contents on page 202.

Setting the host name

Many functions require the system to have a name. You should have set it when you installed the system (see page 81), but if not, or if you entered an incorrect name, you can set it like this:

```
# hostname -s gw.example.org
```

Describing your network

In Table 21-7, on page 400, we saw that systems connect to networks via *network interfaces*. The kernel detects the interfaces automatically when it starts, but you still need to tell it what interfaces are connected to which networks, and even more importantly, which address your system has on each network. In addition, if the network is a *broadcast* network, such as an Ethernet, you need to specify a range of addresses which can be reached directly on that network. As we saw on page 398, we perform this selection with the *network mask*.

Ethernet interfaces

Once we have understood these concepts, it's relatively simple to use the *ifconfig* program to set them. For example, for the Ethernet interface on system *gw*, with IP address 223.147.37.5, we need to configure interface ep0. The network mask is the standard value for a class C network, 255.255.255.0. That's all we need to know:

```
# ifconfig ep0 inet 223.147.37.5 netmask 255.255.255.0 up
```

In fact, this is more than you usually need. The inet tells the interface to use Internet protocols (the default), and up tells it to bring it up (which it does anyway). In addition, this is a class C network address, so the net mask defaults to 255.255.255.0. As a result, you can abbreviate this to:

```
# ifconfig ep0 223.147.37.5
```

Point-to-point interfaces

With a point-to-point interface, the software currently requires you to specify the IP address of the other end of the link as well. As we shall see in Chapter 25, *Configuring PPP*, there is no good reason to do this, but if you omit it, *ifconfig* won't work. In addition, we need the network mask for a non-broadcast medium. The value is obvious:[1] you can reach exactly one address at the other end, so it must be 255.255.255.255. With this information, we could configure the PPP interface on gw:

```
# ifconfig tun0 139.130.136.133 139.130.136.129 netmask 255.255.255.255
```

In fact, even this is frequently not necessary; in Chapter 25, *Configuring PPP* we'll see that the PPP software will usually set the configuration automatically.

The loopback interface

The IP protocols require you to use an address to communicate with every system—even your own system. There's a standard address for your own system, 127.0.0.1. Theoretically, you could associate this address with, say, an Ethernet interface, but this is relatively slow: the data would have to go out on the network and come back in again. Instead, there is a special interface for communicating with other processes in the same system, the *loopback interface*. By convention, its name is *lo0*. It's straightforward enough to configure:

```
# ifconfig lo0 127.0.0.1
```

Checking the interface configuration

ifconfig doesn't just set the configuration: you can also use it to check the configuration by passing it the -a flag.

> The -a flag lists the configuration of all interfaces. Some other UNIX systems, particularly System V, don't understand this flag.

---

1. Well, you'd think it was obvious. We'll see on page 445 that some people think it should be something else.

It's a good idea to do this after you change the configuration:

```
$ ifconfig -a
lp0: flags=8810<POINTOPOINT,SIMPLEX,MULTICAST> mtu 1500
ep0: flags=8843<UP,BROADCAST,RUNNING,SIMPLEX,MULTICAST> mtu 1500
        inet 223.147.37.5 netmask 0xffffff00 broadcast 223.147.37.255
        ether 00:a0:24:37:0d:2b
sl0: flags=c010<POINTOPOINT,LINK2,MULTICAST> mtu 552
tun0: flags=8051<UP,POINTOPOINT,RUNNING,MULTICAST> mtu 1500
        inet 139.130.136.133 --> 139.130.136.129 netmask 0xffffffff
ppp0: flags=8010<POINTOPOINT,MULTICAST> mtu 1500
ppp1: flags=8010<POINTOPOINT,MULTICAST> mtu 1500
lo0: flags=8049<UP,LOOPBACK,RUNNING,MULTICAST> mtu 16384
        inet 127.0.0.1 netmask 0xff000000
```

You'll notice a whole lot more interfaces here: *lp0*, the *PLIP* interface, *sl0*, the *SLIP* interface, and two *ppp* interfaces for kernel PPP. They're not running, but they're present.

The configuration files

The system startup scripts summarize this configuration information in a number of *configuration variables*:

- hostname is the name of the host, which we set above using the *hostname* command.

- network_interfaces is a list of the names of the interfaces which are to be configured.

- For each interface, a variable of the form ifconfig_*interface* contains the parameters to be passed to *ifconfig*.

For *gw*, we put the following information in */etc/rc.conf*:

```
hostname="gw.example.org"
network_interfaces="ep0 tun0 lo0"    # List of network interfaces (lo0 is loopback).
ifconfig_ep0="inet 223.147.37.5  netmask 255.255.255.0"
ifconfig_tun0="inet 139.130.136.133  139.130.136.129  netmask  255.255.255.255"
ifconfig_lo0="inet 127.0.0.1"        # default loopback device configuration.
```

What we can do now

At this point, we have configured the link layer. We can communicate with all directly connected machines. In order to communicate with machines that are not directly connected, we need to set up *routing*. We'll look at that next.

Routing

Looking back at our example network on page 400, we'll reconsider a problem we met there: when a system receives a normal data packet,[1] what does it do with it? There are four possibilities:

---

1. This discussion doesn't apply to *broadcast packets*, which are not routed. Instead, they are sent out on every broadcast interface. It also doesn't apply to *multicast* packets, which we don't consider in this book.

1. If it's addressed to itself, it delivers it locally.

2. If it's addressed to a system to which it has a direct connection, it sends it to that system.

3. If it's not addressed to a system to which it is directly connected, but it knows a system which knows what to do with the packet, it sends the packet to that system.

4. If none of the above apply, it discards the packet.

Table 22-1. The routing table

Destination	Gateway	Net mask	Type	Interface
127.0.0.1	127.0.0.1	255.0.0.0	Host	lo0
223.147.37.0		255.255.255.0	Direct	ep0
139.130.136.129	139.130.136.133	255.255.255.255	Host	tun0
default	139.130.136.129	0.0.0.0	Gateway	tun0

These decisions are the basis of *routing*. The implementation performs them with the aid of a *routing table*, which tells the system which addresses are available where. We've already seen the *net mask* in Chapter 21, *Networks and the Internet*, on page 398. We'll see that it also plays a significant rôle in the routing decision. Table 22-1 shows a symbolic view of the routing table for *gw.example.org*. It looks very similar to the *ifconfig -a* output in the previous section:

- The first entry is the *loopback* entry: it shows that the local host can be reached by the interface lo0, which is the name for the loopback interface on all UNIX systems. You'll notice that, although this entry specifies a single host, the net mask allows for 16,276,778 hosts. The other addresses aren't used.

- The second entry is for the local Ethernet. In this case, we have a direct connection, so we don't need to specify a gateway address. Due to the net mask 255.255.255.0, this entry accounts for all addresses from 223.147.37.0 to 223.147.37.255.

  This entry also emphasizes the difference between the output of *ifconfig* and the routing table. *ifconfig* shows the address of the interface, the address needed to reach our system. For the Ethernet interface, it's 223.147.37.5. The routing table shows the addresses that can be reached *from* this system, so it shows the base address of the Ethernet, 223.147.37.0.

- The third entry represents the PPP interface. It is a host entry, like the loopback entry. This entry allows access to the other end of the PPP link only, so the net mask is set to 255.255.255.255 (only one system).

- Finally, the fourth entry is the big difference. It doesn't have a counterpart in the *ifconfig -a* listing. It specifies how to reach any address not already accounted for—just about the whole Internet. In this case, it refers to the other end address of the PPP link.

And that's all there is to it! Well, sort of. First, we need to see how this works in practice. The Internet is a large network. In our example configuration, we're hidden in one corner, and there's only one way to the network. Things look different when you are connected to more than one network. On page 409 we'll look at the differences we need for the ISP *example.net*. In the middle of the Internet, things are even more extreme. There may be ten different interfaces, and the choice of a route for a particular address may be much more complicated. In such an environment, two problems occur:

- The concept of a default route no longer has much significance. If each interface carries roughly equal traffic, you really need to specify the interface for each network or group of networks. As a result, the routing tables can become enormous.

- There are probably multiple ways to route packets destined for a specific system. Obviously, you should choose the best route. But what happens if it fails or becomes congested? Then it's not the best route any more. This kind of change happens frequently enough that humans can't keep up with it—you need to run *routing software* to manage the routing table.

Adding routes automatically

FreeBSD comes with all the currently available routing software, primarily the dæmons *routed* and *gated*. *routed* is in the base system, and the newer *gated* is in the Ports Collection.

Both dæmons have one thing in common: you don't need them. At any rate, you don't need them until you have at least two different connections to the Internet, and even then it's not sure. As a result, we won't discuss them here. If you do need to run routing dæmons, read all about them in *TCP/IP Network Administration*, by Craig Hunt.

From our point of view, however, the routing protocols have one particular significance: the system expects the routing table to be updated automatically. As a result, it is designed to use the information supplied by the routing protocols to perform the update. This information consists of two parts:

- The address and netmask of the network (in other words, the address range).

- The address of the *gateway* which forwards data for this address range. The gateway is a directly connected system, so it will also figure in the routing table.

Adding routes manually

As we saw in the previous section, the routing software uses only addresses, and not the interface name. In order to add routes manually, we have to give the same information.

The program which adds routes manually is called *route*. We need it to add routes to systems other than those to which we are directly connected.

To set up the routing tables for the systems connected only to our reference network (*freebie*, *presto*, *bumble* and *wait*), we could write:

```
# route add default gw
```

During system startup, the script */etc/rc.network* performs this operation automatically if you set the following variables in */etc/rc.conf*:

```
defaultrouter="223.147.37.5"        # Set to default gateway (or NO).
static_routes=""              # Set to static route list (or leave empty).
```

Note that we enter the address of the default router as an IP address, not a name. This command is executed before the name server is running. We can't change the sequence in which we start the processes: depending on where our name server is, we may need to have the route in place in order to access the name server.

On system gw, the default route goes via the tun0 interface:

```
defaultrouter="139.130.136.133" # Set to default gateway (or NO).
static_routes=""              # Set to static route list (or leave empty).
gateway_enable="YES"          # Set to YES if this host will be a gateway.
```

This is the case for a connection with a static IP address on the PPP interface. If you're forced to use dynamic IP addresses, you don't know the address at this point. We'll see how to address this problem in Chapter 25, *Configuring PPP*, page 446.

We need to enable gateway functionality on this system, since it receives data packets on behalf of other systems. We'll look at this issue in more depth on page 411.

ISP's route setup

At the ISP site, things are slightly more complicated than at *example.org*. The gateway machine *free-gw.example.net* knows the interface to *example.org* and another network, *biguser.com* (the network serviced by interface *ppp0*), but it doesn't know what networks are behind them yet. At some point, you need to issue the commands:

```
# route add -net 223.147.37.0 139.130.136.129
# route add -net 223.147.38.0 139.130.136.9
```

The first line tells the system that the network with the base IP address 223.147.37.0 (*example.org*) can be reached via the interface *ppp3*, and the second line tells it that the network with the base IP address 223.147.38.0 (*biguser.com*) can be reached via the interface *ppp0*.

The procedure to add this information to */etc/rc.conf* is similar to what we did for the interface addresses:

- The variable static_routes contains a list of the static routes which are. to be configured.

- For each route, a variable corresponding to the route name specified in `static_routes`. Unlike the interfaces, you can assign any name you want to them, as long as it starts with `route_`. It makes sense for them to be related to the domain name, but they don't have to. For example, we would have liked to have called our network *freebie.org*, but there's a good chance that this name has been taken, so we called it *example.org* instead. The old name lives on in the name of the route, `route_freebie`. In the case of *biguser.com*, we have called the route variable `route_biguser`.

We put the following entries into */etc/rc.conf*:

```
defaultrouter="139.130.237.117"      # Set to default gateway (or NO).
static_routes="route_freebie route_biguser"    # list of static routes
route_freebie="-net 223.147.37.0 139.130.237.129"
route_biguser="-net 223.147.38.0 139.130.237.9"
```

Looking at the routing tables

You can show the routing tables with the *netstat* tool. Option `-r` shows the routing tables. For example, on `freebie` you might see:

```
# netstat -r
Routing tables

Internet:
Destination      Gateway          Flags     Refs      Use      Netif Expire
default          gw               UGSc        9     8732        ed0
localhost        localhost        UH          0     1255        lo0
223.147.37       link#2           UC          0        0
presto           0:0:c0:44:a5:68  UHLW       13   139702        ed0   1151
freebie          0:a0:24:37:d:2b  UHLW        3    38698        lo0
wait             0:60:97:40:fb:e1 UHLW        6     1062        ed0    645
bumble           8:0:20:e:2c:98   UHLW        2       47        ed0   1195
gw               0:60:97:40:fb:e1 UHLW        6     1062        ed0    645
broadcast        ff:ff:ff:ff:ff:ff UHLWb      2     5788        ed0
```

There's a lot to notice about this information

- The first column is the name of a host or a network to which packets can be sent, or the keyword `default`.

- The second column, the *gateway*, indicates the path to the destination. This field differs significantly even from older versions of UNIX. It can be the name of a host (for example, `gw`), a pointer to an interface (`link#2`, which means the second Internet interface; the output from *ifconfig -a* is in the same sequence), or an Ethernet address (`8:0:20:e:2c:98`). Older versions of UNIX do not use the last two forms.

- We'll look at the flags below. The most important ones to note are `G` (gateway) and `H` (host).

- The fields `Refs`, `Use` and `Expire` are only of interest when you're running a routing protocol. See the man page *netstat(1)* for more details.

- Netif is the name of the interface by which the gateway can be reached. In the case of a link, this is the interface, so the Netif field is empty.

- The order of the entries is not important. The system searches the table for a best fit, not a first fit.

- The default entry points to gw, as we would expect. The interface, ed0, is the interface by which gw can be reached.

Table 22-2. netstat -r flags values

Flag	Name	Meaning
1	RTF_PROTO1	Protocol specific routing flag 1
2	RTF_PROTO2	Protocol specific routing flag 2
3	RTF_PROTO3	Protocol specific routing flag 3
B	RTF_BLACKHOLE	Just discard pkts (during updates)
b	RTF_BROADCAST	The route represents a broadcast address
C	RTF_CLONING	Generate new routes on use
c	RTF_PRCLONING	Protocol-specified generate new routes on use
D	RTF_DYNAMIC	Created dynamically (by redirect)
G	RTF_GATEWAY	Destination requires forwarding by intermediary
H	RTF_HOST	Host entry (net otherwise)
L	RTF_LLINFO	Valid protocol to link address translation
M	RTF_MODIFIED	Modified dynamically (by redirect)
R	RTF_REJECT	Host or net unreachable
S	RTF_STATIC	Manually added
U	RTF_UP	Route usable
W	RTF_WASCLONED	Route was generated as a result of cloning
X	RTF_XRESOLVE	External dæmon translates proto to link address

Flags

Compared to earlier versions of *netstat*, the current version displays many more flags. Table 22-2 gives you an overview.

Packet forwarding

We saw above that when a system receives a packet which is not intended for itself, it will look for a route to the destination. In fact, this is not always the case: by default, FreeBSD just silently drops the packet. This is desirable for security reasons, and indeed it's required by RFC 1122, but if you want to access the Internet via another machine on your local net, it's less than convenient.

The rationale for this is that most systems are only connected to one network, and it doesn't make sense to have packet forwarding enabled. Earlier systems made this a kernel option, so that disabling packet forwarding also made the kernel fractionally smaller. In current versions of FreeBSD, the code is always there, even if it is disabled.

It's straightforward enough to set up your machine as a router (or *gateway*): you can set it with the *sysctl* command:

```
# sysctl -w net.inet.ip.forwarding=1
net.inet.ip.forwarding: 0 -> 1
```

In */etc/rc.conf*, you can set this with the variable `gateway_enable`:

```
gateway_enable="YES"        # Set to YES if this host will be a gateway.
```

Configuration summary

In summary, we need to perform the following steps to configure the networks. We'll use the configuration for *free-gw.example.net* as an example, since it's the most complicated.

- Set your host name:

  ```
  hostname="free-gw.example.net"
  ```

- Decide which interfaces to configure. These are the interfaces *ed0*, *ppp0*, *ppp3* and *lo0*. Enter a line in */etc/rc.conf* listing them:

  ```
  network_interfaces="lo0 ed0 ppp0 ppp3"    # List of network interfaces
  ```

- For each interface, specify IP addresses and possibly net masks for each interface on the machine:

  ```
  ifconfig_ed0="inet 139.130.237.117  netmask 255.255.255.0"
  ifconfig_ppp0="inet 139.130.136.9   139.130.136.134  netmask  255.255.255.255"
  ifconfig_ppp3="inet 139.130.136.129  139.130.136.133  netmask  255.255.255.255"
  ifconfig_lo0="inet 127.0.0.1"               # default loopback device config
  ```

- Decide on a default route. In this case, it will be via the Ethernet interface *ed0*, with the address `139.130.237.117`:

  ```
  defaultrouter="139.130.237.117"      # Set to default gateway (or NO).
  ```

- Decide on other routes. In this case, we have two, to *example.org* and *biguser.com*. List them in the variable `static_routes`:

  ```
  static_routes="route_freebie route_biguser"    # Set to static route list
  ```

- For each static route, create a variable describing the route:

  ```
  route_freebie="-net 223.147.37.0 139.130.136.129"
  route_biguser="-net 223.147.38.0 139.130.136.9"
  ```

- Enable IP forwarding:

```
gateway_enable="YES"                  # Set to YES if this host will be a gateway.
```

Even more briefly, the data are:

```
hostname="gw.example.org"
ifconfig_ed0="inet 139.130.237.117  netmask 255.255.255.0"
ifconfig_ppp0="inet 139.130.136.9  139.130.136.134  netmask  255.255.255.255"
ifconfig_ppp3="inet 139.130.136.129  139.130.136.133  netmask  255.255.255.255"
ifconfig_lo0="inet 127.0.0.1"            # default loopback device configuration.

defaultrouter="139.130.237.117"      # Set to default gateway (or NO).
static_routes="route_freebie route_biguser"    # Set to static route list
route_freebie="-net 223.147.37.0 139.130.136.129"
route_biguser="-net 223.147.38.0 139.130.136.9"
gateway_enable="YES"                  # Set to YES if this host will be a gateway.
```

23

Connecting to the Internet

In order to implement the reference network shown in the previous chapter, we need to do a lot of things which interface with the outside world. They can take some time, so we should look at them first:

- What kind of physical connection should we use? We'll consider that in the next section.

- We may want to *register a domain*. Many people don't, but I strongly recommend it. Find out about that on page 418.

- We may also want to *register a network*. In our example, we have used the network `223.147.37.0`. In real life, we can't choose our own network: we take what is given to us. We'll look at this on page 420.

- We need to find an *Internet Service Provider*. We'll look at what that entails on page 420.

The physical connection

Just two or three years ago, the way to connect to the outside world was simple: a phone line. Since then, things have changed quite a bit, and you may have quite a choice:

- Analogue telephone line connections are still the most cost-effective for small networks in most countries, but their bandwidth is limited to about 7 kB/s at best. You can run SLIP or PPP over this kind of line, though nowadays most ISPs support only PPP.

- *ISDN* stands for *Integrated Systems Digital Network*. It's the new, better, washes whiter telephone system which is replacing POTS (*Plain Old Telephone Service*) in some countries, notably in Europe. We'll look at ISDN in more detail in the next section.

- *Leased lines* form the backbone of the Internet. They're invariably more expensive than dialup lines, but they can provide quite high speeds—in the USA, a *T1* line will give you 1,536 kbps, and in the rest of the world an *E1* will give you 2,048 kbps. We won't look at this kind of line in more detail in this book.

- *Cable modems* use existing cable TV networks to deliver a high speed connection, up to several megabits per second. They use the cable as a broadcast medium, rather like an Ethernet, and suffer from the same load problems: you share the speed with the other users of the cable. There are also some security issues to consider, but if you have a cable service in your area, you'll probably find it superior to telephones. The cable modem is effectively a bridge between the cable and an Ethernet. From the FreeBSD point of view, the cable modem looks like just another Ethernet device.

- *ADSL* (*Asynchronous Digital Subscriber Loop*) and *HDSL* (*High-speed Digital Subscriber Loop*) are the telephone companies' reaction to cable modems. By modifying the way they transmit data over normal phone wires, including the use of special modems, ADSL can get speeds of up to 6 Mb/s downstream (towards the end user), and about 640 kbps upstream. HDSL has similar speeds, but the speed is the same in each direction. In contrast to cable modems, you don't have to share this bandwidth with anybody.

- In some parts of the world, *satellite connections* are a viable alternative. These usually use a telephone line for outgoing data and a satellite receiver for incoming data. The information I have seen so far suggests that they are not very flexible, and others have complained that they are overly expensive.

ISDN

ISDN stands for *Integrated Services Digital Network*, which is a fancy way of saying "digital telephone": it's a new kind of telephone connection based on digital principles. It uses the same old two-wire line you need for a normal analogue phone, but instead it carries digital data. The normal interconnection is called the *Basic Rate Interface* or *BRI*. Deutsche Telekom, the German telephone company, and one of the world leaders in ISDN deployment, calls it S_0 instead.

A Basic Rate ISDN Interface carries three data channels multiplexed on a single pair of wires:

- The *D channel* runs at 16 kbps and is responsible for *signalling*, which is what telephone people call operations like dialling ("call setup") and transmitting charge information. They also carry other information like the phone number of the calling party and the time of day.

- The other two channels are *B channels*, which run at 64 kbps (that's 64,000 bits/second, not 65,536). They are used for telephone conversations or data transmission.

In other words, a Basic Rate Interface is effectively two phone lines, and this is the way most people see it.

Primary Rate Interfaces carry a whole lot more channels on one line. The number is different in the USA and elsewhere. They always carry one D channel, this time at 64 kbps, and in the USA, they carry 23 B channels, which corresponds to the US standard T1 rate of 1536 kbps. In the rest of the world, they have 30 B channels. In each case, the B channels still run at 64 kbps. Deutsche Telekom has found a new name for this interface, too: S_2M or *Primärmultiplexanschluß* (try saying that fast several times in a row).

A Basic Rate Interface is enough for most people. If you need Primary Rate, you'll also have to find equipment which runs on it. The problem here is that most PC hardware is designed to run under Microsoft products, which are not particularly suited to high-speed communications.

ISDN connections have a number of advantages over conventional phone lines:

- They're more reliable. There's no such thing as a noisy line.

- They're faster. Modern analogue modems peak at 56 kbps (the higher speeds base on compression, which doesn't directly relate to the phone line), whereas ISDN runs at 64,000 bps per B channel. These figures are misleading: ISDN always runs at 64 kbps, whereas the analogue modems run a maximum of 56 kbps downstream, and only 33.6 kbps upstream.

- If that's not fast enough, you can often *bundle* ISDN B channels: you transmit the data over multiple B channels at once. This requires that you have a datacomm protocol which can accept datagrams from multiple sources, such as IP.

- Call setup time is very fast, typically in the order of two seconds. This makes it practical to disconnect the ISDN line if the line is idle for a period of time in order to save on costs while you're connected to a remote site: the system can reconnect so fast that you hardly notice the difference.

- It's marginally more secure. Part of the information supplied during call setup is the calling line number, so you can arrange to only accept phone calls from people you know. It's possible to fake the telephone number information, but as this requires configuration access to a PABX or similar telco equipment, it doesn't happen often.

- You don't need a dedicated phone line for the ISDN connection: part of the information supplied with an incoming call request specifies what kind of call it is (data, voice or fax). If it's a data call, your phone won't ring. If it's a voice call, your ISDN datacomm software will ignore it, or, if you wish, log it. This is quite a neat feature: the system log can carry a complete history of who called you and when.

- With a Basic Rate Interface, you can have two calls on the same number, since each gets its own B channel. With appropriate hardware, you can also have multiple numbers attached to a single phone.

These advantages seem to make ISDN an ideal way to connect to the Internet. You can effectively be connected all the time, but you just need to establish a connection when you need to transmit data. This requires your ISP to be prepared to call you when there is data to be transmitted, of course.

To get best results from ISDN, you should use specific software, which can give you speeds of up to 64 kbps (8 kB/s) per line. You can also use *Terminal Adapters*, which perform the same function as modems, and run PPP across them.

The decision for or against ISDN is primarily one of pricing. In Europe, it can cost the same amount as an analogue line; in other countries, it can cost a multiple of the price.

Establishing yourself on the Internet

The first thing you need to decide is the extent of your presence on the net. There are various possibilities:

- You could get a dial-in service where you use your computer just to connect to the ISP, and perform network functions such as reading mail and news on his machine. Since it's a lot faster to perform these functions on your own machine, and you have all the software you need to do so, this isn't very desirable.

- You could perform all the functions on your machine, but using names and addresses assigned to you by the ISP.

- You could perform all the functions on your machine, using addresses assigned to you by the ISP, but you would use your own domain name.

- You get your own address space and use your own domain name.

Does it matter? That's for you to decide. It's certainly a very good idea to have your own domain name. As time goes on, your Email address will become more and more important. If you get a mail address like 4711@flybynight.net, and Flybynight goes broke, or you decide to change to a different ISP, your mail address is gone, and you have to explain that to everybody who might want to contact you. If, on the other hand, your name is Jerry Dunham, and you register a domain dunham.org, you can assign yourself any mail address in that domain that you want to.

But how do you go about it? One way would be to go to your ISP and pay him good money to do it for you. You don't need to do that: it's easy enough to do yourself on the World-Wide Web. You must be connected to the Internet to perform these steps. This implies that you should first connect using your ISP's domain name, then establish your domain name, and change to that domain.

Which domain name?

We'll continue to assume that your name is Jerry Dunham. If you live in, say, Austin, Texas, you have a number of domain names you can choose from: dunham.org, for a non-commercial domain, dunham.com for a commercial domain (this name is, in fact, taken), dunham.net for an ISP (but *not* for his customers!), or even dunham.tx.us if you want to use the geographical domain.

If you live in, say, Capetown, people will probably suggest that you get the domain dunham.za, the geographical domain for South Africa. The problem with that is that you are limiting yourself to that country. If you move to, say, Holland, you would have to change to dunham.nl—a situation which is only fractionally better than being bound to an ISP. The same considerations apply to dunham.tx.us, of course.

Your choice of domain name also affects the way you apply. In the following sections, I assume you take my advice and apply for an organizational rather than a geographical domain.

Preparing for registration

Once upon a time, registration was handled by InterNIC, a professional body. In recent times, it has been delegated to commercial companies, and the quality of service has suffered correspondingly: they don't even appear to know the technical terms. For example, you may find them referring to a domain name as "Web Address". Things are still changing at the time of writing, and additional companies are being allowed to register domain names, so maybe they'll learn to express themselves correctly.

The registration forms ask for information about three kinds of people associated with the records you ask for: the Administrative Contact, Technical Contact, and Billing Contact. These can all be the same person. You can enter the information every time you make a request, but it makes things easier if you have a *NIC handle*, a code by which you can be identified. To apply for a NIC handle, fill in the forms at *http://www.networksolutions.com/cgi-bin/itts/handle/*. This address doesn't appear to be accessible via the home page, and it conveniently calls itself a "Contact Form", hiding the reference to the word "handle" in the fine print. The fields should be self-explanatory, with the exception of the `Country` field, where you should enter the two-letter abbreviation for your country. For example, for the USA, the code is `us`. For Australia, it's `au`. *http://www.ics.uci.edu/pub/websoft/wwwstat/country-codes.txt* gives a list of country codes.

Registering a domain name

The only prerequisites for registering a domain name are:

* The name must be available, though there are some legal implications which suggest that, though you might be able to register a domain such as *microsoft.edu*, it might not be good for you if you do. In fact, *microsoft.edu* is a domain name belonging to the BISPL business school in Hyderabad, India, presumably beyond US jurisdiction.

* You must be able to specify two name servers for it—see Chapter 27, *The Domain Name Service* for further details about name servers.

First, check that the name is available:

```
$ whois dunham.org
No match for "DUNHAM.ORG".

The InterNIC Registration Services Host contains ONLY Internet Information
(Networks, ASN's, Domains, and POC's).
Please use the whois server at nic.ddn.mil for MILNET Information.
$
```

Next, start a web browser and look up the URL *http://www.networksolutions.com/purchase/*. There's no guarantee that this URL may not change, but you should always be able to get it via *http://www.networksolutions.com/*. You must first select a domain name, which for some inexplicable reason Network Solutions call a Web Address. Don't be put off by their apparent ignorance, nor the `www.` to the left of the window: this really is a domain registration, not a Web Address (whatever that may be), and the www appears to be intended to make it clear to you what you're looking at. If the domain is available, you will get another form congratulating you on being so clever. You don't need to enter anything here. Just stop laughing and press the `Continue` button. The next form gives you the choice of reserving or registering the name. When you select `Register` you are finally presented with a form in which you should enter useful data (and they finally admit it's for Domain Name Registration, not "get a Web Address"). The first thing it asks you for is your name and Email address. You must enter these correctly, since you will receive mail from InterNIC at this address. Press *Proceed*, and you will receive another, much longer form. Most of the fields should be obvious, but some may not be. If you have any trouble filling it out, there's a Help button at the top of the form.

When you have filled out the form, you will receive a mail message from `hostmaster@internic.net` with a copy of the form. You should check it for correctness and then reply; after this, it will take a day or two for the domain name to be activated.

Getting IP addresses

Once upon a time it was possible to get IP addresses from InterNIC, but this practice is now restricted to large blocks of at least 16 class C networks, and is intended for ISPs. Instead, get the addresses from your ISP. Routing considerations make it impractical to move IP addresses from one place to another, so if you move a long distance you should expect to change your IP addresses.

Choosing an Internet Service Provider

In most cases, you will get your connection to the Internet from an *Internet Service Provider*, or *ISP*. As the name suggests, an ISP will supply the means for you to connect your system or your local network to the Internet. They will probably also supply other services: ISPs can't live on Internet connections alone.

In this chapter we'll look at the things you need to know about ISPs, and how to get the best deal. We'll concentrate on the most common setup, PPP over a dialup line with a V.34bis modem (56 kbps), which will give you a peak data transfer rate of about 7 kB/s.

Who's that ISP?

As the Internet, and in particular the number of dial-in connections, explodes, a large number of people have had the idea to become involved. Many ISPs are small companies run by very technical people who have seen a market opportunity and have grabbed it. Other ISPs are small companies run by not-so technical people who have jumped on the bandwagon. Still other ISPs are run by large companies, in particular the cable TV companies and the telephone companies. Which is for you? How can you tell to which category an ISP belongs? Do you care?

You *should* care, of course. Let's consider what you want from an ISP, and what he wants from his business. You want a low-cost, high-reliability, high speed connection to the Internet. You may also want technical advice and value-added services such as DNS (see Chapter 27, *The*

Domain Name Service) and web pages.

The main priority of a small ISP (or any other ISP, for that matter) is to get a good night's sleep. Next, he wants to ensure the minimum number of nuisance customers. After that, he wants to ensure that he doesn't go out of business. Only *then* is he interested in the same things that you are.

Questions to ask an ISP

So how do you choose an ISP? Don't forget the value of word-of-mouth—it's the most common way to find an ISP. If you know somebody very technical, preferably a FreeBSD user, who is already connected, ask him—he'll certainly be able to tell you about his ISP. Otherwise, a lot depends on your level of technical understanding. It's easy to know more about the technical aspects of the Internet than your ISP, but it doesn't often help getting good service. Here are a few questions you should ask any prospective ISP:

☐   What kind of connections do you provide?

> See the discussion on page 415.

☐   How do you charge? By volume, by connect time, or flat rate?

> Once most ISPs charged by connect time: you pay whether you transfer data or not. This makes it unattractive to an ISP to provide good service, since that means you can finish your session more quickly. Nowadays, flat rates are becoming more popular: you pay the same no matter how much you use the service. The disadvantage of the flat rate is that there is no incentive to disconnect, so you might find it difficult to establish connections.

> When comparing connect time and volume rates, expect an average data transfer rate of about 600 bytes per second for most connections via a 56 kbps modem. You'll get up to 7 kB per second with traffic-intensive operations like file downloading, but normally, you'll be doing other things as well, and your data rate over the session is more likely to be 600 bytes per second if you're reasonably active, and significantly less if not.

☐   Do you have a cheaper charge for data from your own network?

> Many ISPs maintain ftp archives and network news. If they charge by volume, some will give you free access to their own net. Don't overestimate the value of this free data.

☐   What speed are your modems?

> They should be the fastest, of course, which are currently 56 kbps. Even if you currently have a slower modem, you may want to upgrade. If the ISP currently doesn't have the fastest possible, ask him about his upgrade schedule.

☐   What uplink connections do you have?

> The purpose of this question is twofold: first, see if he understands the question. An uplink connection is the connection that the ISP has to the rest of the Internet. If it's inadequate, your connection to the Internet will also be inadequate. To judge whether the link is fast enough, you also need to know how many people are connected at any one time. See the question about dial-in modems below.

☐ How many hops are there to the backbone?

> Some ISPs are a long way from the Internet backbone. This can be a disadvantage, but it doesn't have to be. If you're connected to an ISP with T3 all the way to the backbone, you're better off than somebody connected directly to the backbone by an ISDN Basic Rate connection. All other things being equal, though, the smaller the number of hops, the better.

☐ How many dial-in modems do you have?

> This question has two points to make as well. On the one hand, the total bandwidth of these modems should not exceed the uplink bandwidth by too much—let's say it shouldn't be more than double the uplink bandwidth. On the other hand, you want to be able to get a free line when you dial in. Nothing is more frustrating than having to try dozens of times before you can get a connection. This phenomenon also causes people not to disconnect when they're finished, especially if there is no hourly rate. This makes the problem even worse. Of course, the problem depends on the number of subscribers, so ask the next question too.

☐ How many subscribers do you have? What is the average time they connect per week?

> Apart from the obvious information, check whether they keep this kind of statistics. They're important for growth.

☐ What's your up-time record? Do you keep availability statistics? What are they?

> ISPs are always nervous to publish their statistics. They're never as good as *I* would like. But if they publish them, you can assume that that fact alone makes them better than their competitors.

☐ What kind of hardware and software are you running?

> This question will sort out the good techie ISPs from the wannabees. The real answers aren't quite as important as the way they explain it. Nevertheless, consider that, since you're running FreeBSD, you'll be better off with an ISP who also runs FreeBSD or BSD/OS.[1] Only small ISPs can afford to use UNIX machines (including FreeBSD) as routers; the larger ones will use dedicated routers.
>
> Next, in my personal opinion, come other UNIX systems (in decreasing order of preference, Solaris 2.X, Linux and IRIX), and finally, a long way behind, Windows NT. If you're looking for technical support as well, you'll be a lot better off with an ISP who uses FreeBSD or BSD/OS. You'll also be something special to them: most ISPs hate trying to solve problems for typical Windows users.

☐ How many name servers do you run?

> The answer should be at least 2. You'll probably be accessing them for your non-local name server information, since that will be faster than sending requests throughout the Internet.

☐ Can you supply primary or secondary DNS for me? How much does it cost?

> I strongly recommend using your own domain name for mail. That way, if your ISP folds, or you have some other reason for wanting to change, you don't need to change your mail ID. In order to do this, you need to have the information available from a name server 24 hours per day. DNS can generate a lot of traffic, and unless you're connected to the network 100% of the time, mail to you can get lost if a system can't find your DNS information. Even if you are connected 100% of the time, it's a good idea to have a backup DNS on the other side of the link. Remember, though, that it

---

1. BSD/OS is a commercial operating system closely related to FreeBSD. If you have a few thousand dollars to spare, you may even find it better than FreeBSD. Check out *http://www.bsdi.com/* for further details.

doesn't have to be your ISP. Many ISPs supply free secondaries to anybody who asks for them, and you might have friends who will also do it for you.

The ISP will also offer to perform the domain registration formalities for you—for a fee. You can just as easily do this yourself: see page 419 for more details. Check the fee, though: in some countries, the ISP may get a discount for the domain registration fees. If it's big enough, registering via the ISP may possibly be cheaper than doing it yourself.

☐ Can you route a class C network for me? What does it cost?

If you're connecting a local area network to the Internet, routing information must be propagated to the net. ISPs frequently consider this usage to be "commercial", and may jack up the prices considerably as a result.

Alternatives to a full class C network are a group of static addresses (say, 8 or 16) out of the ISP's own assigned network addresses. There's no particular problem with taking this route. If you change ISPs, you'll have to change addresses, but as long as you have your own domain name, that shouldn't be a problem.

Another possibility might be to use *IP aliasing*. See page 506 for more details.

☐ Can you supply me with a static address? How much does it cost?

It's highly desirable to have static addresses. See page 445 for more details.

☐ Will you call me if an incoming packet comes for my system? How much does this cost?

This question only makes sense if you have static addresses. Other people (including yourself when you're travelling) can access your system if your ISP is prepared to contact you. In many areas, unfortunately, it's nearly impossible to find an ISP who is prepared to call you.

If the ISP *is* prepared to call you, check what the costs will be. Obviously you'll be liable for any call costs, but some ISPs also add a service charge.

Making the connection

After calling a few ISPs, you should be able to make a decision based on their replies to these questions. The next step is to gather the information needed to connect. Use table 23-1 to collect the information you need. See Chapter 25, *Configuring PPP* for information about authentication, user name and password.

Table 23-1. Information for ISP setup

Information	Fill in specific value
IP address of your end of the link	
IP address of the other end of the link	
Kind of authentication (CHAP, PAP, login)	
User or system name	
Password or key	
Primary Name Server IP name	
Primary Name Server IP address	
Secondary Name Server IP name	
Secondary Name Server IP address	
Pop (Mail) Server Name	
News Server Name	

24

Serial communications and modems

UNIX has always had a high level of support for serial lines, but their purpose has changed dramatically. In the early 70's, the standard "terminal" was a Teletype KSR35, a 10-character-per-second serial printer with keyboard. Early UNIX serial line support was geared towards supporting these devices, either directly connected, or via a modem.

Even in the early 80s, when 4.2BSD introduced network support, things didn't change much, since the network support used different hardware. By this time, the Teletypes had been replaced with *glass tty*s, in other words serial terminals with a monitor instead of a printer. The speeds had gone up from the 110 bps of the Teletype to 9600 bps, but the underlying principles hadn't changed.

It wasn't until the last 10 years that the glass ttys were replaced by display boards directly connected to the system bus, or by other machines connected by Ethernet. The rôle of the serial port has changed completely: nowadays, they're used mainly for mice and dialup Internet connections.

This change in use has invalidated a few basic concepts. Only a few years ago, the standard "high-speed" modem was a V.22bis 2400 bps modem, even then too slow for an Internet connection. The standard data communication line was 56 kb/s, and it was invariably a leased line. As a result, the Internet grew up assuming that connections were leased lines, and therefore permanently connected. Even today, the Internet protocols do not deal well with dialup access.

On the other hand, *UUCP* did use dialup access. As a result, provisions for dialup access in UNIX tend to be derived from *UUCP*. This doesn't make for smooth integration.

In this chapter, we'll look at the way FreeBSD handles serial communications, at how modems work, and how the two fit together.

Terminology

Any serial connection has two ends, which may be computers, terminals, printers or modems. In modem terminology, the computers are *Data Terminal Equipment* or *DTE* (this terminology arose at a time when the device connected to a modem was usually a terminal), and modems are *Data Communication Equipment* or *DCE*. You'll also sometimes hear the name *dataset* for a modem.

Asynchronous and synchronous communication

There are two different ways to transmit serial data, called *synchronous* and *asynchronous* communication. They grew up in different worlds:

Asynchronous communication

Asynchronous communication predates computers. It was originally developed to run *teletypewriters*, electrical typewriters which were run off a serial data stream, the best-known of which were made by the Teletype corporation. These machines were frequently used to provide a remote transcript of what somebody was typing miles away, so they would typically print one character at a time, stop, and wait for the next. In the early days of UNIX, the standard terminal was a Teletype model KSR35, commonly just called *teletype* or *tty* (pronounced "titty").

Here's a picture of a typical byte encoding:

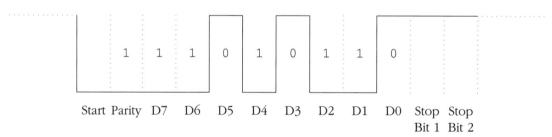

Start Parity D7 D6 D5 D4 D3 D2 D1 D0 Stop Stop
                                          Bit 1 Bit 2

Figure 24-1: Asynchronous byte encoding

This figure shows an encoding for the letter j, in binary `01101011`. We'll see a number of things about it:

- Before the character starts, the line is idle, which shows as a *high* level: this indicates to the teletype that the line is still connected.

- First comes a *start bit*. In the olden days, this bit started the motor of the teletype mechanism. Now it signals that data is coming.

- Next comes a *parity bit*. In order to detect any transmission errors, this character is encoded with *even parity*. The parity bit is set to 1 if the character contains an odd number of bits, and to 0 otherwise, which ensures that the character, including the parity bit, always has an even number of bits.

- Next come the bits of the character, last bit first. We represent 1 with a low level and 0 with a high level.

- Finally come one or two *stop bits*. The stop bits were originally intended to give the teletype time to stop the motor, but they are now largely superfluous. You needed two stop bits for a teletype, but nowadays you should always use one.

- This example also shows something else of importance: there are a number of ways to encode the character. How many bits? How many stop bits? Odd parity? Even parity? No parity? Mark parity (always a 1 bit)? Space parity (always a 0 bit)? How much time from one bit to the next (what bit rate)? They're all set with the *stty* program (see man page *stty(1)*), but if you set them wrongly, you'll run into trouble.

- The encoding isn't very efficient. For every character you send, you also send a start bit and a stop bit. Most communications no longer use the parity bit, but this still means that you have a 25% overhead on communication: for every 8 bits, you send 10, and you could send up to 12, as in this example. We'll see that synchronous communication doesn't have this problem. Users of synchronous communication protocols often refer to asynchronous communication as *start-stop* communication.

Synchronous communication

By contrast with asynchronous communication, synchronous communication comes from the mainframe world, and it assumes that data does not come one byte at a time. Instead, it transmits data in *blocks*. Each block is preceded by one or two *SYN* characters which tell the receiver that data is coming, and which enable it to determine the correct orientation of the bits in the data.

All modern modems use synchronous communication on the phone line, since it is more efficient, and it's the basis of protocols such as SNA and X.25, but you will almost never see any other use of it in UNIX systems.

Serial ports

Nowadays, all PCs come equipped with two serial ports, which are called COM1: and COM2: in the DOS world. UNIX names are different, and FreeBSD calls these same devices sio0 and sio1. It's possible to connect up to four direct serial ports on a standard PC, but due to the design of the board, each one requires a separate IRQ line. If you put two serial ports on the same interrupt line, neither of them will work.

The *GENERIC* kernel contains the following entries:

```
device          sio0 at isa? port "IO_COM1" tty irq 4 vector siointr
device          sio1 at isa? port "IO_COM2" tty irq 3 vector siointr
device          sio2 at isa? disable port "IO_COM3" tty irq 5 vector siointr
device          sio3 at isa? disable port "IO_COM4" tty irq 9 vector siointr
```

The first two devices, *sio0* and *sio1*, are assumed to be at their default IRQs, 4 and 3. By default, however, PC manufacturers put *COM3:* and *COM4:* also at IRQs 4 and 3. How can this work? It can't, if you also have *COM1:* and *COM2:* enabled at those IRQs. However, DOS tends to do only one thing at a time, so you can use different ports at different times on the same IRQ, as long as the interrupts aren't enabled on more than one of the ports at a time. This restriction is unacceptable for UNIX, so we have to put them somewhere else. The only unused interrupts available to 8-bit boards are 2 and 5. As we've seen in Chapter 2, *Before you install*, page 31, you must specify IRQ 2 as IRQ 9.

There's a very good chance that one of these interrupts will already be occupied. What can you do? If one of the boards has a 16-bit or better interface, you can check if one of the interrupts 10 to 15 is available. All EISA and PCI boards fit into this category, and so do ISA boards with two connectors to the motherboard. Unfortunately, a lot of ISA serial cards only have an 8-bit interface. The only alternative is an intelligent serial board which only occupies a single interrupt. In this case, you will probably have to build a custom kernel. See the man page *sio(4)*.

Connecting to the port

Theoretically, a serial line can consist of only three wires: a *Receive Data* line, often abbreviated to *RxD*, a *Transmit Data* line (*TxD*), and a *Signal Ground* line (*SG*). In fact, it is possible to get a link to work like this, but there are a number of problems:

- How do we know when the other end is able to accept data? It may be busy processing data it has already received.

- How do we know when it's even switched on?

- In the case of a modem, how do we know when it is connected to the modem at the other end?

We solve these questions, and more, by the use of additional lines. The most common standard is *RS-232*, also known as *EIA-232*, a standard for DCE to DTE connection. In Europe, it is sometimes confused with the *CCITT V.24* standard, though V.24 does not in fact correspond exactly to RS-232. Most external modems display some of these signals on LED, but modem manufacturers love to create alternative abbreviations for signal names. Here are the signals that RS-232 defines, with some of the more common abbreviations that you may see on external modems.

Table 24-2. RS-232 signals and modem LEDs

RS-232 name	pin	modem LED	purpose
PG	1		Protective ground. Used for electrical grounding only.
TxD	2	TD D1	Transmitted data: data coming from the DTE to the modem.
RxD	3	RD D2	Received data: data coming from the modem to the DTE.
RTS	4		Request to send. Indicates that the device has data to output.
CTS	5		Clear to send. Indicates that the device can receive input.
DSR	6	MR PW ON	Data set ready. Indicates that the modem is powered on and has passed self-test. On some modems, PW indicates that power is on, and MR indicates that it is operative.
SG	7		Signal ground. Return for the other signals.
DCD	8	CD M5	Carrier detect. Indicates that the modem has connection with another modem.
DTR	20	DTR S1	Data terminal ready. Indicates that the terminal or computer is ready to talk to the modem.
RI	22	AA	Ring indicator. Raised by a modem to indicate that an incoming call is ringing. The AA indicator on a modem will usually flash when the incoming call is ringing.
		AA	"Auto Answer". Indicates that the modem will answer an incoming call.
		HS	"High Speed". Indicates that the modem is running at a higher speed than its minimum. Individual modems interpret this differently, but you can assume that something is wrong if your modem has this indicator and it's off during transmission.
		MNP	Indicates that error correction is active.
		OH	"Off hook". Indicates that the modem has some connection with the phone line.
		PW	Indicates that modem power is on. May or may not imply DSR.

The line *DCD* tells the DTE that the modem has established a connection. We'll look at how to use this information on page 435.

In addition to these signals, synchronous modems supply *clocks* on pins 17 and 19. For more details about RS-232, see *RS-232 Made easy* by Martin Seyer.

When can I send data?

There are two ways to determine if the other end is prepared to accept data: *hardware handshaking* and *software handshaking*. Both are also referred to as *flow control*. In each case, the handshaking is symmetrical. We'll look at it from the point of view of the DTE, since this is the more common viewpoint.

In hardware handshaking, the DCE raises *CTS* (*Clear to Send*) when it's ready to accept input. The DTE only transmits data when CTS is asserted from the other end. You'll often see that the DTE asserts RTS (*Request to send*) when it wants to send data. This is a throwback to the days of *half-duplex* modems, which could only transmit in one direction at a time: *RTS* was needed to switch the modem into send mode.

Software handshaking is also called *X-on/X-off*. The DCE sends a character (*X-off*, which corresponds to **CTRL-S**) when the buffer is full, and another (*X-on*, corresponding to **CTRL-Q**) when there is space in the buffer again. You can also use this method on a terminal to temporarily stop the display of a lot of data, and then restart it. It's no longer a good choice for modems.

In order for hardware handshake to work, your modem must be configured correctly, and you must have the correct cables. If it isn't, the symptoms will be very slow response when transferring large quantities of data: at a higher level, TCP can recover from these overruns, but it takes at least a second to do so every time. We'll see how to check that your modem has the correct kind of flow control on page 433.

Modems

A *modem* is a device which transfers digital data into a form suitable for transmission over a transmission line, which is usually a telephone line. Telephone lines are limited to a frequency of about 3.6 kHz, and this limited the speed of older modems to about 1200 bits per second. Modern modems use many sophisticated techniques to increase the speed way beyond this. The current leading edge modems can transmit at up to 56 kilobits per second.

Let's consider the modem connection in the reference network on page 400, which is repeated below. As we can see, there are three connections:

- The connection from the router gw to the local modem, connected at 57,600 bits per second.

- The connection between the modems, at 56,000 bits per second.

- The connection from the ISP's modem to his router, at 115,200 bits per second.

You'll also note another value specified here: the connection between the modems is 2,400 baud. Isn't a *baud* the same thing as a bit per second? No, not always. The term *baud* is a representation of the frequency of data on a serial line. On the connections between the systems and the modem, which handle raw digital data, it corresponds to the bit rate. On the modem line, it doesn't. Here, it indicates that 2,400 units of data are sent per second.

Unfortunately, many people use the term *baud* where *bit rate* should be used. This didn't

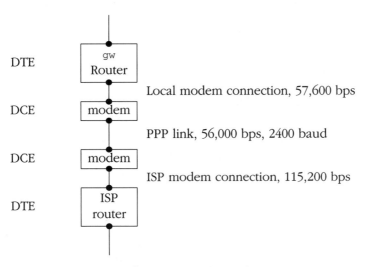

Figure 24-3: Network modem connection

make any difference in the old days with simple modems where the bit rate and baud rate were the same, but nowadays it's confusing.

Modem speeds

Two factors determine the data transmission speed of a modem: the *protocol* and the use of

Table 24-4. Modem protocols

Protocol	Speed (bps)
Bell 203	300
V.21	300
Bell 212	1200
V.22	1200
V.22bis	2400
V.32	9600
V.32bis	14400
V.34	28800
V.34bis	33600
V.90	56000

data compression. Table 24-4 gives an overview of modem protocols and their speeds. Currently, the most popular modem protocol is V.90. V.90 pushes modem technology to the limit, and it only works when the other end of the link is a digital (ISDN) connection. You can't get a 56 kb/s connection with any kind of analogue modem at the other end. As a result, in many areas they can't be used. In addition, the actual speed of the connection depends greatly on the telephone line quality, so the difference between a V.90 and a V.34bis modem may not be as much as it appears.

Data compression

In addition, you usually have a choice of data compression: *V.42bis* or *MNP-5*. The choice depends on what the modem at the other end of the line does. You can set most modems negotiate either protocol. These protocols include related error correction standards, called *V.42* or *MNP2-4* respectively. If you believe the sales claims, these compression protocols will give you up to 100% increase in data throughput. Consider this the upper limit; a lot of data is binary, and when ftp'ing a typical gzipped tar archive, you will probably get almost no speed improvement.

Data compression has one negative side: it increases the data rate, but it also increases *latency*, the time it takes for data to get from the local DTE to the remote DTE. The data doesn't take as long on the line, but it spends more time in the modems being compressed and uncompressed. If you're running a protocol like PPP which supplies optional compression in the software, you may find it advantageous to turn off compression. We'll look at that again in Chapter 25, *Configuring PPP*.

The link speed

The standard PC serial hardware can run at speeds which are a fraction of 115,200 bps (in other words, 115200 divided by a small integer). This gives the following combinations:

Table 24-5. Serial line speeds

Divisor	Speed (bps)
1	115200
2	57600
3	38400
4	28800
5	23040
6	19200

You'll notice that it can't run at 33600 or 56000 bps. Also, looking at the example above, you'll note that all three links run at different speeds. How can that work? Only a few years ago, it wouldn't, but modern modems can *buffer* data. For example, the ISP can send data to the modem far faster than the modem can send it to the other modem. It stores the data in internal memory until it can be transmitted. This can also happen at the other end. If you misconfigure your line so that the local link runs at 9600 bps, things will still work, but of course the total speed is the speed of the slowest link, in this case 9600 bps.

This flexibility brings a problem with it: the modem can't know in advance how fast the connection to the computer is. It needs a way to find out. The modem solves the question of local line speed by a trick: all commands start with AT or at (you're not allowed to mix letters, like aT or At). It can recognize these characters even if they arrive at the wrong speed, and thus it can establish the speed of the connection.

Dialling out

Nowadays, all modems are capable of dialling. That wasn't always the case, and in some old documentation you may find references to an *Auto-Call Unit* or *ACU*, which is simply the dialler part of a modem connected via a separate port. Typically, one ACU could serve multiple modems.

Nearly every modern modem uses a command set designed by Hayes Corporation, which is thus called the *Hayes Command Set*. We'll look at it in the following section. It is also sometimes called the *AT command set*, since nearly all the commands start with the sequence AT. The CCITT also created an autodial recommendation, *V.25*, which was occasionally implemented. Avoid it if you can.

Modem commands

Modern modems store their state in a number of registers, called *S registers*. The register use varies somewhat from manufacturer to manufacturer, but most modems have a number in common. They each store a one-byte value, ranging between 0 and 255. Here's a list of the more important ones for a relatively recent Rockwell V.34 chip set. The name of the chip set is not the same as the name of the modem. You'll note that one of the commands enables you to find out the chip set version, as we'll see in the example which follows.

Table 24-6. Selected S registers

Register number	Purpose
S0	Number of rings until auto-answer. 0 disables auto-answer. Set to 0 for no automatic answer, or 1 for auto-answer.
S2	The *escape character*, which lets you return from on-line mode to command mode. Normally, this character is a +. To return to command mode, wait a second after any previous input, enter +++, and wait a second, after which the modem should reply with OK.
S6	The time, in seconds, to wait before *blind dialling*. If you have set your modem to not wait for a dial tone (maybe because it doesn't understand the dial tone), it will wait this long and then try to dial anyway.
S7	The number of seconds to wait after dialling before DCD must be asserted (before a connection is established). If this is set too short, you will not be able to establish a connection. If it's too long, you will waste time when there is no answer or the line is busy.
S11	The duration of DTMF (dialling) tones. If these are set incorrectly, the telephone exchange may not understand the number you dial.

The AT command set tells the modem to do something specific. Here are some of the more important ones:

Table 24-7. Selected AT commands

Command	Meaning
A/	Redial the last number
ATA	Answer an incoming call manually. This is an alternative to auto-answer by setting S0.
ATD*number*	Dial *number*. This command has a large number of options, but if your modem is set up correctly, you probably won't need any of them.
ATE*number*	Enable command echo if *number* is 1, disable it if *number* is 0. The setting of this command can be important for some chat scripts, which may not respond correctly otherwise.
ATH0	Disconnect the line
ATI*number*	Display modem identification. The values of *number* vary from one modem to the next. See the examples below.
ATL*number*	Set the speaker volume. *number* ranges from 0 to 3. 0 means "speaker off", 3 is the loudest.
ATM*number*	Determine when the speaker is on. 0 means "always off", 1 means "speaker on until connect", 2 means "speaker always on", and 3 means "speaker off during dialling and receiving".
ATO0	Go back on-line from command mode. You don't need this command when dialling: the modem automatically goes on-line when the connection is established.
ATP	Select pulse dial. If your exchange doesn't understand DTMF (tone) dialling, you should set this mode. Never use it if your exchange understands DTMF, since pulse dialling (also known as *steam dialling*) is *much* slower.
ATQ*number*	If *number* is 0, suppress result codes (like OK after every command). If *number* is 1, enable them. This value can be of importance for chat scripts.
ATS*r* =*n*	Set the value of S register *r* to *n*.
ATS*number* ?	Display the contents of an *S* register. See the example below.
ATT	Set tone (DTMF) dialling.
ATV*number*	If *number* is 0, return result codes in numeric form. If it's 1, return text. Don't rely on either form to be consistent from one modem to the next.
ATX*number*	Determine the form of the result codes. This depends a lot on the manufacturer, but it's important for chat scripts. If you run into trouble, with chat scripts, check your modem documentation.
ATZ	Reset modem configuration to default values.

Command	Meaning
AT&K*number*	Select flow control method. Normally, 3 enables RTS/CTS flow control, which is what you want.
AT&R*number*	If *number* is 0, CTS is only asserted if the DTE asserts RTS, even if the modem is able to receive data. If it's set to 1, it behaves normally. Make sure this value is set to 1.
AT&T*number*	Perform modem-specific test *number*. This command is the origin of the statement: "UNIX is a trademark of AT&T in the USA and other countries. AT&T is a modem test command".
AT&V	View the current configuration. See the example below.
AT&W*number*	Store the current configuration as *profile* **number**. Most external modems can store two *profiles*, or configurations. If *number* is not specified, write the profile specified in a previous AT&Y command. See the example below.
AT&Y*number*	Decide which profile (0 or 1) will be loaded when the modem is reset, and which will be written by the command AT&W

Dialling out manually

In this section, we'll look at what needs to be done to establish a dial-out connection. You don't normally do this yourself: some software will do it for you automatically. It's useful to know what goes on, though, since it can be of immense help in solving connection problems.

There are two distinct things that you want to do with the modem: first, you send commands to the modem to set up the link. Once the link is established, you don't want to talk to the modem any more, you want to talk to the system at the other end of the link.

In the old days, the system used a separate ACU to establish the connection, and the solution was simple: the system issued the dialling commands to the ACU and opened the modem in such a manner that the open did not complete until a connection had been established. Nowadays, the modem handles both dialing and the establishment of connection. But to do so, the system has to open the modem before communication has been established.

The terminal parameter clocal enables communication with a device which does is not asserting *DCD* (such as a modem which hasn't established a connection yet). When it starts, the software sets clocal. When it has finished talking to the modem and wants to wait for the connection to be established, it resets (turns off) clocal and waits for *DCD*. You can check this with the *stty* command:

```
# stty -f /dev/cuaa2 -a
ppp disc; speed 57600 baud; 0 rows; 0 columns;
lflags: -icanon -isig -iexten -echo -echoe -echok -echoke -echonl
        -echoctl -echoprt -altwerase -noflsh -tostop -flusho -pendin
        -nokerninfo -extproc
iflags: -istrip -icrnl -inlcr -igncr -ixon -ixoff -ixany -imaxbel ignbrk
        -brkint -inpck ignpar -parmrk
oflags: -opost -onlcr -oxtabs
cflags: cread cs8 -parenb -parodd hupcl -clocal -cstopb crtscts -dsrflow
```

```
           -dtrflow -mdmbuf
cchars: discard = ^O; dsusp = ^Y; eof = ^D; eol = <undef>;
        eol2 = <undef>; erase = ^?; intr = ^C; kill = ^U; lnext = ^V;
        min = 1; quit = ^\; reprint = ^R; start = ^Q; status = ^T;
        stop = ^S; susp = ^Z; time = 0; werase = ^W;
```

This example, taken when the modem is connected, shows clocal reset. As you can see, this is indicated by the text -clocal.

There's a problem here: what if this line is also enabled for dial-in? As we shall see on page 437, there will be a *getty* process in the process of opening the line. It won't succeed until *DCD* is asserted, so we can dial with no problem. But when the connection is established, how do we stop *getty* from being there first?

The FreeBSD solution is to create separate devices for each case. For the second serial port, *sio1*, the system creates a file */dev/cuaa1* for dialling out, and */dev/ttyd1* for dialling in. If *cuaa1* is open, an open on *ttyd1* does not complete when connection is established.

Dialing out–an example

For an example of what you might look at, let's consider a manual dialup to an ISP:

```
# ppp ISP
User Process PPP. Written by Toshiharu OHNO.
Using interface: tun0
Interactive mode
ppp ON freebie> term                    go into direct connect mode
Enter to terminal mode.
Type '~?' for help.
at                                      synchronize with the modem
OK
at&v                                    look at the modem profile
ACTIVE PROFILE:
B0 E1 L0 M1 N1 Q0 T V1 W0 X4 Y0 &C1 &D2 &G0 &J0 &K4 &Q5 &R1 &S0 &T5 &X0 &Y0
S00:000 S01:000 S02:043 S03:013 S04:010 S05:008 S06:002 S07:060 S08:002 S09:006
S10:014 S11:090 S12:050 S18:000 S25:005 S26:001 S36:007 S37:000 S38:020 S44:020
S46:138 S48:007 S95:000

STORED PROFILE 0:
B0 E1 L0 M1 N1 Q0 T V1 W0 X4 Y0 &C1 &D2 &G0 &J0 &K4 &Q5 &R1 &S0 &T5 &X0
S00:000 S02:043 S06:002 S07:060 S08:002 S09:006 S10:014 S11:090 S12:050 S18:000
S36:007 S37:000 S40:104 S41:195 S46:138 S95:000

STORED PROFILE 1:
B0 E1 L1 M1 N1 Q0 T V1 W0 X4 Y0 &C1 &D2 &G0 &J0 &K3 &Q5 &R1 &S0 &T5 &X0
S00:000 S02:043 S06:002 S07:060 S08:002 S09:006 S10:014 S11:090 S12:050 S18:000
S36:007 S37:000 S40:104 S41:195 S46:138 S95:000

TELEPHONE NUMBERS:
0=T1234567890                           1=
2=                                      3=

OK
```

The term *profile* refers to a set of the complete configuration information for the modem. External modems can usually store two different profiles. The AT&V command shows the current configuration ("active profile") and the two stored profiles. The first line reflects the parameters set with AT commands (for example, L0 means that the command ATL0, turn off the speaker, has been issued). The next two or three lines reflect the values of the S registers.

In addition, this modem can store up to four telephone numbers, a feature which is seldom of great interest.

If you look at this profile, you'll notice that the active profile includes the parameter &K4. This means "use XON/XOFF flow control". This is not desirable: it's better to use RTS/CTS flow control. To fix it,

```
at&k3                                      set RTS/CTS flow control
OK
at&w                                       write the active profile
OK
at&v                                       and check
ACTIVE PROFILE:
B0 E1 L0 M1 N1 Q0 T V1 W0 X4 Y0 &C1 &D2 &G0 &J0 &K3 &Q5 &R1 &S0 &T5 &X0 &Y0
S00:000 S01:000 S02:043 S03:013 S04:010 S05:008 S06:002 S07:060 S08:002 S09:006
S10:014 S11:090 S12:050 S18:000 S25:005 S26:001 S36:007 S37:000 S38:020 S44:020
S46:138 S48:007 S95:000

STORED PROFILE 0:
B0 E1 L0 M1 N1 Q0 T V1 W0 X4 Y0 &C1 &D2 &G0 &J0 &K3 &Q5 &R1 &S0 &T5 &X0
S00:000 S02:043 S06:002 S07:060 S08:002 S09:006 S10:014 S11:090 S12:050 S18:000
S36:007 S37:000 S40:104 S41:195 S46:138 S95:000

STORED PROFILE 1:
B0 E1 L1 M1 N1 Q0 T V1 W0 X4 Y0 &C1 &D2 &G0 &J0 &K3 &Q5 &R1 &S0 &T5 &X0
S00:000 S02:043 S06:002 S07:060 S08:002 S09:006 S10:014 S11:090 S12:050 S18:000
S36:007 S37:000 S40:104 S41:195 S46:138 S95:000

TELEPHONE NUMBERS:
0=T1234567890                              1=
2=                                         3=

OK
```

Since the active profile includes the parameter **&Y0**, the AT&W command writes back to stored profile 0.

The **AT&V** command doesn't show all the S registers. Some of them relate to the current state of the modem, and aren't part of the configuration. For example, my modem includes an S register S86, the *Call Failure Reason Code*. If a call fails, it could be interesting to look at it. To do so,

```
ats86?                                     show contents of S86
012                                        Connection dropped by other end
```

With this background, we can now proceed to establish a connection:

```
atd1234567                                 just dial
CONNECT 57600
ppp ON freebie>
PPP ON freebie>
```

Dialling in

Traditionally, UNIX distinguishes between local serial terminals and terminals connected by modem by whether they assert the *DCD* signal. It starts a *getty* (for *Get TTY*) process for each line. *getty* opens the line, but for modems the line state is set in such a way that the call to open does not complete until the DCE asserts *DCD*. This is done by resetting the flag clocal.

If you look at the line state with the *stty* program, it will show -clocal if the flag is reset.

To set up a line for dialing in, add information about the line in the file */etc/ttys*. The default file contains a number of lines like:

```
ttyd0 "/usr/libexec/getty std.9600"   unknown    off secure
```

This information has the following meaning:

- The first column is the name of the terminal special file, relative to */dev* (in other words, this entry represents the file */dev/ttyd0*).

- The next field consists of the text /usr/libexec/getty std.9600. This is the invocation for *getty*: the *getty* program is */usr/libexec/getty*, and it is invoked with the parameter std.9600. This is a label in the file */etc/gettytab*, and describes a standard 9600 bps connection. If you really use it like this, you'll probably want to upgrade to std.57600.

- unknown refers to the terminal type. This is the value to which *getty* sets the environment variable TERM. If you know that only people with VT100 terminals dial in, you might change this string to vt100, but you should do this with care. It can cause a real mess on the screen, and even make it impossible for people to work with it.

- The remaining fields can occur in any order. off means "don't start the *getty* after all". If you want to run a *getty* on this line, change this string to on.

  secure means that only people you trust can access this line, so you can allow a root login on this line. That's fine for a direct connect terminal in the same room, for example. It's not a good idea for a modem which anybody can dial up. If the line is not secure, just omit the string.

It's not enough to edit */etc/ttys*. The *getty*s are actually spawned by *init*, and you must tell *init* that you have changed the file. *init* is always process 1, and you tell it by sending it a *SIGHUP* signal. The unlikely name of the program which sends signals is *kill*, so you write:

```
 # kill -SIGHUP 1
```
or
```
 # kill -1 1
```

These two commands are equivalent: *SIGHUP* has the numeric value 1.

25

Configuring PPP

Two protocols support connection to the Internet via modem: *SLIP* (*Serial Line Internet Protocol*) and *PPP* (*Point to Point Protocol*). As the name suggests, SLIP supports only IP. It is an older, less rugged protocol. Its only advantage is that it may be available where PPP isn't. If you have the choice, always take PPP.

PPP differs from SLIP in being able to handle multiple protocols simultaneously. Since Microsoft discovered the Internet, two things have happened: PPP has become the protocol of choice with nearly every ISP, and Microsoft keeps changing its implementation to make it more difficult for non-Microsoft machines to connect to Microsoft equipment.

In this chapter, we'll look at PPP. We'll consider SLIP, if we have to, in the following chapter.

PPP performs a number of functions:

- It performs the dialling and establishment of a phone connection if necessary. Strictly speaking, this isn't part of the PPP specification, but it is supported by most PPP implementations.

- It performs *authentication* to ensure that you are allowed to use the connection.

- It performs *negotiation* to decide what kind of protocol to use over the link. You might think, "that's OK, I'm just using IP", but in fact there are a number of different ways to transmit IP datagrams over a PPP link. In addition, the other end may be able to handle non-Internet protocols such as X.25, SNA and Novell's IPX.

- It can perform *line quality monitoring* to ensure that the modems are able to understand each other.

FreeBSD supports two versions of PPP:

- Traditional BSD implementations of IP are located in the kernel, which makes for more efficiency. The corresponding implementation of PPP is referred to as *Kernel PPP*. We'll look at it on page 454.

- Although Kernel PPP is more efficient, it's also frequently more difficult to debug. As a result, FreeBSD also supplies an implementation known as *User PPP* or *iijppp*, after the *Internet Institute of Japan*, which supplied it. It uses the *tunnel driver* to pass IP packets up to a user process. It's easier to configure and debug, and though it's not as efficient, the difference is not usually a problem. We'll look at this implementation on page 447.

Quick setup

If you understand how PPP works, and you just want to jump into the setup, look at the configuration summaries on page 453 for User PPP, or page 459 for Kernel PPP. If you run into trouble, come back here and check the details.

How PPP works

To set up a PPP connection, *something* needs to perform most of these steps:

- Set up a serial connection between the two systems. This could be a direct wire connection, but normally it's a modem or ISDN link.

- For a modem link, establish connection, traditionally called *dialling* the other end. The modems then set up a link and assert *DCD* (*Data Carrier Detect*) to tell the machines to which they are connected that the modem connection has been established.

- *Log in.* Traditionally, all UNIX system perform login authentication. Only then do they decide whether you want to run PPP, SLIP, or a simple terminal protocol (the so-called *shell account*). Nowadays, more and more systems are using *PAP* or *CHAP* authentication.

- Start PPP. PPP selects an unused network interface to use for this connection.

- The two PPP processes negotiate details like IP address, protocol, and authentication protocols.

- Establish routes to the systems at the other end of the link.

On the following pages, we'll look at these points in detail.

The interfaces

Most network interfaces are dedicated to networking. For example, an Ethernet adapter can't be used for anything else. PPP and SLIP are different: you're using a serial line which you could also use for a remote terminal, a UUCP connection, or even a mouse. There's another difference, too: you access serial lines via their device names. You access network interfaces via the *ifconfig* program, since they don't usually have device names—in technical jargon, they're in a separate *name space* from files. How do we solve this conflict?

The solution is a little surprising: PPP and SLIP both use two different devices. You decide which serial line you want to use, and the software chooses a network interface for you. For example, your serial line might be called */dev/cuaa0*, */dev/cuaa1* or */dev/cuaa2*, while your interface will be called *tun0* or *tun1* (for User PPP), *ppp0* or *ppp1* (for Kernel PPP), or *sl0* for SLIP. The total number of each kind of network interface is a configurable kernel parameter.

Since User PPP runs in user space, it *does* require a device name for the network interface, for example */dev/tun0*. It uses this device to read and write to the back end of the tunnel interface.

Dialling

Most PPP connections run over a dial-up link. The PPP standard doesn't define dialling, however, since dialling is a modem function.

User PPP includes built-in dialling support, while Kernel PPP supplies a method for invoking an external dialler. In practice, the only difference is the way your configuration files look. We'll look at these when we discuss the individual implementations.

After the modem connection has been set up, the next step depends to a great extent on the system at the other end of the link. You may first have to perform login, or you may find yourself connected directly to a PPP process. The dialling script ("chat script") usually handles login, so when it completes you should be connected to the PPP process. The PPP processes then perform *negotiation*.

Negotiation

Once the modem connection is established and the PPP processes can talk to each other, they negotiate what PPP features they will use. The negotiation is successful if the two sides can agree on a functional subset of the features both would like to have.

For each feature of the link, PPP negotiation can perform up to two actions. User PPP uses the following terms to describe them, viewed from the local end of a link:

- To *enable* a feature means: "request this feature".

- To *disable* a feature means: "do not request this feature".

- To *accept* a feature means: "if the other side requests this feature, accept it".

- To *deny* a feature means: "if the other side requests this feature, refuse it".

Negotiation is successful if each end accepts all the features that the other end has enabled. In some cases, however, non-FreeBSD PPP systems have an alternative (for example, if you accept PAP and deny CHAP, a router may first request CHAP, and when you deny it, it may then request PAP).

Who throws the first stone?

The first step in negotiation is to decide which side starts. One of them starts the negotiation, and the other one responds. If you configure your end wrong, one of two things can happen:

1. You both wait for the other end to start. Nothing happens. After a while, one of you times out and drops the connection.

2. You both fire away and place your demands, and listen for the other one to reply. The software should recognize that the other end is talking, too, and recover, but often enough both ends give up and drop the connection.

In general, systems with login authentication also initiate the negotiation. ISPs with *PAP* or *CHAP* authentication tend to expect the end user to start first, since that's the way Microsoft does it. It's easier for debugging to assume that the other end will start. If it doesn't, and you have an external modem, you'll notice that there is no traffic on the line, and that the line has dropped. Then you can switch to active mode negotiation.

Typical features that require negotiation are:

- *What kind of authentication?* Login authentication doesn't count here, since it's not part of PPP. You may choose to offer *CHAP* or *PAP* negotiation. You may also require the other end to authenticate itself. You can accept both *CHAP* and *PAP* authentication—that way, you can accept whichever the other end asks for. If the other end is an ISP, you will probably not be able to authenticate him, but you should check with the ISP.

- *LQR, Link Quality Requests.* This gives you an overview of your line quality, *if* you don't set your modem to use error correction. If you do use error correction, you're unlikely to see much in the way of LQR problems, since the error correction protocols hide them. Occasionally LQR packets can confuse a PPP implementation, so you shouldn't enable them if you don't intend to use them.

- *Data and header compression.* You have a choice here: modern modems offer various kinds of data compression, and so do the PPP implementations. As we saw on page 432, modem compression increases the data throughput, but also increases the latency. If your ISP supports the same kind of data compression as your PPP software, you might find that it improves matters to disable modem data compression. Both implementations support *Van Jacobson* and *Predictor 1* compression, and Kernel PPP also supports *BSD compression* and *deflate compression.*

  Which do you choose? *Van Jacobson* compression works at the TCP level. It compresses only the headers (see page 389 for more details), and the other compression schemes work at the frame level. You can always enable Van Jacobson compression. As far as the others are concerned, use whatever the other side offers. In case of doubt, use Predictor 1 compression.

  Data and header compression are implemented as a special case of *protocol*: IP with header compression is considered a different protocol from IP without header compression. Other protocols that the remote system might offer include non-IP protocols such as X.25, SNA and IPX.

- *IP addresses.* Dynamic addressing is implemented by making the IP addresses of each end negotiable.

- *Proxy ARP.* Some systems can't understand being at the other end of a PPP link. You can fool them by telling the router to respond to *ARP* requests for machines at the other end of the link. You don't need this subterfuge in FreeBSD.

Authentication

Nearly every PPP link requires some kind of identification to confirm that you are authorized to use the link. On UNIX systems, the authentication traditionally consisted of the UNIX *login* procedure, which also allows you to dial-in either to a shell or to a PPP session, depending on what user ID you use. Login authentication is normally performed by the dial-up chat script.

Microsoft has changed many things in this area. Since their machines don't normally support dæmons or even multiple users, the UNIX login method is difficult to implement. Instead, you connect directly to a PPP server and perform authentication directly with it. There are two different authentication methods currently available, *PAP* (*Password Authentication Protocol*) and *CHAP* (*Challenge Handshake Authentication Protocol*). Both perform similar functions. From the PPP point of view, you just need to know which one you are using. Your ISP should tell you this information, but a surprising number don't seem to know. In case of doubt, accept either of them.

Occasionally you have both login authentication and either *CHAP* or *PAP* authentication. The remote system may require you to start the *ppp* program and perform a second authentication phase. This is part of the information that the system administrator at the other end should give you.

If you're using *PAP* or *CHAP*, you need to specify a system name and an authentication key. These terms may sound complicated, but they're really just a fancy name for a user name and a password. We'll look at how to specify these values when we look at the individual software.

How do you decide whether you use *PAP* or *CHAP*? Maybe you don't—you can leave it to the other end. Typically, though, you will accept the one kind of authentication and deny the other. Most ISPs do not expect you to authenticate *them* (they're beyond reproach), so you should request neither *PAP* nor *CHAP*. For example, for *CHAP* authentication (which seems to be becoming more prevalent), you would accept *CHAP* and not offer anything.

Which IP addresses on the link?

After passing authentication, you may need to negotiate the addresses on the link. At first sight, you'd think that the IP addresses on the link would be very important. In fact, you can often almost completely ignore them. To understand this, we need to consider what the purpose of the IP addresses is.

An IP address is an address placed in the source or the destination field in an IP packet in order to enable the software to route it to its destination. As we saw in Chapter 22, *Configuring the local network*, it is not necessarily the address of the interface to which the packet is sent. If your packet goes through 15 nodes on the way through the Internet, quite a normal number, it will be sent to 14 nodes whose address is not specified in the packet.

The first node is the router at the other end of the PPP link. This is a point-to-point link, so it receives all packets that are sent down the line, so you don't need to do anything special to ensure it gets them. This is in marked contrast to a router on a broadcast medium like an Ethernet: on an Ethernet you must specify the IP address of the router in order for it to receive the packets.

> On an Ethernet, although the IP address in the packets doesn't mention the router, the Ethernet packets do specify the Ethernet address of the router as the destination address. Your local system needs the IP address in order to determine the Ethernet address with the aid of *ARP*, the *Address Resolution Protocol*.

In either case, except for testing, it's very unlikely that you will ever want to address a packet directly to the router, and it's equally unlikely that the router would know what to do with most kinds of packets if they are addressed to itself. So we don't really need to care about the address.

What if we set up the wrong address for the other end of the link? Look at the router gw.example.com in the reference network on page 400. Its PPP link has the local address 139.130.136.133, and the other end has the address 139.130.136.129. What happens if we get the address mixed up and specify the other end as 139.130.129.136? Consider the commands we might enter if we were configuring the interface manually (compare on page 405):

```
# ifconfig tun0  139.130.136.133  139.130.136.129  255.255.255.255
# route add default 139.130.129.136
```

Figure 25-1: Configuring an interface and a route

You need to specify the netmask, because otherwise *ifconfig* chooses one based on the network address. In this case, since it's a class B address, it would choose 255.255.0.0. This tells the system that the other end of the link is 139.130.129.136, which is incorrect. It then tells the system to route all packets which can't be routed elsewhere to this address (the default route). When such a packet arrives, the system checks the routing table, and find that 139.130.129.136 can be reached by sending the packet out from interface *tun0*. It sends the packet down the line.

At this point any memory of the address 139.130.129.136 (or, for that matter, 139.130.136.129) is gone. The packet arrives at the other end, and the router examines it. It still contains only the original destination address, and the router routes it accordingly. In other words, the router never finds out that the packet has been sent to the incorrect "other end" address, and things work just fine.

What happens in the other direction? That depends on your configuration. For any packet to get to your system from the Internet, the routing throughout the Internet must point to your system. Now how many IP addresses do you have? If it's only a single IP address (the address of your end of the PPP link), it must be correct. Consider what would happen if you accidentally changed the octets of your local IP address:

```
# ifconfig tun0  139.130.133.136  139.130.129.136
```

If gw sends out a packet with this source address, it does not prevent it from getting to its destination, since the source address does not play any part in the routing. But when the destination system replies, it sends it to the address specified in the source field, so it will not get back.

So how can this still work? Remember that routers don't change the addresses in the packets they pass. If system bumble sends out a packet, it has the address 223.147.37.3. It passes through the incorrectly configured system gw unchanged, so the reply packet gets back to its source with no problems.

In practice, of course, it's not a good idea to use incorrect IP addresses. If you don't specify an address at either end of the link, PPP can negotiate one for you. What this does mean, though, is that you shouldn't worry too much about what address you get. There is one exception, however: the issue of *dynamic addressing*. We'll look at that below.

The net mask for the link

As we saw on page 398, with a broadcast medium you use a net mask to specify which range of addresses can be addressed directly via the interface. This is a different concept from *routing*, which specifies ranges of addresses which can be addressed indirectly via the interface. By definition, a point-to-point link only has one address at the other end, so the net mask must be 255.255.255.255. Unfortunately, Microsoft software sometimes uses a point-to-point link as if it were an extension of a LAN, and it broadcasts across the link. This is not a good idea, but if you have to use this kind of software, you may need to set a different net mask. In practice, it doesn't matter what net mask you set, as long as it doesn't cause data intended for other interfaces to be sent down the PPP link.

Static and dynamic addresses

Traditionally, each interface has had a specific address. With the increase in the size of the Internet, this has caused significant problems: the Internet is running out of addresses. A solution is on the horizon: version 6 of the Internet Protocol (usually called *IPv6*) has increased the length of an address from 32 bits to 128 bits, increasing the total number of addresses from 4,294,967,296 to 3.4×10^{38}—enough to assign multiple IP addresses to every atom on Earth.[1] In the meantime, ISPs have found a partial solution with *dynamic IP addresses*. With dynamic addresses, every time you dial in, you are assigned a free IP address from the ISP's address space. That way, an ISP only needs as many IP addresses as he has modems. He might have 128 modems and 5000 customers. WIth static addresses, he would need 5000 addresses, but with dynamic addresses he only needs 128.

Dynamic addresses have two very serious disadvantages:

1. IP is a peer-to-peer protocol: there is no master and no slave. Theoretically, any system can initiate a connection to any other, as long as it knows its IP address. This means that your ISP could initiate the connection if somebody was trying to access your system. With dynamic addressing, it is absolutely impossible for the ISP to set up a connection: there is no way for any outside system to know your IP address.

   This may seem unimportant—maybe you consider the possibility of the ISP calling you even dangerous—but consider the advantages. If you're travelling somewhere and need to check on something on your machine at home, you can just *telnet* to it. If you want to let somebody collect some files from your system, there's no problem. In practice, however, very few ISPs are prepared to call you, though that doesn't make it a bad idea.

2. Both versions of PPP support an *idle timeout* feature: if you don't use the link for a specified period of time, it may hang up. Depending on where you live, this may save on phone bills and ISP connect charges. It only disconnects the phone link, and not the TCP sessions. In order to be able to continue the session, however, you need to have the same IP address when the link comes up again. Otherwise, though the session isn't dead, you can't reconnect

---

1. There may still be a limitation when the Internet grows across the entire universe.

to it.

Setting a default route

Very frequently, the PPP link is your only connection to the Internet. In this case, you should set the *default route* to go via the link. You can do this explicitly with the *route add* command, but both versions of PPP can do it for you.

When you do it depends on what kind of addressing you're using. If you're using static addressing, you can specify it as one of the configuration parameters. If you're using dynamic addressing, this isn't possible: you don't know the address at that time. Both versions have a solution for this, which we'll look at when we get to them.

Autodial

A PPP link typically costs money. You may pay some or all of the following charges:

- Telephone call setup charges, a charge made once per call. Unlike the other charges, these make it advantageous to stay connected as long as possible.

- Telephone call duration charges. In some countries, you pay per time unit (for example, per minute), or you pay a fixed sum for a variable period of time.

- ISP connect charges, also per time unit.

- ISP data charges, per unit of data.

Typically, the main cost depends on the connection duration. To limit this cost, both PPP implementations supply methods to dial automatically and to disconnect when the line is idle.

The information you need to know

Whichever PPP implementation you decide upon, you need the following information:

- Who are you going to call? Get the phone number complete with any necessary area codes, in exactly the format the modem needs to dial. If your modem is connected to a PABX, be sure to include the access code for an external line.

- The user identification and password for connection to the ISP system.

- The kind of authentication used (login, *CHAP* or *PAP*).

- Whether you are using static or dynamic addressing.

- If you're using static addressing, what *IP addresses* to use over the link.

- The *net mask* for the link. As we've seen it, you don't need it, but if the provider supplies it, you might as well use it.

You should have collected all this information in the table on page 423.

Setting up User PPP

User PPP uses the *tunnel driver*. You can check this in the configuration file for your system:

```
pseudo-device    tun             1
```

The value (1 in this example) is the number of tunnel devices to provide. Each concurrent PPP connection requires one tunnel driver. The standard GENERIC kernel includes this pseudo-device, so you only have to check if you have already rebuilt a kernel. See page 355 for more details.

It's not enough to have a kernel which supports the tunnel driver: you also need a device node */dev/tun0*. If not, you can create it by:

```
# cd /dev
# ./MAKEDEV tun0
```

Once you have performed these preliminary steps, you can proceed to set up PPP:

- Set up the configuration files in the directory */etc/ppp*.

- Set up the global internet information in */etc/rc.conf*.

The ppp configuration files

After installation, you will find the following files in */etc/ppp*:

```
# ls -l /etc/ppp
  total 21
  drwxr-xr-x   2 root      wheel          512 Aug 17 16:18 .
  drwxr-xr-x   8 root      wheel         1536 Aug 29 18:31 ..
  -rw-r--r--   1 root      wheel         1370 May 20 20:06 ppp.conf.filter.sample
  -rw-r--r--   1 root      wheel         1894 May 20 20:06 ppp.conf.iij.sample
  -rw-r--r--   1 root      wheel         5112 May 20 20:06 ppp.conf.sample
  -rw-r--r--   1 root      wheel         1130 May 20 20:06 ppp.conf.server.sample
  -rw-r--r--   1 root      wheel         1665 May 20 20:06 ppp.dialup.sample
  -rw-r--r--   1 root      wheel         1422 May 20 20:06 ppp.linkup.sample
  -rw-r--r--   1 root      wheel         1705 May 20 20:06 ppp.pap.dialup.sample
  -rw-r--r--   1 root      wheel          313 May 20 20:06 ppp.secret.sample
```

As the names suggest, they are only samples. Most of them are samples for the main configuration file *ppp.conf*. They have the following purposes:

- *ppp.conf* is the main configuration file. We'll look at it in the following section. The files *ppp.conf.sample*, *ppp.conf.iij.sample* and *ppp.conf.server.sample* contain various possible configurations.

- *ppp.conf.filter* is used for packet filtering. We'll look at this feature in Chapter 28, *Firewalls and IP aliasing*.

- *ppp.dialup* is called from *getty* to set up the PPP link for a dial-in connection. *ppp.pap.dialup.sample* is another version which uses *PAP*.

- *ppp.linkup* is invoked after the link has been established when dialling out. We won't discuss it further here.

- *ppp.linkdown* is invoked when the link is dropped after dialling out. There is no sample file for this file, and it's not used very often.

- *ppp.secret* is an alternative file which contains passwords and authentication keys. Putting them in a separate file makes it easier to keep them secure.

- In addition, you may find configuration files for Kernel PPP—unfortunately, both implementations share the same configuration directory. This isn't as bad as it could be: at least there is no clash in the names. See the section on Kernel PPP configuration on page 454 for more details.

We'll look at them in the following sections.

/etc/ppp/ppp.conf

/etc/ppp/ppp.conf is the main configuration file. It consists of a number of entries headed by a label. For example, the `default` entry looks like:

```
default:
  set device /dev/cuaa1                    device to use
  set speed 115200                 connect at 115,200 bps
  set dial "ABORT BUSY ABORT NO\\sCARRIER TIMEOUT 5 \"\" AT \
          OK-AT-OK ATE1Q0 OK \\dATDT\\T TIMEOUT 40 CONNECT"
```

There are a number of things to observe here:

- Note the format: labels begin at the beginning of the line, and other entries must be indented by one character.

- The line `default:` identifies the default entry, which is always run when PPP starts. `set device /dev/cuaa1` tells PPP to use the second serial port (*/dev/cuaa1*), and `set speed` specifies the bit rate at which the connection should be established.

- The *set speed* line sets the speed of the link between the modem and the computer. Some systems have problems at 115,200 bps, but the next slower speed is 57,600 bps, which is too slow to use the full bandwidth when compression is enabled.

- The final line describes a *chat script*, a series of responses and commands to be exchanged with the modem. We'll look at an example of a chat script on page 456.

- The default entry alone does not supply enough information to create a link. In particular, it does not specify who to call. In addition to the default entry, you need an entry describing how to connect to a specific site. The connection for our example system gw (page 400) might look like:

```
ISP:
  set phone 1234567                                    phone number to call
  set login "TIMEOUT 5 login:-\\r-login: ppp word: qqq"   how to log in
  set timeout 120                                      wait up to 120 seconds for connect
  set ifaddr 139.130.136.133  139.130.136.129
  add default HISADDR
```

The second line, set login, includes another chat script. You'll need to change this one. Specifically, this example describes the following exchange of text (text from the remote machine is in constant width, and text sent by the local machine is in **constant bold**):

```
login: ppp
Password: qqq          (doesn't echo)
```

Sometimes the login script goes further, and requires you to start *ppp* as well. Here's an alternative that does that:

```
set login "TIMEOUT 5 login:-\\r-login: foo word: bar BLAZENET> p\\r"
```

In this version, after logging in, your system waits for the prompt BLAZENET> and then sends the sequence p followed by a carriage return to start the *ppp* program.

The line set ifaddr specifies that the PPP interface on the local machine should have the IP address 139.130.136.133 (the first address specified), and the remote machine will answer to the address 139.130.136.129 (the second address). You'll notice that this corresponds almost exactly to the first line of Figure 25-1 on page 444. You use this kind of specification when you have static addressing. We'll look at dynamic addressing below.

Finally, the last line tells *ppp* to set a default route on this interface when the line comes up. HISADDR is a keyword specifying the other end of the link.

Negotiation

As we saw on page 441, you need to decide who starts negotiation. By default, User PPP starts negotiation. If the other end needs to start negotiation, add the following line to your */etc/ppp/ppp.conf*:

```
set openmode passive
```

User PPP uses four keywords to specify how to negotiate:

- To *enable* a feature means: "request this feature".

- To *disable* a feature means: "do not request this feature".

- To *accept* a feature means: "if the other side requests this feature, accept it".

- To *deny* a feature means: "if the other side requests this feature, refuse it".

We'll see examples of this in the following sections.

Requesting LQR

By default, User PPP disables LQR, since it has been found to cause problems under certain circumstances, but it accepts it. If you want to enable it, include the following line in your dial entry:

```
enable lqr
```

Authentication

The configuration file syntax is the same for *PAP* and *CHAP*. Normally, your ISP assigns you both system name and authorization key. Assuming your system name is *BigBird*, and your key is *X4dWg9327*, you would include the following lines in your configuration entry:

```
set authname BigBird
set authkey  X4dWg9327
```

User PPP accepts requests for PAP and CHAP authentication automatically, so this is all you need to do unless you intend to authenticate the other end, which is not normal with ISPs.

/etc/ppp/ppp.secret

The PPP system name and authentication key for PAP or CHAP are important data. Anybody who has this information can connect to your ISP and use the service at your expense. Of course, you should set the permissions of your */etc/ppp/ppp.conf* to -r-------- and the owner to root, but it's easy and costly to make a mistake when changing the configuration. There is an alternative: store the keys in the file */etc/ppp/ppp.secret*. Here's a sample:

```
# Sysname  Secret Key Peer's IP address
oscar      OurSecretKey   192.244.184.34/24
BigBird       X4dWg9327 192.244.184.33/32
gw         localPasswdForControl
```

There are a few things to note here:

- As usual, lines starting with # are comments.

- The other lines contain three values: the system name, the authentication key, and possibly an IP address.

- The last line is a password for connecting to the *ppp* process locally: you can connect to the process by starting:

  ```
  # telnet localhost 3000
  ```

  The local password entry matches the host name. See the man page *ppp(8)* for further details.

We'll look at the IP address in the next section.

Dynamic IP configuration

If you have to accept dynamic IP addresses, User PPP can help. In fact, it provides fine control over which addresses you accept and which you do not. To allow negotiation of IP addresses, you specify how many bits of the IP addresses at each end are of interest to you. In the example above, we specified them exactly (static addresses):

```
set ifaddr 139.130.136.133  139.130.136.129
```

If you have to accept dynamic addressing, you can normally maintain some control over the addressing (in order to ensure that the addresses assigned don't conflict with other network connections, for example). The addresses which are assigned to you when the link comes up are almost invariably part of a single subnet. You can specify that subnet and allow negotiation of the host part of the address. For example, you may say "I don't care what address I get, as long as the first three bytes are 139.130.136, and the address at the other end starts with 139". You can do this by specifying the number of bits that interest you after the address:

```
set ifaddr 139.130.136.133/24  139.130.136.129/8
```

This says that you would prefer the addresses you state, but that you require the first 24 bits of the local interface address and the first eight bits of the remote interface address to be as stated.

If you really don't care which address you get, you can specify this fact by specifying local IP address as 0:

```
set ifaddr 0 0
```

If you do this, you can't use the -auto modes, since you need to send a packet to the interface in order to trigger dialling. Use one of the previous methods in this situation.

Running User PPP

After setting up your PPP configuration, run it like this:

```
$ ppp
User Process PPP. Written by Toshiharu OHNO.
Using interface: tun0
Interactive mode
Warning: No password entry for this host in ppp.secret
Warning: Manipulation is allowed by anyone
ppp ON freebie> dial ISP                    this is the name of the entry in ppp.conf
Dial attempt 1 of 1
Phone: 1234567                              the phone number
dial OK!                                    modem connection established
login OK!                                   authentication complete
ppp ON freebie> Packet mode.                PPP is running
ppp ON freebie>
PPP ON freebie>                             and the network connection is complete
```

You'll notice that the prompt (ppp) changes to upper case (PPP) when the connection is up and running. At the same time, *ppp* writes some messages to the system log:

```
Sep  2 15:12:38 freebie ppp[23679]: Phase: Using interface: tun0
Sep  2 15:12:38 freebie ppp[23679]: Phase: PPP Started.
Sep  2 15:12:47 freebie ppp[23679]: Phase: Phone: 1234567
Sep  2 15:13:08 freebie ppp[23679]: Phase: *Connected!
Sep  2 15:13:11 freebie ppp[23679]: Phase: NewPhase: Authenticate
Sep  2 15:13:11 freebie ppp[23679]: Phase:  his = c223, mine = 0
Sep  2 15:13:11 freebie ppp[23679]: Phase:  Valsize = 16, Name = way3.Adelaide
Sep  2 15:13:11 freebie ppp[23679]: Phase: NewPhase: Network
Sep  2 15:13:11 freebie ppp[23679]: Phase: Unknown protocol 0x8207
Sep  2 15:13:11 freebie ppp[23679]: Link:  myaddr = 139.130.136.133  hisaddr = 139.1
30.136.129
Sep  2 15:13:11 freebie ppp[23679]: Link: OsLinkup: 139.130.136.129
Sep  2 15:14:11 freebie ppp[23679]: Phase: HDLC errors -> FCS: 0 ADDR: 0 COMD: 0 PRO
TO: 1
```

You'll notice a couple of messages there which look like errors. In fact, they're not: Unknown protocol 0x8207 means that the other end requested a protocol which *ppp* doesn't know (and, in fact, is not in the RFCs. This is a real example, and the protocol is in fact Novell's IPX). The other message is HDLC errors -> FCS: 0 ADDR: 0 COMD: 0 PROTO: 1. In fact, this relates to the same "problem".

How long do we stay connected?

Now our PPP connection is up and running. How do we stop it again? There are two possibilities:

- To stop the connection, but to leave the *ppp* process active, enter close:

```
PPP ON freebie> close
ppp ON freebie>
```

- To stop the connection and the *ppp* process, enter q or quit:

```
PPP ON freebie> q
#
```

There are a couple of problems with this method: first, a connection to an ISP usually costs money in proportion to the time you are connected, so you don't want to stay connected longer than necessary. On the other hand, you don't want the connection to drop while you're using it. User PPP approaches these problems with a compromise: when the line has been idle for a certain time (in other words, when no data has gone in either direction during this time), it disconnects. This time is called the *idle timeout*, and by default it is set to 180 seconds. You can set it explicitly:

```
set timeout 300
```

This sets the idle timeout to 300 seconds (5 minutes).

Automating the process

Finally, setting up the connection this way takes a lot of time. You can automate it in a number of ways:

- If you have a permanent connection, you can tell User PPP to stay up all the time. Use the -ddial modifier:

  ```
  $ ppp -ddial ISP
  ```

  This version dials immediately and keeps the connection up regardless of whether traffic is passing or not.

- If you want to be able to connect to the net automatically whenever you have something to say, use the -auto modifer:

  ```
  $ ppp -auto ISP
  ```

  In this case, User PPP does not dial immediately. As soon as you attempt to send data to the net, however, it dials automatically. When the line has been idle for the idle timeout period, it disconnects again and wait for more data before dialling. This only makes sense for static addresses or when you know that no IP connections remain alive after the line disconnects.

- Finally, you can just write

  ```
  $ ppp -background ISP
  ```

  The -background option tells User PPP to dial immediately and stay in the background. After the idle timeout period, the User PPP process disconnects and exits. If you want to connect again, you must restart the process.

Configuration summary

To summarize the examples above: let's assume that the reference network on page 400 uses *CHAP* authentication, and we have to initiate. The */etc/ppp/ppp.conf* for would look like:

```
default:
  set device /dev/cuaa1              device to use
  set speed 115200                   connect at 115,200 bps
  set dial "ABORT BUSY ABORT NO\\sCARRIER TIMEOUT 5 \"\" AT \
          OK-AT-OK ATE1Q0 OK \\dATDT\\T TIMEOUT 40 CONNECT"
ISP:
  set phone 1234567                  phone number to call
  set login "TIMEOUT 5 login:-\\r-login: ppp word: qqq"   how to log in
  set timeout 120                    disconnect after 120 seconds idle time
  set ifaddr 139.130.136.133   139.130.136.129
  add default HISADDR
  accept chap
  deny pap
  disable chap
  disable pap
  set authname BigBird
  set authkey  X4dWg9327
```

If you have to use dynamic addressing, the only thing that changes is the set ifaddr line, so your */etc/ppp/ppp.conf* looks like:

```
default:
  set device /dev/cuaa1              device to use
  set speed 115200                   connect at 115,200 bps
  set dial "ABORT BUSY ABORT NO\\sCARRIER TIMEOUT 5 \"\" AT \
           OK-AT-OK ATE1Q0 OK \\dATDT\\T TIMEOUT 40 CONNECT"
ISP:
  set phone 1234567                  phone number to call
  set login "TIMEOUT 5 login:-\\r-login: ppp word: qqq"   how to log in
  set timeout 120                    disconnect after 120 seconds idle time
  set ifaddr 0 0
  add default HISADDR                negotiate the addresses
  accept chap
  deny pap
  disable chap
  disable pap
  set authname BigBird
  set authkey  X4dWg9327
```

Setting up Kernel PPP

It makes more sense to run PPP in the kernel than in user space, since it's more efficient and theoretically less prone to error. Until recently the implementation had many fewer features than User PPP, so it is not used as much.

The configuration files for Kernel PPP are in the same directory as the User PPP configuration files. You can also set up your own *˜/.ppprc* file, though I don't recommend this: PPP is a system function and should not be manipulated at the user level.

Kernel PPP uses a dæmon called *pppd* to monitor the line when it is active. Kernel PPP interface names start with *ppp* followed by a number. You need one for each concurrent link. You can check for them with *ifconfig -a*:

```
# ifconfig -a                        show the configuration of all interfaces
ze0: flags=8843<UP,BROADCAST,RUNNING,SIMPLEX,MULTICAST> mtu 1500
        inet 223.147.37.1 netmask 0xffffff00 broadcast 223.147.37.255
        ether 00:00:c0:44:a5:68
lp0: flags=8810<POINTOPOINT,SIMPLEX,MULTICAST> mtu 1500
tun0: flags=8051<UP,POINTOPOINT,RUNNING,MULTICAST> mtu 1500
        inet 111.111.111.111 --> 112.222.222.222 netmask 0xff000000
      inet 139.130.136.133 --> 139.130.136.129 netmask 0xffffffff
sl0: flags=c010<POINTOPOINT,LINK2,MULTICAST> mtu 552
ppp0: flags=8010<POINTOPOINT,MULTICAST> mtu 1500
ppp1: flags=8010<POINTOPOINT,MULTICAST> mtu 1500
lo0: flags=8008<LOOPBACK,MULTICAST> mtu 16384
        inet 127.0.0.1 netmask 0xff000000
```

This system has two *ppp* interfaces, called *ppp0* and *ppp1*, so it is capable of maintaining two PPP connections at the same time.

To modify the number of interfaces, change the value in the kernel configuration file and then rebuild the kernel. For example, for four PPP interfaces you need to have the following line in the kernel configuration file:

```
pseudo-device   ppp      4
options PPP_BSDCOMP               #PPP BSD-compress support
options PPP_DEFLATE              #PPP zlib/deflate/gzip support
```

In FreeBSD version 3.0 and later, specify the options `PPP_BSDCOMP` and `PPP_DEFLATE` to enable two kinds of compression. You'll also need to specify the corresponding option in Kernel PPP's configuration file. These options are not available in FreeBSD version 2.

When Kernel PPP starts, it reads its configuration from the file */etc/ppp/options*. Here is a typical example:

```
# Options file for PPPD
defaultroute                     set the default route here when the line comes up
crtscts                          use hardware flow control
modem                            use modem control lines
deflate 12,12                    use deflate compression
user FREEBIE                     our name (index in password file)
lock                             create a UUCP lock file
```

This is quite a short file, but it's full of interesting stuff:

- The `defaultroute` line tells the Kernel PPP to place a default route to the destination IP after it establishes a connection.

- The `crtscts` line tells it to use hardware flow control (necessary to prevent loss of characters). You could also specify `xonxoff`, which uses software flow control, but hardware flow control is preferable.

- The `modem` line says to monitor the modem *DCD* (Carrier detect) line. If the connection is lost without proper negotiation, the only way that Kernel PPP can know about it is because of the drop in *DCD*.

- The line *deflate* tells Kernel PPP to request *deflate* compression, which can increase the effective bandwidth. This only works if your kernel has been built with the `PPP_DEFLATE` option—see above.

- The `user` line tells Kernel PPP the user ID to use. If you don't specify this, it takes the system's name.

- `lock` tells Kernel PPP to create a UUCP-style lock on the serial line. This prevents other programs, such as *getty*, from trying to open the line while it is running PPP.

Dialling

Kernel PPP does not perform dialling, so you need to start a program which does the dialling. In the following example, we use *chat*, a program derived from UUCP which is intended exactly for this purpose. Some people use *kermit*, which is in fact a complete communications program for a PC protocol, to perform this function, but this requires manual intervention. *chat* does the whole job for you.

Chat scripts

chat uses a *chat script* to define the functions to perform when establishing a connection. See the man page *chat(8)* for further details. The chat script consists primarily of alternate *expect strings*, which *chat* waits to receive, followed by *send* strings, which *chat* sends when it receives the *expect* string.

In addition to these strings, the chat script can contain other commands. To confuse things, they are frequently written on a single line, though this is not necessary: *chat* does not pay any attention to line breaks. Our chat script, which we store in */etc/ppp/dial.chat*, looks more intelligible written in the following manner:

```
# Abort the chat script if the modem replies BUSY or NO CARRIER
ABORT BUSY
ABORT 'NO CARRIER'
# Wait up to 5 seconds for the reply to each of these
TIMEOUT 5
'' ATZ
OK ATDT1234567
# Wait 40 seconds for connection
TIMEOUT 40
CONNECT
TIMEOUT 5
gin:-\\r-gin: username
sword: password
```

This script first tells *chat* to abort dial-up on a BUSY or NO CARRIER response from the modem. The next line waits for nothing (' ') and resets the modem with the command ATZ. The following line waits for the modem to reply with OK, and dials the ISP.

Call setup can take a while, almost always more than five seconds for real (analogue) modems, so we need to extend the timeout, in this case to 40 seconds. During this time we must get the reply CONNECT from the modem.

Next, we reset the timeout to five seconds and perform *login* authentication. It's important to reset the timeout, because otherwise a login failure takes 40 seconds to complete. Replace *username* and *password* with your real user name and password. The sequence gin:-\\r-gin: is a shorthand for "expect gin:. If you don't get it, send \\r and expect gin:". The string gin: is, of course, the end of the login: prompt.

Who throws the first stone?

On page 441 we saw how to specify whether we should start negotiating or whether we should wait for the other end to start. By default, Kernel PPP starts negotiation. If you want the other end to start, add the keyword passive in your */etc/ppp/options* file.

Authentication

The previous example assumed *login* authentication. As we have seen, more and more ISPs are expecting *CHAP* or *PAP* authentication. To do this, create a file */etc/ppp/chap-secrets* for *CHAP*, or */etc/ppp/pap-secrets* for *PAP*. The format of either file is:

username systemname password

To match any system name, set *systemname* to *. For example, to authenticate the *BigBird* we saw on page 450, we would enter the following in the file:

```
BigBird * X4dWg9327
```

In addition, you should add a `domain` line to specify your domain for authentication purposes:

```
domain example.org
```

Dynamic IP configuration

By default, Kernel PPP performs dynamic address negotiation, so you don't need to do anything special for dynamic IP. If you have static addresses, add the following line to */etc/ppp/conf*:

```
139.130.136.133:139.130.136.129
```

These are the addresses which you would use on machine `gw.example.org` to set up the PPP link in the middle of Figure 21-7 on page 400. The first address is the local end of the link (the address of the *pppn* device), and the second is the address of the remote machine (`free-gw.example.net`).

Setting the default route

By default, kernel PPP assigns a default route when it brings up a line. If you don't want this to happen, specify the `nodefaultroute` option.

Running Kernel PPP

To run *pppd*, enter:

```
# pppd /dev/cuaa1 115200 connect 'chat -f /etc/ppp/dial.chat' user username
```

This starts Kernel PPP on the serial line */dev/cuaa1* at 115,200 bps. The option `connect` tells Kernel PPP that the following argument is the name of a *program* to execute: it runs *chat* with the options `-f /etc/ppp/dial.chat`, which tells *chat* the name of the chat file. Finally, `username` tells Kernel PPP the user name to use for authentication.

After you run *pppd* with these arguments, the modem starts dialling and then negotiates a connection with your provider, which should complete within 30 seconds. During negotiation, you can observe progress with the *ifconfig* command:

```
$ ifconfig ppp0
ppp0: flags=8010<POINTOPOINT,MULTICAST> mtu 1500
        at this point, the interface has not yet started
$ ifconfig ppp0
ppp0: flags=8810<POINTOPOINT,RUNNING,MULTICAST> mtu 1500
        now the interface has been started
$ ifconfig ppp0
ppp0: flags=8811<UP,POINTOPOINT,RUNNING,MULTICAST> mtu 150
```

457

```
        inet 139.130.136.133 --> 139.130.136.129 netmask 0xffffffff
```
now the connection has been established

Automating the process

You can automate connection setup and disconnection in a number of ways:

- If you have a permanent connection, you can tell Kernel PPP to stay up all the time. Add the following line to */etc/ppp/options*:

  ```
  persist
  ```

  If this option is set, Kernel PPP dials immediately and keeps the connection up regardless of whether traffic is passing or not.

- If you want to be able to connect to the net automatically whenever you have something to say, use the demand option:

  ```
  demand
  ```

  In this case, Kernel PPP does not dial immediately. As soon as you attempt to send data to the net, however, it dials automatically. When the line has been idle for the idle timeout period, it disconnects again and waits for more data before dialling.

- Finally, you can start Kernel PPP without either of these options. In this case, you are connected immediately. After the idle timeout period, Kernel PPP disconnects and exits. If you want to connect again, you must restart the process.

Timeout parameters

A number of options specify when Kernel PPP should dial and disconnect:

- The idle parameter tells Kernel PPP to disconnect if the line has been idle for the specified number of seconds, and if persist (see above) has not been specified. For example, to disconnect after five minutes, you could add the following line to the *//etc/ppp/options* file:

  ```
  idle 300
  ```

- The active-filter parameter may soon be implemented in FreeBSD. It specifies which packets are counted when determining whether the line is idle.

- The holdoff parameter tells Kernel PPP how long to wait before redialling when the line has been disconnected for reasons other than being idle. If the line is disconnected because it was idle, and you have specified demand, it dials as soon as the next valid packet is received.

Configuration summary

To summarize the examples above, we'll show the Kernel PPP versions of the examples on page 453. As before, we assume that the reference network on page 400 uses *CHAP* authentication, and we have to initiate. The */etc/ppp/options* looks like:

```
# Options file for PPPD
crtscts                                   use hardware flow control
modem                                     use modem control lines
domain example.org                        specify your domain name
persist                                   stay up all the time
user FREEBIE                              name to present to ISP
139.130.136.133:139.130.136.129           specify IP addresses of link
idle 120                                  disconnect after two minutes idle time
```

/etc/ppp/dial.chat is unchanged from the example on page 456:

```
# Abort the chat script if the modem replies BUSY or NO CARRIER
ABORT BUSY
ABORT 'NO CARRIER'
# Wait up to 5 seconds for the reply to each of these
TIMEOUT 5
'' ATZ
OK ATDT1234567
# Wait 40 seconds for connection
TIMEOUT 40
CONNECT
TIMEOUT 5
gin:-\\r-gin: username
sword: password
```

/etc/ppp/chap-secrets contains:

```
BigBird * X4dWg9327
```

With Kernel PPP, there's no need to disable *PAP*: that happens automatically if it can't find an authentication for *BigBird* in */etc/pap-secrets*.

The change for dynamic addressing is even simpler: remove the line with the IP addresses from the */etc/ppp/options* file:

```
# Options file for PPPD
crtscts                    use hardware flow control
modem                      use modem control lines
domain example.org         specify your domain name
persist                    stay up all the time
user FREEBIE               name to present to ISP
defaultroute               make this the default route
idle 120                   disconnect after two minutes idle time
```

Nowadays, login authentication is becoming less and less common. If you don't need it, remove the last few lines from */etc/ppp/dial.chat*:

```
# Abort the chat script if the modem replies BUSY or NO CARRIER
ABORT BUSY
ABORT 'NO CARRIER'
# Wait up to 5 seconds for the reply to each of these
TIMEOUT 5
'' ATZ
OK ATDT1234567
# Wait 40 seconds for connection
TIMEOUT 40
CONNECT
```

Dialin PPP

So far, we've looked at how to use PPP to dial in to another system. It's also possible to use both User and Kernel PPP to service dial-ins. The manner in which this is done is currently undergoing revision, so there's no point in describing the method here. See the online handbook for current details.

26

UUCP and SLIP

Before the advent of *PPP*, two other protocols were available for connection to an Internet host: *UUCP* and *SLIP*. They're both poor seconds to *PPP*, but they each have a few advantages. In this chapter, we'll look at how to use these advantages. We'll look at UUCP first, and on page 468 we'll look at SLIP. First, however, we'll consider authentication, which is the same for both protocols.

Login authentication

Authentication is the process of convincing the system into which you are dialling that you are authorized to use the system. It usually also sets default values for the session. As we have seen in Chapter 25, *Configuring PPP*, PPP provides two special kinds of authorization, *PAP* and *CHAP*.

UUCP and SLIP do not support PPP's authentication scheme. You have to log in as a UNIX user. The exact manner differs slightly between UUCP and SLIP:

- UUCP is considered a system function, and it has a special user name uucp. Nevertheless, it's customary to have alias names for each system, since the name determines where the data is stored, and what access rights the system has. For example, we might create a user Ufreebie for system freebie, with the same user number as uucp.

- SLIP users frequently log in as a user rather than a system. There are two common possibilities:

  - Log in as yourself, get a shell, and start *sliplogin*.

  - Use the UUCP approach and create a second user ID with the same user number, and set the shell to *sliplogin*.

  In the SLIP examples, we'll use the second approach.

Adding the users

Let's start with the user norm from the example of */etc/master.passwd* on page 164. We'll use *vipw* to add a second user Snorm for running SLIP, and a second user Ufreebie for UUCP:

```
uucp:*:66:66::0:0:UUCP pseudo-user:/var/spool/uucppublic:/usr/libexec/uucp/uucico
Ufreebie:*:66:66::0:0:UUCP from freebie:/var/spool/uucppublic:/usr/libexec/uucp/uucico
norm::1021:1001::0:0:Norm, Beach of Passionate Love:/home/norm:/bin/bash
Snorm::1021:1001::0:0:Norm, Beach of Passionate Love:/home/norm:/usr/sbin/sliplogin
```

Don't forget to set passwords for the new users when you're finished. For example:

```
# passwd Ufreebie
Changing local password for Ufreebie.
New password:                     doesn't echo
Retype new password:              still doesn't echo
passwd: rebuilding the database...
passwd: done
```

To check them, use *su*. Make sure you're *not* root at the time, so you have to enter a password. For UUCP, you should see:

```
$ su Ufreebie
Password:                         doesn't echo
Shere=uucphost                    uucico prompt
```

The message comes from *uucico*, which is looking for a partner. You can't stop the *uucico*. After about a minute, it will get bored and go away.

For SLIP, you should see *one* of the following error messages:

```
# su Snorm
Password:
su[1871]: /etc/sliphome/slip.hosts: No such file or directory
su[1871]: SLIP access denied for grog
```

You get the first error message if you have not yet created the file */etc/sliphome/slip.hosts*, which is normal at this point. If you have already created it, you get the second error message. This message specifies user grog, not Snorm, since *su* doesn't change the user ID.

UUCP

Before the days of the Internet, UNIX machines communicated with the *UUCP* protocol, which stands for *UNIX to UNIX copy*. It's a much more primitive protocol than IP, and has been largely superseded. In particular, it didn't perform routing, so you had to specify your own route, called a *bang path*. It's only been relatively recently that *USENET*, the network news network, has abandoned bang paths, and occasionally you'll see things like this old news posting:

```
From adagio!unido!Germany.EU.net!mcsun!uunet!news.uiowa.edu!ns-mx!pyrite.cs.uiowa.edu
Wed Jul 29 17:01:27 MST 1992
Article: 26600 of alt.folklore.computers
Path: adagio!unido!Germany.EU.net!mcsun!uunet!news.uiowa.edu!ns-mx!pyrite.cs.uiowa.edu
From: jones@pyrite.cs.uiowa.edu (Douglas W. Jones,201H MLH,3193350740,3193382879)
Newsgroups: comp.arch,alt.folklore.computers,comp.benchmarks
Subject: Re: dinosaur horsepower
Message-ID: <13307@ns-mx.uiowa.edu>
Date: 28 Jul 92 14:48:02 GMT
References: <Bs3oGt.6vp@helios.physics.utoronto.ca>
Sender: news@ns-mx.uiowa.edu
Followup-To: comp.arch
Lines: 32
Xref: adagio alt.folklore.computers:26600 comp.benchmarks:135

>From article <Bs3oGt.6vp@helios.physics.utoronto.ca>,
by sysmark@helios.physics.utoronto.ca (Mark Bartelt):
>
> But, in general, I think it would be fun to see MIPS/MFlops (KIPS/KFlops?
> IPS/Flops?) values (at least, moderately authoritative ballpark estimates)
> for some of the machines we grew up with.

The IBM 701, in 1953, had a fundamental machine cycle time of 12us.  A
memory to accumulator add took 5 cycles (60us) and a multiply took 38
cycles.  IBM claimed an average instruction execution rate of 14,000
instructions per second.  This machine had a 36 bit word.
...etc
```

The first line of this article shows the exact route taken for this message, starting with the destination (`adagio`) and working back to the source system (`pyrite.cs.uiowa.edu`). Each system name is separated by an exclamation mark (`!`), frequently called a *bang*.

Bang paths are now completely obsolete, but it's nice to understand how they work. In particular, *sendmail* may still generate them.

Why use UUCP at all? There are still a couple of reasons:

- It's still used by a number of people who have been using the Internet since the days before the World Wide Web. They have systems which can't run IP, and they're happy with the level of service they get from UUCP.

- UUCP can be faster than *ftp*. In particular, Taylor UUCP, the one we use, can transfer data in both directions at the same time, which is very useful for mail. If you're using an expensive serial link, you might find it preferable to maximize your throughput with UUCP.

Note that in each of these cases, we don't have to worry about routing UUCP. It's always a point to point link.

How UUCP works

UUCP is a *store and forward* network. Viewed from the point of a machine uucphost which communicates with the system freebie,[1] it collects data to be sent to *freebie* in a directory */var/spool/uucp/freebie*. The directory */var/spool/uucp/freebie* contains three subdirectories:

---

1. UUCP systems don't have domain names. In this discussion, we're thinking of system freebie in the reference network, but it identifies itself as freebie, not freebie.example.net.

- */var/spool/uucp/freebie/C.* contains files queued for sending.

- */var/spool/uucp/freebie/D.* contains data files which have arrived from the remote system and are awaiting processing.

- */var/spool/uucp/freebie/X.* contains command files to be executed by UUCP.

Periodically, or when `uucphost` discovers it is necessary, it starts the *uucico* (*UNIX to UNIX Copy In, Copy Out*) program to establish a connection with `freebie`, send the contents of a */var/spool/uucp/freebie*, and get any data that `freebie` has queued to send to it. `freebie` performs the same functions. It doesn't matter to the protocol which end initiates the communication: all data is transferred.

When the data arrives at the machine for which it is destined, it is first queued in the *D.* directory. At the same time, a corresponding command file is stored in the *X.* directory. After the transfer is complete, or when the directory becomes too full, *uucico* starts *uuxqt* to execute the commands in the *X.* directory. Typically, the commands send mail or move the data to where it belongs.

UUCP configuration allows systems to restrict the directories into which and from which the remote system may transfer data. We'll see how this is done in the description of the *sys* file below.

Setting up UUCP

Those of us who were around in the days before the world discovered the Internet remember with horror the trouble it took to set up a UUCP mail link. A lot of that changed when Ian Taylor released his version of UUCP, which rapidly became the version of choice.

Taylor UUCP retains a lot of compatibility with older versions of UUCP (Version 2 and *HoneyDanBer*, which System V calls *BNU* (*Basic Networking Utilities*). Unless you know these versions, there is no reason to use the compatibility. In the rest of this chapter we'll use the native Taylor UUCP configuration.

UUCP configuration files

You don't need to do anything special to install *UUCP*: it's installed with the base system. It uses a number of configuration files, which it stores in the directory */etc/uucp*. The important ones are:

- */etc/uucp/dial* describes how to dial.

- */etc/uucp/port* describes the serial ports you use for UUCP.

- */etc/uucp/sys* describes the systems to which you want to connect.

You'll find a number of sample files in */etc/uucp*.

The dial file

/etc/uucp/dial contains information on how to dial, including the chat scripts for setting up the communication, but not the user name and password for individual sites. Normally you can use the file */etc/uucp/dial.sample* unchanged.

The port file

/etc/uucp/port describes the serial ports you use for UUCP. Again, there is a sample file, but may want to change the defaults. Here's an excerpt from the file:

```
type modem

# This is the name of the port.  This name may be used in the sys file
# to select the port, or the sys file may just specify a baud rate in
# which case the first matching unlocked port will be used.
port port1                           change to sio1

# This is the device name to open to dial out.
device /dev/ttyd0                    change to /dev/cuaa1

# This is the dialer to use, as described in the dialer file.
dialer hayes

# This is the baud rate to dial out at.
speed 2400                           change to 57600

# Here is a second port.  This is like the first, except that it uses
# a different device.  It also permits a range of speeds, which is
# mainly useful if the system specifies a particular baud rate.
port port2
device /dev/ttyd1
dialer hayes
speed-range 2400 9600
```

The `port` starts a port definition and assigns a name to it. Everything down to the next `port` line defines properties of the port. You'll note in this case that the bit rate of the port is set to 2400, something that you'll probably want to raise to 57,600 or even 115,200 bps. In addition, FreeBSD dialout ports are called */dev/cuaa<number>*, so you should change that as well. In this book, we're assuming the serial port on *sio1*, so we should use */dev/cuaa1*. Without the comments, the resultant definition for `port1` should look something like:

```
port sio1
device /dev/cuaa1
dialer hayes
speed 57600
```

The sys file

Most of your configuration will be in the file */etc/uucp/sys*. This is where you store the information you need to login to the remote system. On installation, you will have two files in */etc/uucp*: *sys1.sample* and *sys2.sample*. We'll use a simplified version of *sys1.sample* which doesn't require any further configuration files.

/etc/uucp/sys contains a global portion containing definitions which relate to all systems to be called, followed by information for the individual systems. In our example, there is no global

part. The beginning of the individual parts is signified by the keyword `system`:

```
# The name of the remote system that we call.
system uunet

# The login name and password to use
call-login Ufreebie
call-password foobar

# We can send anything at any time.
time any

# The phone number to call.
phone 7389449

# uunet tends to be slow, so we increase the timeout
chat-timeout 120

# The port we use to dial out.
port sio1

# what we may transfer
# We can send files from /usr/src and /var/spool/uucp
local-send /usr/src   /var/spool/uucp/uucppublic
# And we can receive into /var/spool/uucp/uucppublic
local-receive /var/spool/uucp/uucppublic

# Remote users may send files to our /var/spool/uucp
remote-send /var/spool/uucp
# And they can receive files from /var/spool/uucp and /usr/src
remote-receive /var/spool/uucp /usr/src
```

This information states that you will dial the system `uunet` whenever you want to. When you connect, you will log in as user `Ufreebie` with the password `foobar`. The sample files store the passwords in a different file, */etc/uucp/call*, but that's overkill if you're just calling one or two systems.

Testing the connection

To test whether things work, it's a good idea to send some data to it and see what happens. The program to copy data to the remote system is called *uucp*. It's supposed to look like *cp*, but the syntax for the remote host name is unfortunate: it uses the bang paths we saw at the beginning of the chapter. To send a file */var/spool/uucppublic/foo* to system *uucphost*, you specify the file name as `uucphost!/var/spool/uucppublic/foo`. Unfortunately, the exclamation mark (`!`) has since taken on a special significance when used in a shell, so we have to precede it with an escape character (`\`):

```
$ uucp -r foo uucphost\!/var/spool/uucp/uucppublic/foo
```

The `-r` option tells *uucp* to queue the file and not to start a session immediately.

Next, run the script *Uutry*. *Uutry* is a standard script on System V machines, but for some reason it's not supplied with Taylor UUCP. You'll find a copy on */book/scripts/Uutry*. *Uutry* starts *uucico* and displays the log files as they are written. We might see something like this:

```
# Uutry uucphost
uucico uucphost - (1997-09-25 15:46:33.90 27571) DEBUG: fcsend: Writing "atz\r" sleep
uucico uucphost - (1997-09-25 15:46:34.94 27571) DEBUG: icexpect: Looking for 2 "OK"
uucico uucphost - (1997-09-25 15:46:34.94 27571) DEBUG: icexpect: Got "atz\r\r\nOK" (found it)
uucico uucphost - (1997-09-25 15:46:34.94 27571) DEBUG: fcsend: Writing "atdt" \T "83888725\r"
uucico uucphost - (1997-09-25 15:46:34.94 27571) DEBUG: icexpect: Looking for 7 "CONNECT"
uucico uucphost - (1997-09-25 15:46:34.94 27571) DEBUG: icexpect: Got "\r\natdt83888725\r\r\nCONNE
CT" (found it)
uucico uucphost - (1997-09-25 15:46:54.54 27571) DEBUG: fcsend: Writing "\r"
uucico uucphost - (1997-09-25 15:46:54.54 27571) DEBUG: icexpect: Looking for 5 "ogin:"
uucico uucphost - (1997-09-25 15:46:54.54 27571) DEBUG: icexpect: Got " 57600\r\nLEMIS Modem (3840
0 bps) login:" (found it)
uucico uucphost - (1997-09-25 15:46:59.65 27571) DEBUG: fcsend: Writing login "Ufreebie\r"
uucico uucphost - (1997-09-25 15:46:59.65 27571) DEBUG: icexpect: Looking for 5 "word:"
uucico uucphost - (1997-09-25 15:46:59.65 27571) DEBUG: icexpect: Got " UfreebPassword:" (found it)
uucico uucphost - (1997-09-25 15:46:59.85 27571) DEBUG: fcsend: Writing password "freedom!\r"
uucico uucphost - (1997-09-25 15:46:59.85 27571) DEBUG: zget_uucp_cmd: Got "\r\nLast login: Thu Se
p 25 15:28:18 on ttyd1\r\nCopyright (c) 19"
uucico uucphost - (1997-09-25 15:47:00.31 27571) Login successful
```

This log shows the chat script. You'll notice the echo in the receive strings: it sees what it has just written out (the user name, for example). Then *login* produces the message of the day (most of which has been omitted) and starts *uucico*. The two *uucico*s negotiate a protocol, and come out with protocol G.

> We're not going to discuss protocols. They're described in the documentation for *UUCP*, but for our purposes it can be simplified to one line: "Use the G protocol".

```
uucico uucphost - (1997-09-25 15:47:00.31 27571) DEBUG: fsend_uucp_cmd: Sending "Sfreebie -R -N07"
uucico uucphost - (1997-09-25 15:47:00.31 27571) DEBUG: zget_uucp_cmd: Got "\020ROKN07\000"
uucico uucphost - (1997-09-25 15:47:00.70 27571) DEBUG: zget_uucp_cmd: Got "\020PiagGjfvy\000"
uucico uucphost - (1997-09-25 15:47:00.70 27571) DEBUG: fsend_uucp_cmd: Sending "UG"
uucico uucphost - (1997-09-25 15:47:00.70 27571) DEBUG: fgsend_control: Sending control INITA 7
uucico uucphost - (1997-09-25 15:47:00.70 27571) DEBUG: fgwait_for_packet: Need 6 bytes
uucico uucphost - (1997-09-25 15:47:00.82 27571) DEBUG: fgprocess_data: Got control INITA 7
uucico uucphost - (1997-09-25 15:47:00.82 27571) DEBUG: fgsend_control: Sending control INITB 1
uucico uucphost - (1997-09-25 15:47:00.82 27571) DEBUG: fgwait_for_packet: Need 6 bytes
uucico uucphost - (1997-09-25 15:47:00.90 27571) DEBUG: fgprocess_data: Got control INITB 1
uucico uucphost - (1997-09-25 15:47:00.90 27571) DEBUG: fgsend_control: Sending control INITC 7
uucico uucphost - (1997-09-25 15:47:00.90 27571) DEBUG: fgwait_for_packet: Need 6 bytes
uucico uucphost - (1997-09-25 15:47:00.98 27571) DEBUG: fgprocess_data: Got control INITC 7
uucico uucphost - (1997-09-25 15:47:00.98 27571) Handshake successful (protocol 'G' sending packet
/window 64/7 receiving 64/7)
```

Here the two *uucico*s have agreed on using the G protocol. Next, our *uucico* starts sending the file */home/grog/foo*. It also logs each packet as it sends it:

```
uucico uucphost grog (1997-09-25 15:47:00.98 27571) DEBUG: fgsendcmd: Sending command "S /home/gro
g/foo /var/spool/uucp/uucppublic/foo grog -Cd D.0001 0600 "" 0x2be8"
uucico uucphost grog (1997-09-25 15:47:00.98 27571) DEBUG: fgsenddata: Sending packet 1 (64 bytes)
uucico uucphost grog (1997-09-25 15:47:00.98 27571) DEBUG: fgsenddata: Sending packet 2 (64 bytes)
uucico uucphost - (1997-09-25 15:47:00.98 27571) DEBUG: floop: Waiting for data
uucico uucphost - (1997-09-25 15:47:00.98 27571) DEBUG: fgwait_for_packet: Need 6 bytes
uucico uucphost - (1997-09-25 15:47:01.19 27571) DEBUG: fgprocess_data: Got control RR 1
uucico uucphost - (1997-09-25 15:47:01.19 27571) DEBUG: fgwait_for_packet: Need 6 bytes
uucico uucphost - (1997-09-25 15:47:01.20 27571) DEBUG: fgprocess_data: Got control RR 2
```

```
uucico uucphost - (1997-09-25 15:47:01.20 27571) DEBUG: fgwait_for_packet: Need 6 bytes
```

After many more such messages, the file has been transferred. *uucico* finds that it has nothing else to do. The *uucico* at the other end didn't have anything to transmit, so they stop.

```
uucico uucphost grog (1997-09-25 15:47:08.02 27571) DEBUG: fgot_data: Charging 669641 to S /home/g
rog/foo /var/spool/uucp/uucppublic/foo
uucico uucphost - (1997-09-25 15:47:08.16 27571) DEBUG: floop: No work for master
uucico uucphost - (1997-09-25 15:47:08.16 27571) DEBUG: fgsendcmd: Sending command "H"
uucico uucphost - (1997-09-25 15:47:08.16 27571) DEBUG: fgsenddata: Sending packet 4 (64 bytes)
uucico uucphost - (1997-09-25 15:47:08.16 27571) DEBUG: floop: Waiting for data
uucico uucphost - (1997-09-25 15:47:08.16 27571) DEBUG: fgwait_for_packet: Need 6 bytes
uucico uucphost - (1997-09-25 15:47:08.28 27571) DEBUG: fgprocess_data: Got control RR 4
uucico uucphost - (1997-09-25 15:47:08.28 27571) DEBUG: fgwait_for_packet: Need 49 bytes
uucico uucphost - (1997-09-25 15:47:08.30 27571) DEBUG: fgprocess_data: Got packet 3
uucico uucphost - (1997-09-25 15:47:08.30 27571) DEBUG: fgsend_control: Sending control RR 3
uucico uucphost - (1997-09-25 15:47:08.30 27571) DEBUG: ftadd_cmd: Got command "HY"
uucico uucphost - (1997-09-25 15:47:08.30 27571) DEBUG: fgsendcmd: Sending command "HY"
uucico uucphost - (1997-09-25 15:47:08.30 27571) DEBUG: fgsenddata: Sending packet 5 (64 bytes)
uucico uucphost - (1997-09-25 15:47:08.30 27571) DEBUG: fgsend_control: Sending control CLOSE 0
uucico uucphost - (1997-09-25 15:47:08.30 27571) DEBUG: fgsend_control: Sending control CLOSE 0
uucico uucphost - (1997-09-25 15:47:08.30 27571) Protocol 'G' packets: sent 181, resent 0, receive
d 3
uucico uucphost - (1997-09-25 15:47:08.30 27571) DEBUG: fsend_uucp_cmd: Sending "OOOOOO"
uucico uucphost - (1997-09-25 15:47:08.30 27571) DEBUG: fsend_uucp_cmd: Sending "OOOOOO"
uucico uucphost - (1997-09-25 15:47:08.30 27571) DEBUG: zget_uucp_cmd: Got "\020\002kl$!HY\000"
uucico uucphost - (1997-09-25 15:47:08.30 27571) DEBUG: zget_uucp_cmd: Got "\000\000\000\000\000\0
00\000\000\000\000\000\000\000\000\000\000\000\000\000\000\000\000\000\000\000\000
uucico uucphost - (1997-09-25 15:47:08.32 27571) DEBUG: zget_uucp_cmd: Got "\000\020\011\"*\010\01
1\020\011\"*\010\011\0200000000\000"
uucico uucphost - (1997-09-25 15:47:08.33 27571) Call complete (9 seconds 11240 bytes 1248 bps)
uucico uucphost - (1997-09-25 15:47:08.33 27571) DEBUG: fcsend: Writing sleep sleep "+++" sleep sl
eep "ATH\r"
```

The lines with the many \000\000\000\000s are, in fact, noise after the line hangs up.

Uutry does stop when the communication is finished; the last line is typical of the end of the communication. When you've seen enough, hit **Ctrl-C** to stop *Uutry*. This won't stop the transfer even if it is still running.

Once you get this far, your UUCP link is functional.

SLIP

As we saw in Chapter 25, *Configuring PPP*, SLIP is a poor choice if you can use PPP. Still, you may find a need to do so, so in this chapter we'll look at how to configure SLIP.

Setting up a SLIP connection involves the same kind of steps as in setting up a PPP connection. If you haven't read the description of how PPP setup works, you might like to read it now—see page 440. If you know all about SLIP, you can skip the following sections and go straight to the summary on page 473.

What we need to know

Most SLIP implementations can't handle dynamic IP addresses, so if you have a SLIP connection, you're likely to have a static address. This is the only configuration we will consider. We obviously need to know the addresses of each end of the link, and we also need a form of authentication.

You set the interface addresses with the *ifconfig* program. In our example, we'll assume we're setting up a connection from gw.example.org to free-gw.example.net.

Dialling out with SLIP

Use the *slattach* program to establish a connection with a SLIP server, *slattach* does only some of the things that the PPP programs do. In particular, it doesn't set up the interfaces, and it doesn't dial.

Setting the interface addresses

Set the interface address with *ifconfig*. On gw.example.org, you could enter:

```
# ifconfig sl0  139.130.136.133  139.130.136.129
```

The addresses are the addresses of gw.example.org and free-gw.example.net. We use the IP addresses and not the names because it's unlikely that your name dæmon will be able to resolve the names until the link is up. It doesn't matter whether you configure the interface before or after dialling, but it won't work until you have done so. In practice, it's easiest to have the dial script perform this function, as we'll see below.

How to dial

Like Kernel PPP, *slattach* doesn't dial, but it is able to invoke a dialer. We'll use *chat* again in the following example. Dialling for a SLIP link is essentially the same as for a PPP link. We'll use the same chat script we used for Kernel PPP. See page 456 for more details about chat scripts.

```
# Abort the chat script if the modem replies BUSY or NO CARRIER
ABORT BUSY
ABORT 'NO CARRIER'
# Wait up to 5 seconds for the reply to each of these
TIMEOUT 5
'' ATZ
OK ATDT1234567
# Wait 40 seconds for connection
TIMEOUT 40
CONNECT
TIMEOUT 5
gin:-\r-gin: Snorm
sword: Oh!No!
```

We'll put this script and everything else we need for SLIP in the directory */etc/sliphome*, which we may have to create. We'll call this script */etc/sliphome/slip.chat*. It first tells chat to abort dialup on a BUSY or NO CARRIER response from the modem. The next line waits for nothing

(' ') and resets the modem. The following line waits for the modem to reply with OK, and dials the ISP.

Call setup can take a while, almost always more than 5 seconds for real (analogue) modems, so we need to extend the timeout, in this case to 40 seconds. During this time we must get the reply CONNECT from the modem.

Next, we reset the timeout to 5 seconds and perform *login* authentication. It's important to reset the timeout, because otherwise a login failure will take 40 seconds to complete. The sequence gin:-\r-gin: is a shorthand for "expect gin:. If you don't get it, send \r and expect "gin:", the end of the login: prompt.

One of the weaknesses of the current SLIP configuration is that it is difficult to control the assignment of network interfaces to serial lines. This is, of course, not a problem if you only have one SLIP interface. See the man page *slattach(8)* for details of how to handle multiple interfaces.

Invoking slattach

To the SLIP link, first place the following commands in a file */etc/sliphome/startslip*:

```
#!/bin/sh
# Dial a slip link
ifconfig  sl0  139.130.136.133  139.130.136.129  netmask 255.255.255.255
route delete default
route add default 139.130.136.129
slattach -h -r'chat -f /etc/sliphome/slip.chat' -s 57600 -L /dev/cuaa1
```

The *ifconfig* line first configures the addresses of the link, and the *slattach* line establishes the connection:

- The -h option sets hardware handshaking (see page 430).

- According to the man page, the -r option specifies what to do on *redial*. In fact, it is what to do if *slattach* finds that the modem is not asserting *DCD*, so if it is started in this condition, it will dial immediately.

  The chat script invokes the script */etc/sliphome/slip.chat*, which we saw above, to perform the dialling.

- The option -s 57600 sets the bit rate of the local link to the modem.

- The option -L tells *slattach* to create a UUCP lock file. See page 455 for more details.

- Finally, */dev/cuaa1* is the name of the serial line to use.

You'll notice that this invocation doesn't specify the name of the network interface. There is an option (-S) which does this, but normally the interface is chosen automatically. If you use -S, you need to find a way to determine which interface is available.

Starting the link

Once we have set up */etc/startslip* and */etc/slip.chat*, we proceed to set up the connection. That's simple:

```
# /etc/sliphome/startslip
```

The prompt returns immediately, but that doesn't mean the link is up. First, *slattach* discovers that there is no modem connection, and that it needs to dial. At this point, it logs the following message to the console and */var/log/messages*:

```
Sep 24 13:24:04 freebie slattach[2680]: SIGHUP on /dev/cuaa1 (sl-1); running 'chat -v
-f /etc/sliphome/slip.chat'
```

After a successful connection—about 30 seconds—it logs another message:

```
Sep 24 13:24:35 freebie slattach[2681]: sl0 connected to /dev/cuaa1 at 57600 baud
```

At this point, you can check the configuration:

```
# ifconfig sl0
sl0: flags=8011<UP,POINTOPOINT,MULTICAST> mtu 552
        inet 139.130.136.133 --> 139.130.136.129 netmask 0xffffffff
# netstat -rn
Routing tables

Internet:
Destination        Gateway            Flags     Refs     Use     Netif Expire
default            139.130.136.129    UGSc      22       13032   sl0
139.130.136.129    139.130.136.133    UH        20       2       sl0
... other entries
```

SLIP dialin

Like PPP, SLIP is a symmetrical protocol, but you wouldn't know this from the way you have to configure SLIP dialin.

Accepting calls and authentication

SLIP uses the standard program that handles dialin, *getty*. We've seen how to set up *getty* on page 128. In our example, we'll put a *getty* on the serial line */dev/ttyd1*. We put the following line in */etc/ttys*:

```
ttyd1 "/usr/libexec/getty 38400"unknown          on
```

Then we get *init* to re-read */etc/ttys* and start the *getty*:

```
# kill -1 1
```

getty provides *login authentication*, so we don't need to perform any additional steps for authentication. In this example, we chose for the user Snorm to automatically start */usr/sbin/sliplogin* on login.

sliplogin first searches a file */etc/sliphome/slip.hosts* for an entry which matches the logged in user. If it finds one, it performs the following steps:

- It checks for the existance of a file */etc/sliphome/slip.slparms*. If it finds it, it loads certain operational parameters from it.

- It changes the line parameters to run SLIP.

- It selects a SLIP interface on which to run the network connection.

- It configures the interface with the addresses specified in the */etc/sliphome/slip.hosts* entry.

The slip.hosts file

/etc/sliphome/slip.hosts contains one entry for each user which is entitled to use SLIP. On page 462 we saw the error message that it produces if it doesn't find a user in this file. The entries have the following format:

user   local system   remote system net mask   options

The *local system* and *remote system* addresses and the net mask are used to simulate an *ifconfig* entry. As we have seen above, these should be numeric values.

The *options* can be `normal` (use normal line discipline), `compress` (enable Van Jacobsen header compression), `noicmp` (throw away ICMP packets), or `autocomp` (auto enable Van Jacobsen header compression). If you throw away ICMP packets, you won't be able to ping across the link, since *ping* produces ICMP packets. In general, the only interesting parameter is `autocomp`, which gives you compression if it's possible. The only valid reason to omit this parameter would be if your machine is very slow, and the compression would slow it down further. Nowadays, that's hardly possible.

```
Snorm136.130.139.133 136.130.139.133 255.255.255.255 autocomp
```

slip.slparms options

The file */etc/sliphome/slip.slparms* contains a single line with up to three parameters:

keepalive   outfill   slunit

keepalive is the line idle time after which the connection should be dropped to save costs. *outfill* is more or less the opposite: it's the time after which the link should generate traffic in order to avoid the line at the other end dropping. Both units are in seconds.

slunit is the SLIP network interface unit number to use. For example, if you put a 2 here, *sliplogin* connects to interface *sl2*. It does this even if *sl2* is active, so use this parameter with great care.

In our example, we don't want to keep the line up unnecessarily. Instead, we'll drop the line after five minutes of no activity. Our */etc/sliphome/slip.slparms* contains only:

Accepting a call

After setting up the files as above, we're ready to accept incoming calls. When one arrives, we notice it by the activity on the system console:

```
Sep 24 13:24:35 gw -sliplogin[5658]: attaching slip unit 0 for Snorm
```

After this has occurred, you can check the network configuration:

```
$ ifconfig sl0
sl0: flags=8011<UP,POINTOPOINT,MULTICAST> mtu 552
        inet 139.130.136.129 --> 139.130.136.133 netmask 0xffffffff
$ netstat -rn
Routing tables

Internet:
Destination       Gateway           Flags    Refs    Use    Netif Expire
192.109.197.197   192.109.197.156   UH       0       3      sl0
...etc
```

sliplogin doesn't create a default route, and normally you won't want it to. If you need one, you can create it with the *route add* command, as we have seen on page 470.

Putting it all together

In this section we'll summarize the steps above.

Calling out

To call out, perform these steps:

☐ Create a dial script */etc/sliphome/startslip*:

```
#!/bin/sh
# Dial a slip link
ifconfig  sl0  139.130.136.133  139.130.136.129  netmask 255.255.255.255
route delete default
route add default 139.130.136.129
slattach -h -r'chat -f /etc/sliphome/slip.chat' -s 57600 -L /dev/cuaa1
```

☐ Create a chat script */etc/sliphome/slip.chat*:

```
# Abort the chat script if the modem replies BUSY or NO CARRIER
ABORT BUSY
ABORT 'NO CARRIER'
# Wait up to 5 seconds for the reply to each of these
TIMEOUT 5
'' ATZ
OK ATDT1234567
# Wait 40 seconds for connection
TIMEOUT 40
CONNECT
TIMEOUT 5
gin:-\r-gin: Snorm
sword: Oh!No!
```

□   Start the link:

```
# /etc/sliphome/startslip
```

If you are using the SLIP link for a permanent connection, you should put the invocation of */etc/sliphome/startslip* in */etc/rc.local.*

Calling in

To accept incoming calls, perform these steps:

□   Create a user name for the connection (`Snorm` in this example) with *vipw*:

```
Snorm::1021:1001::0:0:Norm, Beach of Passionate Love:/home/norm:/usr/sbin/sliplogin
```

□   Ensure that `Snorm` has the correct password.

□   Enable a serial line in */etc/ttys*:

```
ttyd1 "/usr/libexec/getty 38400"unknown          on
```

□   Get *init* to read */etc/ttys*:

```
# kill -1 1
```

□   Create a file */etc/sliphome/slip.hosts* containing the following line:

```
Snorm136.130.139.133 136.130.139.133 255.255.255.255 autocomp
```

The addresses are in the same sequence that they are used in *ifconfig*.

□   Create a file */etc/sliphome/slip.slparms* with the timeout value 300 seconds:

```
300
```

Problems

This description looks pretty straightforward, but consider it more like a description of a safe path through a minefield: leave the path and all hell breaks loose. Here are some possible pitfalls:

•   *The chat script starts complaining, and you get lots of error messages on the console*

Check your chat script. You can invoke *chat* manually. If you give it the correct input, it should give you the appropriate output.

•   *You can't stop* slattach—*it keeps restarting.*

Stop it with:

```
# killall slattach
```

This kills any SLIP session, so use it with care if you have more than one running.

- *The modems dial, and you get a connection, and* slattach *says that the connection is up, but you can't get any data across. After about a minute, the line drops.*

  Probably authentication is failing at the other end. There's no way to feed this information back to the caller, so it just dies. Check that the passwords are correct.

27

The Domain Name Service

Ever since the beginning of the ARPAnet, systems have had both names and IP addresses. UNIX systems, as well as a lot of others who have copied the BSD IP implementation, used the file */etc/hosts* to convert between names to addresses.

It's clearly impossible to have an */etc/hosts* which describes the complete Internet. Even if you had disk space, the number of updates would overload your network. The only viable solution is a distributed database.

The solution to this problem is the *Domain Name System*, or *DNS*. The primary implementation of the DNS is *BIND*, the *Berkeley Internet Name Domain*.[1] You'll notice the word *Berkeley* in there. BIND is part of BSD, and it's about the only game in town. Despite these names, the program you use to perform the resolution is called *named* (the *name dæmon*, pronounced "name-dee").

DNS provides the information needed to connect to remote systems in the form of *Resource Records*, or *RRs*. Unfortunately, the names of the records aren't as intuitive as you may like. If you find the names confusing, don't worry: they're not that important.

- *A (address) records* provide a translation from name to IP address. These are what most people think of when they hear the name DNS. The name specified in the A record is called the *canonical* name of the interface, and it should be the one to which the PTR record (see below) refers.

- *PTR (pointer) records* provide a translation from IP address to name. This process is also called *reverse lookup*. Very many systems don't have this set up correctly.

- *MX (mail exchange) records* don't relate to IP addresses at all. They specify where to send mail for a specific name.

- *SOA (start of authority) records* give information about *zones*, which roughly correspond to domains.

---

1. Does this sound like an acronym in search of a name? Yes, I think so too.

- *NS (name server) records* describe the address of a name server for a zone.

- *HINFO (hardware information) records* describe the hardware and software which runs on a particular system.

- *CNAME (canonical name) records* describe alternative names for a system.

FreeBSD provides the possibility of using both */etc/hosts* and DNS. There's no reason to do so, however, and I'm not going to discuss it any further. See the online handbook and the man page for *resolver(5)* if you want to do this anyway. There is only one reason for not running DNS somewhere on your network: if you're not connected to a network. Otherwise, you should be running it.

Many people find objections to running DNS:

- It's supposedly difficult to set up DNS configuration files.

- DNS supposedly generates a lot of network traffic.

- DNS supposedly can cause a dial-on-demand system to dial all the time.

These statements are all untrue. We'll look at them in the rest of this chapter as we set up DNS for our reference network.

Domains and zones

In Internet parlance, a *domain* is a group of names ending with a specific *domain name*. We looked at domain names in Chapter 23, *Connecting to the Internet*, page 419. Note that, like file names, there are two kinds of domain names:

- A *fully-qualified domain name* (*FQDN*) ends in a period (.). This domain name relates to the root domain ..

- A *relative domain name* relates to the current domain. You'll see them occasionally in the configuration files.

Most times, when you write a domain name, it's fully-qualified. But if you write it without the terminating period, DNS will frequently append your own domain name. For example, if you specify a name like *freebie.example.org*, there's a very good chance that DNS will first look for a name *freebie.example.org.example.org*. It won't find it, of course, but it'll spend a long time trying. The moral is simple: when writing DNS configuration, always put a period at the end of names which are fully qualified.

Zones

In many ways, a *zone* is the same thing as a domain: it's the subset of the DNS name space which is maintained by a specific set of name servers—in DNS-speak, name servers are *authoritative* for the zone. The difference is mainly in the way it's used. There is one exception, however: usually, a *subdomain* will have a different name server. This subdomain is part of the domain, but not of the zone.

For example, in our reference network, the name servers on *freebie* and *presto* are authoritative for *example.org*. The owner of the domain might give permission for somebody, maybe in a different country, to run a subdomain *china.example.org*, with nameservers *beijing.china.example.org* and *xianggang.china.example.org*. Because there are different name servers, there are two zones: *freebie.example.org* would be authoritative for the zone *example.org*, but not for *china.example.org*. *beijing.china.example.org* and *xianggang.china.example.org* would be authoritative for the zone *china.example.org*, but not for *example.org*.

Setting up a name server

DNS service is supplied by the *name dæmon, named*. *named* can be run in a number of different modes. In this chapter, we'll concentrate on setting the appropriate configurations for our reference network. If you want to go further, check the following documents:

- The *BIND Operations Guide*, in the source distribution in the directory */usr/src/contrib/bind/doc/bog*. To make a printable version, change to that directory and type `make` to create an ASCII version *file.lst*, or `make file.psf` to create the printable PostScript version *file.psf*.

- *TCP/IP Network Administration*, by Craig Hunt.

- *DNS and BIND*, by Paul Albitz and Cricket Liu.

BIND has recently undergone some significant changes, partially as a result of abuse on the net. The current version is 8.1.2, but most documentation refers to version 4 (there were no versions 5, 6 or 7). The main configuration file has changed its format completely since version 4; even the name has changed. We'll look at how to convert the formats on page 493. Before using the documentation above, make sure that it refers to version 8 of BIND (at the time of writing the BIND Operations Guide didn't, for example).

Passive DNS usage

Not every system needs to run its own name dæmon. If you have another machine on the same network, you can send requests to it. For example, in the reference network, *freebie* and *presto* may be running name servers. There's no particular reason for *bumble* and *wait*, both presumably slower machines, to do so as well. Instead, you can tell them to use the name servers on the other two machines.

To do this, make sure that the following line is set in your */etc/defaults/rc.conf*, and that there is nothing in */etc/rc.conf* which overrides it. This is the normal situation.

```
named_enable="NO"                        # Run named, the DNS server (or NO).
```

Create a file */etc/resolv.conf* with the following contents:

```
domain example.org
nameserver 223.147.37.1          # freebie
nameserver 223.147.37.2          # presto
```

Note that you need to specify IP addresses here. This is a classic chicken-and-egg problem: you can't access the name server to get its address until you know its address.

With this file in place, this machine will send all name server requests to *freebie* or *presto*. We'll look at their configuration later.

Name server on a standalone system

If you only have a single machine connected to the network via a PPP link, and your own machine is part of the ISP's zone, you can use the *resolv.conf* method as well. But it's not a good idea. Every lookup goes over the link, which is relatively slow. Since the results of the lookup aren't stored anywhere locally, you can end up performing the same lookup again and again. The answer is obvious: save the information locally. You can do this with a *caching-only name server*. As the name suggests, the caching-only name server doesn't have any information of its own, but it stores the results of any queries it makes to other systems, so if a program makes the same request again—which happens very frequently—it presents the results much more quickly on subsequent requests.

- Either rename or remove */etc/resolv.conf*, and create a new one with the following contents:

```
nameserver 127.0.0.1             local name server
nameserver 139.130.237.3         ISP's first name server
nameserver 139.130.237.17        ISP's second name server
```

  /etc/resolv.conf isn't necessary, but if you have one like in the example, lookups will still succeed (but a little more slowly) if your name server should fail for any reason.

- Put this line in */etc/rc.conf*:

```
named_enable="YES"                       # Run named, the DNS server (or NO).
```

  If */etc/rc.conf* doesn't exist, just create one with this content.

- Create a file */etc/namedb/localhost.rev* containing:

```
@       IN SOA    @host@. root.@host@.  (
                                @date@    ; Serial
                                3600      ; Refresh
                                300       ; Retry
                                3600000   ; Expire
                                3600 )    ; Minimum
        IN NS     @host@.
1       IN PTR    localhost.@domain@.
```

To create the file, you can start with the file */etc/namedb/PROTO.localhost.rev*, which contains a template for this file. Replace @host@ with the FQDN of your host (*freebie.example.org* in this example), @date@ (the serial number) with the date in the form *yyyymmddxx*,[1] and @domain@ with *example.org.*. Make sure that the FQDNs end with a trailing period. Alternatively, you can run the script */etc/namedb/make-localhost.*

- Edit the file */etc/namedb/named.conf* to contain:

```
options {
      directory "/etc/namedb";

      forwarders {
            139.130.237.3;    139.130.237.17;
      };
zone "0.0.127.in-addr.arpa" {
      type master;
      file "localhost.rev";
};
```

/etc/namedb/named.conf should already be present on your system as well. It contains a lot of comments, but at the end there's a similar zone definition, which you can edit if you want. The address 139.130.237.3 is the ISP's name server address. The forwarders line contains up to ten name server addresses. In this case, we're assuming that an additional name server exists with the address 139.130.237.17.

- Start *named*:

  # **named**

Name server on an end-user network

Of course, a simple caching-only name server won't work when you have your own domain. In fact, most of the authorities who allocate domain names won't even let you register an Internet domain unless you specify two functional name servers, and they'll check them before the registration can proceed. In this section, we'll look at what you need to do to run a "real" name server.

The first thing we need to do is to create a configuration file for our zone *example.org*. We'll put it and all other configuration files in a directory */etc/namedb* and call it */etc/namedb/db.example.org.*

The SOA record

The first thing we need is a record describing the *Start of Authority*. This defines a new zone. Write:

---

1. We'll look at the serial number on page 482.

```
example.org.    IN   SOA  freebie.example.org. grog.example.org.  (
                1997010902 ; Serial (date, 2 digits version of day)
                86400    ; refresh (1 day)
                7200     ; retry (2 hours)
                8640000  ; expire (100 days)
                86400 )  ; minimum (1 day)
```

The name on the left is the name of the zone. The keyword IN means *Internet*, in other words the Internet Protocols. The BIND software includes support for multiple network types, most of which have now been forgotten. The keyword SOA defines the type of record. *freebie.example.org* is called the *origin* of the zone. It should be the primary name server.

The next field, *grog.example.org*, is the mail address of the DNS administrator. Wait a minute, you may say, that's not a mail address. There should be a @ there, not a .. That's right. Unfortunately, DNS uses the @ sign for other purposes, and it would be a syntax error in this position. So the implementors resorted to this kludge. To generate the mail ID, replace the first . with a @, to give you *grog@example.org*.

The *serial number* identifies this version of the zone configuration. Remote name servers first retreive the SOA record and check if the serial number has incremented before deciding whether to load the whole zone, which could be large. Make sure you increment this field every time you edit the file. If you don't, your updates will not propagate to other name servers. It's a good idea to use a format which reflects the date, as here: the format gives four digits for the year (so that you don't run into problems in the year 2000), two digits for the month, two for the day, and two for the number of the modification on a particular day. The serial number in this example shows it to be the second modification to the zone configuration on 9 September 1997.

The remaining parameters describe the timeout characteristics of the zone. All parameters are specified in seconds.

- The *refresh* time is the time after which a remote name server will check whether the zone configuration has changed. 1 day is reasonable here unless you change your configuration several times per day.

- The *retry* time is the time to wait if an attempt to load the zone fails.

- The *expire* time is the time after which a secondary name server will drop the information about a zone if it has not been able to reload it from the primary name server. You probably want to make this large.

- The *minimum time to live* is the minimum time that a remote name server should cache records from this zone.

The A records

The most obvious thing you need are the IP addresses of the systems on the network. In the zone *example.org*, you define the A records like this:

```
freebie        IN   A    223.147.37.1
presto         IN   A    223.147.37.2
bumble         IN   A    223.147.37.3
wait           IN   A    223.147.37.4
gw             IN   A    223.147.37.5
```

In practice, as we will see in the completed configuration file, we tend to put the A records further towards the end of the list, since they are usually the most numerous. It makes the file easier to read if we put them after the short entries.

The NS records

For efficiency's sake, DNS uses a special kind of record to tell where your name servers are. In our case, we're running name servers on *freebie* and *presto*. We could write:

```
               IN   NS   freebie.example.org.
               IN   NS   presto.example.org.
```

This would work just fine, but in fact, we'll do it a little differently, as we'll see in the next section.

Nicknames

We're running a whole lot of services on the reference network, in particular a Web server and an ftp server. By convention, a web server machine is called *www*, an ftp server is called *ftp*, and a name server is called *ns*. But we don't have machines like that. What do we do? We give our machines nicknames:

```
www            IN   CNAME    freebie
ftp            IN   CNAME    presto
```

We'd like to do the same with the name servers, but unfortunately DNS doesn't like that, and will complain about your DNS configuration all over the world if you make *ns* a CNAME. There's a good reason for this: if you use CNAME records to define your name servers, remote systems have to perform two lookups to find the address of the name server, one to retreive the CNAME and one to get the corresponding A record for the CNAME. Define new A records for them:

```
               IN   NS   ns
               IN   NS   ns1

ns             IN   A    223.147.37.1
ns1            IN   A    223.147.37.2
```

You'll note that we're using relative domain names here. They are taken to be relative to the name which starts the SOA record.

The MX records

As we will see on page 555, you can send mail to hosts listed in an A record, but it's not a good idea. Instead, you should have some MX records to tell SMTP what to do with mail for your domain. This method has an added advantage: it allows you to rename individual machines without having to change the users' mail IDs. We'll take this advice and assume that all mail is sent to *user@example.org*. In addition, we'll use the ISP's mail server *mail.example.net* as a backup in case our mail server is down. That way, when it comes back up, the delivery will be expedited. The resulting MX records look like:

```
        IN   MX   50  bumble.example.org.
        IN   MX   100 mail.example.net.
```

The numbers 50 and 100 are called *preferences*. Theoretically you can make them 0 and 1, except that you might want to put others in between. A mail transfer agent sends mail to the system with the lowest preference unless it does not respond—then it tries the MX record with the next-lowest preference, and so on.

The HINFO records

Finally, you may want to tell the world about your hardware and this great operating system you're running. You can do that with the HINFO record:

```
freebie      IN   HINFO   "Intel Pentium/133"   "FreeBSD 4.0-CURRENT (4.4BSD)"
presto       IN   HINFO   "Intel Pentium II /233" "FreeBSD 3.2 (4.4BSD)"
bumble       IN   HINFO   "Intel Pentium/133"   "SCO OpenServer"
wait         IN   HINFO   "Intel Pentium Pro 266"  "Microsoft Windows 95%"
gw           IN   HINFO   "Intel 486/33"        "FreeBSD 3.2 (4.4BSD)"
```

Of course, telling the world the truth about your hardware also helps crackers choose the tools to use if they want to break in to your system. If this worries you, either don't use HINFO, or put in incorrect information. It's still the exception to see HINFO records.

Putting it all together

In summary, our configuration file */etc/namedb/db.example.org* looks like:

```
; Definition of zone example.org
example.org.    IN   SOA   freebie.example.org. grog.example.org.  (
                           1997010902 ; Serial (date, 2 digits version of day)
                           86400    ; refresh (1 day)
                           7200     ; retry (2 hours)
                           8640000  ; expire (100 days)
                           86400 ) ; minimum (1 day)

; name servers
                IN   NS        ns
                IN   NS        ns1
ns              IN   A         223.147.37.1
ns1             IN   A         223.147.37.2
; MX records
                IN   MX        50  bumble.example.org.
                IN   MX        100 mail.example.net.
```

```
; Hosts
freebie         IN    A         223.147.37.1
presto          IN    A         223.147.37.2
bumble          IN    A         223.147.37.3
wait            IN    A         223.147.37.4
gw              IN    A         223.147.37.5

; nicknames
www             IN    CNAME     freebie
ftp             IN    CNAME     presto

; System information
freebie         IN    HINFO     "Intel Pentium/133"    "FreeBSD 4.0-CURRENT (4.4BSD)"
presto          IN    HINFO     "Intel Pentium II/233" "FreeBSD 3.2 (4.4BSD)"
bumble          IN    HINFO     "Intel Pentium/133"    "SCO OpenServer"
wait            IN    HINFO     "Intel Pentium Pro 266" "Microsoft Windows 95%"
gw              IN    HINFO     "Intel 486/33"         "FreeBSD 3.2 (4.4BSD)"
```

You'll notice that comment lines start with ; , and not with the more usual #.

That's all the information we need for our zone *example.org*. But we're not done yet, we need another zone. Read on.

Reverse lookup

/etc/hosts is a file, so it can allow you to perform lookup in either direction. Not so with DNS: how can you know which name server is authoritative for the domain if you don't know its name? You can't, of course, so DNS uses a trick: it fabricates a name from the address. For the address 223.147.37.4, it creates a domain name *37.147.223.in-addr.arpa* and looks up the name *4.37.147.223.in-addr.arpa*. You'll note that the digits of the address are reversed, and the last digit is missing, since it is considered the host part of the address. This is one of the remaining cases where the Internet address classes we discussed on page 399 still apply.

In order to resolve the names, we need another zone, then. That means another file, which we'll call */etc/namedb/example-reverse*. It's not quite as bad as the forward file:

```
@               IN    SOA       freebie.example.org. grog.example.org. (
                                1996110801 ; Serial (date, 2 digits version of day)
                                86400    ; refresh (1 day)
                                7200     ; retry (2 hours)
                                8640000 ; expire (100 days)
                                86400 ) ; minimum (1 day)
                IN    NS        ns.example.org.
                IN    NS        ns1.example.org.

1               IN    PTR       freebie.example.org.
2               IN    PTR       presto.example.org.
3               IN    PTR       bumble.example.org.
4               IN    PTR       wait.example.org.
5               IN    PTR       gw.example.org.
```

In this case, the SOA record is identical to that in */etc/namedb/db.example.org*, with two exceptions: instead of the zone name at the beginning of the line, we have the @ symbol, and the serial number is different: you don't normally need to update reverse lookup domains so often. This @ symbol represents the name of the zone, in this case *37.147.223.in-addr.arpa.*.

We'll see how that works when we make the */etc/named/named.root* file below. We also use the same name server entries. This time they need to be fully qualified, since they are in a different zone.

Finally, we have the PTR (reverse lookup) records. They specify only the last digit (the host part) of the IP address, so this will be prepended to the zone name. The host name at the end of the line is in fully-qualified form, since it's in another zone. For example, in fully-qualified form, the entry for *wait* could be written:

```
4.37.147.223.in-addr.arpa.     IN    PTR   wait.example.org.
```

The distant view: the outside world

So far, we have gone to a lot of trouble to describe our own tiny part of the Internet. What about the rest? How can the name server find the address of, say, *freefall.FreeBSD.org*? So far, it can't.

What we need now is some information about other name servers who can help us, specifically the thirteen *root name servers*. These are named *A.ROOT-SERVERS.NET.* through *M.ROOT-SERVERS.NET.*. They are described in a file which you can get from *ftp://ftp.rs.internic.net/domain/named.root* if necessary, but you shouldn't need to: after installing FreeBSD, it should be present in */etc/namedb/named.root*. This file has hardly changed in years—the names have changed (only once), but the addresses have stayed the same. Of course, it's always a good idea to check from time to time.

The named.conf file

So far, we have two files, one for each zone for which our name server is authoritative. In a large system, there could be many more. What we need now is to tell the name server which files to use. That's the main purpose of *named.conf*. There's already a skeleton in */etc/namedb/named.conf*. With most of the comments stripped, it looks like:

```
options {
     directory "/etc/namedb";
     forwarders {
          127.0.0.1;
     };
zone "." {
     type hint;
     file "named.root";
};

zone "0.0.127.IN-ADDR.ARPA" {
     type master;
     file "localhost.rev";
};

zone "domain.com" {
     type slave;
     file "s/domain.com.bak";
     masters {
          192.168.1.1;
     };
```

```
};
zone "0.168.192.in-addr.arpa" {
     type slave;
     file "s/0.168.192.in-addr.arpa.bak";
     masters {
          192.168.1.1;
     };
};
```

Each entry consists of a keyword followed by text in braces ({}). These entries have the following significance:

- The `directory` entry tells *named* where to look for the configuration files.

- The first zone is the top-level domain, .. It's a hint: it tells *named* to look in the file *named.root* in its configuration directory. *named.root* contains the IP addresses of the 13 top-level name servers.

- We've seen the entry for `0.0.127.IN-ADDR.ARPA` already on page 481: it's the reverse lookup for the localhost address.

- The `hint` entry specifies the name of the file describing the root servers (domain .).

- The zone entries for *domain.com* and *0.168.192.in-addr.arpa* define *slave name servers*. A slave name server addresses all queries to one of the specified *master name servers*. In earlier versions of DNS, a slave name server is called a *secondary name server*, and the master name server was called a *primary name server*. Since this is still current usage outside BIND, and the documentation is not yet available, expect this to change. In this chapter, we'll retain the old terminology.

This file already contains most of the information we need. The only things we need to add is the information about the names of our zones and the location of the description file:

```
zone "example.org" {
       type master;
       file "db.example.org";
};
zone "37.147.223.in-addr.arpa" {
       type master;
       file "example-reverse";
};
```

When we've done that, we can start the name server:

```
# named
```

If it's already running, we can restart it with a `SIGHUP` signal:

```
# ps aux | grep named
 root      55 0.0 1.0 1140  928 ??  Is   Thu12PM   0:25.66 named
# kill -1 55
```

Alternatively we can use the a file */var/run/named.pid*, which contains the PID of *named*, and write:

```
# kill -1 'cat /var/run/named.pid'
```

Note the backquotes (' '): they tell the shell to run the program enclosed inside and replace the text with the standard output of the program. If */var/run/named.pid* contains the text 55, this will effectively reduce to kill -1 55. The disadvantage of this method is that it's easier to use *ps* to find the PID (and to confirm that it's correct) than remember the name of the file (is it */etc/named.pid*? Is it */var/run/named.pid*? Is it */var/run/pid.named*?

Starting or restarting the name server doesn't mean it will work, of course. If you make a mistake in your configuration files, it may not work at all. Otherwise it might start, but refuse to load specific zones. *named* logs messages with *syslog*, and if you are using the standard *syslog* configuration they will be written to the console and to the file */var/log/messages*. After starting *named*, you should check what it said. You should see something like:

```
May 10 14:18:35 freebie named[1360]: starting.  named 8.1.2 Sun May  9 13:04:13 CST 1
999  grog@freebie.example.org:/usr/obj/usr.sbin/named
May 10 14:18:35 freebie named[1360]: master zone "example.org" (IN) loaded (serial 19
97010902)
May 10 14:18:35 freebie named[1360]: master zone "37.147.223.in-addr.arpa" (IN) loade
d (serial 1996110801)
May 10 14:18:35 freebie named[1360]: listening on [223.147.37.2].53 (ep0)
May 10 14:18:35 freebie named[1360]: listening on [127.0.0.1].53 (lo0)
May 10 14:18:35 freebie named[1360]: Forwarding source address is [0.0.0.0].1063
May 10 14:18:35 freebie named[1361]: Ready to answer queries.
```

What you don't want to see are error messages like:

```
May 10 14:26:37 freebie named[1361]: db.example.org: Line 28: Unknown type: System.
May 10 14:26:37 freebie named[1361]: db.example.org:28: Database error (System)
May 10 14:26:37 freebie named[1361]: master zone "example.org" (IN) rejected due to e
rrors (serial 1997010902)
```

Funny: if you look at line 28 of */etc/namedb/db.example.org*, it looks straightforward enough:

```
# System information
freebie        IN    HINFO     "Intel Pentium/133"  "FreeBSD 3.0-CURRENT (4.4BSD)"
presto         IN    HINFO     "Intel Pentium II/233" "FreeBSD 2.2.5 (4.4BSD)"
```

The problem here is that *named* doesn't use the standard UNIX convention for comments: the comment character is a semicolon (;), not a hash mark (#).

Most other configuration errors should be self-explanatory. On page 492 we'll look at messages that *named* produces during normal operation.

Secondary name servers

A lot of software relies on name resolution. If for any reason a name server is not accessible, it can cause serious problems. This is one of the reasons why InterNIC insists on at least two name servers before it will register a domain.

If you run multiple name servers, it doesn't really matter which one answers. So why a distinction between *primary* and *secondary* name servers? It's purely organizational: a primary name server loads its data from the configuration files you create, as we saw above. A secondary name server loads its data from a primary name server if it is running. It saves the information in a private file so that if it is restarted while the primary name server isn't running, it can reload information about the zones it is serving from this file. This makes it a lot easier to configure a secondary name server, of course: all we need is in */etc/namedb/named.conf*:

```
zone "." {
      type hint;
      file "named.root";
};

zone "example.org" {
      type slave;
      file "backup.example.org";
      masters {
            223.147.37.1;
      };
};

zone "37.147.223.in-addr.arpa" {
      type slave;
      file "backup.example-reverse";
      masters {
            223.147.37.1;
      };
};

zone "0.0.127.in-addr.arpa" {
      type slave;
      file "localhost.rev";
      masters {
            223.147.37.1;
      };
};
```

Recall that BIND version 8 uses the terms *master* and *slave* for primary and secondary name servers.

The numerical address is for *freebie.example.org*, the name server from which the zone is to be loaded. We use the numerical address because the name server needs the address before it can perform resolution. You can specify multiple name servers if you want. The *backup file* is the name of the file where the zone information should be saved in case the name server is restarted when the primary name server is not accessible.

The next level up: delegating zones

In the previous example, we configured a name server for a single zone with no subzones. We did briefly consider what would happen if we created a subdomain *china.example.org*. In this section, we'll create the configuration files for this subzone.

china.example.org

For the subdomain *china.example.org*, the same considerations apply as in our previous example: we have a domain without subdomains. Only the names and the addresses change.

In the following examples, let's assume that *china.example.org* has two name servers, *beijing.china.example.org* and *xianggang.china.example.org*. Let's look at the files we might have on these systems, starting with */etc/namedb/db.china.example.org*:

```
; Definition of zone example.org
@               IN    SOA  beijing.china.example.org. zhang.china.example.org.  (
                           1997070101 ; Serial (date, 2 digits version of day)
                           86400   ; refresh (1 day)
                           7200    ; retry (2 hours)
                           8640000 ; expire (100 days)
                           86400 ) ; minimum (1 day)

; name servers
                IN    NS   ns
                IN    NS   ns1
ns              IN    A    223.169.23.1
ns1             IN    A    223.169.23.2
; MX records
                IN    MX   50  xianggang.china.example.org.
                IN    MX   70  bumble.example.org.
                IN    MX   100 mail.example.net.

; Hosts
beijing         IN    A    223.169.23.1
xianggang       IN    A    223.169.23.2
shanghai        IN    A    223.169.23.3
guangzhou       IN    A    223.169.23.4
gw              IN    A    223.169.23.5

; nicknames
www             IN    CNAME     shanghai
ftp             IN    CNAME     shanghai
```

Then, */etc/namedb/china-reverse*:

```
; Definition of zone china.example.org
@               IN    SOA  beijing.china.example.org. zhang.china.example.org.  (
                           1997090501 ; Serial (date, 2 digits version of day)
                           86400   ; refresh (1 day)
                           7200    ; retry (2 hours)
                           8640000 ; expire (100 days)
                           86400 ) ; minimum (1 day)

; name servers
                IN    NS   ns.china.example.org.
                IN    NS   ns1.china.example.org.

; Hosts
```

```
1                    IN    PTR    beijing
2                    IN    PTR    xianggang
3                    IN    PTR    shanghai
4                    IN    PTR    guangzhou
5                    IN    PTR    gw
```

and finally */etc/namedb/named.conf*:

```
zone "." {
        type hint;
        file "named.root";
};

zone "0.0.127.IN-ADDR.ARPA" {
        type master;
        file "localhost.rev";
};

zone "china.example.org" {
        type master;
        file "db.china.example.org";
};

zone "23.169.233.IN-ADDR.ARPA" {
        type master;
        file "china-reverse";
};
```

These files look very much like the corresponding files for *example.org*. The real difference happens in the configuration for *example.org*, not for *china.example.org*. We'll look at it next.

example.org with delegation

What does *example.org*'s name server need to know about *china.example.org*? You might think, "nothing, they're separate zones", but that's not completely true. The parent domain maintains name server records for the subdomain, since any query for *china.example.org* first goes via *example.org*. It's obviously a good idea for the name servers for *example.org* to maintain a secondary name server for *china*, since that way we can save a lookup to the primary name servers for *china.example.org* most of the time. To do so, we add the following line to */etc/namedb/named.conf*:

```
zone "china.example.org" {
        type slave;
        file "backup.china";
        masters {
                223.169.23.1;
                223.169.23.2;
        };
};

zone "23.169.223.in-addr.arpa" {
        type slave;
        file "backup.china-reverse";
        masters {
                223.169.23.1;
                223.169.23.2;
        };
};
```

We add the following information to */etc/namedb/db.example.org*:

```
@               IN    SOA   freebie.example.org. grog.example.org. (
                            1997090501 ; Serial (date, 2 digits version of day)
                            86400   ; refresh (1 day)
                            7200    ; retry (2 hours)
                            8640000 ; expire (100 days)
                            86400 ) ; minimum (1 day)
china           IN    NS    ns.china.example.org.
china           IN    NS    ns1.china.example.org.
china           IN    NS    ns.example.org.

ns.china        IN    A     223.169.23.1
ns1.china       IN    A     223.169.23.2
```

Since we changed the information, we also change the serial number of the SOA record so that the secondary name servers for *example.org* will reload the updated information.

We need to specify the addresses of the name servers as well, although strictly speaking they belong to the zone *china*, because there is no way to find these addresses from *china.example.org*: these are the addresses to which we need to send any kind of query.

After changing the configuration like this, we restart the name server and check the output, either by looking on the system console, or by using the command `tail /var/log/mes-sages`. We'll see something like:

```
May 10 15:03:36 freebie named[1408]: starting.  named 8.1.2 Sun May  9 13:04:13 CST 1
999  grog@freebie.example.org:/usr/obj/usr.sbin/named
May 10 15:03:36 freebie named[1408]: cache zone "" (IN) loaded (serial 0)
May 10 15:03:36 freebie named[1408]: master zone "0.0.127.IN-ADDR.ARPA" (IN) loaded (
serial 97091501)
May 10 15:03:36 freebie named[1408]: master zone "example.org" (IN) loaded (serial 19
97090501)
May 10 15:03:36 freebie named[1408]: master zone "37.147.223.in-addr.arpa" (IN) loade
d (serial 1996110801)
May 10 15:03:36 freebie named[1408]: listening on [223.147.37.1].53 (ep0)
May 10 15:03:36 freebie named[1408]: listening on [127.0.0.1].53 (lo0)
May 10 15:03:36 freebie named[1408]: Forwarding source address is [0.0.0.0].1072
May 10 15:03:36 freebie named[1409]: Ready to answer queries.
```

Messages from named

Once your *named* is up and running, it may still produce a number of messages. Here are some examples:

```
May 10 15:09:06 freebie named[124]: approved AXFR from [223.147.37.5].2872 for "ex
ample.org"
May 10 15:09:06 freebie named[124]: zone transfer of "example.org" (IN) to [192.10
9.197.137].2872
```

These messages indicate that another name server has loaded the zone specified. This will typically be one of your secondary name servers. This should happen about as often as you have specified in your *refresh* parameter for the zone.

```
Sep 13 10:17:04 freebie named[55]: ns_resp: query(example.org) contains our address (F
REEBIE.example.org:223.147.37.1) learnt (A=198.41.0.4:NS=198.41.0.4)
```

This message indicates that the server indicated by the A record has asked us to forward a query whose nameserver list includes our own name or address(es). This used to be called a *lame delegation*. It's interesting that the address in this (real) message was *a.root-servers.net*, one of the nine base servers for the whole Internet, which was probably forwarding a query from some other system. The server doesn't check the validity of the queries it forwards, so it's quite possible that they could be in error.

```
Sep 14 03:33:18 freebie named[55]: ns_forw: query(goldsword.com) NS points to CNAME (n
s-user.goldsword.com:) learnt (CNAME=199.170.202.100:NS=199.170.202.100)
```

As we saw above, a name server address should be an A record. The administrator of this system didn't know this, and pointed it to a CNAME record.

```
Sep 14 15:55:52 freebie named[55]: ns_forw: query(219.158.96.202.in-addr.arpa) A RR ne
gative cache entry (ns.gz.gdpta.net.cn:) learnt (NODATA=202.96.128.68:NS=202.12.28.129)
```

This message indicates that the name server has already found that the name server specified cannot be found, and has noted that fact in a *negative cache entry*.

Upgrading a version 4 configuration

Since the last edition of this book, version 8 of *named*, the DNS dæmon, has been released. Since the previous version (version 4[1]) the format of the main configuration file has changed dramatically. The previous section described version 8. If you have an existing DNS configuration from version 4, the main configuration file will be called */etc/named.boot* or */etc/named/named.boot*. You can convert it to the *named.conf* format with the script */usr/sbin/named-bootconf*:

```
# named-bootconf < /etc/namedb/named.boot > /etc/namedb/named.conf
```

DNS tools

A number of tools are available for manipulating DNS entries:

- You can use *nslookup* or *dig* to look up name information. It's a matter of preference which you use. I use *nslookup* because the output format of *dig* gets on my nerves. Others prefer *dig* because its output is more suited as input to *named*. For example, the command `dig @a.root-servers.net . axfr` produces a *named.root* file that *named* understands.

---

1. Don't ask what happened to versions 5, 6 and 7. Rumour has it that the next version will be version 16.

- You can use *named-xfer* to download complete zones.

- You can use *ndc* to communicate with *named*.

We'll look briefly at each of these in the following sections.

nslookup

nslookup is a program which performs DNS queries. Here are some examples:

```
$ nslookup
Default Server:  freebie.example.org
Address:  0.0.0.0                              this appears to be a bug in nslookup—see below

> 199.170.202.100                              what was that address in the printout above?
Server:  freebie.example.org
Address:  0.0.0.0

Name:     ns.goldsword.com
Address:  199.170.202.100

> hub.freebsd.org                              get the address of the system
Server:  freebie.example.org
Address:  0.0.0.0

Name:     hub.freebsd.org
Address:  204.216.27.18

> ftp.freebsd.org                              get another address
Server:  freebie.example.org
Address:  0.0.0.0

Non-authoritative answer:                      this means that the name server
                                               had the result cached
Name:     wcarchive.cdrom.com                  this is a CNAME record: it points
Address:  165.113.121.81                       to another system
Aliases:  ftp.freebsd.org

> set type=soa                                 look for SOA records
> freebsd.org                                  for freebsd.org
Server:  freebie.example.org
Address:  0.0.0.0

Non-authoritative answer:
freebsd.org                                    this is the SOA record
        origin = implode.root.com
        mail addr = hostmaster.freebsd.org
        serial = 97090900
        refresh = 3600 (1 hour)
        retry   = 600 (10 mins)
        expire  = 604800 (7 days)
        minimum ttl = 3600 (1 hour)

Authoritative answers can be found from:       and these are the name servers
freebsd.org     nameserver = WHO.CDROM.com
freebsd.org     nameserver = NS1.CRL.com
freebsd.org     nameserver = NS2.CRL.com
WHO.CDROM.com   internet address = 204.216.27.3     and their addresses
NS1.CRL.com     internet address = 165.113.1.36
NS2.CRL.com     internet address = 165.113.1.37
```

The server IP address in these examples looks funny. It   was on the same machine, so it uses a different method to communicate with the name server (UNIX domain transport instead of

Internet domain transport). UNIX domain transport doesn't need addresses, but *nslookup* leaves a null address there anyway. This appears to be a harmless bug which has been in *nslookup* for a long time.

In this last example, the local name server at *example.org* already had the SOA record for *FreeBSD.org* in its cache. As a result, it didn't need to ask the name server which was authoritative for the zone. It indicates this fact with the message `Non-authoritative answer`, and tells you where you can get a valid answer. We can do that like this:

```
> server who.cdrom.com              select an authoritative name server
Default Server:  who.cdrom.com
Address:  204.216.27.3              this time the address is correct

> freebsd.org.                      and repeat the query
Server:  who.cdrom.com
Address:  204.216.27.3

freebsd.org
        origin = implode.root.com
        mail addr = hostmaster.freebsd.org
        serial = 97090900
        refresh = 3600 (1 hour)
        retry   = 600 (10 mins)
        expire  = 604800 (7 days)
        minimum ttl = 3600 (1 hour)
freebsd.org       nameserver = who.cdrom.com
freebsd.org       nameserver = ns1.crl.com
freebsd.org       nameserver = ns2.crl.com
freebsd.org       nameserver = ns.gnome.co.uk
who.cdrom.com     internet address = 204.216.27.3
ns1.crl.com       internet address = 165.113.1.36
ns2.crl.com       internet address = 165.113.1.37
ns.gnome.co.uk    internet address = 193.243.228.142
```

Interestingly, though the serial number is the same, the information returned is not: we have an additional name server. This is probably an administrative problem: one of the name servers has not been registered.

Continuing,

```
> set type=mx                       look for MX records
> freebsd.org
Server:  who.cdrom.com
Address:  204.216.27.3

freebsd.org       preference = 10, mail exchanger = hub.freebsd.org
freebsd.org       nameserver = who.cdrom.com
freebsd.org       nameserver = ns1.crl.com
freebsd.org       nameserver = ns2.crl.com
freebsd.org       nameserver = ns.gnome.co.uk
hub.freebsd.org internet address = 204.216.27.18
who.cdrom.com     internet address = 204.216.27.3
ns1.crl.com       internet address = 165.113.1.36
ns2.crl.com       internet address = 165.113.1.37
ns.gnome.co.uk  internet address = 193.243.228.142
> set type=hinfo                    look for HINFO records
> hub.freebsd.org
Server:  who.cdrom.com
Address:  204.216.27.3

*** No host information (HINFO) records available for hub.freebsd.org
```

For some reason, *hub.freebsd.org* didn't have any HINFO records. Oh well, let's look at another system:

```
> freefall.freebsd.org
Server:  who.cdrom.com
Address:  204.216.27.3

freefall.freebsd.org    CPU = Pentium    OS = FreeBSD
```

But how did we know about this system? So far, we've been looking up individual systems. *nslookup* also includes a command to download a zone:

```
> ls freebsd.org
[who.cdrom.com]
 FreeBSD.org.               server = who.cdrom.com
 FreeBSD.org.               server = ns1.crl.com
 FreeBSD.org.               server = ns2.crl.com
 FreeBSD.org.               server = ns.gnome.co.uk
 FreeBSD.org.               204.216.27.18
 www2                       206.109.20.118
 hub                        204.216.27.18
 lv                         server = ns.lv.freebsd.org
 ns.lv                      199.125.215.66
 www5                       207.90.181.14
 localhost                  127.0.0.1
 www6                       137.112.206.126
 nl                         server = ns1.IAEhv.nl
 nl                         server = ns2.IAEhv.nl
 nl                         server = who.cdrom.com
 no                         server = skarven.itea.ntnu.no
 no                         server = who.cdrom.com
 ns                         198.145.90.17
 (etc)
```

This command lists the zone, along with a whole lot of information which it considers interesting, but which doesn't belong to the zone. To get the real information, use *named-xfer*, which we'll look at next.

named-xfer

nslookup is useful for performing lookups. As we saw in the previous section, it's not ideal for transferring zones. If that's what you want to do, it's easier to use the tool that *named* uses.

named-xfer is intended to be started only by *named*, so it lives in */usr/libexec*, a directory which is not usually on a PATH. To start it, you need to tell it the name of a zone, the name of the name server, the name of a file to store the zone, and the lowest serial number which interests you.

The serial number is required because that's the way *named* avoids useless transfers. When using it outside *named*, you can accept any serial number, so you set this value to 0.

We run *named-xfer* like this:

```
# /usr/libexec/named-xfer -s 0 -z freebsd.org -f /tmp/foo who.cdrom.com
# cat /tmp/foo
; BIND version named 4.9.6-REL Wed Aug 27 12:54:15 CST 1997
; BIND version grog@freebie.example.org:/usr/obj/src/FREEBIE/libexec/named-xfer
; zone 'freebsd.org'   last serial 0
; from 204.216.27.3    at Wed Sep 17 12:45:48 1997
$ORIGIN org.
freebsd           IN   SOA     implode.root.com. hostmaster.FreeBSD.org. (
                  97090900 3600 600 604800 3600 )
                  IN   NS      who.cdrom.com.
                  IN   NS      ns1.crl.com.
                  IN   NS      ns2.crl.com.
                  IN   NS      ns.gnome.co.uk.
                  IN   MX      10 hub.FreeBSD.org.
                  IN   A       204.216.27.18
$ORIGIN FreeBSD.org.
(etc)
```

You'll notice the format of this file: it's effectively a configuration file, except for the added $ORIGIN statements. This is the file that a secondary name server saves for restart (see page 489).

Checking DNS for correctness

Several programs are available for diagnosing DNS configuration problems. They're outside the scope of this book, but if you're managing large DNS configurations, you should take a look at the collection at *ftp://ftp.isc.org/isc/bind/src/8.1.1/bind-contrib.tar.gz*.

28

Firewalls and IP aliasing

The Internet was developed by a relatively small community of computer scientists, who were for the most part responsible people. Since the Internet has been opened to the general public, two problems have become evident:

- A large number of people have sought to abuse its relatively lax security.

- The address space is no longer adequate for the number of machines connecting to the network.

What do these problems have to do with each other? Nothing much, but we'll see that the solutions do, so we'll look at them together. More specifically, we'll consider:

- How to set up an *Internet Firewall* to keep intruders out of your network.

- Security tools which will ensure that nobody can steal your password from a node through which it passes.

- Tools for *IP aliasing*, which translate IP addresses to make them appear to come from the gateway machine. The way this is done makes it impossible to set them up from outside, so they also represent a kind of security device.

Security and firewalls

Recall from Chapter 21, *Networks and the Internet*, that incoming packets need to connect to an IP port, and that some process on the machine must accept them. By default, this process is *inetd*. You can limit the vulnerability of your machine by limiting the number of services it supports. Do you need to supply both a *telnet* and an *rlogin* service? You might be able to get rid of one or both by commenting out the appropriate line in *inetd.conf*. Obviously, careful system configuration can minimize your vulnerability, but it also reduces your accessibility: intruders can't get in, but neither can the people who need to access the machine.

Obviously, you need a tool which passes authorized data and refuses to pass unauthorized data. Such a tool is called a *firewall*. In this section, we'll look at *packet filtering firewalls*: the firewall examines each incoming packet and uses a set of predefined walls to decide whether to pass it unchanged, whether to change it, or whether to simply discard it. An alternative approach is a *proxy firewall*, which analyzes each packet and creates new requests based on its content. We won't look at proxy firewalls in this book.

In this section, we'll look at the FreeBSD kernel firewall code. Don't consider this description to be sufficient: if you want to set up a firewall, check the references in Appendix C, *Bibliography*.

See page 350 for details of how to configure the kernel for a firewall. Before you reboot your machine, make sure you understand how to set the firewall options. Until you do so, you will not be able to communicate with *any* other machine (unless you use the IPFIREWALL_DE-FAULT_TO_ACCEPT option). Read the following section, then reboot your machine.

Table 28-1. *ipfw* packet types

Keyword	Description
ip	All IP packets
tcp	TCP packets
udp	UDP packets
icmp	ICMP packets
service name or number	A packet destined for one of the services described in */etc/services*.
src *IP address range*	A packet with a source address which matches *IP address*. See below for the interpretation of *IP address range*.
dst *IP address range*	A packet with a destination address which matches *IP address*. See below for the interpretation of *IP address range*.
via *interface*	All packets going by the specified interface. *interface* may be an interface name or an IP address associated with only one interface.
recv *interface*	All packets arriving by the specified interface. *interface* may be an interface name or an IP address associated with only one interface.
xmit *interface*	All packets going out by the specified interface. *interface* may be an interface name or an IP address associated with only one interface.
IP address	This is an IP address. It specifies a match for exactly this address.
IP address/ bits	*bits* is a value between 0 and 32. This form matches the first *bits* bits of *IP address*.
IP address : mask	*mask* is a 32-bit value. This form matches those bits of *IP address* which are specified in *mask*. This is the same concept as a net mask—see Chapter 21, *Networks and the Internet*, page 398, for a description of net masks.

ipfw: defining access rules

The program *ipfw* defines access rules for the firewall. The default is to allow no traffic. The rules define particular kinds of packet, and what to do with them.

Table 28-1 shows the keywords you can use to define the packets and the forms that *IP address range* can take. These options can be combined with a few restrictions:

- The `recv` interface can be tested on either incoming or outgoing packets, while the `xmit` interface can only be tested on outgoing packets. This means that you must specify the keyword `out` (and you may not specify `in`) when you use `xmit`. You can't specify `via` together with `xmit` or `recv`.

- A packet which originates from the local host does not have a receive interface. A packet destined for the local host has no transmit interface.

There are other tests which you can also apply, but these are the most important.

Actions

So far, we've seen how to identify packets. Next, we need to decide what to do with any packet that we single out. In some cases, we can do more than one thing with them: after performing a rule, the firewall code may continue searching the remaining rules. We'll note which of them do this below. Table 28-2 shows the possibilities.

Writing rules

The sequence in which rules are applied is *not* necessarily the sequence in which they are read. Instead, each rule can have a *line number* between 1 and 65534. Rules are applied from the lowest to the highest line number. If you enter a rule without a line number, however, it is automatically numbered 100 higher than the previous rule.

The highest-numbered rule is number 65535, which is always present:

```
65535 deny all from any to any
```

In other words, if no other rules are present, or they don't match the packet, it will be dropped. If you build a kernel with the option `IPFIREWALL_DEFAULT_TO_ACCEPT`, this rule is changed to its opposite:

```
65535 allow all from any to any
```

These two rulesets implicitly illustrate two basic security strategies. You may note parallels to certain political systems:

- The first takes the attitude "everything is forbidden unless explicitly allowed".

- The second takes the attitude "everything is allowed unless explicitly forbidden".

It goes without saying that the first policy is more restrictive—and, many argue, safer. If you make a mistake with the first (more restrictive) ruleset, you're more likely to lock people out of

501

your system accidentally than you are to let them in when you don't want them.

Table 28-2. Actions on packets

Keyword	Description
allow	Allow a packet to pass. Stop processing the rules.
deny	Discard the packet. Stop processing the rules.
unreach	Discard the packet and send an ICMP *host unreachable* message to the sender. Stop processing the rules.
reset	Discard the packet and send a TCP reset message. This can only apply to TCP packets. Stop processing the rules.
count	Count the packet and continue processing the rules.
divert *port*	Divert the packet to the *divert socket* bound to port *port*. See the man page *ipfw(8)* for more details. Stop processing the rules.
tee *port*	Send a copy of the packet to the *divert socket* bound to port *port*. Continue processing the rules.
skipto *rule*	Continue processing the rules at rule number *rule*.

Configuration files

The main configuration file is */etc/rc.firewall*. You will need to do a lot of customization to get this to do what you want, so we'll just look at some parts of it. It starts with:

```
/sbin/ipfw add 1000 pass all from 127.0.0.1 to 127.0.0.1
```

This rule allows all local traffic.

To set up the firewall, first decide the kind of profile you need. The current version of */etc/rc.firewall* defines three kinds of usage profile:

* The *open* profile is effectively a disabled firewall. It allows all traffic.

* The *client* profile is a good starting point for a system which does not provide many publicly accessible services to the net.

* The *simple* profile, despite its name, is intended for systems which do provide a number of publicly accessible services to the net.

We'll look at them individually:

The *open* profile

```
# Prototype setups.
if [ "${firewall}" = "open" ]; then

    /sbin/ipfw add 65000 pass all from any to any
```

In other words, everything is allowed.

The *client* profile

```
elif [ "${firewall}" = "client" ]; then

    ############
    # This is a prototype setup that will protect your system somewhat against
    # people from outside your own network.
    ############

    # set these to your network and netmask and ip
    net="223.147.37.0"
    mask="255.255.255.0"
    ip="223.147.37.1"              freebie.example.org
```

In the current version of */etc/rc.firewall*, you need to set these values yourself. This may change—check the addenda.

```
    # Allow any traffic to or from my own net.
    /sbin/ipfw add pass all from ${ip} to ${net}:${mask}
    /sbin/ipfw add pass all from ${net}:${mask} to ${ip}
```

The preceding rules allow any traffic in the local network.

```
    # Allow TCP through if setup succeeded
    /sbin/ipfw add pass tcp from any to any established
```

If a TCP connection has already been established, allow it to continue. Establishing a TCP connection requires other rules, which we shall see below.

```
    # Allow setup of incoming email
    /sbin/ipfw add pass tcp from any to ${ip} 25 setup

    # Allow setup of outgoing TCP connections only
    /sbin/ipfw add pass tcp from ${ip} to any setup

    # Disallow setup of all other TCP connections
    /sbin/ipfw add deny tcp from any to any setup
```

The preceding three rules allow external systems to establish a TCP connection for delivering mail (first rule), but nothing else (third rule). The second rule allows setup of TCP connections to the outside world.

```
    # Allow DNS queries out in the world
    /sbin/ipfw add pass udp from any 53 to ${ip}
    /sbin/ipfw add pass udp from ${ip} to any 53

    # Allow NTP queries out in the world
    /sbin/ipfw add pass udp from any 123 to ${ip}
    /sbin/ipfw add pass udp from ${ip} to any 123

    # Everything else is denied as default.
```

These two rules allow DNS and NTP queries. Since these are all the rules, the default *deny* rule prevents any other kind of traffic.

The *simple* profile

Despite the name, the *simple* profile is really a simple server profile. It assumes that the machine is a gateway, and that it will supply DNS and NTP services to the outside world (for example, to the *client* machine we just looked at. This profile is more appropriate for the system *gw.example.org*, so we'll use its addresses.

```
elif [ "${firewall}" = "simple" ]; then
        # set these to your outside interface network and netmask and ip
        oif="tun0"
        onet="139.130.136.0"
        omask="255.255.255.0"
        oip="139.130.136.133"

        # set these to your inside interface network and netmask and ip
        iif="ep0"
        inet="223.147.37.0"
        imask="255.255.255.0"
        iip="223.147.37.0"
```

These addresses and networks correspond to the PPP link and the local ethernet, respectively.

```
        # Stop spoofing
        /sbin/ipfw add deny all from ${inet}:${imask} to any in via ${oif}
        /sbin/ipfw add deny all from ${onet}:${omask} to any in via ${iif}
```

These two rules stop any packets purporting to come from the local network which arrive via the external network, and any packets purporting to come from the remote network which arrive via the local interface. These packets would have been faked, an action known as *spoofing*.

```
        # Stop RFC1918 nets on the outside interface
        /sbin/ipfw add deny all from 192.168.0.0:255.255.0.0 to any via ${oif}
        /sbin/ipfw add deny all from 172.16.0.0:255.240.0.0 to any via ${oif}
        /sbin/ipfw add deny all from 10.0.0.0:255.0.0.0 to any via ${oif}
```

RFC 1918 defines networks which should not be routed. These rules enforce that requirement.

```
        # Allow TCP through if setup succeeded
        /sbin/ipfw add pass tcp from any to any established

        # Allow setup of incoming email
        /sbin/ipfw add pass tcp from any to ${oip} 25 setup

        # Allow access to our DNS
        /sbin/ipfw add pass tcp from any to ${oip} 53 setup

        # Allow access to our WWW
        /sbin/ipfw add pass tcp from any to ${oip} 80 setup
```

These rules add to what we saw for the *client* profile: in addition to email, we will allow incoming DNS and WWW connections.

Do you want to allow *anybody* to load your zone information? See page 496 for more details. If you don't want them to, you can stop them by disallowing tcp connections from the outside world: *named-xfer* uses TCP to load zone information, but *named* uses UDP to get individual records.

```
# Reject&Log all setup of incoming connections from the outside
/sbin/ipfw add deny log tcp from any to any in via ${oif} setup

# Allow setup of any other TCP connection
/sbin/ipfw add pass tcp from any to any setup
```

Here, we don't just reject TCP setup requests from the outside world, we log them as well.

```
# Allow DNS queries out in the world
/sbin/ipfw add pass udp from any 53 to ${oip}
/sbin/ipfw add pass udp from ${oip} to any 53

# Allow NTP queries out in the world
/sbin/ipfw add pass udp from any 123 to ${oip}
/sbin/ipfw add pass udp from ${oip} to any 123

# Everything else is denied as default.
```

Finally, we allow DNS and NTP queries via UDP, and deny everything else from the outside world.

user-defined profiles

If the profile isn't one of the recognized keywords, */etc/rc.firewall* checks if there's a file with that name. If so, it uses it as a command file to pass to *ipfw*:

```
elif [ "${firewall}" != "NONE" -a -r "${firewall}" ]; then
    /sbin/ipfw ${firewall}
```

Note that you can't put comment lines in the file defined by ${firewall}.

/etc/rc.conf

Once you have decided what kind of firewall configuration best suits your network, note the fact in */etc/rc.conf*. Set the value of firewall_enable to **YES** to enable the firewall, and the value of firewall_type to indicate the type of firewall. For our example network, client is probably the most appropriate type:

```
firewall_enable="YES"       # Set to YES to enable firewall functionality
firewall_type="client"      # Firewall type (see /etc/rc.firewall)
```

Trying it out

You'll probably find that your first attempt at firewall configuration won't be the optimum, to put it mildly. You'll probably discover requirements that you hadn't thought of which are now being denied by the default rule. Be prepared to spend some time getting everything to work, and *do this at the system console*. There's no good alternative, not even X in this case: if you mess up your localhost rule, you won't be able to use X either.

IP aliasing

In our reference network on page 400, we assumed that our local network had a valid assigned IP address. Sometimes, this isn't possible. In fact, in the Real World it's pretty well impossible to get a complete class C network for a system with only five systems on it. You have the alternative of getting a subset of a class C network (in this case, 8 addresses would do) from your ISP, or using just one address and running software which makes all traffic from the network to the outside world look as if it's coming from that system. The latter approach, called *IP aliasing*, can be significantly cheaper: ISPs usually charge good money for additional addresses.

IP aliasing software

FreeBSD has a number of packages which provide IP aliasing. If you're connecting to the outside world via User PPP (see Chapter 25, *Configuring PPP*, page 447), you can use the `-alias` keyword to tell PPP to alias *all* packets coming from the network to the address of the tunnel interface. In our reference network, this would be the address `139.130.136.133`.

There are some good reasons not to use this particular form of IP aliasing: it only works for a single User PPP connection to the outside world, and it's global in its functionality. One alternative is the *Network Address Translation Dæmon*, or *natd*, which uses divert sockets to translate addresses. It works well in conjunction with the firewall software we looked at above.

natd

To set up *natd*, perform the following steps:

- Even if you don't plan to run an IP firewall, build a custom kernel with the following options:

    ```
    options IPFIREWALL
    options IPDIVERT
    ```

    If you are running a firewall, configure the firewall normally, but be sure to include the `IPDIVERT` option.

- Ensure that your machine is acting as a gateway. See Chapter 22, *Configuring the local network*, page 411 for further details.

- Make sure your interface is running. For example, if you're running User PPP, and you want to specify *tun0* as your interface, start *ppp* before starting *natd*.

- Make sure you have the following entry in */etc/services*:

```
natd           6668/divert  # Network Address Translation socket
```

- Adjust the */etc/rc.firewall* script as shown above. If you're not using a firewall, the following lines will be enough:

```
/sbin/ipfw -f flush
/sbin/ipfw add divert natd all from any to any via tun0
/sbin/ipfw add pass all from any to any
```

Make sure you have the correct interface name in the second line. This is the name of the interface to the external world, not the LAN.

Older versions of *natd* didn't look up the names in */etc/services*. If you run into problems, consider putting the service in as a number rather than a name.

If you specify real firewall rules, it's best to specify line 2 at the start of the script so that natd sees all packets before they are dropped by the firewall. After *natd* translates the IP addresses, the firewall rules will be run again on the translated packet, with the exception of the divert rules.

- Enable your firewall as shown above in the firewall section. If you don't wish to reboot now, just run */etc/rc.firewall* this by hand from the console:

```
# firewall=client sh /etc/rc.firewall
```

The expression `firewall=client` tells the Bourne shell to set the value of the variable `firewall` just for this command. If you're using *csh* or *tcsh*, use the following sequence:

```
(setenv firewall=client; sh /etc/rc.firewall)
```

Never start this script from an X terminal or across the network. If you do, you can lock yourself out of the session in the middle of the script, and */etc/rc.firewall* will stop at this point, blocking all accesses permanently.

- Add the following to */etc/rc.conf*:

```
natd_enable="YES"                # Enable natd (if firewall_enable == YES).
natd_interface="tun0"            # Public interface or IPaddress to use.
```

See the man page *natd(8)* for the meanings of the flags. In particular, `-unregistered_only` tells *natd* to only modify packets with *unregistered* source addresses. We'll look at them in the next section.

Choosing an IP address for the LAN

One freedom that *natd* gives you is the choice of an IP address for the LAN. Theoretically, you can choose just about anything. Of course, Murphy's law dictates that you will then find that you need to communicate with the real owner of that IP address. The address will usually be hidden in a name (a URL, for example), and finding out the problem can be quite complicated.

There's no need for this problem. We saw above that RFC 1918 defines networks which should not be routed, so-called *unregistered* IP addresses. Choose one of the address ranges `192.168.0.0` to `192.168.255.255`, `172.16.0.0` to `172.31.255.255`, or `10.0.0.0` to `10.255.255.255`. In practice, it's best to choose `192.168.0.0` to `192.168.255.255`, since that address range is least likely to give you problems with net masks.

29

Network debugging

The chances are that you'll have some problems somewhere when you set up your network. FreeBSD gives you a large number of tools with which to find and solve the problem.

In this chapter, we'll first look some of the more useful tools. In particular, in the next section we'll look at the *ping* program, on page 510 we'll look at *traceroute*, and on page 512 we'll look at the *tcpdump* program. After that, on page 514, we'll consider a methodology of debugging network problems.

Network debug tools

We've already seen a number of tools which can also be of use to us in debugging network problems, in particular *ifconfig* (page 405), *route* (page 408), and *netstat* (page 410). In addition, we have three tools which are used specifically for debugging: *ping*, *tcpdump* and *traceroute*. It will help to have your finger in Chapter 21, *Networks and the Internet* while reading this section.

ping

ping is a relatively simple program which sends a packet to a specific IP address and checks the reply. The packet is an *ICMP echo packet*. *ICMP* is the *Internet Control Message Protocol*—see *TCP/IP Illustrated*, by Richard Stevens, for more information.

A typical *ping* session might look like:

```
$ ping daemon
PING bumble.example.org (223.147.37.156): 56 data bytes
64 bytes from 223.147.37.156: icmp_seq=0 ttl=255 time=1.137 ms
64 bytes from 223.147.37.156: icmp_seq=1 ttl=255 time=0.640 ms
64 bytes from 223.147.37.156: icmp_seq=2 ttl=255 time=0.671 ms
64 bytes from 223.147.37.156: icmp_seq=3 ttl=255 time=0.612 ms
^C
--- bumble.example.org ping statistics ---
4 packets transmitted, 4 packets received, 0% packet loss
round-trip min/avg/max/stddev = 0.612/0.765/1.137/0.216 ms
```

In this case, we are sending the messages to the system *bumble.example.org*. By default, *ping* will send messages of 56 bytes. With the IP header, this makes packets of 64 bytes. When started without parameters, *ping* continues until you stop it—notice the ^C indicating that this invocation was stopped by pressing **Ctrl-C**.

The information that *ping* gives you isn't much, but it's useful:

- It tells you how long it takes for each individual packet to get to its destination and back.

- It tells you how many didn't make it.

- It also prints a summary of packet statistics.

But what if this doesn't work? You enter your ping command, and all you get is:

```
$ ping wait
PING wait.example.org (223.147.37.4): 56 data bytes
^C
--- wait.example.org ping statistics ---
5 packets transmitted, 0 packets received, 100% packet loss
```

Obviously, something's wrong here. We'll look at it in more detail below. This is *very* different, however, from this situation:

```
$ ping presto
^C
```

In the second case, even after waiting a reasonable amount of time, nothing happened at all. *ping* didn't print the PING message, and when we hit **Ctrl-C** there was no further output. This is indicative of a name resolution problem: *ping* can't print the first line (PING presto...) until it has found the IP address of the system, in other words until it has performed a DNS lookup. If we wait long enough, it will time out, and we get the message ping: cannot resolve presto: Unknown host.

If this happens, use the IP address instead of the name. As we'll see below, we will solve name lookup problems later in the day.

traceroute

ping is a useful tool for telling you whether data is getting through to the destination, and if so, how much is getting through. If nothing gets through, there are two possibilities:

- If both systems are on the same network, you need to look at the network connections.

- If the systems are on two different networks, we don't know which network to look at. It could be either of the networks on which the systems are located, or it could also be a problem with one of the networks on the way. How do you find out where your packets get lost?

Another problem: you're losing 40% of your packets to *foo.bar.org*, and the remaining ones are taking up to 5 *seconds* to get through. Where's the problem? Based on the recent "upgrade" your ISP performed, and the fact that you've had trouble getting to other sites, you suspect that the performance problems might be occurring in the ISP's net. How can you find out?

In each case, it's difficult, but frequently *traceroute* can help. *traceroute* sends UDP packets to the destination, but it modifies the *time-to-live* field (see page 390) so that, initially at any rate, they don't get there. As we saw on page 21-2, the time-to-live field specifies the number of hops that a packet can go before it is discarded. When it is, the system which discards it *should* send back an *ICMP destination unreachable* message. *traceroute* uses this feature and sends out packets with time-to-live set first to one, then to two, and so on. It prints the IP address of the system which sends the "destination unreachable" message, and the time it took, thus giving something like a three-dimensional *ping*. Here's an example to *hub.FreeBSD.org*:

```
$ traceroute hub.freebsd.org
traceroute to hub.freebsd.org (204.216.27.18), 30 hops max, 40 byte packets
 1  gw (223.147.37.5)  1.138 ms  0.811 ms  0.800 ms
 2  free-gw.example.net (139.130.136.129)  131.913 ms  122.231 ms  134.694 ms
 3  Ethernet1-0.way1.Adelaide.telstra.net (139.130.237.65)  118.229 ms  120.040 ms  118.723 ms
 4  Fddi0-0.way-core1.Adelaide.telstra.net (139.130.237.226)  171.590 ms  117.911 ms  123.513 ms
 5  Serial5-0.lon-core1.Melbourne.telstra.net (139.130.239.21)  129.267 ms  226.927 ms  125.547 ms
 6  Fddi0-0.lon5.Melbourne.telstra.net (139.130.239.231)  144.372 ms  133.998 ms  136.699 ms
 7  borderx2-hssi3-0.Bloomington.mci.net (204.70.208.121)  962.258 ms  482.393 ms  754.989 ms
 8  core2-fddi-1.Bloomington.mci.net (204.70.208.65)  821.636 ms  *  701.920 ms
 9  bordercore3-loopback.SanFrancisco.mci.net (166.48.16.1)  424.254 ms  884.033 ms  645.302 ms
10  pb-nap.crl.net (198.32.128.20)  435.907 ms  438.933 ms  451.173 ms
11  E0-CRL-SFO-02-E0X0.US.CRL.NET (165.113.55.2)  440.425 ms  430.049 ms  447.340 ms
12  T1-CDROM-00-EX.US.CRL.NET (165.113.118.2)  553.624 ms  460.116 ms  *
13  hub.FreeBSD.ORG (204.216.27.18)  642.032 ms  463.661 ms  432.976 ms
```

By default, *traceroute* tries each hop three times and prints out the times as they happen, so if the reponse time is more than about 300 ms, you'll notice it as it happens. If there is no reply after a timeout period, *traceroute* will print an asterisk (*). You'll also occasionally notice a significant delay at the beginning of a line, although the response time seems reasonable. In this case, the delay is probably caused by a DNS reverse lookup for the name of the system.

If you look more carefully at the times in the example above, you'll see three groups of times:

1. The times to *freebie* are round 1 ms. This is typical of an Ethernet.

2. The times for hops 2 to 6 are in the order of 100 to 150 ms. This is indicative of the fact that the link between *gw.example.org* and *free-gw.example.net* is running PPP at 33.6 kb/s. The delay between *free-gw.example.net* and *Fddi0-0.lon5.Melbourne.telstra.net* is negligible compared to the delay across the PPP link, so you don't see much difference.

3. The times from *borderx2-hssi3-0.Bloomington.mci.net* to *hub.FreeBSD.ORG* are significantly higher, between 400 and 1000 ms. We also note a couple of dropped packets. This is indicative of the fact that the line between *Fddi0-0.lon5.Melbourne.telstra.net* and *borderx2-hssi3-0.Bloomington.mci.net* is overloaded. The length of the link (about 8,000 miles) is *not* relevant.

tcpdump

tcpdump is a program which monitors a network interface and displays selected information which passes through it. It uses the *Berkeley Packet Filter* (*bpf*), an optional component of the kernel which is not included in the GENERIC kernel: see Chapter 18, *Configuring the kernel*, page 355, for information on how to configure it.

If you don't configure the Berkeley Packet Filter, you will get a message like

```
tcpdump: /dev/bpf0: device not configured
```

If you forget to create the devices for bpf, you will get a message like:

```
tcpdump: /dev/bpf0: No such file or directory
```

Since *tcpdump* poses a potential security problem, you must be root in order to run it. The simplest way to run it is without any parameters. This will cause *tcpdump* to monitor and display all traffic on the first active network interface, normally Ethernet:

```
# tcpdump
tcpdump: listening on ep0
1: 13:27:57.757157 arp who-has wait.example.org tell presto.example.org
2: 13:28:06.740047 0:4c:a5:0:0:0 2:0:0:0:45:0 4011 80:
                       c93c c06d c589 c06d c5ff 007b 007b 0038
                       5ccb 1d03 06ee 0000 5613 0000 1093 cb15
                       2512 b7e2 de6b 0ead c000 0000 0000 0000
                       0000 0000 0000
3: 13:28:06.740117 freebie.example.org.ntp > 223.147.37.255.ntp: v3 bcast strat 3 p
oll 6  prec -18
4: 13:28:08.004715 arp who-has wait.example.org tell presto.example.org
5: 13:28:10.987453 bumble.example.org.who > 223.147.37.255.who: udp 84
6: 13:28:13.790106 freebie.example.org.6000 > presto.example.org.1089: P 536925467:
   536925851(384) ack 325114346 win 17280 <nop,nop,timestamp 155186 1163778,nop,no
   p,[|tcp]> (DF)
7: 13:28:13.934336 arp who-has freebie.example.org tell presto.example.org
8: 13:28:13.934444 arp reply freebie.example.org is-at 0:a0:24:37:d:2b
9: 13:28:13.935903 presto.example.org.1089 > freebie.example.org.6000: . ack 536925
851 win 16896 <nop,nop,timestamp 1190189 155186,nop,nop,[|tcp]> (DF)
10: 13:28:13.936313 freebie.example.org.6000 > presto.example.org.1089: P 536925851
   :536926299(448) ack 325114346 win 17280 <nop,nop,timestamp 155186 1190189,nop,no
   p,[|tcp]> (DF)
```

This output looks confusing at first. Let's look at it in more detail:

* The first message shows the interface on which *tcpdump* listens. By default, it is the first running interface that it finds in its list. The sequence of the list is the same that *ifconfig -a* displays, but generally you can assume it to be the Ethernet interface. If you want to listen on another interface, specify it on the command line. For example, to listen on a PPP interface, you would enter

```
# tcpdump -i tun0
```

- At the beginning of each message is a timestamp, with a resolution of 1 μs. These times are relatively accurate; you'll frequently see time differences of less than 1 ms. In this example, the last two messages are 108 μs apart. These times are important: a lot of network problems are performance problems, and there's a big difference in performance between a net where a reply takes 100 μs and one in which a reply takes 100 ms.

- To make things easier, I have put a line number in *italics* at the beginning of each line. This line does not appear in the *tcpdump* printout.

- Line 1 shows an *ARP* request: system *presto* is looking for the Ethernet address of *wait*. It would appear that *wait* is currently not responding, since there is no reply.

- Line 2 is not an IP message at all. *tcpdump* shows the Ethernet addresses and the beginning of the packet. We don't consider this kind of request in this book.

- Line 3 is a broadcast *ntp* message. We looked at *ntp* on page 186.

- Line 4 is another attempt by *presto* to find the IP address of *wait*.

- Line 5 is a broadcast message from *bumble* on the rwho port, giving information about its current load averages and how long it has been up. See the man page *rwho(1)* for more information.

- Line 6 is from a TCP connection between port 6000 on *freebie* and port 1089 on *presto*. It is sending 384 bytes (with the sequence numbers 536925467 to 536925851; see page 391), and is acknowledging that the last byte it received from *presto* had the sequence number 325114346. The window size is 17280.

- Line 7 is another ARP request. *presto* is looking for the Ethernet address of *freebie*. How can that happen? We've just seen that they have a TCP connection. In fact, ARP information expires after 20 minutes. It's quite possible that all connections between *presto* and *freebie* have been dormant for this period, so *presto* needs to find *freebie*'s IP address again.

- Line 8 is the ARP reply from *freebie* to *presto* giving its Ethernet address.

- Line 9 shows a reply from *presto* on the connection to *freebie* that we saw on line 6. It acknowledges the data up to sequence number 536925851, but doesn't send any itself.

- Line 10 shows another 448 bytes of data from *freebie* to *presto*, and acknowledging the same sequence number from *presto* as in line 6.

How to approach network problems

You will recall from Chapter 21, *Networks and the Internet*, that network software and hardware operate at at least four layers. If one layer doesn't work, the ones on top won't either. It obviously makes sense to start at the bottom and work up.

Most people understand this up to a point. Nobody expects a PPP connection to the Internet to work if the modem can't dial the ISP. On the other hand, a large number of messages to the `FreeBSD-questions` mailing list show that many people seem to think that once this connection has been established, everything else will work automatically. If it doesn't, they're puzzled.

Unfortunately, the Net isn't that simple. In fact, it's too complicated to give a hard-and-fast methodology at all. Much network debugging can look more like magic than anything rational. Nevertheless, a surprising number of network problems can be solved by using the steps below. Even if they don't solve your problem, read through them. They might give you some ideas about where to look.

The link layer

The first thing to do is to ensure that the link layer is running. You can do this by *ping*ing another address on the same link. In the case of a PPP link, you don't get any choice: ping the address at the other end of the link. In the case of an Ethernet, you have a choice of addresses. In either case, be sure to use the IP address, not the name: in order to get the address from the name, you may need to issue a DNS query, which runs at the application layer. The chances that the name resolution will fail are much higher than the chances that the *ping* will fail.

A successful ping, here from *gw.example.org* to *free-gw.example.net*, will look like this:

```
$ ping 139.130.136.129
PING 139.130.136.129 (139.130.136.129): 56 data bytes
64 bytes from 139.130.136.129: icmp_seq=0 ttl=255 time=145.203 ms
64 bytes from 139.130.136.129: icmp_seq=1 ttl=255 time=140.743 ms
64 bytes from 139.130.136.129: icmp_seq=2 ttl=255 time=138.039 ms
64 bytes from 139.130.136.129: icmp_seq=3 ttl=255 time=139.783 ms
64 bytes from 139.130.136.129: icmp_seq=4 ttl=255 time=136.698 ms
64 bytes from 139.130.136.129: icmp_seq=5 ttl=255 time=138.753 ms
64 bytes from 139.130.136.129: icmp_seq=6 ttl=255 time=208.389 ms
64 bytes from 139.130.136.129: icmp_seq=7 ttl=255 time=187.463 ms
64 bytes from 139.130.136.129: icmp_seq=8 ttl=255 time=128.463 ms
64 bytes from 139.130.136.129: icmp_seq=9 ttl=255 time=333.895 ms
64 bytes from 139.130.136.129: icmp_seq=10 ttl=255 time=180.670 ms
^C                    stop by hitting Ctrl-C
--- 139.130.136.129 ping statistics ---
11 packets transmitted, 11 packets received, 0% packet loss
round-trip min/avg/max/stddev = 128.463/170.736/333.895/57.179 ms
```

When we looked at this display on page 509, we were just interested in whether we got a reply or not. This time, however, we need to look a little more carefully:

- Check if *all* packets got there. Lost packets could mean line quality problems. In fact, there's an uncertainty here: you might hit **Ctrl-C** after last packet went out, but before it came back.

- Check that each packet comes back only once. If not, there's definitely something wrong.

- Check the times. A *ping* across an Ethernet should take between about 0.5 and 4 ms, a *ping* across an ISDN connection should take about 30 ms, and a *ping* across a 33.6 kb/s analogue connection should take about 150 ms. All of these times are for idle lines, and the time can go up to about 1.5 seconds for a line transferring large blocks of data (for example, *ftp*ing a file). In this example, some line traffic delayed the response to individual pings.

If you get results like these, you can assume that the link layer is working correctly, and you can continue at the next section, "The network layer". Otherwise read on.

Link layer problems

But maybe your *ping* output didn't look like the example above. Let's look at a couple of possibilities:

- Maybe your interface hasn't been configured correctly. Check the output of *ifconfig*:

```
ifconfig ep0
ep0: flags=8843<UP,BROADCAST,RUNNING,SIMPLEX,MULTICAST> mtu 1500
        inet 223.147.37.1 netmask 0xffffff00 broadcast 223.147.37.255
        ether 00:a0:24:37:0d:2b
```

The second line is the important one: check that the IP address, net mask and broadcast address are correct. Don't rely on the fact that this is a class C address: if somebody else than you is administering the network, check with him that the net mask is what he has implemented.

- If your interface is configured correctly, check whether you are using the correct connection to the network. Many modern Ethernet boards support multiple physical connections (for example, both BNC and UTP). For example, if your network runs on RG58 thin Ethernet, and your interface is set to receive from a AUI, you may still be able to send data on the RG58, but you won't be able to receive any.

The method of setting the connection depends on the board you are using. In the case of some older boards, such as the Western Digital 8003, you may need to set jumpers. In others, you may need to run the setup utility under DOS,[1] and with other you can set it with the *link* flags to *ifconfig*. For example, on a 3Com 3c509 "combo" board, you can set the connection like this:

---

1. An old joke claims that *DOS* stands for *Diagnostic Operational Support*, since many UNIX people use it only to run diagnostics.

515

```
# ifconfig ep0 -link0              set BNC
# ifconfig ep0 link0 -link1        set AUI
# ifconfig ep0 link0 link1         set UTP
```

Don't assume that these flags work the same way for other Ethernet boards: each board has its own flags. Read the man page for the board for the correct flags.

- If your interface looks OK, check whether you can *ping* other machines on the network. If so, of course, you should continue your search on the machine that isn't responding.

- If you can't get any response, check whether you can communicate between other machines on the network. If none are working, you probably have a cabling problem. On an RG58 network, the solution to this one is "divide and conquer": divide the network into two by disconnecting a segment in the middle and placing terminators at each side of the division:

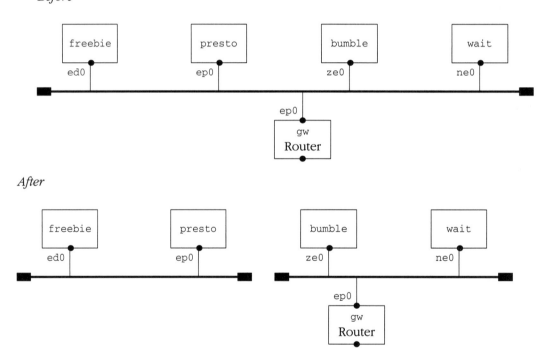

Typically, you will then find that one of the resultant networks will work, and the other will not. Repartition the network to find which one works, and continue until you find the cabling fault.

The network layer

After you are sure that the link layer is functional,, check the network layer. Try to ping a system which is not directly connected. Typically, you'll have been having communication problems with a specific system, so try to ping that system. If you don't have a specific machine, use one of the root name servers, since we'll probably be performing a name server lookup later on. The addresses are in the file */etc/namedb/named.root*, but you can usually rely on the address of *A.ROOT-SERVERS.NET.* to be 198.41.0.4. The *ping* looks much as before:

```
$ ping 198.41.0.4
PING 198.41.0.4 (198.41.0.4): 56 data bytes
64 bytes from 198.41.0.4: icmp_seq=0 ttl=244 time=496.426 ms
64 bytes from 198.41.0.4: icmp_seq=1 ttl=244 time=491.334 ms
64 bytes from 198.41.0.4: icmp_seq=2 ttl=244 time=479.077 ms
64 bytes from 198.41.0.4: icmp_seq=3 ttl=244 time=473.774 ms
64 bytes from 198.41.0.4: icmp_seq=4 ttl=244 time=733.429 ms
64 bytes from 198.41.0.4: icmp_seq=5 ttl=244 time=644.726 ms
64 bytes from 198.41.0.4: icmp_seq=7 ttl=244 time=490.331 ms
64 bytes from 198.41.0.4: icmp_seq=8 ttl=244 time=839.671 ms
64 bytes from 198.41.0.4: icmp_seq=9 ttl=244 time=773.764 ms
64 bytes from 198.41.0.4: icmp_seq=10 ttl=244 time=553.067 ms
64 bytes from 198.41.0.4: icmp_seq=11 ttl=244 time=454.707 ms
64 bytes from 198.41.0.4: icmp_seq=12 ttl=244 time=472.212 ms
64 bytes from 198.41.0.4: icmp_seq=13 ttl=244 time=448.322 ms
64 bytes from 198.41.0.4: icmp_seq=14 ttl=244 time=441.352 ms
64 bytes from 198.41.0.4: icmp_seq=15 ttl=244 time=455.595 ms
64 bytes from 198.41.0.4: icmp_seq=16 ttl=244 time=460.040 ms
64 bytes from 198.41.0.4: icmp_seq=17 ttl=244 time=476.943 ms
64 bytes from 198.41.0.4: icmp_seq=18 ttl=244 time=514.615 ms
64 bytes from 198.41.0.4: icmp_seq=23 ttl=244 time=538.232 ms
64 bytes from 198.41.0.4: icmp_seq=24 ttl=244 time=444.123 ms
64 bytes from 198.41.0.4: icmp_seq=25 ttl=244 time=449.075 ms
^C
--- 198.41.0.4 ping statistics ---
27 packets transmitted, 21 packets received, 22% packet loss
round-trip min/avg/max/stddev = 441.352/530.039/839.671/113.674 ms
```

In this case, we have a connection. What about the packet loss rate? How high a packet drop rate is still acceptable? 1% or 2% is probably still all right, and you'll see that often enough. By the time you get to 10%, though, things look a lot worse. 10% packet drop rate doesn't mean that your connection slows down by 10%. For every dropped packet, you have a minimum delay of one second until TCP retries it. If that retried packet gets dropped too—which it will every 10 dropped packets if you have a 10% drop rater—the second retry takes another 3 seconds. If you're transmitting packets of 64 bytes over a 33.6 kb/s link, you can normally get about 60 packets through per second. With 10% packet loss, the time to get these packets through will be about 8 seconds: a throughput loss of 87.5%.

With 20% packet loss, the results are even more dramatic. Now 12 of the 60 packets have to be retried, and 2.4 of them will be retried a second time (for 3 seconds delay), and 0.48 of them will be retried a third time (6 seconds delay). This makes a total of 22 seconds delay, a throughput degradation of nearly 96%.

Theoretically, you might think that the degradation would not be as bad for big packets, such as you might have with file transfers with *ftp*. In fact, the situation is worse then: the packet drop rate rises sharply with the packet size, and it's common enough that *ftp* will time out completely before it can transfer a file.

The following example shows the result of sending some text on a less-than-perfect *ssh* connection to *hub.FreeBSD.org*. To make things more readable, the names have been truncated to *freebie* and *hub*. In real-life output, they would be reported as *freebie.example.org* and *hub.FreeBSD.org*.

```
# tcpdump -i ppp0 host hub.freebsd.org
14:16:35.990506 freebie.1019 > hub.22: P 20:40(20) ack 77 win 17520 (DF) [tos 0x10]
14:16:36.552149 hub.22 > freebie.1019: P 77:97(20) ack 40 win 17520 (DF) [tos 0x10]
14:16:36.722290 freebie.1019 > hub.22: . ack 97 win 17520 (DF) [tos 0x10]
14:16:39.344229 freebie.1019 > hub.22: P 40:60(20) ack 97 win 17520 (DF) [tos 0x10]
14:16:41.321850 freebie.1019 > hub.22: P 40:60(20) ack 97 win 17520 (DF) [tos 0x10]
```

The previous two lines are retries of the same acknowledgement, since *hub* did not respond in time.

```
14:16:42.316150 hub.22 > freebie.1019: P 97:117(20) ack 60 win 17520 (DF) [tos 0x10]
```

This was the missing acknowledgement—it came another second later.

```
14:16:42.321773 freebie.1019 > hub.22: . ack 117 win 17520 (DF) [tos 0x10]
14:16:47.428694 freebie.1019 > hub.22: P 60:80(20) ack 117 win 17520 (DF) [tos 0x10]
14:16:48.590805 freebie.1019 > hub.22: P 80:100(20) ack 117 win 17520 (DF) [tos 0x10]
14:16:49.055735 freebie.1019 > hub.22: P 100:120(20) ack 117 win 17520 (DF) [tos 0x10]
14:16:49.190703 hub.22 > freebie.1019: P 137:157(20) ack 100 win 17520 (DF) [tos 0x10]
```

Here, *freebie* has sent data to *hub*, and *hub* has replied with an acknowledgement up to serial number 100. Unfortunately, the data it sent (serial numbers 137 to 157) don't line up with the last previously received data (serial number 117 at 14:16:42.316150). *freebie* thus repeats the previous acknowledgement and then continues sending its data:

```
14:16:49.190890 freebie.1019 > hub.22: . ack 117 win 17520 (DF) [tos 0x10]
14:16:49.538607 freebie.1019 > hub.22: P 120:140(20) ack 117 win 17520 (DF) [tos 0x10]
14:16:49.599395 hub.22 > freebie.1019: P 157:177(20) ack 120 win 17520 (DF) [tos 0x10]
```

Here, *hub* has sent yet more data, now acknowledging the data that *freebie* sent at 14:16:49.055735. It still hasn't sent the data in the serial number range 117 to 136, so *freebie* resends the last acknowledgement again and continues sending data:

```
14:16:49.599538 freebie.1019 > hub.22: . ack 117 win 17520 (DF) [tos 0x10]
14:16:49.620506 freebie.1019 > hub.22: P 140:160(20) ack 117 win 17520 (DF) [tos 0x10]
14:16:50.066698 hub.22 > freebie.1019: P 177:197(20) ack 140 win 17520 (DF) [tos 0x10]
```

Again *hub* has sent more data, still without sending the missing packet. *freebie* tries yet again, and then continues sending data:

```
14:16:50.066868 freebie.1019 > hub.22: . ack 117 win 17520 (DF) [tos 0x10]
14:16:51.820708 freebie.1019 > hub.22: P 140:160(20) ack 117 win 17520 (DF) [tos 0x10]
14:16:52.308992 hub.22 > freebie.1019: . ack 160 win 17520 (DF) [tos 0x10]
14:16:55.251176 hub.22 > freebie.1019: P 117:217(100) ack 160 win 17520 (DF) [tos 0x10]
```

Finally, *hub* resends the missing data, with serial numbers from 117 to 217. *freebie* is now happy, and acknowledges receipt of all the data up to 217. That's all we transmitted, so after about 1.5 seconds the two systems exchange final acknowledgements:

```
14:16:55.251358 freebie.1019 > hub.22: . ack 217 win 17420 (DF) [tos 0x10]
14:16:56.690779 hub.login > freebie.1015: . ack 3255467530 win 17520
14:16:56.690941 freebie.1015 > hub.login: . ack 1 win 17520 (DF) [tos 0x10]
```

This example shows us that the connection is less than perfect. Why? You can use *traceroute* to find out where it's happening, but unless the place is within your ISP's network, you can't do much about it.

No connection

But maybe you don't get anything back. You see something like this:

```
$ ping rider.fc.net
PING rider.fc.net (207.170.123.194): 56 data bytes
^C
--- rider.fc.net ping statistics ---
8 packets transmitted, 0 packets received, 100% packet loss
```

tcpdump shows:

```
# tcpdump -i ppp0 host rider.fc.net
13:30:32.336432 freebie.example.org > rider.fc.net: icmp: echo request
13:30:33.355045 freebie.example.org > rider.fc.net: icmp: echo request
13:30:34.374888 freebie.example.org > rider.fc.net: icmp: echo request
13:30:35.394728 freebie.example.org > rider.fc.net: icmp: echo request
13:30:36.414769 freebie.example.org > rider.fc.net: icmp: echo request
```

For some reason, *rider.fc.net* is not reachable. But why? We know it's not the local link, but somewhere the data isn't getting through. Where? *traceroute* can help:

```
# traceroute rider.fc.net
traceroute to rider.fc.net (207.170.123.194), 30 hops max, 40 byte packets
 1  Cont0.way3.Adelaide.telstra.net (139.130.136.129)  359.252 ms  138.754 ms  380.136 ms
 2  Ethernet1-0.way1.Adelaide.telstra.net (139.130.237.65)  417.399 ms  641.075 ms  654.572 ms
 3  Fddi0-0.way-core1.Adelaide.telstra.net (139.130.237.226)  653.558 ms  807.843 ms  820.315 ms
 4  Serial5-5.pad-core2.Sydney.telstra.net (139.130.249.209)  861.472 ms  165.041 ms  149.836 ms
 5  Fddi0-0.pad8.Sydney.telstra.net (139.130.249.228)  163.000 ms  207.969 ms  448.134 ms
 6  bordercore4-hssi0-0.SanFrancisco.mci.net (166.48.19.249)  347.656 ms  404.727 ms  342.072 ms
 7  core2.Dallas.mci.net (204.70.4.69)  383.040 ms  639.875 ms  560.789 ms
 8  borderx1-fddi-1.Dallas.mci.net (204.70.114.52)  436.243 ms  575.502 ms  388.719 ms
 9  smart-technologies.Dallas.mci.nct (204.70.114.110)  1025.478 ms  936.228 ms  1213.072 ms
10  freeside-100Mb.smart-nap.net (208.10.195.146)  1166.775 ms  1216.596 ms  1245.616 ms
11  6jane.fc.net (207.170.70.133)  1235.122 ms  398.822 ms  458.958 ms
12  * * *
13  *^C
```

This example shows that the data gets through fine as far as *6jane.fc.net*, after which it disappears completely. This is a pretty good sign that the problem lies in the network *fc.net*. If, as in this case, *rider* is connected via PPP, it's a good assumption that it's currently not connected.

On the other hand, you might see something like:

```
# traceroute rider.fc.net
traceroute to rider.fc.net (207.170.123.194), 30 hops max, 40 byte packets
 1  gw (223.147.37.5)  1.519 ms  1.168 ms  1.100 ms
 2  * * *
 3  * * *
```

In this case, there is obviously something wrong on the local network. You can get the data as far as *gw*, but that's as far as it goes.

There are more possible reasons for this than meet the eye. Here are some of them:

- The link to the next system may be down. The solution's obvious: bring it up and try again.

- *gw* may not be configured as a gateway. You can check this with

  ```
  $ sysctl net.inet.ip.forwarding
  net.inet.ip.forwarding: 1
  ```

  For a router, this value should be 1. If it's 0, change it with:

  ```
  # sysctl -w net.inet.ip.forwarding=1
  net.inet.ip.forwarding: 0 -> 1
  ```

  See page 411 for further details.

- You may be using a non-routable IP address such as those in the range $192.168.x.x$. You can't do that. You'll need to run some kind of aliasing package. See page 506 for further details.

- Maybe there is something wrong with routing to your network. This is a difficult one to check, but one possibility is to repeat the *traceroute* from the machine *gw*. The packets there will go out with the address $139.130.136.133$, which belongs to another network, so they will not be affected by a routing problem for network $223.147.37.x$. If this proves to be the case, contact your ISP to solve it.

Another possibility might be that you get messages like these:

```
# ping rider.fc.net
PING rider.fc.net (207.170.123.194): 56 data bytes
36 bytes from gw.example.org (223.147.37.5): Destination Host Unreachable
Vr HL TOS  Len   ID Flg  off TTL Pro  cks      Src      Dst
 4  5  00 6800 c5da   0 0000  fe  01 246d 223.147.37.2  207.170.123.194

36 bytes from gw.example.org (223.147.37.5): Destination Host Unreachable
Vr HL TOS  Len   ID Flg  off TTL Pro  cks      Src      Dst
 4  5  00 6800 c5e7   0 0000  fe  01 2460 223.147.37.2  207.170.123.194

^C
--- rider.fc.net ping statistics ---
```

```
2 packets transmitted, 0 packets received, 100% packet loss
# traceroute rider.fc.net
traceroute to rider.fc.net (207.170.123.194), 30 hops max, 40 byte packets
 1  gw (223.147.37.5)  1.519 ms  1.168 ms  1.100 ms
 2  gw (223.147.37.5)  1.244 ms !H  1.242 ms !H  0.955 ms !
```

These messages are caused by ICMP messages returned from *gw* indicating that it does not know where to send the data. This is almost certainly a problem of the routing tables: on *gw* you'll probably see something like

```
$ netstat -rn
Routing tables
```

Internet: Destination	Gateway	Flags	Refs	Use	Netif	Expire
127.0.0.1	127.0.0.1	UH	3	16671	lo0	
139.130.136.129	223.147.37.5	UH	17	2	tun0	
223.147.37	link#2	UC	0	0		
223.147.37.1	0:0:c0:44:a5:68	UHLW	4	21375	ep0	1172
223.147.37.5	127.0.0.1	UGHS	1	90	lo0	
223.147.37.255	ff:ff:ff:ff:ff:ff	UHLWb	2	3357	ep0	
224/4	link#2	UCS	0	0		

The problem here is that there is no `default` route. Add it with the *route* command:

```
# route add default 139.130.136.129
# netstat -rn
Routing tables
```

Internet: Destination	Gateway	Flags	Refs	Use	Netif	Expire
127.0.0.1	127.0.0.1	UH	3	16671	lo0	
default	139.130.136.129	UGSc	18	221	tun0	
139.130.136.129	223.147.37.5	UH	17	2	tun0	
223.147.37	link#2	UC	0	0		
223.147.37.1	0:0:c0:44:a5:68	UHLW	4	21375	ep0	1172
223.147.37.5	127.0.0.1	UGHS	1	90	lo0	
223.147.37.255	ff:ff:ff:ff:ff:ff	UHLWb	2	3357	ep0	
224/4	link#2	UCS	0	0		

See Chapter 22, *Configuring the local network*, page 408, for more details, including how to ensure that the routes will be added automatically at boot time.

Transport and Application layers

If you have got this far, the chances are that things will now work. About the only things that can still cause problems are the individual applications. We'll look at some of these in the relevant chapters.

One particular problem are is the Domain Name Service. This is such an integral part of the Internet Protocols that people tend to forget that it's really an application. If you get a timeout accessing a Web URL, for example, there's a good chance that DNS is causing the problem. Take a look at Chapter 27, *The Domain Name Service* for some ideas.

The Network File System

Setting up NFS

The *Network File System*, or *NFS*, is the standard way to share UNIX files across a network.

We've already seen that UNIX file systems are accessible in a single tree by *mount*ing them on a specific directory. NFS continues this illusion across the network.

From a user point of view, there is little difference: you use the same *mount* command, and it performs what looks like the same function. For example, if system *presto*'s system administrator wants to mount *freebie*'s file systems */*, */usr* and */home*, he could enter:

```
# mkdir /freebie /freebie/usr /freebie/home
# mount freebie:/ /freebie
# mount freebie:/usr /freebie/usr
# mount freebie:/home /freebie/home
```

You'll note how to specify the file systems: the system name, a colon (:), and the file system name. This terminology predates URLs; nowadays, people would probably write `nfs://freebie/usr`.

If you look at NFS more closely, things don't look quite as similar. You access local file systems via the disk driver, which is part of the kernel. You access NFS file systems via the NFS processes.

Older implementations of NFS had a plethora of processes. If you're used to such systems, don't let the lack of processes make you think that there's something missing.

NFS

NFS runs in two directions:

- When you mount a file system from another system on your system, your system is an *NFS Client*.

- When another system mounts one of your system's file system, your system is an *NFS Server*.

A system can, and often does, perform both of these functions at the same time. A certain amount of setup is required, however. We'll look at both in more detail in the following sections, but the simple answer is: */etc/rc.conf* does it for you. Just set these two lines:

```
nfs_client_enable="YES"      # This host is an NFS client (or NO).
nfs_server_enable="YES"      # This host is an NFS server (or NO).
```

There are also a few other NFS-related flags you can put in */etc/rc.conf.* We'll look at them later.

NFS client

You don't need any particular software to run as an NFS client, but the program *nfsiod* greatly improves performance. It's started at bootup time if you specify `nfs_client_en-able="YES"` in your */etc/rc.conf*, but you can also start it manually if it's not running:

```
# nfsiod -n 4
```

The parameter `-n 4` tells *nfsiod* how many copies of itself to start. The default is four. Each *nfsiod* can handle a concurrent I/O request, so if you find that your performance isn't what you would like it to be, and the CPU time used by each *nfsiod* is similar, then you might like to increase this value. To ensure it's done automatically at boot time, change the value of this line in */etc/rc.network*:

```
        echo -n ' nfsiod';          nfsiod -n 4
```

There is currently no way to configure this value from */etc/rc.conf.*

Mounting remote file systems

As we've seen, we mount NFS file with the same *mount* command which we use for local file systems. This is another illusion: *mount* is just a front-end program which determines which program to start. In the case of local file systems, it will start *mount_ufs*, and for NFS file systems it will start *mount_nfs*.

Unfortunately, the documentation isn't very clear about how it passes its parameters. You can mount a file system as we saw above, but there are a number of parameters that you should consider:

Table 30-1. NFS mount options

mount option	*mount_nfs* option	Meaning
bg	-b	Continue attempting the mount in the background if it doesn't complete immediately. This is a very good idea in */etc/fstab*, since otherwise the boot process will wait until all mounts have completed. If you've just had a power failure, this can cause deadlocks otherwise.
kerb	-K	Pass Kerberos authenticators to the server for client-to-server user-credential mapping.
nfsv2	-2	Use NFS version 2 protocol. By default, *mount_nfs* will try NFS version 3 protocol first, and fall back to version 2 if the other end can't handle version 3.
retry=*num*	-R*num*	Retry up to *num* times before aborting an I/O operation.
-o ro	-o ro	Mount the file system for read-only access.
-o rw	-o rw	Mount the file system for read and write access.
-R *num*	-R *num*	Retry the mount operation up to *num* times. If you have chosen soft mounting, fail I/O operations after *num* retries. The default value is 10.
-r *size*	-r *size*	Set the read data block size to *size* bytes. *size* should be a power of 2 between 1024 and 32768. The default value is 8192. Use smaller block sizes for UDP mounts if you have frequent "fragments dropped due to timeout" messages on the client.
soft	-s	If operations on the file system time out, don't retry for ever. Instead, give up after *Retry* timeouts. See option -R.
-t *num*	-t *num*	Time out and retry an operation if it doesn't complete with in *num*/10 seconds. The default value is 10 (1 second).
tcp	-T	Use TCP instead of UDP for mounts. This is more reliable, but slightly slower. In addition, not all implementations of NFS support TCP transport.
-w *size*	-w *size*	Set the write data block size to *size* bytes. *size* should be a power of 2 between 1024 and 32768. The default value is 8192 Use smaller block sizes for UDP mounts if you have frequent "fragments dropped due to timeout" messages on the server.

Normally, the only options that are of interest are -o ro, if you specifically want to restrict write access to the file system, and soft, which you should always use.

> Purists claim that `soft` compromises data integrity, because it may leave data on the server machine in an unknown state. That's true enough, but in practice the alternative to soft mounting is to reboot the client machine. This is not only a nuisance, it *also* compromises data integrity. The only solution which doesn't always compromise data integrity is to wait for the server machine to come back on line again. It's unlikely that anybody will wait more than a few hours at the outside for a server to come back.

A typical mount operation might be:

```
# mount -o soft presto:/usr /presto/usr
```

Where to mount NFS file systems

You can mount an NFS file system just about anywhere you would mount a local file system. Still, a few considerations will make life easier. In this discussion, we'll assume that we have a large number of file systems mounted on *freebie*, and we want to make them accessible to *presto*.

- If you have a "special" file system which you want to mount on multiple systems, it makes sense to mount them on the same mount point on every system. *freebie* has two file systems, */S* and */src*, which contain source files and are shared between all systems on the network. It makes sense to mount the file system on the same directory.

- *freebie* has a CD-ROM changer, and mounts the disks on */cdrom/1* to */cdrom/7*. *presto* finds that too confusing, and mounts one of them on */cdrom*.

- Some other file systems can't be mounted in the same place. For example, *freebie:/usr* can't be mounted on */usr*. Mount them on directories which match the system name. For example, mount *freebie:/usr* on */freebie/usr*.

Having done this, you might find the following file systems mounted on *freebie*:

```
# df
Filesystem     1024-blocks      Used     Avail Capacity  Mounted on
/dev/wd0a           30206     26830       960      97%   /
/dev/wd0s1e       1152422   1016196     44034      96%   /usr
/dev/da0h          931630    614047    243052      72%   /src
/dev/da1h         2049812   1256636    629192      67%   /home
procfs                  4         4         0     100%   /proc
/dev/cd0a          656406    656406         0     100%   /cdrom/1
/dev/cd1a          664134    664134         0     100%   /cdrom/2
/dev/cd2a          640564    640564         0     100%   /cdrom/3
/dev/cd3a          660000    660000         0     100%   /cdrom/4
/dev/cd4a          525000    525000         0     100%   /cdrom/5
/dev/cd5a          615198    615198         0     100%   /cdrom/6
/dev/cd6a          278506    278506         0     100%   /cdrom/7
```

On *presto*, you might see:

```
# df
Filesystem     1024-blocks      Used     Avail Capacity  Mounted on
/dev/da0a           29727     20593      6756      75%   /
/dev/da0s1e       1901185    742884   1006207      42%   /usr
procfs                  4         4         0     100%   /proc
freebie:/           30206     26830       960      97%   /freebie
freebie:/usr      1152422   1016198     44032      96%   /freebie/usr
freebie:/home     2049812   1256638    629190      67%   /home
```

526

```
freebie:/src        931630   614047   243052    72%   /src
freebie:/S         3866510  1437971  2119219    40%   /S
freebie:/cdrom/1    656406   656406        0   100%   /cdrom
```

Mounting NFS file systems automatically

If you want to mount NFS files automatically at boot time, make an entry for them in the file
/etc/fstab. You can even do this if you don't necessarily want to mount them: just add the
keyword `noauto`, and *mountall* will ignore them at boot time. The advantage is that you then
just need to specify, say,

```
# mount /src
```

instead of

```
# mount -s freebie:/src /src
```

See the description of */etc/fstab* on page 212 for more information.

NFS server

A number of processes are needed to provide NFS server functionality:

- The *NFS dæmon, nfsd,* provides the NFS server capability.

- The *mount dæmon, mountd,* processes mount requests from clients.

- The *NFS lock dæmon, rpc.lockd,* processes lock requests for NFS file systems. There are still
  a lot of problems with this function on all platforms. It's best to avoid it if you can.

- The *Status monitoring dæmon, rpc.statd,* provides a status monitoring service.

In addition,

- since NFS uses *Remote procedure calls (RPC)*, the *portmap* dæmon must be running.
  portmap is not part of NFS, but it is required to map RPC port numbers to IP service
  numbers.

- The server needs a file */etc/exports* to define which file systems to export and how to export
  them. We'll look at this in the next section.

/etc/exports

A number of security implications are associated with NFS. Without some kind of authentication, you could mount any file system on the Internet.

NFS was developed at a time when users were relatively trusted. As a result, the security
precautions are not overly sophisticated. */etc/exports* describes one file system per line. The
format is:

file system   options   systems

systems is a list of systems which are allowed to mount the file system. The only required field is the name of the file system, but if you're on the Internet, you should at least limit the number of systems which can mount your file systems. If you don't, any system on the net can mount your file systems.

There are a number of options. Here are the more important ones:

- The -maproot option describes how to treat root. By default, root does not have special privileges on the remote system. Instead, NFS changes the user ID to user nobody, which is user 65534 (or -2). You can change this with the -maproot option. For example, to map root to the real root user for a specific file system, you would add -maproot=0 to the line describing the file system.

- The -mapall option maps the user IDs of other users. This is relatively uncommon. See the man page *exports(5)* for more details.

- The -ro option restricts access to read-only.

- The *-network* option restricts the access to systems on the specified network.

If you come from a System V background, you'll notice that the mechanism is different. */etc/exports* corresponds in concept roughly to System V's */etc/dfs/dfstab* file, except that the *share* statement does not exist.

Updating */etc/exports*

It's not enough to change the contents of */etc/exports*: you also need to tell *mountd* that you have done so. You do this by the relatively common method of sending a SIGHUP to *mountd*:

```
# ps waux | grep mountd
root      103  0.0  0.0   636     0 ??  Is    Sat05PM   0:00.55 mountd -n
# kill -1 103
```

A typical */etc/exports* for *presto* might be:

```
/ -maproot=0 presto bumble wait gw
/usr -maproot=0 -network 223.147.37.0
```

Setup in */etc/rc.conf*

A number of parameters in */etc/rc.conf* relate to NFS server setup:

- Set nfs_server_enable to YES to enable the system as an NFS server.

- Set weak_mountd_authentication if you your network includes Microsoft machines which can't provide a login. This will cause the system to start *mountd* with the -n option.

- Set nfs_reserved_port_only to YES if you want to provide NFS only on a secure port.

- Set `rpc_lockd_enable` to `YES` to start *rpc.lockd*.

- Set `rpc_statd_enable` to `YES` to start *rpc.statd*.

- Set `portmap_enable` to `YES` to start *portmap*. You don't have any choice: you must do this to run an NFS server. This parameter is only supplied here separately because you may want to run *portmap* without the NFS server.

- If you have special flags for *portmap*, set `portmap_flags` to them.

On a typical system, this section of */etc/rc.conf* might look like:

```
nfs_server_enable="YES"            # This host is an NFS server (or NO).
weak_mountd_authentication="NO" # Running PCNFSD / other non-root nfsd (or NO).
nfs_reserved_port_only="NO"     # Provide NFS only on secure port (or NO).
rpc_lockd_enable="NO"           # Run NFS rpc.lockd (*broken!*) if nfs_server.
rpc_statd_enable="YES"          # Run NFS rpc.statd if nfs_server (or NO).
portmap_enable="YES"            # Run the portmapper service (or NO).
portmap_flags=""                # Flags to portmap (if enabled).
```

NFS strangenesses

NFS mimics a local file system across the network. It does a pretty good job, but it's not perfect. Here are some things that you should consider:

No devices

NFS handles disk files and directories, but not devices. Well, in fact, it handles devices too, but not the way you would expect.

In a UNIX file system, a device is more correctly known as a *device node*: it's an inode that *describes* a device in terms of its major and minor numbers (see page 231). The device itself is implemented by the device driver. NFS exports the device nodes, but it doesn't interpret the fact that these devices are on another system. If you refer to the devices, one of three things will happen:

- If a driver for the specified major number exists on your local system, and the devices are the same on both systems, you will access the local device. Depending on which device it is, this could create some subtle problems which could go undetected for quite a while.

- If a driver for the for the specified major number exists on your local system, and the devices are different on the two systems, you will still access the local device. The results could be very confusing.

- If no driver for the specified major number exists on your local system, the request will fail. This can still cause considerable confusion.

Just one file system

NFS exports file systems, not directory hierarchies. Consider the example on page 526. *presto* has mounted both *freebie:/* and *freebie:/usr*. If it were just to mount *freebie:/*, we would see the directory */freebie/usr*, but it would be empty.

Things can get even stranger: you can mount a local file system on a directory which is not empty. Consider the following scenario:

- You install FreeBSD on system *freebie*. In single user mode, before mounting the other file systems, you create a directory */usr/bin* and a file */usr/bin/vi*. Since the */usr* file system isn't mounted, this file goes onto the root file system.

- You go to multiuser mode and mount the other file systems, including the file system for */usr*. You can no longer see the */usr/bin/vi* you put there in single user mode. It hasn't gone away, it's just masked.

- On *presto*, you mount the file system *freebie:/* on */freebie*. If you list the contents of the directory */freebie/usr*, you will see the original file *vi*, and not the contents that the users on *freebie* will see.

31

Basic network access

Finally we have set up the network connections, and everything is working. What can we do with the network? In this part of the book, we'll take a look at some of the more important services which make up the application layer:

- In the rest of this chapter, we'll look at the old diehards: *telnet* and *rlogin*, which give you interactive shell access to other systems, and *ftp* and *rcp*, which transfer files across the network. We'll also look at *ssh*, a secure *rsh* lookalike.

- In Chapter 32, *Electronic Mail*, we'll look at electronic mail.

- In Chapter 33, *The World-Wide Web*, we'll look at the *World Wide Web*, how to access it, and how to provide services.

- In Chapter 34, *HylaFAX*, we'll look at how to send and receive faxes via computer.

When the Internet Protocols were first implemented, *telnet* and *ftp* were some of the most important protocols, and considerable time was expended in "getting them right". This was too long for the people at Berkeley, who produced their own "quick and dirty" tools: *rlogin* does what *telnet* was supposed to do, and *rcp* does what *ftp* was supposed to do. In addition, there is a command *rsh* which executes batch commands on a remote machine. These so-called *r* commands were supposed to be replaced by *telnet* and *ftp*, but as the old rhyme goes:

> *K* is the kludge that you say
> You require to avoid some delay.
> But that interim fix
> forms a habit that sticks,
> And you'll find that it's in there to stay.

Thus *rlogin* and *rcp* are still around, and they still get a lot of use.

telnet **and** *rlogin*

telnet and *rlogin* both perform the same function: they allow you to start an interactive shell on another machine. They are relatively similar in use, but there are some differences. In addition, *rsh* is a variant of *rlogin* that will allow you to start a non-interactive shell on another machine. There's no direct *telnet* relative which will do this.

telnet

Start *telnet* with the name of the system you want to connect to:

```
$ telnet freebie
Trying 223.147.37.1...
Connected to freebie.example.org.
Escape character is '^]'.

    FreeBSD (freebie.example.org) (ttyp9)

login: grog
Password:
Last login: Thu Oct  9 16:19:54 from unix:0.0
Copyright (c) 1980, 1983, 1986, 1988, 1990, 1991, 1993, 1994
        The Regents of the University of California.  All rights reserved.

FreeBSD 3.0-CURRENT (FREEBIE) #37: Thu Oct  9 04:36:32 CST 1997

You have mail.
It is always preferable to visit home with a friend.  Your parents will
not be pleased with this plan, because they want you all to themselves
and because in the presence of your friend, they will have to act like
mature human beings ...
                -- Playboy, January 1983
$ tty
/dev/ttyp9
$
```

Once you get this far, you are connected to the machine in almost identical manner as if you were directly connected. This is particularly true if you are running X. As the output of the *tty* command shows, your "terminal" is a *pseudo-tty* or *pty* (pronounced "pity"). This is the same interface that you will have with an *xterm*.

It's worth looking in more detail at how the connection is established:

- The first line (*Trying...*) appears as soon as *telnet* has resolved the IP address.

- The next three lines appear as soon as it has a reply from the other end. At this point, there can be a marked delay before *telnet* continues. *telnet* performs a reverse DNS lookup to find the name of your system. If you get a delay here, it could indicate that your reverse lookup is not working correctly. After DNS times out, it will continue normally, but the delay is a nuisance.

- Logging in is almost exactly the same as logging in locally. Normally you won't be able to log in directly as root, unless you have set */dev/ptyx* as secure in your */etc/ttys* (see page 240 for further details). It's not a good idea to set your *pty*s as secure. Use su instead if you want to become root.

When you log in via *telnet*, there's a good chance that your TERM environment variable will be set incorrectly. See table 11-7 on page 178 for more details. Remember that TERM describes the display at your end of the display, not the other end. If you're running an *xterm*, this shouldn't be a problem: probably the name xterm will propagate to the other end. If you're using a character-oriented display (*/dev/ttyvx*), however, your TERM variable will probably be set to cons25, which many systems don't know. If you have problems where systems refuse to start full-screen modes when you connect from a virtual terminal, try setting the TERM variable to ansi.

To exit *telnet*, you just log off. If you run into problems, however, like a hung network, you can also hit **Ctrl-]** to enter *telnet* command mode, and from there enter quit:

```
$ ^]
telnet> quit
$
```

If you hit **Ctrl-]** by accident, just hit **Enter**, and you will be returned to the telnet session.

rlogin

You can run *rlogin* in almost exactly the same way as *telnet*. By default, *rlogin* makes a few assumptions, though: for example, it assumes that you want to log in with the same user ID. What you see is:

```
$ rlogin freebie
Password:
Last login: Fri Oct 10 14:58:43 from allegro
Copyright (c) 1980, 1983, 1986, 1988, 1990, 1991, 1993, 1994
        The Regents of the University of California.  All rights reserved.

FreeBSD 3.0-CURRENT (FREEBIE) #37: Thu Oct  9 04:36:32 CST 1997

You have mail.
A witty saying proves nothing, but saying something pointless gets
people's attention.
```

This saves a little effort, since you don't need to type in your user ID. You can even eliminate the need to type in the password: create a file *.rhosts* in your home directory on the destination system, specifying the names of the systems from which your user ID allows access without password:

```
$ cat > .rhosts
freebie
presto
bumble
wait
gw
^D                              press CTRL-D
$ chmod 600 .rhosts             and set accessible by you alone
$ ls -l .rhosts
-rw-------  1 grog  bin  30 Oct 10 16:01 .rhosts
```

It's important to set the permissions of *.rhosts* to -rw-------, since otherwise *rlogin* won't look at it.

Once you have done this, you can connect to the system with *rlogin* with no further problems:

```
$ rlogin freebie
Last login: Fri Oct 10 15:57:05 from daemon
Copyright (c) 1980, 1983, 1986, 1988, 1990, 1991, 1993, 1994
        The Regents of the University of California.  All rights reserved.

FreeBSD 3.0-CURRENT (FREEBIE) #37: Thu Oct  9 04:36:32 CST 1997

You have mail.
My mother loved children -- she would have given anything if I had been
one.
                -- Groucho Marx
$
```

The file *.rhosts* works on a per-user basis. You may be allowed access to *freebie*, while user *norm* may not. If all users on the system are allowed access to the machines in *.rhosts*, you can rename it to */etc/hosts.equiv*, and all users will be able to access the system.

There's more to *.rhosts* and */etc/hosts.equiv* than shown here—look at the man page *hosts.equiv(4)*.

Stopping *rlogin*

As with *telnet*, you usually stop *rlogin* by exiting the shell. If the net hangs, however, you have an alternative. In this case, enter the sequence ˜ . at the beginning of the line:

```
$ ˜.
rlogin: closed connection.
$
```

When you enter this sequence, the ˜ does not echo until you enter the next character. This is because the ˜ character is a special escape character. If you really *want* to enter a ˜ at the beginning of the line, you must enter it twice, and it will only echo the second time. Read the man page *rsh(1)* for other functions of the ˜ character.

rsh

rsh is closely related to *rlogin*, so much so that you could mistake them. *rsh* executes a single command on a remote system. At one time, you couldn't use *rsh* to run programs which use full-screen capabilities, but this is no longer the case: *rsh* without a command now performs the same function as *rlogin*. For a more typical example, to show the status of processes running on *freebie* you might enter:

```
$ rsh freebie ps waux
USER     PID %CPU %MEM   VSZ  RSS  TT  STAT STARTED      TIME COMMAND
grog   25722  0.0  0.3   700  316  ??  R       4:13PM 0:00.17 ps -waux
grog   24902  0.0  0.0     0    0  v0  Z       -      0:00.00 (rsh)
grog   25594  0.0  0.0     0    0  v0  Z       -      0:00.00 (rsh)
root       0  0.0  0.0     0    0  ??  DLs     7:43PM 0:00.71 (swapper)
root       1  0.0  0.1   480   96  ??  Ss      7:43PM 0:00.42 /sbin/init --
root       2  0.1  0.0     0    0  ??  DL      7:43PM 8:42.55 (pagedaemon)
(etc)
```

In order for this to work, you *must* have an entry in *.rhosts* or */etc/hosts.equiv*. If you don't, you will get the following message:

```
$ rsh freebie ps waux
Permission denied.
```

Using *telnet* for other services

The way we have used *telnet* so far, it connects to the default port, `telnet` (number 23, as you can see in the file */etc/services*). This isn't the only possibility, though: you can tell *telnet* which port to connect to. In Chapter 32, *Electronic Mail*, we'll see how to communicate with *sendmail* using *telnet* on port `smtp` page 557, and how to communicate with *POP* on port `pop`, page 559. You'll find many other such uses as well.

ftp and *rcp*

The other basic function involves copying files between systems. In this area, *ftp* has a number of advantages over *rcp*.

ftp

ftp is the Internet File Transfer Program, and is the standard way to transfer large files long distances across the net. It works for small files and short distances too, but you may find thet *rcp* or *NFS* are better alternatives in these areas.

One serious drawback in duplicating files across the net is that you need to have permission to access the remote system. Traditionally, you need a user id to access a system. Of course, the file server could have a specific user ID without a password, but that would throw the system open to attack from crackers.

> The term *cracker* is used to indicate people who try to crack computer system security. The tabloid press users the word *hacker*, much to the annoyance of dyed-in-the-wool UNIX hackers. See the Jargon file entries on *hacker* and *cracker* for much more information.

ftp solves this problem by recognizing the special user name `ftp`. This user name used to be `anonymous`, but it turned out to be a problem to spell. *ftp* servers still accept the name `anonymous` as well. The user `ftp` doesn't really exist, but *ftp* can be set up to allow access to the system if the user name `ftp` is specified—see page 539 for more details. By convention, to help the system administrators with their bookkeeping, you should enter your real user ID in place of the password when logging in as `ftp`. A typical session might look like:

```
$ ftp ftp.tu-darmstadt.de
Connected to rs3.hrz.th-darmstadt.de.
220 rs3.hrz.th-darmstadt.de FTP server (Version 4.1) ready.
Name (grog): ftp
331 Guest login ok, send ident as password.
Password:                    username does not echo
230 Guest login ok, access restrictions apply.
ftp> cd /pub/gnu
250 CWD command successful.
```

```
ftp> bin                           to ensure binary transfer
200 Type set to I.
ftp> get gdb-4.12.tar.gz    start the transfer
200 PORT command successful.
150 Opening data connection for gdb-4.12.tar.gz (3682855 bytes).
3682855 bytes received in 1.1e+04 seconds (0.34 Kbytes/s)
ftp>
```

There are a couple of things to note about this transfer:

- The server may have multiple names, and the one you use may not be its canonical name (the name specified in the server's DNS A record—see page 477). By convention, the first part of the name of an FTP server is *ftp*. Here we opened the server `ftp.tu-darmstadt.de`, but the canonical name of the server is `rs3.hrz.th-darmstadt.de`.

- Some versions of *ftp* transmit in ASCII mode by default: they change every incidence of the ASCII line feed character (the C language constant `\n`) to the sequence `\r\n` (they prepend an ASCII carriage return character). This permits you to print the results on normal printers, but makes a terrible mess of binary files. Transmitting in binary form always works. The message `Type set to I.` is *ftp*'s way of telling you that it has set binary transmission mode.

This transmission is fairly typical (though the transfer rates are appalling). In real life, you might find some of the other of *ftp*'s 60-odd commands of use. We'll look at the most useful commands in the following sections.

mget

Frequently you need to copy more than a single file. For example, if you currently have *gcc-2.5.0* and want to get *gcc-2.5.8*, you will discover the following files on the file server:

```
ftp> ls
200 PORT command successful.
150 Opening ASCII mode data connection for /bin/ls.
-rw-rw-r-- 1 117 1001    43367 Nov  1 02:37 gcc-2.5.0-2.5.2.diff.gz
-rw-rw-r-- 1 117 1001     1010 Nov  1 02:37 gcc-2.5.1-2.5.2.diff.gz
-rw-rw-r-- 1 117 1001    78731 Nov 11 13:53 gcc-2.5.2-2.5.3.diff.gz
-rw-rw-r-- 1 117 1001    13931 Nov 17 09:27 gcc-2.5.3-2.5.4.diff.gz
-rw-rw-r-- 1 117 1001    76271 Nov 27 16:48 gcc-2.5.4-2.5.5.diff.gz
-rw-rw-r-- 1 117 1001     8047 Dec  3 09:22 gcc-2.5.5-2.5.6.diff.gz
-rw-rw-r-- 1 117 1001  5994481 Nov 27 16:49 gcc-2.5.5.tar.gz
-rw-rw-r-- 1 117 1001    10753 Dec 12 19:15 gcc-2.5.6-2.5.7.diff.gz
-rw-rw-r-- 1 117 1001    14726 Jan 24 09:02 gcc-2.5.7-2.5.8.diff.gz
-rw-rw-r-- 1 117 1001  5955006 Dec 22 14:16 gcc-2.5.7.tar.gz
-rw-rw-r-- 1 117 1001  5997896 Jan 24 09:03 gcc-2.5.8.tar.gz
226 Transfer complete.
ftp>
```

In other words, you have the choice of transferring 6 megabytes of software in *gcc-2.5.8.tar.gz* or 7 incremental patch files with a total of less than 250 kilobytes. On the other hand, copying the diffs requires typing all these long, complicated file names, so you might decide it's easier just to duplicate the whole 6 MB.

There is an easier way: `mget` (multiple get) duplicates files matching a wild card. You could perform the complete transfer with

```
ftp> mget gcc-2*diff.gz
mget gcc-2.5.0-2.5.2.diff.gz?y
200 PORT command successful.
150 Opening BINARY mode data connection for
    gcc-2.5.0-2.5.2.diff.gz (43667 bytes).
226 Transfer complete.
43667 bytes received in 19 seconds (2.298 Kbytes/s)
mget gcc-2.5.1-2.5.2.diff.gz?n  we don't need this one
mget gcc-2.5.2-2.5.3.diff.gz?y
200 PORT command successful.
150 Opening BINARY mode data connection for
    gcc-2.5.2-2.5.3.diff.gz (78731 bytes).
226 Transfer complete.
78731 bytes received in 33 seconds (2.835 Kbytes/s)
... etc
```

prompt

Using mget saves a lot of network bandwidth and copies the files faster, but it has one disadvantage: *ftp* prompts you for each file name, so you have to wait around to answer the prompts. If you don't, *ftp* disconnects after 15 minutes of inactivity. It would be simpler to perform all the gets without any intervention. This is where the prompt command comes in.

The prompt command specifies whether to issue certain prompts or not—the mget command is one example. This command is a toggle—in other words, if prompting is on, prompt turns it off, and if prompting is off, prompt turns it on. If prompting is off, the mget command in the previous example would have gone through with no interruptions.

In the previous example, you don't really want to transfer the file *gcc-2.5.1-2.5.2.diff.gz*, since you don't need it to perform the patches: you can upgrade from 2.5.0 to 2.5.2 directly with the file *gcc-2.5.0-2.5.2.diff.gz*. On the other hand, not copying the file would mean sitting around for the duration of the transfer and answering the prompt for each file, and the file is only 1 kilobyte long. In this case, it is reasonable to copy it as well—in other cases, you may need to consider other alternatives.

reget

Sooner or later, you will lose a connection in the middle of a transfer. According to Murphy's law, this will usually happen with a file like *gcc-2.5.8.tar.gz* in the previous example, and it will be shortly before the transfer is finished. If you notice this in time, it may be sufficient to reestablish connection: TCP is a remarkably resilient protocol, and you may find that it just continues as if nothing had happened. If this isn't successful, you may be able to save the day with reget, which picks up the transfer where it left off. The semantics are the same as for get.

Unfortunately, not all versions of *ftp* have the reget command, and on many systems that do have the command, it doesn't work correctly. If you *do* decide to use it, you should first make a copy of the partially copied file, in case something goes wrong.

user

Normally, *ftp* attempts to log in using the user name of the user who started the *ftp* program. To make establishing connections easier, *ftp* checks for a file called *.netrc* when perfoming a login sequence. *.netrc* contains information on how to log in to specific systems. A typical *.netrc* might look like:

```
machine freebie        login grog password foo
machine presto         login grog password bar
machine bumble         login grog password baz
machine wait           login grog password zot
default                login ftp  password grog@example.org
```

Lines starting with the keyword *machine* specify login name (*grog* in this example) and password for each system. The last line is the important one: if the system is not mentioned by name, *ftp* attempts a login with user name `ftp` and password `grog@example.org`. Though this may be of use with systems you don't know, it causes a problem: you *must* have an entry for each system on which you have accounts. Otherwise you will be unable to log in to them as yourself: you will be user *ftp* instead.

ftp is not overly clear about login failures. For example,

```
$ ftp ftp.tu-darmstadt.de
Connected to ftp.tu-darmstadt.de.
220 rs3.hrz.th-darmstadt.de FTP server (Version 4.1) ready.
331 Password required for grog.
530 Login incorrect.
Login failed.
Remote system type is UNIX.
Using binary mode to transfer files.
ftp>
```

This error message is not very obvious: although you're not logged in, you still get the same prompt, and *ftp* produces enough verbiage that it's easy to oversee that the login attempt failed. In order to complete the login, you need to use the *user* command:

```
ftp> user ftp
331 Guest login ok, send ident as password.
Password:               username does not echo
230 Guest login ok, access restrictions apply.
```

Be aware that the *.netrc* file is a security risk: it contains all your passwords in readable form. If you use a *.netrc* file, make sure it is secured so that only you can read or write it.

idle

By default *ftp* closes a connection if nothing happens for 15 minutes (900 seconds). The `idle` command can modify this time, up to a limit of 2 hours, which can occasionally be of use on a local net. ***Don't use this option with an Internet file server!***—it ties up valuable and scarce resources that other people might be able to use.

rcp

rcp is the Berkeley alternative to *ftp*. Like *rlogin* and *rcp*, it provides simpler services, but they're easier to use. If you have set up an *.rhosts* or */etc/hosts.equiv* file as described on page 533, you can use *rcp* almost like *cp*. For example, to copy the file *beowulf* from your home directory on *presto* to your home directory on the current machine (*bumble*), you could do:

```
$ rsh presto ls -l beowulf
-rw-------  1 grog  wheel  1526 Oct  8 13:56 beowulf
$ rcp presto:beowulf .
$ ls -l beowulf
-rw-------  1 grog  wheel  1526 Oct 11 11:55 beowulf
$
```

telnet and *ftp* servers

In the first half of this chapter, we saw how to use clients to access other systems. This is only half the picture, of course. At the other end of the link, we need *servers* to provide this service. Most of the time, the servers are relatively trivial. For each client, there is a server (a dæmon) whose name is usually derived from the client name by adding a d to it:

Table 31-1. Basic services dæmons

Client	Dæmon
telnet	telnetd
rsh	rshd
rlogin	rlogind
ftp	ftpd
rcp	rshd

rcp does not have its own dæmon. Instead, it uses *rshd* to start another instance of *rcp* at the other end.

In most cases, these dæmons will be started by *inetd*. If you are running an *ftp* server, however, it makes more sense to have the dæmon running all the time, since this saves overhead.

To run *ftpd* directly,

- Add the following line in */etc/rc.local*:

  ```
  echo -n 'starting local daemons:'
  # put your local stuff here
  echo " ftpd" && ftpd -D
  ```

The option -D tells *ftpd* to run as a dæmon. You will possibly want other options as well; see the discussion below.

- Comment out the *ftp* line in */etc/inetd.conf* by adding a hash mark (#) in front of it:

```
# ftp stream   tcp  nowait    root /usr/libexec/ftpd    ftpd -l
```

- Either reboot, or cause *inetd* to re-read its configuration file:

```
# ps waux | grep inetd         find the PID of inetd (2nd column)
root    7818  3.1  0.7   252  644 p6  S+   10:56AM   0:00.03 grep inetd
root     118  0.0  0.1   200   92 ??  Is   Thu10AM   0:01.78 inetd
# kill -1 118                   send a SIGHUP
```

As shown above, you can run *ftpd* either directly or from *inetd*. For security reasons, you will probably want to add options such as logging and anonymous *ftp*. We'll look at how to do that in the next two sections.

anonymous *ftp*

Anonymous *ftp* gives you a number of security options:

- It restricts access to the home directory of user *ftp*. From the point of view of the user, *ftp*s home directory is the root directory, and he cannot access any files outside this directory. Note that this means that you can't use symbolic links outside the *ftp* directory, either.

- It restricts access to the machine generally: the user doesn't learn any passwords, so he has no other access to the machine.

In addition, you can start *ftpd* in such a manner that it will allow only anonymous *ftp* connections.

There are a number of preparations for anonymous *ftp*:

- Decide on a directory for storing anonymous ftp files. The location will depend on the amount of data you propose to store there. A good choice is */var/spool/ftp*.

- Create a user *ftp*, with the anonymous *ftp* directory as the home directory and the shell */dev/null*. Using */dev/null* as the shell makes it impossible to log in as user *ftp*, but does not interfere with the use of anonymous *ftp*. *ftp* can be a member of group *bin*, or you can create a new group *ftp* by adding the group to */etc/group*. See page 164 for more details of adding users, and the man page *group(5)* for adding groups.

- Create subdirectories ˜*ftp/bin* and ˜*/ftp/pub*. If you want to allow incoming data, create a directory ˜*ftp/incoming* as well. Set the ownership of the directories like this:

```
dr-xr-xr-x   2 ftp    ftp       512 Feb 28 12:57 bin
drwxr-xr-x   2 ftp    ftp       512 Oct  7 05:55 incoming
drwxrwxr-x  20 ftp    ftp       512 Jun  3 14:03 pub
```

- Copy the following files to ˜*ftp/bin*: */usr/bin/compress*, */usr/bin/gzip*, */usr/bin/gunzip*, */bin/ls*, */usr/bin/tar* and */usr/bin/uncompress*. Since the view of anonymous *ftp* users is restricted to the home directory, all programs which are to be executed must also be in this directory.

  You can hard link the files if you want (and if you can, in other words if the directory is on the same file system), but symbolic links will fail, since they contain path names which do not point to the correct place when running in the anonymous *ftp* environment.

Restricting access and logging

A number of *ftpd* options make it easier to control and monitor *ftp* access:

- The -1 option logs each session, whether successful or not, to *syslogd* with the facility LOG_FTP. In order to enable this logging, your */etc/syslog.conf* should contain a line like

```
ftp.*                          /var/log/ftpd
```

In addition, the file */var/log/ftpd* must exist. If it doesn't, create it with:

```
# touch /var/log/ftpd
```

- The -S option logs all anonymous transfers to the file */var/log/ftpd*.
- You can restrict access to *only* anonymous *ftp* with the -A option.

There are a number of other options; see the man page *ftpd(8)* for further details.

In addition to these options, when a real user establishes a connection, *ftpd* checks the user's shell. If it is not listed in */etc/shells*, *ftpd* will deny the connection. This can be useful if you don't want specific users to access the system: give them a different shell, such as */usr/bin/sh* instead of */bin/sh*, and ensure that */usr/bin/sh* is not in */etc/shells*.

Log file format

The format of the log files is a little unusual. You'll see things like:

```
Oct 12 16:32:03 freebie ftpd[8691]: connection from adam.adonai.net
Oct 12 16:32:04 freebie ftpd[8691]: ANONYMOUS FTP LOGIN FROM adam.adonai.net, leec@ado
nainet
Oct 12 18:33:32 freebie ftpd[9007]: connection from gateway.smith.net.au
Oct 12 18:33:37 freebie ftpd[9007]: ANONYMOUS FTP LOGIN FROM gateway.smith.net.au, mik
e
Oct 12 21:36:28 freebie ftpd[9369]: connection from grisu.bik-gmbh.de
Oct 12 21:36:29 freebie ftpd[9369]: ANONYMOUS FTP LOGIN FROM grisu.bik-gmbh.de, harves
t@
Oct 12 21:36:37 1997!harvest@!grisu.bik-gmbh.de!/pub/cfbsd/README!9228!1
Oct 12 21:37:05 freebie ftpd[9371]: connection from grisu.bik-gmbh.de
Oct 12 21:37:06 freebie ftpd[9371]: ANONYMOUS FTP LOGIN FROM grisu.bik-gmbh.de, harves
t@
Oct 13 09:38:19 freebie ftpd[13514]: connection from 151.197.101.46
Oct 13 09:38:21 freebie ftpd[13514]: ANONYMOUS FTP LOGIN FROM 151.197.101.46, bmc@hove
rcraft.willscreek.com
Oct 13 09:38:58 1997!bmc@hovercraft.willscreek.com!151.197.101.46!/pub/cfbsd/dear-revi
ewer!8890!1
Oct 13 09:41:42 1997!bmc@hovercraft.willscreek.com!151.197.101.46!/pub/cfbsd/txt/26-ne
tdebug.txt.gz!12188!1
Oct 13 09:42:05 1997!bmc@hovercraft.willscreek.com!151.197.101.46!/pub/cfbsd/txt/C-pac
kages.txt.gz!37951!1
Oct 13 09:59:07 freebie ftpd[14117]: connection from 151.197.101.46
Oct 13 09:59:08 freebie ftpd[14117]: ANONYMOUS FTP LOGIN FROM 151.197.101.46, bmc@hove
rcraft.willscreek.com
Oct 13 09:59:24 1997!bmc@hovercraft.willscreek.com!151.197.101.46!/pub/cfbsd/txt/D-bib
```

```
lio.txt.gz!1815!1
```

This log excerpt shows three kinds of message:

- The messages starting with the text `connection from` occur when an *ftp* connection is made. They don't mean that any permission to access has been given. These messages are logged by the `-l` option.

- The `ANONYMOUS FTP LOGIN` messages show that somebody has logged in anonymously. The name follows, not always in the required username format. The standard *ftpd* does not enforce this requirement; you may find something which does in the Ports Collection. These messages are logged by the `-S` option.

- The lines full of ! marks show files being transferred. The ! marks delimit the fields, which are:

  - The year, as an extension of the timestamp.

  - The user ID.

  - The IP address of the system to which the data is transferred.

  - The name of the file transferred.

  - The number of bytes transferred.

Secure interactive connections

The traditional interactive connections between two machines on the Internet have a serious disadvantage: it's relatively easy to wiretap them on the way between source and destination. From time to time cases become known where an employee of an ISP does this and extracts confidential data, including passwords.

One answer to this problem is the *secure shell, ssh*. You can use *ssh* as a drop-in replacement for *rlogin*. Unlike *rlogin* and *telnet*, however, all data transferred is encrypted. Due to US export restrictions on cryptology, there is no package for *ssh* on the CD-ROM. Instead, you'll have to build it from the port.

> In order to build the port, you must set the variable USA_RESIDENT to YES or NO. This is a remnant of the times when it was prohibited to export freely available cryptology from the USA. Currently, this export is under review, and may change. There's no problem for USA residents to get the software from outside the country: you're allowed to import it into the USA, only *exporting* it is prohibited. If you understand this, please explain it to me.

For example, you might enter:

```
# USA_RESIDENT=NO make install
```

What *ssh* does

The *ssh* package works a lot like the traditional BSD *r* commands (*rsh*, *rlogin* and *rcp*): there's a set of client programs (*ssh*, *scp* and *slogin*) that you run on the local machine to connect to a remote machine, and there's a dæmon on the remote system (*sshd*) to which the clients connect to establish the remote session. From your viewpoint, the main difference between the BSD *r* commands and *ssh* suite is that the network traffic between the *ssh* clients and *sshd* is encrypted.

Encrypted remote login sessions protect against the following dangers:

- IP spoofing and IP source routing, two techniques used by attackers to make IP packets appear to come from host that is implicitly trusted by a local machine.

- DNS spoofing, where an attacker forges name server records.

- Interception of cleartext passwords and other data by intermediate hosts.

- Manipulation of data by people in control of intermediate hosts.

- Attacks based on listening to X authentication data and spoofed connection to the X11 server.

ssh uses encryption to protect against IP-spoofing and public-key authentication to protect against DNS and routing spoofing.

To illustrate, consider these two real-world scenarios:

- Someone is "sniffing" network traffic (for example, with *tcpdump*), either at your site, at the remote site to which you're connected, or at an ISP in between. Suppose you connect to the remote system with *rlogin* or *telnet*. When the remote system prompts you for your password, you type your password, and it is transmitted *in the clear*. The attacker now has your login name and password on the remote system and can log in as you. Worse, you might *su* to root on the remote system once you've logged in. If that happens, the attacker now has the keys to the store.

  Compare this to what happens when you log into the remote system using *ssh*. All traffic between your machine in the remote host is encrypted. Even if you *su* to root and type in root's password, the data on the wire is encrypted and is of no use to the attacker who's sniffing the IP packets.

- In another scenario, someone is sniffing network traffic, but only because he wants to be able to tell when you initiate an *rlogin* session to the remote host. This time, however, he starts sniffing *after* you've already logged in. No problem: he simply hijacks your TCP connection, effectively stealing it out from under you. What you see is a connection that mysteriously drops; however, the attacker is now using *your* login session, and he's probably putting in a back door to allow him to get in later from anywhere he wants.

Both kinds of attacks can, and do, happen. You can find prebuilt cracker kits on the Internet and on various BBSs to make those sorts of attacks easier. Using *ssh* to encrypt your login sessions goes a long way toward thwarting that kind of attack.

Running *ssh*

To use ssh, the remote system must be capable of accepting incoming *ssh* connections, which usually means that it should be running *sshd*. You can start it directly:

```
# sshd
```

You'll probably find it easier to add the following line to your */etc/rc.local*:

```
echo -n 'starting local daemons:'

# put your local stuff here
echo " sshd"; /usr/local/sbin/sshd
```

When you run *sshd* for the first time, it will log the following messages to */var/log/messages*, shown here when running *sshd* on *freebie*:

```
Nov 28 09:57:31 freebie sshd[28796]: log: Server listening on port 22.
Nov 28 09:57:31 freebie sshd[28796]: log: Generating 768 bit RSA key.
Nov 28 09:57:34 freebie sshd[28796]: log: RSA key generation complete.
```

After that, it's ready to accept connections. On the requesting machine, enter:

```
$ ssh freebie
Host key not found from the list of known hosts.
Are you sure you want to continue connecting (yes/no)? yes
Host 'freebie' added to the list of known hosts.
grog's password:                        doesn't echo
Last login: Fri Nov 28 10:07:50 1997 from hub.freebsd.org
Copyright (c) 1980, 1983, 1986, 1988, 1990, 1991, 1993, 1994
        The Regents of the University of California.   All rights reserved.

FreeBSD 3.0-CURRENT (FREEBIE) #1: Sun Nov 23 18:53:11 CST 1997

You have mail.
The universe does not have laws -- it has habits, and habits can be
broken.
=== grog@freebie (/dev/ttyp8) ~ 1 ->
```

You only get the first three lines the first time you log in from a specific system.

32

Electronic Mail

Before the advent of the World-Wide Web, the two most important uses of the Internet from the popular point of view were electronic mail and Usenet news. Both of these systems have roughly the same purpose: they are means of personal communications. Electronic mail is more personal, whereas News is a free-for-all. Nowadays, Email is going from strength to strength, while the increase in the size of the Internet has reduced the viability of News, which is increasingly showing signs of age. In this chapter, we'll look at how to set up Email. Due to lack of interest, this book does not cover Internet News.

Electronic mail

One of the most important applications on the Internet is *electronic mail*, usually called *Email*, *E-mail* or simply *Mail*, the ability to send messages to other people on the Net. In this chapter, we'll look at some ways to set up and run mail.

There are two kinds of mail software:

- The part of the mail system that most users know is the *Mail User Agent*, or *MUA*, the program that interacts with the user and handles incoming and outgoing mail. We'll look at my favourite MUA, *mutt*, in the next section, and we'll briefly touch on what others are available.

- The *Mail Transfer Agent*, or *MTA*. As the name suggests, it is responsible for moving mail from one system to another. We'll look at the most popular MTA, *sendmail*, on page 555.

Mail user agents

A *mail user agent* is a program which interfaces between the user and the mail system. It allows the user to read, forward and reply to incoming mail, and to send his own mail. Beyond that, it usually has facilities for creating and maintaining *folders*, where you can keep received mail messages. For most UNIX MUAs, a folder is the same thing as a file.

mail

The oldest MUA you're likely to meet is *mail*. It's a very primitive, character-oriented program, but nevertheless it has its advantages. You can use it in scripts to send mail. For example, if you have a job running and producing copious output, where you want to save the output, you might normally write something like

```
$ longjob 2>&1 > logfile
```

This command runs *longjob*. The sequence `2>&1` redirects the error output to the standard output, and the `>` writes them to the file *logfile*. While this is a good way to solve the problem, you might find that you have a lot of such jobs, or that you tend to forget the log files and leave them cluttering up your disks. An alternative would be to send yourself mail. You could do this with the following command:

```
$ longjob 2>&1 | mail me
```

In this case, **me** represents your user ID. When the job finishes, you will get a mail message with the output of the commands. *cron* (see page 184) uses this method to send you its output.

Other MUAs

The trouble with *mail* is that it can't deal very well with long mail messages, and it's difficult to keep an overview of large quantities of mail, like most people seem to accumulate. Many more sophisticated mailers have been written since *mail* Some of the more popular ones, which are also available in the Ports Collection, are:

- *elm* is one of the oldest full-screen mailers. Its age is showing: it has a few annoying problems which make it less desirable now that there's a choice.

- *pine* is not *elm*—that's what the acronym means. It's quite like *elm*, nonetheless.

- *mutt* is also similar to *elm* and *pine*. It's my current favourite, and we'll look at it in the next section.

- *exmh* is built on Rand's *mh* MUA. Some people like it, but it has a mailbox format incompatible with most of the others. It also seems relatively easy to configure it to mutilate messages.

- *xfmail* is an X-based mailer, which you might prefer to the text-based mailers we're talking about here. It also has an incompatible mailbox format, so if you try it out, be sure first to back up any mail you might want to keep.

mutt

In this section, we'll take a detailed look at *mutt*. Start it just by typing in its name. Like most UNIX mailers, *mutt* runs on a character-oriented terminal, including of course an *xterm*. We'll take a look into my mailbox. When I start it up, I get a full-screen display like the one shown in figure 32-1.

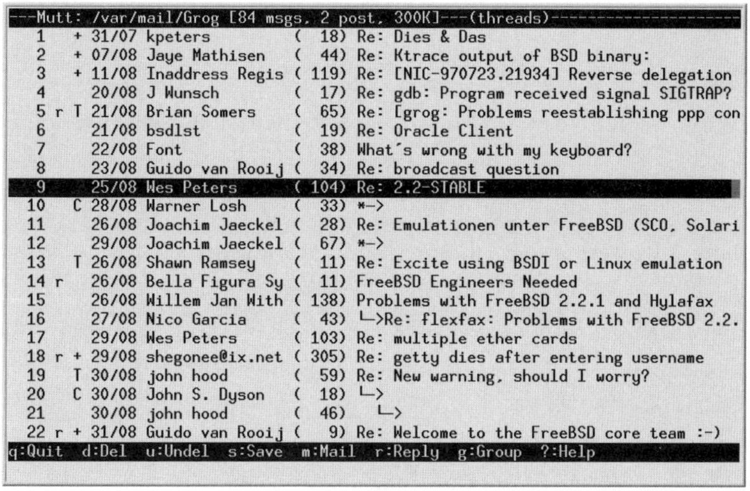

```
---Mutt: /var/mail/Grog [84 msgs, 2 post, 300K]---(threads)------------
  1   + 31/07 kpeters        ( 18) Re: Dies & Das
  2   + 07/08 Jaye Mathisen   ( 44) Re: Ktrace output of BSD binary:
  3   + 11/08 Inaddress Regis ( 119) Re: [NIC-970723.21934] Reverse delegation
  4     20/08 J Wunsch        ( 17) Re: gdb: Program received signal SIGTRAP?
  5 r T 21/08 Brian Somers    ( 65) Re: [grog: Problems reestablishing ppp con
  6     21/08 bsdlst          ( 19) Re: Oracle Client
  7     22/08 Font            ( 38) What's wrong with my keyboard?
  8     23/08 Guido van Rooij ( 34) Re: broadcast question
  9     25/08 Wes Peters      ( 104) Re: 2.2-STABLE
 10   C 28/08 Warner Losh     ( 33) *->
 11     26/08 Joachim Jaeckel ( 28) Re: Emulationen unter FreeBSD (SCO, Solari
 12     29/08 Joachim Jaeckel ( 67) *->
 13   T 26/08 Shawn Ramsey    ( 11) Re: Excite using BSDI or Linux emulation
 14 r   26/08 Bella Figura Sy ( 11) FreeBSD Engineers Needed
 15     26/08 Willem Jan With ( 138) Problems with FreeBSD 2.2.1 and Hylafax
 16     27/08 Nico Garcia     ( 43) └─>Re: flexfax: Problems with FreeBSD 2.2.
 17     29/08 Wes Peters      ( 103) Re: multiple ether cards
 18 r + 29/08 shegonee@ix.net ( 305) Re: getty dies after entering username
 19   T 30/08 john hood       ( 59) Re: New warning, should I worry?
 20   C 30/08 John S. Dyson   ( 18) └─>
 21     30/08 john hood       ( 46)   └─>
 22 r + 31/08 Guido van Rooij ( 9) Re: Welcome to the FreeBSD core team :-)
q:Quit  d:Del  u:Undel  s:Save  m:Mail  r:Reply  g:Group  ?:Help
```

Figure 32-1: *mutt* main menu

This display shows a number of things:

- The line at the top specifies the name of the folder (*/var/mail/grog*), the number of messages in the folder, and its size. It also states the manner in which the messages are sorted: by *threads*. We'll look at threads further down.

- The bottom line gives a brief summary of the most common commands. Each command is a single character. You don't need to press **Enter** to execute the command.

- The rest of the screen contains information about the messages in the folder. The first column gives the message a number, then come some flags:

  - In the first column, we can see r next to some messages. This indicates that I have already replied to these messages.

  - In the same column, N signalizes a *new* message (an unread message which has arrived after the last invocation of *mutt* finished).

  - O signalizes an *old* message (an unread message which arrived before the last invocation of *mutt* finished).

  - The symbol D means that the message has been marked for deletion. It won't be deleted until you leave *mutt* or update the display with the $ command, and until then you can undelete it with the u command

  - The symbol + means that the message is addressed to me, and only to me.

  - The symbol T means that the message is addressed to me and also to other people.

- The symbol C means that the message is addressed to other people, and that I have been copied.

- The symbol F means that the message is from me.

- The next column is the date (in international notation in this example, but it can be changed).

- The next column is the name of the sender, or, if I'm the sender, the name of the recipient.

- The next column gives the size of the message. The format is variable: you can specify the size in kilobytes (as in the example), or the number of lines.

- The last column is usually the subject. We'll see alternatives when we discuss *threading* below.

```
--- Wes Peters <softweyr@xmission.com> Re: 2.2-STABLE        -- (15%)
Date: Mon, 25 Aug 1997 23:16:41 -0600 (MDT)
From: Wes Peters <softweyr@xmission.com>
To: rdkeys@csemail.cropsci.ncsu.edu
CC: questions@FreeBSD.ORG
Subject: Re: 2.2-STABLE

rdkeys@csemail.cropsci.ncsu.edu writes:
 > Not to pick at nits.... but, I am still confused as to what EXACTLY
 > is the ``stable'' FreeBSD.  Please enlighten me, and tell me the
 > reasoning behind it.
 >
 > I read all the various manuals, faq's, .txt's and everything else
 > that I can find, but it still is not clear.
 >
 > That will help clarify the waters for me, and I am sure others,
 > tremendously.

OK, I'll take a shot at this.  To really understand what 2.2-STABLE is,
you have to have some idea of how the FreeBSD team uses `branches'.  In
particular, we are talking about branches as implemented by the CVS
source code control system, but other SCCS are similar.

i:Exit  -:PrevPg  SPC:NextPg  v:Attach  d:Del  r:Reply  j:Next  ?:Help
```

Figure 32-2: *mutt* **message display**

You'll notice that message 9 has been represented in reverse video. This indicates that this message has been *selected*: certain commands, such as r (reply) or **Enter** (read) will apply to this message. For example, Figure 32-2 shows the display you get by pressing **Enter** at this point. Here, the display has changed to show the contents of the message. The top line now tells you the name and mail ID of the message, the subject, and the percentage of the message that is displayed: 15%. As before, the bottom line tells you the most common commands you might need in this context: they're not all the same as in the menu display.

The message itself is divided into three parts: the first 5 lines are called the *headers*. They include information on how the message got here, when it was sent, who sent it, who it was sent to, and much more. The display here shows only a selection of the headers.

After the header comes an empty line to signalize the end of the headers, and then the message itself. The first part, which *mutt* displays in **bold face**, is *quoted* text: by putting a > character before each line, the sender has signalized that the text was written by the person to whom it is addressed: this message is a reply, and the text is what he is replying to.

To read the rest of the message, press **SPACE**. A 25 line display is obviously inadequate for this kind of message. On an X display, choose as high a window as you can.

Replying to a message

To reply to a message, simply press r. *mutt* will start your favourite editor for you. How does it know which one? If you set your EDITOR environment variable to the name of your editor, it will start that editor, otherwise it will start *vi*. See page 176 for more details. You can also specify it in the file *.muttrc*.

```
╔═══════════════════════════════════════════════════════════════╗
║  _ ▁                emacs@freebie.lemis.com            ⁊ ⌐      ║
╟───────────────────────────────────────────────────────────────╢
║ Buffers  Files  Tools  Edit  Search  Help                     ║
╟───────────────────────────────────────────────────────────────╢
║ From: Greg Lehey <grog@lemis.com>                          █   ║
║ To: Wes Peters <softweyr@xmission.com>                     █   ║
║ Cc:                                                        █   ║
║ Bcc:                                                           ║
║ Subject: Re: 2.2-STABLE                                        ║
║ Reply-To:                                                      ║
║ In-Reply-To: <199708260516.XAA22495@obie.softweyr.ml.org>; from Wes Peters on M\ ║
║ on, Aug 25, 1997 at 11:16:41PM -0600                          ║
║ Organisation:   LEMIS, PO Box 460, Echunga SA 5153, Australia ║
║ Phone:          +61-8-8388-8250                               ║
║ Fax:            +61-8-8388-8250                               ║
║ Mobile:         +61-41-739-7062                               ║
║ WWW-Home-Page:  http://www.lemis.com/~grog                    ║
║ Fight-Spam-Now: http://www.cauce.org                          ║
║                                                               ║
║ On Mon, Aug 25, 1997 at 11:16:41PM -0600, Wes Peters wrote:   ║
║ > rdkeys@csemail.cropsci.ncsu.edu writes:                     ║
║ > > Not to pick at nits.... but, I am still confused as to what EXACTLY ║
║ > > is the ``stable'' FreeBSD.  Please enlighten me, and tell me the ║
║ > > reasoning behind it.                                      ║
║ > >                                                           ║
║ > > I read all the various manuals, faq's, .txt's and everything else ║
║ > > that I can find, but it still is not clear.               ║
║ ----Emacs: mutt-freebie-25721-6     (Fundamental)--L1--Top------------ ║
╟───────────────────────────────────────────────────────────────╢
║ None                                                      ■    ║
╚═══════════════════════════════════════════════════════════════╝
```

Figure 32-3: Replying to a message

In this case, we start Emacs. Figure 32-3 shows the resultant screen before entering any text. See page 316 for more information on the Emacs editor. You'll notice that *mutt* automatically "quotes" the text. For example, the original text started with:

```
rdkeys@csemail.cropsci.ncsu.edu writes:
> Not to pick at nits.... but, I am still confused as to what EXACTLY
> is the ``stable'' FreeBSD.  Please enlighten me, and tell me the
> reasoning behind it.
(lines omitted)
OK, I'll take a shot at this.  To really understand what 2.2-STABLE is,
you have to have some idea of how the FreeBSD team uses 'branches'.  In
particular, we are talking about branches as implemented by the CVS
```

This message itself starts with quoted text, which indicates that it was written by somebody else (rdkeys@csemail.cropsci.ncsu.edu). The text from the submitter starts with OK, I'll have a shot at this. When you reply, however, all this text is quoted, so what you see on the screen is:

```
> rdkeys@csemail.cropsci.ncsu.edu writes:
> > Not to pick at nits.... but, I am still confused as to what EXACTLY
> > is the ''stable'' FreeBSD.  Please enlighten me, and tell me the
> > reasoning behind it.
(lines omitted)
> OK, I'll take a shot at this.  To really understand what 2.2-STABLE is,
> you have to have some idea of how the FreeBSD team uses 'branches'.  In
> particular, we are talking about branches as implemented by the CVS
```

This is the standard way to reply to mail messages.

How to send and reply to mail

In the impersonal world of the Internet, your mail messages are the most tangible thing about you. Send out a well thought out, clear and legible message, and you will leave a good impression. Send out a badly formulated, badly formatted and badly spelt message, and you will leave a bad impression.

So what's good and what's bad? That's a matter of opinion (and self-expression), of course. We've seen some of the following things already:

- Unless there's a very good reason, avoid proprietary formats. Most mailers can handle them nowadays, but some can't. For example, some people set up Microsoft mailers to use HTML as the standard format. Most other mailers have difficulty with HTML (*mutt* can display it, however, with the help of *Netscape*). Other Microsoft mailers send out mail in Microsoft Word format, which is illegible to just about anybody without a Microsoft system.

- When sending "conventional" mail, ensure that you adhere to the standards. Again, Microsoft mailers are often bad in this respect: without telling you, they either transform paragraphs into one long line, or they break lines into two, one long and one short. The resulting appearance of the message looks like (taking this paragraph as an example):

```
When sending ''conventional'' mail, ensure that you adhere to the standards. Agai
n, Microsoft mailers are often bad in this respect: without telling you, they eit
her transform paragraphs into one long line, or they break lines into two, one lo
ng and one short.  The resulting appearance of the message looks like (taking thi
s paragraph as an example):
```

Figure 32-4: One line per paragraph

```
When sending ''conventional'' mail, ensure that you adhere to the
standards.
Again, Microsoft mailers are often bad in this respect: without telling
you,
they either transform paragraphs into one long line, or they break
lines into
two, one long and one short.  The resulting appearance of the message
looks like
(taking this paragraph as an example):
```

Figure 32-5: Alternate long and short lines

The insidious thing about these conversions is that you may not be aware of them. If you get messages from other people which appear to be garbled, your mailer may be reformatting them on arrival, in which case it is possibly reformatting them before transmission.

- When replying, ensure that you use a quote convention as shown above. Place your reply text directly below the part of the text to which you are replying.

- Messages tend to grow as more and more replies get added. If large parts of the original text are irrelevant, remove them from the reply.

- Leave an empty line between the original text and your reply, and leave a space after the > quote character. Both make the message more legible. For example, compare these two fragments:

```
> rdkeys@csemail.cropsci.ncsu.edu writes:
>>Not to pick at nits.... but, I am still confused as to what EXACTLY
>>is the ''stable'' FreeBSD.  Please enlighten me, and tell me the
>>reasoning behind it.
>OK, I'll take a shot at this.  To really understand what 2.2-STABLE is,
>you have to have some idea of how the FreeBSD team uses 'branches'.  In
>particular, we are talking about branches as implemented by the CVS
```

Figure 32-6: Less legible reply

```
> rdkeys@csemail.cropsci.ncsu.edu writes:
>> Not to pick at nits.... but, I am still confused as to what EXACTLY
>> is the ''stable'' FreeBSD.  Please enlighten me, and tell me the
>> reasoning behind it.

> OK, I'll take a shot at this.  To really understand what 2.2-STABLE is,
> you have to have some idea of how the FreeBSD team uses 'branches'.  In
> particular, we are talking about branches as implemented by the CVS
```

Figure 32-7: More legible reply

- What about salutations? You'll see a lot of messages out there which don't start with "Dear Fred", and either aren't even signed or just have the name of the author. This looks rather rude at first, but it has become pretty much a standard on the net. There's a chance that this will change in the course of time, but at the moment it's the way things are, and you shouldn't assume any implicit rudeness on the part of people who write in this manner.

- At the other end of the scale, some people add a standard signature block to each message. You can do this automatically by storing the text in a file called ˜/.*signature*. If you do this, consider that it appears in *every* message you write, and that it can get on people's nerves if it's too long or too scurrile.

- Make sure that your user ID states who you are. It doesn't make a very good impression to see mail from `foobar` (The greatest guru on Earth), especially if he happens to make an incorrect statement. There are better ways to express your individuality.

mutt configuration

Like most mailers, there are a lot of things that you can change about *mutt*'s behaviour. They are described in a file *˜/.muttrc* (in other words, the file *.muttrc* in your home directory). You'll find the *.muttrc* file that created these examples in */book/mutt/.muttrc*. Read the *mutt* documentation (installed in HTML in *file:/usr/local/share/doc/mutt/manual.html*) for details on how to customize the configuration.

Mail aliases

You'll find that some people have strange mail IDs: they are unusual, confusing, or just plain difficult to type. Most mailers give you the option of setting up *aliases*, short names for people you often contact. In *mutt*, you can put the aliases in the *˜/.muttrc* file, or you can put them in a separate file and tell *mutt* when to find them in the *˜/.muttrc* file. You'll find a sample file which uses the latter method in */book/mutt/.mail_aliases*. Figure 32-8 shows a typical entry:

```
alias questions questions@FreeBSD.org (FreeBSD Questions)
alias stable FreeBSD Stable Users <freebsd-stable@freebsd.org>
```

Figure 32-8: Mail aliases

The format is straightforward:

- First comes the keyword alias. Aliases can be placed in *˜/.muttrc*, so the word alias is used to distinguish them from other commands.

- Next is the alias name (questions and stable in this example).

- Next comes the mail ID in one of two forms: either the name followed by the mail ID in angle brackets (<>), or the mail ID followed by the name in parentheses (()).

Mail headers

In the message display above we saw only a selection of the mail headers that a message might contain. Sometimes it's interesting to look at them in more detail, especially if you're having mail problems. To look at the complete headers, press the h key. The previous message (now saved in a different folder) is shown in figure 32-9. These headers show:

- The first line shows the name of the sender and the date it arrived at this machine. The date is in local time.

- The next line (Received:) shows the most recent step of the message's journey to its destination. It shows that it was receive from *smyrno.sol.net* by *freebie.lemis.com*, and that *freebie.lemis.com* was running version 8.8.5 of *sendmail*, and that the configuration files were made at version 8.6.12. It also shows the time the message arrived at *freebie*, 15:13:03 on 26 August 1997. The time zone is 9½ hours ahead of UTC. The message ID is PAA09815.

  This line is continued over two screen lines. *mutt* shows this by starting the continuation lines with the + character.

```
1/2 r   Wes Peters      (r) Re: 2.2-STABLE                      -- (22%)
From owner-freebsd-questions@FreeBSD.ORG Tue Aug 26 15:13:08 1997
Received: from smyrno.sol.net (smyrno.sol.net [206.55.64.117]) by
+freebie.lemis.com (8.8.7/8.6.12) with ESMTP
        id PAA09815 for <grog@lemis.com>; Tue. 26 Aug 1997 15:13:03 +0930 (CST)
Received: from hub.freebsd.org (hub.FreeBSD.ORG [204.216.27.18]) by
+smyrno.sol.net (8.8.5/8.6.12) with ESMTP id AAA09389; Tue. 26 Aug 1997 00:42:26
+-0500 (CDT)
Received: from localhost (daemon@localhost)
          by hub.freebsd.org (8.8.7/8.8.7) with SMTP id WAA08079;
          Mon, 25 Aug 1997 22:06:35 -0700 (PDT)
Received: (from root@localhost)
          by hub.freebsd.org (8.8.7/8.8.7) id WAA08051
          for questions-outgoing; Mon, 25 Aug 1997 22:06:25 -0700 (PDT)
Received: from obie.softweyr.ml.org ([199.104.124.49])
          by hub.freebsd.org (8.8.7/8.8.7) with ESMTP id WAA08046
          for <questions@freebsd.org>; Mon, 25 Aug 1997 22:06:19 -0700 (PDT)
Received: (from wes@localhost) by obie.softweyr.ml.org (8.7.5/8.6.12) id
+XAA22495; Mon, 25 Aug 1997 23:16:41 -0600 (MDT)
Date: Mon, 25 Aug 1997 23:16:41 -0600 (MDT)
Message-Id: <199708260516.XAA22495@obie.softweyr.ml.org>
From: Wes Peters <softweyr@xmission.com>
To: rdkeys@csemail.cropsci.ncsu.edu
CC: questions@FreeBSD.ORG
Subject: Re: 2.2-STABLE
In-Reply-To: <9708251522.AA128968@csemail.cropsci.ncsu.edu>
References: <19970825195938.31646@lemis.com>
            <9708251522.AA128968@csemail.cropsci.ncsu.edu>
Sender: owner-freebsd-questions@FreeBSD.ORG
X-Loop: FreeBSD.org
Precedence: bulk
Status: RO
X-Status: A
Content-Length: 5491
Lines: 104

rdkeys@csemail.cropsci.ncsu.edu writes:
i:Exit  -:PrevPg  SPC:NextPg  v:Attach  d:Del  r:Reply  j:Next  ?:Help
```

Figure 32-9: Mail message with all headers

- The next line shows that the message arrived at *smyrno.sol.net* from *hub.freebsd.org* at 00:42:26 local time on 26 August 1997, and that the local time was 5 hours behind UTC. *smyrno.sol.net* was running *sendmail* version 8.8.5, and its configuration files were also version 8.6.12. The message ID is AAA09389.

- The next header is split into three lines, a modification due to more recent version of the configuration files. It shows that the message was received locally by *hub.FreeBSD.org* at 22:06:35 on 25 August 1997. *hub.FreeBSD.org* is running version 8.8.7 of *sendmail*, and its configuration files are also at version 8.8.7, which may explain the slight difference in format. The local time is 7 hours behind UTC. The message ID is WAA08079.

- The next header shows that the message was received again by *hub.freebsd.org*, this time at 22:06:35 (ten seconds earlier), with the message ID WAA08051. This is the header associated with distributing the message to questions@FreeBSD.org.

- The next header shows the message being received by *hub.FreeBSD.org* for the first of three times, this time at 22:06:19. It came from *obie.softweyr.ml.org*. This time the message ID is WAA08046.

- Finally (or initially), the message was received from a mail user agent on the local host by *obie.softweyr.ml.org*, which is running *sendmail* version `8.7.5` with configuration files of release `8.6.12`. The message was sent at 23:16:41 local time, which is 6 hours before UTC. On careful comparison, you'll notice that this is a little more than ten minutes after it was supposed to have arrived at *hub.FreeBSD.org*. It's reasonable to assume that this means that the timekeeping on one of these two machines is incorrect. Since this is the original message, this is also the time allocated to the message. The message ID is `XAA22495`.

- The next header is the date. We saw this in the previous example.

- We've just seen six different message IDs. So why the header `Message-Id:`? That's exactly the reason: the other six IDs are local to the system they pass through. The line beginning with `Message-Id:` gives a definitive message ID which can be used for references.

- The next four headers are the same as we have seen before. They can appear in any order, and may be interspersed with other headers, like the `Date:` header we saw before.

- The `In-Reply-To:` header shows the ID of the message to which this is a reply. This is used for threading. You'll notice that the *Emacs* screen of the reply in figure 32-3 shows an `In-Reply-To:` header referring to this message.

- The `References:` header shows a list of messages to which this message refers. The `Sender:` header is the address of the *real sender*. Although this message is `From:` Wes Peters, it was resent from the `FreeBSD-questions` mailing list. This header documents the fact.

- Headers starting with `X-` are *official custom headers*. *sendmail* doesn't process them. `X-Loop` is another indication that the message went through `FreeBSD-questions`. The `X-Status` header isn't documented.

- The `Precedence:` header is used internally by *sendmail* to determine the order in which messages should be sent. `bulk` is a low priority.

- The final headers are added by *mutt* when it updates the mail folder, for example when it exits. Other MUAs add similar headers.

  The `Status:` flag is used by the MUA to set flags in the display. The letters each have their own meaning: `R` means that the message has been read, and `O` means that it is old (in other words, it was already in the mail folder when the MUA last exited).

- The `Content-Length:` header specifies the *approximate* length of the message (without the headers) in bytes. It is used by some MUAs to speed things up.

- The `Lines:` header states the length of the message in lines.

Who gets the mail?

According to RFC 822, a mail ID is something like `grog@lemis.com`. This looks very much like a user ID, the `@` sign, and the name of a machine. This similarity is intended, but it's still only a similarity. Consider the system manager of *example.org*. At different times he might send mail from *freebie.example.org*, *bumble.example.org*, and *wait.example.org*. If the mail ID were associated with the machine, he would have three different mail IDs: `fred@freebie.example.org`, `fred@bumble.example.org` and `fred@wait.example.org`. It would make things a whole lot simpler (and easier to type) if his mail ID were simply `fred@example.org`. *sendmail* calls this name change *masquerading*.

One way to do this would be to associate the name `example.org` as a `CNAME` with one of the machines—say *wait.example.org*. This would work, but it would mean that mail would always have to come from and go to *wait.example.org*. In addition, this is purely a mail function. DNS solves this problem with a special class of record, the `MX` record (*mail exchanger*). We saw how to add them on page 484. MX records are not directly associated with any particular machine, though they point to the names of machines which handle mail.

sendmail

Mail has been around for a long time now, at least 20 years. In that time, many mail systems have come and gone. One seems to have been around for ever: the *sendmail* MTA. *sendmail* has an unparalleled reputation. On the one hand, it can do just about anything, but on the other hand, its configuration file is one of the most arcane ever to be seen. Still, nothing has appeared to even come close to it, and it is still actively being developed.

The definitive book on *sendmail* was written by Bryan Costales and others—see Appendix C, *Bibliography* for more details. It is over 1000 pages long. Obviously this book can't compete with it.

The good news about *sendmail* is: it works. It is possible to install *sendmail* and run it with no configuration whatsoever. Nevertheless, there are a couple of things that you might like to do with it.

There are two ways to change the *sendmail* configuration: you can change the template files supplied as part of *sendmail*, and then reinstall */etc/sendmail.cf*, or you can edit */etc/sendmail.cf* directly. There's not much difference in complexity, and it's easier to edit */etc/sendmail.cf* directly, so that's the method I'll show here. Let's look at some of the more likely things you will want to change:

- By default, *sendmail* accepts mail sent to the local system only, and in the headers it sends out, it shows the name of the local system. If we want to masquerade as the domain name, as we discussed above, we have to modify */etc/sendmail.cf*. Find the line beginning with `DM` and add the masquerade name:

```
# who I masquerade as (null for no masquerading) (see also $=M)
DMexample.org
```

- You may also want to receive mail for other domains. This is also sometimes called *masquerading*, but there's a difference: you accept mail for these domains, but when you send mail, it's given the name specified in the DM line above.

  To accept mail for other domains, create a file */etc/sendmail.cw* (by default it doesn't exist), and enter the domain names, one per line:

  ```
  freebsd.example.org
  example.com
  ```

  This file would cause *sendmail* to accept mail addressed to names like fred@example.com and beastie@freebsd.example.org.

- Finally, you may find it convenient to let some other system handle all your mail delivery for you: you just send anything you can't deliver locally to this other host, which *sendmail* calls a *smart host*. This is particularly convenient if you send your mail with *UUCP*.

  To tell *sendmail* to use a smart host (in our case, *mail.example.net*), find the following line in *sendmail.cf*:

  ```
  # "Smart" relay host (may be null)
  DS
  ```

  Change it to:

  ```
  # "Smart" relay host (may be null)
  DSmail.example.net
  ```

After changing the *sendmail* configuration, restart *sendmail* by sending it a SIGHUP signal.

```
# ps waux | grep sendmail
root    9137  2.3  0.7  252  636  p6  S+   4:13PM   0:00.02 grep sendmail
root     136  0.0  0.3  552  284  ??  Ss   Thu10AM  0:11.99 sendmail: accepting connections on p
root    9135  0.0  0.5  552  504  ??  S    4:13PM   0:00.01 sendmail: startup with 194.93.177.11
# kill -1 136                         choose the one which is accepting connections
# ps waux | grep sendmail
root    9144  2.3  0.9  600  892  ??  S    4:13PM   0:00.02 sendmail: server relay.ucb.crimea.ua
root    9135  0.1  0.8  600  764  ??  S    4:13PM   0:00.04 sendmail: server relay.ucb.crimea.ua
root    9142  0.0  0.9  552  888  ??  Ss   4:13PM   0:00.01 sendmail: accepting connections on p
```

In this example, the other *sendmail* processes are handling individual incoming mail messages. As you can see, unlike some other programs, *sendmail* doesn't just read the configuration files: it really does restart.

Running *sendmail* at boot time

By default, the system starts *sendmail* at boot time. You don't need to do anything special. There are two parameters in */etc/rc.conf*:

```
sendmail_enable="YES"   # Run the sendmail daemon (or NO).
sendmail_flags="-bd -q30m" # -bd is pretty mandatory
```

The flags have the following meanings:

- -bd means *become dæmon*: *sendmail* will run as a dæmon.

- -q30m means "try to send queued messages every 30 minutes" (30m). If you wanted to try to send them every 2 hours, you would write -q2h. The default */etc/sendmail.cf* file tries to send messages immediately, but if they can't be delivered immediately, this interval specifies how often *sendmail* will try to send the message.

Talking to *sendmail*

The *Simple Mail Transfer Protocol*, or *SMTP*, is a text-based protocol. If you want, you can talk to *sendmail* directly on the smtp port. Try this with *telnet*:

```
$ telnet localhost smtp
Trying 127.0.0.1...
Connected to localhost.example.org.
Escape character is '^]'.
220 freebie.example.org ESMTP Sendmail 8.8.8/8.8.5; Fri, 28 Nov 1997 11:35:09 +1030 (CST)
ehlo freebie.example.org                        say who you are
250-freebie.example.org Hello localhost.example.org [127.0.0.1], pleased to meet you
250-EXPN                                         short list of possible commands
250-VERB
250-8BITMIME
250-SIZE
250-DSN
250-ONEX
250-ETRN
250-XUSR
250 HELP
mail from: grog@example.org                      say who the mail is from
250 grog@example.org... Sender ok
rcpt to: grog@example.org                        and who it goes to
250 grog@example.org... Recipient ok
data                                             start the body of the message
354 Enter mail, end with "." on a line by itself
Test data                                        the message itself
250 LAA01997 Message accepted for delivery
quit                                             and exit
221 freebie.example.org closing connection
Connection closed by foreign host.
```

This rather cumbersome method is useful if you're having trouble with *sendmail*.

Aliases revisited

On page 552 we looked at how to set up individual aliases for use with *mutt*. *sendmail* also has an alias facility, this time at the system level. The file is called */etc/aliases*. The default */etc/aliases* looks like:

```
# Basic system aliases -- these MUST be present
MAILER-DAEMON: postmaster
postmaster: root

# General redirections for pseudo accounts
bin:       root
daemon: root
games:  root
ingres: root
nobody: root
system: root
toor:      root
uucp:      root

# Well-known aliases -- these should be filled in!
# root:
# manager:
# dumper:
# operator:

root: grog
```

Each line contains the name of an alias, followed by the name of the user which should receive it. In this case, mail addressed to the users bin, daemon, games, ingres, nobody, system, toor and uucp will be sent to root instead. Note that the last line redefines root to send all mail to a specific user.

After changing */etc/aliases*, you must run the *newaliases* program to rebuild the aliases database. Don't confuse this with the *newalias* program, which is part of the *elm* mail reader.

Downloading mail from your ISP

As we saw before, the Internet wasn't designed for dialup use. Most protocols assume that systems are up a large proportion of the time: down time indicates some kind of failure. This can cause problems delivering mail if you are not permanently connected to the Internet.

As we saw above, if you have an MX record which points to another system which is permanently connected, this doesn't seem to be a problem: the mail will be sent to that system instead. When you connect, the mail can be sent to you.

How does the mail system know when you connect? Normally it doesn't. That's the first problem. Most systems set up *sendmail* to try to deliver mail every 30 to 120 minutes. If you are connected that long, the chances are good that the mail will be delivered automatically, but you don't know when.

One possibility here is to tell the remote *sendmail* when you're connected. You can do this with the *sendmail* ETRN command. Telnet to the smtp port on the system where the mail is queued:

```
$ telnet mail.example.net  smtp
Trying 139.130.237.17...
Connected to mail.example.net.
Escape character is '^]'.
220 freebie.example.org ESMTP Sendmail 8.8.7/8.8.7 ready at Mon, 5 May 1997
12:55:10 +0930 (CST)

etrn freebie.example.org
250 Queuing for node freebie.example.org started
```

```
quit
221 mail.example.net closing connection
Connection closed by foreign host.
```

The mail will start coming after the message `Queuing for node freebie.example.org started`. Depending on how much mail it is, it might take a while, but you don't need to wait for it.

Another alternative is the *Post Office Protocol*, or *POP*. POP was designed originally for Microsoft-style computers which can't run dæmons, so they have to explicitly request the other end to download the data. POP is an Internet service, so you need the cooperation of the other system in order to run it. We'll look at POP in the next section.

POP: the Post Office Protocol

The Post Office Protocol is a means for transferring already-delivered mail to another site. It consists of two parts, the client and the server. A number of both clients and servers are available. In this discussion, we'll look at the server *popper* and the client *popclient*, both of which are in the Ports Collection.

popper: the server

To install *popper*, you need to define a user pop. The installation procedure suggests that you define the user with *vipw* (see page 164) as follows:

```
pop:*:68:1::0:0:Post Office Owner:/nonexistent:/nonexistent
```

This assumes that user number 68 is free; otherwise use any other available number.

popper is designed to be started only via *inetd*. To enable it,

- Edit */etc/inetd.conf*. By default, it should contain the following line commented out with a # character:

  ```
  pop3   stream    tcp   nowait    root  /usr/local/libexec/popper    popper
  ```

  Remove the # or add the line.

- Either reboot, or cause *inetd* to re-read its configuration file:

  ```
  # ps waux | grep inetd              find the PID of inetd (2nd column)
  root    7818  3.1  0.7   252  644 p6  S+   10:56AM   0:00.03 grep inetd
  root     118  0.0  0.1   200   92 ??  Is   Thu10AM   0:01.78 inetd
  # kill -1 118                       send a SIGHUP
  #
  ```

To test the server, telnet to the pop3 port. You can't do much like this, but at least you can confirm that the server is answering:

```
$ telnet localhost pop3
Trying 127.0.0.1...
Connected to localhost.example.org.
Escape character is '^]'.
+OK QPOP (version 2.3) at freebie.example.org starting.
<12061.876903437@freebie.exam
ple.org>
quit
+OK Pop server at freebie.example.org signing off.
Connection closed by foreign host.
```

popclient: the client

Install *popclient* from the Ports Collection. To run it, just specify the name of the server from which you want to load the mail.

```
$ popclient hub
querying hub
Enter mailserver password:              doesn't echo
QPOP (version 2.3) at hub.freebsd.org starting.  <27540.876902406@hub.freebsd.org>
7 messages in folder, 6 new messages.
reading message 1...
flushing message 2
reading message 2....
flushing message 3
reading message 3...
flushing message 4
reading message 4...
flushing message 5
reading message 5....
flushing message 6
reading message 6..
flushing message 7
```

popclient and *popper* are relatively simple to use. My main objections to them are that they add another level of complexity to the mail system, and that they require manual intervention in a system which is designed to be automatic. In addition, *popclient* is not a speed demon: if you have a lot of mail to transfer, be prepared to wait much longer than *sendmail* would take.

Mailing lists: majordomo

majordomo is a mail list manager. If you run mailing lists, you probably want to use majordomo: it saves you manually modifying the mailing lists.

As usual, you can find *majordomo* in the Ports Collection, in the directory */usr/ports/mail/majordomo*. When installing, you'll notice a message:

```
To finish the installation, 'su' to root and type:

        make install-wrapper

If not installing the wrapper, type

        cd /usr/local/majordomo; ./wrapper config-test

(no 'su' necessary) to verify the installation.
./install.sh -o root -g 54  -m 4755 wrapper /usr/local/majordomo/wrapper
```

With the exception of the last line, this comes from the original *majordomo* installation procedure. The last line is the port performing the `make install-wrapper` for you. You

560

don't need to do anything else, and you can ignore the messages.

After installation, you still need to perform some configuration:

- Customize */usr/local/majordomo/majordomo.cf*. This should be easy enough to read, and you may not need to change anything. Once you have it up and running, you might like to consider changing the `default_subscribe_policy`.

- Define your lists in */usr/local/majordomo/aliases.majordomo*. This file contains a single list, `test-l`, which you should remove once you have things up and running.

- Ensure that there is a mail user `majordomo-owner` on the system. Probably the best way to handle this is to add an entry in */etc/aliases* (see page 557):

```
majordomo-owner:  root
```

  Since `root` should be an alias for your mail ID, this will mean that you get the mail for `majordomo-owner` as well. Don't run *newaliases* yet.

- Add */usr/local/majordomo/aliases.majordomo* to the *sendmail* aliases. Find the following line in */etc/sendmail.cf*, and add the text in **bold type**:

```
O AliasFile=/etc/aliases,/usr/local/majordomo/aliases.majordomo
```

- Run *newaliases*. You may get the following message:

```
/etc/aliases: 12 aliases, longest 14 bytes, 146 bytes total
hash map "Alias1": unsafe map file /usr/local/majordomo/aliases.majordomo: Permissi
on denied
WARNING: cannot open alias database /usr/local/majordomo/aliases.majordomo
Cannot create database for alias file /usr/local/majordomo/aliases.majordomo: Opera
tion not supported by device
```

  If this happens, perform the following steps:

```
# cd /usr/local/majordomo
# chmod 777 .
# newaliases
/etc/aliases: 12 aliases, longest 14 bytes, 146 bytes total
WARNING: writable directory /usr/local/majordomo
WARNING: writable directory /usr/local/majordomo
WARNING: writable directory /usr/local/majordomo
/usr/local/majordomo/aliases.majordomo: 16 aliases, longest 235 bytes, 890 bytes to
tal
# chmod 755 .
# newaliases
/etc/aliases: 12 aliases, longest 14 bytes, 146 bytes total
/usr/local/majordomo/aliases.majordomo: 16 aliases, longest 235 bytes, 890 bytes to
tal
```

  This will create the files with the correct permissions.

- Restart *sendmail*—see page 556. You don't need to do this if you're planning to reboot before using *majordomo*.

That's all you need to do. You don't need to start any processes to run *majordomo*: it gets started automatically when a mail message is received.

Mailing lists: majordomo

33

The World-Wide Web

For the vast majority of the public, the Internet and the *World-Wide Web* are the same thing. FreeBSD is an important contender in this area. Some of the world's largest Web sites, including Yahoo! (*http://www.yahoo.com/*) run FreeBSD. FreeBSD's web performance appears to be at least an order of magnitude better than that of Microsoft NT, not to mention other Microsoft platforms.

We'll look at web browsers first, then on page 566 we'll look at how to set up a web server.

Uniform Resource Locators

Another term has become widely known in connection with the World Wide Web: the concept of a *Uniform Resource Locator* or *URL*, the means by which resources are located on the Internet. The most usual kind of URL can consist of up to 6 components, although most contain only 3. The syntax is (roughly translated into UNIX terminology):

service : / / *user* : *password* @ *host* : *port* / *path*

These names have the following meaning:

Table 33-1. URL syntax

Component	Meaning
service	An IP service, normally described in */etc/services*. See page 393 for more details. Some exceptions are the string `mailto`, which identifies the *user* and *host* components as a mail ID, and `file`, which identifies the following pathname as the name of a local file. The most common services are *http*, *ftp* and *telnet*.
user	The name of a user on whose behalf the operation is performed. For example, when using the *ftp* service, this would be the user name to use for logging in to the FTP server. We've seen that it represents the name of the recipient for mail. From a UNIX perspective, the *user* information comes from */etc/passwd*.

Component	Meaning
password	Where authentication is needed, the password to use. You'll see this occasionally in FTP URLs. Traditionally, this information is stored in */etc/passwd*, but FreeBSD stores it in a separate file, */etc/spwd.db*, which is accessible only to `root`.
host	The DNS name of the system on which the resource is located. Some non-UNIX sites also use an IP address here. This information is stored in a file such as */etc/namedb/db.domain* for the local system, and retrieved via DNS.
path	A UNIX path name, in other words a complete file name. Unlike other UNIX path names, the root is not normally the root file system. For the *http* service, the root is implementation defined. For Apache on FreeBSD, it's normally */usr/local/www/data/*. If you use the ˜ notation to mean *home directory* (see page 163), you will get ˜*user/public_html/*.
	For *ftp*, it's the directory which belongs to *user*. If you omit *user* for *ftp*, you'll get the user *ftp*, so the pathname */pub* maps to the UNIX file name ˜*ftp/pub*.

As you'll see, all of these components are intimately related to UNIX. See RFC 1738 at *http://www.cis.ohio-state.edu/htbin/rfc/rfc1738.html* for a precise definition.

Web browsers

A *web browser* is a piece of software which retrieves documents from the Web and displays them. FreeBSD does not include a web browser, but a large number are available in the Ports Collection. The most important are:

- *lynx* is a web browser for people who don't use X. It displays text only.

- *mosaic* was the original web browser. It's looking a bit dated now.

- *netscape* is the most popular browser available. We'll look at it in more detail later.

You'll note one exception on this list: Microsoft's *Internet Explorer* is not available for FreeBSD. Nobody seems to have missed it. In view of the fact that Microsoft appears to be trying to fragment the web market, I can't recommend it even for those platforms for which it is available.

Netscape

Until recently, there was no native version of Netscape for FreeBSD, but both BSDI and Linux versions work. The BSDI version is preferable, since it doesn't have any particular prerequisites. The Linux version requires Linux emulation, of course—see page 384 for more details. Now Netscape also has a FreeBSD version, so that's the one to choose.

Theoretically you could download Netscape in the same way you download any other version of Netscape. The installation instructions are rather complicated, however, so FreeBSD provides an installation procedure in the Ports Collection. This doesn't compile Netscape—the sources are not all available—but it does ensure that the installation completes correctly. Installation looks like this:

```
# cd /usr/ports/web/netscape4
# make install
>> communicator-v403b8-export.x86-unknown-freebsd.tar.gz doesn't seem to exist on this
system.
>> Attempting to fetch from file:/cdrom/ports/distfiles//.
cp: /cdrom/ports/distfiles//communicator-v403b8-export.x86-unknown-freebsd.tar.gz: No
such file or directory
>> Attempting to fetch from ftp://ftp.netscape.com/pub/communicator/4.03/4.03b8/englis
h/unix/freebsd/base_install/.
Receiving communicator-v403b8-export.x86-unknown-freebsd.tar.gz (7639662 bytes)
7639662 bytes transfered in 2547.6 seconds  (2.93 Kbytes/s)
>> Checksum OK for communicator-v403b8-export.x86-unknown-freebsd.tar.gz.
===>   Extracting for netscape-4.03b8
===>   Patching for netscape-4.03b8
===>   Applying FreeBSD patches for netscape-4.03b8
===>   Configuring for netscape-4.03b8
===>   Installing for netscape-4.03b8
===>   Warning: your umask is "0000".
       If this is not desired, set it to an appropriate value
       and install this port again by ''make reinstall''.
... lots of information

Installing Communicator files...
Installing Communicator Java files...
Installing additional component files...
Registering Communicator 4.03b8...

The Netscape Communicator software installation is complete.
... more information

Note: If Java applets fail to display.  Type this as root:
        cd /usr/X11R6/lib/X11/fonts/misc
        /usr/X11R6/bin/mkfontdir
        chmod 444 fonts.dir
     And then exit and restart your X server.
===>   Registering installation for netscape-4.03b8
```

Running Netscape

To run Netscape, just enter the name:

```
$ netscape &
```

Netscape starts in a separate window. The & character after the name is not essential, but if you don't specify it, you won't be able to use the window in which you start it until netscape terminates.

Figure 33-2 shows the default netscape display. There are many configuration possibilities—see the instructions for further information. One thing is not immediately apparent, however: when entering text to Netscape, you can use most Emacs **Ctrl-** keys, such as **Ctrl-A** to go to the beginning of the line, **Ctrl-D** to delete the next character after the cursor, and so on.

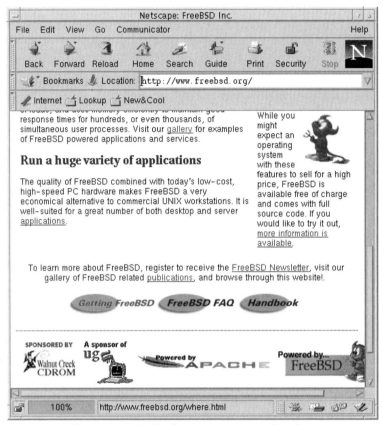

Figure 33-2: Default netscape display

Setting up a web server

FreeBSD is a system of choice for running web servers, so it's not surprising that a large number are available. Probably the most popular is *apache*, which is available in the Ports Collection. Install with:

```
# pkg_add /cdrom/packages/www/apache-1.2.4.tgz
```

In future versions, the name *apache-1.2.4* will change. Apache comes with a lot of documentation in HTML format (of course), but the port doesn't install it anywhere. You can access the current documentation at *http://www.apache.org/manual-index/docs*.

Configuring apache

The Apache port uses the following directories:

- The configuration files are in the directory hierarchy */usr/local/etc/apache*. The port installs prototype configuration files, but they need to be modified.

- Web pages are in */usr/local/www/data*. This is the "root" directory for the web pages: the file */usr/local/www/data/foo.html* on *www.example.org* will have the URL *http://www.example.org/foo.html*. You can change it by changing the entry `DocumentRoot` in */usr/local/etc/apache/access.conf*.

- Icons are stored in */usr/local/www/icons*.

- CGI scripts are stored in */usr/local/www/cgi-bin*.

The configuration files

There are three configuration files in */usr/local/etc/apache*: *access.conf*, which controls access to the system, *httpd.conf*, which defines most server parameters, and *srm.conf*, which defines the mapping between the file names and URLs. *httpd.conf* is the only one you must change. See the *apache* documentation if you need to change the other files.

httpd.conf

Probably the best way to understand *httpd.conf* is to read through it. Most entries can be left the way there are. We'll look at the ones that may need change.

- `ServerAdmin` is the mail ID of the system administrator. It's set to `you@your.address`, which obviously needs to be changed.

- The comments about `ScoreBoardFile` suggest that you should check to see if the system creates one. Don't bother: FreeBSD doesn't create this file.

- You don't need to set `ServerName`, but it may be a good idea. For example, *www.example.org* is a CNAME for *freebie.example.org* (see page 483), and if we don't set this value, clients will access *www.example.org*, but the server will return the name *freebie.example.org*.

- If you set the parameter `CacheNegotiatedDocs`, Apache tells proxy servers to cache any documents it receives. This improves performance if the page is referenced again. It is disabled (commented out) in the original configuration file. Unfortunately, you can't specify this parameter for individual pages: it's either on or off for all pages.

- The Keep-Alive extension to HTTP, as defined by the `HTTP/1.1 draft`, allows persistent connections. These long-lived HTTP sessions allow multiple requests to be sent over the same TCP connection, and in some cases have been shown to result in an almost 50% speedup in latency times for HTML documents with lots of images.

- The parameters `MinSpareServers`, `MaxSpareServers`, `StartServers`, `MaxClients` and `MaxRequestsPerChild` are used for server tuning. The default values should work initially, but if you have a lot of Web traffic, you should consider changing them.

- The parameter `ProxyRequests` allows Apache to function as a *proxy server*. We'll look at this in more detail below.

- The parameters starting with `Cache` apply only to proxy servers, so we'll look at them below as well.

- The `Listen` parameter defines alternate ports on which Apache listens.

- `VirtualHost` allows Apache to serve as multiple hosts. This feature is important enough that we'll talk about it in its own section on page 568.

Proxy web servers

Apache is capable of operating as a proxy server: it can accept requests for web pages of other systems. This can be an alternative to a general IP aliasing package such as *natd* (see page 506) if you need it only for Web access. It's also useful in conjunction with *caching*.

Unfortunately, by default the current version of Apache does not support proxy servers. You need to rebuild the package manually after enabling it in the configuration file—see the file */usr/ports/www/apache/work/apache-1.2.4/src/INSTALL* for more details. In addition to reinstalling the server with code for proxy serving, you must set `ProxyRequests` to `On` in order to enable the proxy server.

Caching

One reason for enabling the proxy server is in order to *cache* data requests. Caching keeps pages which have been requested through the proxy and presents them again if they are requested again. This is particularly useful if the server serves a large number of people who communicate with each other and are thus likely to request many of the same pages.

The `Cache` parameters are commented out by default. If you uncomment them, you should uncomment them all execpt possibly `NoCache`. When setting these values, change the name of the directory `CacheRoot`. A good name might be */usr/local/www/proxy*.

Virtual hosts

Running and maintaining a web server is enough work that you might want to use the same server to host several sets of web pages, for example for a number of different organizations. For example, at *example.org* you may run your own web pages and also a set of pages for *biguser.com* (see page 409). To do this, you add the following section to */usr/local/etc/apache/httpd.conf*:

```
<VirtualHost www.biguser.com>
ServerAdmin grog@example.org
DocumentRoot /usr/local/www/biguser          where we put the web pages
ServerName www.biguser.com                   the name that the server will claim to be
ErrorLog /var/log/biguser/error_log
TransferLog /var/log/biguser/access_log
</VirtualHost>
```

The log files don't contain any information about the names by which the data was invoked, so it's important to have separate log files for each virtual domain. In this case we've put them in a subdirectory of */var/log*, */var/log/biguser*. You must create this directory before restarting the server.

After restarting *apache*, it handles any requests to *www.biguser.com* with these parameters. If you don't define a virtual host, the server will access the main web pages (defined by the entry `DocumentRoot` in */usr/local/etc/apache/access.conf*).

Running apache

Depending on the origin of your port, the server is stored either in */usr/local/sbin/httpd* or in the rather unusual location */usr/local/www/server/httpd*. You can run it with no parameters:

```
# /usr/local/www/server/httpd
```

It automatically starts 7 other processes.

To start *apache* automatically at boot time, add the following entry to */etc/rc.local*:

```
echo -n 'starting local daemons:'
# put your local stuff here

echo " httpd"; /usr/local/www/server/httpd
```

Stopping apache

One of the disadvantages of the number of processes is that it's confusing to stop *apache*. In fact, it's not as difficult as it looks. The original *httpd* process belongs to `root`, and the others belong to `nobody`. Use *ps* to find the first one, and kill it gently (without `-9`) so that it can close its files:

```
root    29322  0.0  0.2   520  192  ??  Ss   10:42AM   0:01.79 httpd
nobody  29323  0.0  0.2   556  168  ??  I    10:42AM   0:00.02 httpd
nobody  29324  0.0  0.2   568  172  ??  I    10:42AM   0:00.04 httpd
nobody  29325  0.0  0.2   568  172  ??  I    10:42AM   0:00.03 httpd
nobody  29326  0.0  0.2   568  172  ??  I    10:42AM   0:00.04 httpd
nobody  29327  0.0  0.2   556  168  ??  I    10:42AM   0:00.02 httpd
nobody    281  0.0  0.2   520  168  ??  I    10:54AM   0:00.00 httpd
nobody    282  0.0  0.2   520  168  ??  I    10:54AM   0:00.00 httpd
root     4748  0.0  0.7   252  644  p5  S+    1:05PM   0:00.02 grep http
# kill 29322                            the one belonging to root
# ps waux | grep http
root     4793  0.0  0.7   252  644  p5  S+    1:06PM   0:00.02 grep http
```

34

HylaFAX

HylaFAX is a free fax software packet written by Sam Leffler, one of the authors of *The Design and the Implementation of the 4.3BSD UNIX Operating System.* It is supplied in the Ports Collection—see page 111 for details of how to install a port.

Setting up HylaFAX

HylaFAX consists of two parts, a *client* and a *server*. As a user, you use the client to send and display faxes. The server is responsible for the delivery to or from another system. A server system usually runs at least two server processes, the scheduler process *faxq* and server *hfaxd*. Server systems may also use *faxgetty* to monitor modems and possibly receive incoming fax calls. If you're running a send-only system, you would run *faxq* and *hfaxd* but not *faxgetty*.

In addition to the server processes that operate all the time, *HylaFAX* comes with two programs that are intended to be run periodically. On a server, *faxqclean* removes unwanted files from the spooling area, and *faxcron* monitors the spooling area and performs routine maintenance tasks such as truncating log files. These programs are usually invoked by *cron*.

In the remainder of this chapter we'll look at the basic steps required to set up *HylaFAX*. They are:

- Install the *HylaFAX* software.

- Select a facsimile modem for use.

- Check your modem is functional.

- Select a flow control scheme to use for facsimile communication.

- Select a TTY device to use.

- Use *faxsetup* to configure a server machine.

- Use *faxaddmodem* to configure modems.

- Start up outbound service.

Selecting a fax modem

HylaFAX has drivers for Class 1, Class 2, and Class 2.0 fax modems. Avoid Class 1 modems, which are now obsolete. Class 2 modems are the most common, but compatibility can be a problem. In addition, the quality of Class 2 modems varies significantly. Class 2.0 modems follow the latest standard, a ratified version of the specification used in implementing Class 2 modems. There are significantly fewer Class 2.0 modems available, and the quality of these modems also varies. The *HylaFAX* distribution includes a list of modems that have been tried with *HylaFAX*, including several modems that have been found to be reliable for use in sending and receiving.

Flow control

Modern fax modems can run at speeds of up to 14,400 bps. At these speeds, you should use hardware flow control to avoid data loss—see page 430. Some modems only implement hardware flow control correctly when doing data communication, and may not support hardware flow control during fax communication. Consult the modem information supplied with the distribution for specifics on some modems. If the *HylaFAX* distribution includes a prototype configuration file for your modem, then use the appropriate default flow control scheme defined for the modem. In case of doubt, or if you have trouble, configure the modem to use software flow control for fax use.

Choosing a *tty* device

As we saw in Chapter 24, *Serial communications and modems*, your choice of *tty* device depends on the way you want to use it. Choose */dev/cuaan* for dialout connections and *dev/ttydn* for dialin connections.

Using *faxsetup* to configure a server machine

Before using any *HylaFAX* software, run the *faxsetup* script to verify the software installation to carry out a number of one-time tasks to prepare the system for use. It's especially important to run *faxsetup* if you install the *HylaFAX* package, because it checks that the parameters set up at the time the package was built are correct for your machine.

After testing, *faxsetup* writes configuration information to two files in the *HylaFAX* spool directory. */var/spool/fax/etc/setup.cache* contains the parameter settings used by *HylaFAX* command scripts, and */var/spool/fax/etc/setup.modem* contains settings and shell functions used by command scripts that communicate with modems.

> *The setup.cache and setup.modem files must be present for HylaFAX to function properly. If these files do not exist then HylaFAX server applications will terminate with an error message.*

faxsetup performs the following tasks. It always prompts for permission before doing anything that might affect normal system operation (for example adding a new user to the password file).

- It verifies that the pathnames compiled into *HylaFAX* applications are correct and that the directory hierarchy is present and set up correctly. If any of these checks fails then it is assumed that *HylaFAX* has not been installed or that there is a misconfiguration problem such as might occur when a binary distribution is loaded in an unexpected location.

- It verifies that the TIFF software distribution is properly installed on the server machine. *HylaFAX* uses certain of the TIFF tools in normal server operation.

- It verifies that the configured PostScript RIP is present and that it has the necessary functionality to use it with *HylaFAX*. If you're using Ghostscript, make sure to configure the *tiffg3* device driver when building Ghostscript for use with *HylaFAX*.

- It verifies that a user `fax` exists. If it doesn't find one, it will create it. The user `fax` is used in various places in *HylaFAX*. You should set it up to have the same user number as that of `uucp` so that UUCP lock files can be shared.

- It verifies that */etc/services* contains suitable entries for the `hylafax` and `snpp`. If no entries are present then they may optionally be set up, though the software will still work correctly without them.

- It verifies that *hfaxd* is started when the system is brought up multi-user, or that *hfaxd* is started by the *inetd* dæmon. *hfaxd* is the central *HylaFAX* dæmon. It operates most efficiently when started standalone, but it may also be invoked through *inetd*.

- It verifies that the mail aliases database contains an entry `FaxMaster`. This alias is equivalent to the normal `postmaster` alias used to deliver mail-related problems. *HylaFAX* directs notices about problems and received fax to this alias. The FaxMaster alias should list those system administrators that will handle *HylaFAX*-specific problems. If this alias is not present, *faxsetup* creates one.

Next, *faxsetup* prompts to create a configuration file for the *HylaFAX* scheduler process and for any modems on the system that are to be used by *HylaFAX*. Finally it starts the *HylaFAX* server processes, or restarts them if an existing installation is being updated or reconfigured, and any modem configuration work is performed. In the following sections we'll look at this process in more detail.

Using *faxaddmodem* to configure modems

faxaddmodem configures modems for use. It walks you through the configuration and installation of a new or existing modem. Even if you have a previous version of *HylaFAX* or *FlexFAX* installed, it's a good idea to run *faxaddmodem* to update the configuration information for your modems after installing a new distribution.

You can *faxaddmodem* directly from the command line, but for a first-time installation it's better to run it via *faxsetup*.

The remainder of this section shows a sample configuration session and describes the work done. *faxaddmodem* displays the current or default setting for a configuration parameter enclosed in "[ ]". To accept the current value, type **Enter**.

```
# faxsetup
Setup program for HylaFAX (tm) v4.0pl1.

Created for i386-unknown-freebsd3.0 on Fri Jun  6 17:01:48 CST 1997.

Checking system for proper client configuration.
Checking system for proper server configuration.

Warning: /bin/vgetty does not exist or is not an executable program!

The file:

    /bin/vgetty

does not exist or this file is not an executable program.  The
HylaFAX software optionally uses this program and the fact that
it does not exist on the system is not a fatal error.  If the
program resides in a different location and you do not want to
install a symbolic link for /bin/vgetty that points to your program
then you must reconfigure and rebuild HylaFAX from source code.
```

There is in fact no program called *vgetty*: if you want a *getty* which understands voice calls as well, you should install it and create the symbolic link *vgetty* to point to it.

Next, *faxsetup* repeats this message almost exactly for *egetty*, an external program which determines the type of the call. Then it continues:

```
Make /var/spool/fax/bin/ps2fax a link to /var/spool/fax/bin/ps2fax.gs.

You do not appear to have a "fax" user in the password file.
HylaFAX needs this to work properly, add it [yes]? ENTER
Added user "fax" to /etc/master.passwd.

Warning: No hylafax service entry found!

No entry was found for the hylafax service in the YP/NIS database
or in the /etc/services file.  The software should work properly
without one (except if you want to start hfaxd from inetd), but you
will see warning messages whenever you run a HylaFAX client
application.  If you want to manually add an entry the following
information should be used:

hylafax 4559/tcp                # HylaFAX client-server protocol

Should a hylafax entry be added to /etc/services [yes]?  ENTER

Warning: /etc/inetd.conf is setup wrong!

The /etc/inetd.conf file is set up to start /home/Book/FreeBSD
instead of /usr/local/sbin/hfaxd.  You will need to correct
this before client requests to submit jobs will be properly serviced.

Should the entry in /etc/inetd.conf be corrected [yes]?  ENTER
?

FATAL ERROR: Unable to correct HylaFAX entry in /etc/inetd.conf!

We were unable to edit the /etc/inetd.conf file to correct the entry
for starting up the HylaFAX client-server protocol process.  You
must manually correct this entry so that it reads:

hylafax stream  tcp     nowait  fax     /usr/local/sbin/hfaxd   hfaxd -I

and then rerun faxsetup.
```

What went wrong now? I don't know either: it looks like a bug in *faxsetup*. The

/etc/inetd.conf file looks just fine, but *faxsetup* somehow thought it specified the home directory (*/home/Book/FreeBSD* in this case).

At this point, you have two choices: find out what is wrong with *faxsetup* (and let Sam Leffler know when you fix it), or modify */etc/inetd.conf* manually, as suggested. We'll take the latter approach. After that, we restart *faxsetup*. After the messages about the missing *getty*s, we see:

```
# faxsetup
Make /var/spool/fax/bin/ps2fax a link to /var/spool/fax/bin/ps2fax.gs.

Modem support functions written to /var/spool/fax/etc/setup.modem.
Configuration parameters written to /var/spool/fax/etc/setup.cache.

No scheduler config file exists, creating one from scratch.
```

The next few questions ask about phone numbers and prefixes.

```
Country code [1]? 61                              Australia
Area code []? 8                                   Adelaide area
Long distance dialing prefix [1]? 0
International dialing prefix [011]? 0011
Dial string rules file (relative to /var/spool/fax) ["etc/dialrules"]? ENTER
Tracing during normal server operation [1]? ENTER
Default tracing during send and receive sessions [0xffffffff]? ENTER
Continuation cover page (relative to /var/spool/fax) []? ENTER
Timeout when converting PostScript documents (secs) [180]? ENTER
Maximum number of concurrent jobs to a destination [1]? ENTER
Define a class of modems []? ENTER
Time of day restrictions for outbound jobs ["Any"]? ENTER
Pathname of destination controls file (relative to /var/spool/fax) []? ENTER
Timeout before purging a stale UUCP lock file (secs) [30]? ENTER
Max number of pages to permit in an outbound job [0xffffffff]? ENTER
Syslog facility name for ServerTracing messages [daemon]? ENTER

The non-default scheduler parameters are:

CountryCode:            61
AreaCode:               8
LongDistancePrefix:     0

Are these ok [yes]? ENTER

Creating new configuration file /var/spool/fax/etc/config...

Restarting HylaFAX server processes.
```

At this point, the *HylaFAX* dæmon and any other processes have been restarted. Next, you need to configure your modem. If you're connecting to the standard serial ports, use the devices */dev/cuaa0* to */dev/cuaa3*. Enter the just the filename part, since the script automatically adds the */dev/* to the beginning of the name:

```
You do not appear to have any modems configured for use.  Modems are
configured for use with HylaFAX with the faxaddmodem(1M) command.
Do you want to run faxaddmodem to configure a modem [yes]? ENTER
Serial port that modem is connected to []? cuaa0
Hmm, there does not appear to be an fuser command on your machine.
This means that I am unable to insure that all processes using the
modem have been killed.  I will keep going, but beware that you may
have competition for the modem.

Ok, time to setup a configuration file for the modem.  The manual
page config(4F) may be useful during this process.  Also be aware
that at any time you can safely interrupt this procedure.

Reading scheduler config file /var/spool/fax/etc/config.
```

```
No existing configuration, let's do this from scratch.
```

This claim is not quite correct: it refers only to the modem configuration file. It does use the information in the configuration file */var/spool/fax/etc/config*, including the phone number information we added above, and it uses it:

```
Country code [61]? ENTER
Area code [8]? ENTER
Phone number of fax modem [+1.999.555.1212]? +61-8-8388-8725
```

This is the phone number of the modem, and is used to insert on the header line of the fax.

```
Local identification string (for TSI/CIG) ["NothingSetup"]? LEMIS, Echunga
```

The local identification string is passed to peer fax machines during communication. If it is not specified, or set to a null string, then *HylaFAX* uses the canonical phone number of the fax modem instead.

```
Long distance dialing prefix [0]? ENTER
International dialing prefix [0011]? ENTER
Dial string rules file (relative to /var/spool/fax) ["etc/dialrules"]? ENTER
Tracing during normal server operation [1]? ENTER
Tracing during send and receive sessions [11]? ENTER
Protection mode for received facsimile [0600]? ENTER
Protection mode for session logs [0600]? ENTER
Protection mode for cuaa0 [0660]? ENTER
Rings to wait before answering [1]? ENTER
Modem speaker volume [off]? ENTER
Command line arguments to getty program ["std.%s"]? ENTER
Pathname of TSI access control list file (relative to /var/spool/fax) [""]? ENTER
Pathname of Caller-ID access control list file (relative to /var/spool/fax) [""]? ENTER
Tag line font file (relative to /var/spool/fax) [etc/lutRS18.pcf]? ENTER
Tag line format string ["From %%l|%c|Page %%p of %%t"]? ENTER
Time before purging a stale UUCP lock file (secs) [30]? ENTER
Hold UUCP lockfile during inbound data calls [Yes]? ENTER
Hold UUCP lockfile during inbound voice calls [Yes]? ENTER
Percent good lines to accept during copy quality checking [95]? ENTER
Max consecutive bad lines to accept during copy quality checking [5]? ENTER
Max number of pages to accept in a received facsimile [25]? ENTER
Syslog facility name for ServerTracing messages [daemon]? ENTER
Set UID to 0 to manipulate CLOCAL [""]? ENTER

The non-default server configuration parameters are:

CountryCode:            61
AreaCode:               8
FAXNumber:              +61-8-8388-8725
LongDistancePrefix:     0
InternationalPrefix:    0011
DialStringRules:        "etc/dialrules"
SessionTracing:         11
DeviceMode:             0660
RingsBeforeAnswer:      1
SpeakerVolume:          off
GettyArgs:              "std.%s"
LocalIdentifier:        LEMIS, Echunga
TagLineFont:            etc/lutRS18.pcf
TagLineFormat:          "From %%l|%c|Page %%p of %%t"
MaxRecvPages:           25

Are these ok [yes]? ENTER
```

Some of the questions above merit more discussion:

- *HylaFAX* includes a trace facility. We won't look at this in this book; check the documentation supplied with *HylaFAX* for more detail.

- The default number of rings before answering is 1. You might think that you could speed things up further by setting this value to 0, but this will disable answering altogether. See page 433 for more details.

- The *tag line* is the line across the top of most faxes which gives information on the date and origin of the fax. *HylaFAX* supplies a number of utilities to configure this line to your liking—see the documentation for further information.

- By default, Hylafax uses the *UUCP* locking scheme to ensure that only one process accesses the serial port at a time. This is a good choice, since most other programs, including just about every flavour of *getty* and *ppp*, do so as well. It doesn't mean that *HylaFAX* has anything to do with UUCP except that they could conceivably both want to access the same serial port.

- The *percent good lines* and *maximum consecutive bad lines* can be set to control the minimum acceptable quality of a page when receiving a fax. The term *line* applies to a line of data, about 1/50" in normal mode, and 1/100" in fine mode. The values given are probably the minimum quality you should accept: 5 consecutive bad lines would make a line of text almost unreadable.

Testing the modem

The next step is to test the modem to determine its capabilities. This carries straight on from the previous section:

```
Now we are going to probe the tty port to figure out the type
of modem that is attached.  This takes a few seconds, so be patient.
Note that if you do not have the modem cabled to the port, or the
modem is turned off, this may hang (just go and cable up the modem
or turn it on, or whatever).

Probing for best speed to talk to modem: 38400 OK.
[1]+  Terminated              ( trap 0 1 2 15; while true; do
    sleep 10; echo ""; echo "Hmm, something seems to be hung, check your modem eh?";
done )&

This modem looks to have support for both Class 1 and 2;
how should it be configured [2]? ENTER

Hmm, this looks like a Class 2 modem.
Modem manufacturer is "ROCKWELL".
Modem model is "AC/V34".
DTE-DCE flow control scheme [default]? ENTER
```

The results you see above may look surprising. In all probability, you don't have a Rockwell modem, and the model number may also look completely different from what is written on the modem. In fact, the manufacturer and model stated often refer to the modem chipset, and not the modem itself.

```
Using prototype configuration file rc288dpi...

The modem configuration parameters are:

ModemAnswerFaxBeginCmd: "<19200><xon>"
ModemDialCmd:           ATDT%s
ModemFlowControl:       rtscts
ModemHardFlowCmd:       AT&K3
ModemNoFlowCmd:         AT&K0
ModemRate:              38400
ModemRecvFillOrder:     MSB2LSB
ModemSendFillOrder:     LSB2MSB
ModemSetupAACmd:        AT+FAA=1
ModemSetupDCDCmd:       AT&C1
ModemSetupDTRCmd:       AT&D3
ModemSoftFlowCmd:       AT&K4
Class2RecvDataTrigger:  " 22"

Are these ok [yes]? ENTER

Creating new configuration file /var/spool/fax/etc/config.cuaa0...
Creating fifo /var/spool/fax/FIFO.cuaa0 for faxgetty... done.
Done setting up the modem configuration.

Checking /var/spool/fax/etc/config for consistency...
...everything looks ok; leaving existing file unchanged.

Don't forget to run faxmodem(1M) (if you have a send-only environment)
or configure init to run faxgetty on cuaa0.
Do you want to run faxaddmodem to configure another modem [yes]? no

You do not appear to be using faxgetty to notify the HylaFAX scheduler
about new modems and/or their status.  This means that you must use the
faxmodem program to inform the new faxq process about the modems you
want to have scheduled by HylaFAX.  Beware that if you have modems that
require non-default capabilities specified to faxmodem then you should
read faxmodem(1M) manual page and do this work yourself (since this
script is not intelligent enough to automatically figure out the modem
capabilities and supply the appropriate arguments).

Should I run faxmodem for each configured modem [yes]? ENTER
/usr/local/sbin/faxmodem cuaa0

Done verifying system setup.
```

Starting HylaFAX

When you configured *HylaFAX* in the previous section, you also started it, and set it up to run automatically when the system is booted. Normally, there's nothing more you need to do.

Checking fax system status

You may have occasion to want to find out what the current status of the fax system is. You do this with *faxstat*. Typically, you just enter the name:

```
# faxstat
HylaFAX scheduler on freebie.example.org: Running
Modem cuaa0 (+61-8-8388-8725): Sending job 1
```

Restarting the *hfaxd* dæmon

Sometimes you may find that the *hfaxd* dæmon is not running, and it can't be restarted. You can restart it (as root) with the following:

```
# hfaxd -i hylafax
```

You will not get any messages, even if it dies: it logs its messages via *syslogd*, and you will normally find them on the console or in the log file */var/log/messages*.

Sending a fax

Finally your fax configuration is complete. So how do you go about sending a fax?

The simple part is: the program is called *sendfax*. Unfortunately, it takes a plethora of parameters, so you'll probably want to write a small script to take care of some of the aspects. In this section, we'll look at the information needed to complete a fax.

Whenever you send a fax, whether with a computer or with an old-fashioned fax machine, you need the following information:

- The destination to which you want to send the fax. Normally this is a phone number, but *HylaFAX* gives you the opportunity to send faxes over the Internet. We'll look at this below as well.

- The document or documents you want to send. This seems straightforward enough, but with a computer, you need to consider the format. We'll look at this in detail below.

- Possibly a *fax cover sheet*. There are a number of ways to create a cover sheet. We'll look at some of them further down.

The destination

If the destination is a phone number, you just need to specify it with the -d option:

```
$ sendfax -d+49-6637-919122
```

This will send a fax to the number specified, in this case an international connection.

The document

Faxes are transmitted in a special format which is not used anywhere else One of *HylaFAX*'s functions is to convert documents into this format. It recognizes a number of other formats and performs the conversion automatically. To send a document, you just specify the names of the document on the command line. For example, to send the documents *logfile.txt* and *example.ps*, which are in plain ASCII text and PostScript respectively, to the fax machine in the previous example, you could enter:

```
$ sendfax -d+49-6637-919122 logfile.txt example.ps
```

This example will send a single fax containing both documents and a default cover sheet.

The cover sheet

HylaFAX supplies a default cover sheet, */usr/local/lib/fax/faxcover.ps*. You will probably not want to use the cover sheet in this form, since it includes a Silicon Graphics logo. If you do, however, you will need to fill out a number of fields:

- To specify the name of the recipient, include it in the dialling information supplied to the -d option, with an @ sign in between:

  ```
  $ sendfax -d"Mister Never There@+49-6637-919122" wakeupcall.ps
  ```

- The fax number. This is done automatically from the -d option.

- The destination company name. Set this with the -x option:

  ```
  $ sendfax -d"Mister Never There@+49-6637-919122" -x "Yoyodyne Cosmetics" \
  > wakeupcall.ps
  ```

  This line has been continued over two lines. The second line has a different prompt.

- Optionally, you may specify a name for the "from" line with the -f option. If you don't specify one, it will be generated automatically from your user entry in */etc/passwd* (the so-called GECOS field, which is also used for mail). In this example, we'll leave out this option, as people will normally do.

- You may also specify a "regarding" field, which is in fact abbreviated to "Re", with the -r option. For example, you might write:

  ```
  $ sendfax -d"Mister Never There@+49-6637-919122" -x "Yoyodyne Cosmetics" \
  > -r "Your voice mail yesterday" wakeupcall.ps
  ```

- Finally, if you haven't had enough already, you can send up to five lines of comments. We might write:

  ```
  $ sendfax -d"Mister Never There@+49-6637-919122" -x "Yoyodyne Cosmetics" \
  > -r "Your voice mail yesterday" -c "I've been trying to call you for the
  last 8 hours.  Where have you been?" wakeupcall.ps
  ```

The examples above will generate the following line on the cover sheet:

To: Mister Never There
Fax Number: +49-6637-919122
Company: Yoyodyne cosmetics
From: Greg Lehey
Re: Your voice mail yesterday
Today's date: Tue Jun 10 1997 11:50:55 CST
# of pages to follow this sheet: 3

Comments: I've been trying to call you for the last 8 hours. Where have you been?

You'll notice a couple of fields that get filled in automatically. The date and the "number of pages" field are determined automatically. Unfortunately, the "number of pages" field doesn't include the cover sheet, which is not normal practice.

How to omit the cover sheet

Of course, a cover sheet may not be for you. It costs time and money to transmit, especially for a non-local call. Alternatively, you may include a cover sheet along with the document. In this case, you can omit the automatic cover sheet generation by using the -n option to *sendfax*:

```
$ sendfax -n -d5551212 enquiry.ps
```

This will send just the document *enquiry.ps* to the specified number.

35

Connecting to non-IP networks

BSD UNIX and the Internet grew up together, but it took other vendors a long time to accept the Internet Protocols. In that time, a number of other protocols arose. We've already mentioned X.25 and SNA, currently both not supported by FreeBSD. The protocols that grew up in the DOS world are more important: *SMB* (*System Message Block*), which is often also known by names like *LanManager* and *NetBIOS*, and Novell's *IPX*.

IPX support is relatively rudimentary. FreeBSD includes an IPX routing dæmon, *IPXrouted*. See the man page *IPXrouted(8)* for further information. In the rest of this chapter we'll look at a more extensive networking implementation, *samba*.

Samba

Samba is a collection of software components which implement the SMB protocol over TCP/IP. You can use it to interface with Microsoft environments such as Windows for Workgroups, Windows 95 and Windows NT. It is part of the Ports Collection, in */usr/ports/net/samba*, and you can get more information, including support, from *http://samba.anu.edu.au*. There's also a mailing list—see the web page for details.

Samba consists of the following components:

- *smbd*, a dæmon which provides file and print services to SMB clients.

- *nmbd* provides name services for NetBIOS.

- *smbclient* is a simple ftp-like client which is useful for accessing SMB shared files on other servers, such as Windows for Workgroups. You can also use it to allow a UNIX box to print to a printer attached to any SMB server.

- *testparm* tests the *samba* configuration file, *smb.conf.*

- *smbstatus* tells you who is using the *smbd* dæmon.

Installing the *samba* software

Install *samba* from the port:

```
# cd /usr/ports/net/samba
# make install
```

This operation installs the binaries *addtosmbpass, nmblookup, smbclient, smbpasswd, smbrun, smbstatus, smbtar, testparm* and *testprns* in */usr/local/bin*, the standard location for additional binaries on a BSD system, and the dæmons *smbd* and *nmbd* in */usr/local/sbin*. These are appropriate for FreeBSD, but they are *not* the locations that the Samba documentation recommends. It also installs the man pages in */usr/local/man*, where the *man* program can find them. That is all that the port installs. In particular, it does not install a sample configuration file. We'll see how to do that further down.

There are a number of security implications for the server, since it handles sensitive data. To maintain an adequate security level,

- Ensure that the software is readable by all and writeable only by `root`. *smbd* should be executable by all. Don't make it *setuid*. If an individual user runs it, it runs with their permissions.

- Put server log files in a directory readable and writable only by `root`, since they may contain sensitive information.

- Put the *smbd* configuration file in */usr/local/etc/smb.conf*, and ensure that it is secured so that only `root` can change it.

  The Samba documentation recommends setting the directory readable and writeable only by `root`. Depending on what other configuration files you have in */etc/local/etc*, this could cause problems.

smbd and *nmbd*: the Samba dæmons

The main component of Samba is *smbd*, the SMB dæmon. In addition, you need the Samba name dæmon, *nmbd*, which supplies NetBIOS name services for Samba. *smbd* requires a configuration file, which we'll look at below, while you don't normally need one for *nmbd*. By default, *nmbd* maps DNS host names (without the domain part) to NetBIOS names, though it can perform other functions if you need them. In this chapter we'll assume the default behaviour. See the man page *nmbd(8)* for other possibilities.

You have two choices of how to run *smbd* and *nmbd*: you can start them from */etc/rc.local* at boot time, or you can let *inetd* start them.

To start *smbd* at boot time, put the following lines (shown in **bold face**) in */etc/rc.local*:

```
echo -n 'starting local daemons:'
# put your local stuff here
echo " smbd" && /usr/local/sbin/smbd -D
echo " nmbd" && /usr/local/sbin/nmbd -D
```

The option -D tells the dæmons to run as a dæmon; otherwise they expect to have a connection and exit when the connection closes.

The man page for *smbd* gives a number of parameters to specify the configuration file and the log file. As long as you stick to the specified file names, you shouldn't need this: by default, *smbd* looks for the configuration file at */usr/local/etc/smb.conf*, and this file contains the names of the other files.

Running the dæmons from *inetd*

To run the dæmons from *inetd*,

- Edit */etc/inetd.conf*. You should find the following two lines towards the bottom of the file with a # in front. Remove the # to show the lines as they are here. If your *inetd.conf* doesn't contain these lines, add them.

```
netbios-ssn      stream   tcp    nowait   root   /usr/local/sbin/smbd   smbd
netbios-ns       dgram    udp    wait     root   /usr/local/sbin/nmbd   nmbd
```

- Either reboot, or cause *inetd* to re-read its configuration file:

```
# ps waux | grep inetd                        find the PID of inetd (2nd column)
root     7818  3.1  0.7   252  644 p6 S+   10:56AM  0:00.03 grep inetd
root      118  0.0  0.1   200   92 ?? Is   Thu10AM  0:01.78 inetd
# kill -1 118                                 send a SIGHUP
```

The configuration file

The Samba configuration file describes the services that the dæmon offers. These are primarily printer and file access services.

The configuration file is divided into sections identified by a label in brackets. Most labels correspond to a service, but there are also three special labels: [global], [homes] and [printers], all of which are optional. We'll look at them in the following sections.

The [global] section

As the name suggests, the [global] section defines parameters which either apply to the server as a whole, or which are defaults for the other services. The interesting ones for us are:

- socket options is hardly mentioned in the documentation, but it's very important: many Microsoft implementations of TCP/IP are inefficient and establish a new TCP more often than necessary. Select the socket options TCP_NODELAY and IPTOS_LOWDELAY, which can speed up the response time of such applications by over 95%.

- `printing` describes the kind of printing services the system offers. Choose `bsd`, the default.

- `printcap name` is the name of the *printcap* file. Choose the default */etc/printcap*.

- `guest account` is the account (in UNIX terms: user ID) to use if no password is supplied. You probably want to define a guest account, since many Microsoft clients don't use user IDs. Ensure that the privileges are set appropriately.

- `lock directory` is a directory in which Samba places file locks for concurrent access. If you have concurrent write access to files, you should enable this option: by default it is commented out. The default directory name is */usr/local/samba/var/locks*, which doesn't get created automatically. If you use this option, create the directory:

```
# mkdir -p /usr/local/samba/var/locks
```

The [homes] section

The [homes] section allows clients to connect to their home directories without needing an entry in the configuration file. If this section is present, and an incoming request specifies a service which is not defined in the configuration file, Samba checks if it matches a user ID. If it does, and if the specified password is correct, Samba creates a service which supplies the user's home directory.

The following options are of interest in the [homes] section:

- `writeable` can be `yes` or `no`, and specifies whether the user is allowed to write to the directory.

- `create mode` specifies the permission bits (in octal) to set for files which are created.

- `public` specifies whether other users are allowed access to this directory. In combination with a `guest` user, this can be a serious security liability.

The [printers] section

The [printers] section describes printing services. It doesn't need the names of the printers: if it doesn't find the specified service, either in the configuration file or in the [homes] section, if it exists, it looks for them in the */etc/printcap* file.

You probably don't want to change anything in this section. In particular, don't change the `printable` option. If you do, *smbd* will refuse to run.

Other sections: service descriptions

Samba takes any section name except for [global], [homes] or [printers] as the definition of a service. A typical example might be:

```
[ftp]
  comment = ftp server file area
  path = /var/spool/ftp/pub
  read only = yes
  public = yes
  write list = grog
```

This entry defines access to the anonymous *ftp* section. Anybody can read it, but only user `grog` can write to it.

Creating the configuration file

The port does not currently install a configuration file, but there is a sample file in the port. To install it, perform the following steps manually:

* Copy the sample configuration file to the correct location:

```
# cp /usr/ports/net/samba/work/samba-1.9.16p11/examples/simple/smb.conf \
> /usr/local/etc
```

Sorry about the name of the directory, especially as it will change in the next version of Samba: the section *samba-1.9.16p11* will change to reflect the new version number. Note also that this is *not* the location mentioned in the Samba documentation.

* Create a directory */var/log/samba* readable and writeable only by `root`. This is for the log files, which may contain confidential data, so you shouldn't put them in the publicly readable */var/log* directory.

Next, edit the configuration file to suit FreeBSD and your personal needs. There's also a fair amount of commentary in the file. Consider the following:

* Either create a user `pcguest` (see Chapter 11, *Making friends with FreeBSD*, page 164), or change the entry `guest_account` to point to an existing account.

* Change the entry `log file` in the `[global]` section to point to */var/log/samba/log.%m*.

Testing the installation

Once you have performed the steps described above, you can proceed to test the installation. First, run *testparm* to check the correctness of the configuration file:

```
$ testparm
Load smb config files from /usr/local/etc/smb.conf
Processing section "[homes]"
Processing section "[printers]"
No path in service printers - using /tmp
Processing section "[tmp]"
Processing section "[ftp]"
Processing section "[grog]"
Loaded services file OK.
Press enter to see a dump of your service definitions          Press Enter

Global parameters:
lots of information which could be of use in debugging
```

```
Service parameters [homes]:
        comment: Home Directories
        browseable: No
        read only: No
        create mask: 0750

Service parameters [printers]:
        comment: All Printers
        browseable: No
        path: /tmp
        create mask: 0700
        print ok: Yes

Service parameters [tmp]:
        comment: Temporary file space
        path: /usr/tmp
        read only: No
        create mask: 01775
        guest ok: Yes

Service parameters [ftp]:
        comment: ftp server file area
        path: /var/spool/ftp/pub
        write list: grog
        guest ok: Yes

Service parameters [lp]:
        comment: local LaserJet 6MP printer
        path: /tmp
        create mask: 0700
        print ok: Yes
        printer: lp

Service parameters [IPC$]:
        comment: IPC Service (Samba 1.9.16p11)
        path: /tmp
        status: No
        guest ok: Yes
$
```

As you see, *testparm* spells out all the parameters which have been created, whether explicitly or by default. If you run into problems, this is the first place to which to return.

Next, test the functionality with *smbclient*. If you're running the servers as dæmons, start them now. If you're starting them from *inetd*, you don't need to do anything.

Samba services are specified in Microsoft format: *system**service*. To make this worse, UNIX interprets the \ character specially, so you need to repeat the character. For example, to access the ftp service on *freebie*, you must enter \\\\freebie\\ftp. To test, start *smbclient* from another system:

```
$ smbclient \\\\freebie\\ftp
Added interface ip=223.147.37.4 bcast=223.147.37.4 nmask=255.255.255.255
Server time is Thu Oct 16 12:36:13 1997
Timezone is UTC+9.5
Password:                               leave empty: it's a public service
Domain=[WORKGROUP] OS=[Unix] Server=[Samba 1.9.16p11]
smb: \> ls                              list the files
  cfbsd                     D        0  Thu Oct 16 10:57:28 1997
  elm.irix5.gz              A   184318  Fri Jan 31 04:40:25 1997
  muscan.tar.gz                 53812  Tue Jul 29 12:18:25 1997
  scan.tar.gz                   45418  Tue Jul 29 12:18:55 1997
  pppd                     AR    94208  Fri Sep 19 12:58:38 1997
  libc.so.3.0.gz            R   198583  Tue May 20 20:00:22 1997
  fvwm-1.23b-core.tar.gz        212920  Sat Sep 13 18:55:48 1997
  fvwm-1.23b-icons.tar.gz        17881  Sat Sep 13 18:55:50 1997
  fvwm-1.23b-modules.tar.gz     158579  Sat Sep 13 18:55:55 1997
  ppp-chapter               D        0  Thu Oct  9 16:08:23 1997
  mail.local               AR    12288  Fri Oct  3 14:36:29 1997
```

```
xterm                        R     151552  Thu Aug  7 20:55:54 1997
                  64056 blocks of size 32768. 18093 blocks available
smb: \>
```

If you get this far, Samba is working. The next step is to attach to the services from the Microsoft machines. That's not a topic for this book. Note, however, that Samba only works with TCP/IP transport, not with NetBEUI.

Displaying Samba status

You can display the status of Samba connections with *smbstatus*. For example,

```
$ smbstatus

Samba version 1.9.16p11
Service      uid      gid      pid      machine
---------------------------------------------
ftp          guest    guest    17820    wait     (223.147.37.4) Thu Oct 16 12:36:17 1997

No locked files
```

Part II: Selected man pages

This section of the book contains a selection of those manual pages that you might find useful when installing the system. They have been formatted approximately as you will find them when using the *man* program.

Previous editions of this book contained many more man pages, but they proved to be unpopular: they made the book much bigger and heavier, and they were never as up to date as the version installed on the system.

We discussed man pages on page 13. If you're new to *man*, you'll find these pages considerably more difficult to read than the first half of the book. Nevertheless, they have the advantage of being the second-best reference you can get for a program (the best is, of course, the source code, but most people find that even more difficult to read).

Unlike the rest of this book, the conventions used in the man pages differ slightly from one man page to the next. This is an unfortunate result of the fact that the man pages have all been written by different authors. Some of them have spelling errors, or the formatting is unusual. In addition, in the index, you will notice that there are often two index entries, one with the command name spelt correctly, and one with the name spelt with an Initial Capital. I have deliberately not changed the pages: their advantage is their authority, not their beauty.

Printing other man pages

If you prefer to have the remaining man pages in print, rather than on the screen, you can do this in two different ways:

- The simpler way is to redirect the output to the spooler:

```
$ man ls | lpr
```

This gives you a printed version which looks pretty much like the original on the screen, except that you may not get bold or underlined text.

- You can typeset with *troff*:

```
$ man -t ls | lpr
```

This gives you a properly typeset version of the man page, similar to the appearance in the following pages, but it requires that your spooling system understand PostScript—see page 300 for more details of printing PostScript, even on printers which don't understand PostScript.

NAME

bad144 – read/write dec standard 144 bad sector information

SYNOPSIS

bad144 [**-c**] [**-f**] [**-v**] *disk* [*sno* [*bad* ...]]
bad144 **-a** [**-c**] [**-f**] [**-v**] *disk* [*bad* ...]
bad144 [**-s**] [**-v**] *disk*

DESCRIPTION

Bad144 can be used to inspect the information stored on a disk that is used by the disk drivers to implement bad sector forwarding.

Available options:

-a The argument list consists of new bad sectors to be added to an existing list. The new sectors are sorted into the list, which must have been in order. Replacement sectors are moved to accommodate the additions; the new replacement sectors are cleared.

-c Forces an attempt to copy the old sector to the replacement, and may be useful when replacing an unreliable sector.

-f For a RP06, RM03, RM05, Fujitsu Eagle, or SMD disk on a Massbus, the **-f** option may be used to mark the new bad sectors as "bad" by reformatting them as unusable sectors. This option is *required unless* the sectors have already been marked bad, or the system will not be notified that it should use the replacement sector. This option may be used while running multiuser; it is no longer necessary to perform format operations while running single-user.

-s The entire disk is scanned for bad blocks.

-v The entire process is described as it happens in gory detail if **-v** (verbose) is given.

The format of the information is specified by DEC standard 144, as follows. The bad sector information is located in the first 5 even numbered sectors of the last track of the disk pack. There are five identical copies of the information, described by the *dkbad* structure.

Replacement sectors are allocated starting with the first sector before the bad sector information and working backwards towards the beginning of the disk. A maximum of 126 bad sectors are supported. The position of the bad sector in the bad sector table determines the replacement sector to which it corresponds. The bad sectors must be listed in ascending order.

The bad sector information and replacement sectors are conventionally only accessible through the "c" file system partition of the disk. If that partition is used for a file system, the user is responsible for making sure that it does not overlap the bad sector information or any replacement sectors. Thus, one track plus 126 sectors must be reserved to allow use of all of the possible bad sector replacements.

The bad sector structure is as follows:

```
struct dkbad {
        long    bt_csn;         /* cartridge serial number */
        u_short bt_mbz;         /* unused; should be 0 */
        u_short bt_flag;        /* -1 => alignment cartridge */
        struct bt_bad {
                u_short bt_cyl;     /* bad sector cylinder number */
                u_short bt_trksec; /* track and sector number */
        } bt_bad[126];
};
```

Unused slots in the *bt_bad* array are filled with all bits set, a putatively illegal value.

Bad144 is invoked by giving a device name (e.g. hk0, hp1, etc.). With no optional arguments it reads the first sector of the last track of the corresponding disk and prints out the bad sector information. It issues a warning if the bad sectors are out of order. **Bad144** may also be invoked with a serial number for the pack and a list of bad sectors. It will write the supplied information into all copies of the bad-sector file, replacing any previous information. Note, however, that **bad144** does not arrange for the specified sectors to be marked bad in this case. This procedure should only be used to restore known bad sector information which was destroyed.

It is no longer necessary to reboot to allow the kernel to reread the bad-sector table from the drive.

SEE ALSO

badsect(8)

BUGS

It should be possible to format disks on-line under UNIX.

It should be possible to mark bad sectors on drives of all type.

On an 11/750, the standard bootstrap drivers used to boot the system do not understand bad sectors, handle ECC errors, or the special SSE (skip sector) errors of RM80-type disks. This means that none of these errors can occur when reading the file /kernel to boot. Sectors 0-15 of the disk drive must also not have any of these errors.

The drivers which write a system core image on disk after a crash do not handle errors; thus the crash dump area must be free of errors and bad sectors.

HISTORY

The **bad144** command appeared in 4.1BSD.

NAME

badsect – create files to contain bad sectors

SYNOPSIS

badsect *bbdir sector ...*

DESCRIPTION

Badsect makes a file to contain a bad sector. Normally, bad sectors are made inaccessible by the standard formatter, which provides a forwarding table for bad sectors to the driver; see bad144(8) for details. If a driver supports the bad blocking standard it is much preferable to use that method to isolate bad blocks, since the bad block forwarding makes the pack appear perfect, and such packs can then be copied with dd(1). The technique used by this program is also less general than bad block forwarding, as **badsect** can't make amends for bad blocks in the i-list of file systems or in swap areas.

On some disks, adding a sector which is suddenly bad to the bad sector table currently requires the running of the standard DEC formatter. Thus to deal with a newly bad block or on disks where the drivers do not support the bad-blocking standard **badsect** may be used to good effect.

Badsect is used on a quiet file system in the following way: First mount the file system, and change to its root directory. Make a directory BAD there. Run **badsect** giving as argument the *BAD* directory followed by all the bad sectors you wish to add. (The sector numbers must be relative to the beginning of the file system, but this is not hard as the system reports relative sector numbers in its console error messages.) Then change back to the root directory, unmount the file system and run fsck(8) on the file system. The bad sectors should show up in two files or in the bad sector files and the free list. Have fsck remove files containing the offending bad sectors, but *do not* have it remove the BAD/*nnnnn* files. This will leave the bad sectors in only the BAD files.

Badsect works by giving the specified sector numbers in a mknod(2) system call, creating an illegal file whose first block address is the block containing bad sector and whose name is the bad sector number. When it is discovered by fsck(8) it will ask "HOLD BAD BLOCK ?" A positive response will cause fsck(8) to convert the inode to a regular file containing the bad block.

SEE ALSO

bad144(8), fsck(8)

DIAGNOSTICS

Badsect refuses to attach a block that resides in a critical area or is out of range of the file system. A warning is issued if the block is already in use.

BUGS

If more than one sector which comprise a file system fragment are bad, you should specify only one of them to **badsect**, as the blocks in the bad sector files actually cover all the sectors in a file system fragment.

HISTORY

The **badsect** command appeared in 4.1BSD.

NAME

boot – system bootstrapping procedures

DESCRIPTION

Power fail and crash recovery. Normally, the system will reboot itself at power-up or after crashes. An automatic consistency check of the file systems will be performed, and unless this fails, the system will resume multi-user operations.

Cold starts. Most i386 PCs attempt to boot first from floppy disk drive 0 (sometimes known as drive A:) and, failing that, from hard disk drive 0 (sometimes known as drive C:, or as drive 0x80 to the BIOS). Some BIOSes allow you to change this default sequence, and may also include a CD-ROM drive as a boot device.

By default, a three-stage bootstrap is employed, and control is automatically passed from the boot blocks (bootstrap stages one and two) to a separate third-stage bootstrap program, /boot/loader. This third stage provides more sophisticated control over the booting process than it is possible to achieve in the boot blocks, which are constrained by occupying limited fixed space on a given disk or slice.

However, it is possible to dispense with the third stage altogether, either by specifying a kernel name in the boot block parameter file, /boot.config, or by hitting a key during a brief pause (while one of the characters -, \, |, or / is displayed) before /boot/loader is invoked. Booting will also be attempted at stage two, if the third stage cannot be loaded.

The remainder of this subsection deals only with the boot blocks. At present, documentation of the third stage is chiefly available through online help in the /boot/loader program itself.

After the boot blocks have been loaded, you should see a prompt similar to the following:

```
>> FreeBSD/i386 BOOT
Default: 0:wd(0,a)/kernel
boot:
```

The automatic boot will attempt to load /kernel from partition 'a' of either the floppy or the hard disk. This boot may be aborted by typing any character on the keyboard at the boot: prompt. At this time, the following input will be accepted:

?   Give a short listing of the files in the root directory of the default boot device, as a hint about available boot files. (A ? may also be specified as the last segment of a path, in which case the listing will be of the relevant subdirectory.)

bios_drive:interface(unit,part) filename [**-aCcDdghPrsv**]
>   Specify boot file and flags.
>   bios_drive
>>   The drive number as recognized by the BIOS. 0 for the first drive, 1 for the second drive, etc.
>
>   interface
>>   The type of controller to boot from. Note that the controller is required to have BIOS support since the BIOS services are used to load the boot file image.
>>
>>   The supported interfaces are:
>>   wd   ST506, IDE, ESDI, RLL disks on a WD100[2367] or lookalike controller
>>   fd   5 1/4" or 3 1/2" High density floppies
>>   da   SCSI disk on any supported SCSI controller
>
>   unit The unit number of the drive on the interface being used. 0 for the first drive, 1 for the second drive, etc.
>
>   part The partition letter inside the BSD portion of the disk. See disklabel(8). By convention, only partition 'a' contains a bootable image. If sliced disks are used ("fdisk partitions"), any slice can be booted from, with the default being the active slice or, otherwise, the first FreeBSD slice.
>
>   filename
>>   The pathname of the file to boot (relative to the root directory on the specified partition). Defaults to /kernel. Symbolic links are not supported (hard links are).

-acCdDghPrsv
>   Boot flags:
>   **-a**   during kernel initialization, ask for the device to mount as as the root file system.
>   **-C**   boot from CDROM.
>   **-c**   run UserConfig to modify hardware parameters for the loaded kernel. If the kernel was built with the USERCONFIG_BOOT option, remain in UserConfig regardless of any **quit** commands present in the script.
>   **-D**   toggle single and dual console configurations. In the single configuration the console will be either the internal display or the serial port, depending on the state of the **-h** option below. In the dual console configuration, both the internal display and the serial port will become the console at the same time, regardless of the state of the **-h** option. However, the dual console configuration takes effect only during the boot prompt. Once the kernel is loaded, the console specified by the

-h option becomes the only console.

-d   enter the DDB kernel debugger (see ddb(4)) as early as possible in kernel initialization.

-g   use the GDB remote debugging protocol.

-h   toggle internal and serial consoles. You can use this to switch console devices. For instance, if you boot from the internal console, you can use the **-h** option to force the kernel to use the serial port as its console device. Alternatively, if you boot from the serial port, you can use this option to force the kernel to use the internal display as the console instead. This option has no effect if the kernel was compiled with *options COMCONSOLE.*

-P   probe the keyboard. If no keyboard is found, the **-D** and **-h** options are automatically set.

-r   use the statically configured default for the device containing the root file system (see config(8)). Normally, the root file system is on the device that the kernel was loaded from.

-s   boot into single-user mode; if the console is marked as "insecure" (see ttys(5)), the root password must be entered.

-v   be verbose during device probing (and later).

You may put a BIOS drive number, a controller type, a unit number, a partition, a kernel file name, and any valid option in /boot.config to set defaults. Enter them in one line just as you type at the boot: prompt.

FILES

/boot.config	parameters for the boot blocks (optional)
/boot/loader	third-stage bootstrap
/kernel	default kernel
/kernel.old	typical non-default kernel (optional)

SEE ALSO

ddb(4), ttys(5), btxld(8), config(8), disklabel(8), halt(8), reboot(8), shutdown(8)

BUGS

The disklabel format used by this version of BSD UNIX is quite different from that of other architectures.

Some features are not yet documented.

NAME

boot0cfg – boot manager installation/configuration utility

SYNOPSIS

boot0cfg [**-Bv**] [**-b** *boot0*] [**-d** *drive*] [**-f** *file*] [**-o** *options*] [**-t** *ticks*]
disk

DESCRIPTION

The FreeBSD 'boot0' boot manager permits the operator to select from which disk and which slice an i386 machine (PC) is booted.

Note that what are referred to here as "slices" are typically called "partitions" in non-BSD documentation relating to the PC. Typically, only non-removable disks are sliced.

The **boot0cfg** utility optionally installs the 'boot0' boot manager on the specified *disk*; and allows various operational parameters to be configured.

On PCs, a boot manager typically occupies sector 0 of a disk, which is known as the Master Boot Record (MBR). The MBR contains both code (to which control is passed by the PC BIOS) and data (an embedded table of defined slices).

The options are:

-B   Install the 'boot0' boot manager. This option causes MBR code to be replaced, but without affecting the embedded slice table.

-v   Verbose: display information about the slices defined, etc.

-b *boot0*
       Specify which 'boot0' image to use. The default is /boot/boot0.

-d *drive*
       Specify the drive number used by the PC BIOS in referencing the drive which contains the specified *disk*. Typically this will be 0x80 for the first hard drive, 0x81 for the second hard drive, and so on; however any integer between 0 and 0xff is acceptable here.

-f *file*
       Specify that a backup copy of the preexisting MBR should be written to *file*. This file is created if it does not exist, and truncated if it does.

-o *options*
       A comma-separated string of any of the following options may be specified

(with "no" prepended as necessary):

packet　　Use the disk packet (BIOS Int 0x13 extensions) interface rather than the conventional (CHS) interface, when accessing disk-related BIOS services. The default is 'nopacket'.

setdrv　　Forces the drive containing the disk to be referenced using drive number definable by means of the -d option. The default is 'nosetdrv'.

update　　Allow the MBR to be updated by the boot manager. (The MBR may be updated to flag slices as 'active', and to save slice selection information.) This is the default; a 'noupdate' option causes the MBR to be treated as read-only.

-t *ticks*

Set the timeout value to *ticks*. (There are approximately 18.2 ticks per second.)

SEE ALSO

boot(8), fdisk(8).

DIAGNOSTICS

Exit status is 0 on success and >0 on error.

AUTHORS

Robert Nordier <rnordier@FreeBSD.org>.

BUGS

Use of the 'packet' option may cause 'boot0' to fail, depending on the nature of BIOS support.

Use of the 'setdrv' option with an incorrect -d operand may cause the MBR to be written to the wrong disk. Be careful!

NAME

camcontrol – CAM control program

SYNOPSIS

camcontrol \<command> [generic args] [command args]
camcontrol devlist [**-v**]
camcontrol periphlist [**-n** *dev_name*] [**-u** *unit_number*]
camcontrol tur [generic args]
camcontrol inquiry [generic args] [**-D**] [**-S**] [**-R**]
camcontrol start [generic args]
camcontrol stop [generic args]
camcontrol eject [generic args]
camcontrol rescan \<bus[:target:lun]>
camcontrol reset \<bus[:target:lun]>
camcontrol defects [generic args] \< **-f** *format*> [**-P**] [**-G**]
camcontrol modepage [generic args] \< **-m** *page*> [**-P** *pgctl*] [**-e**] [**-d**]
camcontrol cmd [generic args] \< **-c** *cmd* [args]> [**-i** *len fmt*]
　　　　[**-o** *len fmt* [args]]
camcontrol debug [**-I**] [**-T**] [**-S**] [**-c**] \<all | off | bus[:target[:lun]]>
camcontrol tags [generic args] [**-N** *tags*] [**-q**] [**-v**]
camcontrol negotiate [generic args] [**-c**] [**-D** *enable/disable*] [**-O** *offset*]
　　　　[**-q**] [**-R** *syncrate*] [**-T** *enable/disable*] [**-U**] [**-W**
　　　　bus_width] [**-v**]

DESCRIPTION

camcontrol is a utility designed to provide a way for users to access and control the FreeBSD CAM subsystem.

camcontrol can cause a loss of data and/or system crashes if used improperly. Even expert users are encouraged to exercise caution when using this command. Novice users should stay away from this utility.

camcontrol has a number of primary functions, most of which take some generic arguments:

-C *count*　　　　SCSI command retry count. In order for this to work, error recovery (**-E**) must be turned on.

-E　　　　Instruct the kernel to perform generic SCSI error recovery for the given command. This is needed in order for the retry count (**-C**) to be honored. Other than retrying commands, the generic error recovery in the code will generally attempt to spin up drives that are not spinning. It may take some other actions, depending upon the sense code returned from the command.

-n *dev_name*   Specify the device type to operate on. The default is *da*.

-t *timeout*   SCSI command timeout in seconds. This overrides the default time-out for any given command.

-u *unit_number*

Specify the device unit number. The default is 0.

-v   Be verbose, print out sense information for failed SCSI commands.

Primary command functions:

devlist   List all physical devices (logical units) attached to the CAM subsystem. This also includes a list of peripheral drivers attached to each device. With the **-v** argument, SCSI bus number, adapter name and unit numbers are printed as well.

periphlist   List all peripheral drivers attached to a given physical device (logical unit).

tur   Send the SCSI test unit ready (0x00) command to the given device. **camcontrol** will report whether the device is ready or not.

inquiry   Send a SCSI inquiry command (0x12) to a device. By default, **camcontrol** will print out the standard inquiry data, device serial number, and transfer rate information. The user can specify that only certain types of inquiry data be printed:

    -D   Get the standard inquiry data.

    -S   Print out the serial number. If this flag is the only one specified, **camcontrol** will not print out "Serial Number" before the value returned by the drive. This is to aid in script writing.

    -R   Print out transfer rate information.

start   Send the SCSI Start/Stop Unit (0x1B) command to the given device with the start bit set.

stop   Send the SCSI Start/Stop Unit (0x1B) command to the given device with the start bit cleared.

eject   Send the SCSI Start/Stop Unit (0x1B) command to the given device with the start bit cleared and the eject bit set.

rescan   Tell the kernel to scan the given bus (XPT_SCAN_BUS), or bus:target:lun (XPT_SCAN_LUN) for new devices or devices that have gone away. The user may only specify a bus to scan, or a lun. Scanning all luns on a target isn't supported.

reset   Tell the kernel to reset the given bus (XPT_RESET_BUS) by issuing a SCSI bus reset for that bus, or to reset the given bus:target:lun (XPT_RE-SET_DEV), typically by issuing a BUS DEVICE RESET message after connecting to that device. Note that this can have a destructive impact on the system.

defects   Send the SCSI READ DEFECT DATA (10) command (0x37) to the given device, and print out any combination of: the total number of defects, the primary defect list (PLIST), and the grown defect list (GLIST).

      -f *format*   The three format options are: *block*, to print out the list as logical blocks, *bfi*, to print out the list in bytes from index format, and *phys*, to print out the list in physical sector format. The format argument is required. Most drives support the physical sector format. Some drives support the logical block format. Many drives, if they don't support the requested format, return the data in an alternate format, along with sense information indicating that the requested data format isn't supported. **camcontrol** attempts to detect this, and print out whatever format the drive returns. If the drive uses a non-standard sense code to report that it doesn't support the requested format, **camcontrol** will probably see the error as a failure to complete the request.

      -G   Print out the grown defect list. This is a list of bad blocks that have been remapped since the disk left the factory.

      -P   Print out the primary defect list.

      If neither **-P** nor **-G** is specified, **camcontrol** will print out the number of defects given in the READ DEFECT DATA header returned from the drive.

modepage   Allows the user to display and optionally edit a SCSI mode page. The mode page formats are located in /usr/share/misc/scsi_modes. This can be overridden by specifying a different file in the SCSI_MODES environment variable. The modepage command takes several arguments:

-d   Disable block descriptors for mode sense.

-e   This flag allows the user to edit values in the mode page.

-m *mode_page*
                  This specifies the number of the mode page the user would like to view and/or edit. This argument is mandatory.

-P *pgctl*   This allows the user to specify the page control field. Possible values are:
                  0   Current values
                  1   Changeable values
                  2   Default values
                  3   Saved values

cmd   Allows the user to send an arbitrary SCSI CDB to any device. The cmd function requires the **-c** argument to specify the CDB. Other arguments are optional, depending on the command type. The command and data specification syntax is documented in cam(3). NOTE: If the CDB specified causes data to be transfered to or from the SCSI device in question, you MUST specify either **-i** or **-o**.

-c *cmd* [args]   This specifies the SCSI CDB. CDBs may be 6, 10, 12 or 16 bytes.

-i *len fmt*   This specifies the amount of data to read, and how it should be displayed. If the format is '-', *len* bytes of data will be read from the device and written to standard output.

-o *len fmt* [args] This specifies the amount of data to be written to a device, and the data that is to be written. If the format is '-', *len* bytes of data will be read from standard input and written to the device.

debug   Turn on CAM debugging printfs in the kernel. This requires options CAMDEBUG in your kernel config file. WARNING: enabling debugging printfs currently causes an EXTREME number of kernel printfs. You may have difficulty turning off the debugging printfs once they start, since the kernel will be busy printing messages and unable to service other requests quickly. The debug function takes a number of arguments:

-I   Enable CAM_DEBUG_INFO printfs.

-T   Enable CAM_DEBUG_TRACE printfs.

-S   Enable CAM_DEBUG_SUBTRACE printfs.

-c   Enable CAM_DEBUG_CDB printfs. This will
                          cause the kernel to print out the SCSI CDBs
                          sent to the specified device(s).

all   Enable debugging for all devices.

off   Turn off debugging for all devices

bus[:target[:lun]]   Turn on debugging for the given bus, target or
                          lun. If the lun or target and lun are not speci-
                          fied, they are wildcarded. (i.e., just specifying a
                          bus turns on debugging printfs for all devices
                          on that bus.)

tags   Show or set the number of "tagged openings" or simultaneous transac-
               tions we attempt to queue to a particular device. By default, the 'tags'
               command, with no command-specific arguments (i.e. only generic argu-
               ments) prints out the "soft" maximum number of transactions that can be
               queued to the device in question. For more detailed information, use the
               -v argument described below.

               -N *tags*
                          Set the number of tags for the given device. This must be be-
                          tween the minimum and maximum number set in the kernel
                          quirk table. The default for most devices that support tagged
                          queueing is a minimum of 2 and a maximum of 255. The min-
                          imum and maximum values for a given device may be deter-
                          mined by using the **-v** switch. The meaning of the **-v** switch
                          for this **camcontrol** subcommand is described below.

               -q   Be quiet, and don't report the number of tags. This is general-
                          ly used when setting the number of tags.

               -v   The verbose flag has special functionality for the *tags* argu-
                          ment. It causes **camcontrol** to print out the tagged queueing
                          related fields of the XPT_GDEV_TYPE CCB:

dev_openings   This is the amount of capacity for transactions queued to a given device.

dev_active   This is the number of transactions currently queued to a device.

devq_openings   This is the kernel queue space for transactions. This count usually mirrors dev_openings except during error recovery operations when the device queue is frozen (device is not allowed to receive commands), the number of dev_openings is reduced, or transaction replay is occurring.

devq_queued   This is the number of transactions waiting in the kernel queue for capacity on the device. This number is usually zero unless error recovery is in progress.

held   The held count is the number of CCBs held by peripheral drivers that have either just been completed or are about to be released to the transport layer for service by a device. Held CCBs reserve capacity on a given device.

mintags   This is the current "hard" minimum number of transactions that can be queued to a device at once. The *dev_openings* value above cannot go below this number. The default value for *mintags* is 2, although it may be set higher or lower for various devices.

maxtags   This is the "hard" maximum number of transactions that can be queued to a device at one time. The *dev_openings* value cannot go above this number. The default value for *maxtags* is 255, although it may be set higher or lower for various devices.

negotiate   Show or negotiate various communication parameters. Some controllers may not support setting or changing some of these values. For instance, the Adaptec 174x controllers do not support changing a device's sync rate or offset. **camcontrol** will not attempt to set the parameter if the controller indicates that it does not support setting the parameter. To find out what the controller supports, use the **-v** flag. The meaning of the **-v** flag for the 'negotiate' command is described below. Also, some controller drivers don't support setting negotiation parameters, even if the underlying controller supports negotiation changes. Some controllers, such as the Advansys wide controllers, support enabling and disabling synchronous negotiation for a device, but do not support setting the synchronous negotiation rate.

-a　　　　　　　　Attempt to make the negotiation settings take effect immediately by sending a Test Unit Ready command to the device.

-c　　　　　　　　Show or set current negotiation settings. This is the default.

-D *enable/disable*
　　　　　　　　　　Enable or disable disconnection.

-O *offset*　　　Set the command delay offset.

-q　　　　　　　　Be quiet, don't print anything. This is generally useful when you want to set a parameter, but don't want any status information.

-R *syncrate*　　Change the synchronization rate for a device. The sync rate is a floating point value specified in MHz. So, for instance, '20.000' is a legal value, as is '20'.

-T *enable/disable*
　　　　　　　　　　Enable or disable tagged queueing for a device.

-U　　　　　　　　Show or set user negotiation settings. The default is to show or set current negotiation settings.

-v　　　　　　　　The verbose switch has special meaning for the 'negotiate' subcommand. It causes **camcontrol** to print out the contents of a Path Inquiry (XPT_PATH_INQ) CCB sent to the controller driver.

-W *bus_width*　　Specify the bus width to negotiate with a device. The bus width is specified in bits. The only useful values to specify are 8, 16, and 32 bits. The controller must support the bus width in question in order for the setting to take effect.

In general, sync rate and offset settings will not take effect for a device until a command has been sent to the device. The **-a** switch above will automatically send a Test Unit Ready to the device so negotiation parameters will take effect.

ENVIRONMENT

The SCSI_MODES variable allows the user to specify an alternate mode page format file.

The EDITOR variable determines which text editor **camcontrol** starts when editing mode pages.

FILES

/usr/share/misc/scsi_modes is the SCSI mode format database.
/dev/xpt0   is the transport layer device.
/dev/pass*   are the CAM application passthrough devices.

EXAMPLES

```
camcontrol eject -n cd -u 1 -v
```

Eject the CD from cd1, and print SCSI sense information if the command fails.

```
camcontrol tur
```

Send the SCSI test unit ready command to da0. **camcontrol** will report whether the disk is ready, but will not display sense information if the command fails since the **-v** switch was not specified.

```
camcontrol tur -n da -u 1 -E -C 4 -t 50 -v
```

Send a test unit ready command to da1. Enable kernel error recovery. Specify a retry count of 4, and a timeout of 50 seconds. Enable sense printing (with the **-v** flag) if the command fails. Since error recovery is turned on, the disk will be spun up if it is not currently spinning. **camcontrol** will report whether the disk is ready.

```
camcontrol cmd -n cd -u 1 -v -c "3C 00 00 00 00 00 00 00 0e 00"
        -i 0xe "s1 i3 i1 i1 i1 i1 i1 i1 i1 i1 i1 i1"
```

Issue a READ BUFFER command (0x3C) to cd1. Display the buffer size of cd1, and display the first 10 bytes from the cache on cd1. Display SCSI sense information if the command fails.

```
camcontrol cmd -n cd -u u -v -c "3B 00 00 00 00 00 00 00 0e 00" \
    -o 14 "00 00 00 00 1 2 3 4 5 6 v v v v" 7 8 9 8
```

Issue a WRITE BUFFER (0x3B) command to cd1. Write out 10 bytes of data, not including the (reserved) 4 byte header. Print out sense information if the command fails. Be very careful with this command, improper use may cause data corruption.

```
camcontrol modepage -n da -u 3 -m 1 -e -P 3
```

Edit mode page 1 (the Read-Write Error Recover page) for da3, and save the settings on the drive. Mode page 1 contains a disk drive's auto read and write reallocation settings, among other things.

```
camcontrol rescan 0
```

Rescan SCSI bus 0 for devices that have been added, removed or changed.

```
camcontrol rescan 0:1:0
```

Rescan SCSI bus 0, target 1, lun 0 to see if it has been added, removed, or changed.

```
camcontrol tags -n da -u 5 -N 24
```

Set the number of concurrent transactions for da5 to 24.

```
camcontrol negotiate -n da -u 4 -T disable
```

Disable tagged queueing for da4.

```
camcontrol negotiate -n da -u 3 -R 20.000 -O 15 -a
```

Negotiate a sync rate of 20MHz and an offset of 15 with da3. Then send a Test Unit Ready command to make the settings take effect.

```
camcontrol cmd -n da -u 3 -v -t 7200 -c "4 0 0 0 0 0"
```

Send the FORMAT UNIT (0x04) command to da3. This will low-level format the disk. Print sense information if the command fails, and set the timeout to two hours (or 7200 seconds).

WARNING! WARNING! WARNING!

Low level formatting a disk will destroy ALL data on the disk. Use extreme caution when issuing this command. Many users low-level format disks that do not really need to be low-level formatted. There are relatively few scenarios that call for low-level formatting a disk. One reason for low-level formatting a disk is if you want to change the physical sector size of the disk. Another reason for low-level formatting a disk is to revive the disk if you are getting "medium format corrupted" errors from the disk in response to read and write requests.

Some disks take longer than others to format. Users should specify a timeout long enough to allow the format to complete. Some hard disks will complete a format operation in a very short period of time (on the order of 5 minutes or less). This is often because the drive doesn't really support the FORMAT UNIT command -- it just accepts the command, waits a few minutes and then returns it.

SEE ALSO
cam(3), cam_cdbparse(3), pass(4), cam(9), xpt(9)

HISTORY
The **camcontrol** command first appeared in FreeBSD 3.0.

The mode page editing code and arbitrary SCSI command code are based upon code in the old scsi(8) utility and scsi(3) library, written by Julian Elischer and Peter Dufault. The scsi(8) program first appeared in 386BSD 0.1.2.4, and first appeared in FreeBSD in FreeBSD 2.0.5.

AUTHORS
Kenneth Merry <ken@FreeBSD.ORG>

BUGS
Most of the man page cross references don't exist yet. This will be fixed soon.

The code that parses the generic command line arguments doesn't know that some of the subcommands take multiple arguments. So if, for instance, you tried something like this:

```
camcontrol -n da -u 1 -c "00 00 00 00 00 v" 0x00 -v
```

The sense information from the test unit ready command would not get printed out, since the first getopt(3) call in **camcontrol** bails out when it sees the second argument to **-c** (0x00), above. Fixing this behavior would take some gross code, or changes to the getopt(3) interface. The best way to circumvent this problem is to always make sure to specify generic **camcontrol** arguments before any command-specific arguments.

It might be nice to add a way to allow users to specify devices by bus/target/lun or by device string (e.g. "da1").

NAME
     disklabel – read and write disk pack label

SYNOPSIS
     disklabel [**-r**] *disk*
     disklabel -w [**-r**] *disk disktype* [*packid*]
     disklabel -e [**-r**] *disk*
     disklabel -R [**-r**] *disk protofile*
     disklabel [**-NW**] *disk*

     disklabel -B [**-b** *boot1* [**-s** *boot2*]] *disk* [*disktype*]
     disklabel -w -B [**-b** *boot1* [**-s** *boot2*]] *disk disktype* [*packid*]
     disklabel -R -B [**-b** *boot1* [**-s** *boot2*]] *disk protofile* [*disktype*]

DESCRIPTION
     Disklabel can be used to install, examine or modify the label on a disk drive or pack.
     When writing the label, it can be used to change the drive identification, the disk parti-
     tions on the drive, or to replace a damaged label. On some systems, **disklabel** can
     be used to install bootstrap code as well. There are several forms of the command that
     read (display), install or edit the label on a disk. Each form has an additional option,
     -r, which causes the label to be read from or written to the disk directly, rather than go-
     ing through the system's in-core copy of the label. This option may allow a label to be
     installed on a disk without kernel support for a label, such as when labels are first in-
     stalled on a system; it must be used when first installing a label on a disk. The specific
     effect of **-r** is described under each command. The read and install forms also support
     the **-B** option to install bootstrap code. These variants are described later.

     The first form of the command (read) is used to examine the label on the named disk
     drive (e.g. da0 or /dev/rda0c). It will display all of the parameters associated with the
     drive and its partition layout. Unless the **-r** flag is given, the kernel's in-core copy of
     the label is displayed; if the disk has no label, or the partition types on the disk are in-
     correct, the kernel may have constructed or modified the label. If the **-r** flag is given,
     the label from the raw disk will be displayed rather than the in-core label.

     The second form of the command, with the **-w** flag, is used to write a standard label on
     the designated drive. The required arguments to **disklabel** are the drive to be labeled
     (e.g. da0), and the drive type as described in the disktab(5) file. The drive parameters
     and partitions are taken from that file. If different disks of the same physical type are to
     have different partitions, it will be necessary to have separate disktab entries describing
     each, or to edit the label after installation as described below. The optional argument is
     a pack identification string, up to 16 characters long. The pack id must be quoted if it

contains blanks. If the **-r** flag is given, the disk sectors containing the label and bootstrap will be written directly. A side-effect of this is that any existing bootstrap code will be overwritten and the disk rendered unbootable. If **-r** is not specified, the existing label will be updated via the in-core copy and any bootstrap code will be unaffected. If the disk does not already have a label, the **-r** flag must be used. In either case, the kernel's in-core label is replaced.

For a virgin disk that is not known to disktab(5), *disktype* can be specified as "auto". In this case, the driver is requested to produce a virgin label for the disk. This might or might not be successful, depending on whether the driver for the disk is able to get the required data without reading anything from the disk at all. It will likely succeed for all SCSI disks, most IDE disks, and vnode devices. Writing a label to the disk is the only supported operation, and the *disk* itself must be provided as the canonical name, i.e. not as a full path name.

An existing disk label may be edited by using the **-e** flag. The label is read from the in-core kernel copy, or directly from the disk if the **-r** flag is also given. The label is formatted and then supplied to an editor for changes. If no editor is specified in an EDITOR environment variable, vi(1) is used. When the editor terminates, the formatted label is reread and used to rewrite the disk label. Existing bootstrap code is unchanged regardless of whether **-r** was specified.

With the **-R** flag, **disklabel** is capable of restoring a disk label that was formatted in a prior operation and saved in an ascii file. The prototype file used to create the label should be in the same format as that produced when reading or editing a label. Comments are delimited by # and newline. As with **-w**, any existing bootstrap code will be clobbered if **-r** is specified and will be unaffected otherwise.

The **-NW** flags for **disklabel** explicitly disallow and allow, respectively, writing of the pack label area on the selected disk.

The final three forms of **disklabel** are used to install bootstrap code on machines where the bootstrap is part of the label. The bootstrap code is comprised of one or two boot programs depending on the machine. The **-B** option is used to denote that bootstrap code is to be installed. The **-r** flag is implied by **-B** and never needs to be specified. The name of the boot program(s) to be installed can be selected in a variety of ways. First, the names can be specified explicitly via the **-b** and **-s** flags. On machines with only a single level of boot program, **-b** is the name of that program. For machines with a two-level bootstrap, **-b** indicates the primary boot program and **-s** the secondary boot program. If the names are not explicitly given, standard boot programs will be used. The boot programs are located in /boot. The names of the programs are taken from the "b0" and "b1" parameters of the disktab(5) entry for the disk if *disktype* was given and its disktab entry exists and includes those parameters. Otherwise, the default boot image names are used, these being: /boot/boot1 and

/boot/boot2 for the standard stage1 and stage2 boot images (details may vary on architectures like the Alpha, where only a single-stage boot is used).

The first of the three boot-installation forms is used to install bootstrap code without changing the existing label. It is essentially a read command with respect to the disk label itself and all options are related to the specification of the boot program as described previously. The final two forms are analogous to the basic write and restore versions except that they will install bootstrap code in addition to a new label.

FILES

```
/etc/disktab
/boot/
/boot/boot<n>
```

EXAMPLES

```
disklabel da0
```

Display the in-core label for da0 as obtained via /dev/rda0c.

```
disklabel -w -r /dev/rda0c da2212 foo
```

Create a label for da0 based on information for "da2212" found in /etc/disktab. Any existing bootstrap code will be clobbered.

```
disklabel -e -r da0
```

Read the on-disk label for da0, edit it and reinstall in-core as well as on-disk. Existing bootstrap code is unaffected.

```
disklabel -r -w da0 auto
```

Try to auto-detect the required information from da0, and write a new label to the disk. Use another disklabel -e command to edit the partitioning and file system information.

```
disklabel -R da0 mylabel
```

Restore the on-disk and in-core label for da0 from information in mylabel. Existing bootstrap code is unaffected.

```
disklabel -B da0
```

Install a new bootstrap on da0. The boot code comes from /boot/boot1 and possibly /boot/boot2. On-disk and in-core labels are unchanged.

```
disklabel -w -B /dev/rda0c -b newboot da2212
```

Install a new label and bootstrap. The label is derived from disktab information for "da2212" and installed both in-core and on-disk. The bootstrap code comes from the file /boot/newboot.

SEE ALSO

disklabel(5), disktab(5)

DIAGNOSTICS

The kernel device drivers will not allow the size of a disk partition to be decreased or the offset of a partition to be changed while it is open. Some device drivers create a label containing only a single large partition if a disk is unlabeled; thus, the label must be written to the "a" partition of the disk while it is open. This sometimes requires the desired label to be set in two steps, the first one creating at least one other partition, and the second setting the label on the new partition while shrinking the "a" partition.

On some machines the bootstrap code may not fit entirely in the area allocated for it by some filesystems. As a result, it may not be possible to have filesystems on some partitions of a "bootable" disk. When installing bootstrap code, **disklabel** checks for these cases. If the installed boot code would overlap a partition of type FS_UNUSED it is marked as type FS_BOOT. The newfs(8) utility will disallow creation of filesystems on FS_BOOT partitions. Conversely, if a partition has a type other than FS_UNUSED or FS_BOOT, **disklabel** will not install bootstrap code that overlaps it.

BUGS

When a disk name is given without a full pathname, the constructed device name uses the "a" partition on the Tahoe, the "c" partition on all others.

For the i386 architecture, the primary bootstrap sector contains an embedded *fdisk* table. **Disklabel** takes care to not clobber it when installing a bootstrap only (**-B**), or when editing an existing label (**-e**), but it unconditionally writes the primary bootstrap program onto the disk for **-w** or **-R**, thus replacing the *fdisk* table by the dummy one in the bootstrap program. This is only of concern if the disk is fully dedicated, so that the BSD disklabel starts at absolute block 0 on the disk.

NAME

dmesg – display the system message buffer

SYNOPSIS

dmesg [**-M** *core*] [**-N** *system*]

DESCRIPTION

Dmesg displays the contents of the system message buffer.

The options are as follows:

-M   Extract values associated with the name list from the specified core instead of the default /dev/kmem.

-N   Extract the name list from the specified system instead of the default /kernel.

SEE ALSO

syslogd(8)

FILES

```
/dev/mem
/dev/kmem
/dev/drum
/kernel
```

HISTORY

The **dmesg** command appeared in 4.0BSD.

NAME
     fdformat – format floppy disks

SYNOPSIS
     fdformat [**-q**] [**-v** | **-n**] [**-f** *capacity*] [**-c** *cyls*] [**-s** *secs*] [**-h** *heads*]
             [**-r** *rate*] [**-g** *gap3len*] [**-i** *intleave*] [**-S** *secshft*] [**-F**
             fillbyte] [**-t** *steps_per_track*] *device_name*

DESCRIPTION
     Fdformat formats a floppy disk at device *device_name*. *Device_name* should be a
     character device; it may be given either with a full path name of a raw device node for a
     floppy disk drive (e. g. /dev/rfd0), or default name in an abbreviated form (e. g.
     fd0). In the latter case, the name is constructed by prepending /dev/r and appending
     a *.capacity* to the *device_name*. Note that any geometry constraints of the device node
     (minor device number) are meaningless, since they're overridden by **fdformat**.

     The options are as follows:

     -q   Suppress any normal output from the command, and don't ask the
                user for a confirmation whether to format the floppy disk at
                device_name.

     -f *capacity*
                The normal way to specify the desired formatting parameters.
                Capacity is the number of kilobytes to format. Valid choices are
                360, 720, 800, 820, 1200, 1440, 1480 or 1720.

     -n   Don't verify floppy after formatting.

     -v   Don't format, verify only.

     -c *cyls*   Number of cylinders: 40 or 80.

     -s *secs*   Number of sectors per track: 9, 10, 15 or 18.

     -h *heads* Number of floppy heads: 1 or 2.

     -r *rate*   Data rate: 250, 300 or 500 kbps.

     -g *gap3len*
                Gap length.

     -i *intleave*

Interleave factor.

-S *secshft*
> Sector size: 0=128, 1=256, 2=512 bytes.

-F *fillbyte*
> Fill byte.

-t *steps_per_track*
> Number of steps per track. An alternate method to specify the geometry data to write to the floppy disk.

If the **-q** flag has not been specified, the user is asked for a confirmation of the intended formatting process. In order to continue, an answer of "y" must be given.

Note that **fdformat** does only perform low-level formatting. In case you wish to create a file system on the medium, see the commands newfs(8) for an *ufs* file system, or newfs_msdos(8) for an *MS-DOS (FAT)* file system.

DIAGNOSTICS

Unless **-q** has been specified, a single letter is printed to standard output to inform the user about the progress of work. First, an 'F is printed when the track(s) is being formatted, then a 'V while it's being verified, and if an error has been detected, it will finally change to 'E.

An exit status of 0 is returned upon successful operation. Exit status 1 is returned on any errors during floppy formatting, and an exit status of 2 reflects invalid arguments given to the program (along with an appropriate information written to diagnostic output).

SEE ALSO

fdc(4), newfs(8), newfs_msdos(8)

HISTORY

Fdformat has been developed for 386BSD 0.1 and upgraded to the new fdc(4) floppy disk driver. It later became part of the FreeBSD 1.1 system.

AUTHORS

The program has been contributed by Jörg Wunsch, Dresden, with changes by Serge Vakulenko and
Andrey A. Chernov, Moscow.

NAME

fdisk – DOS partition maintenance program

SYNOPSIS

fdisk [**-i**] [**-u**] [**-a**] [**-b**] [**-1234**] [*disk*]

fdisk [**-f** *configfile*] [**-i**] [**-v**] [**-t**] [*disk*]

PROLOGUE

In order for the BIOS to boot the kernel, certain conventions must be adhered to. Sector 0 of the disk must contain boot code, a partition table, and a magic number. BIOS partitions can be used to break the disk up into several pieces. The BIOS brings in sector 0 (does it really use the code?) and verifies the magic number. It then searches the 4 BIOS partitions described by sector 0 to determine which of them is *active*. This boot then brings in the secondary boot block from the *active* partition and runs it. Under DOS, you could have one or more partitions with one *active*. The DOS **fdisk** program can be used to divide space on the disk into partitions and set one *active*.

DESCRIPTION

The FreeBSD program **fdisk** serves a similar purpose to the DOS program. The first form is used to display partition information or to interactively edit the partition table. The second is used to write a partition table using a *configfile* and is designed to be used by other scripts/programs.

Options are:

-u　　Is used for updating (editing) sector 0 of the disk. Ignored if **-f** is given.

-i　　Initialize sector 0 of the disk. This implies **-u**, unless **-f** is given.

-a　　Change the active partition only. Ignored if **-f** is given.

-b　　Reinitialize the boot code contained in sector 0 of the disk. Ignored if **-f** is given. It should be noted, however, that the standard boot code written by **fdisk** is suitable for booting only from hard drive 0 (BIOS drive 0x80).

-1234

Operate on a single fdisk entry only. Ignored if **-f** is given.

-f *configfile*

Set partition values using the file *configfile*. The *configfile* always modifies existing partitions, unless **-i** is also given, in which case all existing partitions are deleted (marked as "unused") before the *configfile* is read. The *configfile* can be "-", in which case *stdin* is read. See CONFIGURATION FILE, below, for file syntax.

>　*WARNING*: when **-f** is used, you are not asked if you really want to write the partition table (as you are in the interactive mode).　Use with caution!

-t　　Test mode; do not write partition values.　Generally used with the **-f** option to see what would be written to the partition table.　Implies **-v**.

-v　　Be verbose.　When **-f** is used, **fdisk** prints out the partition table that is written to the disk.

The final disk name can be provided as a 'bare' disk name only, e.g. da0, or as a fully qualified device node under /dev. If omitted, the disks wd0, da0, and od0 are being searched in that order, until one is being found responding.

When called with no arguments, it prints the sector 0 partition table.　An example follows:

```
******* Working on device /dev/rwd0 *******
parameters extracted from in-core disklabel are:
cylinders=769 heads=15 sectors/track=33 (495 blks/cyl)

parameters to be used for BIOS calculations are:
cylinders=769 heads=15 sectors/track=33 (495 blks/cyl)

Warning: BIOS sector numbering starts with sector 1
Information from DOS bootblock is:
The data for partition 1 is:
sysid 165,(FreeBSD/NetBSD/386BSD)
    start 495, size 380160 (185 Meg), flag 0
        beg: cyl 1/ sector 1/ head 0;
        end: cyl 768/ sector 33/ head 14
The data for partition 2 is:
sysid 164,(unknown)
    start 378180, size 2475 (1 Meg), flag 0
        beg: cyl 764/ sector 1/ head 0;
        end: cyl 768/ sector 33/ head 14
The data for partition 3 is:
<UNUSED>
The data for partition 4 is:
sysid 99,(ISC UNIX, other System V/386, GNU HURD or Mach)
    start 380656, size 224234 (109 Meg), flag 80
        beg: cyl 769/ sector 2/ head 0;
        end: cyl 197/ sector 33/ head 14
```

The disk is divided into three partitions that happen to fill the disk. The second partition overlaps the end of the first. (Used for debugging purposes)

sysid	is used to label the partition. FreeBSD reserves the magic number 165 decimal (A5 in hex).
start and size	fields provide the start address and size of a partition in sectors.
flag 80	specifies that this is the active partition.
cyl, sector and head	fields are used to specify the beginning address and end address for the partition.
Note:	these numbers are calculated using BIOS's understanding of the disk geometry and saved in the bootblock.

The flags **-i** or **-u** are used to indicate that the partition data is to be updated, unless the **-f** option is used. If the **-f** option is not used, the **fdisk** program will enter a conversational mode. This mode is designed not to change any data unless you explicitly tell it to. **Fdisk** selects defaults for its questions to guarantee the above behavior.

It displays each partition and ask if you want to edit it. If you say yes, it will step through each field showing the old value and asking for a new one. When you are done with a partition, **fdisk** will display it and ask if it is correct. **Fdisk** will then proceed to the next entry.

Getting the *cyl, sector,* and *head* fields correct is tricky. So by default, they will be calculated for you; you can specify them if you choose.

After all the partitions are processed, you are given the option to change the *active* partition. Finally, when the all the data for the first sector has been accumulated, you are asked if you really want to rewrite sector 0. Only if you answer yes, will the data be written to disk.

The difference between the **-u** flag and **-i** flag is that the **-u** flag just edits the fields as they appear on the disk. While the **-i** flag is used to "initialize" sector 0; it will setup the last BIOS partition to use the whole disk for FreeBSD; and make it active.

NOTES

The automatic calculation of starting cylinder etc. uses a set of figures that represent what the BIOS thinks is the geometry of the drive. These figures are by default taken from the incore disklabel, but the program initially gives you an opportunity to change them. This allows the user to create a bootblock that can work with drives that use geometry translation under the BIOS.

If you hand craft your disk layout, please make sure that the FreeBSD partition starts on a cylinder boundary. A number of decisions made later may assume this. (This might not be necessary later.)

Editing an existing partition will most likely cause you to lose all the data in that partition.

You should run this program interactively once or twice to see how it works. This is completely safe as long as you answer the last question in the negative. There are subtleties that the program detects that are not fully explained in this manual page.

CONFIGURATION FILE

When the **-f** option is given, a disk's partition table can be written using values from a *configfile*. The syntax of this file is very simple. Each line is either a comment or a specification, and whitespace (except for newlines) are ignored:

*comment ...*
> Lines beginning with a "#" are comments and are ignored.

g *spec1 spec2 spec3*
> Set the BIOS geometry used in partition calculations. There must be three values specified, with a letter preceding each number:
>
> **c***num*   Set the number of cylinders to *num*.
>
> **h***num*   Set the number of heads to *num*.
>
> **s***num*   Set the number of sectors/track to *num*.
>
> These specs can occur in any order, as the leading letter determines which value is which; however, all three must be specified.
>
> This line must occur before any lines that specify partition information.
>
> It is an error if the following is not true:
>
>> 1 <= number of cylinders
>> 1 <= number of heads <= 256
>> 1 <= number of sectors/track < 64
>
> The number of cylinders should be less than or equal to 1024, but this is not enforced, although a warning will be output. Note that bootable FreeBSD partitions (the "/" filesystem) must lie completely within the first 1024 cylinders; if this is not true, booting may fail. Non-bootable partitions do not have this restriction.
>
> Example (all of these are equivalent), for a disk with 1019 cylinders, 39 heads, and 63 sectors:

```
g     c1019  h39    s63
g     h39    c1019  s63
g     s63    h39    c1019
```

p *partition type start length*

Set the partition given by *partition* (1-4) to type *type*, starting at sector *start* for *length* sectors.

Only those partitions explicitly mentioned by these lines are modified; any partition not referenced by a "p" line will not be modified. However, if an invalid partition table is present, or the **-i** option is specified, all existing partition entries will be cleared (marked as unused), and these "p" lines will have to be used to explicitly set partition information. If multiple partitions need to be set, multiple "p" lines must be specified; one for each partition.

These partition lines must occur after any geometry specification lines, if one is present.

The *type* is 165 for FreeBSD partitions. Specifying a partition type of zero is the same as clearing the partition and marking it as unused; however, dummy values (such as "0") must still be specified for *start* and *length*.

Note: the start offset will be rounded upwards to a head boundary if necessary, and the end offset will be rounded downwards to a cylinder boundary if necessary.

Example: to clear partition 4 and mark it as unused:

```
p    4    0    0    0
```

Example: to set partition 1 to a FreeBSD partition, starting at sector 1 for 2503871 sectors (note: these numbers will be rounded upwards and downwards to correspond to head and cylinder boundaries):

```
p    1    165    1    2503871
```

a *partition*

Make *partition* the active partition. Can occur anywhere in the config file, but only one must be present.

Example: to make partition 1 the active partition:

```
a    1
```

SEE ALSO
disklabel(8)

BUGS

The entire program should be made more user-friendly.

Throughout this man page, the term 'partition' is used where it should actually be 'slice', in order to conform with the terms used elsewhere.

You cannot use this command to completely dedicate a disk to FreeBSD. The disklabel(8) command must be used for this.

NAME
　　fsck – filesystem consistency check and interactive repair

SYNOPSIS
　　fsck –p [**-f**] [**-m** *mode*] [*filesystem*] ...
　　fsck [**-ny**] [**-b** *block#*] [**-c** *level*] [**-l** *maxparallel*] [**-m** *mode*]
　　　　[*filesystem*] ...

DESCRIPTION
　　The first form of **fsck** preens a standard set of filesystems or the specified filesystems.
　　It is normally used in the script /etc/rc during automatic reboot. Here **fsck** reads the
　　table /etc/fstab to determine which filesystems to check. Only partitions in fstab
　　that are mounted "rw," "rq" or "ro" and that have non-zero pass number are checked.
　　Filesystems with pass number 1 (normally just the root filesystem) are checked one at a
　　time. When pass 1 completes, all remaining filesystems are checked, running one pro-
　　cess per disk drive. The disk drive containing each filesystem is inferred from the
　　longest prefix of the device name that ends in a digit; the remaining characters are as-
　　sumed to be the partition designator.

　　In "preen" mode the clean flag of each filesystem's superblock is examined and only
　　those filesystems that are not marked clean are checked. Filesystems are marked clean
　　when they are unmounted, when they have been mounted read-only, or when **fsck**
　　runs on them successfully. If the **-f** option is specified, the filesystems will be checked
　　regardless of the state of their clean flag.

　　The kernel takes care that only a restricted class of innocuous filesystem inconsistencies
　　can happen unless hardware or software failures intervene. These are limited to the fol-
　　lowing:

　　　　Unreferenced inodes
　　　　Link counts in inodes too large
　　　　Missing blocks in the free map
　　　　Blocks in the free map also in files
　　　　Counts in the super-block wrong

　　These are the only inconsistencies that **fsck** with the **-p** option will correct; if it en-
　　counters other inconsistencies, it exits with an abnormal return status and an automatic
　　reboot will then fail. For each corrected inconsistency one or more lines will be printed
　　identifying the filesystem on which the correction will take place, and the nature of the
　　correction. After successfully correcting a filesystem, **fsck** will print the number of files
　　on that filesystem, the number of used and free blocks, and the percentage of fragmenta-
　　tion.

If sent a QUIT signal, **fsck** will finish the filesystem checks, then exit with an abnormal return status that causes an automatic reboot to fail. This is useful when you want to finish the filesystem checks during an automatic reboot, but do not want the machine to come up multiuser after the checks complete.

Without the **-p** option, **fsck** audits and interactively repairs inconsistent conditions for filesystems. If the filesystem is inconsistent the operator is prompted for concurrence before each correction is attempted. It should be noted that some of the corrective actions which are not correctable under the **-p** option will result in some loss of data. The amount and severity of data lost may be determined from the diagnostic output. The default action for each consistency correction is to wait for the operator to respond yes or no. If the operator does not have write permission on the filesystem **fsck** will default to a **-n** action.

Fsck has more consistency checks than its predecessors *check*, *dcheck*, *fcheck*, and *icheck* combined.

The following flags are interpreted by **fsck**.

-b   Use the block specified immediately after the flag as the super block for the filesystem. Block 32 is usually an alternate super block.

-c   Convert the filesystem to the specified level. Note that the level of a filesystem can only be raised. There are currently four levels defined:

0   The filesystem is in the old (static table) format.

1   The filesystem is in the new (dynamic table) format.

2   The filesystem supports 32-bit uid's and gid's, short symbolic links are stored in the inode, and directories have an added field showing the file type.

3   If maxcontig is greater than one, build the free segment maps to aid in finding contiguous sets of blocks. If maxcontig is equal to one, delete any existing segment maps.

In interactive mode, **fsck** will list the conversion to be made and ask whether the conversion should be done. If a negative answer is given, no further operations are done on the filesystem. In preen mode, the conversion is listed and done if possible without user interaction. Conversion in preen mode is best used when all the filesystems are being converted at once. The format of a filesystem can be determined from the first line of output from dumpfs(8).

-f   Force **fsck** to check 'clean' filesystems when preening.

-l   Limit the number of parallel checks to the number specified in the following argument. By default, the limit is the number of disks, running one process per disk. If a smaller limit is given, the disks are checked round-robin, one filesystem at a time.

-m   Use the mode specified in octal immediately after the flag as the permission bits to use when creating the lost+found directory rather than the default 1777. In particular, systems that do not wish to have lost files accessible by all users on the system should use a more restrictive set of permissions such as 700.

-n   Assume a no response to all questions asked by **fsck** except for CONTINUE?, which is assumed to be affirmative; do not open the filesystem for writing.

-p   Preen filesystems (see above).

-y   Assume a yes response to all questions asked by **fsck**; this should be used with great caution as this is a free license to continue after essentially unlimited trouble has been encountered.

If no filesystems are given to **fsck** then a default list of filesystems is read from the file /etc/fstab.

Inconsistencies checked are as follows:
1. Blocks claimed by more than one inode or the free map.
2. Blocks claimed by an inode outside the range of the filesystem.
3. Incorrect link counts.
4. Size checks:
    Directory size not a multiple of DIRBLKSIZ.
    Partially truncated file.
5. Bad inode format.
6. Blocks not accounted for anywhere.
7. Directory checks:
    File pointing to unallocated inode.
    Inode number out of range.
    Directories with unallocated blocks (holes).
    Dot or dot-dot not the first two entries of a directory or having the wrong inode number.
8. Super Block checks:
    More blocks for inodes than there are in the filesystem.

Bad free block map format.
Total free block and/or free inode count incorrect.

Orphaned files and directories (allocated but unreferenced) are, with the operator's concurrence, reconnected by placing them in the `lost+found` directory. The name assigned is the inode number. If the `lost+found` directory does not exist, it is created. If there is insufficient space its size is increased.

Because of inconsistencies between the block device and the buffer cache, the raw device should always be used.

FILES

`/etc/fstab` contains default list of filesystems to check.

DIAGNOSTICS

The diagnostics produced by **fsck** are fully enumerated and explained in Appendix A of *Fsck − The UNIX File System Check Program.*

SEE ALSO

`fs`(5), `fstab`(5), `fsdb`(8), `newfs`(8), `reboot`(8)

NAME

fsdb – FFS debugging/editing tool

SYNOPSIS

fsdb [**-d**] [**-f**] [**-r**] *fsname*

DESCRIPTION

Fsdb opens *fsname* (usually a raw disk partition) and runs a command loop allowing manipulation of the file system's inode data. You are prompted to enter a command with **fsdb (inum X)>** where *X* is the currently selected i-number. The initial selected inode is the root of the filesystem (i-number 2). The command processor uses the editline(3) library, so you can use command line editing to reduce typing if desired. When you exit the command loop, the file system superblock is marked dirty and any buffered blocks are written to the file system.

The following options are available:

-d	Enable additional debugging output (which comes primarily from fsck(8)-derived code).

-f	Left for historical reasons and has no meaning.

-r	Open the filesystem read/only, and disables all commands that would write to it.

COMMANDS

Besides the built-in editline(3) commands, **fsdb** supports these commands:

help	Print out the list of accepted commands.

inode *i-number*
Select inode *i-number* as the new current inode.

back	Revert to the previously current inode.

clri	Clear the current inode.

lookup *name*
cd *name*
Find *name* in the current directory and make its inode the current inode. *Name* may be a multi-component name or may begin with slash to indicate that the root inode should be used to start the lookup. If some component along the pathname is not found, the last valid directory encountered is left as the active inode.
This command is valid only if the starting inode is a directory.

active

print　　Print out the active inode.

uplink　Increment the active inode's link count.

downlink
> Decrement the active inode's link count.

linkcount *number*
> Set the active inode's link count to *number*.

ls　　　List the current inode's directory entries. This command is valid only if the current inode is a directory.

rm *name*
del *name*
> Remove the entry *name* from the current directory inode. This command is valid only if the current inode is a directory.

ln *ino name*
> Create a link to inode *ino* under the name *name* in the current directory inode. This command is valid only if the current inode is a directory.

chinum *dirslot inum*
> Change the i-number in directory entry *dirslot* to *inum*.

chname *dirslot name*
> Change the name in directory entry *dirslot* to *name*. This command cannot expand a directory entry. You can only rename an entry if the name will fit into the existing directory slot.

chtype *type*
> Change the type of the current inode to *type*. *Type* may be one of: *file*, *dir*, *socket*, or *fifo*.

chmod *mode*
> Change the mode bits of the current inode to *mode*. You cannot change the file type with this subcommand; use **chtype** to do that.

chflags *flags*
> Change the file flags of the current inode to *flags*.

chown *uid*
> Change the owner of the current inode to *uid*.

chgrp *gid*
> Change the group of the current inode to *gid*.

chgen *gen*
> Change the generation number of the current inode to *gen*.

mtime *time*
ctime *time*
atime *time*
> Change the modification, change, or access time (respectively) on the current inode to *time*. *Time* should be in the format *YYYYMMDDHHMMSS[.nsec]* where *nsec* is an optional nanosecond specification. If no nanoseconds are specified, the *mtimensec, ctimensec,* or *atimensec* field will be set to zero.

quit, q, exit, *<EOF>*
> Exit the program.

SEE ALSO
editline(3), fs(5), clri(8), fsck(8)

BUGS
Manipulation of "short" symlinks doesn't work (in particular, don't try changing a symlink's type).

You must specify modes as numbers rather than symbolic names.

There are a bunch of other things that you might want to do which **fsdb** doesn't implement.

HISTORY
Fsdb uses the source code for fsck(8) to implement most of the file system manipulation code. The remainder of **fsdb** first appeared in NetBSD, written by John T. Kohl. Peter Wemm ported it to FreeBSD.

WARNING
Use this tool with extreme caution--you can damage an FFS file system beyond what fsck(8) can repair.

NAME

fstab – static information about the filesystems

SYNOPSIS

#include <fstab.h>

DESCRIPTION

The file **fstab** contains descriptive information about the various file systems. **fstab** is only read by programs, and not written; it is the duty of the system administrator to properly create and maintain this file. Each filesystem is described on a separate line; fields on each line are separated by tabs or spaces. The order of records in **fstab** is important because fsck(8), mount(8), and umount(8) sequentially iterate through **fstab** doing their thing.

The first field, (*fs_spec*), describes the block special device or remote filesystem to be mounted. For filesystems of type *ufs*, the special file name is the block special file name, and not the character special file name. If a program needs the character special file name, the program must create it by appending a "r" after the last "/" in the special file name.

The second field, (*fs_file*), describes the mount point for the filesystem. For swap partitions, this field should be specified as "none".

The third field, (*fs_vfstype*), describes the type of the filesystem. The system can support various filesystem types. Only the root, /usr, and /tmp filesystems need be statically compiled into the kernel; everything else will be automatically loaded at mount time. (Exception: the UFS family - FFS, MFS, and LFS cannot currently be demand-loaded.) Some people still prefer to statically compile other filesystems as well.

ufs	a local UNIX filesystem
mfs	a local memory-based UNIX filesystem
nfs	a Sun Microsystems compatible "Network File System"
swap	a disk partition to be used for swapping
msdos	a DOS compatible filesystem
cd9660	a CD-ROM filesystem (as per ISO 9660)

procfs   a file system for accessing process data

kernfs   a file system for accessing kernel parameter

The fourth field, (*fs_mntops*), describes the mount options associated with the filesystem. It is formatted as a comma separated list of options. It contains at least the type of mount (see *fs_type* below) plus any additional options appropriate to the filesystem type.

If the options "userquota" and/or "groupquota" are specified, the filesystem is automatically processed by the quotacheck(8) command, and user and/or group disk quotas are enabled with quotaon(8). By default, filesystem quotas are maintained in files named quota.user and quota.group which are located at the root of the associated filesystem. These defaults may be overridden by putting an equal sign and an alternative absolute pathname following the quota option. Thus, if the user quota file for /tmp is stored in /var/quotas/tmp.user, this location can be specified as:

    userquota=/var/quotas/tmp.user

If the option "noauto" is specified, the filesystem will not be automatically mounted at system startup.

The type of the mount is extracted from the *fs_mntops* field and stored separately in the *fs_type* field (it is not deleted from the *fs_mntops* field). If *fs_type* is "rw" or "ro" then the filesystem whose name is given in the *fs_file* field is normally mounted read-write or read-only on the specified special file. If *fs_type* is "sw" then the special file is made available as a piece of swap space by the swapon(8) command at the end of the system reboot procedure. The fields other than *fs_spec* and *fs_type* are unused. If *fs_type* is specified as "xx" the entry is ignored. This is useful to show disk partitions which are currently unused.

The fifth field, (*fs_freq*), is used for these filesystems by the dump(8) command to determine which filesystems need to be dumped. If the fifth field is not present, a value of zero is returned and **dump** will assume that the filesystem does not need to be dumped.

The sixth field, (*fs_passno*), is used by the fsck(8) program to determine the order in which filesystem checks are done at reboot time. The root filesystem should be specified with a *fs_passno* of 1, and other filesystems should have a *fs_passno* of 2. Filesystems within a drive will be checked sequentially, but filesystems on different drives will be checked at the same time to utilize parallelism available in the hardware. If the sixth field is not present or is zero, a value of zero is returned and fsck(8) will assume that the filesystem does not need to be checked.

```
#define FSTAB_RW        "rw"    /* read/write device */
#define FSTAB_RQ        "rq"    /* read/write with quotas */
#define FSTAB_RO        "ro"    /* read-only device */
#define FSTAB_SW        "sw"    /* swap device */
#define FSTAB_XX        "xx"    /* ignore totally */

struct fstab {
        char    *fs_spec;       /* block special device name */
        char    *fs_file;       /* filesystem path prefix */
        char    *fs_vfstype;    /* File system type, ufs, nfs */
        char    *fs_mntops;     /* Mount options ala -o */
        char    *fs_type;       /* FSTAB_* from fs_mntops */
        int     fs_freq;        /* dump frequency, in days */
        int     fs_passno;      /* pass number on parallel fsck */
};
```

The proper way to read records from fstab is to use the routines getfsent(3), getfsspec(3), getfstype(3), and getfsfile(3).

FILES

　　/etc/fstab The file **fstab** resides in /etc.

SEE ALSO

　　getfsent(3), getvfsbyname(3), dump(8), fsck(8), mount(8), quotacheck(8), quotaon(8), swapon(8), umount(8).

HISTORY

　　The **fstab** file format appeared in 4.0BSD.

NAME

getty – set terminal mode

SYNOPSIS

getty [*type* [*tty*]]

DESCRIPTION

The **getty** program is called by init(8) to open and initialize the tty line, read a login name, and invoke login(1).

The argument *tty* is the special device file in /dev to open for the terminal (for example, "ttyh0"). If there is no argument or the argument is ' - ', the tty line is assumed to be open as file descriptor 0.

The *type* argument can be used to make **getty** treat the terminal line specially. This argument is used as an index into the gettytab(5) database, to determine the characteristics of the line. If there is no argument, or there is no such table, the *default* table is used. If there is no /etc/gettytab a set of system defaults is used. If indicated by the table located, **getty** will clear the terminal screen, print a banner heading, and prompt for a login name. Usually either the banner or the login prompt will include the system hostname.

Most of the default actions of **getty** can be circumvented, or modified, by a suitable gettytab table.

The **getty** program can be set to timeout after some interval, which will cause dial up lines to hang up if the login name is not entered reasonably quickly.

DIAGNOSTICS

ttyxx: No such device or address.
ttyxx: No such file or address.

A terminal which is turned on in the ttys file cannot be opened, likely because the requisite lines are either not configured into the system, the associated device was not attached during boot-time system configuration, or the special file in /dev does not exist.

FILES

/etc/gettytab
/etc/ttys

SEE ALSO
    login(1), ioctl(2), tty(4), gettytab(5), ttys(5), init(8)

HISTORY
    A **getty** program appeared in Version 6 AT&T UNIX.

NAME

gettytab – terminal configuration data base

SYNOPSIS

gettytab

DESCRIPTION

The **gettytab** file is a simplified version of the termcap(5) data base used to describe terminal lines. The initial terminal login process getty(8) accesses the **gettytab** file each time it starts, allowing simpler reconfiguration of terminal characteristics. Each entry in the data base is used to describe one class of terminals.

There is a default terminal class, *default*, that is used to set global defaults for all other classes. (That is, the *default* entry is read, then the entry for the class required is used to override particular settings.)

CAPABILITIES

Refer to termcap(5) for a description of the file layout. The *default* column below lists defaults obtained if there is no entry in the table obtained, nor one in the special *default* table.

Name	Type	Default	Description
ac	str	unused	expect-send chat script for modem answer
al	str	unused	user to auto-login instead of prompting
ap	bool	false	terminal uses any parity
bk	str	0377	alternate end of line character (input break)
c0	num	unused	tty control flags to write messages
c1	num	unused	tty control flags to read login name
c2	num	unused	tty control flags to leave terminal as
ce	bool	false	use crt erase algorithm
ck	bool	false	use crt kill algorithm
cl	str	NULL	screen clear sequence
co	bool	false	console - add '\n' after login prompt
ct	num	10	chat timeout for ac/ic scripts
dc	num	0	chat debug bitmask
de	num	0	delay secs and flush input before writing first prompt
ds	str	'^Y'	delayed suspend character

dx	bool	false	set DECCTLQ
ec	bool	false	leave echo OFF
ep	bool	false	terminal uses even parity
er	str	'^?'	erase character
et	str	'^D'	end of text (EOF) character
ev	str	NULL	initial environment
f0	num	unused	tty mode flags to write messages
f1	num	unused	tty mode flags to read login name
f2	num	unused	tty mode flags to leave terminal as
fl	str	'^O'	output flush character
hc	bool	false	do NOT hangup line on last close
he	str	NULL	hostname editing string
hn	str	hostname	hostname
ht	bool	false	terminal has real tabs
hw	bool	false	do cts/rts hardware flow control
i0	num	unused	tty input flags to write messages
i1	num	unused	tty input flags to read login name
i2	num	unused	tty input flags to leave terminal as
ic	str	unused	expect-send chat script for modem initialization
if	str	unused	display named file before prompt, like /etc/issue
ig	bool	false	ignore garbage characters in login name
im	str	NULL	initial (banner) message
in	str	'^C'	interrupt character
is	num	unused	input speed
kl	str	'^U'	kill character
l0	num	unused	tty local flags to write messages
l1	num	unused	tty local flags to read login name
l2	num	unused	tty local flags to leave terminal as
lm	str	login:	login prompt
ln	str	'^V'	"literal next" character
lo	str	/usr/bin/login	program to exec when name obtained
mb	bool	false	do flow control based on carrier
nl	bool	false	terminal has (or might have) a newline character
np	bool	false	terminal uses no parity (i.e. 8-bit characters)
nx	str	default	next table (for auto speed selection)
o0	num	unused	tty output flags to write messages
o1	num	unused	tty output flags to read login name
o2	num	unused	tty output flags to leave terminal as

op	bool	false	terminal uses odd parity
os	num	unused	output speed
pc	str	'\0'	pad character
pe	bool	false	use printer (hard copy) erase algorithm
pf	num	0	delay between first prompt and following flush (seconds)
pp	str	unused	PPP authentication program
ps	bool	false	line connected to a MICOM port selector
qu	str	'^\'	quit character
rp	str	'^R'	line retype character
rt	num	unused	ring timeout when using ac
rw	bool	false	do NOT use raw for input, use cbreak
sp	num	unused	line speed (input and output)
su	str	'^Z'	suspend character
tc	str	none	table continuation
to	num	0	timeout (seconds)
tt	str	NULL	terminal type (for environment)
ub	bool	false	do unbuffered output (of prompts etc)
we	str	'^W'	word erase character
xc	bool	false	do NOT echo control chars as '^X'
xf	str	'^S'	XOFF (stop output) character
xn	str	'^Q'	XON (start output) character
Lo	str	C	the locale name used for %d in the banner message

The following capabilities are no longer supported by getty(8):

bd	num	0	backspace delay
cb	bool	false	use crt backspace mode
cd	num	0	carriage-return delay
fd	num	0	form-feed (vertical motion) delay
lc	bool	false	terminal has lower case
nd	num	0	newline (line-feed) delay
uc	bool	false	terminal is known upper case only

If no line speed is specified, speed will not be altered from that which prevails when getty is entered. Specifying an input or output speed will override line speed for stated direction only.

Terminal modes to be used for the output of the message, for input of the login name, and to leave the terminal set as upon completion, are derived from the boolean flags specified. If the derivation should prove inadequate, any (or all) of these three may be overridden with one of the *c0, c1, c2, i0, i1, i2, l0, l1, l2, o0, o1,* or *o2* numeric specifications, which can be used to specify (usually in octal, with a leading '0') the exact values of the flags. These flags correspond to the termios *c_cflag*, *c_iflag*, *c_lflag*, and *c_oflag* fields, respectively. Each these sets must be completely specified to be effective. The *f0*, *f1*, and *f2* are excepted for backwards compatibility with a previous incarnation of the TTY sub-system. In these flags the bottom 16 bits of the (32 bits) value contain the sgttyb *sg_flags* field, while the top 16 bits represent the local mode word.

Should getty(8) receive a null character (presumed to indicate a line break) it will restart using the table indicated by the *nx* entry. If there is none, it will re-use its original table.

Delays are specified in milliseconds, the nearest possible delay available in the tty driver will be used. Should greater certainty be desired, delays with values 0, 1, 2, and 3 are interpreted as choosing that particular delay algorithm from the driver.

The *cl* screen clear string may be preceded by a (decimal) number of milliseconds of delay required (a la termcap). This delay is simulated by repeated use of the pad character *pc*.

The initial message, login message, and initial file; *im*, *lm* and *if* may include any of the following character sequences, which expand to information about the environment in which getty(8) is running.

%d	The current date and time in the locale's representation as of the *Lo* string (the %+ format of strftime(3)).
%h	The hostname of the machine, which is normally obtained from the system using gethostname(3), but may also be overridden by the *hn* table entry. In either case it may be edited with the *he* string. A '@' in the *he* string causes one character from the real hostname to be copied to the final hostname. A '#' in the *he* string causes the next character of the real hostname to be skipped. Each character that is neither '@' nor '#' is copied into the final hostname. Surplus '@' and '#' characters are ignored.
%t	The tty name.
%m, %r, %s, %v	The type of machine, release of the operating system, name of the operating system, and version of the kernel, respectively, as returned by uname(3).
%%	A "%" character.

When getty execs the login process, given in the *lo* string (usually "/usr/bin/login"), it will have set the environment to include the terminal type, as indicated by the *tt* string (if it exists). The *ev* string, can be used to enter additional data into the environment. It is a list of comma separated strings, each of which will presumably be of the form *name=value*.

If a non-zero timeout is specified, with *to*, then getty will exit within the indicated number of seconds, either having received a login name and passed control to login(1), or having received an alarm signal, and exited. This may be useful to hangup dial in lines.

Output from getty(8) is even parity unless *op* or *np* is specified. The *op* string may be specified with *ap* to allow any parity on input, but generate odd parity output. Note: this only applies while getty is being run, terminal driver limitations prevent a more complete implementation. Getty(8) does not check parity of input characters in RAW mode.

If *pp* string is specified and a PPP link bring up sequence is recognized, getty will invoke the program referenced by the pp option. This can be used to handle incoming PPP calls.

Getty provides some basic intelligent modem handling by providing a chat script feature available via two capabilities:

ic	Chat script to initialize modem.
ac	Chat script to answer a call.

A chat script is a set of expect/send string pairs. When a chat string starts, **getty** will wait for the first string, and if it finds it, will send the second, and so on. Strings specified are separated by one or more tabs or spaces. Strings may contain standard ascii characters and special 'escapes', which consist of a backslash character followed by one or more characters which are interpreted as follows:

\a	bell character.
\b	backspace.
\n	newline.
\e	escape.
\f	formfeed.
\p	half-second pause.
\r	carriage return.
\S, \s	space character.
\t	tab.
\xNN	hexadecimal byte value.
\0NNN	octal byte value.

Note that the '\p' sequence is only valid for send strings and causes a half-second pause between sending the previous and next characters. Hexidecimal values are, at most, 2 hex digits long, and octal values are a maximum of 3 octal digits.

The *ic* chat sequence is used to initialize a modem or similar device. A typical example of an init chat script for a modem with a hayes compatible command set might look like this:

```
:ic="" ATE0Q0V1\r OK\r ATS0=0\r OK\r:
```

This script waits for nothing (which always succeeds), sends a sequence to ensure that the modem is in the correct mode (suppress command echo, send responses in verbose mode), and then disables auto-answer. It waits for an "OK" response before it terminates. The init sequence is used to check modem responses to ensure that the modem is functioning correctly. If the init script fails to complete, **getty** considers this to be fatal, and results in an error logged via syslogd(8), and exiting.

Similarly, an answer chat script is used to manually answer the phone in response to (usually) a "RING". When run with an answer script, **getty** opens the port in non-blocking mode, clears any extraneous input and waits for data on the port. As soon as any data is available, the answer chat script is started and scanned for a string, and responds according to the answer chat script. With a hayes compatible modem, this would normally look something like:

```
:ac=RING\r ATA\r CONNECT:
```

This causes the modem to answer the call via the "ATA" command, then scans input for a "CONNECT" string. If this is received before a *ct timeout, then a normal login sequence commences.*

The *ct* capability specifies a timeout for all send and expect strings. This timeout is set individually for each expect wait and send string and must be at least as long as the time it takes for a connection to be established between a remote and local modem (usually around 10 seconds).

In most situations, you will want to flush any additional input after the connection has been detected, and the *de* capability may be used to do that, as well as delay for a short time after the connection has been established during which all of the connection data has been sent by the modem.

SEE ALSO
　　login(1), gethostname(3), uname(3), termcap(5), getty(8), telnetd(8).

BUGS

The special characters (erase, kill, etc.) are reset to system defaults by login(1). In *all* cases, '#' or '^H' typed in a login name will be treated as an erase character, and '@' will be treated as a kill character.

The delay stuff is a real crock. Apart form its general lack of flexibility, some of the delay algorithms are not implemented. The terminal driver should support sane delay settings.

The *he* capability is stupid.

The termcap(5) format is horrid, something more rational should have been chosen.

HISTORY

The **gettytab** file format appeared in 4.2BSD.

NAME

ifconfig – configure network interface parameters

SYNOPSIS

ifconfig *interface address_family* [*address* [*dest_address*]]
        [*parameters*]
ifconfig -a [**-d**] [**-u**] [*address_family*]
ifconfig -l [**-d**] [**-u**] [*address_family*]

DESCRIPTION

Ifconfig is used to assign an address to a network interface and/or configure network interface parameters. **Ifconfig** must be used at boot time to define the network address of each interface present on a machine; it may also be used at a later time to redefine an interface's address or other operating parameters.

The following options are available:

address

> For the DARPA-Internet family, the address is either a host name present in the host name data base, hosts(5), or a DARPA Internet address expressed in the Internet standard "dot notation".

address_family

> Specify the *address family* which affects interpretation of the remaining parameters. Since an interface can receive transmissions in differing protocols with different naming schemes, specifying the address family is recommended. The address or protocol families currently supported are "inet", "atalk", and "ipx".

dest_address

> Specify the address of the correspondent on the other end of a point to point link.

interface

> This parameter is a string of the form "name unit", for example, "en0".

The following parameters may be set with **ifconfig**:

alias   Establish an additional network address for this interface. This is sometimes useful when changing network numbers, and one wishes to accept packets addressed to the old interface.

arp   Enable the use of the Address Resolution Protocol in mapping between net-
             work level addresses and link level addresses (default). This is currently imple-
             mented for mapping between DARPA Internet addresses and 10Mb/s Ethernet
             addresses.

-arp   Disable the use of the Address Resolution Protocol.

broadcast
             (Inet only) Specify the address to use to represent broadcasts to the network.
             The default broadcast address is the address with a host part of all 1's.

debug   Enable driver dependent debugging code; usually, this turns on extra console
             error logging.

-debug
             Disable driver dependent debugging code.

delete   Remove the network address specified. This would be used if you incorrectly
             specified an alias, or it was no longer needed. If you have incorrectly set an
             NS address having the side effect of specifying the host portion, removing all
             NS addresses will allow you to respecify the host portion.

down   Mark an interface "down". When an interface is marked "down", the system
             will not attempt to transmit messages through that interface. If possible, the in-
             terface will be reset to disable reception as well. This action does not automat-
             ically disable routes using the interface.

media *type*
             If the driver supports the media selection system, set the media type of the in-
             terface to *type*. Some interfaces support the mutually exclusive use of one of
             several different physical media connectors. For example, a 10Mb/s Ethernet
             interface might support the use of either AUI or twisted pair connectors. Setting
             the media type to "10base5/AUI" would change the currently active connector
             to the AUI port. Setting it to "10baseT/UTP" would activate twisted pair. Refer
             to the interfaces' driver specific documentation or man page for a complete list
             of the available types.

mediaopt *opts*
             If the driver supports the media selection system, set the specified media op-
             tions on the interface. *Opts* is a comma delimited list of options to apply to
             the interface. Refer to the interfaces' driver specific man page for a complete
             list of available options.

-mediaopt *opts*
             If the driver supports the media selection system, disable the specified media

options on the interface.

metric *n*

Set the routing metric of the interface to *n*, default 0. The routing metric is used by the routing protocol (routed(8)). Higher metrics have the effect of making a route less favorable; metrics are counted as addition hops to the destination network or host.

mtu *n*   Set the maximum transmission unit of the interface to *n*, default is interface specific. The mtu is used to limit the size of packets that are transmitted on an interface. Not all interfaces support setting the mtu, and some interfaces have range restrictions.

netmask *mask*

(Inet only) Specify how much of the address to reserve for subdividing networks into sub-networks. The mask includes the network part of the local address and the subnet part, which is taken from the host field of the address. The mask can be specified as a single hexadecimal number with a leading 0x, with a dot-notation Internet address, or with a pseudo-network name listed in the network table networks(5). The mask contains 1's for the bit positions in the 32-bit address which are to be used for the network and subnet parts, and 0's for the host part. The mask should contain at least the standard network portion, and the subnet field should be contiguous with the network portion.

range   Under appletalk, set the interface to respond to a *netrange.* of the form start-net-endnet. Appletalk uses this scheme instead of netmasks though FreeBSD implements it internally as a set of netmasks.

phase   The argument following this specifies the version (phase) of the Appletalk network attached to the interface. Values of 1 or 2 are permitted.

link[0-2]

Enable special processing of the link level of the interface. These three options are interface specific in actual effect, however, they are in general used to select special modes of operation. An example of this is to enable SLIP compression, or to select the connector type for some Ethernet cards. Refer to the man page for the specific driver for more information.

-link[0-2]

Disable special processing at the link level with the specified interface.

up   Mark an interface "up". This may be used to enable an interface after an "ifconfig down". It happens automatically when setting the first address on an interface. If the interface was reset when previously marked down, the hardware will be re-initialized.

Ifconfig displays the current configuration for a network interface when no optional parameters are supplied. If a protocol family is specified, **ifconfig** will report only the details specific to that protocol family.

If the driver does supports the media selection system, the supported media list will be included in the output.

Optionally, the **−a** flag may be used instead of an interface name. This flag instructs **ifconfig** to display information about all interfaces in the system. The **−d** flag limits this to interfaces that are down, and **−u** limits this to interfaces that are up.

The **−l** flag may be used to list all available interfaces on the system, with no other additional information. Use of this flag is mutually exclusive with all other flags and commands, except for **−d** (only list interfaces that are down) and **−u** (only list interfaces that are up).

Only the super-user may modify the configuration of a network interface.

NOTES

The media selection system is relatively new and only some drivers support it (or have need for it).

DIAGNOSTICS

Messages indicating the specified interface does not exist, the requested address is unknown, or the user is not privileged and tried to alter an interface's configuration.

SEE ALSO

netstat(1), netintro(4), rc(8), routed(8)

HISTORY

The **ifconfig** command appeared in 4.2BSD.

NAME
　　　inetd – internet "super-server"

SYNOPSIS
　　　inetd [**-d**] [**-l**] [**-c** *maximum*] [**-C** *rate*] [**-a** *address*] [**-p** *filename*] [**-R**
　　　　　rate] [*configuration file*]

DESCRIPTION
　　　The **inetd** program should be run at boot time by /etc/rc (see rc(8)). It then listens
　　　for connections on certain internet sockets. When a connection is found on one of its
　　　sockets, it decides what service the socket corresponds to, and invokes a program to ser-
　　　vice the request. The server program is invoked with the service socket as its standard
　　　input, output and error descriptors. After the program is finished, **inetd** continues to
　　　listen on the socket (except in some cases which will be described below). Essentially,
　　　inetd allows running one daemon to invoke several others, reducing load on the sys-
　　　tem.

　　　The following options are available:

　　　-d　　　Turn on debugging.

　　　-l　　　Turn on logging.

　　　-c *maximum*
　　　　　　　Specify the default maximum number of services that can be invoked. May be
　　　　　　　overridden on a per-service basis with the "max-child" parameter.

　　　-C *rate*
　　　　　　　Specify the default maximum number of times a service can be invoked from a
　　　　　　　single IP address in one minute; the default is unlimited. May be overridden
　　　　　　　on a per-service basis with the "max-connections-per-ip-per-minute" parameter.

　　　-R *rate*
　　　　　　　Specify the maximum number of times a service can be invoked in one minute;
　　　　　　　the default is 256.

　　　-a　　　Specify a specific IP address to bind to.

　　　-p　　　Specify an alternate file in which to store the process ID.

　　　Upon execution, **inetd** reads its configuration information from a configuration file
　　　which, by default, is /etc/inetd.conf. There must be an entry for each field of the
　　　configuration file, with entries for each field separated by a tab or a space. Comments
　　　are denoted by a "#" at the beginning of a line. There must be an entry for each field.
　　　The fields of the configuration file are as follows:

service name
socket type
protocol
{wait | nowait}[/max-child[/max-connections-per-ip-per-minute]]
user[:group][/login-class]
server program
server program arguments

To specify an ONC RPC-based service, the entry would contain these fields:

service name/version
socket type
rpc/protocol
user[:group][/login-class]
server program
server program arguments

There are two types of services that **inetd** can start: standard and TCPMUX. A standard service has a well-known port assigned to it; it may be a service that implements an official Internet standard or is a BSD-specific service. As described in RFC 1078, TCPMUX services are nonstandard services that do not have a well-known port assigned to them. They are invoked from **inetd** when a program connects to the "tcpmux" well-known port and specifies the service name. This feature is useful for adding locally-developed servers. TCPMUX requests are only accepted when the multiplexor service itself is enabled, above and beyond and specific TCPMUX-based servers; see the discussion of internal services below.

The *service-name* entry is the name of a valid service in the file /etc/services. For "internal" services (discussed below), the service name *must* be the official name of the service (that is, the first entry in /etc/services). When used to specify an ONC RPC-based service, this field is a valid RPC service name in the file /etc/rpc. The part on the right of the "/" is the RPC version number. This can simply be a single numeric argument or a range of versions. A range is bounded by the low version to the high version - "rusers/1-3". For TCPMUX services, the value of the *service-name* field consists of the string "tcpmux" followed by a slash and the locally-chosen service name. The service names listed in /etc/services and the name "help" are reserved. Try to choose unique names for your TCPMUX services by prefixing them with your organization's name and suffixing them with a version number.

The *socket-type* should be one of "stream", "dgram", "raw", "rdm", or "seqpacket", depending on whether the socket is a stream, datagram, raw, reliably delivered message, or sequenced packet socket. TCPMUX services must use "stream".

The *protocol* must be a valid protocol as given in /etc/protocols. Examples might be "tcp" or "udp". If it is desired that the service is reachable via T/TCP, one should specify "tcp/ttcp". Rpc based services are specified with the "rpc/tcp" or "rpc/udp" service type. TCPMUX services must use "tcp".

The *wait/nowait* entry specifies whether the server that is invoked by **inetd** will take over the socket associated with the service access point, and thus whether **inetd** should wait for the server to exit before listening for new service requests. Datagram servers must use "wait", as they are always invoked with the original datagram socket bound to the specified service address. These servers must read at least one datagram from the socket before exiting. If a datagram server connects to its peer, freeing the socket so **inetd** can received further messages on the socket, it is said to be a "multi-threaded" server; it should read one datagram from the socket and create a new socket connected to the peer. It should fork, and the parent should then exit to allow **inetd** to check for new service requests to spawn new servers. Datagram servers which process all incoming datagrams on a socket and eventually time out are said to be "single-threaded". Comsat(8), (biff(1)) and talkd(8) are both examples of the latter type of datagram server. Tftpd(8) is an example of a multi-threaded datagram server.

Servers using stream sockets generally are multi-threaded and use the "nowait" entry. Connection requests for these services are accepted by **inetd**, and the server is given only the newly-accepted socket connected to a client of the service. Most stream-based services operate in this manner. Stream-based servers that use "wait" are started with the listening service socket, and must accept at least one connection request before exiting. Such a server would normally accept and process incoming connection requests until a timeout. TCPMUX services must use "nowait".

The maximum number of outstanding child processes (or "threads") for a "nowait" service may be explicitly specified by appending a "/" followed by the number to the "nowait" keyword. Normally (or if a value of zero is specified) there is no maximum. Otherwise, once the maximum is reached, further connection attempts will be queued up until an existing child process exits. This also works in the case of "wait" mode, although a value other than one (the default) might not make sense in some cases. You can also specify the maximum number of connections per minute for a given IP address by appending a "/" followed by the number to the maximum number of outstanding child processes. Once the maximum is reached, further connections from this IP address will be dropped until the end of the minute.

The *user* entry should contain the user name of the user as whom the server should run. This allows for servers to be given less permission than root. Optional *group* part separated by ":" allows to specify group name different than default group for this user. Optional *login-class* part separated by "/" allows to specify login class different than default "daemon" login class.

The *server-program* entry should contain the pathname of the program which is to be executed by **inetd** when a request is found on its socket. If **inetd** provides this service internally, this entry should be "internal".

The *server program arguments* should be just as arguments normally are, starting with argv[0], which is the name of the program. If the service is provided internally, the word "internal" should take the place of this entry.

The **inetd** program provides several "trivial" services internally by use of routines within itself. These services are "echo", "discard", "chargen" (character generator), "daytime" (human readable time), and "time" (machine readable time, in the form of the number of seconds since midnight, January 1, 1900). All of these services are available in both TCP and UDP versions; the UDP versions will refuse service if the request specifies a reply port corresponding to any internal service. (This is done as a defense against looping attacks; the remote IP address is logged.) For details of these services, consult the appropriate RFC document.

The TCPMUX-demultiplexing service is also implemented as an internal service. For any TCPMUX-based service to function, the following line must be included in inetd.conf:

```
    tcpmux  stream  tcp     nowait  root    internal
```

When given the **-l** option **inetd** will log an entry to syslog each time an accept(2) is made, which notes the service selected and the IP-number of the remote requestor.

The **inetd** program rereads its configuration file when it receives a hangup signal, SIGHUP. Services may be added, deleted or modified when the configuration file is reread. Except when started in debugging mode, **inetd** records its process ID in the file /var/run/inetd.pid to assist in reconfiguration.

Support is provided for TCP Wrappers; see the relevant documentation (hosts_access(5)). The tcpd daemon is not required, as that functionality is builtin. This also allows the "internal" services to be wrapped.

TCPMUX

RFC 1078 describes the TCPMUX protocol: "A TCP client connects to a foreign host on TCP port 1. It sends the service name followed by a carriage-return line-feed <CRLF>. The service name is never case sensitive. The server replies with a single character indicating positive (+) or negative (−) acknowledgment, immediately followed by an optional message of explanation, terminated with a <CRLF>. If the reply was positive, the selected protocol begins; otherwise the connection is closed." The program is passed the TCP connection as file descriptors 0 and 1.

If the TCPMUX service name begins with a "+", **inetd** returns the positive reply for the program. This allows you to invoke programs that use stdin/stdout without putting any special server code in them.

The special service name "help" causes **inetd** to list TCPMUX services in inetd.conf.

FILES

/etc/inetd.conf	configuration file.
/etc/rpc	translation of service names to RPC program numbers.
/etc/services	translation of service names to port numbers.
/var/run/inetd.pid	the pid of the currently running **inetd**.

EXAMPLES

Here are several example service entries for the various types of services:

```
ftp            stream  tcp   nowait root  /usr/libexec/ftpd         ftpd -l
ntalk          dgram   udp   wait   root  /usr/libexec/ntalkd       ntalkd
tcpmux/+date   stream  tcp   nowait guest /bin/date                 date
tcpmux/phonebook stream tcp nowait guest /usr/local/bin/phonebook phonebook
rstatd/1-3     dgram   rpc/udp wait root  /usr/libexec/rpc.rstatd   rpc.rstatd
```

ERROR MESSAGES

The **inetd** server logs error messages using syslog(3). Important error messages and their explanations are:

service/protocol server failing (looping), service terminated.
The number of requests for the specified service in the past minute exceeded the limit. The limit exists to prevent a broken program or a malicious user from swamping the system. This message may occur for several reasons:

1. There are many hosts requesting the service within a short time period.

2. A broken client program is requesting the service too frequently.

3. A malicious user is running a program to invoke the service in a denial-of-service attack.

4. The invoked service program has an error that causes clients to retry quickly.

Use the **-R** *rate* option, as described above, to change the rate limit. Once the limit is reached, the service will be reenabled automatically in 10 minutes.

service/protocol: No such user *user*, service ignored

service/protocol: getpwnam: *user*: No such user
No entry for *user* exists in the passwd(5) database. The first message occurs when **inetd** (re)reads the configuration file. The second message occurs when the service is invoked.

service: can't set uid *uid*
service: can't set gid *gid*
The user or group ID for the entry's *user* field is invalid.

setsockopt(SO_PRIVSTATE): Operation not supported
The **inetd** program attempted to renounce the privileged state associated with a socket
but was unable to.

SEE ALSO

hosts_access(5), hosts_options(5), login.conf(5), passwd(5), rpc(5),
services(5), comsat(8), fingerd(8), ftpd(8), portmap(8), rexecd(8),
rlogind(8), rshd(8), telnetd(8), tftpd(8)

HISTORY

The **inetd** command appeared in 4.3BSD. TCPMUX is based on code and documentation by Mark Lottor. Support for ONC RPC based services is modeled after that provided
by SunOS 4.1. The FreeBSD TCP Wrappers support first appeared in

NAME

init – process control initialization

SYNOPSIS

init

DESCRIPTION

The **init** program is the last stage of the boot process. It normally runs the automatic reboot sequence as described in reboot(8), and if this succeeds, begins multi-user operation. If the reboot scripts fail, **init** commences single user operation by giving the super-user a shell on the console. The **init** program may be passed parameters from the boot program to prevent the system from going multi-user and to instead execute a single user shell without starting the normal daemons. The system is then quiescent for maintenance work and may later be made to go to multi-user by exiting the single-user shell (with ^D). This causes **init** to run the /etc/rc start up command file in fastboot mode (skipping disk checks).

If the *console* entry in the ttys(5) file is marked "insecure", then **init** will require that the superuser password be entered before the system will start a single-user shell. The password check is skipped if the *console* is marked as "secure".

The kernel runs with four different levels of security. Any superuser process can raise the security level, but only **init** can lower it. The security levels are:

-1   Permanently insecure mode – always run the system in level 0 mode. This is the default initial value.

0   Insecure mode – immutable and append-only flags may be turned off. All devices may be read or written subject to their permissions.

1   Secure mode – the system immutable and system append-only flags may not be turned off; disks for mounted filesystems, /dev/mem, and /dev/kmem may not be opened for writing.

2   Highly secure mode – same as secure mode, plus disks may not be opened for writing (except by mount(2)) whether mounted or not. This level precludes tampering with filesystems by unmounting them, but also inhibits running newfs(8) while the system is multi-user.

3   Network secure mode – same as highly secure mode, plus IP packet filter rules (see ipfw(8) and ipfirewall(4)) can not be changed and dummynet configuration can not be adjusted.

If the security level is initially -1, then **init** leaves it unchanged. Otherwise, **init** arranges to run the system in level 0 mode while single user and in level 1 mode while multiuser. If level 2 mode is desired while running multiuser, it can be set while single user, e.g., in the startup script /etc/rc, using sysctl(8) to set the "kern.securelevel" variable to the required security level.

In multi-user operation, **init** maintains processes for the terminal ports found in the file ttys(5). **Init** reads this file, and executes the command found in the second field. This command is usually getty(8); **getty** opens and initializes the tty line and executes the login(1) program. The **login** program, when a valid user logs in, executes a shell for that user. When this shell dies, either because the user logged out or an abnormal termination occurred (a signal), the **init** program wakes up, deletes the user from the utmp(5) file of current users and records the logout in the wtmp(5) file. The cycle is then restarted by **init** executing a new **getty** for the line.

Line status (on, off, secure, getty, or window information) may be changed in the ttys(5) file without a reboot by sending the signal SIGHUP to **init** with the command "kill -HUP 1". On receipt of this signal, **init** re-reads the ttys(5) file. When a line is turned off in ttys(5), **init** will send a SIGHUP signal to the controlling process for the session associated with the line. For any lines that were previously turned off in the ttys(5) file and are now on, **init** executes a new **getty** to enable a new login. If the getty or window field for a line is changed, the change takes effect at the end of the current login session (e.g., the next time **init** starts a process on the line). If a line is commented out or deleted from ttys(5), **init** will not do anything at all to that line. However, it will complain that the relationship between lines in the ttys(5) file and records in the utmp(5) file is out of sync, so this practice is not recommended.

Init will terminate multi-user operations and resume single-user mode if sent a terminate (TERM) signal, for example, "kill -TERM 1". If there are processes outstanding that are deadlocked (because of hardware or software failure), **init** will not wait for them all to die (which might take forever), but will time out after 30 seconds and print a warning message.

Init will cease creating new **getty**'s and allow the system to slowly die away, if it is sent a terminal stop (TSTP) signal, i.e. "kill -TSTP 1". A later hangup will resume full multi-user operations, or a terminate will start a single user shell. This hook is used by reboot(8) and halt(8).

Init will terminate all possible processes (again, it will not wait for deadlocked processes) and reboot the machine if sent the interrupt (INT) signal, i.e. "kill -INT 1". This is useful for shutting the machine down cleanly from inside the kernel or from X when the machine appears to be hung.

When shutting down the machine, **init** will try to run the `/etc/rc.shutdown` script. This script can be used to cleanly terminate specific programs such as **innd** (the Inter-NetNews server).

The role of **init** is so critical that if it dies, the system will reboot itself automatically. If, at bootstrap time, the **init** process cannot be located, the system will panic with the message "panic: "init died (signal %d, exit %d)".

DIAGNOSTICS

getty repeating too quickly on port %s, sleeping A process being started to service a line is exiting quickly each time it is started. This is often caused by a ringing or noisy terminal line. *Init will sleep for 10 seconds, then continue trying to start the process.*

some processes would not die; ps axl advised. A process is hung and could not be killed when the system was shutting down. This condition is usually caused by a process that is stuck in a device driver because of a persistent device error condition.

FILES

`/dev/console`	system console device
`/dev/tty*`	terminal ports found in ttys(5)
`/var/run/utmp`	record of current users on the system
`/var/log/wtmp`	record of all logins and logouts
`/etc/ttys`	the terminal initialization information file
`/etc/rc`	system startup commands
`/etc/rc.shutdown`	
	system shutdown commands

SEE ALSO

kill(1), login(1), sh(1), ipfirewall(4), ttys(5), crash(8), getty(8), halt(8), ipfw(8), rc(8), reboot(8), shutdown(8), sysctl(8)

HISTORY

A **init** command appeared in Version 6 AT&T UNIX.

CAVEATS

Systems without `sysctl` behave as though they have security level −1.

Setting the security level above 1 too early in the boot sequence can prevent fsck(8) from repairing inconsistent filesystems. The preferred location to set the security level is at the end of `/etc/rc` after all multi-user startup actions are complete.

NAME

ipfw – controlling utility for IP firewall

SYNOPSIS

ipfw [**-q**] [**-p** *preproc* [**-D** *macro*[=value]] [**-U** *macro*]] file
ipfw [**-f** | **-q**] flush
ipfw [**-q**] zero [*number* ...]
ipfw delete *number* ...
ipfw [**-aftN**] list [*number* ...]
ipfw [**-ftN**] show [*number* ...]
ipfw [**-q**] add [*number*] *action* [log] *proto* from *src* to *dst* [via *name* | *ipno*]
    [*options*]

DESCRIPTION

If used as shown in the first synopsis line, the *file* will be read line by line and applied as arguments to the **ipfw** command.

Optionally, a preprocessor can be specified using **-p** *preproc* where *file* is to be piped through. Useful preprocessors include cpp(1) and m4(1). If *preproc* doesn't start with a slash as its first character, the usual PATH name search is performed. Care should be taken with this in environments where not all filesystems are mounted (yet) by the time **ipfw** is being run (e. g. since they are mounted over NFS). Once **-p** has been specified, optional **-D** and **-U** specifications can follow and will be passed on to the preprocessor. This allows for flexible configuration files (like conditionalizing them on the local hostname) and the use of macros to centralize frequently required arguments like IP addresses.

Each packet that has been received or is about to be sent goes through the **ipfw** rules. In the case of a host acting as a gateway, packets that are forwarded by the host are processed by **ipfw** twice (once when entering, and once when leaving). Each packet can be filtered based on the following information that is associated with it:

    Receive Interface (*recv*)
        Interface over which the packet was received
    Transmit Interface (*xmit*)
        Interface over which the packet would be transmitted
    Incoming (*in*)
        Packet was just received
    Outgoing (*out*)

Packet would be transmitted
Source IP Address
Sender's IP Address
Destination IP Address
Target's IP Address
Protocol
IP protocol, including but not limited to IP (*ip*), UDP (*udp*), TCP (*tcp*), or ICMP (*icmp*)
Source Port
Sender's UDP or TCP port
Destination Port
Target's UDP or TCP port
Connection Setup Flag (*setup*)
This packet is a request to setup a TCP connection
Connection Established Flag (*established*)
This packet is part of an established TCP connection
All TCP Flags (*tcpflags*)
One or more of the TCP flags: close connection (*fin*), open connection (*syn*), reset connection (*rst*), push (*psh*), acknowledgment (*ack*), and urgent (*urg*)
Fragment Flag (*frag*)
This packet is a fragment of an IP packet
IP Options (*ipoptions*)
One or more of the IP options: strict source route (*ssrr*), loose source route (*lsrr*), record route (*rr*), and timestamp (*ts*)
ICMP Types (*icmptypes*)
One or more of the ICMP types: echo reply (*0*), destination unreachable (*3*), source quench (*4*), redirect (*5*), echo request (*8*), router advertisement (*9*), router solicitation (*10*), time-to-live exceeded (*11*), IP header bad (*12*), timestamp request (*13*), timestamp reply (*14*), information request (*15*), information reply (*16*), address mask request (*17*), and address mask reply (*18*)

Note that may be dangerous to filter on the source IP address or source TCP/UDP port because either or both could easily be spoofed.

The **ipfw** code works by going through the rule-list for each packet until a match is found. All rules have two associated counters, a packet count and a byte count. These counters are updated when a packet matches the rule.

The rules are ordered by a "line-number" from 1 to 65534 that is used to order and delete rules. Rules are tried in increasing order, and the first rule that matches a packet applies. Multiple rules may share the same number and apply in the order in which they were added.

If a rule is added without a number, it is numbered 100 higher than the highest defined rule number, unless the highest defined rule number is 65435 or greater, in which case new rules are given that same number.

The delete operation deletes the first rule with number *number*, if any.

The list command prints out the current rule set.

The show command is equivalent to 'ipfw -a list'.

The zero operation zeroes the counters associated with rule number *number*.

The flush operation removes all rules.

Any command beginning with a '#', or being all blank, is ignored.

One rule is always present:

```
65535 deny all from any to any
```

This rule is the default policy, i.e., don't allow anything at all. Your job in setting up rules is to modify this policy to match your needs.

However, if the kernel option "IPFIREWALL_DEFAULT_TO_ACCEPT" is active, the rule is instead:

```
65535 allow all from any to any
```

This variation lets everything pass through. This option should only be activated in particular circumstances, such as if you use the firewall system as an on-demand denial-of-service filter that is normally wide open.

The following options are available:

-a While listing, show counter values. See also "show" command.

-f Don't ask for confirmation for commands that can cause problems if misused (i.e. flush). *Note*, if there is no tty associated with the process, this is implied.

-q While adding, zeroing or flushing, be quiet about actions (implies '-f'). This is useful for adjusting rules by executing multiple **ipfw** commands in a script (e.g., 'sh /etc/rc.firewall'), or by processing a file of many **ipfw** rules, across a remote login session. If a flush is performed in normal (verbose) mode (with the default kernel configuration), it prints a message. Because all rules are flushed, the message cannot be delivered to the login session. This causes the remote login session to be closed and the remainder of the ruleset is not processed. Access to the console is required to recover.

-t   While listing, show last match timestamp.

-N   Try to resolve addresses and service names in output.

action:

     allow   Allow packets that match rule. The search terminates. Aliases are *pass*, *permit*, and *accept*.

     deny   Discard packets that match this rule. The search terminates. *Drop* is an alias for *deny*.

     reject   (Deprecated.) Discard packets that match this rule, and try to send an ICMP host unreachable notice. The search terminates.

     unreach code   Discard packets that match this rule, and try to send an ICMP unreachable notice with code *code*, where *code* is a number from zero to 255, or one of these aliases: *net, host, protocol, port, needfrag, srcfail, net-unknown, host-unknown, isolated, net-prohib, host-prohib, tosnet, toshost, filter-prohib, host-precedence,* or *precedence-cutoff*. The search terminates.

     reset   TCP packets only. Discard packets that match this rule, and try to send a TCP reset (RST) notice. The search terminates.

     count   Update counters for all packets that match rule. The search continues with the next rule.

     divert port   Divert packets that match this rule to the divert(4) socket bound to port *port*. The search terminates.

     tee port   Send a copy of packets matching this rule to the divert(4) socket bound to port *port*. The search continues with the next rule. This feature is not yet implemeted.

   fwd ipaddr [,port] Change the next-hop on matching packets to *ipaddr*, which can be an IP address in dotted quad or a host name. If *ipaddr* is not a directly-reachable address, the route as found in the local routing table for that IP is used instead. If *ipaddr* is a local address, then on a packet entering the system from a remote host it will be diverted to *port* on the local machine, keeping the local address of the socket set to the original IP address the packet was destined for. This is intended for use with transparent proxy servers. If the IP is not a local address then the port number (if specified) is ignored and the rule only applies to packets leaving the system. This will also map addresses to local ports when packets are generated locally. The search terminates if this rule matches. If the port number is not given then the port number in the packet is used, so that a packet for an external machine port Y would be forwarded to local port Y. The kernel must have been compiled with optiions IPFIRE-WALL_FORWARD.

`skipto number`   Skip all subsequent rules numbered less than *number*. The search continues with the first rule numbered *number* or higher.

If a packet matches more than one *divert* and/or *tee* rule, all but the last are ignored.

If the kernel was compiled with `IPFIREWALL_VERBOSE`, then when a packet matches a rule with the *log* keyword a message will be printed on the console. If the kernel was compiled with the `IPFIREWALL_VERBOSE_LIMIT` option, then logging will cease after the number of packets specified by the option are received for that particular chain entry. Logging may then be re-enabled by clearing the packet counter for that entry.

Console logging and the log limit are adjustable dynamically through the sysctl(8) interface.

proto:

   `ip`   All packets match. The alias *all* has the same effect.

   `tcp`   Only TCP packets match.

   `udp`   Only UDP packets match.

   `icmp`   Only ICMP packets match.

   <number|*name>*   Only packets for the specified protocol matches (see `/etc/protocols` for a complete list).

src and *dst*:

   <address/mask> [*ports*]

The *<address/mask>* may be specified as:

`ipno`	An ipnumber of the form 1.2.3.4. Only this exact ip number match the rule.
`ipno/bits`	An ipnumber with a mask width of the form 1.2.3.4/24. In this case all ip numbers from 1.2.3.0 to 1.2.3.255 will match.
`ipno:mask`	An ipnumber with a mask width of the form 1.2.3.4:255.255.240.0. In this case all ip numbers from 1.2.0.0 to 1.2.15.255 will match.

The sense of the match can be inverted by preceding an address with the "not" modifier, causing all other addresses to be matched instead. This does not affect the selection of port numbers.

With the TCP and UDP protocols, optional *ports* may be specified as:

{port | port-port}[,port[,...]]

Service names (from `/etc/services`) may be used instead of numeric port values. A range may only be specified as the first value, and the length of the port list is limited to `IP_FW_MAX_PORTS` (as defined in `/usr/src/sys/netinet/ip_fw.h`) ports.

Fragmented packets which have a non-zero offset (i.e. not the first fragment) will never match a rule which has one or more port specifications. See the `frag` option for details on matching fragmented packets.

Rules can apply to packets when they are incoming, or outgoing, or both. The `in` keyword indicates the rule should only match incoming packets. The `out` keyword indicates the rule should only match outgoing packets.

To match packets going through a certain interface, specify the interface using `via`:

`via ifX`	Packet must be going through interface `ifX`.
`via if*`	Packet must be going through interface `ifX`, where X is any unit number.
`via any`	Packet must be going through *some* interface.
`via ipno`	Packet must be going through the interface having IP address `ipno`.

The `via` keyword causes the interface to always be checked. If `recv` or `xmit` is used instead of `via`, then the only receive or transmit interface (respectively) is checked. By specifying both, it is possible to match packets based on both receive and transmit interface, e.g.:

```
ipfw add 100 deny ip from any to any out recv ed0 xmit ed1
```

The *recv* interface can be tested on either incoming or outgoing packets, while the *xmit* interface can only be tested on outgoing packets. So *out* is required (and *in* invalid) whenver *xmit* is used. Specifying *via* together with *xmit* or *recv* is invalid.

A packet may not have a receive or transmit interface: packets originating from the local host have no receive interface. while packets destined for the local host have no transmit interface.

Additional *options*:

frag	Matches if the packet is a fragment and this is not the first fragment of the datagram. *frag* may not be used in conjunction with either *tcpflags* or TCP/UDP port specifications.
in	Matches if this packet was on the way in.
out	Matches if this packet was on the way out.
ipoptions *spec*	Matches if the IP header contains the comma separated list of options specified in *spec*. The supported IP options are: *ssrr* (strict source route), *lsrr* (loose source route), *rr* (record packet route), and *ts* (timestamp). The absence of a particular option may be denoted with a "!".
established	Matches packets that have the RST or ACK bits set. TCP packets only.
setup	Matches packets that have the SYN bit set but no ACK bit. TCP packets only.
tcpflags *spec*	Matches if the TCP header contains the comma separated list of flags specified in *spec*. The supported TCP flags are: *fin*, *syn*, *rst*, *psh*, *ack*, and *urg*. The absence of a particular flag may be denoted with a "!". A rule which contains a *tcpflags* specification can never match a fragmented packet which has a non-zero offset. See the *frag* option for details on matching fragmented packets.
icmptypes *types*	Matches if the ICMP type is in the list *types*. The list may be specified as any combination of ranges or individual types separated by commas.

CHECKLIST

Here are some important points to consider when designing your rules:

- Remember that you filter both packets going in and out. Most connections need packets going in both directions.

- Remember to test very carefully. It is a good idea to be near the console when doing this.

- Don't forget the loopback interface.

FINE POINTS

There is one kind of packet that the firewall will always discard, that is an IP fragment with a fragment offset of one. This is a valid packet, but it only has one use, to try to circumvent firewalls.

If you are logged in over a network, loading the KLD version of **ipfw** is probably not as straightforward as you would think. I recommend this command line:

```
kldload /modules/ipfw.ko && \
ipfw add 32000 allow all from any to any
```

Along the same lines, doing an

```
ipfw flush
```

in similar surroundings is also a bad idea.

The IP filter list may not be modified if the system security level is set to 3 or higher (see init(8) for information on system security levels).

PACKET DIVERSION

A divert socket bound to the specified port will receive all packets diverted to that port; see divert(4). If no socket is bound to the destination port, or if the kernel wasn't compiled with divert socket support, diverted packets are dropped.

EXAMPLES

This command adds an entry which denies all tcp packets from *cracker.evil.org* to the telnet port of *wolf.tambov.su* from being forwarded by the host:

```
ipfw add deny tcp from cracker.evil.org to wolf.tambov.su
23
```

This one disallows any connection from the entire crackers network to my host:

```
ipfw add deny all from 123.45.67.0/24 to my.host.org
```

Here is a good usage of the *list* command to see accounting records and timestamp information:

```
ipfw -at l
```

or in short form without timestamps:

```
ipfw -a l
```

This rule diverts all incoming packets from 192.168.2.0/24 to divert port 5000:

```
ipfw divert 5000 all from 192.168.2.0/24 to any in
```

SEE ALSO

cpp(1), m4(1), divert(4), ip(4), ipfirewall(4), protocols(5), services(5), init(8), kldload(8), reboot(8), sysctl(8), syslogd(8).

BUGS

WARNING!!WARNING!!WARNING!!WARNING!!WARNING!!WARNING!!WARNING!!

This program can put your computer in rather unusable state. When using it for the first time, work on the console of the computer, and do *NOT* do anything you don't understand.

When manipulating/adding chain entries, service and protocol names are not accepted.

Incoming packet fragments diverted by *divert* are reassembled before delivery to the socket, whereas fragments diverted via *tee* are not.

Port aliases containing dashes cannot be first in a list.

The "tee" action is unimplemented.

AUTHORS

Ugen J. S. Antsilevich,
Poul-Henning Kamp,
Alex Nash,
Archie Cobbs. API based upon code written by
Daniel Boulet for BSDI.

HISTORY

ipfw first appeared in FreeBSD 2.0.

NAME
     kbdcontrol – a utility for manipulating the syscons keyboard driver section

SYNOPSIS
     kbdcontrol [**-dFx**] [**-b** *duration.pitch* | *[quiet.]belltype*] [**-r**
     delay.repeat | *speed*] [**-l** *mapfile*] [**-f** *# string*] [**-h** *size*] [**-L**
     mapfile]

DESCRIPTION
     The **kbdcontrol** command is used to set various keyboard related options for the
     syscons console driver, such as keymap, keyboard repeat & delay rates, bell characteris-
     tics etc.

     The following command line options are supported:

     -b *duration.pitch* | *[quiet.]belltype*
          Set the bell duration in miliseconds and pitch in hertz. If a *belltype* argu-
          ment is specified, it may be one of *normal* which set sound parameters back
          to normal values, or *visual* which set the bell to visual mode, i.e. flashes the
          screen instead. If *belltype* is preceded by the word *quiet.*, the bell will
          not be rung when the ringing process is in the background vty.

     -r *delay.repeat* | *speed*
          Set keyboard *delay (250, 500, 750, 1000)* and *repeat (34, 38,
          42, 46, 50, 55, 59, 63,* 136, 152, 168, 184, 200, 220, 236, 252, 272, 304,
          336, 368, 400, 440, 472, 504) rates, or if a *speed* argument is specified, it may
          be one of *slow* (1000.504), *fast* (250.34) or *normal* (500.126).

     -l *mapfile*
          Install keyboard map file from *mapfile*.

     -d   Dump the current keyboard map onto stdout.

     -f *# string*
          Set function key number # to send *string*.

     -F   Set function keys back to the standard definitions.

     -x   Use hexadecimal numbers in keyboard map dump.

     -h *size*
          Set history buffer size to *size* lines.

-L *mapfile*
> Load keyboard map file from *mapfile* and write the *struct keymap* compiled from it to stdout.

FILES
/usr/share/syscons/keymaps

BUGS
Report when found.

SEE ALSO
vidcontrol(1), keyboard(4), screen(4)

AUTHORS
Søren Schmidt <sos@FreeBSD.org>

NAME

ld.so – run-time link-editor

DESCRIPTION

ld.so is a self-contained, position independent program image providing run-time support for loading and link-editing shared objects into a process' address space. It uses the data structures (see link(5)) contained within dynamically linked programs to determine which shared libraries are needed and loads them at a convenient virtual address using the mmap(2) system call.

After all shared libraries have been successfully loaded, **ld.so** proceeds to resolve external references from both the main program and all objects loaded. A mechanism is provided for initialization routines to be called, on a per-object basis, giving a shared object an opportunity to perform any extra set-up, before execution of the program proper begins. This is useful for C++ libraries that contain static constructors.

ld.so is itself a shared object that is initially loaded by the startup module *crt0*. Since a.out(5) formats do not provide easy access to the file header from within a running process, *crt0* uses the special symbol *_DYNAMIC* to determine whether a program is in fact dynamically linked or not. Whenever the linker ld(1) has relocated this symbol to a location other than 0, *crt0* assumes the services of **ld.so** are needed (see link(5) for details) . *crt0* passes control to **ld.so** 's entry point before the program's **main**() routine is called. Thus, **ld.so** can complete the link-editing process before the dynamic program calls upon services of any dynamic library.

To quickly locate the required shared objects in the filesystem, **ld.so** may use a "hints" file, prepared by the ldconfig(8) utility, in which the full path specification of the shared objects can be looked up by hashing on the 3-tuple <library-name, major-version-number, minor-version-number> .

ld.so recognizes a number of environment variables that can be used to modify its behaviour as follows:

LD_LIBRARY_PATH   A colon separated list of directories, overriding the default search path for shared libraries. This is ignored for set-user-ID and set-group-ID programs.

LD_PRELOAD   A colon separated list of shared libraries, to be linked in before any other shared libraries. If the directory is not specified then the directories specified by LD_LIBRARY_PATH will be searched first followed by the set of built-in standard directories. This is ignored for set-user-ID and set-group-ID programs.

LD_BIND_NOW   When set to a nonempty string, causes **ld.so** to re-
                           locate all external function calls before starting exe-
                           cution of the program. Normally, function calls are
                           bound lazily, at the first call of each function.
                           LD_BIND_NOW increases the start-up time of a pro-
                           gram, but it avoids run-time surprises caused by un-
                           expectedly undefined functions.

LD_WARN_NON_PURE_CODE   When set to a nonempty string, issue a warning
                           whenever a link-editing operation requires modifica-
                           tion of the text segment of some loaded object. This
                           is usually indicative of an incorrectly built library.

LD_SUPPRESS_WARNINGS   When set to a nonempty string, no warning messages
                           of any kind are issued. Normally, a warning is given
                           if satisfactorily versioned library could not be found.

LD_IGNORE_MISSING_OBJECTS When set to a nonempty string, makes it a nonfatal
                           condition if one or more required shared objects can-
                           not be loaded. Loading and execution proceeds us-
                           ing the objects that are available. A warning is pro-
                           duced for each missing object, unless the environ-
                           ment variable LD_SUPPRESS_WARNINGS is set to a
                           nonempty string.

                           This is ignored for set-user-ID and set-group-ID pro-
                           grams.

                           Missing shared objects can be ignored without errors
                           if all the following conditions hold:

                           • They do not supply definitions for any required
                             data symbols.

                           • No functions defined by them are called during
                             program execution.

                           • The environment variable LD_BIND_NOW is unset
                             or is set to the empty string.

LD_TRACE_LOADED_OBJECTS   When set to a nonempty string, causes **ld.so** to exit
                           after loading the shared objects and printing a sum-
                           mary which includes the absolute pathnames of all

objects, to standard output.

LD_TRACE_LOADED_OBJECTS_FMT1

LD_TRACE_LOADED_OBJECTS_FMT2

When set, these variables are interpreted as format strings a la printf(3) to customize the trace output and are used by ldd(1)'s **-f** option and allows ldd(1) to be operated as a filter more conveniently. The following conversions can be used:

%a   The main program's name (also known as"__progname").

%A   The value of the environment variable LD_TRACE_LOADED_OBJECTS_PROGNAME

%o   The library name.

%m   The library's major version number.

%n   The library's minor version number.

%p   The full pathname as determined by **rtld**'s library search rules.

%x   The library's load address.

Additionally, **\n** and **\t** are recognized and have their usual meaning.

FILES

/var/run/ld.so.hints

SEE ALSO

ld(1), link(5), ldconfig(8)

HISTORY

The shared library model employed first appeared in SunOS 4.0

NAME
ldconfig – configure the shared library cache

SYNOPSIS
ldconfig [**-aout** | **-elf**] [**-Rmrsv**] [**-f** *hints_file*] [*directory* | *file*
...]

DESCRIPTION
ldconfig is used to prepare a set of "hints" for use by the dynamic linker to facilitate
quick lookup of shared libraries available in multiple directories. It scans a set of built-in
system directories and any *directories* specified on the command line (in the given
order) looking for shared libraries and stores the results in a system file to forestall the
overhead that would otherwise result from the directory search operations the dynamic
linker would have to perform to load the required shared libraries.

Files named on the command line are expected to contain directories to scan for shared
libraries. Each directory's pathname must start on a new line. Blank lines and lines
starting with the comment character '#' are ignored.

The shared libraries so found will be automatically available for loading if needed by the
program being prepared for execution. This obviates the need for storing search paths
within the executable.

The LD_LIBRARY_PATH environment variable can be used to override the use of directories (or the order thereof) from the cache or to specify additional directories where
shared libraries might be found. LD_LIBRARY_PATH is a ':' separated list of directory
paths which are searched by the dynamic linker when it needs to load a shared library. It
can be viewed as the run-time equivalent of the **-L** switch of ld(1).

Ldconfig is typically run as part of the boot sequence.

The following options recognized by **ldconfig**:

-aout   Generate the hints for a.out format shared libraries.

-elf   Generate the hints for ELF format shared libraries.

-R   Rescan the previously configured directories. This opens the previous hints file
and fetches the directory list from the header. Any additional pathnames on
the command line are also processed.

-f *hints_file*
Read and/or update the specified hints file, instead of the standard file. This

option is provided primarily for testing.

-m   Instead of replacing the contents of the hints file with those found in the directories specified, "merge" in new entries. Directories recorded in the hints file by previous runs of **ldconfig** are also rescanned for new shared libraries.

-r   List the current contents of the hints file on the standard output. The hints file is not modified. The list of directories stored in the hints file is included.

-s   Do not scan the built-in system directory ("/usr/lib") for shared libraries.

-v   Switch on verbose mode.

Security

Special care must be taken when loading shared libraries into the address space of set-user-Id programs. Whenever such a program is run, the dynamic linker will only load shared libraries from the hints file. In particular, the LD_LIBRARY_PATH is not used to search for libraries. Thus, the role of ldconfig is dual. In addition to building a set of hints for quick lookup, it also serves to specify the trusted collection of directories from which shared objects can be safely loaded. It is presumed that the set of directories specified to **ldconfig** are under control of the system's administrator.

ENVIRONMENT

OBJFORMAT   Overrides /etc/objformat (see below) to determine whether **-aout** or **-elf** is the default. If set, its value should be either aout or elf.

FILES

/var/run/ld.so.hints	Standard hints file for the a.out dynamic linker.
/var/run/ld-elf.so.hints	Standard hints file for the ELF dynamic linker.
/etc/ld.so.conf	Conventional configuration file containing directory names for invocations with **-aout**.
/etc/ld-elf.so.conf	Conventional configuration file containing directory names for invocations with **-elf**.
/etc/objformat	Determines whether **-aout** or **-elf** is the default. If present, it must consist of a single line containing either OBJFORMAT=aout or OBJFORMAT=elf.

SEE ALSO

ld(1), link(5)

HISTORY

A **ldconfig** utility first appeared in SunOS 4.0, it appeared in its current form in FreeB-
SD 1.1.

NAME
     loader.4th – loader.conf processing tools

DESCRIPTION
     The file that goes by the name of **loader.4th** is a set of commands designed to ma-
     nipulate loader.conf(5) files. The default /boot/loader.rc includes **loader.4th**
     and uses one of it's commands to automatically read and process the standard load-
     er.conf(5) files. Other commands exists to help the user specify alternate configura-
     tions.

     The commands of **loader.4th** by themselves are not enough for most uses. Please re-
     fer to the examples below for the most common situations, and to loader(8) for addi-
     tional commands.

     Before using any of the commands provided in **loader.4th**, it must be included
     through the command:

          include loader.4th

     This line is present on the default /boot/loader.rc file, so it isn't needed (and
     should not be re-issued) in a normal setup.

     The commands provided by it are:

          boot-conf   Boot as specified by the loader.conf(5) files
                                      read. It uses **autoboot**, so it can be stopped.

          start   Reads /boot/defaults/loader.conf, all other
                                      loader.conf(5) files specified in it, and then pro-
                                      ceeds to boot as specified in them. This is com-
                                      mand used on the default /boot/loader.rc file,
                                      and it uses the autoboot command (see
                                      loader(8)), so it can be stopped for further inter-
                                      action with loader(8).

          read-conf *filename*   Reads and processes a loader.conf(5) file. Does
                                      not proceeds to boot.

          enable-module *module* Enables the loading of *module*.

          disable-module *module* Disables the loading of *module*.

          toggle-module *module* Toggles the loading of *module* on and off.

show-module *module*   Shows the information gathered in the load-
                         er.conf(5) files about the module *module*.

retry   Used inside loader.conf(5) files to specify the
                         action after a module loading fails.

ignore   Used inside loader.conf(5) files to specify the
                         action after a module loading fails.

FILES
    /boot/loader   The loader(8).
    /boot/loader.4th **loader.4th** itself.
    /boot/loader.rc   loader(8) bootstrapping script.
    /boot/defaults/loader.conf
                      File loaded by the **start** command.

EXAMPLES
    Standard /boot/loader.rc:

        include /boot/loader.4th
        start

    Loads a different kernel with the standard configuration:

        set kernel="kernel.old"
        unload
        boot-conf

    Reads an additional configuration file and then proceeds to boot:

        unload
        read-conf /boot/special.conf
        boot-conf

    Disable the loading of the splash screen module and bitmap and then proceeds to boot:

        unload
        disable-module splash_bmp
        disable-module bitmap
        boot-conf

SEE ALSO

`loader.conf(5)`, `loader(8)`

HISTORY

loader.4th first appeared in

AUTHORS

loader.4th was written by Daniel C. Sobral <dcs@freebsd.org>.

BUGS

A british espionage series.

NAME

loader – system bootstrap stage three

DESCRIPTION

The program called **loader** is the third stage of FreeBSD's three stage bootstrap. It is a BTX client linked statically to libstand(3) and usually located in the directory /boot.

It provides a scripting language that can be used to automate tasks, do pre-configuration or assist in recovery procedures. This scripting language is roughly divided in two main components. The smaller one is a set of commands designed for direct use by the casual user, called "builtin commands" for historical reasons. The main drive behind these commands is user-friendlyness. The bigger component is an ANS Forth compatible Forth interpreter based on ficl, by John Sadler.

During initialization, **loader** will probe for a console and set the *console* variable, or set it to serial console ("comconsole") if the previous boot stage used that. Then, devices are probed, *currdev* and *loaddev* are set, and *LINES* is set to 24 . Next, FICL is initialized, the builtin words are added to it's vocabulary, and /boot/boot.4th will be processed if it exists. No disk switching is possible while that file is being read. The inner interpreter **loader** will use with FICL is then set to **interpret**, which is FICL's default. After that, /boot/loader.rc is processed if available, and, failing that, /boot/boot.conf will be read for historical reasons. These files are processed through the **include** command, which read all of them into memory before processing them, making disk changes possible.

At this point, if an **autoboot** has not been tried, and if *autoboot_delay* is not set to "NO" (not case sensitive), then an **autoboot** will be tried. If the system gets past this point, *prompt* will be set and **loader** will engage interactive mode.

BUILTIN COMMANDS

Loader's builtin commands take it's parameters from the command line. Presently, the only way to call them from a script is by using evaluate on a string. If an error condition occurs, an exception will be generated, which can be intercepted using ANS Forth exception handling words. If not intercepted, an error message will be displayed and the interpreter's state will be reset, emptying the stack and restoring interpreting mode.

The builtin commands available are:

autoboot [*seconds*]
> Proceeds to bootstrap the system after a number of seconds, if not interrupted by the user. Displays a countdown prompt warning the user the system is about to be booted, unless interrupted by a key press. The kernel will be loaded first if necessary. Defaults to 10 seconds.

bcachestat
> Displays statistics about disk cache usage. For depuration only.

boot
boot *kernelname* [...]
boot **-flag** **...**
> Immediately proceeds to bootstrap the system, loading the kernel if necessary. Any flags or arguments are passed to the kernel, but they must precede the kernel name, if a kernel name is provided.

echo [**-n**] [<message>]
> Displays a text on the screen. A new line will be printed unless **-n** is specified.

heap   Displays memory usage statistics. For debugging purposes only.

help [topic [subtopic]]
> Shows help messages read from /boot/loader.help. The special topic *index* will list the topics available.

include *file* [*file* ...]
> Process script files. Each file is, at a turn, completely read into memory, and then have each of it's lines passed to the command line interpreter. If any error is returned by the interpreter, the include commands aborts immediately, without reading any other files, and returns an error itself (see ERRORS).

load [**-t** *type*] *file* **...**
> Loads a kernel, kernel loadable module (kld), or a file of opaque contents tagged as being of the type *type*. Kernel and modules can be either in a.out or elf format. Any arguments passed after the name of the file to be loaded will be passed as arguments to that file. Notice, though, that, at the present, this does not work for the kernel.

ls [**-l**] [*path*]
> Displays a listing of files in the directory *path*, or the root directory if *path* is not specified. If **-l** is specified, file sizes will be shown too.

lsdev [**-v**]
> Lists all of the devices from which it may be possible to load modules. If **-v** is specified, more details are printed.

lsmod [**-v**]
> Displays loaded modules. If **-v** is specified, more details are shown.

more *file* [*file* ...]
> Display the files specified, with a pause at each *LINES* displayed.

pnpscan [**-v**]
> Scans for Plug-and-Play devices. This is not functional at the present.

read [**-t** *seconds*] [**-p** *prompt*] [*variable*]
> Reads a line of input from the terminal, storing it in *variable* if specified. A timeout can be specified with **-t**, though it will be canceled at the first key pressed. A prompt may also be displayed through the **-p** flag.

reboot
> Immediately reboots the system.

set *variable*
set *variable=value*
> Set loader's environment variables.

show [*variable*]
> Displays the specified variable's value, or all variables and their values if *variable* is not specified.

unload
> Remove all modules from memory.

unset *variable*
> Removes *variable* from the environment.

?
> Same as "help index".

BUILTIN ENVIRONMENT VARIABLES

The **loader** has actually two different kinds of 'environment' variables. There are ANS Forth's *environmental queries*, and a separate space of environment variables used by builtins, which are not directly available to Forth words. It is the later ones that this session covers.

Environment variables can be set and unset through the use of the **set** and **unset** builtins, and have their value interactively examined through the use of the **show** builtin. Their values can also be accessed as described in BUILTIN PARSER.

Notice that this environment variables are not inherited by any shell after the system has been booted.

A few variables are set automatically by . Others can affect either **loader** or kernel's behavior at boot. While some of these may require a value, others define behavior just by being set. These are described below.

autoboot_delay

> Number of seconds **autoboot** will wait before booting. If this variable is not defined, **autoboot** will default to 10 seconds.
>
> If set to "NO", no **autoboot** will be automatically attempted after processing `/boot/loader.rc`, though explicit **autoboot**'s will be processed normally, defaulting to 10 seconds delay.

boot_askname

> Instructs the kernel to prompt the user for the name of the root device when the kernel is booted.

boot_ddb Instructs the kernel to start in the DDB debugger, rather than proceeding to initialise when booted.

boot_gdb Selects gdb-remote mode for the kernel debugger by default.

boot_single Prevents the kernel from initiating a multi-user startup, single-user mode will be entered when the kernel has finished device probes.

boot_userconfig

> Requests that the kernel's interactive device configuration program be run when the kernel is booted.

boot_verbose

> Setting this variable causes extra debugging information to be printed by the kernel during the boot phase.

bootfile List of semicolon-separated search path for bootable kernels. The default is "kernel;kernel.old".

console   Defines the current console.

currdev   Selects the default device. Syntax for devices is odd.

interpret Has the value "ok" if the Forth's current state is interpreting.

LINES   Define the number of lines on the screen, to be used by the pager.

module_path

> Sets the list of directories which will be searched in for modules named in a load command or implicitly required by a dependancy. The default value for this variable is "/;/boot;/modules".

num_ide_disks

> Sets the number of IDE disks as a work around for some problems in finding the root disk at boot. This has been deprecated in favour of

　　　　　　　　　　　　root_disk_unit.

prompt　　　　　Value of **loader**'s prompt. Defaults to "${currdev}>".

root_disk_unit
　　　　　　　　　　If the code which detects the disk unit number for the root disk is
　　　　　　　　　　confused, eg. by a mix of SCSI and IDE disks, or IDE disks with gaps
　　　　　　　　　　in the sequence (eg. no primary slave), the unit number can be
　　　　　　　　　　forced by setting this variable.

rootdev　　　　By default the value of *currdev* is used to set the root filesystem
　　　　　　　　　　when the kernel is booted. This can be overridden by setting *rootdev*
　　　　　　　　　　explicitly.

Other variables are used to override kernel tunnable parameters. The following tunables
are available:

kern.ipc.nmbclusters
　　　　　　　　　　Set the number of mbuf clusters to be allocated. The value cannot
　　　　　　　　　　be set below the default determined when the kernel was com-
　　　　　　　　　　piled. Modifies *NMBCLUSTERS*.

kern.vm.kmem.size
　　　　　　　　　　Sets the size of kernel memory (bytes). This overrides completely
　　　　　　　　　　the value determined when the kernel was compiled. Modifies
　　　　　　　　　　VM_KMEM_SIZE.

machdep.pccard.pcic_irq
　　　　　　　　　　Overrides the IRQ normally assigned to a PCCARD controller.
　　　　　　　　　　Typically the first available interrupt will be allocated, which may
　　　　　　　　　　conflict with other hardware. If this value is set to 0, an interrupt
　　　　　　　　　　will not be assigned and the controller will operate in polled mode
　　　　　　　　　　only.

net.inet.tcp.tcbhashsize
　　　　　　　　　　Overrides the compile-time set value of *TCBHASHSIZE* or the pre-
　　　　　　　　　　set default of 512. Must be a power of 2.

BUILTIN PARSER
　　　　When a builtin command is executed, the rest of the line is taken by it as arguments, and
　　　　it's processed by a special parser which is not used for regular Forth commands.

　　　　This special parser applies the following rules to the parsed text:

1. All backslash characters are preprocessed.

   - \b , \f , \r , \n and \t are processed as by C's **printf()**.

   - \s is converted to a space.

   - \v is converted to ASCII 11.

   - \z is just skipped. Useful for things like "\0xf\z\0xf".

   - \0xN and \0xNN are replaced by the hex N or NN.

   - \NNN is replaced by the octal NNN ASCII character.

   - \" , \' and \$ will escape these characters, preventing them from receiving special semantics on the step 2 described below.

   - \\ will be replaced with a single \ .

   - In any other occurance, backslash will just be removed.

2. Every string between non-escaped quotes or double-quotes will be treated as a single word for the purposes of the remaining steps.

3. Replace any $VARIABLE or ${VARIABLE} with the value of the environemnt variable *VARIABLE*.

4. Passes multiple space-delimited arguments to the builtin command called. Spaces can also be escaped through the use of \\ .

An exception to this parsing rule exists, and is described in BUILTINS AND FORTH.

BUILTINS AND FORTH

All builtin words are state-smart, immediate words. If interpreted, they behave exactly as described previously. If they are compiled, though, they extract their arguments from the stack instead of the command line.

If compiled, the builtin words expect to find, at execution time, the following parameters on the stack:

    addrN lenN ... addr2 len2 addr1 len1 N

where *addrX lenX* are strings which will compose the command line that will be parsed into the builtin's arguments. Internally, these strings are concatenated in from 1 to N, with a space put between each one.

If no arguments are passed, a 0 *must* be passed, even if the builtin accepts no arguments.

While this behavior has benefits, it has it's trade-offs. If the execution token of a builtin is acquired (through ' or [']), and then passed to **catch** or **execute**, the builtin behavior will depend on the system state *at the time* **catch** *or* **execute** *is processed* ! This is particular annoying for programs that want or need to treat exceptions. In this case, it is recommended the use of a proxy. For example:

```
: (boot) boot;
```

FICL

FICL is a Forth interpreter written in C, in the form of a forth virtual machine library that can be called by C functions and vice versa.

In **loader**, each line read interactively is then fed to FICL, which may call **loader** back to execute the builtin words. The builtin **include** will also feed FICL, one line at a time.

The words available to FICL can be classified in four groups. The ANS Forth standard words, extra FICL words, extra words, and the builtin commands. The later were already described. The ANS Forth standard words are listed in the STANDARDS section. The words falling in the two other groups are described in the following subsections.

FICL EXTRA WORDS

      .env

      .ver

      -roll

      2constant

      >name

      body>

      compare   This the STRING word set's **compare**.

      compile-only

      endif

      forget-wid

      parse-word

      sliteral   This is the STRING word set's **sliteral**.

      wid-set-super

w@

w!

x.

empty

cell-

-rot

FREEBSD EXTRA WORDS

tib> *(-- addr len)*
> Returns the remainder of the input buffer as a string on the stack.

% *(--)* Evaluates the remainder of the input buffer under a **catch** exception guard.

$ *(--)* Evaluates the remainder of the input buffer, after having printed it first.

fopen *(addr len -- fd)*
> Open a file. Returns a file descriptor, or -1 in case of failure.

fclose *(fd --)*
> Closes a file.

fread *(fd addr len -- len')*
> Tries to read *len* bytes from file *fd* into buffer *addr*. Returns the actual number of bytes read, or -1 in case of error or end of file.

fload *(fd --)*
> Process file *fd*.

fkey *(fd -- char)*
> Reads a single character from a file.

key *(-- char)*
> Reads a single character from the console.

key? *(-- flag)*
> Returns **true** if there is a character available to be read from the console.

ms *(u --)*

Waits *u* microseconds.

seconds (*-- u*)
    Returns the number of seconds since midnight.

trace! (*flag --*)
    Activates or deactivates tracing. Does not work with **catch**.

outb (*port char --*)
    Writes a byte to a port.

inb (*port -- char*)
    Reads a byte from a port.

FREEBSD DEFINED ENVIRONMENTAL QUERIES

arch-i386
    TRUE if the architecture is IA32.

arch-alpha
    TRUE if the architecture is AXP.

FreeBSD_version
    version at compile time.

loader_version
    loader version.

SYSTEM DOCUMENTATION

FILES

/boot/loader	**loader** itself.
/boot/boot.4th	Additional FICL initialization.
/boot/boot.conf	**loader** bootstrapping script. Deprecated.
/boot/loader.rc	**loader** bootstrapping script.
/boot/loader.help	Loaded by **help**. Contains the help messages.

EXAMPLES

Boot in single user mode:

```
boot -s
```

Loads kernel's user configuration file. Notice that a kernel must be loaded before any other **load** command is attempted.

```
load kernel
load -t userconfig_script /boot/kernel.conf
```

Loads the kernel, a splash screen, and then autoboots in five seconds.

```
load kernel
load splash_bmp
load -t splash_image_data /boot/chuckrulez.bmp
autoboot 5
```

Sets the disk unit of the root device to 2, and then boots. This would be needed in the case of a two IDE disks system, with the second IDE hardwired to wd2 instead of wd1.

```
set root_disk_unit=2
boot /kernel
```

See also:

`/boot/loader.4th`	Extra builtin-like words.
`/boot/support.4th`	`loader.conf` processing words.
`/usr/share/examples/bootforth/`	Assorted examples.

ERRORS

The following values are thrown by :

100	Any type of error in the processing of a builtin.
-1	**Abort** executed.
-2	**Abort**" executed.
-56	**Quit** executed.
-256	Out of interpreting text.
-257	Need more text to succeed -- will finish on next run.
-258	**Bye** executed.
-259	Unspecified error.

SEE ALSO

libstand(3), loader.conf(5), boot(8), btxld(8)

STANDARDS

For the purposes of ANS Forth compliance, loader is an *ANS Forth System with Environmental Restrictions, Providing* .(, :noname, ?do, parse, pick, roll, refill, to, value, \, false, true, <>, 0<>, compile, , erase, nip, tuck *and* marker *from the Core Extensions word set, Providing the Exception Extensions word set, Providing the Locals Extensions word set, Providing the Memory-Allocation Extensions word set, Providing* .s , bye, forget, see, words, [if] , [else] *and* [then] *from the Programming-Tools extension word set, Providing the Search-Order extensions word set.*

HISTORY

loader first appeared in

AUTHORS

loader was written by Michael Smith <msmisth@freebsd.org>.

FICL was written by
John Sadler <john_sadler@alum.mit.edu>.

BUGS

FICL is case sensitive. Though this is not a standard violation, all Forth words are lower cased, which would result in a standard violation. Do not rely on this bug.

The **expect** and **accept** words will read from the input buffer instead of the console. The later will be fixed, but the former will not.

NAME

`login.conf` – login class capability database

SYNOPSIS

`/etc/login.conf, ~/.login_conf`

DESCRIPTION

login.conf contains various attributes and capabilities of login classes. A login class (an optional annotation against each record in the user account database, `/etc/master.passwd`) determines session accounting, resource limits and user environment settings. It is used by various programs in the system to set up a user's login environment and to enforce policy, accounting and administrative restrictions. It also provides the means by which users are able to be authenticated to the system and the types of authentication available.

A special record "default" in the system user class capability database `/etc/login.conf` is used automatically for any non-root user without a valid login class in `/etc/master.passwd`. A user with a uid of 0 without a valid login class will use the record "root" if it exists, or "default" if not.

In FreeBSD, users may individually create a file called `.login_conf` in their home directory using the same format, consisting of a single entry with a record id of "me". If present, this file is used by `login(1)` to set user-defined environment settings which override those specified in the system login capabilities database. Only a subset of login capabilities may be overridden, typically those which do not involve authentication, resource limits and accounting.

Records in a class capabilities database consist of a number of colon-separated fields. The first entry for each record gives one or more names that a record is to be known by, each separated by a '|' character. The first name is the most common abbreviation. The last name given should be a long name that is more descriptive of the capability entry, and all others are synonyms. All names but the last should be in lower case and contain no blanks; the last name may contain upper case characters and blanks for readability.

See `getcap(3)` for a more in-depth description of the format of a capability database.

CAPABILITIES

Fields within each record in the database follow the `getcap(3)` conventions for boolean, type string '=' and type numeric '#', although type numeric is depreciated in favour of the string format and either form is accepted for a numeric datum. Values fall into the following categories:

file   Path name to a data file

program   Path name to an executable file

list   A list of values (or pairs of values) separated by commas or spaces

path   A space or comma separated list of path names, following the usual csh con-
            ventions (leading tilde with and without username being expanded to home
            directories etc.)

number   A numeric value, either decimal (default), hexadecimal (with leading 0x), or
            octal (with a leading 0). With a numeric type, only one numeric value is al-
            lowed. Numeric types may also be specified in string format (ie. the capabili-
            ty tag being delimited from the value by '=' instead of '#'). Whichever method
            is used, then all records in the database must use the same method to allow
            values to be correctly overridden in interpolated records.

size   A number which expresses a size. The default interpretation of a value is the
            number of bytes, but a suffix may specify alternate units:
                b   explicitly selects 512-byte blocks
                k   selects kilobytes (1024 bytes)
                m   specifies a multiplier of 1 megabyte (1048576 bytes),
                g   specifies units of gigabytes, and
                t   represents terabytes.
            A size value is a numeric quantity and case of the suffix is not significant.
            Concatenated values are added together.

time   A period of time, by default in seconds. A prefix may specify a different unit;
                y   indicates the number of 365 day years,
                w   indicates the number of weeks,
                d   the number of days,
                h   the number of hours,
                m   the number of minutes, and
                s   the number of seconds.
            Concatenated values are added together. For example, 2 hours and 40 min-
            utes may be written either as 9600s, 160m or 2h40m.

The usual convention to interpolate capability entries using the special *tc=value* notation
may be used.

RESOURCE LIMITS

Name	Type	Notes	Description

cputime	time		CPU usage limit.
filesize	size		Maximum file size limit.
datasize	size		Maximum data size limit.
stacksize	size		Maximum stack size limit.
coredumpsize	size		Maximum coredump size limit.
memoryuse	size		Maximum of core memory use size limit.
memorylocked	size		Maximum locked in core memory size limit.
maxproc	number		Maximum number of processes.
openfiles	number		Maximum number of open files per process.

These resource limit entries actually specify both the maximum and current limits (see getrlimit(2)). The current (soft) limit is the one normally used, although the user is permitted to increase the current limit to the maximum (hard) limit. The maximum and current limits may be specified individually by appending a -max or -cur to the capability name.

ENVIRONMENT

Name	Type	Notes	Description
charset	string		Set $MM_CHARSET environment variable to the specified value.
hushlogin	bool	false	Same as having a ˜/.hushlogin file.
ignorenologin	bool	false	Login not prevented by nologin.
lang	string		Set $LANG environment variable to the specified value.
manpath	path		Default search path for manpages.
nologin	file		If the file exists it will be displayed and the login session will be terminated.
path	path	/bin /usr/bin	Default search path.
priority	number		Initial priority (nice) level.
requirehome	bool	false	Require a valid home directory to login.
setenv	list		A comma-separated list of environment variables and values to which they are to be set.
shell	prog		Session shell to execute rather than the shell specified in the passwd file. The SHELL environment variable will contain the shell specified in the password file.
term	string	su	Default terminal type if not able to determine from other means.

timezone	string		Default value of $TZ environment variable.
umask	number	022	Initial umask. Should always have a leading 0 to ensure octal interpretation.
welcome	file	/etc/motd	File containing welcome message.

AUTHENTICATION

Name	Type	Notes	Description
minpasswordlen	number	6	The minimum length a local password may be.
auth	list	passwd	Allowed authentication styles. The first value is the default style.
auth-<type>	list		Allowed authentication styles for the authentication type 'type'.
copyright	file		File containing additional copyright information
host.allow	list		List of remote host wildcards from which users in the class may access.
host.deny	list		List of remote host wildcards from which users in the class may not access.
times.allow	list		List of time periods during which logins are allowed.
times.deny	list		List of time periods during which logins are disallowed.
ttys.allow	list		List of ttys and ttygroups which users in the class may use for access.
ttys.deny	list		List of ttys and ttygroups which users in the class may not use for access.

These fields are intended to be used by passwd(1) and other programs in the login authentication system.

Capabilities that set environment variables are scanned for both '~' and '$' characters, which are substituted for a user's home directory and name respectively. To pass these characters literally into the environment variable, escape the character by preceding it with a backslash '\'.

The *host.allow* and *host.deny* entries are comma separated lists used for checking remote access to the system, and consist of a list of hostnames and/or IP addresses against which remote network logins are checked. Items in these lists may contain wildcards in the form used by shell programs for wildcard matching (See fnmatch(3) for details on the implementation). The check on hosts is made against both the remote system's Internet address and hostname (if available). If both lists are empty or not specified, then logins from any remote host are allowed. If host.allow contains one or more hosts, then only remote systems matching any of the items in that list are allowed to log in. If host.deny contains one or more hosts, then a login from any matching hosts will be disallowed.

The *times.allow* and *times.deny* entries consist of a comma-separated list of time periods during which the users in a class are allowed to be logged in. These are expressed as one or more day codes followed by a start and end times expressed in 24 hour format, separated by a hyphen or dash. For example, MoThSa0200-1300 translates to Monday, Thursday and Saturday between the hours of 2 am and 1 p.m.. If both of these time lists are empty, users in the class are allowed access at any time. If *times.allow* is specified, then logins are only allowed during the periods given. If *times.deny* is specified, then logins are denied during the periods given, regardless of whether one of the periods specified in *times.allow* applies.

Note that login(1) enforces only that the actual login falls within periods allowed by these entries. Further enforcement over the life of a session requires a separate daemon to monitor transitions from an allowed period to a non-allowed one.

The *ttys.allow* and *ttys.deny* entries contain a comma-separated list of tty devices (without the /dev/ prefix) that a user in a class may use to access the system, and/or a list of ttygroups (See getttyent(3) and ttys(5) for information on ttygroups). If neither entry exists, then the choice of login device used by the user is unrestricted. If only *ttys.allow* is specified, then the user is restricted only to ttys in the given group or device list. If only *ttys.deny* is specified, then the user is prevented from using the specified devices or devices in the group. If both lists are given and are non-empty, the user is restricted to those devices allowed by ttys.allow that are not available by ttys.deny.

ACCOUNTING LIMITS

Name	Type	Notes	Description
accounted	bool	false	Enable session time accounting for all users in this class.
autodelete	time		Time after expiry when account is auto-deleted.
bootfull	bool	false	Enable 'boot only if ttygroup is full' strategy when terminating sessions.
daytime	time		Maximum login time per day.
expireperiod	time		Time for expiry allocation.
graceexpire	time		Grace days for expired account.
gracetime	time		Additional grace login time allowed.
host.accounted	list		List of remote host wildcards from which login sessions will be accounted.
host.exempt	list		List of remote host wildcards from which login session accounting is exempted.

idletime	time	Maximum idle time before logout.
monthtime	time	Maximum login time per month.
passwordtime	time	Used by passwd(1) to set next password expiry date.
refreshtime	time	New time allowed on account refresh.
refreshperiod	str	How often account time is refreshed.
sessiontime	time	Maximum login time per session.
sessionlimit	number	Maximum number of concurrent login sessions on ttys in any group.
ttys.accounted	list	List of ttys and ttygroups for which login accounting is active.
ttys.exempt	list	List of ttys and ttygroups for which login accounting is exempt.
warnexpire	time	Advance notice for pending account expiry.
warnpassword	time	Advance notice for pending password expiry.
warntime	time	Advance notice for pending out-of-time.
weektime	time	Maximum login time per week.

These fields are used by the time accounting system, which regulates, controls and records user login access.

The *ttys.accounted* and *ttys.exempt* fields operate in a similar manner to *ttys.allow* and *ttys.deny* as explained above. Similarly with the *host.accounted* and *host.exempt* lists.

SEE ALSO

login(1), getcap(3), getttyent(3), login_cap(3), login_class(3), passwd(5), ttys(5)

NAME
     mount – mount file systems

SYNOPSIS
     mount [**-adfpruvw**] [**-t** *ufs* | *lfs* | *external_type*]
     mount [**-dfpruvw**] *special* | *node*
     mount [**-dfpruvw**] [**-o** *options*] [**-t** *ufs* | *lfs* | *external_type*] *special*
           node

DESCRIPTION
     The **mount** command calls the mount(2) system call to prepare and graft a *special
     device* or the remote node (rhost:path) on to the file system tree at the point *node*. If
     either *special* or *node* are not provided, the appropriate information is taken from the
     fstab(5) file.

     The system maintains a list of currently mounted file systems. If no arguments are given
     to **mount**, this list is printed.

     The options are as follows:

     -a   All the filesystems described in fstab(5) are mounted. Exceptions are those
              marked as "noauto", excluded by the **-t** flag (see below), or if they are al-
              ready mounted (except the root filesystem which is always remounted to pre-
              serve traditional single user mode behavior).

     -d   Causes everything to be done except for the actual system call. This option is
              useful in conjunction with the **-v** flag to determine what the **mount** command
              is trying to do.

     -f   Forces the revocation of write access when trying to downgrade a filesystem
              mount status from read-write to read-only. Also forces the R/W mount of an
              unclean filesystem (dangerous; use with caution).

     -o   Options are specified with a **-o** flag followed by a comma separated string of
              options. The following options are available:

              async   All I/O to the file system should be done asynchronously. This is a
                      dangerous flag to set, and should not be used unless you are pre-
                      pared to recreate the file system should your system crash.

              force   The same as **-f**; forces the revocation of write access when trying to
                      downgrade a filesystem mount status from read-write to read-only. Al-
                      so forces the R/W mount of an unclean filesystem (dangerous; use

with caution).

noatime   Do not update the file access time when reading from a file. This op-
          tion is useful on filesystems where there are large numbers of files
          and performance is more critical than updating the file access time
          (which is rarely ever important). This option is currently only support-
          ed on local filesystems.

noauto   This filesystem should be skipped when mount is run with the **-a**
          flag.

noclusterr
          Disable read clustering.

noclusterw
          Disable write clustering.

nodev   Do not interpret character or block special devices on the file system.
          This option is useful for a server that has file systems containing spe-
          cial devices for architectures other than its own.

noexec   Do not allow execution of any binaries on the mounted file system.
          This option is useful for a server that has file systems containing bina-
          ries for architectures other than its own.

nosuid   Do not allow set-user-identifier or set-group-identifier bits to take ef-
          fect. Note: this option is worthless if a public available suid or sgid
          wrapper like suidperl(1) is installed on your system.

nosymfollow
          Do not follow symlinks on the mounted file system.

rdonly   The same as **-r**; mount the file system read-only (even the super-user
          may not write it).

sync   All I/O to the file system should be done synchronously.

suiddir   A directory on the mounted filesystem will respond to the SUID bit
          being set, by setting the owner of any new files to be the same as the
          owner of the directory. New directories will inherit the bit from their
          parents. Execute bits are removed from the file, and it will not be
          given to root.

          This feature is designed for use on fileservers serving PC users via ftp,
          SAMBA, or netatalk. It provides security holes for shell users and as
          such should not be used on shell machines, especially on home direc-
          tories. This option requires the SUIDDIR option in the kernel to

work. Only UFS filesystems support this option. See chmod(2) for more information.

update   The same as **-u**; indicate that the status of an already mounted file system should be changed.

union   Causes the namespace at the mount point to appear as the union of the mounted filesystem root and the existing directory. Lookups will be done in the mounted filesystem first. If those operations fail due to a non-existent file the underlying directory is then accessed. All creates are done in the mounted filesystem.

Any additional options specific to a filesystem type that is not one of the internally known types (see the **-t** option) may be passed as a comma separated list; these options are distinguished by a leading "-" (dash). Options that take a value are specified using the syntax -option=value. For example, the **mount** command:

```
mount -t mfs -o nosuid,-N,-s=4000 /dev/dk0b /tmp
```

causes **mount** to execute the equivalent of:

```
/sbin/mount_mfs -o nosuid -N -s 4000 /dev/dk0b /tmp
```

-p   Print mount information in fstab format. Implies also the **-v** option.

-r   The file system is to be mounted read-only. Mount the file system read-only (even the super-user may not write it). The same as the "rdonly" argument to the **-o** option.

-t *ufs | lfs | external type*
    The argument following the **-t** is used to indicate the file system type. The type *ufs* is the default. The **-t** option can be used to indicate that the actions should only be taken on filesystems of the specified type. More than one type may be specified in a comma separated list. The list of filesystem types can be prefixed with "no" to specify the filesystem types for which action should *not* be taken. For example, the **mount** command:

```
mount -a -t nonfs,mfs
```

mounts all filesystems except those of type NFS and MFS.

If the type is not one of the internally known types, **mount** will attempt to execute a program in /sbin/mount_*XXX* where *XXX* is replaced by the type name. For example, nfs filesystems are mounted by the program /sbin/mount_nfs.

Most filesystems will be dynamically loaded by their mount programs if not already present in the kernel, using the vfsload(3) subroutine. Because this mechanism requires writable temporary space, the filesystem type containing /tmp must be compiled into the kernel, and the filesystems containing /tmp and /usr/bin/ld must be listed in /etc/fstab before any filesystems which might be dynamically loaded.

-u The **-u** flag indicates that the status of an already mounted file system should be changed. Any of the options discussed above (the **-o** option) may be changed; also a file system can be changed from read-only to read-write or vice versa. An attempt to change from read-write to read-only will fail if any files on the filesystem are currently open for writing unless the **-f** flag is also specified. The set of options is determined by first extracting the options for the file system from the fstab(5) table, then applying any options specified by the **-o** argument, and finally applying the **-r** or **-w** option.

-v Verbose mode.

-w The file system object is to be read and write.

The options specific to NFS filesystems are described in the mount_nfs(8) manual page.

DIAGNOSTICS

Various, most of them are self-explanatory.

```
XXXXX filesystem is not available
```

The kernel doesn't support the respective filesystem type. Note that support for a particular filesystem might be provided either on a static (kernel compile-time), or dynamic basis (loaded as a kernel module by kldload(8)). Normally, **mount** or its subprocesses attempt to dynamically load a filesystem module if it hasn't been configured statically, using vfsload(3). In this case, the above error message can also mean that you didn't have permission to load the module.

FILES

/etc/fstab file system table

SEE ALSO

mount(2), vfsload(3), fstab(5), kldload(8), mount_cd9660(8), mount_devfs(8), mount_fdesc(8), mount_kernfs(8), mount_lfs(8), mount_mfs(8), mount_msdos(8), mount_nfs(8), mount_null(8), mount_portal(8), mount_procfs(8), mount_umap(8), mount_union(8), umount(8)

BUGS

It is possible for a corrupted file system to cause a crash.

Switching a filesystem back and forth between asynchronous and normal operation or between read/write and read/only access using "mount -u" may gradually bring about severe filesystem corruption.

CAVEATS

After a successful mount, the permissions on the original mount point determine if . . is accessible from the mounted file system. The minimum permissions for the mount point for traversal across the mount point in both directions to be possible for all users is 0111 (execute for all).

HISTORY

A **mount** command appeared in Version 1 AT&T UNIX.

NAME

mount_cd9660 – mount an ISO-9660 filesystem

SYNOPSIS

mount_cd9660 [**-egrv**] [**-o** *options*] [**-s** *startsector*] *special* | *node*

DESCRIPTION

The **mount_cd9660** command attaches the ISO-9660 filesystem residing on the device special to the global filesystem namespace at the location indicated by node. This command is normally executed by mount(8) at boot time.

The options are as follows:

-e   Enable the use of extended attributes.

-g   Do not strip version numbers on files. (By default, if there are files with different version numbers on the disk, only the last one will be listed.) In either case, files may be opened without explicitly stating a version number.

-j   Do not use any Joliet extensions included in the filesystem.

-o   Options are specified with a **-o** flag followed by a comma separated string of options. See the mount(8) man page for possible options and their meanings.

-r   Do not use any Rockridge extensions included in the filesystem.

-s *startsector*
         Start the filesystem at *startsector*. Normally, if the underlying device is a CD-ROM drive, **mount_cd9660** will try to figure out the last track from the CD-ROM containing data, and start the filesystem there. If the device is not a CD-ROM, or the table of contents cannot be examined, the filesystem will be started at sector 0. This option can be used to override the behaviour. Note that *startsector* is measured in CD-ROM blocks, with 2048 bytes each. This is the same as for example the **info** command of cdcontrol(8) is printing.

-v   Be verbose about the starting sector decisions made.

SEE ALSO

mount(2), unmount(2), fstab(5), cdcontrol(8), mount(8)

BUGS

POSIX device node mapping is currently not supported.

Version numbers are not stripped if Rockridge extensions are in use. In this case, accessing files that don't have Rockridge names without version numbers gets the one with the lowest version number and not the one with the highest.

There is no ECMA support.

HISTORY

The **mount_cd9660** utility first appeared 4.4BSD.

NAME

newfs, **mount_mfs** – construct a new file system

SYNOPSIS

newfs [-NO] [**-S** *sector-size*] [**-T** *disktype*] [**-a** *maxcontig*] [**-b**
block-size] [**-c** *cylinders*] [**-d** *rotdelay*] [**-e** *maxbpg*] [**-f**
frag-size] [**-i** *bytes*] [**-k** *skew*] [**-l** *interleave*] [**-m** *free
space*] [**-n** *rotational positions*] [**-o** *optimization*] [**-p**
sectors] [**-r** *revolutions*] [**-s** *size*] [**-t** *tracks*] [**-u** *sectors*]
[**-v**] [**-x** *sectors*] *special*

mount_mfs [**-N**] [**-F** *file*] [**-T** *disktype*] [**-a** *maxcontig*] [**-b** *block-size*]
[**-c** *cylinders*] [**-d** *rotdelay*] [**-e** *maxbpg*] [**-f** *frag-size*] [**-i**
bytes] [**-m** *free space*] [**-n** *rotational positions*] [**-o** *options*]
[**-s** *size*] *special node*

DESCRIPTION

Newfs replaces the more obtuse mkfs(8) program. Before running **newfs** or
mount_mfs, the disk must be labeled using disklabel(8). **Newfs** builds a file system
on the specified special file. (We often refer to the "special file" as the "disk", although
the special file need not be a physical disk. In fact, it need not even be special.) Typically the defaults are reasonable, however **newfs** has numerous options to allow the defaults to be selectively overridden.

Mount_mfs is used to build a file system in virtual memory and then mount it on a
specified node. **Mount_mfs** exits and the contents of the file system are lost when the
file system is unmounted. If **mount_mfs** is sent a signal while running, for example
during system shutdown, it will attempt to unmount its corresponding file system. The
parameters to **mount_mfs** are the same as those to **newfs**. If the **-T** flag is specified
(see below), the special file is unused. Otherwise, it is only used to read the disk label
which provides a set of configuration parameters for the memory based file system. The
special file is typically that of the primary swap area, since that is where the file system
will be backed up when free memory gets low and the memory supporting the file system has to be paged.

The following options define the general layout policies:

-T *disktype*
> For backward compatibility and for **mount_mfs**.

-F *file*
> **Mount_mfs** will use this file for the image of the filesystem. When

mount_mfs exits, this file will be left behind.

-N   Cause the file system parameters to be printed out without really creating the file system.

-O   Create a 4.3BSD format filesystem. This options is primarily used to build root filesystems that can be understood by older boot ROMs.

-T   Use information for the specified disk from /etc/disktab instead of trying to get the information from a disklabel.

-a *maxcontig*

Specify the maximum number of contiguous blocks that will be laid out before forcing a rotational delay (see the **-d** option). The default value is 1. See tunefs(8) for more details on how to set this option.

-b *block-size*

The block size of the file system, in bytes. It must be a power of 2. The default size is 8192 bytes, and the smallest allowable size is 4096 bytes.

-c *#cylinders/group*

The number of cylinders per cylinder group in a file system. The default value is 16. The maximum value is dependent on a number of other parameters, in particular the block size. The best way to find the maximum value for a specific file system is to attempt to specify a value which is far too large: **newfs** will print out the maximum value.

-d *rotdelay*

This parameter once specified the minimum time in milliseconds required to initiate another disk transfer on the same cylinder. It was used in determining the rotationally optimal layout for disk blocks within a file. Modern disks with read/write-behind achieve higher performance with this feature disabled, so this value should be left at the default value of 0 milliseconds. See tunefs(8) for more details on how to set this option.

-e *maxbpg*

Indicate the maximum number of blocks any single file can allocate out of a cylinder group before it is forced to begin allocating blocks from another cylinder group. The default is about one quarter of the total blocks in a cylinder group. See tunefs(8) for more details on how to set this option.

-f *frag-size*

The fragment size of the file system in bytes. It must be a power of two ranging in value between *blocksize/8* and *blocksize*. The default is 1024 bytes.

-i *number of bytes per inode*

Specify the density of inodes in the file system. The default is to create an inode for every (4 * frag-size) bytes of data space. If fewer inodes are desired, a larger number should be used; to create more inodes a smaller number should be given. One inode is required for each distinct file, so this value effectively specifies the average file size on the file system.

-m *free space %*

The percentage of space reserved from normal users; the minimum free space threshold. The default value used is defined by MINFREE from <ufs/ffs/fs.h>, currently 8%. See tunefs(8) for more details on how to set this option.

-n *number of distinguished rotational positions*

UFS has the ability to keep track of the availability of blocks at different rotational positions, so that it could lay out the data to be picked up with minimum rotational latency. This parameter specifies the default number of rotational positions to distinguish.

Nowadays this value should be set to 1 (which essentially disables the rotational position table) because modern drives with read-ahead and write-behind do better without the rotational position table.

-o *optimization preference*

("space" or "time") The file system can either be instructed to try to minimize the time spent allocating blocks, or to try to minimize the space fragmentation on the disk. If the value of minfree (see above) is less than 8%, the default is to optimize for space; if the value of minfree is greater than or equal to 8%, the default is to optimize for time. See tunefs(8) for more details on how to set this option.

-s *size*

The size of the file system in sectors. This value defaults to the size of the raw partition specified in *special* (in other words, **newfs** will use the entire partition for the file system).

-v

Specify that the disk does not contain any partitions, and that **newfs** should build a file system on the whole disk. This option is useful for synthetic disks such as **vinum.**

The following options override the standard sizes for the disk geometry. Their default values are taken from the disk label. Changing these defaults is useful only when using **newfs** to build a file system whose raw image will eventually be used on a different type of disk than the one on which it is initially created (for example on a write-once disk). Note that changing any of these values from their defaults will make it impossible for fsck(8) to find the alternate superblocks if the standard superblock is lost.

-S *sector-size*
> The size of a sector in bytes (almost never anything but 512).

-k *sector 0 skew, per track*
> Used to describe perturbations in the media format to compensate for a slow controller. Track skew is the offset of sector 0 on track N relative to sector 0 on track N-1 on the same cylinder. This option is of historical importance only; modern controllers are always fast enough to handle operations back-to-back.

-l *hardware sector interleave*
> Used to describe perturbations in the media format to compensate for a slow controller. Interleave is physical sector interleave on each track, specified as the denominator of the ratio:
> > sectors read/sectors passed over
> Thus an interleave of 1/1 implies contiguous layout, while 1/2 implies logical sector 0 is separated by one sector from logical sector 1. This option is of historical importance only; the physical sector layout of modern disks is not visible from outside.

-p *spare sectors per track*
> Spare sectors (bad sector replacements) are physical sectors that occupy space at the end of each track. They are not counted as part of the sectors/track (**-u**) since they are not available to the file system for data allocation. This option is of historical importance only. Modern disks perform their own bad sector allocation.

-r *revolutions/minute*
> The speed of the disk in revolutions per minute. This value is no longer of interest, since all the parameters which depend on it are usually disabled.

-t *#tracks/cylinder*
> The number of tracks/cylinder available for data allocation by the file system. The default is 1. If zero is specified, the value from the disklabel will be used.

-u *sectors/track*
> The number of sectors per track available for data allocation by the file system. The default is 4096. If zero is specified, the value from the disklabel will be used. This does not include sectors reserved at the end of each track for bad

block replacement (see the **-p** option).

-x *spare sectors per cylinder*
Spare sectors (bad sector replacements) are physical sectors that occupy space at the end of the last track in the cylinder. They are deducted from the sectors/track (**-u**) of the last track of each cylinder since they are not available to the file system for data allocation. This option is of historical importance only. Modern disks perform their own bad sector allocation.

The options to the **mount_mfs** command are as described for the **newfs** command, except for the **-o** option.

That option is as follows:

-o   Options are specified with a **-o** flag followed by a comma separated string of options. See the mount(8) man page for possible options and their meanings.

EXAMPLES
        mount_mfs -s 131072 -o nosuid,nodev /dev/da0s1b /tmp

Mount a 64 MB large memory file system on /tmp, with mount(8) options nosuid and nodev.

BUGS
The boot code of FreeBSD assumes that the file system that carries the kernel has blocks of 8 kilobytes and fragments of 1 kilobyte. You will not be able to boot from a file system that uses another size.

SEE ALSO
fdformat(1), disktab(5), fs(5), disklabel(8), diskpart(8), dumpfs(8), fsck(8), mount(8), scsiformat(8), tunefs(8), vinum(8)

M. McKusick, W. Joy, S. Leffler, and R. Fabry, "A Fast File System for UNIX,", *ACM Transactions on Computer Systems 2*, 3, pp 181-197, August 1984, (reprinted in the BSD System Manager's Manual).

HISTORY
The **newfs** command appeared in 4.2BSD.

NAME

reboot, **halt** – stopping and restarting the system

SYNOPSIS

halt [**-nqp**]
reboot [**-nqp**]
fasthalt [**-nqp**]
fastboot [**-nqp**]

DESCRIPTION

The **halt** and **reboot** utilities flush the file system cache to disk, send all running processes a SIGTERM (and subsequently a SIGKILL) and, respectively, halt or restart the system. The action is logged, including entering a shutdown record into the login accounting file.

The options are as follows:

-n　　　The file system cache is not flushed. This option should probably not be used.

-q　　　The system is halted or restarted quickly and ungracefully, and only the flushing of the file system cache is performed. This option should probably not be used.

-p　　　The system will turn off the power if it can. This is of course likely to make **reboot** rather similar to **halt**.

The **fasthalt** and **fastboot** utilities are nothing more than aliases for the **halt** and **reboot** utilities.

Normally, the shutdown(8) utility is used when the system needs to be halted or restarted, giving users advance warning of their impending doom.

SEE ALSO

utmp(5), boot(8), shutdown(8), sync(8)

HISTORY

A **reboot** command appeared in Version 6 AT&T UNIX.

NAME

swapon – specify additional device for paging and swapping

SYNOPSIS

swapon -a
swapon *special_file ...*

DESCRIPTION

Swapon is used to specify additional devices on which paging and swapping are to take place. The system begins by swapping and paging on only a single device so that only one disk is required at bootstrap time. Calls to **swapon** normally occur in the system multi-user initialization file /etc/rc making all swap devices available, so that the paging and swapping activity is interleaved across several devices.

Normally, the first form is used:

-a   All devices marked as "sw" swap devices in /etc/fstab are made available unless their "noauto" option is also set.

The second form gives individual block devices as given in the system swap configuration table. The call makes only this space available to the system for swap allocation.

SEE ALSO

swapon(2), fstab(5), init(8), pstat(8), rc(8), vnconfig(8)

FILES

/dev/[ru][pk]?b standard paging devices
/etc/fstab   ascii filesystem description table

BUGS

There is no way to stop paging and swapping on a device. It is therefore not possible to make use of devices which may be dismounted during system operation.

HISTORY

The **swapon** command appeared in 4.0BSD.

NAME
   sync – force completion of pending disk writes (flush cache)

SYNOPSIS
   sync

DESCRIPTION
   Sync can be called to insure that all disk writes have been completed before the processor is halted in a way not suitably done by reboot(8) or halt(8). Generally, it is
   preferable to use reboot(8) or halt(8) to shut down the system, as they may perform
   additional actions such as resynchronizing the hardware clock and flushing internal
   caches before performing a final **sync**.

   Sync utilizes the sync(2) function call.

SEE ALSO
   fsync(2), sync(2), update(4), halt(8), reboot(8)

HISTORY
   A **sync** command appeared in Version 6 AT&T UNIX.

NAME
     umount – unmount filesystems

SYNOPSIS
     umount [**-fv**] *special* | *node*
     umount -a | **-A** [**-fv**] [**-h** *host*] [**-t** *type*]

DESCRIPTION
     The **umount** command calls the unmount(2) system call to remove a *special*
     device or the remote node (rhost:path) from the filesystem tree at the point *node*. If ei-
     ther *special* or *node* are not provided, the appropriate information is taken from the
     fstab(5) file.

     The options are as follows:

     -a   All the filesystems described in fstab(5) are unmounted.

     -A   All the currently mounted filesystems except the root are unmounted.

     -f   The filesystem is forcibly unmounted. Active special devices continue to work,
              but all other files return errors if further accesses are attempted. The root
              filesystem cannot be forcibly unmounted.

     -h *host*
              Only filesystems mounted from the specified host will be unmounted. This op-
              tion implies the **-A** option and, unless otherwise specified with the **-t** option,
              will only unmount NFS filesystems.

     -t *type*
              Is used to indicate the actions should only be taken on filesystems of the speci-
              fied type. More than one type may be specified in a comma separated list.
              The list of filesystem types can be prefixed with "no" to specify the filesystem
              types for which action should *not* be taken. For example, the **umount** com-
              mand:

                   umount -a -t nfs,mfs

              umounts all filesystems of the type NFS and MFS.

     -v   Verbose, additional information is printed out as each filesystem is unmounted.

FILES

`/etc/fstab` filesystem table

SEE ALSO

unmount(2), fstab(5), mount(8)

BUGS

When using union filesystems, umount(8) cannot always determine the node which is the mountpoint. In this case, it is necessary to specify the relevant directory to be unmounted in the same form as that displayed by mount(8). For example, given a mount entry like this:

<above>/tmpdir on /cdrom (local, user mount)

then the command:

umount '<above>/tmpdir'

would unmount /tmpdir from the mountpoint /cdrom.

HISTORY

A **umount** command appeared in Version 6 AT&T UNIX.

NAME
     vidcontrol – a utility for manipulating the syscons video driver.

SYNOPSIS
     vidcontrol [**-r** *fg bg*] [**-b** *color*] [**-c** *appearance*] [**-d**] [**-i**
     adapter/mode] [**-l** *scrmap*] [**-L**] [**-m** *on/off*] [**-f** *size file*] [**-s** *number*]
     [**-t** *N/off*] [**-x**] [mode] [fgcol [bgcol]] [show]

DESCRIPTION
     The **vidcontrol** command is used to set various options for the syscons video driver,
     such as video mode, colors, cursors, scrnmaps, font and screensaver timeout.

     The following command line options are supported:

     mode   Select a new video mode. The modes currently recognized are: *40x25*, *80x25*,
               80x30, *80x43*, *80x50*, *80x60*, *132x25*, *132x30*, *132x43*, *132x50*,
               132x60, *VGA_40x25*, *VGA_80x25*, *VGA_80x30*, *VGA_80x50*, *VGA_80x60*,
               EGA_80x25, *EGA_80x43*, *VESA_132x25*, *VESA_132x30*, *VESA_132x43*,
               VESA_132x50, *VESA_132x60*. The graphic mode *VGA_320x200* and
               VESA_800x600 can also be chosen. Note that not all modes listed above may
               be supported by the video hardware, and that the VESA BIOS support must be
               linked to the kernel or loaded as a KLD if you wish to use VESA video modes
               or 132 column modes.

     fgcol [bgcol]
               Change colors when displaying text. Specify the foreground color (e.g. "vidcon-
               trol white"), or both a foreground & background color (e.g. "vidcontrol yellow
               blue").

     show   See the supported colors on a given platform.

     -r *foreground background*
               Change reverse mode colors to *foreground* and *background*.

     -b *color*
               Set border color to *color* (only supported on VGA hardware).

     -c *normal/blink/destructive*
               Change the cursor appearance. The cursor is either an inverting block (normal)
               that eventually can "blink". Or it can be like the old hardware cursor (destruc-
               tive). The latter is actually a simulation.

-d   Print out current screen output map.

-l *scrmap*
           Install screen output map file from *scrmap*

-L   Install default screen output map.

-i *adapter*
           Shows info about the current videoadapter.

-i *mode*
           Shows the possible videomodes with the current video hardware.

-m *on/off*
           Switch the mousepointer *on* or *off*. Used together with the moused daemon
           for textmode cut & paste functionality.

-f *size file*
           Load font *file* for *size* (currently, only 8x8, 8x14 or 8x16). The font file can
           be either uuencoded or in raw binary format.

-s *number*
           Set the current vty to *number*.

-t *N/off*
           Set the screensaver timeout to *N* seconds, or turns it *off*.

-x   Use hexadecimal digits for output.

FILES
```
/usr/share/syscons/fonts
/usr/share/syscons/scrnmaps
```

SEE ALSO
kbdcontrol(1), keyboard(4), screen(4), moused(8)

AUTHORS
Søren Schmidt <sos@FreeBSD.org>

NAME

vipw – edit the password file

SYNOPSIS

vipw

DESCRIPTION

Vipw edits the password file after setting the appropriate locks, and does any necessary processing after the password file is unlocked. If the password file is already locked for editing by another user, **vipw** will ask you to try again later. The default editor for **vipw** is vi(1).

Vipw performs a number of consistency checks on the password entries, and will not allow a password file with a "mangled" entry to be installed. If **vipw** rejects the new password file, the user is prompted to re-enter the edit session.

Once the information has been verified, **vipw** uses pwd_mkdb(8) to update the user database. This is run in the background, and, at very large sites could take several minutes. Until this update is completed, the password file is unavailable for other updates and the new information is not available to programs.

ENVIRONMENT

If the following environment variable exists it will be utilized by **vipw**:

EDITOR The editor specified by the string EDITOR will be invoked instead of the default editor vi(1).

SEE ALSO

chpass(1), passwd(1), passwd(5), adduser(8), pwd_mkdb(8)

HISTORY

The **vipw** command appeared in 4.0BSD.

Terminology

Table A-1. Networking terms

ARPANET	The old name of what became the Internet. The name refers to *DARPA* (see below).
Baud Rate	The number of electrical state transitions that may be made in a period of time. Modem designers use this term to describe the data transmission capabilities of a modem. Since it doesn't specify how many bits are transferred at a time, however, it is almost meaningless to computer users, who frequently quote it incorrectly. For example, a modem which transmits data at 28,800 bps has a baud rate of 2400.
BNU	The System V name for *UUCP*.
bps	Bits per Second, the rate at which data is transmitted over a modem.
CCITT	Commité Consultatif International de Téléphones et Télégraphes. The old name for the ITU-T.
DARPA	The US *Defence Advanced Research Projects Agency*, which developed the Internet Protocols.
DTE	Data Terminal Equipment, for example, a computer.
DCE	Data Communications Equipment, for example a modem
Ethernet	A broadcast network of computers which are geographically close to each other.
HTTP	The *Hypertext Transfer Protocol*, the basis of the World-Wide Web.
ICMP	Internet Control Message Protocol, a protocol primarily for testing and error messages.
Internet	The world's leading computer network. The name comes from the concept of *routing*, seen as an *Inter*connection of *Net*works.
IP	Internet Protocol—the basic protocol on the Internet.
ISO	The International Standards Organization.
Link Layer	The lowest layer of the Internet Protocols, concerned with the physical interconnection of computers.

LKM
: A *loadable kernel module*, software which runs in kernel space, but which can be loaded separately after the system is running.

Network layer
: The part of the Internet protocols concerned with transferring data between systems which are not connected to each other.

OSI
: *Open Systems Interconnect*, a series of protocols produced by the ISO. Largely obsolescent.

RS-232
: EIA standard for serial communications via hardware

SNA
: IBM's *Systems Network Architecture*. An early networking implementation.

TCP
: Transmission Control Protocol, the reliable internet transport protocol.

TSR
: MS-DOS term for *Terminate and Stay Resident*: programs that are started by MS-DOS and which remain in memory after they stop. Typical examples are mouse drivers and memory managers.

UART
: *Universal Asynchronous Receiver-Transmitter*, the chip that converts parallel data into serial asynchronous data.

UDP
: User Datagram Protocol, the unreliable internet transport protocol.

UUCP
: *UNIX to UNIX Copy*, a primitive UNIX data communication protocol.

WWW
: The *World-Wide Web*, an abstract structure built on top of the *HTTP* protocol.

X.25
: A CCITT/ITU-T recommendation for package switched networks.

B

Command equivalents

A number of simple utility commands have an equivalent on just about every system. Table B-1 lists the more frequent MS-DOS commands and suggests UNIX commands which might be able to achieve the same purpose. In many cases, there is no direct equivalent, and the UNIX commands are very different. For more details of the FreeBSD commands, look at the corresponding man page.

Table B-1. MS-DOS and UNIX command comparison

MS-DOS Command	UNIX Equivalent	Description
APPEND	*ln*	Add files from other directories to current directory. This works in a very different way in UNIX: use the *ln* command to create a link to the file.
ASSIGN	*ln, mount*	Reassign drive letters. Obsolete.
ATTRIB	*chmod*	Change file attributes. The attributes themselves differ significantly, of course.
BACKUP	*tar, cpio, dump*	Back up data
CD	*cd*	Change the current directory. FreeBSD has the concept of a *home directory* (see page 163), and invoking *cd* without parameters will change to the home directory. To find the current directory, use *pwd*.
CHKDSK	*fsck*	Check a file system for errors. To display disk usage, use *du* or *df*.
COMMAND	*sh, bash, csh, tcsh, zsh*	Command interpreter or shell. See page 163 for more details.
COMP	*cmp*	Compare two files

MS-DOS Command	UNIX Equivalent	Description
COPY	cp	Copy files from one place to another.
CTTY	getty	Change controlling tty. In MS-DOS, this transfers control to another line, usually a serial line. In FreeBSD, *getty* activates another line without losing access to the first. Read the man page for *ttys(5)* for further information.
	COMCONSOLE	To redirect the system console, use the COMCONSOLE option in the kernel. See Chapter 18, *Configuring the kernel*, page 340, for further details.
DATE	date	Show or change the date
DEBUG	gdb	Debug programs
DEL	rm	Delete (remove) files. *rm* only physically removes the file when it removes the last hard link—otherwise it just removes the directory entry.
DIR	ls	List the contents of directories
DISKCOMP	cmp	Compare floppy disk contents
DISKCOPY	dd	Copy disks. *dd* will also copy files.
DOSKEY	(none)	Enable command line editing and history. In UNIX, this function is performed by the shell. See pages 171 and 174 for more details.
ECHO	echo	Echo text to the output. In MS-DOS, this is also used for the unrelated function of enabling or disabling echoing of command files. FreeBSD shells typically do this with *set -v*— see the man pages for your shell.
EDIT	emacs, vi	Start an editor. Many editors are supplied with FreeBSD— see the Ports Collection for more details.
EDLIN	ed	Primitive line editor
EXPAND	gunzip	Expand compressed data. *gunzip* expands data compressed with *gzip*, not MS-DOS compressed data, but it corresponds in function.
FC	diff	Compare files and display the differences between them
FDISK	fdisk	Partition disks—see Chapter 2, *Before you install*, page 38.
FIND	grep	Search for a string in a group of files. UNIX *grep* is very powerful—see *UNIX Power Tools* for a number of ideas.
FORMAT	fdformat, newfs	Format a disk. See Chapter 14, *Disks*, page 243, for more details.

MS-DOS Command	UNIX Equivalent	Description
JOIN	*mount*	Mount the contents of a partition in a directory
KEYB	*kbdcontrol*	Set keyboard mapping. FreeBSD stores keyboard maps in files in the directory */usr/share/syscons/keymaps*. See the contents of this directory for your favourite keyboard layout.
MD (or MKDIR)	*mkdir*	Create a directory.
MORE	*more, less*	Paginate output. *more* and *less* can take command line arguments specifying the files to paginate.
PATH	*PATH*	Specify a search path for executables. In FreeBSD, PATH is an environment variable (see the description of your shell).
PRINT	*lpr*	Print a file in the background
RENAME	*mv*	Rename a file. *mv* ("move") also moves files to a different directory.
RMDIR	*rmdir*	Remove a directory
TIME	*date*	Display or set the time
TYPE	*cat*	Display the contents of a file. FreeBSD has a *type* command, but it has a different purpose: it displays the type of a file.
UNDELETE	*(none)*	Undelete a deleted file. ***YOU CAN'T DO THIS*** in FreeBSD. Once you delete a file, it's gone.
UNFORMAT	*(none)*	Restore a disk erased by *FORMAT*. ***YOU CAN'T DO THIS*** in FreeBSD. Once you format a disk, the old contents are gone. If you lose the beginning of a disk only, however, the *fsck* program may help you recover the contents via a backup super block.
VER	*uname*	Display the operating system version information
XCOPY	*cp*	Copy files

C

Bibliography

While the manual pages provide the definitive reference for individual pieces of the FreeBSD operating system, they are notorious for not illustrating how to put the pieces together to make the whole operating system run smoothly. For this, there is no substitute for a good book on UNIX system administration, and a good users' manual.

The 4.4BSD manuals

The original 4.4BSD manual set includes the man pages and a number of documents on various aspects of programming, user programs and system administration. With the exception of some historical documents with AT&T copyright, you can find the latest versions in */usr/share/man* (the man pages) and */usr/share/doc* (the other documents). If you want the original 4.4BSD versions, you can check them out of the repository.

If you prefer a bound version, O'Reilly and Associates publish the original five-volume set of documentation for 4.4BSD as released by the CSRG in 1994, including the AT&T historical documents. Compared to FreeBSD, much of this documentation is severely out of date. It comprises the following volumes:

- *4.4BSD Programmer's Reference Manual.* These are sections 2, 3, 4 and 5 of the man pages for 4.4BSD.

- *4.4BSD Programmer's Supplementary Documents.* You can find the latest versions of most of these documents in */usr/share/doc/psd.*

- *4.4BSD User's Reference Manual.* This book contains sections 1, 6 and 7 of the 4.4BSD man pages.

- *4.4BSD User's Supplementary Documents.* You can find the latest versions of most of these documents in */usr/share/doc/usd.*

- *4.4BSD System Manager's Manual.* Contains section 8 of the manual and a number of other documents. You can find the latest versions of most of these documents in */usr/share/doc/smm.*

Users' guides

UNIX Power Tools. Jerry Peek, Tim O'Reilly, and Mike Loukides, O'Reilly and Associates, Inc., 1993. A superb collection of interesting information, including a CD-ROM. Recommended for everybody, from beginners to experts.

UNIX for the Impatient, by Paul W. Abrahams and Bruce R. Larson. Second Edition, Addison-Wesley, 1996. An excellent not-too-technical introduction to UNIX in general. Includes a section on X11.

UNIX in a Nutshell for 4.3BSD. O'Reilly and Associates, Inc., 1990. Somewhat outdated.

Administrators' guides

Building Internet Firewalls, by D. Brent Chapman and Elizabeth Zwicky. O'Reilly & Associates, Inc., 1995.

DNS and BIND, by Paul Albitz and Cricket Liu. O'Reilly and Associates, Inc., 1993.

Essential System Administration, by Æleen Frisch. Second edition, O'Reilly and Associates, Inc., 1995.

Firewalls and Internet Security: Repelling the Wily Hacker, by William R. Cheswick and Steven M. Bellovin. Addison-Wesley, 1994.

Sendmail, by Bryan Costales, et al. O'Reilly and Associates, Inc., 1993.

TCP/IP Network Administration, by Craig Hunt. O'Reilly and Associates, Inc., 1992.

UNIX System Administration Handbook, by Evi Nemeth, Garth Snyder, Scott Seebass, and Trent R. Hein. 2nd edition, Prentice Hall, 1995. An excellent coverage of 6 real-life systems, including BSD/OS, which is very close to FreeBSD.

Programmers' guides

X Window System Toolkit, by Paul Asente. Digital Press.

The Annotated C++ Reference Manual, by Margaret A. Ellis and Bjarne Stroustrup. Addison-Wesley, 1990.

C: A Reference Manual, by Samuel P. Harbison and Guy L. Steele, Jr. 3rd edition, Prentice Hall, 1991.

"Porting UNIX to the 386" in *Dr. Dobb's Journal*, William Jolitz. January 1991-July 1992.

The Design and the Implementation of the 4.3BSD UNIX Operating System. Samuel J. Leffler, Marshall Kirk McKusick, Michael J. Karels, John S. Quarterman. Addison-Wesley, 1990. The definitive description of the 4.3BSD kernel and communications.

Porting UNIX Software, by Greg Lehey. O'Reilly and Associates, 1995.

The Standard C Library, by P. J. Plauger. Prentice Hall, 1992.

Writing Serial Drivers for UNIX, by Bill Wells. *Dr. Dobb's Journal*, 19(15), December 1994. pp 68-71, 97-99.

Hardware reference

ISA System Architecture, by Tom Stanley. 3rd edition, Addison-Wesley, 1995.

PCI System Architecture, by Tom Stanley. 3rd edition, Addison-Wesley, 1995.

RS-232 made easy, second edition. Martin D. Seyer, Prentice-Hall 1991. A discussion of the RS-232 standard.

The Undocumented PC, by Frank Van Gilluwe. Addison-Wesley, 1994.

Resources on the net

In addition to the books above, a number of web sites have information on FreeBSD. They have the potential to be much more up-to-date than the books above, but not all of them are kept up to date.

Annelise Anderson has a tutorial "For People New to Both FreeBSD and UNIX" at *http://www.freebsd.org/tutorials/newuser/newuser.html.*

Chris Coleman and Mark Mayo are currently writing a book called *NewBie FreeBSD*. Drafts are available on-line at *http://www.vmunix.com/fbsd-book/.*

Finally, take a look at *http://www.FreeBSD.org*. There's a lot of stuff of interest there.

D

License agreements

As we have already seen, FreeBSD is *not* public domain software. It resembles commercial software in that its use is subject to a license agreement (in fact, each component is subject to a license agreement). It differs from commercial software only in the content of these license agreements. They all state that you may distribute the software without paying anything to the owners of the licenses. They also state a lot of legalese which I am not going to try to interpret. Instead, here's the text of the two most important license agreements:

- The Berkeley license agreement covers most of the core software and the kernel.

- The GNU General Public license covers most of the GNU software, and many others.

The Berkeley License

All of the documentation and software included in the 4.4BSD and 4.4BSD-Lite Releases is copyrighted by The Regents of the University of California.

Copyright © 1979, 1980, 1983, 1986, 1988, 1989, 1991, 1992, 1993, 1994
    The Regents of the University of California. All rights reserved.

Redistribution and use in source and binary forms, with or without modification, are permitted provided that the following conditions are met:
1. Redistributions of source code must retain the above copyright notice, this list of conditions and the following disclaimer.
2. Redistributions in binary form must reproduce the above copyright notice, this list of conditions and the following disclaimer in the documentation and/or other materials provided with the distribution.
3. All advertising materials mentioning features or use of this software must display the following acknowledgement:

    This product includes software developed by the University of California, Berkeley and its contributors.

4. Neither the name of the University nor the names of its contributors may be used to endorse or promote products derived from this software without specific prior written permission.

THIS SOFTWARE IS PROVIDED BY THE REGENTS AND CONTRIBUTORS "AS IS" AND ANY EXPRESS OR IMPLIED WARRANTIES, INCLUDING, BUT NOT LIMITED TO, THE IMPLIED WARRANTIES OF MERCHANTABILITY AND FITNESS FOR A PARTICULAR PURPOSE ARE DISCLAIMED. IN NO EVENT SHALL THE REGENTS OR CONTRIBUTORS BE LIABLE FOR ANY DIRECT, INDIRECT, INCIDENTAL, SPECIAL, EXEMPLARY, OR CONSEQUENTIAL DAMAGES (INCLUDING, BUT NOT LIMITED TO, PROCUREMENT OF SUBSTITUTE GOODS OR SERVICES; LOSS OF USE, DATA, OR PROFITS; OR BUSINESS INTERRUPTION) HOWEVER CAUSED AND ON ANY THEORY OF LIABILITY, WHETHER IN CONTRACT, STRICT LIABILITY, OR TORT (INCLUDING NEGLIGENCE OR OTHERWISE) ARISING IN ANY WAY OUT OF THE USE OF THIS SOFTWARE, EVEN IF ADVISED OF THE POSSIBILITY OF SUCH DAMAGE.

The Institute of Electrical and Electronics Engineers and the American National Standards Committee X3, on Information Processing Systems have given us permission to reprint portions of their documentation.

In the following statement, the phrase "this text" refers to portions of the system documentation.

Portions of this text are reprinted and reproduced in electronic form in the second BSD Networking Software Release, from IEEE Std 1003.1-1988, IEEE Standard Portable Operating System Interface for Computer Environments (POSIX), copyright © 1988 by the Institute of Electrical and Electronics Engineers, Inc. In the event of any discrepancy between these versions and the original IEEE Standard, the original IEEE Standard is the referee document.

In the following statement, the phrase "This material" refers to portions of the system documentation.

This material is reproduced with permission from American National Standards Committee X3, on Information Processing Systems. Computer and Business Equipment Manufacturers Association (CBEMA), 311 First St., NW, Suite 500, Washington, DC 20001-2178. The developmental work of Programming Language C was completed by the X3J11 Technical Committee.

The views and conclusions contained in the software and documentation are those of the authors and should not be interpreted as representing official policies, either expressed or implied, of the Regents of the University of California.

The GNU General Public License

GNU GENERAL PUBLIC LICENSE
Version 2, June 1991

Preamble
The licenses for most software are designed to take away your freedom to share and change it. By contrast, the GNU General Public License is intended to guarantee your freedom to share and change free software—to make sure the software is free for all its users. This General Public License applies to most of the Free Software Foundation's software and to any other program whose authors commit to using it. (Some other Free Software Foundation software is covered by the GNU Library General Public License instead.) You can apply it to your programs, too.

When we speak of free software, we are referring to freedom, not price. Our General Public Licenses are designed to make sure that you have the freedom to distribute copies of free software (and charge for this service if you wish), that you receive source code or can get it if you want it, that you can change the software or use pieces of it in new free programs; and that you know you can do these things.

To protect your rights, we need to make restrictions that forbid anyone to deny you these rights or to ask you to surrender the rights. These restrictions translate to certain responsibilities for you if you distribute copies of the software, or if you modify it.

For example, if you distribute copies of such a program, whether gratis or for a fee, you must give the recipients all the rights that you have. You must make sure that they, too, receive or can get the source code. And you must show them these terms so they know their rights.

We protect your rights with two steps: (1) copyright the software, and (2) offer you this license which gives you legal permission to copy, distribute and/or modify the software.

Also, for each author's protection and ours, we want to make certain that everyone understands that there is no warranty for this free software. If the software is modified by someone else and passed on, we want its recipients to know that what they have is not the original, so that any problems introduced by others will not reflect on the original authors' reputations.

Finally, any free program is threatened constantly by software patents. We wish to avoid the danger that redistributors of a free program will individually obtain patent licenses, in effect making the program proprietary. To prevent this, we have made it clear that any patent must be licensed for everyone's free use or not licensed at all.

The precise terms and conditions for copying, distribution and modification follow.
GNU GENERAL PUBLIC LICENSE
TERMS AND CONDITIONS FOR COPYING, DISTRIBUTION

AND MODIFICATION

0. This License applies to any program or other work which contains a notice placed by the copyright holder saying it may be distributed under the terms of this General Public License. The "Program", below, refers to any such program or work, and a "work based on the Program" means either the Program or any derivative work under copyright law: that is to say, a work containing the Program or a portion of it, either verbatim or with modifications and/or translated into another language. (Hereinafter, translation is included without limitation in the term "modification".) Each licensee is addressed as "you".

Activities other than copying, distribution and modification are not covered by this License; they are outside its scope. The act of running the Program is not restricted, and the output from the Program is covered only if its contents constitute a work based on the Program (independent of having been made by running the Program). Whether that is true depends on what the Program does.

1. You may copy and distribute verbatim copies of the Program's source code as you receive it, in any medium, provided that you conspicuously and appropriately publish on each copy an appropriate copyright notice and disclaimer of warranty; keep intact all the notices that refer to this License and to the absence of any warranty; and give any other recipients of the Program a copy of this License along with the Program.

You may charge a fee for the physical act of transferring a copy, and you may at your option offer warranty protection in exchange for a fee.

2. You may modify your copy or copies of the Program or any portion of it, thus forming a work based on the Program, and copy and distribute such modifications or work under the terms of Section 1 above, provided that you also meet all of these conditions:

> a) You must cause the modified files to carry prominent notices stating that you changed the files and the date of any change.

> b) You must cause any work that you distribute or publish, that in whole or in part contains or is derived from the Program or any part thereof, to be licensed as a whole at no charge to all third parties under the terms of this License.

> c) If the modified program normally reads commands interactively when run, you must cause it, when started running for such interactive use in the most ordinary way, to print or display an announcement including an appropriate copyright notice and a notice that there is no warranty (or else, saying that you provide a warranty) and that users may redistribute the program under these conditions, and telling the user how to view a copy of this License. (Exception: if the Program itself is interactive but does not normally print such an announcement, your work based on the Program is not required to print an announcement.)

These requirements apply to the modified work as a whole. If identifiable sections of that work are not derived from the Program, and can be reasonably considered independent and separate works in themselves, then this License, and its terms, do not apply to those sections when you distribute them as separate works. But when you distribute the same sections as part of a whole which is a work based on the Program, the distribution of the whole must be on the terms of this License, whose permissions for other licensees extend to the entire whole, and thus to each and every part regardless of who wrote it.

Thus, it is not the intent of this section to claim rights or contest your rights to work written entirely by you; rather, the intent is to exercise the right to control the distribution of derivative or collective works based on the Program.

In addition, mere aggregation of another work not based on the Program with the Program (or with a work based on the Program) on a volume of a storage or distribution medium does not bring the other work under the scope of this License.

3. You may copy and distribute the Program (or a work based on it, under Section 2) in object code or executable form under the terms of Sections 1 and 2 above provided that you also do one of the following:

a) Accompany it with the complete corresponding machine-readable source code, which must be distributed under the terms of Sections 1 and 2 above on a medium customarily used for software interchange; or,

b) Accompany it with a written offer, valid for at least three years, to give any third party, for a charge no more than your cost of physically performing source distribution, a complete machine-readable copy of the corresponding source code, to be distributed under the terms of Sections 1 and 2 above on a medium customarily used for software interchange; or,

c) Accompany it with the information you received as to the offer to distribute corresponding source code. (This alternative is allowed only for noncommercial distribution and only if you received the program in object code or executable form with such an offer, in accord with Subsection b above.)

The source code for a work means the preferred form of the work for making modifications to it. For an executable work, complete source code means all the source code for all modules it contains, plus any associated interface definition files, plus the scripts used to control compilation and installation of the executable. However, as a special exception, the source code distributed need not include anything that is normally distributed (in either source or binary form) with the major components (compiler, kernel, and so on) of the operating system on which the executable runs, unless that component itself accompanies the executable.

If distribution of executable or object code is made by offering access to copy from a designated place, then offering equivalent access to copy the source code from the same place counts as distribution of the source code, even though third parties are not compelled to copy the source along with the object code.

4. You may not copy, modify, sublicense, or distribute the Program except as expressly provided under this License. Any attempt otherwise to copy, modify, sublicense or distribute the Program is void, and will automatically terminate your rights under this License. However, parties who have received copies, or rights, from you under this License will not have their licenses terminated so long as such parties remain in full compliance.

5. You are not required to accept this License, since you have not signed it. However, nothing else grants you permission to modify or distribute the Program or its derivative works. These actions are prohibited by law if you do not accept this License. Therefore, by modifying or distributing the Program (or any work based on the Program), you indicate your acceptance of this License to do so, and all its terms and conditions for copying, distributing or modifying the Program or works based on it.

6. Each time you redistribute the Program (or any work based on the Program), the recipient automatically receives a license from the original licensor to copy, distribute or modify the Program subject to these terms and conditions. You may not impose any further restrictions on the recipients' exercise of the rights granted herein. You are not responsible for enforcing compliance by third parties to this License.

7. If, as a consequence of a court judgment or allegation of patent infringement or for any other reason (not limited to patent issues), conditions are imposed on you (whether by court order, agreement or otherwise) that contradict the conditions of this License, they do not excuse you from the conditions of this License. If you cannot distribute so as to satisfy simultaneously your obligations under this License and any other pertinent obligations, then as a consequence you may not distribute the Program at all. For example, if a patent license would not permit royalty-free redistribution of the Program by all those who receive copies directly or indirectly through you, then the only way you could satisfy both it and this License would be to refrain entirely from distribution of the Program.

If any portion of this section is held invalid or unenforceable under any particular circumstance, the balance of the section is intended to apply and the section as a whole is intended to apply in other circumstances.

It is not the purpose of this section to induce you to infringe any patents or other property right claims or to contest validity of any such claims; this section has the sole purpose of protecting the integrity of the free software distribution system, which is implemented by public license practices. Many people have made generous contributions to the wide range of software distributed through that system in reliance on consistent application of that system; it is up to the author/donor to decide if he or she is willing to distribute software through any other system and a licensee cannot impose that choice.

This section is intended to make thoroughly clear what is believed to be a consequence of the rest of this License.

8. If the distribution and/or use of the Program is restricted in certain countries either by patents or by copyrighted interfaces, the original copyright holder who places the Program under this License may add an explicit geographical distribution limitation excluding those countries, so that distribution is permitted only in or among countries not thus excluded. In such case, this License incorporates the limitation as if written in the body of this License.

9. The Free Software Foundation may publish revised and/or new versions of the General Public License from time to time. Such new versions will be similar in spirit to the present version, but may differ in detail to address new problems or concerns.

Each version is given a distinguishing version number. If the Program specifies a version number of this License which applies to it and "any later version", you have the option of following the terms and conditions either of that version or of any later version published by the Free Software Foundation. If the Program does not specify a version number of this License, you may choose any version ever published by the Free Software Foundation.

10. If you wish to incorporate parts of the Program into other free programs whose distribution conditions are different, write to the author to ask for permission. For software which is copyrighted by the Free Software Foundation, write to the Free Software Foundation; we sometimes make exceptions for this. Our decision will be guided by the two goals of preserving the free status of all derivatives of our free software and of promoting the sharing and reuse of software generally.

NO WARRANTY

11. BECAUSE THE PROGRAM IS LICENSED FREE OF CHARGE, THERE IS NO WARRANTY FOR THE PROGRAM, TO THE EXTENT PERMITTED BY APPLICABLE LAW. EXCEPT WHEN OTHERWISE STATED IN WRITING THE COPYRIGHT HOLDERS AND/OR OTHER PARTIES PROVIDE THE PROGRAM "AS IS" WITHOUT WARRANTY OF ANY KIND, EITHER EXPRESSED OR IMPLIED, INCLUDING, BUT NOT LIMITED TO, THE IMPLIED WARRANTIES OF MERCHANTABILITY AND FITNESS FOR A PARTICULAR PURPOSE. THE ENTIRE RISK AS TO THE QUALITY AND PERFORMANCE OF THE PROGRAM IS WITH YOU. SHOULD THE PROGRAM PROVE DEFECTIVE, YOU ASSUME THE COST OF ALL NECESSARY SERVICING, REPAIR OR CORRECTION.

12. IN NO EVENT UNLESS REQUIRED BY APPLICABLE LAW OR AGREED TO IN WRITING WILL ANY COPYRIGHT HOLDER, OR ANY OTHER PARTY WHO MAY MODIFY AND/OR REDISTRIBUTE THE PROGRAM AS PERMITTED ABOVE, BE LIABLE TO YOU FOR DAMAGES, INCLUDING ANY GENERAL, SPECIAL, INCIDENTAL OR CONSEQUENTIAL DAMAGES ARISING OUT OF THE USE OR INABILITY TO USE THE PROGRAM (INCLUDING BUT NOT LIMITED TO LOSS OF DATA OR DATA BEING RENDERED INACCURATE OR LOSSES SUSTAINED BY YOU OR THIRD PARTIES OR A FAILURE OF THE PROGRAM TO OPERATE WITH ANY OTHER PROGRAMS), EVEN IF SUCH HOLDER OR OTHER PARTY HAS BEEN ADVISED OF THE POSSIBILITY OF SUCH DAMAGES.

END OF TERMS AND CONDITIONS

Appendix: How to Apply These Terms to Your New Programs

If you develop a new program, and you want it to be of the greatest possible use to the public, the best way to achieve this is to make it free software which everyone can redistribute and change under these terms.

To do so, attach the following notices to the program. It is safest to attach them to the start of each source file to most effectively convey the exclusion of warranty; and each file should have at least the "copyright" line and a pointer to where the full notice is found.

<one line to give the program's name and a brief idea of what it does.> Copyright © 19yy <name of author>

This program is free software; you can redistribute it and/or modify it under the terms of the GNU General Public License as published by the Free Software Foundation; either version 2 of the License, or (at your option) any later version.

This program is distributed in the hope that it will be useful, but WITHOUT ANY WARRANTY; without even the implied warranty of MERCHANTABILITY or FITNESS FOR A PARTICULAR PURPOSE. See the GNU General Public License for more details.

You should have received a copy of the GNU General Public License along with this program; if not, write to the Free Software Foundation, Inc., 675 Mass Ave, Cambridge, MA 02139, USA.

Also add information on how to contact you by electronic and paper mail.

If the program is interactive, make it output a short notice like this when it starts in an interactive mode:

Gnomovision version 69, Copyright © 19yy name of author Gnomovision comes with ABSOLUTELY NO WARRANTY; for details type 'show w'. This is free software, and you are welcome to redistribute it under certain conditions; type 'show c' for details.

The hypothetical commands 'show w' and 'show c' should show the appropriate parts of the General Public License. Of course, the commands you use may be called something other than 'show w' and 'show c'; they could even be mouse-clicks or menu items—whatever suits your program.

You should also get your employer (if you work as a programmer) or your school, if any, to sign a "copyright disclaimer" for the program, if necessary. Here is a sample; alter the names:

Yoyodyne, Inc., hereby disclaims all copyright interest in the program 'Gnomovision' (which makes passes at compilers) written by James Hacker.

<signature of Ty Coon>, 1 April 1989 Ty Coon, President of Vice

This General Public License does not permit incorporating your program into proprietary programs. If your program is a subroutine library, you may consider it more useful to permit linking proprietary applications with the library. If this is what you want to do, use the GNU Library General Public License instead of this License.

Index

About the author

Greg Lehey is an independent computer consultant specializing in UNIX. Born in Australia, he was educated in Malaysia and England before studying Chemistry in Germany and Chemical Engineering in England. He spent most of his professional career in Germany, where he worked for computer manufacturers such as Univac, Tandem, and Siemens-Nixdorf, the German space research agency, nameless software houses and a large user before deciding to work for himself. In the course of 25 years in the industry he has performed most jobs, ranging from kernel development to product marketing, from systems programming to systems administration, from processing satellite data to programming gasoline pumps, from the production of CD-ROMs of ported free software to DSP instruction set design. Apart from this book, he is also the author of "Porting UNIX Software" (O'Reilly and Associates, 1995). About the only thing he hasn't done is writing commercial applications software. He has recently returned to Australia. He is available for short-term contracts and can be reached by mail at grog@FreeBSD.ORG or grog@lemis.com. Alternatively, browse his home page at *http://www.lemis.com/~grog/.*

When he can drag himself away from his shed full of UNIX workstations, he is involved in performing baroque and classical woodwind music on his collection of original instruments, exploring the Australian countryside with his family on their Arabian and Peruvian horses, or exploring new cookery techniques or ancient and obscure European languages.